THE ROUGH GUIDE TO

St Petersburg

There are more than two hundred Rough Guide titles
covering destinations from Alaska to Zimbabwe
and subjects from Acoustic Guitar to Travel Health

Forthcoming travel guides include

Devon & Cornwall • Dordogne • Malta
Tenerife • Thai Beaches & Islands • Vancouver

Forthcoming reference guides include

Cuban Music • Personal Computers
Pregnancy & Birth • Trumpet & Trombone

Rough Guides Online
www.roughguides.com

Rough Guide Credits

Text Editor:	Gavin Thomas
Series Editor:	Mark Ellingham
Editorial:	Martin Dunford, Jonathan Buckley, Jo Mead, Kate Berens, Amanda Tomlin, Ann-Marie Shaw, Paul Gray, Helena Smith, Judith Bamber, Orla Duane, Olivia Eccleshall, Ruth Blackmore, Geoff Howard, Claire Saunders, Alexander Mark Rogers, Polly Thomas, Joe Staines, Andrew Tomičić, Richard Lim, Duncan Clark, Peter Buckley, Sam Thorne, Lucy Ratcliffe, Clifton Wilkinson, David Glen (UK); Andrew Rosenberg, Mary Beth Maioli, Stephen Timblin, Yuki Takagaki (US)
Online:	Kelly Cross, Anja Mutić-Blessing, Jennifer Gold, Audra Epstein, Suzanne Welles (US)
Production:	Susanne Hillen, Andy Hilliard, Link Hall, Helen Ostick, Julia Bovis, Michelle Draycott, Katie Pringle, Robert Evers, Mike Hancock, Zoë Nobes
Cartography:	Melissa Baker, Maxine Repath, Ed Wright, Katie Lloyd-Jones
Picture Research:	Louise Boulton, Sharon Martins
Finance:	John Fisher, Gary Singh, Edward Downey, Mark Hall, Tim Bill
Marketing & Publicity:	Richard Trillo, Niki Smith, David Wearn, Chloë Roberts, Birgit Hartmann, Claire Southern (UK); Simon Carloss, David Wechsler, Kathleen Rushforth (US)
Administration:	Tania Hummel, Demelza Dallow, Julie Sanderson

Acknowledgements

The author would like to thank all those in **Russia** for their help and hospitality: Tanya, Masha and Sergei for many fun evenings and caring for Sonia; Lena Yefimovich and Nikolai Nikolaiovich for all their kindness; Dima for the loan of his computer; Andrei Khlabystin for laughs and wisdom; Alexei Larionov for many sage corrections at the Hermitage; Elvina Builova at Gatchina Palace; Yelena Nikiforova at the Beloselskiy-Belozerskiy Palace; Olga Voronina at the Nabokov Museum; Olga Utochkina at the Yusupov Palace; and the staff of the St Petersburg tourist office. In **Finland**, many thanks to Arto Tarkkonen and Natasha Lundisheva for a wonderful time in Joensuu. In **England**, thanks to Gavin Thomas at Rough Guides for sensitive and erudite editing, Irina Gaylard at CIS Travel Services; and Olga Scott at Scott's Tours.

The editor would also like to thank Olivia Eccleshall for sharing the editorial load, Ruth Blackmore for language tuition, Amy Brown and Narrell Leffman for additional Basics research, Anne Hegerty for proofreading, Link Hall for typesetting, and Mandy Muggridge and Maxine Repath for cartography.

This third edition published April 2001 by Rough Guides Ltd, 62–70 Shorts Gardens, London WC2H 9AH.

Distributed by the Penguin Group:
Penguin Books Ltd, 27 Wrights Lane, London W8 5TZ.
Penguin Putnam, Inc. 375 Hudson Street, New York, NY 10014, USA.
Penguin Books Australia Ltd, 487 Maroondah Highway, PO Box 257, Ringwood, Victoria 3134, Australia.
Penguin Books Canada Ltd, 10 Alcorn Avenue, Toronto, Ontario M4V 1E4, Canada.
Penguin Books (NZ) Ltd, 182–190 Wairau Road, Auckland 10, New Zealand.

Printed in England by Clays Ltd, St Ives PLC.
Typography and original design by Jonathan Dear and The Crowd Roars.
Illustrations throughout by Edward Briant.

ISBN 1-85828-693-X

THE ROUGH GUIDE TO

St Petersburg

Written and researched by
Dan Richardson

with additional research by Lena Parizhskaya
and Anna Parizhskaya

THE ROUGH GUIDES

Help us update

We've gone to a lot of trouble to ensure that this fourth edition of *The Rough Guide to St Petersburg* is accurate and up-to-date. However, things inevitably change, and if you feel we've got it wrong or left something out, we'd like to know: any suggestions, comments or corrections would be much appreciated. We'll credit all contributions and send a copy of the next edition – or any other *Rough Guide* if you prefer – for the best correspondence.

Please mark letters "Rough Guide to St Petersburg" and send to: Rough Guides, 62–70 Shorts Gardens, London WC2H 9AH or Rough Guides, 4th Floor, 345 Hudson St, New York, NY 10014.

Email should be sent to:
mail@roughguides.co.uk

Online updates about Rough Guide titles can be found on our Web site at *www.roughguides.com*

The Authors

Dan Richardson was born in England in 1958. Before joining Rough Guides in 1984, he worked as a sailor on the Red Sea and lived in Peru. Since then he has travelled extensively in Russia and Eastern Europe, and is also the author of *The Rough Guide to Moscow* and co-author of *The Rough Guide to Romania*. While in St Petersburg in 1992 he met his future wife, Anna; they have a daughter, Sonia.

Readers' letters

Many thanks to all the readers of the last edition who took the time to write in with their comments and suggestions (and apologies to anyone whose name has been omitted or misspelt): Penny Barr, Jessica Barrick, K. Behr, Benjamin Brierley, Zanichelli Bruno, M.J. Carty, Miriam Clincy, Elspeth Christie, Julie Coleman & Mark Phillips, Kate Emmett, Dr J.F. de P. Farrugia, Anne Fawcett, Steven Garside, Jill Gaston, Cyrus Ginwala, Stephen Goldby, Barry Greenaway, Iryna Grygorenko, Richard Hardy, Simon Hetzel, Chris Himsworth, Johan Hedborg, P. Hind, Arthur R. Hollbach, Larissa Howlett, Kate Jervis, Clare Jones, Anne Keetley, Neil Kerr, Nika Kim, George Kollias, Tarja Kuhne, Linda G. Lasker, Rebekka H. Lake, Lucy Mallows, Ahilleas Maurellis, Elizabeth Sinclair Miller, Massimo Minella, Sinead McPhillips, S. Newcombe, G.A. Parish, Robert Procope, Ian Renfrew, Joan & Bill Robbins, George Roberson, Rosemary Roberts & Mark A. Prelas, Steve Robinson, David Rosen, Robert Sayers, Kim Skerton, G. Silcock, Holger Spamann, Veronika Streitwieser, Tim Sykes, Sylvia Temple, C. Till, Radim Vovesny, Paul Ware, Rich Wilson, Esther Wolff.

Our apologies to anyone whose name has been omitted or misspelt.

Rough Guides

Travel Guides • Phrasebooks • Music and Reference Guides

We set out to do something different when the first *Rough Guide* was published in 1982. Mark Ellingham, just out of university, was travelling in Greece. He brought along the popular guides of the day, but found they were all lacking in some way. They were either strong on ruins and museums but went on for pages without mentioning a beach or taverna. Or they were so conscious of the need to save money that they lost sight of Greece's cultural and historical significance. Also, none of the books told him anything about Greece's contemporary life – its politics, its culture, its people, and how they lived.

So with no job in prospect, Mark decided to write his own guidebook, one which aimed to provide practical information that was second to none, detailing the best beaches and the hottest clubs and restaurants, while also giving hard-hitting accounts of every sight, both famous and obscure, and providing up-to-the-minute information on contemporary culture. It was a guide that encouraged independent travellers to find the best of Greece, and was a great success, getting shortlisted for the Thomas Cook travel guide award, and encouraging Mark, along with three friends, to expand the series.

The Rough Guide list grew rapidly and the letters flooded in, indicating a much broader readership than had been anticipated, but one which uniformly appreciated the Rough Guides' mix of practical detail and humour, irreverence and enthusiasm. Things haven't changed. The same four friends who began the series are still the caretakers of the Rough Guide mission today: to provide the most reliable, up-to-date and entertaining information to independent-minded travellers of all ages, on all budgets.

We now publish 100 titles and have offices in London and New York. The travel guides are written and researched by a dedicated team of more than 100 authors, based in Britain, Europe, the USA and Australia. We have also created a unique series of phrasebooks to accompany the travel series, along with the acclaimed series of music guides, and a best-selling pocket guide to the Internet and World Wide Web. We also publish comprehensive travel information on our Web site: *http://www.roughguides.com*

Contents

List of maps

MAP SYMBOLS

═══	Road	⚓	Hydrofoil/boat station
━●━	Railway	★	Bus stop
-----	Path	✕	Airport
— —	Ferry/hydrofoil route	ⓘ	Tourist office
─────	Waterway	✉	Post office
– – –	Chapter division boundary	ℭ	Telephone
ⵜ	Fountain	◼	Building
⊙	Statue	➕	Church (town maps)
♖	Fort	⁺⁺⁺	Christian cemetery
⸸	Church (regional maps)	✡	Jewish cemetery
♜	Mosque	▓	Park
♠	Buddhist temple	⬚	Forest
Ⓜ	Metro station		

Introduction

Where were you born?
St Petersburg.
Where did you go to school?
Petrograd.
Where do you live now?
Leningrad.
And where would you like to live?
St Petersburg.

St Petersburg, Petrograd, Leningrad and now, again, St Petersburg – as this tongue-in-cheek Russian catechism suggests, the city's succession of names mirrors Russia's turbulent history. Founded in 1703 as a "window on the West" by Peter the Great, St Petersburg was for two centuries the capital of the Tsarist Empire, synonymous with hubris, excess and magnificence. During World War I the city renounced its Germanic-sounding name and became Petrograd, and as such was the cradle of the revolutions that overthrew Tsarism and brought the Bolsheviks to power in 1917. Later, as Leningrad, it epitomized the Soviet Union's heroic sacrifices in the war against Fascism, withstanding almost nine hundred days of Nazi siege. Finally, in 1991 – the year that Communism and the USSR collapsed – the change of name, back to St Petersburg, proved deeply symbolic, infuriating the wartime generation and die-hard Communists,

---

The city has been known by several names throughout its brief history; in our accounts of events and sights we have used whichever name was in use at the time:

Until August 31, 1914 – St Petersburg
August 31, 1914 to January 26, 1924 – Petrograd
January 26, 1924 to September 1991 – Leningrad
From September 1991 to the present day – St Petersburg

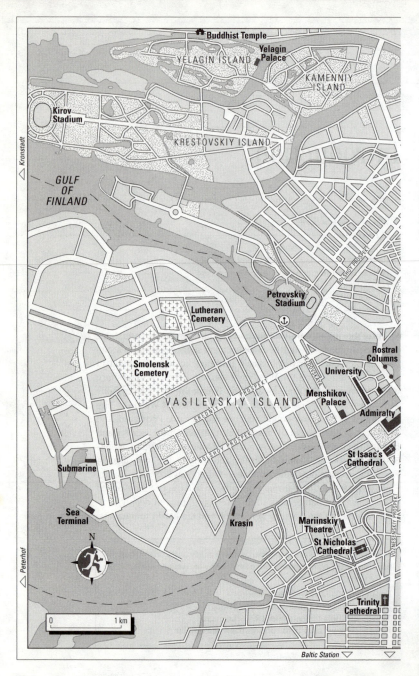

Buddhist Temple

Yelagin Palace

YELAGIN ISLAND

KAMENNIY ISLAND

Kirov Stadium

KRESTOVSKIY ISLAND

△ Kronstadt

GULF OF FINLAND

Petrovskiy Stadium

BOLSHOY PROSPEKT

Lutheran Cemetery

Rostral Columns

University

Smolensk Cemetery

SREDNIY PROSPEKT

VASILEVSKIY ISLAND

Menshikov Palace

Admiralty

SREDNIY PROSPEKT

St Isaac's Cathedral

BOLSHOY PROSPEKT

Submarine

VOZNESENSKIY PROSPEKT

Sea Terminal

N

Krasin

Mariinskiy Theatre

St Nicholas Cathedral

△ Peterhof

Trinity Cathedral

0   1 km

Baltic Station ▽   ▽

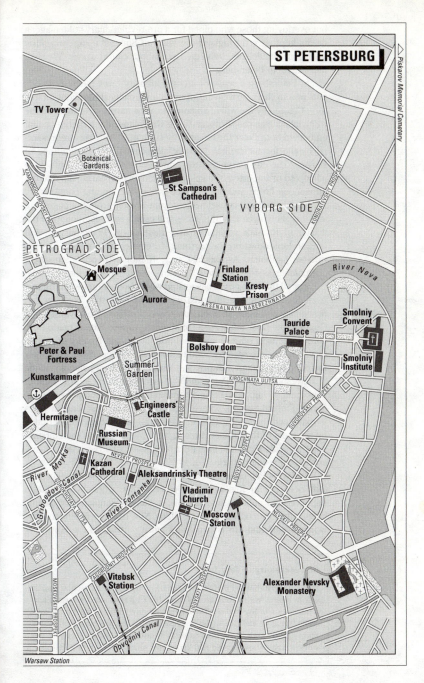

ST PETERSBURG

but overjoying those who pined for a pre-revolutionary golden age; a dream kept alive throughout the years of Stalinist terror, when the poet Osip Mandelstam (who died in a labour camp) wrote: "We shall meet again in Petersburg . . ."

St Petersburg's sense of its own **identity** owes much to its origins and to the interweaving of myth and reality throughout its history. Created by the will of an autocrat, on a barren river delta on the same latitude as the southern tip of Greenland, the Imperial capital embodied both Peter the Great's rejection of Old Russia – represented by the former capital, "Asiatic" Moscow – and his embrace of Europe. The city's architecture, administration and social life were all copied or imported, the splendid buildings appearing alien to the indigenous forms and out of place in the surrounding countryside. Artificiality and self-consciousness were present from the beginning and this showpiece city of palaces and canals soon decreed itself the arbiter of Russia's sensibility and imagination. Petersburgers still tend to look down on the earthier Muscovites, who regard them in turn as snobbish. As the last tsar, Nicholas II, once remarked, "Remember, St Petersburg is Russian – but it is not Russia."

For all that, the city is associated with a host of renowned figures from Russian culture and **history**. It was here that Tchaikovsky, Stravinsky and Shostakovich composed; Pushkin, Dostoyevsky and Gogol wrote their masterpieces; Mendeleyev and Pavlov made their contributions to science; and Rasputin, Lenin and Trotsky made history. So, too, are various buildings and sites inseparable from their former occupants or visitors: the amazing Imperial palaces outside St Petersburg, where Peter and Catherine the Great led the field in exuberant living; the Yusupov Palace, where Rasputin was murdered; Finland Station, where Lenin returned from seventeen years in exile; and the Winter Palace, the storming of which was heralded by the guns of the cruiser *Aurora*, now moored along the embankment from the Peter and Paul Fortress – itself a Tsarist prison to generations of revolutionaries.

Today, St Petersburg is coming to terms with the seismic changes that occurred in Russia in the early 1990s, when hyperinflation impoverished millions and the Mafia was so rampant that people likened the city to Chicago in the 1920s. Now there's a feeling that the worst is past and life is becoming more normal, as the consumer

---

St Petersburg: A few facts

St Petersburg (Sankt Peterburg – Санкт Петербург) is the second largest city in Russia, with a total area of more than 1400 square kilometres and a population of five million. The city is built on 44 islands, interlaced with some 50 canals and rivers (the River Neva alone has five branches): water makes up a tenth of its total area. It is also the most northerly of the world's large cities, located 800 kilometres south of the Arctic Circle.

Transliteration

The problem with transliterating Russian from the Cyrillic alphabet into the Roman alphabet is that there is no agreed way to do it. In addition to the German, French and American systems, there are several English systems. In this book we've used the Revised English System, with a few minor modifications to help pronunciation and readability. All proper names appear as they are best known, not as they would be transliterated (for example Tchaikovsky not Chaykovskiy). For more information on transliteration and pronunciation, see p.441.

goods and services enjoyed by other nations become commonplace, and politics is a matter of balancing budgets rather than averting mayhem. Even so, visitors are confused by the city's paradoxes: beautiful yet filthy, both progressive and stagnant, sophisticated and cerebral, industrial and maritime. Echoes of an anachronistic character are everywhere, from the sailors who look like they've just walked off the battleship *Potemkin*, to the promenading and champagne-quaffing that accompanies performances at the Mariinskiy (formerly the Kirov Ballet). Grandiose facades conceal warrens of communal apartments where disparate lifestyles flourish behind triple-locked doors, and courtyards where *babushki* gossip and drunkards philosophize, just as in stories by Dostoyevsky and Gogol.

Although the city is impossible to understand without some knowledge of its history, it is easy for visitors to enjoy – not least for its magnificent **architecture**. Planned on a grandiose scale, the city centre is awash with palaces and cathedrals calculated to impress, their colonnaded facades painted in bold Mediterranean colours and reflected in the dark waters of St Petersburg's canals and rivers. Its **cultural life** is equally abundant, embracing the staggering riches of the Hermitage art collection and the Russian Museum, the Mariinskiy, all kinds of music and drama, offbeat pursuits and wild nightlife. The people and the seasons provide the rest of the city's entertainment, as visitors are sucked in by the intensity of life – at its most intoxicating during the midsummer "White Nights", when the city barely sleeps and darkness never falls. It's easy to make friends in St Petersburg and anyone staying for more than just a few days is sure to be initiated into such Russian pleasures as going to the bathhouse or spending an evening talking round the kitchen table over a plateful of snacks washed down with vodka.

When to go

St Petersburg lies on the same latitude as the Shetland Islands and Anchorage, Alaska, but its **climate** is less harsh than you'd imagine, being moderated by warm air blowing in from the Atlantic Ocean. Summers are hot and while winters may be cold by Western European standards, they rarely compare with the ferocious cold of winter in Moscow, let alone Siberia.

See p.45 for advice on what to bring.

The most popular time to go is **summer**, lasting from the beginning of June to early September, when the city celebrates the famous "White Nights" (mid-June to mid-July) with a special festival and weeks of partying. Days are baking hot and nights sultry with the occasional downpour providing relief from the humidity. In August, everyone who can afford to leaves the city, if only to stay in a *dacha* (cottage) in the surrounding countryside. Although tourism is at its height in the summer, ballet fans should bear in mind that the Mariinskiy is closed in August. By mid-September **autumn** is under way, with cloudy skies and falling temperatures. October sees the first frosts (and sometimes snowfalls), though it's not unknown for there to be warm and sunny days, when the city looks especially beautiful in the soft northern light.

Subzero temperatures and snow can set in weeks before **winter** officially begins in December. The canals and rivers soon freeze over and a blanket of snow creates enchanting vistas that almost make you forget the cold. The secular New Year occasions shopping and merrymaking, much as Christmas in the West, though you need to stick around a while longer to catch the traditional Russian Orthodox Church celebrations of both holidays, in early January. While temperatures rarely fall below -15°C, the snow soon loses its charm as it compacts into black ice which lingers on until March, by which time everyone is longing for **spring**. Like winter, its arrival is somewhat unpredictable – the fabulous sight of the Neva ice floes breaking up and flowing through the heart of the city may not occur until April, or even early May.

Monthly temperatures and average monthly rainfall in St Petersburg

	Jan	Feb	Mar	Apr	May	Jun	Jul	Aug	Sep	Oct	Nov	Dec
Max °C	-7	-5	0	8	15	20	21	20	15	9	2	-3
Min °C	-13	-12	-8	0	6	11	13	13	9	4	-2	-8
mm	35	30	31	36	45	50	72	78	64	76	46	40

Changes in the new Russia

Inevitably, the speed of **change** in Russian society means that certain sections of this book are going to be out of date by the time you read them, not to mention the more humdrum but frequent changes to opening times, phone numbers, and suchlike. More positively, the prospect of political uncertainty has receded for the time being, and the apocalyptic scenarios of civil war that were popular in the media a few years ago now look ridiculous.

Basics

Getting there from Britain

By far the most convenient way to reach St Petersburg is by plane. Scheduled flights from London take just three hours (compared to over 48 hours by train), and there are direct daily services on Aeroflot or British Airways. If you have more time to devote to the journey itself, then the train becomes a more attractive proposition, since you can travel through the Baltic States or via Finland. Although it's possible to economize by taking a cheap flight to Central Europe and then a bus to St Petersburg, independent overland travel won't always save much money in comparison to going on a package tour once you've taken account of the cost of visa arrangements – but under optimum conditions, it's possible to travel part of the way by air and the rest overland via Helsinki for as little as £67, or via Berlin for £72 (one-way).

By plane

The Russian airline Aeroflot and British Airways (BA) between them operate up to nine scheduled **direct flights** a week from London to St Petersburg. Aeroflot flies from Heathrow (Sat) and Gatwick (Sun), and may have extra flights from Gatwick (Wed & Fri) in the summer, while BA flies from Gatwick daily except Tuesday and Thursday. **Fares** on BA flights can range anywhere from around £350 to £750 – though fares in January and February can occasionally fall as low as

£300. Aeroflot's prices are generally lower than BA's, but also vary widely throughout the year – note that neither BA nor Aeroflot's Web sites are of much help in working out fares.

A third option is to take an **indirect flight** with the Russian airline Transaero, which flies daily from Heathrow to Moscow with onward connections to St Petersburg on Monday and Wednesday after a two-hour stopover – the price of a return ticket is £247 year round. Other indirect flights to St Petersburg via various European cities can also work out cheaper than a direct flight: possible routings include flying with Lufthansa via Frankfurt, KLM via Amsterdam, Air France via Paris, Austrian Airlines or Lauda Air via Vienna, CSA via Prague, SAS via Stockholm, Sabena via Brussels, or Finnair via Helsinki. Some airlines also offer connections from cities other than London: Lufthansa from Birmingham and Manchester; Sabena from Manchester, Newcastle, Glasgow and Edinburgh; SAS and Finnair from Manchester; and KLM UK from all of them.

Rather than getting bogged down dealing directly with the airlines themselves, check out the **specialist travel agencies** listed in the box on p.5, who usually get the best discounts going on all routings to St Petersburg. Aside from Transaero's rock-bottom price, you can fly Aeroflot to St Petersburg through CIS Travel from £238, IMS Travel from £239, or Interchange from £249. For indirect flights, Benz Travel offers Finnair flights to St Petersburg from Gatwick (£229) or Manchester (£249), Interchange has SAS or Swissair flights from Manchester (£319) and Finnair (£272) or Austrian Airlines (£293) flights from London, while Farnley Travel offers Swissair flights from Manchester (£300). Interchange also offers a one-way ticket from London to St Petersburg via Vienna on Lauda Air/Austrian Airlines (£188).

It's also worth checking with **discount ticket agents** (see box on p.4), such as the youth-and-student specialists Usit Campus or STA, and exploring **Web sites** such as *www.atab.co.uk*, *www.cheapflights.com* and *www.lastminute.com* (but be aware that the search engine on www.cheapflights.com can't distinguish between St Petersburg in Russia and St Petersburg in Florida, even if you enter the right airport code – LED – in the destination slot).

You might also want to investigate **low-cost airlines** such as Buzz, easyJet and Ryanair, which sometimes offer amazingly cheap fares to cities from where cheap onward connections to St

AIRLINES

Aeroflot ☎ 020/7355 2233, *www.aeroflot.co.uk*

Air Baltic ☎ 020/7393 1207

Austrian Airlines ☎ 020/7434 7300, *www.aua.com*

British Airways ☎ 0345/222111, *www.british-airways.com*

Buzz ☎ 0870/240 7070, *www.buzzaway.com*

CSA ☎ 020/7255 1898, *www.csa.cz*

easyJet ☎ 0870/600 0000, *www.easyjet.com*

Estonian Air ☎ 020/7333 0196, *www.estonian-air.ee*

Finnair London ☎ 020/7408 1222, Manchester ☎ 0161/499 0294, *www.finnair.com*

KLM UK ☎ 08705/074074, *www.klmuk.com*

Lufthansa ☎ 0345/737747, *www.lufthansa.co.uk*

Ryanair ☎ 0870/156 9569, *www.ryanair.com*

Sabena ☎ 0845/601 0933, *www.sabena.com*

SAS ☎ 0845/607 2772, *www.sas.se*

Swissair 020/7434 7300, *www.swissair.com*

Transaero ☎ 020/7436 6767

DISCOUNT TICKET AGENTS

Airborn Travel, 50a Fenchurch St, London EC3M 3JY ☎ 020/7929 3616, *www.airborn.co.uk*

Benz Travel, 83 Mortimer St, London W1R 7PV ☎ 020/7462 0000, *www.benztravel.co.uk*

Farnley Travel, 4 Royal Opera Arcade, Haymarket, London SW1Y 4UY ☎ 020/7930 7679

North South Travel, Moulsham Mill Centre, Parkway, Chelmsford, Essex CM2 7PX ☎ 01245/608291

STA Travel (*www.statravel.co.uk*), 86 Old Brompton Rd, London SW7 3LH; 117 Euston Rd, London NW1 2SX; 38 Store St, London WC1E 7BZ ☎ 020/7361 6161; 25 Queens Rd, Bristol BS8 1QE ☎ 0117/929 4399; 38 Sidney St, Cambridge CB2 3HX ☎ 01223/366966; 75 Deansgate, Manchester M3 2BW ☎ 0161/834 0668; 88 Vicar Lane, Leeds LS1 7JH ☎ 0113/244 9212; 78 Bold St, Liverpool L1 4HR ☎ 0151/707 1123; 9 St Mary's Place, Newcastle-upon-Tyne NE1 7PG ☎ 0191/233 2111; 36 George St, Oxford OX1 2OJ ☎ 01865/792800; 30 Upper Kirkgate St, Aberdeen ☎ 0122/465 8222; and branches on university campuses in Birmingham, Canterbury, Cardiff, Coventry, Durham, Glasgow, Loughborough, Nottingham, Warwick and Sheffield

Trailfinders (*www.trailfinders.co.uk*), 1 Threadneedle Street, London EC2R 8JX ☎ 020/7628 7628; 215 Kensington High St, London W6 6BD ☎ 020/7937 5400; 58 Deansgate, Manchester M3 2FF ☎ 0161/839 6969; 254–284 Sauchiehall St, Glasgow G2 3EH ☎ 0141/353 2224; 22–24 The Priory, Queensway, Birmingham B4 6BS ☎ 0121/236 1234; 48 Corn St, Bristol BS1 1HQ ☎ 0117/929 9000

Travel Bug, 597 Cheetham Hill Rd, Manchester M8 5EJ ☎ 0161/721 4000; 125a Gloucester Road, London SW7 4SF ☎ 020/7835 2000

Travel Cuts, 295a Regent St, London W1R 7YA ☎ 020/7255 1944; *www.travelcuts.co.uk*

Usit Campus (*www.usitcampus.co.uk*), national call centre ☎ 0870/240 1010; 52 Grosvenor Gardens, London SW1W 0AG ☎ 020/7730 3402; 541 Bristol Rd, Selly Oak, Birmingham B29 6AU ☎ 0121/414 1848; 61 Ditchling Rd, Brighton BN1 4SD ☎ 01273/570 226; 37–39 Queen's Rd, Clifton, Bristol BS8 1QE ☎ 0117/929 2494; 5 Emmanuel St, Cambridge CB1 1NE ☎ 01223/324 283; 53 Forest Rd, Edinburgh EH1 2QP ☎ 0131/225 6111, telesales 668 3303; 122 George St, Glasgow G1 1RF ☎ 0141/553 1818; 166 Deansgate, Manchester M3 3FE ☎ 0161/833 2046, telesales 273 1721; 105–106 St Aldates, Oxford OX1 1DO ☎ 01865/242 067.

Usit Council, 28a Poland St, London W1V 3DB ☎ 020/7287 3337 or 437 7767.

SPECIALIST TRAVEL AGENTS AND TOUR OPERATORS

CIS Travel Services, 5 Hobart Place, London SW1W 0HU ☎ 020/7393 1212, *cistravel@chapman-freeborn.co.uk*
Agent for Aeroflot, Air Baltic, Transaero and other CIS airlines. Visa services.

Findhorn EcoTravels, The Park, Forres, Morayshire, IV36 OTZ ☎ 01309/690995, *www.rmplc.co.uk/eduweb/sites/ecoliza*
Affiliated to the Ecologia Trust, a charity running youth exchanges and a summer language school at the Kitezh children's community, Kaluga. Can arrange visa support, flights, flat rental, homestays and hostel accommodation in St Petersburg.

GW Travel, 6 Old Market Place, Altrincham, Cheshire WA14 4NP ☎ 0161/928 9410, *www.gwtravel.co.uk*
Private railway tours of the CIS, including St Petersburg and the Baltic States by steam train.

IMS Travel, 9 Mandeville Place, London W1U 3AU ☎ 020/7224 4678, *info@imstravel.co.uk*
General sales agent for Aeroflot.

Inntel-Moscow Travel Co. Ltd, Orchard House, 167–169 High St Kensington, London W8 6SH ☎ 020/7937 7207, *www.russia-travel.com*
Visa support, flights and hotel bookings within the CIS.

Interchange, Interchange House, 27 Stafford Rd, Croydon CR0 4NG ☎ 020/8681 3612, *interchange@interchange.uk.com*
Tailored short breaks, flights, hotel and homestay bookings; tours to Georgia and Armenia.

Intourist, 219 Marsh Wall, London E14 9PD ☎ 020/7538 8600; Suite 2f, Central Buildings, 211 Deansgate, Manchester M3 3NW ☎ 0161/834 0230; *www.intourist.com*
St Petersburg–Moscow cruises and two-centre

breaks; St Petersburg and Helsinki city breaks; Trans-Siberian packages; independent travel (no homestays).

Norvista, 227 Regent St, London W1R 8PD ☎ 020/7409 7334, *www.norvista.co.uk*
Scandinavian and Baltic specialists, acting as ferry and rail agents in the region and also offering packages including two Baltic cruises featuring St Petersburg, and trips combining Helsinki and St Petersburg.

Progressive Tours, 12 Porchester Place, London W2 2BS ☎ 020/7262 1676, *101533.513@compuserve.com*
Flights, accommodation and services.

Scott's Tours, 141 Whitfield St, London W1T 5EV ☎ 020/7383 5353, *www.scottstours.co.uk*
Specialists in discount flights to the CIS, visa support, accommodation and other services.

The Russia Experience, Research House, Fraser Rd, Perivale, Middx UB6 7AQ ☎ 020/8566 8846, *www.trans-siberian.co.uk*
Trans-Siberian specialists in individual and small group travel, from B&B in St Petersburg to exploring Tuva, Mongolia and China. During summer, they operate the Beetroot Bus between Moscow and St Petersburg (see p.10).

The Russia House Ltd, 50 Southwark St ,London SE1 1RU ☎ 020/7450 3262, *www.therussiahouse.ltd.co*
Visa support, hotel bookings and other services, mainly for business travellers.

Voyages Jules Verne, 21 Dorset Square, London NW1 6QG ☎ 020/7616 1000, *www.vjv.co.uk*
Two Baltic cruises including St Petersburg, and a cruise combining it with Moscow, Uglich and Kizhi.

Petersburg are available. Although these deals are subject to restrictions and you'll also have to sort out an onward flight – which you'll probably have to buy on the spot abroad – they can be economical for those flying from regional airports. Possible routings include Ryanair from Glasgow to Frankfurt or Paris, and from London to Stockholm or Frankfurt; easyJet to Amsterdam from Edinburgh or Liverpool; and Buzz from Stansted to Frankfurt, Berlin, Vienna or Helsinki.

If you have more time for the journey, it's feasible to use Finland, Estonia or Latvia as jumping-off points for overland travel to St Petersburg. Helsinki is the obvious choice given Buzz's one-way fare, or you might go via the beautiful city of Tallinn with a return flight on Estonian Air (£265) or the Latvian capital Riga on Air Baltic (from £244). Estonian Air flies from Gatwick (daily except Sat) and Air Baltic from Heathrow (daily). The Riga flight involves a stopover at

Copenhagen or Stockholm, and uses SAS for the initial leg. See "Approaches from Finland, Estonia and Latvia" (p.9) for information on overland travel to St Petersburg.

Package tours

Given the price of flights to and hotels in St Petersburg, there's a strong incentive to look for a **package tour** – an easy way of cutting the cost and trouble of organizing a trip. There are all kinds of tours, from city breaks to Trans-Siberian tours and luxury cruises. Unless otherwise stated, all prices below are for one person in a twin share; where two prices are given, these refer to low- and high-season rates.

The former Soviet travel agency, **Intourist**, offers a range of packages that include flights, hotels and escorted visits. You can spend three nights in St Petersburg in a three-star (£345–499) or de luxe (£599–859) hotel, go for a Moscow/St Petersburg package featuring three nights in each city in de luxe hotels (£1099–1349), or combine St Petersburg with Helsinki in a seven-night package (from £615). By comparison, **Interchange** does three nights in St Petersburg for £395–539, while **Norvista**'s week-long St Petersburg/Moscow package costs £844–906. Neither features any guided tours.

Other operators' packages cover accommodation, transfers and the services of a guide, but not flights, since it's assumed that clients are travelling to Russia under their own steam – though flights and visas can be arranged if needed. **The Russia Experience** does an eight-day twin-centre deal starting in St Petersburg and ending in Moscow, with an overnight train journey between the two, using either hotels (£500) or half-board in a Russian home (£360), or a tri-centre package including Novgorod (£465), based on half-board homestay accommodation.

From May to September, a luxuriously laid-back option is **to cruise** from St Petersburg to Moscow via the magical Kizhi Island and the historic Volga towns of Yaroslavl, Kostroma and Uglich. All the packages on offer include return flights and last eleven or twelve days. Intourist's cruise (£989–£1035) features the monastic island of Valaam on its itinerary, unlike the otherwise similar Voyages Jules Verne (£995–1085), Norvista and Noble Caledonia cruises. Alternatively, you could visit St Petersburg as part of a two-week odyssey around the "Great Cities of the Baltic", on one of two itineraries offered by Voyages Jules Verne (£895 or £995). Another

Baltic itinerary is offered by GW Travel, whose twelve-day tour (£2295) by private steam train starts and finishes in St Petersburg and includes Tallinn and Riga on its list of stops.

The other main area of Russian tourism is **Trans-Siberian railway packages** and "soft adventure" spin-offs in Siberia or Mongolia. Although most tourists heading eastwards on the Trans-Sib are bound for Beijing rather than the Russian Pacific port city of Vladivostok, the attractions en route are identical until the lines diverge at Ulan Ude in the Buryat region of Siberia. Intourist's sixteen-day Moscow–Beijing trip includes visits to Irkutsk, Lake Baikal, the Great Wall and the Ming Tombs, plus return flights from Britain (£1379–1499), while The Russia Experience offers numerous land-only trips starting in Moscow or St Petersburg and ending up in China, Mongolia or Vladivostok, from a basic fifteen-day trip to Beijing that includes cycling by Lake Baikal and staying in a felt tent on the Mongolian steppes (£860) to a mega-trip (£1570) featuring jeep trekking in the Karakorum Desert, with forays into Buryatia or Tuva to witness Buddhist and shamanistic traditions or the Altay Mountains to go white-water rafting as add-on extras.

By train

Travelling **by train** from London to St Petersburg takes two nights and three days. Still, if you've got the time to spare and a taste for adventure, it can be an enjoyable way of getting there.

Train information

European Rail Ltd, Tavistock House North, Tavistock Square, London WC1H 9HR ☎ 020/7387 04444, *www.inter-rail.co.uk* Agents for InterRail, Eurostar and European railways.

Eurostar, Eurostar House, Waterloo Station, London SE1 8SE ☎ 0990/186186, *www.eurostar.com*

Wasteels, Platform #2, Victoria Station, London SW1V 1JY ☎ 020/7834 7066 Agent for Polrail (Polish) and Scandinavian rail passes.

Eurotunnel, Customer Service Centre, jct #12 off M20, PO Box 300, Folkestone, Kent CT19 4DQ ☎ 0990/353535, *www.eurotunnel.com*

VISA REQUIREMENTS FOR OVERLAND TRAVEL

The following list covers requirements for nationals of Britain, Ireland, the US, Canada, Australia and New Zealand. Nationals of other countries should consult the relevant embassy (see list below).

Belarus

All foreigners need visas.

Australia/New Zealand No embassies or consulates; contact the Russian Embassy (see p.22). Online visas can be obtained from *www.visitrussia.com*. Single-entry tourist visas US$75.

Canada 130 Albert St, Suite 600, Ottawa, ON K1R 5G4 ☎ 613/233-9994, *www.belarusembassy.org* Single-entry tourist/transit visas CDN$35, double-entry CDN$62.

UK 6 Kensington Court, London W8 5DL ☎ 020/7937 3288 or 020/7938 3677, *http://belemb.port5.com* Double-entry transit visa £20 (allow 5–10 working days).

US 1619 New Hampshire Ave NW, Washington, DC 20009 ☎ 202/986-1606, *www.belarusembassy.org* Transit visa $50 (allow 5 working days).

Estonia

Visa required by Canadians.

Australia/New Zealand 86 Louisa Road, Birchgrove, NSW 2141 ☎ 02/9810 7468

Canada 958 Broadview Ave, Toronto, ON M4K 2R6 ☎ 416/461-0764, *www.estemb.org* Single-entry tourist visa CDN$21, double-entry CDN$42.

UK 16 Hyde Park Gate, London SW7 5DG ☎ 020/7589 3428, *Embassy.London@estonia.gov.uk*

US 2131 Massachusetts Ave NW, Washington, DC 20008 ☎ 202/588-0101, *www.estemb.org*

Latvia

Canadians, Australians and New Zealanders require visas.

Australia/New Zealand 32 Parnell Street, Strathfield, NSW 2135 ☎ 02/9744 5981 Single-entry tourist visa A$40/NZ$50.

Canada 280 Albert St, Suite 300, Ottawa, ON K1P 5G8 ☎ 613/238-6868 Single-entry tourist visa CDN$20, double-entry CDN$30. Single-entry transit visa CDN$10, double-entry CDN$20.

UK 45 Nottingham Place, London W1M 3FE ☎ 020/7312 0040..

US 4325 17th St NW, Washington, DC 20011 ☎ 202/726-8213

Lithuania

No visa required.

Australia/New Zealand No embassy.

Canada 235 Yorkland Blvd, Suite 502, Willowdale, ON M2J 4Y8 ☎ 416/538-2992

UK 84 Gloucester Place, London W1H 3HN ☎ 020/7486 6401

US 2622 16th St NW, Washington, DC 20009 ☎ 202/234-5860, *www.ltembassyus.org*

Poland

Canadians, Australians and New Zealanders require visas.

Australia 7 Turrana St, Yarralumla, Canberra, ACT 2600 ☎ 06/6273 1208 Single-entry tourist visa A$85, multiple-entry A$155.

Canada 443 Daly Ave, Ottawa, ON K1N 6H3 ☎ 613/789-0468, *www.polonianet.com/pol/ambasada* Single-entry tourist visa CDN$89, multiple-entry CDN$207. Single-entry transit visa CDN$33, multiple-entry CDN$96.

Ireland 5 Ailesbury Rd, Dublin 4 ☎ 01/283 0855

New Zealand 17 Upland Rd, Kelburn, Wellington ☎ 04/475 9453 Single-entry tourist visa NZ$85, multiple-entry NZ$155

UK 73 Cavendish St, London W1M 8LS ☎ 020/7580 0476 or 0900/1600 0358 (premium line rates); 4 Palmerston Rd, Sheffield S1D 2TE ☎ 014/276-6513

US 2640 16th St NW, Washington, DC 20009 ☎ 202/234 3800, *www.polishworld.com/polemb*; 12400 Wilshire Blvd, Suite 555, Los Angeles, CA 90025 ☎ 310/442-8500; a list of other US consulates can be found on *www.pan.net/konsulat*

A regular second-class return **ticket** from London (bookable through some high-street travel agents or with International Rail at London's Victoria Station) will currently set you back £370 via the Channel Tunnel – the fare includes a surcharge (£75) for a sleeper on the outward journey, but not for the return journey, which must be paid for in St Petersburg.

A more flexible option is the **InterRail pass**, available in under-26 and over-26 versions, both covering 28 European countries (including Turkey and Morocco) grouped together in zones. The one-zone pass is valid for 22 days and costs £129 for under-26s, £179 for those 26 and over. The two-zone, three-zone and all-zone passes are all valid for a month: two zones cost £169 for under-26s, £235 for 26s and over; three zones £195/£269; and the all-zone pass costs £219/£309. Sadly, none of them are valid in Russia, Belarus, Ukraine or the Baltic States, though they can still be useful if you're including St Petersburg as part of a longer European trip. Passes are available from major train stations or travel agents and must be purchased at least 14 days in advance; there's a £5 discount for online bookings and a £3 charge for credit card bookings. To qualify for the pass you must have been resident in one of the participating countries for at least six months.

The journey

There are no direct train services from London to St Petersburg, but four times a week there's an overnight train from Brussels to Berlin that connects with an onward service to St Petersburg. The train departs from Brussels at 11.30pm, so passengers travelling on Eurostar via the Channel Tunnel need to catch the 7.27pm Eurostar from London – which gives you 25 minutes to make the connection – or an earlier service to be on the safe side. Arriving at Berlin Ostbahnhof at 8am next day, you must change trains or take the U-Bahn to Berlin-Lichtenberg, whence the train to St Petersburg departs at 3pm, arriving at St Petersburg's Vitebsk Station around dawn two days later.

The route goes through Germany, Poland and Belarus. The most stringent customs check comes at Brest on the Polish–Belarus border, where trains are jacked up in order to change to the wide-gauge Russian railtracks (which were designed to make it difficult for invaders to use the network). It's a good idea to bring food and

drink for the whole journey, since there's nothing available in Russian wagons except hot water from the samovar, and the odd can of beer.

Besides transit **visas** for Poland and Belarus (see "Visa requirements for overland travel" box) you'll need to obtain a Russian visa before you leave (p.21), as they are not issued at border crossings.

By coach

Though it's a route that's unlikely to appeal to many, you can reach St Petersburg **by coach from Berlin or Frankfurt** – both cities which are readily accessible from Britain by low-cost airlines (see p.4). The service is operated by Eurolines Russia (www.eurolines.ru), an affiliate of the European-wide bus company Eurolines, and is mainly used by Russians travelling to Germany. Their coaches leave the central bus station in Frankfurt and Berlin on Tuesdays and Fridays, and arrive outside St Petersburg's Baltic Station two days later. It's cheaper to travel from Berlin (£37/$52 one-way, £61/$87 return) than from Frankfurt (£43/$61, £73/$104). Tickets can be booked through BEX (☎030/3022 5294) in Berlin's central bus station, or DTG (☎069/790 3250) at Mannheimerstr. 4, in Frankfurt.

Another, more roundabout route is to go from Germany **via Estonia**. Eurolines Estonia (www.eurolines.ee) run coaches to Tallinn from Berlin (Tues, Wed & Sat; 28hr; £50/$71 one-way, £89/$127 return), Munich (Wed; 38hr; £61/$87, £110/$156) and Cologne (Tues, Wed & Sat; 38hr; £61/$87, £110/$156). From Tallinn, you can continue on to St Petersburg by Eurolines Russia coach or by train (see "Approaches via Finland, Estonia and Latvia", p.10).

A still longer route is from Germany **via Latvia**, using the Eurolines Estonia service to Riga from Berlin (Sat, Sun & Tues, plus Fri during summer; 22hr; £43/$61 one-way, £79/$113 return), Hamburg (Sun & Tues; 26hr; £49/$69, £90/$128), Munich (Sat; 32hr; £52/$74, £95/$135) or Cologne (Fri summer only; 33hr; £52/$74, £95/$135). From Riga there's a Eurolines Russia coach to St Petersburg (see "Approaches via Finland, Estonia and Latvia", p.10).

Although coach fares are extremely cheap, you have to consider the cost of transit visas for Poland or Belarus (see "Visa requirements for overland travel" box on p.7). You'll also need to obtain a Russian visa in advance (see p.21).

By car

It doesn't make a lot of sense to travel from Britain to St Petersburg **by car**, especially since Western vehicles are so vulnerable to unwelcome attention in Russia, but if you're intent on doing so, the easiest and most economical route is **via Sweden and Finland**. The ferry companies (see box on below) encourage customers to book well ahead, since it would be awful to reach Sweden and find all ferries to Finland booked up for days to come.

The first stage involves taking a DFDS Seaways car ferry from Newcastle to Gothenburg (Mon & Fri; 27hr). A standard return costs from £108 per person (car included), but you can economize by booking at least 21 days ahead for a "Seapex" ticket (from £84) or four months ahead for a "Superseapex" (from £69). Three or four people travelling together by car might do better with an all-in-car fare (from £319 per vehicle), which can be purchased at any time.

From Gothenburg you drive to Stockholm to board one of the huge and lavishly equipped Silja or Viking ferries to Helsinki (daily 9am & 5pm; 16–17hr). The high-season fare for a single person sharing a four-berth cabin is £38/$55; a car costs £14/$20. From Helsinki, it's 350km by road to St Petersburg, a journey of about six hours – expect to be stuck in a queue of vehicles for an hour or more on both the Finnish and Russian sides of the border, which has several checkpoints over 15km of road, before Vyborg. While the main road to Petersburg is now far safer than it was in the early 1990s, it still pays to be careful for whom you stop.

Ferry Companies and agents

DFDS Seaways ☎ 0990/333000 or 0191/296 0101, *www.dfds.co.uk*
Newcastle to Gothenburg.

Emagine UK Ltd ☎ 01942/262662, *res@emagine-travel.co.uk*
Agents for Viking ferries from Stockholm to Helsinki.

Norvista ☎ 020/7409 7334, *www.norvista.co.uk*
Agents for Silja and Viking ferries from Stockholm to Helsinki.

Tallink *www.tallink.ee*
Helsinki to Tallinn.

A more roundabout way is to travel **via Estonia** – if only to see the stunning medieval centre of Tallinn. There are regular Tallink car ferries from Helsinki to Tallinn throughout the year (5 daily; 4hr; £9/$14 one-way, car £5/$8), while Tallink's Express Autocatamarans zip across in one hour forty minutes (2–3 daily; £16 one-way, car £5/$8). A third company, Lindaline, operates a daily hydrofoil that cuts another twenty minutes off the journey (£12/$18) – but it doesn't carry vehicles.

Driving licence and insurance requirements in Russia are covered on p.33.

Approaches via Finland, Estonia and Latvia

Travelling **from Helsinki** to St Petersburg offers the widest choice of transportation, and was for many years the most popular approach with those travelling around Europe **by train**. Although none of the European rail passes are valid for services to St Petersburg, the second-class fare (£29/$41 one way, £58/$82 return) isn't exorbitant, and tickets are easily available in Helsinki. There are two trains daily: the Finnish *Sibelius* (early in the morning) and the Russian *Repin* (in the afternoon) – both are comfortable and do the 350km journey in seven hours, stopping at Vyborg (see p.385) en route to St Petersburg's Finland Station. Details of both can be obtained from Finnish Railways' Web site (*www.vr.fi/heo/itaane.htm*).

Alternatively, there are two daily **coaches** operated by Finnord and Saimaan Liikenne Oy. These two companies share offices in Helsinki's main bus station (☎3580/607718) and at Vyborg and St Petersburg (see box on p.10), have identical fares, routes, stopovers and coaches (with airconditioning, toilets and videos) – the only difference is the colour of their vehicles. They leave Helsinki at 9am and 11pm, arriving in St Petersburg eight hours later, where they stop at Finnord's office and the *Astoria Hotel* before terminating at the *Pulkovskaya Hotel*. Tickets should be booked one or two days ahead; the one-way fare to St Petersburg is about £28/$40; returns cost double.

One final option is to join one of the "booze cruises" to St Petersburg (from one to several days' duration) that sail **from Kotka**, west of Helsinki. The main organiser is Kristina Cruises, based in Helsinki. You are required to submit

Coach and ferry agents in St Petersburg

Eurolines Russia ul. Shkapina 10 ☎168 27 40, *www.eurolines.ru*
Coach operators to the Baltic States and Germany.

Finnord Italyanskaya ul. 37 ☎314 89 51
Ticket agents (and the point of departure) for both coach lines to Helsinki.

Norvista Kazanskaya ul. 44 ☎326 18 50
Agents for Silja line and other Scandinavian ferries.

passport details to the ferry operator five to fourteen days before departure to be registered with the Russian authorities, but you don't need a visa providing you sleep on the boat. In Britain, Norvista can arrange tickets.

Travelling **from Tallinn**, the Estonian capital, is increasingly popular with backpackers and a major route for commercial travellers and smugglers, so most vehicles are packed with luggage and the border formalities are long and rigorous. Eurolines Russia runs five coaches daily from Tallinn (5–7 hr; £7/$11 one-way), terminating outside St Petersburg's Baltic Station, near their office on ulitsa Shkapina. For bookings in Tallinn, contact MootoReisi AS, Lastekadu 46 (☎372/601 0700). Alternatively, there's the daily EVR express train leaving at 11pm and arriving at St Petersburg's Baltic Station at 8am next day. A second-class sleeper costs £10/$15 one-way. Tickets are sold by EVR Ekspress Reisid in Tallinn station.

Travelling **from Riga**, the Latvian capital, is the longest of the three journeys to St Petersburg. There is a daily Eurolines Russia coach at 6pm, arriving at 8am next day outside the Baltic Station. The one-way fare is about £7/$11. Book in Riga on ☎371/750 3135. There is also an overnight train taking twelve hours (£45/$63 one-way first class).

Anyone approaching St Petersburg via Finland, Estonia or Latvia should be sure to obtain a **Russian visa** beforehand, as they are not issued at border crossings, and may not be easily available from the Russian consulates in Helsinki, Tallinn or Riga either. Citizens of some nationalities might also require an Estonian or Latvian visa, again only obtainable in advance.

Onward travel to Moscow

From St Petersburg, many tourists **travel on to Moscow by train**. Of the fifteen trains from St Petersburg's Moscow Station, the fastest are daytime services, the *ER-200* (Mon & Thurs; 5hr) and the *Aurora* (daily; 6hr), which have comfortable seating and provide a fine view of the countryside en route. However, most people prefer to travel overnight (8–9hr) on the *Krasnaya Strela Express*, the *Nikolaevskiy*, the *Express* or the *Afanasiy Nikitin* (all daily), which arrive in Moscow at a reasonable hour in the morning. Though unjustly notorious for robberies, the risk is slight providing you secure the door handle with the plastic device provided, or insert a wedge into the flip-lock in the upper left corner of the door. Shortly after leaving St Petersburg the sleeping-car attendant will come around dispensing

---

THE BEETROOT BUS

The **Beetroot Bus** is an agreeable compromise between packaged and independent travel, which enables foreigners to see something of provincial Russia without all the usual hassles. From July to September, the bus runs once a week between St Petersburg and Moscow, visiting or staying overnight at Novgorod, Kostroma and other places of interest. The trip includes guided tours of monasteries and museums, and experiences such as a *banya* beside the River Volga. Passengers can join the tour in either St Petersburg or Moscow at a few days' notice.

There's a full fifteen-day tour ($750) starting and finishing in Moscow, or an eight-day "half" tour ($395) beginning in either city and ending in the other one. The price includes accommodation en route and two or three nights at either end, but not meals.

Full details appear on *www.beetroot.org*. For bookings contact The Russia Experience in London (see p.5) or Moscow (☎095/453 43 68, fax 095/456 66 06, *info@trans-siberian.co.uk*). The bus departs from the *St Petersburg International Hostel* (see p.274) and the *Travellers Guesthouse* in Moscow.

sheets (for a surcharge), and offering tea to passengers in first class.

While the journey is easy enough, buying **tickets** is another matter, as speculators often purchase them en masse for resale at a profit, and there are usually long queues at the ticket offices in Moscow Station or the Railway Bookings Office at nab. kanala Gribeoedova 24 (Mon–Sat 8am–8pm, Sun 8am–4pm), which has a special section for foreigners (upon entering turn right immediately, right again and head upstairs to the second floor). You might have more luck at the Business Centre (daily 8am–11.45pm; ☎279 89 62) on the second floor of Moscow Station, or there's a service where you can book by phone (☎162 44 55) and have the tickets delivered to your address (payable on delivery); both options involve a surcharge ($3–5). Always bring your passport along, since tickets are sold to named individuals only, and conductors invariably make identity checks before allowing passengers on board the train.

Alternatively, you could consider a more leisurely journey to Moscow, with stopovers in historic towns en route, aboard the Beetroot Bus (see box opposite).

Getting there from Ireland

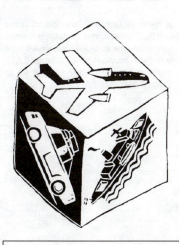

At present there are **no direct flights** to St Petersburg from Ireland, so the best you can hope for is an indirect flight via another hub city. The Russian airline Aeroflot flies to Moscow from Dublin (Sun) and Shannon (Wed & Sun), and sometimes has an onward connection to St Petersburg the same day. Return fares start at IR£280 for an Apex return booked fourteen days in advance for a stay of six days (including a Saturday night) to a month, with unchangeable outward and return dates. Indirect flights on other airlines are generally more expensive than on Aeroflot (excluding special offers or youth/student discounts). Dublin to St Petersburg via Vienna on Austrian Airlines, for example, cost IR£379, while Belfast to St Petersburg via Zurich on Swissair is IR£315.

AIRLINES

Aer Lingus Dublin airport ☎01/844 4777, Belfast ☎0645/737747, Cork ☎021/327155, Limerick ☎061/474239, *www.aerlingus.ie*

Aeroflot Dublin ☎01/844 6166, Shannon Airport ☎061/472 299

British Airways Eire (c/o Aer Lingus) ☎0141/222 2345, Northern Ireland ☎0345/222111, *www.british-airways.com*

British Midland Dublin ☎01/283 8833, Belfast ☎0345/554554, *www.iflybritishmidland.com*

Lufthansa Dublin ☎01/844 5544

Ryanair Dublin ☎01/609 7800, *www.ryanair.com*

Sabena Dublin ☎01/844 5440

SAS Dublin ☎01/844 5440

TRAIN INFORMATION

Continental Rail Desk Dublin ☎ 01/836 6222.
InterRail passes and tickets to Moscow.

Northern Ireland Railways Belfast
☎ 028/9023 0621.
InterRail passes and tickets to Moscow.

TRAVEL AGENTS AND TOUR OPERATORS

Joe Walsh Tours, 8 Lower Baggot St, Dublin 2
☎ 01/676 3053; 69 Upper O'Connell St, Dublin 1
☎ 01/872 2555; 117 St Patrick St, Cork
☎ 021/277111.
General budget fares agent.

Thomas Cook, 11 Donegall Place, Belfast
☎ 028/9055 4555; 118 Grafton St, Dublin 2
☎ 01/677 0469.
Package holiday and flight agent, with occasional discount offers.

Trailfinders, 4–5 Dawson Street, Dublin 2
☎ 01/677 7888.

USIT Now, Fountain Centre, Belfast BT1 6ET
☎ 028/9032 4073; O'Connell Bridge, 19 Aston
Quay, Dublin 2 ☎ 01/602 1777 or 677 8117;
10–11 Market Parade, Patrick St, Cork
☎ 021/270900; 33 Ferryquay St, Derry
☎ 01504/371888; Victoria Place, Eyre Square,
Galway ☎ 091/565177; Central Buildings,
O'Connell St, Limerick ☎ 061/415064; 36–37
George's St, Waterford ☎ 051/72601.
Student and youth travel specialists.

Other possibilities include KLM via Amsterdam
or Lufthansa via Frankfurt.

It's worth checking also to see if you're better off
flying via London and picking up a connecting flight
or package from there. There are numerous daily
flights from Dublin or Shannon to London, operated
by Ryanair, Aer Lingus and British Midland. Ryanair
have IR£29 midweek returns to Luton or Stansted.
From Belfast, there are BA and British Midland flights
to Heathrow, but you may well be better off flying
easyJet to Amsterdam (IR£32 one-way) for an
onward connection on KLM.

Getting there from North America

There are no direct flights to St Petersburg from the US or Canada; if you travel on Aeroflot (usually the cheapest option) you'll have to go via Moscow – a total flying time of around ten hours, plus any stopovers. Aeroflot flies from Montréal and several US gateways, but for more choice you may wish to travel with another carrier to a European city and get an onward flight or make your way overland there. Helsinki is the closest Western European city to St Petersburg, just seven hours away by train; Berlin is a cheaper, but more distant (36 hours by train or coach), gateway. See "Getting there from Britain" for a complete rundown of the trans-European options. Note that all flight fares quoted are exclusive of tax.

Shopping for tickets

Barring special offers, the cheapest of the airlines' published fares is usually an **Apex** (Advance Purchase Excursion) ticket, although these carry certain restrictions: you will, most likely, have to book – and pay – 21 days before departure, spend at least seven days abroad and limit your stay to between one and three months. Moreover, you will probably get penalized if you change your schedule, and get only a percentage

refund, if any, should you cancel. Check all the restrictions carefully before buying a ticket.

You can normally cut costs further by going through a **specialist flight agent** – either a **consolidator**, who buys up blocks of tickets from the airlines and sells them at a discount, or a discount agent, who in addition to dealing with discounted flights may also offer special student and youth fares and a range of other travel-related services such as travel insurance, rail passes, car rentals, tours and the like. Bear in mind, though, that penalties for changing your plans can be stiff. Remember too that these companies make their money by dealing in bulk – don't expect them to answer lots of questions. If you travel a lot, **discount travel clubs** are another option – the annual membership fee may be worth it for benefits such as cut-price air tickets and car rental.

Don't automatically assume that tickets purchased through a travel specialist will be cheapest – once you get a quote, check with the airlines and you may turn up an even better deal. Be advised also that the pool of travel companies is swimming with sharks – exercise caution and never deal with a company that demands cash up front or refuses to accept payment by credit card.

All ticket prices quoted below are round-trip and exclusive of taxes. Where applicable, fares are for midweek travel. Weekend flights cost around $50–70 extra.

Flights from the US

Aeroflot flies from New York, Miami, Washington DC, Chicago, San Francisco, Seattle and Anchorage to Moscow, from where you can catch a flight on to St Petersburg. The Anchorage flight usually requires an overnight stay in Khabarovsk.

Fares vary according to the time of year, with prices divided into three seasons: **low** (Nov–March, except Christmas/New Year), **shoulder** (April–May, mid-Sept to Oct), and **high** (June

AIRLINES

Aeroflot US ☎1-888/340-6400; Canada ☎514/288-2125, *www.aeroflot.com*
Although you can make reservations directly with Aeroflot, travellers flying from the US will probably find it easier dealing with their agents, Commonwealth Express (US ☎1-800/995-5555, Canada ☎514/288-2125). Aeroflot flies daily to Moscow from New York; twice weekly from Miami and Seattle; three times weekly from Chicago, Washington DC, Anchorage, San Francisco and Montréal.

Air Canada Canada ☎1-800/776-3000, *www.aircanada.ca*

Air France US ☎1-800/237-2747, Canada ☎1-800/667-2747, *www.airfrance.com*
Daily flights from New York JFK and Newark, Washington Dulles, Miami, Houston, Chicago, Los Angeles and San Francisco. Some routes involve overnight stopovers in Paris.

British Airways US ☎1-800/247-9297, Canada ☎1-800/668-1059, *www.britishairways.com*
Daily flights from all their gateways.

CSA Czech Airlines US ☎1-800/223-2365 or 212/765-6022, Canada ☎416/363-3174 (Toronto) and ☎514/844-6376 (Montréal), *www.czechairlines.com*
Four flights weekly from New York, twice weekly from Toronto and once weekly from Montréal.

Delta US and Canada ☎1-800/241-4141, Canada ☎1-800/221-1212, *www.delta.com*
Daily from New York via Vienna or Zurich.

Finnair US ☎1-800/950-5000, Canada ☎1-800/461-8651, *www.finnair.com*
Five flights weekly from New York via Helsinki.

KLM US ☎1-800/447-4747, Canada ☎1-800/361-5370, *www.klm.com*
Daily via Amsterdam.

Lufthansa US ☎1-800/645-3880, Canada ☎1-800/563-5954, *www.lufthansa.com*
Daily via Frankfurt.

DISCOUNT FLIGHT AGENTS, TRAVEL CLUBS AND CONSOLIDATORS

Council Travel (*www.counciltravel.com*), Head Office, 205 E 42nd St, New York, NY 10017 ☎1-888/COUNCIL or 212/822-2700; 530 Bush St, Suite 700, San Francisco, CA 94108 ☎415/421-3473; 3301 M St NW, 2nd Floor, Washington, DC 20007 ☎202/337-6464; 1160 N. State St, Chicago, IL 60610 ☎312/951-0585; 273 Newbury St, Boston, MA 02116 ☎617/266-1926.
Mostly, but by no means exclusively, specializes in student travel.

New Frontiers/Nouvelles Frontières (*www.newfrontiers.com*), 12 E 33rd St, New York, NY 10016 ☎1-800/366-6387 or 212/779-0600; 1001 Sherbrook East, Suite 720, Montréal, PQ H2L 1L3 ☎514/526-8444; plus branches in Los Angeles, San Francisco and Quebec City.
Discount travel firm.

STA Travel (*www.statravel.com*), 10 Downing St, New York, NY 10014 ☎1-800/777-0112 or 212/627-3111; 7202 Melrose Ave, Los Angeles, CA 90046 ☎213/934-8722; 36 Geary St, San Francisco, CA 94108 ☎415/391-8407; 297 Newbury St, Boston, MA 02115 ☎617/266-6014;

429 S Dearborn St, Chicago, IL 60605 ☎312/786 9050; 1905 Walnut St, Philadelphia, PA 19103 ☎215/382-2928; 317 14th Ave SE, Minneapolis, MN 55414 ☎612/615-1800.
Specialists in independent travel.

Travac, 989 6th Ave, New York, NY 10018 ☎1-800/872-8800, *www.travac.com*
Consolidator and charter broker.

Travel Avenue, 10 S Riverside, Suite 1404, Chicago, IL 60606 ☎1-800/333-3335, *www.travelavenue.com*
Discount travel company.

Travel Cuts (*www.travelcuts.com*), 187 College St, Toronto, ON M5T 1P7 ☎1-800/667-2887; 1613 Rue St Denis, Montréal, PQ H2X 3K3 ☎514/843-8511; 555 W 8th Ave, Vancouver, BC V5Z 1C6 ☎888/FLY CUTS or 604/822-6890; plus branches at Calgary, Edmonton and Winnipeg.
Canadian student travel organization.

Unitravel, 11737 Administration Drive, St Louis, MO 63146 ☎1-800/325-2222, *www.unitravel.com*
Consolidator.

SPECIALIST TOUR OPERATORS

Abercrombie and Kent ☎ 1-800/323-7308, *www.abercrombieandkent.com*
Luxury tours and accommodation; nine days in St Petersburg and Moscow from $6975 (flights included).

Adventure Center ☎ 1-800/227-8747, *www.adventurecenter.com*
US division of the UK-based Overland Travel dealing mostly in active holidays. Their 15-day "Treasures of the Tsars" tour (June–Aug; $1455) features Tallinn, Moscow, Suzdal, Yaroslavl, St Petersburg and Finland.

Delta Dream Vacations Eastern Europe ☎ 1-800/872-7786 or 221-2216, *www.general-tours.com*
City breaks and a six-day Moscow–St Petersburg escorted tour package (from $1129, flight included) with an overnight train journey between the two cities.

Elderhostel ☎ 1-877/426-8056, *www.elderhostel.org*
Specialists in educational and activity programmes, cruises and homestays for senior travellers, offering a two-week "Treasures of Russian Art and Literature" tour (from $3347) focused on St Petersburg and Moscow.

Host Families Association (HOFA) ☎ 202/333-9343, *www.webcenter.re/~hofa*
US contact for St Petersburg firm offering private rooms and services in St Petersburg, Moscow and other cities in the former Soviet Union.

IBV Bed and Breakfast Systems ☎ 301/942-3770, fax 933-0024.
Arranges B&B accommodation (singles $75, doubles $85) and visa support in Russia.

International Gay Travel Association ☎ 954/776-3303.
Trade group with lists of gay-owned or gay-friendly travel agents, accommodation and other travel businesses.

International Market Place Tours ☎ 1-800/641-3456, *www.imp-world-tours*
Nine-day journey between Moscow and St Petersburg from $2049 (flight included).

Intourist USA ☎ 1-800/556-5305, *www2.intourist.com*
Individual, group, special-interest and educational tours. "The Wonders of Russian Art and Culture" tours include six days in Petersburg (from $679, depending on level of accommodation, flights not included).

Intours Corporation Canada ☎ 1-800/268-1785 or 416/766-4720, *www.intourist.ru*
Canadian affiliate of Intourist, with tours featuring St Petersburg, Moscow, the Golden Ring, Siberia and the Russian Far East. Their Web site belongs to Intourist in Russia, and is years out of date.

Mir Corporation ☎ 1-800/424-7289, *www.mircorp.com*
Seattle-based company offering a huge range of small group tours on diverse themes such as Siberian shamanism or the Gulag Archipelago, besides more mainstream St Petersburg and Moscow packages, including homestays.

Pioneer Tours and Travel ☎ 1-800/369-1322, *www.pioneerrussia.com*
Customized individual tours, special-interest and educational tours to suit a wide range of budgets, plus homestays (half-board $37.50 per person per night) and Trans-Siberian Railway trips (approximately $4000).

Russiatours, Inc ☎ 1-800/633-1008, *www.exeterinternational.com*
Offers four de luxe tours focused on St Petersburg, including a thirteen-day cruise featuring Uglich, Kostroma and Kizhi ($3500) and a ten-day trip with three days in Moscow and one day in Helsinki (from $4250).

Russia House ☎ 202/986-6010, fax 667-4244, *www.russiahouse.org*
Arranges visas, registration, tickets and accommodation in Russia, mainly for business travellers.

Russian Travel Bureau ☎ 1-800/847-1800 or 212/986-1500, *www.russiantravelbureau.com*
Eight-day stays in Moscow and St. Petersburg from $899 (including flight).

Russian Travel Service ☎ & fax 603/585-6534.
Arranges visas, B&B accommodation and other services.

Saga Holidays ☎ 1-877/265-6862, *www.sagaholidays.com*
Specialists in group travel for seniors, with a four-teen-night Baltic cruise featuring St Petersburg during May, June & Sept (from $3099).

to mid-September & Christmas/New Year). Aeroflot fares from New York start from $700/$850 (low/high seasons). Fares from Chicago for the different seasons are around $700/$800 and, from San Francisco and Seattle, $800/$900. **European carriers** usually offer more flexibility, although they tend to be pricier than Aeroflot. Excluding special offers, expect to pay around $850/$1150 (low/high season) from New York, $950/$1050 from Chicago, and $1070/$1400 from LA.

Flights from Canada

Aeroflot flies once a week to St Petersburg from Montréal via Moscow (CDN$900–$1000, depending on the time of year), while British Airways flies daily from Montréal and Toronto (CDN$1100–$1400) and Vancouver (CDN$1405–1950) via London. KLM, Air France and Lufthansa all fly daily from Toronto and Montréal via their home bases, with similar fares to those of British Airways. Air Canada fly from a wide variety of Canadian gateways to Paris, London or Frankfurt, where you can connect with a European carrier. Whether you're a student or not, it's worth checking with the student/youth agency Travel Cuts (see p.14) for their latest flight deals.

Package tours

Given the current changeable situation in the Russian Federation, it's hardly surprising that **agencies specializing in Russian travel** tend to come and go. Pioneer Tours and Travel (see p.15) is an excellent source of up-to-date advice, and also has information on cheap flight deals, while the Russian National Tourist Office (☎212/758-1162) can also be helpful if you can get them to answer the phone. Several companies offer **package tours** to St Petersburg, either as a single destination or as part of a longer itinerary – see the box on p.15 for details. For example, Delta Dream Vacations Eastern Europe offers a five-day, three-night tour of St Petersburg, starting from $999 in low season. The Russian Travel Bureau and the Mir Corporation are specialists in the area and offer a variety of tours.

Travelling by train

If you have the time, travelling by train from Britain or elsewhere in Europe to Russia (see p.6 for full details) can be a rewarding experience. Unfortunately, the various types of **Eurail pass**, valid for unlimited travel in sixteen European countries, are not valid in Russia, Belarus, Poland, Ukraine or the Baltic States, so it's only worth getting one if you plan to travel fairly extensively around Europe by train in addition to visiting St Petersburg.

The **Eurail Youthpass** (for under-26s) costs US$388 for 15 days, US$499 for 21 days; $623 for one month or $882 for two months; if you're 26 or over you'll have to buy a **first-class pass**, available in 15-day ($554), 21-day ($718), one-month ($890), two-month ($1260) or three-month ($1558) forms.

You stand a better chance of getting your money's worth out of a **Eurail Flexipass**, which is good for a certain number of days' travel within a two-month period. This also comes in under-26 and over-26 versions: a pass valid for ten days' travel costs $458/$654, for fifteen days, $599/$862. If you're travelling with at least one other person, your best option is probably the **Eurail Saverpass**, which covers two to five peo-

---

RAIL CONTACTS

CIT Tours, 9501 W Devon Ave, Suite 502, Rosemont, IL 60018 ☎1-800/CIT-RAIL, *www.cit-tours.com*

DER Tours/GermanRail, US: 9501 W Devon Ave, Suite 400, Rosemont, IL 60018 ☎1-800/421-2929; Canada: 904 East Mal, Etobicoke, ON M9B 6K2 ☎416/695-1209, *www.dertravel.com*

Nouvelles Frontières, 1001 Sherbrook East, Suite 720, Montréal, PQ H2L 1L3 ☎514/526-8444, *www.newfrontiers.com*

Rail Europe, 226 Westchester Ave, White Plains, NY 10604 ☎1-800/4EURAIL (US), ☎1-800/361-RAIL (Canada), *www.raileurope.com* Agents for Eurail passes and rail tickets within Russia.

ScanTours, 1535 6th St, Suite 205, Santa Monica, CA 90401 ☎1-800/223-7226, *www.scantours.com*

ple travelling together and costs $470 for 15 consecutive days' travel, $610 for 21 days, $756 for a month, $1072 for two months, or $1324 for three. Another version of this pass, the **Saver Flexipass**, also valid for two to five people trav-elling together, costs $556 for ten days or $732 for fifteen days' travel within a two-month period.

Details of **visa requirements** for Belarus, Poland, the Baltic States and Ukraine are given on p.7.

Getting there from Australia and New Zealand

There are no direct flights from Australia or New Zealand to St Petersburg; all involve either a transfer or a stopover in the airline's home city and can take up to 24 hours in all. If you have plenty of time and an adventurous spirit there are several plane–train combinations that will get you to St Petersburg and beyond, such as the Trans-Siberian deals available from specialist tour operators (see box on p.19).

Flights

Air **fares** reflect the time of year you travel in, being divided into low season (mid-Jan to Feb and Oct–Nov), high season (mid-May to Aug and Dec to mid-Jan) and shoulder season (rest of the year). Tickets purchased direct from the airlines tend to be expensive; **discount flight agents**, such as Flight Centres, STA and Trailfinders (see box on p.14), offer much better deals on fares, have the latest information on any special deals and can also help with visas, travel insurance and tours. You might also want to have a look on the Internet: *www.travel.com.au* offers discounted fares online, as does *www.sydneytravel.com*.

Qantas and Air New Zealand team up with a number of European carriers to provide a reliable connecting service from major Australian and New Zealand cities to St. Petersburg. The cheapest fares are with Aeroflot, via Singapore and Moscow (from A$1600/NZ$2000 low season to A$2200/NZ$2600 high season), while for a more comfortable flight, KLM fly via Amsterdam and Lufthansa via Frankfurt (from A$1899/NZ$2199 to A$2499/NZ$2999), and SAS and Finnair via Stockholm and Helsinki respectively, from where you can continue on to St Petersburg by air or overland (see p.9 for details of the various routes) from around A$2099/NZ$2399 to A$2699/NZ$2899; British Airways flies daily from Sydney via Asia and from Auckland via LA to London, with onward connections to St. Petersburg for A$2099/NZ$2399–A$2899/NZ$3100.

If you want to take in St. Petersburg as part of a longer trip, another option is a **round-the-world** ticket. Of the ever-increasing choices available, Qantas-Air France's is the cheapest, allowing six stopovers from A$1699/NZ$2099, while the most flexible are offered by the "One World" (Qantas and British Airways) and "Star Alliance" (Air New Zealand and Lufthansa) consortiums; prices are mileage-based, from A$2500/NZ$2700 for a maximum of 29,000 miles up to

AIRLINES

Aeroflot Australia ☎ 02/9262 2233, *www.aeroflot.com* (no NZ office)
Three times weekly to Moscow: teams up with Qantas from Australian and New Zealand cities, with onward connections to St Petersburg from Singapore.

British Airways Australia ☎ 02/8904 8800, New Zealand ☎ 09/356 8690, *www.british-airways.com*
Daily from Sydney, Melbourne, Brisbane and Perth to London via Singapore, and from Auckland via LA, with onward connections to St Petersburg.

Cathay Pacific Australia ☎ 13 1747 or 02/9931 5500, New Zealand ☎ 09/379 0861, *www.cathaypacific.com*
Several flights weekly to Hong Kong and Beijing, where you can connect with the Trans-Siberian network, from major Australian and New Zealand cities.

Finnair Australia ☎ 02/9244 2299, New Zealand ☎ 09/308 3365, *www.finnair.com*
Four flights weekly (in conjunction with Qantas/Singapore Airlines) from Sydney via Bangkok/Tokyo to Helsinki and twice weekly

from Auckland via Singapore to Helsinki, with daily onward flights to St Petersburg.

Garuda Australia ☎ 1300/365330, New Zealand ☎ 09/366 1862 or ☎ 1800/128510.
Several flights weekly from major Australian and New Zealand cities to Frankfurt via Denpasar or Jakarta.

KLM Australia ☎ 1300/303747, New Zealand ☎ 09/309 1782, *www.klm.com*
Several flights weekly from Sydney to Amsterdam via Singapore, with connections to St Petersburg.

Qantas Australia ☎ 13 1313, New Zealand ☎ 09/357 8900 or 0800/808767, *www.qantas.com.au*
Daily flights from major Australasian cities to London and Frankfurt via Singapore/Bangkok; an onward connection with another airline is required to St Petersburg.

SAS Australia ☎ 02/9299 9800 or 1800/251157, New Zealand ☎ 0800/737000 or 09/357 3000, *www.flysas.com*
Several flights weekly from Sydney and Auckland to Stockholm via Bangkok, with onward connections to St Petersburg.

DISCOUNT FLIGHT AGENTS

Anywhere Travel, 345 Anzac Parade, Kingsford, Sydney ☎ 02/9663 0411, *anywhere@ozemail.com.au*

Budget Travel, 16 Fort St, Auckland, plus branches around the city ☎ 09/366 0061 or 0800/808040

Destinations Unlimited, 220 Queen St, Auckland ☎ 09/373 4033

Flight Centre (*www.flightcentre.com.au*) Australia: 82 Elizabeth St, Sydney ☎ 02/9235 3522, plus branches nationwide (for the location of your nearest branch, call ☎ 13 1600); New Zealand: 350 Queen St, Auckland ☎ 09/358 4310, plus branches nationwide

Northern Gateway, 22 Cavenagh St, Darwin ☎ 08/8941 1394, *oztravel@norgate.com.au*

STA Travel (*www.statravel.com.au*) Australia: 855 George St, Sydney ☎ 1300/360960; 256 Flinders St, Melbourne ☎ 1300/360960; plus offices nationwide (for the location of your nearest branch, call ☎ 13 1776); New Zealand: 10 High St, Auckland ☎ 09/309 0458 (fastfare telesales ☎ 09/366 6673), plus branches nationwide

Student Uni Travel, 92 Pitt St, Sydney ☎ 02/9232 8444, *sydney@backpackers.net*, plus branches in Brisbane, Cairns, Darwin, Melbourne and Perth

Thomas Cook (*www.thomascook.com.au*), Australia: 175 Pitt St, Sydney ☎ 02/9231 2877; 257 Collins St, Melbourne ☎ 03/9282 0222; plus branches in other state capitals (for the

A$3500/NZ$3700 for 39,000 miles. Alternatively, Cathay Pacific fly several times a week to Hong Kong and Beijing, where you can connect with the Trans-Siberian network, from around A$1299.

Package tours

The **package tours** to Russia which are available in Australia don't usually include flights, as it's assumed that you'll be making your own way location of your nearest branch, call ☎13 1771; telesales ☎1800/801002); New Zealand: 191 Queen St, Auckland ☎09/379 3920

Trailfinders, 8 Spring St, Sydney ☎02/9247 7666; 91 Elizabeth St, Brisbane ☎07/3229 0887; Hides Corner, Shield St, Cairns ☎07/4041 1199

Travel.com.au, 76–80 Clarence St, Sydney ☎02/9249 5444 or 1800/000447, *www.travel.com.au*

USIT Beyond, cnr Shortland St and Jean Batten Place, Auckland ☎09/379 4224 or 0800/788336, *www.usitbeyond.co.nz*, plus branches in Christchurch, Dunedin, Palmerston North, Hamilton and Wellington

SPECIALIST TRAVEL AGENTS

The Adventure Specialists, 69 Liverpool St, Sydney ☎02/9261 2927.
Agents for a wide range of adventure travel companies including Sundowners Trans-Siberian and Trans-Kazakhstan "Silk Route" rail journeys to or from St Petersburg.

Adventure World
(*www.adventureworld.com.au*), Australia: 73 Walker St, North Sydney ☎02/9956 7766 or 1300/363 055, plus branches in Adelaide, Brisbane, Melbourne and Perth; New Zealand: 101 Great South Rd, Remuera, Auckland ☎09/524 5118.
Accommodation, and small group adventure tours.

Gateway Travel, 48 The Boulevard, Strathfield, Sydney ☎02/9745 3333, *www.russian-gate-way.com.au*
Russian specialists whose packages (flights not included) feature eight-day stays in St Petersburg and Moscow (A$675–1599) or B&Bs (A$675), a twelve-day Volga cruise (A$1840), and eight days in St Petersburg, Novgorod and Pskov (A$980).

Croydon Travel 34 Main St, Croydon, Vic ☎03/9725 8555.
Homestays with English-speaking families, plus hotel accommodation and river cruises.

Moonsky Tours Ltd, Chungking Mansions, E-block, 4th floor, flat 6, Nathan Rd 36–44, Kowloon, Hong Kong ☎852/2723 1376
Passport Travel Services, Suite 11a, 401 St Kilda Rd, Melbourne ☎03/9867 3888, *www.travelcentre.com.au*

Rail itineraries from Beijing to Moscow/St Petersburg via Manchuria (A$658) or Mongolia (A$685), with extensions including a bike tour of Lake Baikal from June to mid-Sept (A$282). Also seven-night homestays in St Petersburg/Moscow (A$339), with a day-trip to Tsarskoe Selo and Pavlovsk (A$128).

Eastern European Travel Bureau/Russian Travel Centre, 5/75 King St, Sydney ☎02/9262 1144, *eetb@ozimail.com.au*, plus branches in Melbourne, Brisbane and Perth.
Trans-Siberian and twin-centre packages, plus homestays in St Petersburg and Moscow.

Russia and Beyond, 191 Clarence St, Sydney ☎02/9299 5799.
Specialists in trips to western Russia and the Baltic States. Packages include city breaks in St Petersburg and a Volga cruise.

Silke's Travel, 263 Oxford St, Darlinghurst, Sydney ☎1800/807860 or 02/9380 5835, *www.silkes.com.au*
Specially tailored holidays for gay and lesbian travellers.

Sundowners Adventure Travel, Suite 15, 600 Lonsdale St, Melbourne ☎03/9600 1934 or 1800/337089, *www.sundowners.com.au*
Rail trips from Beijing (A$3870) or Vladivostok (A$2930) to St Petersburg via Lake Baikal, plus add-ons such as fourteen days' trekking in the Pamirs ($2190).

Topdeck Travel, 65 Grenfell St, Adelaide ☎08/8232 7222.
City stays and escorted coach and river tours from St Petersburg to Moscow.

there – though most specialist agents listed in the box above will also be able to arrange them if required. The main reason to take a tour is to avoid the hassle of booking train tickets and accommodation. All the prices given are for a single person sharing a double room.

The most popular tours link Beijing, Moscow and St Petersburg with a journey on the **Trans-**

Siberian railway. The Eastern European Travel Bureau's tour (from A$2099) includes stopovers at Ulan Bator and Lake Baikal, five nights in St Petersburg and the same in Moscow. Sundowners Adventure Travel packages range from an eleven-day tour between Vladivostok and St Petersburg (A$770) to an extensive, all-inclusive 39-day journey from Vietnam through China, Mongolia and Russia (A$9900). Russian Specialists' "Beijing–Moscow Express" (A$800) comes with two nights' accommodation at each end, and an overnight train journey to St Petersburg as an optional extra (A$85). This train journey also features in Moscow–St Petersburg packages such as the Eastern European Travel Bureau's eight-day tour (A$895), and Russia and Beyond's eight-day "Grand Russia" package (A$1280). From May to September, both these operators also offer eleven-day Volga cruises (A$1500), with two nights in Moscow and three in St Petersburg. All these deals are fully inclusive, except for flights.

If you just want **accommodation**, you can arrange B&B lodgings in St Petersburg with the Eastern European Travel Bureau (A$95 a night) or Russian Specialists (A$75 a night), or hotel rooms through Russia and Beyond (two nights from A$280 twin-share). There are also short city-stays with Gateway Travel (four nights from A$295 twin-share) and Sundowners Adventure Travel (from A$392 twin-share).

Lastly, it's worth knowing that you can also arrange a Trans-Siberian itinerary terminating in St Petersburg through the Hong Kong specialist travel agency Moonsky Tours Ltd, which also maintains an office in Beijing during the summer.

Travelling by train

If you're planning to visit St Petersburg as an extension to a European trip it may be worth looking into the various European **rail passes** which are available – though sadly none of them is valid for travel in Russia itself. You'll need to buy a pass in your home country before you leave. The **Eurail Youthpass** for under-26s, valid for rail travel in sixteen European countries, is available for periods of fifteen days (A$733/NZ$915), 21 days (A$942/NZ$1175), one month (A$1176/NZ$1470), two months (A$1665/NZ$2080) and three months (A$2055/NZ$2570); if you're 26 or over you'll have to buy a **First-Class Pass**, available for the same durations but costing roughly thirty percent more.

The **Eurail Flexipass** is good for a certain number of days' travel within a two-month period in the same countries, and also comes in youth and first-class versions. Ten days' travel costs A$865/1234 (youth) or NZ$1080/1542 (first class), fifteen days A$1131/1627 or NZ$1415/2033. A scaled-down version of the Flexipass, the **Europass**, allows travel in France, Germany, Italy, Spain and Switzerland only for A$440/$657 (youth/first class) or NZ$550/821 for five days in two months, rising to A$968/1374 or NZ$1210/1717 for fifteen days in two months. There's also the option of adding adjacent "associate" countries (Austria, Hungary, Benelux, Portugal and Greece) for around A$85/NZ$110 per country.

Red tape and visas

Bureaucracy has long been the bane of visitors to Russia, and despite the collapse of the USSR, little has changed. All foreign nationals visiting Russia require a full passport and a visa, which must be obtained in advance from a Russian embassy or consulate abroad. Each embassy sets its own visa prices according to the speed of delivery (see p.23). Although the cheapest method is to apply independently a month in advance, this involves a lot of hassle, and it's worth spending another £30/$50 to have the entire business done through a visa agency or tour operator. If you foresee having to register yourself or extend your visa in St Petersburg, be sure that the agency has a bona fide address there. Note too that your passport must be valid for at least three months after your intended date of departure from Russia.

Visas

There are several types of visa available, so it's important to know which one you want. The most common one is a straight **tourist visa**, valid for a precise number of days up to a maximum of thirty. To get this, you must have proof of pre-booked accommodation in St Petersburg. If you're going on a package tour, all the formalities can be sorted out for you by the travel agency, though they may charge extra for this. If you're travelling independently, local tourist

agencies can supply B&B lodgings and visa support, as can most of St Petersburg's hostels, for their guests (see Chapter 9, "Accommodation"). You have to fax or email the hostels the following information: nationality, date of birth, passport number and date of expiry, length of stay at the hostel, date of arrival and departure from Russia, and credit card details. The visa support documentation should be faxed to you the following day. If you're applying through tourist agencies the procedure is essentially the same.

A **business visa** is more flexible in that it is automatically valid for up to a month (occasionally longer) and doesn't require you to pre-book accommodation. You don't actually have to be involved in any business in order to get one; you simply need to provide the embassy/consulate with a stamped letter of invitation (or fax) from a registered business organization in Russia. This can be arranged by firms like Scott's Tours in Britain (see box on p.5). The cost may depend on whether or not you also book a tour and/or accommodation with them, but is likely to be around £50/$80.

If you don't have a business visa, and wish to stay with Russian friends, you'll need a **private individual visa**, which is the most difficult kind to obtain. This requires a personal invitation (*izveschenie*) from your Russian host – cleared through the PVS (see p.23) – guaranteeing to look after you for the duration of your stay. The whole process can take three or four months to complete.

If you are only planning to pass through Russia en route to another country, you must apply for a **transit visa**, valid for a 24-hour stopover in one city (usually Moscow). Since travellers without a visa are liable to be confined until their flight leaves Moscow, it pays to get one from a Russian consulate beforehand; you'll need to show a ticket for your onward journey from Russia.

With all these visas, what you get is a document to slip into your passport. With the single-entry visas, one half (the entry visa) is collected on arrival, the other half (the exit visa) on departure. Multiple-entry visas are stamped, as is your passport, on arrival and departure. Lost visas must be reported to the main PVS office in St Petersburg (see p.23), which should eventually issue you with a replacement.

Note that if you intend to travel between Russia and any other republics of the former Soviet Union, you need a separate visa for each independent state, and also a multiple-entry visa to get back into Russia. Foreigners wishing to stay in Russia for longer than three months must obtain a doctor's letter certifying that they are not HIV-positive, and bring it with them to Russia (the original, *not* a photocopy).

Applying for a visa

Although all applications require that you submit your passport, three photos (signed on the back), the fee (cash or money order only, no cheques) and a prepaid SAE envelope (for postal applications), the finer points differ from country to country.

In Britain, the Edinburgh consulate is more helpful than the London one, so better for applications by post (or in person, if you live in Scotland). Application forms can be downloaded from *www.russialink.couk.com/embassy* or faxed on request. Applying for a tourist, business or

---

RUSSIAN EMBASSIES AND CONSULATES ABROAD

Australia
Embassy: 78 Canberra Ave, Griffith, Canberra, ACT 2603 ☎ 02/6295 9474

Consulate: 7–9 Fullerton St, Woollahra, Sydney, NSW 2000 ☎ 02/9326 1866

Canada
Embassy: 52 Range Rd, Ottawa, Ontario K1N 8J5 ☎ 613/236-0920, *www.russianembassy.net*

Consulate: 3655 Ave du Musée, Montréal, Quebec H3G 2E1 ☎ 514/842-5343, *www.intranet.ca/~rusemb*

Ireland
Embassy: 186 Orwell Rd, Rathgar, Dublin 14 ☎ 01/492 3492

New Zealand
Embassy: 57 Messines Rd, Karori, Wellington ☎ 04/476 6742

UK
www.russialink.couk.com/embassy

Consulates: 5 Kensington Palace Gdns, London W8 4QS ☎ 020/7229 8027, fax 020/7229 3215; 58 Melville St, Edinburgh EH3 7HF ☎ 0131/225 7098

US
www.ruscon.com.

Consulates: 2641 Tunlaw Rd, NW, Washington, DC 20007 ☎ 202/939-8907, fax 202/483-7579; 9 East 91st St, New York, NY 10128 ☎ 212/348-0926, fax 212/831-9162; 2790 Green St, San Francisco, CA 94123 ☎ 415/928-6878, fax 415/929-0306; 2323 Westin Bldg, 2001 6th Ave, Seattle, WA 981121 ☎ 206/728-1910, fax 206/728-1871

FOREIGN CONSULATES IN ST PETERSBURG

Canada Malodetskoselsky pr.32 ☎ 325 84 48, fax 325 83 93

UK pl. Proletarskoy diktatury 5 ☎ 320 32 00, fax 320 32 11, *www.britain.spb.ru*

US Furshtadtskaya ul. 15 ☎ 275 17 01 (emergencies 274 86 92), fax 110 70 22

FOREIGN EMBASSIES IN MOSCOW

Australia, Ireland and New Zealand do not have consulates in St Petersburg. Citizens of those countries should contact their embassy in Moscow. To call Moscow from St Petersburg dial ☎ 8-095.

Australia Kropotkinskiy per. 13, Moscow ☎ 956 60 70

Ireland Grokholskiy per. 5, Moscow ☎ 442 09 07

New Zealand Povarskaya ul. 44, Moscow ☎ 956 26 42, fax 956 35 83, *www.nzembassy.msk.ru*

transit visa, it's acceptable to enclose a fax or photocopy of your accommodation voucher, invitation or ticket for onward travel. The visa fee is directly related to the speed of processing your application: £30 for six or more working days; £50 for three working days; £70 for two days; £80 for one day; and £120 for one hour.

In the US, you can download the application form from *www.ruscon.com*, which specifies the consulate to which residents of each US state need to apply, and the firms that must deliver the application if you're not doing so in person (regular postal or messenger service deliveries are not accepted). You must supply the *original* voucher, invitation or tickets to support your application for a tourist, business or transit visa (not faxes or photocopies), and payment must be in the form of a bank or postal order – not cash. Again, fees are related to the speed of issue: $70 for two weeks, $80 for one week, $110 for three working days, $150 for the next day, and $300 for the same day.

In Canada, the consular Web site doesn't provide downloadable application forms, you're not required to deliver your application by a specified agency, and you should enclose a photocopy of the information pages of your passport rather than the passport itself. Fees likewise reflect the speed of issue: two weeks CDN$75, one week CDN$135, three days CDN$165.

Registration and the PVS

By law, all foreigners are supposed to register within three days of arrival at the **PVS** (Passport and Visa Service – still universally known by its old title, **OVIR**) and obtain a stamp on their exit visa to that effect. Anyone coming on a tour or staying at any form of pre-booked accommodation should have this done for them automatically, so it only applies to those staying in some form of "unofficial" accommodation. If you're lodging with a Russian family, they'll probably offer to sort it out on your behalf, although if you're on a business visa it will have to be done by the firm that invited you (who will probably charge a fee for the service). Should you need to do it yourself, this entails going to the PVS office of the district in which you're staying, with your passport and visa, and hanging around for ages to get it stamped (free of charge). Although officials don't always enforce the rule, anyone found *not* to have registered can be fined $200 upon leaving Russia. Moreover, it's vital to register if

---

Main PVS office

Kirochnaya ul. 4 ☎ 278 34 86; open to foreigners Mon, Wed & Fri 10am–noon.

District PVS offices

Admiralteyskiy, Sadovaya ul. 55/57 ☎ 310 74 21

Frunzenskiy, nab. Obvodnovo kanala 48 ☎ 166 14 68

Kalinskiy, Mineralnaya ul. 3 ☎ 540 39 87

Kirovskiy, ul. Avtovskaya 22 ☎ 183 44 14

Krasnogvardeyskiy, Zanevskiy pr. 22 ☎ 528 67 67

Moskovskiy, Blagodatnaya ul. 34 ent. 11 ☎ 298 18 27

Nevskiy, ul. Sedova 86 ☎ 262 20 70

Petrograd Side, ul. Grota 1 ☎ 230 83 60

Primorskiy, ul. Savushkina 83 ☎ 430 15 09

Tsentralniy, per. Krylova 5 ☎ 315 79 36

Vasilevskiy Island, 19ya Liniya 12 ☎ 321 75 24

Vyborg Side, Lesnoy pr. 20 ☎ 542 94 52

---

you think you may need to renew or extend your visa (both of which are handled by the main PVS office). To extend a business visa, you'll need written confirmation from the same institution that arranged your initial invitation.

The opening hours of PVS offices are short, and change frequently. Bring a Russian along to help out if at all possible. The box above lists the addresses of the main and district PVS offices.

Customs and allowances

Border controls have relaxed considerably since Soviet times. Bags are no longer searched for "subversive" literature, but simply passed through an X-ray machine. However, you should declare all foreign currency that you bring into the country, plus any laptops or mobile phones, and you will be asked to do the same when you leave (see p.40 for details).

Export controls are more of a problem, as the rules change so frequently that even customs officials aren't sure how things stand. The main restriction is on exporting antiques and contemporary art, though it's unclear where they draw the line between artwork and ordinary souvenirs (which aren't liable to controls). However, you can be fairly sure of encountering problems if you try to take out icons, antique samovars or anything of that ilk. You can export 250 grams of black caviar and any amount of red, and there are no limits on alcohol or cigarettes – though the last two are subject to allowances set by other countries.

Permission to export contemporary art and antiques (anything pre-1960, in effect) must be applied for to the Ministry of Culture at nab. kanala Griboedova 107 (Mon–Fri 11am–2pm), but you would be advised to ask the seller to do the paperwork for you. If the export is approved, you can be liable for tax of up to one hundred percent of the object's value. Pre-1960 books must be approved by the Public Library, using the entrance on Sadovaya ulitsa by the crossroads with Nevskiy prospekt (Tues 3–6pm, Thurs 4–6pm & Fri 10am–noon).

Insurance

A typical travel insurance policy usually provides cover for the loss of baggage, tickets and – up to a certain limit – cash or cheques, as well as cancellation or curtailment of your journey. Most of them exclude so-called "dangerous" sports unless an extra premium is paid. Read the small print and benefits tables of prospective policies carefully; coverage can vary wildly for roughly similar premiums. Many policies can be chopped and changed to exclude coverage you don't need.

If you do take medical coverage, ascertain whether benefits will be paid as treatment proceeds or only after return home, and whether there is a 24-hour medical emergency number. When securing baggage cover, make sure that the per-article limit – typically under £500 equivalent – will cover your most valuable possession.

If you need to make a claim, you should keep receipts for medicines and medical treatment, and in the event you have anything stolen, you must obtain an official statement from the police. Bank and credit cards often have certain levels of medical or other insurance included and you may automatically get travel insurance if you use a major credit card to pay for your trip.

In the **UK and Ireland**, travel agents and tour operators are likely to require some sort of insurance when you book a package holiday, though according to UK law they can't make you buy their own (other than a £1 premium for "schedule airline failure"). If you have a good all-risks home insurance policy it *may* cover your possessions against loss or theft even when overseas. Many private medical schemes such as BUPA or PPP also offer coverage plans for abroad, including baggage loss, cancellation or curtailment and cash replacement as well as sickness or accident.

Americans and Canadians should also check that they're not already covered. Canadian provincial health plans usually provide partial cover for medical mishaps overseas. Holders of official student/teacher/youth cards are entitled to meagre accident coverage and hospital in-patient benefits. Students will often find that their student health coverage extends during the vacations and for one term beyond the date of last enrollment. Homeowners' or renters' insurance often covers theft or loss of documents, money and valuables while overseas, though conditions and maximum amounts vary from company to company.

Health

Because of previous health scares, visitors to St Petersburg and other cities in western Russia are advised to get booster-shots for diphtheria, polio and tetanus, but there's no need to be inoculated against typhoid and hepatitis A unless you're planning to visit remote rural areas. Though there's no danger of malaria, mosquitoes can be fierce during the summer months, so a good repellent is advisable. The most likely hazard for a visitor, however, is an upset stomach, as giardia in the water supply is a major problem (see below). To play safe, wash fresh fruit and vegetables in boiled water; treat dairy products with caution in the summer; and watch out for bootleg liquor (see p.282).

Giardia and heavy metals

St Petersburg's water supply is extracted from the polluted River Neva, and its antiquated filtration plants are unable to deliver tap water free of the parasitic bacteria **Giardia lamblia** (to which the locals are largely immune). To avoid giardia, use only bottled water for drinking and cleaning your teeth, or use tap water that has been boiled for fifteen minutes. If ingested, giardia causes acute diarrhoea, which should be treated with 200mg of Metronidazole three times daily for fourteen days. In Russia this drug is called Trikapol and comes in 250mg tablets; it's used by Russians for treating body lice, so you may get a funny look when you ask for it.

Also present in the water supply are **heavy metals** such as lead, cadmium and mercury. Brief exposure to these substances shouldn't do you any harm, but long-term residents may suffer from skin complaints and apathy as a result. Simply boiling the water is not enough: you need to leave it to stand for a day and avoid drinking the dregs. If you're staying for a long period of time, a proper water filter makes life easier; imported models are sold all over town. Alternatively, you can buy spring water in five-litre bottles from most food stores, either Russian brands or Finnish imports.

Pharmacies, doctors and hospitals

For minor complaints, it's easiest to go to a high-street **pharmacy** (aptéka), which now stock a wide range of Western and Russian products; most are open daily from 8am to 9pm and identifiable by the green cross sign. It goes without saying, however, that if you are on any prescribed medication, you should bring enough supplies for your stay. This is particularly true for diabetics, who should ensure that they have enough needles.

The standard of **doctors** varies enormously, so seek recommendations from friends or acquaintances before consulting one. Some Russian specialists are highly skilled diagnosticians who charge far less for a private consultation than you'd pay in the West, while private **dentistry** is so much cheaper that savvy foreigners often get their teeth fixed while they're here. Information on private clinics, consultants and all-night pharmacies can be obtained by calling ☎003.

If your condition is serious, public **hospitals** will provide free emergency treatment to foreigners on production of a passport (but may charge for medication). However, standards of hygiene and care are low by Western standards and horror stories abound. Aside from routine shortages of

---

USEFUL NUMBERS

For a public ambulance call ☎03. Alternatively, the American Medical Centre (☎326 1730) has a fleet of ambulances (see below).

Medical centres

American Medical Centre, Serpukhovskaya ul. 10 (Mon–Fri 8.30am–6pm; 24hr emergency number ☎326 17 30). A team of Western doctors offering a full range of medical treatments including prenatal and paediatric care, and AIDS tests. Prices are apt to induce a heart attack, though most insurance plans are accepted.

First Medical Institute, ul. Lva Tostovo 6/8 ☎238 70 66 (daily 9am–6pm). Some of the best treatment in town, at reasonable rates. Director Larisa Koncharova speaks fluent English (☎234 09 89).

Clinical and dental treatment

Poliklinika #2, Moskovskiy pr. 22 (Mon–Fri 9am–8pm, Sat 9am–3pm; 24hr emergency service ☎316 62 72). Prices in US dollars but payment in ruble equivalent. A regular visit costs $27; emergency appointments and home visits $45–80.

Dental clinics

Dental Classik, ul. Marata 4 ☎315 85 74.

Medi Up-to-date chain of dental polyclinics, with several branches: the one at Nevskiy pr. 82 is open 24hr (☎327 32 32); all other branches Mon–Fri 8am–9.30pm. Accept all credit cards except Union Card.

Pharmacies

Homeopathic pharmacies, Nevskiy pr. 50; Svechnoy per. 7/11; Bolshoy pr. 2, P.S.

Petropharm, Nevskiy pr. 22, 50, 66 and 83. The branch at no. 22, on the corner of Bolshaya Konyushennaya ul., is open 24hr (☎311 20 70). The night entrance (9pm–8am) is in the courtyard, entered via the arch next door.

Opticians

Vision Express, ul. Lomonosova 5 ☎310 15 95 (daily 10–8pm).

24-hour Eye Trauma Clinic, Liteyniy pr. 25 ☎272 59 55.

---

anaesthetics and drugs, nurses are usually indifferent to their patients unless bribed to care for them properly. Anyone found to be HIV-positive or carrying an infectious disease, such as hepatitis, risks being incarcerated in a locked isolation ward and treated like a subhuman.

On the whole, foreigners tend to rely on special polyclinics with imported drugs and equipment, and American-standard charges – a powerful reason to take out insurance. As a last resort, Helsinki is only an hour's flight or six hours' drive from St Petersburg.

Travellers with disabilities

The needs of disabled citizens in Russia were largely ignored in the past, and the chronic shortage of funds has hindered progress even now in places where attitudes have changed. Wheelchair access to most of the major international hotels in St Petersburg is possible with some assistance, but only the *Grand Hotel Europe* and the *Nevsky Palace* (the city's most expensive hotels) are fully wheelchair-accessible.

Transport is a major problem, since buses, trams and trolleybuses are virtually impossible to get onto with a wheelchair, and the metro and suburban train systems only slightly better. Of the theatres and museums, only the Teatr na Liteynom is wheelchair-accessible. It's worth noting that disabled customers (along with war veterans) are permitted to jump the queues in all shops.

CONTACTS FOR TRAVELLERS WITH DISABILITIES

Australia and New Zealand

ACROD (Australian Council for Rehabilitation of the Disabled), Box 60, Curtin, ACT 2605 ☎ 02/6282 4333.
Provides lists of travel agencies and tour operators for people with disabilities.

Disabled Persons Assembly, 173–175 Victoria St, Wellington ☎ 04/801 9100.
Resource centre with lists of travel agencies and tour operators for people with disabilities.

UK and Ireland

Disability Action Group, 2 Arnedale Ave, Belfast BT7 3JH ☎ 028/9049 1011.
Voluntary organization for people with disabilities, including services for holiday-makers.

Holiday Care, 2nd floor, Imperial Building, Victoria Rd, Horley, Surrey RH6 7PZ ☎ 01293/774535, fax 784647, minicom ☎ 01293/776943,
www.freespace.virgin.net/hol-care

Provides free lists of accessible accommodation abroad.

Irish Wheelchair Association, Blackheath Drive, Clontarf, Dublin 3 ☎ 01/833 8241, *iwa@iol.ie*
National voluntary organization for people with disabilities, including services for holidaymakers.

RADAR (Royal Association for Disability and Rehabilitation), 12 City Forum, 250 City Rd, London EC1V 8AF ☎ 020/7250 3222, minicom ☎ 020/7250 4119, *www.radar.org.uk*
A good source of advice on holidays and travel abroad, with an annual *Getting There* guide ($5) and a useful Web site.

Tripscope, Brentford Community Resource Centre, Alexandra House, Brentford High Street, Brentford, Middlesex TW8 0NE ☎ 08457/585641,
www.justmobility.co.uk/tripscope
Free advice on UK and international transport for those with a mobility problem.

US and Canada contacts overleaf

US and Canada

Directions Unlimited, 720 N Bedford Rd, Bedford Hills, NY 10507 ☎ 1-800/533-5343. Travel agency specializing in custom tours for people with disabilities.

Jewish Rehabilitation Hospital, 3205 Place Alton Goldbloom, Chomedy Laval, Quebec H7V 1R2 ☎ 514/688-9550 ext. 226. Guidebooks and travel information.

Mobility International US, PO Box 10767, Eugene, OR 97440, voice and TDD ☎ 541/343-1284, *www.miusa.org* Information and referral services, access guides, tours and exchange programmes. Annual membership $35 (includes quarterly newsletter).

Society for the Advancement of Travel for the Handicapped (SATH), 347 5th Ave, New York, NY 10016 ☎ 212/447-7284, *www.sath.org*

Non-profit-making travel industry referral service that passes queries on to its members as appropriate.

Travel Information Service ☎ 215/456-9600. Telephone-only information and referral service for disabled travellers.

Twin Peaks Press, Box 129, Vancouver, WA 98666 ☎ 360/694-2462 or 1-800/637-2256, *www.disabilitybookshop.virtualave.net* Publisher of the *Directory of Travel Agencies for the Disabled* ($19.95), listing more than 370 agencies worldwide, and *Wheelchair Vagabond* ($19.95), loaded with personal tips.

Wheels Up ☎ 1-888/389-4335, *www.wheelsup.com* Provides discount air fares, tours and cruises for disabled travellers, and publishes a free monthly newsletter.

Points of arrival

Most visitors arrive by air and enter the city via one of the grand Stalinist thoroughfares that whets your appetite for the historic centre. If you're not being met at the airport, the taxi ride will be your first introduction to Russian-style haggling and manic driving. Arriving by coach from Helsinki, you'll cross Petrograd Side and the River Neva – another scenic curtain-raiser. The sea approach holds some appeal, with vistas of shipyards as you steam towards the Sea Terminal on Vasilevskiy Island. Arriving by train, you'll be pitched straight into the heart of things.

Airports

St Petersburg's **international airport**, Pulkovo-2 (☎ 104 34 44), is 17km south of the city centre. In the baggage reclaim hall of the Arrivals building there's a hard-currency duty-free shop and an exchange machine which takes US dollars,

Deutschmarks and French francs, while the lobby beyond customs contains a Hertz car rental desk and a bureau de change (daily 10.30am–9.30pm). If you arrive after the latter has closed, there's another exchange in the nearby Departures building that's open until later. BCL phonecards (see p.43) are sold from the trolley-rental point in the luggage hall.

There are several ways of getting into the city. A cheap **bus** service (#13) and a slightly more expensive **minibus** (#T-13) run every twenty minutes or so to Moskovskaya ploshchad, from where you can continue your journey by metro. For both the bus and minibus, you'll need rubles to buy a ticket once on board. Services depart from outside the Arrivals building and the journey to Moskovskaya ploshchad takes about twenty minutes.

If you have a lot of luggage or don't feel up to dealing with public transport immediately, there are always plenty of **taxis** waiting outside –

both licensed and unofficial (see p.32), You're expected to pay in hard currency (or at a very disadvantageous exchange rate), and the price is negotiable: $20 is fair for a ride into the centre, but drivers usually open the bidding at $60. Package tourists and guests with reservations at the *Astoria Hotel, Hotel Pribaltiyskaya* or *Grand Hotel Europe* will be met by the particular hotel's own minibus. There's also a **taxi limousine service**, Svit (☎356 93 29), which can provide Fords with English-speaking drivers for $20–35 an hour.

Should you fly to St Petersburg from Moscow or somewhere else in the Russian Federation, you'll arrive at the **domestic airport**, Pulkovo, 15km south of the city, from where buses #39 and #339 run regularly to Moskovskaya metro station. Taxi drivers might accept rubles rather than dollars from foreigners who speak passable Russian, but otherwise charges are much the same as from Pulkovo-2.

Leaving St Petersburg

When leaving St Petersburg, allow plenty of time to get to the international airport in order to arrive at least an hour and a half before your flight is scheduled to depart. Using public transport, give yourself at least an hour from the centre: catch bus #13, or one of the minibuses that depart from outside Moskovskaya metro, but make sure that the latter is going to Pulkovo *mezhdunarodniy aeroport* (the international one).

Check-in opens ninety minutes before take-off for Western airlines and two hours before for Aeroflot flights; beware that check-in desks close forty minutes before departure. Passengers often have to queue for thirty minutes in order to pass through the only working metal detector, before they can submit their baggage for inspection and then join a queue at check-in. The customs officer will expect to see your original currency declaration (see p.40) and a duplicate form detailing what you're taking out of the country (forms are available in the hall).

Train stations

All St Petersburg's train stations are linked to the city centre by the fast and efficient metro system. Arriving by train from Berlin or Warsaw, you'll end up at **Vitebsk Station** (Vitebskiy vokzal), near Pushkinskaya metro station, or **Warsaw Station** (Varshavskiy vokzal), a short distance east of Baltiyskaya metro. Trains from Helsinki arrive at the famous **Finland Station** (Finlyandskiy vokzal), served by Ploshchad Lenina metro, while services from Moscow culminate at **Moscow Station** (Moskovskiy vokzal), which is linked to Ploshchad Vosstaniya metro.

Bus terminals

Eurolines Russia coaches from Berlin, Frankfurt, Tallinn and Riga drop passengers on the square outside the Baltic Station (Baltiyskaya metro), near the Eurolines office, while **Finnish coaches**

AIRLINE OFFICES IN ST PETERSBURG

Besides the following offices, you can book tickets for international or domestic flights on any airline on ☎316 31 35 or 316 21 33.

Aeroflot, Nesvkiy pr. 7–9 ☎315 00 72

Air France, Bolshaya Morskaya ul. 35 ☎325 82 52

Austrian Airways, Nesvkiy pr. 57 (*Nevsky Palace Hotel*) ☎325 32 60

Balkan, Bolshaya Morskaya ul. 36 ☎315 50 30

British Airways, Malaya Konyushennaya ul. 1/3 ☎329 25 65

CSA, Bolshaya Morskaya ul. 36 ☎315 52 59

Delta, Bolshaya Morskaya ul. 36 ☎311 58 20

El Al, Baskov per. 21 ☎275 17 20

Finnair, Kazanskaya ul. 44 ☎326 18 70

KLM, Zagorodniy pr. 5 ☎325 89 89

LOT, Karavannaya ul. 1 ☎273 57 21

Lufthansa, Voznesenskiy pr. 7 ☎325 70 00

Malév, Voznesenskiy pr. 7 ☎314 54 55

SAS, Nesvkiy pr. 57 (*Nevsky Palace Hotel*) ☎325 32 55

Swissair, Nesvkiy pr. 57 (*Nevsky Palace Hotel*) ☎325 32 50

Transaero, Nevskiy pr. 42 ☎325 85 29

---

from Helsinki (and Vyborg) drop them at the Finnord office on Italyanskaya ulitsa, the *Astoria Hotel* in the centre, and the *Pulkovskaya Hotel* in the southern suburbs. In the unlikely event of you arriving on a coach run by a different company, from the Baltic States or another Russian city, you could arrive at either of two terminals near the Obvodniy Canal. **Bus Station #1** lurks around the eastern side of Warsaw Station (see above), while **Bus Station #2** is 1.5km further east. To reach the centre from there, catch any bus or tram up Ligovskiy prospekt, alighting either at the metro station of the same name, or further north at Ploshchad Vosstaniya.

Cruise boat moorings

Finnish "booze cruise" vessels usually dock at the **Sea Terminal** (morskoy vokzal) on the Gulf coast of Vasilevskiy Island, some 4km west of the centre. Other than taking a taxi (you're likely to be charged at least $10, though Russians pay only $4), the best way of getting into the centre is to catch a #T-128 minibus to Vasileostrovskaya metro station on Bolshoy prospekt, and then continue by metro. More upmarket Baltic cruise ships moor in the **Neva basin** instead – usually within fifteen minutes' walk of the Winter Palace, off the Angliyskaya naberezhnaya to the west of the Admiralty.

City transport and tours

St Petersburg is a big city, which means that sooner or later you're going to want to make use of its cheap and relatively efficient public transport system. As well as the fast metro network, there are minibuses, buses, trolleybuses and trams (in that order of usefulness). Although the transport maps in the colour section of this book should help you out, they can't compare with larger, fold-out maps of the municipal transport system (*marshruty gorodsko transporta*) sold from street kiosks and in bookshops – the best being the one sponsored by *McDonald's*.

Tickets

In an effort to stamp out fare evasion on buses, trams and trolleybuses, the authorities have replaced the old system whereby passengers were trusted to buy tickets in batches of ten and punch them using a gadget aboard the vehicle, with conductors selling individual tickets. As there is a **flat fare** on all routes there's no need to state your destination. On minibuses you simply pay the driver; no ticket is issued.

Unless you're going to be in St Petersburg for a long time and make regular use of particular services, it's not worth buying a one- or three-month pass for any combination of the above vehicles,

though you might purchase a one-month **yediniy bilet**, valid for up to seventy journeys on buses, trolleybuses, trams and the metro, simply to avoid buying *talony* or metro tokens all the time. The *yediniy bilet* goes on sale in metro stations and kiosks towards the end of the calendar month, for a few days only; there is also a half-monthly version that goes on sale during the middle of the month.

The system on **the metro** is different, insofar as you can either buy metro **tokens** (*zhetony*) from the cashier (each token is valid for one journey, with as many changes of line as you wish), or various kinds of machine-readable **tickets**. There is a *prisnoy bilet* valid for ten, twenty or sixty journeys within a thirty-day period, or a one-month *prisnoy bilet* valid for up to seventy journeys. Alternatively, you can buy a **transport card** (*transportnaya karta*) valid for an unlimited number of journeys within a one-month (*na mesats*) or three-month (*tri mesyatsa*) period, or even an entire year (*na god*), starting from the date of issue. With all of these, you feed the ticket or card into the slot of the turnstile, wait for the light to switch from red to green, and retrieve it from the other slot. If you're using a *yediniy bilet*, you simply show it as you walk past the guardian at the end of the row of turnstiles.

Although the price of tickets and passes is liable to increase in line with inflation, public transport is still affordable for the locals and amazingly good value for tourists. At the time of writing, a *talon* costs the equivalent of 5p/7¢, a one-month *prisnoy bilet* £4/$6, a monthly *yediniy bilet* £8/$11, and a one-year *transportnaya karta* £53/$75. A single metro ride costs the equivalent of 10p/15¢.

The metro

The metro's former name, "The Leningrad Metro in the name of Lenin with the Order of Lenin", gives you an idea of the pride that accompanied its construction, which began in the 1930s and is still continuing. There are four **lines** in operation (see the colour map at the back of this book), though further construction is hampered by a lack of funds and the sheer difficulty of tunnelling through St Petersburg's marshy subsoil. To add to the metro's woes, a section of tunnel on the oldest line – the Kirovsko-Vyborgskaya – collapsed in 1996, since when the gap between Lesnaya and Ploshchad Muzhestva metro stations has been served by bus #80. Stations are marked with a large "M" and have separate doors for incoming and outgoing passengers.

All **signs and maps** on the metro are in the Cyrillic alphabet; the colour metro map in this book gives the Cyrillic characters for each station and the common signs you will come across. Although each metro line is numbered and colour-coded, the shade of colour varies widely according to which map you buy. The colours on our map are as representative as any.

The metro covers most parts of the city you're likely to visit, except for the Smolniy district and the western end of the downtown area within the Fontanka. Depending on the line, trains run daily from about 5.45am till midnight or slightly later, with **services** every one to two minutes during peak periods (8–10am and 5–7pm), and every three to five minutes at night. Note, however, that certain underground walkways linking crucial **interchange stations** may close earlier – in particular, between Mayakovskaya and Ploshchad Vosstaniya, or Gostiniy Dvor and Nevskiy Prospekt. Where two lines intersect, the station may have two separate names, one for each line, or, alternatively be numbered (as at Tekhnologicheskiy Institut or Ploshchad Aleksandra Nevskovo).

Due to the city's many rivers and swampy subsoil, most of the lines were built extremely deep

underground, with vertiginous **escalators** that almost nobody walks up, although the left-hand side is designated for that purpose. The older lines also boast a system of "horizontal lifts", whereby the **platforms** are separated from the tracks by automatic doors that open in alignment with those of the incoming trains – a bit of Stalinist wizardry that's been abandoned on the newer lines. Many of the station vestibules and platforms are notable for their **decor**, especially those on the downtown section of the Kirovsko–Vyborgskaya line, adorned with marble, granite, bas-reliefs and mosaics. It's worth travelling almost to the end of the line to see the glass columns at Avtovo station.

Since the platforms carry few signs indicating which station you are in, it's advisable to pay attention to the tannoy **announcements** (in Russian only) in the carriages. As the train pulls into each station, you'll hear its name, immediately followed by the words *Sléduyushchaya stántsiya* – and then the name of the *next* station. Most importantly, be sure to heed the words *Ostorózhno, dvéry zakryváyutsya* – "Caution, doors closing" – since they slam shut with great force.

Minibuses

The biggest improvement to the transport system in recent years has been the spread of **minibuses** (*marsrutnoe taxi*, or *marshrutki*). Besides being faster than buses, trolleybuses or trams, they only carry as many passengers as there are seats, and can be flagged down or drop you off at any point along their route, making them both comfortable and convenient. There are **flat fares** on all routes, which are only fractionally higher than on other forms of surface transport, while the services running out from suburban metro stations to outlying points of interest such as Peterhof, Tsarskoe Selo and Pavlovsk are not only a faster and easier way of getting there than by suburban train, but cheaper, too.

Minibuses are usually numbered, with the prefix T, and carry a **signboard** listing their termini and the main points along the route. However, you should never assume that this is the same as the one followed by buses or trolleybuses with the same route number, although in some cases it is. The most useful *marshrutka* routes are marked on the transport map at the back of this book, and listed where appropriate in the text.

Buses, trams and trolleybuses

Since there are few destinations of interest to tourists that can't be reached by minibus, visitors have less reason than they did to use the city's antiquated, overcrowded **buses**, **trolleybuses** and **trams** – the last being the slowest of the lot, though many visitors enjoy riding them at least once, purely for the experience. Whilst foreigners are often discouraged by the pushing and shoving, Russians rarely take this personally, and once inside the vehicle will cheerfully help each other to punch tickets or buy them from the driver. Should anyone ask if you are getting off at the next stop – *Vy vykhodíte?* – it means that they are, and need to squeeze past. The other big problem is that **routes** are often altered due to roadworks, so that even the most recent transport maps can't be relied upon.

As a rule, the system is supposed to operate daily from 5.30am to 1am, although cutbacks may see these **hours** reduced on some lines after 9pm. Some buses operate only during peak periods (daily 6–9am and 4–7pm), though these generally serve outlying factories and are of little use to visitors. **Trolleybuses #1, #7 and #10** offer a sedate sightseeing trip up Nevskiy prospekt and onto the Strelka; catch one from opposite Ploshchad Vosstaniya metro. Even better for sightseeing are **trams #2 and #54**, which run along Sadovaya ulitsa, past the Engineer's Castle and across the Neva to the Peter and Paul Fortress, with wonderful views all the way. During summer, **antique trams** run from Finland Station, along Liteyniy prospekt and through the centre to ploshchad Turgeneva.

Stops are relatively few and far between, so getting off at the wrong one can mean a lengthy walk. Bus stops are marked with an "A" (for *avtobus*); trolleybus stops with what resembles a squared-off "m", but is in fact a handwritten Cyrillic "т" (for *trolleybus*). Both are usually attached to walls, and therefore somewhat inconspicuous, whereas the signs for tram stops (bearing a "Т", for *tramvay*), are suspended from the overhead cables above the road.

In addition to the services outlined above, there are special **express buses** (*ekspress*) on certain routes prefixed by an Э. These tend to leave from metro or mainline stations and serve the airport and other outlying destinations. Passengers pay the driver instead of using a *talon*, and the fares are double those on regular buses.

Taxis

Officially registered taxis are run by many different companies. They are usually Volgas or Fords, painted bright yellow with a chequered logo on the doors. If the domed light on the roof is on, the taxi is unoccupied. At the time of writing, taxis no longer use meters, and one simply pays the going rate per kilometre, or five minutes' travel (roughly 20¢). Though obviously open to abuse, this *laissez faire* system is kept within bounds by strong competition from ordinary vehicles acting as taxis (see below), except at airports and hotels, where the "taxi mafia" has a stranglehold and drivers have agreed on fixed rates for certain journeys.

Besides official taxis, there are unmarked **private taxis** that have a near monopoly at the airport and certain big hotels. They too are unmetered and charge whatever they think they can get away with, especially if you're a foreigner – avoid them if at all possible.

Most Russians ignore both types of taxi and favour **hitching rides in private vehicles**, which enables ordinary drivers to earn extra money as *chastniki* (moonlighters). It's especially common after the public transport system closes down; you'll see people flagging down anything that moves. You simply state your destination and what you're willing to pay ("*Mozhno -- za -- rubley?*"); the driver may haggle a bit, but there's so much competition that it's a buyer's market. As a rule of thumb, one pays about 20¢ per five minutes' journey time, with a minimum fare of 60¢. Foreigners may be asked for more, but can usually get the same price by remaining firm – though if travelling with Russian friends, it's best not to speak until the deal is concluded.

As the above system is unregulated, it's as well to observe some **precautions**. Don't get into a vehicle which has more than one person in it, and never accept lifts from anyone who approaches you, particularly outside restaurants and nightclubs. Instances of drunken foreigners being robbed in the back of private cars are not uncommon, and women travelling alone would be best advised to give the whole business a miss.

Taxis can be called out 24 hours on ☎ 068 or 312 00 22 (50¢ call-out charge).

Driving and car rental

Traffic in St Petersburg is relatively heavy and many Russian motorists act like rally drivers, swerving at high speed to avoid potholes and tramlines, with a reckless disregard for pedestrians and other cars. Bear in mind also that many drivers are likely to have purchased their licence, rather than passed a test. Driving yourself, therefore, requires a fair degree of skill and nerve.

To drive a car in St Petersburg you are required to carry with you all of the following **documents**: your home driving licence and an international driving permit (available from motoring organizations) with a Russian-language insert; an insurance certificate from your home insurer, and one from a Russian insurance company, such as Ingosstrakh (details from their St Petersburg branch on ☎275 44 60, or from your travel company); your passport and visa; the vehicle registration certificate; and a customs document asserting that you'll take the car back home when you leave (unless, of course, you rented it in St Petersburg).

Rules of the road – and the GIBDD

Although keeping in lane goes by the board, other **rules of the road** are generally observed.

Traffic coming from the right has **right of way** – something that's particularly important to remember at roundabouts – while **left turns** are (theoretically) only allowed in areas indicated by a broken centre line in the road, and an overhead sign. If you are turning into a side street, pedestrians crossing the road have right of way. **Trams** have right of way at all times, and you are not allowed to overtake them when passengers are getting on and off, unless there is a safety island.

Unless otherwise specified, **speed limits** are 60km (37 miles) per hour in the city and 80km (50 miles) per hour on highways. It is illegal to drive after having consumed *any* **alcohol** – the rule is stringently enforced, with heavy fines for offenders. **Safety-belt use** is mandatory (though many Russians only drape the belt across their lap), and **crash helmets** are obligatory for motorcyclists. Take extra care when driving in **winter** (between Oct and March), when snow and ice make for hazardous road conditions.

Rules are enforced by a branch of the Militia, the **GIBDD** (see p.51), recognizable by their white plastic wands tipped with a light, which they flourish to signal drivers to pull over. Their reputation for taking bribes derives from the fact

---

BEWARE OF THE BRIDGES

Whether travelling by car or on foot, you should always bear in mind that, between April and November, the **Neva bridges** are raised late at night to allow ships to pass through, severing the islands from the mainland. Should you inadvertently get stuck on the wrong side of the Neva, you can either wait for the bridge to reopen or look for a small boat prepared to take you across. Given that you're in no position to haggle, this is likely to cost you a packet – unless you happen to find a second boatman who's willing to undercut the first.

The following opening times apply only when the Neva is navigable; in **winter**, when the river is frozen over, the bridges remain permanently lowered. Always allow an extra five minutes if aiming to get across a bridge, as they can open or close early and there is invariably a tailback of cars waiting to race across during the brief interval that some of them come down again around 3am. Conversely, they may stay open all night if there's a naval holiday or too many ships. For up-to-date **information** on bridge opening hours (in Russian), phone ☎063 (9am–8pm).

Dvortsoviy most 1.55–3.05am & 3.15–4.45am.	**Most Aleksandra Nevskovo** 2.35–4.50am
Birzhevoy most 2.25–3.20am & 3.40–4.40am	**Sampsonievskiy most** 2.10–2.45am & 3.20–4.25am
Troitskiy most 2–4.40am	
Most Leytenanta Shmidta 1.55–4.50am	**Tuchkov most** 2.20–3.10am & 3.40–4.40am
Liteyniy most 2.10–4.35am	**Grenaderskiy most** 2.45–3.45am & 4.20–4.50am
Kamennoostrovskiy most 2.15–3am & 4.05–4.55am	
Most Petra Velikovo 1.25–5.05am	**Volodarskiy most** 2–3.45am & 4.25–5.45am
	Most Svobody 2.10–2.45am & 3.20–4.25am

---

that they are allowed to levy on-the-spot fines, which are open to negotiation. If you're unlucky enough to get such a fine, it's easier to pay it there and then: if not, you'll have to surrender your licence and reclaim it when you pay the fine at the local police station. The GIBDD regards cars driven by foreigners as a prime source of income, so unless your Russian is fluent it's better not to argue, but simply concentrate on negotiating a lower fine. Officers may try to extract hard currency, but will probably settle for rubles in the end.

Fuel and breakdowns

Petrol (*benzin*) is fairly easy to come by, but the decent stuff – 95 (3-star) or 98 (4-star) – is nearly as expensive as in the West. If you're driving your own car, avoid 76. **Lead-free petrol** and high-octane fuel suitable for cars fitted with catalytic converters are sold at Neste-Petro service stations at the following addresses: Moskovskiy prospekt 102, in the southern suburbs; Maily prospekt 68, Vasilevskiy Island; Pulkovskoe shosse 32 and 38, en route to the airport; and ul. Savushkina 87, Vyborg Side. They all take rubles and major credit cards. If you **break down**, emergency repairs or a tow-away service is provided by A24 (☎ 320 90 00) and LAT (☎ 001).

Car rental

Various **car rental agencies** offer Western models, mostly with a driver. Hiring a driver deserves serious consideration: it could spare you a lot of anxiety and may not cost much more than straightforward car rental – rates for driver and car range from approximately $17/hr to $30/hr. If you're driving yourself, it's best to stick to Western-model cars and reputable agencies. Many rental agencies prefer payment by credit card and require the full range of documentation (see p.33) for self-drive rental. Interavto-Hertz and Svit offer a 24-hour service, which you can reserve through the *Grand Hotel Europe* or the *Moskva*. Addresses are given in the box below.

Coach and minibus tours

Numerous local tourist agencies offer **coach tours** of the city and its environs, with commentary in Russian. The most accessible firms have kiosks outside Gostiniy dvor (see p.74), where you can buy tickets and check schedules. Davranov Travel (☎ 311 01 60) is the largest operator and the best bet for foreigners, as its tours are partly translated into English. They do day-trips ($5–8) to four of the Imperial palaces, plus Novgorod, Kronstadt and Schlüsselburg – destinations also offered by Eklektika (☎ 279 24 10), whose tours are slightly cheaper but don't have any English translation. Other Russian-only tours are provided by Tur Servis (☎ 315 26 41), whose destinations include Vyborg ($7) and Oranienbaum ($6).

Other firms offer more expensive **minibus tours** of the city with commentary in English, such as Antis Tour, based in the *Sovetskaya Hotel* (☎ 329 02 84), whose three-hour tour costs $30 for one person or $9 per person for a group of five, with the option of visiting one of the city's major museums ($3–9 extra per head); and similar, pricier tours from Intourist (☎ 314 60 69) and Interexpo (☎ 275 66 35).

CAR RENTAL AGENCIES IN ST PETERSBURG

Astoria-Service, Borovaya ul. 11/13, office 65, room 1 ☎ 112 15 83, fax 164 96 22
Cars with driver only. CCs.

Auto-Mobile, Borovaya ul. 11/13 ☎ 164 60 66 or 164 91 73.
Cars with or without drivers. CCs only (Visa, MC, Eurocash).

Hertz, Pulkovo-2 airport ☎ 324 32 42.
Cars with or without driver. CCs only (Amex, Visa, MC, DC, EC, JCB).

Ingosstrakh, Zacharievskaya ul. 17 ☎ 275 44 60, fax 275 77 12.

You must have had a driving licence for a minimum of three years.

Interavto-Hertz, Perekupnoy per. 4 ☎ 277 40 32; pl. Aleksandra Hevskovo 2 (*Moskva Hotel*) ☎ 274 20 60.
Cars with drivers. Cash only. Open 24hr.

Limuzin-Servis SPB, Ligovskiy pr. 10 (*Oktyabyrskaya Hotel*) ☎ 118 24 36 or 118 11 28.
Cars with or without driver.

Svit, ul. Korabelstroiteley 14, V.O. ☎ 325 93 29.
Fords with or without drivers. CCs. Open 24hr.

Boat and yacht tours

One of the pleasures of St Petersburg in summer is **to cruise on the canals and rivers**, which are navigable from mid-April till mid-October. The cheapest trips are aboard the large, enclosed boats that Russians call **kater** (cutters) – their disadvantage is that you have to endure a non-stop commentary in Russian. The main operator is Bark (☎315 56 06), with departures every half hour from the pier at nab. reki Fontanki 44, near the Anichkov most on the River Fontanka. Tours last just over an hour, taking in the Fontanka, the Kryukov Canal, the River Moyka and the Neva basin, and cost $4 per person. Bark also do two-hour **night cruises** (1am–3am; $8 per person). Alternatively, Neva Cruises' tours (10am–10pm; $4 per person) depart from the pier outside the Hermitage and cruise up and down the Neva for an hour. If you fancy hosting your own private boat party, you can rent larger and more luxurious vessels from Mir (☎311 83 20; ask for Yelena Krashnikova).

It's also possible to rent a small motorboat, advertised as **"water-taxis"**, from the moorings alongside the Politseyskiy most, where Nevskiy prospekt crosses the Moyka. You hire the entire boat (plus driver) for a negotiable price in hard currency; $45 an hour for a four-seater is standard, but a ten-seater is better value at $55 if you can get a group together. The route is pretty much the same as the tours mentioned above, though you can combine elements of the two if desired. The advantage of the water-taxis is that there's no commentary, the itinerary is much more flexible, and you can bring along champagne and caviar to complete the experience, particularly during the White Nights, when the boats work into the small hours. Call ☎230 77 47 to book in advance or go down to the bridge and pay a small deposit. If you do go boating at night, stick to the canals rather than cruising around the Neva basin, where collisions with larger ships are possible, especially in the not completely unlikely event that your motorboat captain happens to be drunk.

For a completely different experience, you might enjoy **yachting** on the Gulf of Finland. Trips range from a few hours' sailing on the Gulf to overnight excursions to the sea forts beyond Kronstadt, beauty spots along the northern coast as far as Vyborg, or even further afield into Lake Lagoda or Lake Onega. Prices depend on the destination and the company involved, so it definitely pays to shop around. The three main outfits are Sunny Sailing, the River Yacht Club and the Kronstadt Yacht Club – see p.316 for details. The cost will include crew hire and all meals.

Helicopter and plane tours

Helicopter trips provide an amazing view of the city, though the only operator at present is Baltic Air (Nevskiy pr. 7/9, office 12 ☎311 00 84), who offer fifteen-minute trips over the city centre at weekends (April–Oct), and the Imperial palace at Peterhof (July only) for $35 per person. You can also go for a ride in an Ilyushin-103 **propeller plane**, seating three passengers, from Rzhevka Airfield on the city's eastern outskirts to Peterhof, for a total cost of $120 (☎104 15 72). In the event that **balloon trips** resume (they're currently suspended for security reasons), the firms to contact are Aerotour Balloons (☎265 50 18, fax 264 63 58) or Oparin Balloons (☎264 63 58 or 264 50 18).

Information, maps and addresses

At long last, St Petersburg has a tourist office to fill the vacuum left by the collapse of the old state tourist monopoly, Intourist. There are also quite a few useful publications for visitors, while anyone with access to the Internet can tap into numerous more-or-less relevant Web sites. All in all, it's easier now to find out what's what and what's on in St Petersburg than it has ever been.

Information

After nearly a decade when the city had no centralized source of information, there's finally a **tourist information centre** (daily 10am–7pm; ☎311 28 43 or 311 29 43, www.tourism.spb.ru), at Nevskiy prospekt 41, through the doorway of the Beloselskiy-Belozerskiy Palace furthest from Anichkov most over the River Fontanka (see map on p.67). Though still finding their feet and unresponsive to emails (though you could always try on tourism@gov.spb.ru), the staff are keen to help tourists who drop by and are slowly increasing their stock of free leaflets and brochures. Among the services on offer are hotel (but not hostel or homestay) reservations, guided tours and even armed bodyguards (only $9 an hour, if you want to look butch). Over summer they also have a branch in the lobby of the Oktyabrskaya

Hotel, opposite Moscow Station, that supposedly works the same hours but in reality is less reliable.

Another new service is the **Eldofon enquiry line** (☎326 96 96), which in theory has English-speaking staff who can supply current information on city transport, entertainment, business and much else free of charge – but may not be able to deliver in practice. Alternatively, there's the old standby of using the service desks at such hotels as the Astoria, Pribaltiyskaya, Pulkovskaya and (best of all) the Grand Hotel Europe – or their counterparts at St Petersburg's hostels (for addresses, see Chapter 9) – which are usually willing to help out even if you're not staying there.

Certain **publications** are also useful. If you're planning to stay a while, it's worth investing in the pocket-sized St Petersburg Traveller's Yellow Pages, which lists all kinds of businesses and services, with lots of maps and advice on diverse aspects of life. It's regularly updated, and is sold at leading hotels and Pulkovo-2 airport; there is also an online version. For reviews of restaurants, clubs, concerts and exhibitions, check out the free English-language bi-weekly St Petersburg Times, and the free monthly magazines Pulse and Where St Petersburg (see p.45) – available in the tourist office and hotels, restaurants, bars and shops frequented by Westerners.

For those with Internet access, there are scores of **Web sites** belonging to tourist agencies, museums, hotels and hostels – as well as online editions of the St Petersburg Times and Pulse. Budget travellers in particular should find lots of useful information on the St Petersburg International Hostel and International Holiday Hostel sites, which tend to be kept up to date rather more than some of the tourist-oriented sites devoted to the city itself. The box on p.37 lists some of the most useful sites; others are given in the text as appropriate.

Russian friends or acquaintances are often generous with their help and time, and know their city well. News of good places to eat, shop

USEFUL WEB SITES

www.300.spb.ru
Online calendar of festivals, exhibitions and events in the city, throughout the year.

www.alexanderpalace.org
Lavishly illustrated site devoted to the Imperial palaces and the Romanov dynasty.

www.all-hotels.ru
Probably Russia's most comprehensive online accommodation booking service.

www.cityvision2000.com
One of the best St Petersburg tourist sites, with online booking facilities and a noticeboard.

www.gay.ru
Gay advice and contact listings.

www.glasnost.apc.org.ru
Ecological, educational and aid projects, and links.

www.glasweb.ru
Info on visas, hotels and transport, aimed at business travellers.

www.hotels.spb.ru
Accommodation in St Petersburg and online bookings.

www.hro.ru
Internet bulletin on art and culture in St Petersburg.

www.infoservices.com
Online Traveller's Yellow Pages for St Petersburg, Moscow, Novgorod and Vyborg.

www.online.ru
Russia-On-Line, the leading Internet service provider in the CIS.

www.other.spb.ru
Excerpts from John Nicholson's entertaining book *The Other St Petersburg*.

www.pavlovskart.spu.ru
Official site of Pavlovsk Palace.

www.spb.ru/horis
Digital map of St Petersburg.

www.spb.ru
Official city site with links to tourist services, hotels and museums.

www.tourism.spb.ru
The official site of the city's tourist information centre.

www.travel-labs.com
Online hotel reservations and other services.

www.travelto.spb.ru
Tourist site with links to others.

or have fun was traditionally spread by word of mouth rather than the media, and old habits die hard, despite there being less need for a grapevine nowadays. Alternatively, visitors can hire guides or interpreters from the tourist office, hotel service bureaux, the Guides and Interpreters Association (Serpukhovskaya ul. 30 ☎112 76 99) or most of the tour and travel agencies listed in the *St Petersburg Traveller's Yellow Pages*.

Maps

The **maps** in this guide should be sufficient for most purposes, but if you need more detail, or are staying outside the centre, it's worth investing in a detailed street plan. If you can understand the Cyrillic alphabet, the most useful is the *Polyplan Map of St Petersburg*, which is updated annually and shows all the transport routes; it is recognizable in bookshops and on street stalls

in St Petersburg by the McDonald's logo on the cover, and costs about $1.50 (considerably more in map shops abroad). Unless they improve them, it's not worth buying the dated, unwieldy *Falk plan* or *Freytag & Berndt's* map, which are more commonly found in bookshops abroad. At a pinch, visitors can also use the English colour maps in the free magazine *Where St Petersburg*. For serious map buffs who intend to make a lot of excursions outside the city, it's also worth buying the *Polyplan Map of St Petersburg's Environs*, featuring plans of the towns surrounding the Imperial palaces, Kronstadt and Schlüsselburg – while anyone with access to the Internet can download useful, if somewhat dated, maps of Vyborg, Novgorod, Strelna and Gatchina from the online *Traveller's Yellow Pages* (*www.infoservices.com*), or browse through the Horis digital map of St Petersburg (*www.spb.ru/horis*).

MAP OUTLETS

Australia

Mapland, 372 Little Bourke St, Melbourne ☎03/9670 4383

Perth Map Centre, 1/884 Hay St, Perth ☎08/9322 5733

The Map Shop, 6 Peel St, Adelaide ☎08/8231 2033

Travel Bookshop, Shop 3, 175 Liverpool St, Sydney ☎02/9261 8200

Worldwide Maps and Guides, 187 George St, Brisbane ☎07/3221 4330

Canada

Open Air Books and Maps, 25 Toronto St, Toronto, ON M5C 2R1 ☎416/363-0719

Ulysses Travel Bookshop, 4176 St-Denis, Montréal, PQ H2W 2M5 ☎514/843 9447, *www.ulyssesguides.com*

World Wide Books and Maps, 1247 Granville St, Vancouver, BC V6Z 1G3 ☎604/687-3320

New Zealand

Mapworld, 173 Gloucester Street, Christchurch ☎03/374 5399, fax 03/374 5633, *www.mapworld.co.nz*

Specialty Maps, 46 Albert St, Auckland ☎09/307 2217

St Petersburg

Anglia, nab. reki Fontanki 40 ☎279 82 84, *info@anglia-books.spb.ru*

Dom knigi, Nevskiy pr. 28, 2nd floor.

UK and Ireland

Easons Bookshop, 40 O'Connell St, Dublin 1 ☎01/873 3811, *www.eason.ie*

John Smith and Sons, 57–61 St Vincent St, Glasgow G2 5TB ☎0141/221 7472, *www.johnsmith.co.uk*

Newcastle Map Centre, 55 Grey St, Newcastle upon Tyne NE1 6EF ☎0191/261 5622, *www.newtraveller.com*

Stanfords, 12–14 Long Acre, London WC2E 9LP ☎020/7836 1321, *sales@stanfords.co.uk*; plus branches in Campus Travel, 52 Grosvenor Gardens, London SW1W 0AG ☎020/7730 1314; British Airways, 156 Regent St, London W1R 5TA ☎020/7434 4744; 29 Corn Street, Bristol BS1 1HT ☎0117/929 9966

The Map Shop, 30a Belvoir St, Leicester LE1 6QH ☎0116/247 1400

Waterstone's, 91 Deansgate, Manchester M3 2BW ☎0161/837 3000, *enquiries@waterstones -manchester-deansgate.co.uk*; Queens Bldg, 8 Royal Ave, Belfast BT1 1DA ☎028/9024 7355

US

The Complete Traveler Bookstore, 3207 Fillmore St, San Francisco, CA 92123 ☎415/923-1511

The Complete Traveller Bookstore, 199 Madison Ave, New York, NY 10016 ☎212/685-9007

Elliott Bay Book Company, 101 S Main St, Seattle, WA 98104 ☎1-800/962-5311 or 206/624-6600, *www.elliottbaybooks.com*

Rand McNally, 444 N Michigan Ave, Chicago, IL 60611 ☎312/321-1751; 150 E 52nd St, New York, NY 10022 ☎212/758-7488; 595 Market St, San Francisco, CA 94105 ☎415/777-3131; plus more than twenty stores across the US (call ☎1-800/333-0136 ext 2111 or check *www.randmcnally.com* for your nearest branch, and mail order)

Addresses

In Russian usage, the street name is always written before the number in **addresses**. When addressing letters, Russians start with the country, followed by a six-digit postal code, then the street, house and apartment number, and finally the addressee's name; the sender's details are usually written on the bottom of the envelope. The number of the house, building or complex may be preceded by *dom*, abbreviated to *d.* Two numbers separated by an oblique dash (for example, 16/21) usually indicate that the building is on a corner; the second figure is the street number on the smaller side street. However, if a building occupies more than one number (for example, 4/6), it is also written like this; you can usually tell when this is the case as the numbers will be close to each other and will both be even or odd. *Korpus* or *k.* indicates a building within a complex, *podezd* (abbreviated to *pod.*), an entrance number, *etazh* (*et.*) the floor and *kvartira* (*kv.*) the apartment. **Floors** are numbered in American or Continental fashion, starting with the ground floor, which Russians would call *etazh 1*. To avoid confusion we have followed the Russian usage throughout this book.

The main **abbreviations** used in St Petersburg (and in this book) are: ul. (for *ulitsa*, street); nab. (for *naberezhnaya*, embankment); pr. (for *prospekt*, avenue); per. (for *pereulok*, lane) and pl. (for *ploshchad*, square). Other common terms include *most* (bridge), *bulvar* (boulevard), *shosse* (highway), *alleya* (alley) and *sad* (garden).

Since 1992 many **street names** have officially reverted to their former (mostly pre-revolutionary) titles, though you'll still hear the old Soviet names used in everyday speech. In this book, streets are referred to by their "correct" name at the time of going to press, but don't be surprised at the occasional difference between the names in this book, and those on the ground. In the city centre most of the streets now have **bilingual signs** (Cyrillic and Latin script), which make it easier to find your way around.

Visitors should also be aware of the quintessentially St Petersburg distinction between the **main entrance stairway** (*paradnaya lesnitsa*) of an apartment building, and the subsidiary entrances off the **inner courtyard** or *dvor*. Traditionally the former was for show, with handsome mirrors and carpets, while the real life of the apartments revolved around the *dvor*. In Soviet times the grand stairways were gradually reduced to the darkened, shabby stairwells of today, but the *dvor* never lost its role as the spiritual hearth of St Petersburg life.

CYRILLIC ADDRESSES

alleya	аллея	*naberezhnaya*	набережная
bulvar	бульвар	*pereulok*	переулок
dom	дом	*ploshchad*	площадь
dvor	двор	*podezd*	подъезд
etazh	этаж	*prospekt*	проспект
kvartira	квартира	*sad*	сад
korpus	корпус	*shosse*	шоссе
most	мост	*ulitsa*	улица

Costs, money and banks

Successive booms and slumps during the 1990s have shown the folly of trying to predict the future of Russia's economy. However, one feature that's likely to remain is the infuriating two-tier price system used by museums, hotels and theatres, and on long-distance trains and internal flights, whereby foreigners are charged anything from two to ten times the price that locals pay. In other spheres, they pay the same and competition prevails, so it's worth shopping around for all consumer goods and services. The following will give you a general idea of how much you're likely to spend during a visit – for more detail, refer to the relevant listings sections of the book.

Package tourists with prepaid accommodation including full- or half-board really only need money for tickets to museums and palaces, buying gifts and grabbing the odd snack or drink. Unless you go overboard in expensive places, £20/$30 a day should suffice. **Independent travellers** will of course have to add accommodation costs and food on top of this figure. If you stay in a hotel, though, and frequent upmarket restaurants and bars, you'll be lucky to get by on less than you would spend in the average European or American city – say £55/$90 a day and one. Alternatively, if you stay with a family and live as the Russians do, you could spend £30/$48 a day or less on the whole works, including lodging, food and drink.

Currency

Since **the ruble** was revalued in 1998, the denominations in circulation have comprised coins of 5, 10 and 50 kopeks (100 kopeks equals one ruble) and 1, 2 and 5 rubles; and notes of 5, 10, 50, 100 and 500 rubles. In the unlikely event of you being palmed off with "old" rubles (recognizable by their strings of noughts), these are supposedly exchangeable in banks until the end of 2002, but have already vanished from circulation and are no longer legal tender.

Given that anything might happen to the ruble during the lifetime of this edition, **all prices given in this book are quoted in US dollars**, calculated at the rate of exchange at the time of writing (approximately 28 rubles to the dollar) – but you'll be expected to pay in rubles at the current rate, unless the transaction is with a private individual, such as a landlord, who may well prefer to receive hard currency. To find out the exchange rate set by the Central Bank, check at any bank or in the financial section of the *St Petersburg Times*.

Although almost everywhere specifies prices in rubles, a few restaurants, bars and hotels quote them in so-called **"standard units"** (*uslovnye yedenitsy*, abbreviated to УЕ in Cyrillic), which basically means dollars, converted into rubles. So far as restaurants go – and sometimes hotels and bars as well – this is often an indication that the establishment is way overpriced, and best avoided.

Currency declaration

Despite talk of abolishing the system, visitors arriving in Russia should still assume that they'll have to fill in a **currency declaration form** stating exactly how much money they are carrying and listing valuables such as gold jewellery, video cameras, laptop computers and mobile phones (the latter under the heading "high-frequency radio-electronic devices and means of communication"). Forms are often handed out on the plane shortly before landing, and can be obtained at Pulkovo-2 airport or any border crossing. The form will be stamped at customs.

Upon **leaving Russia**, you're obliged to fill in a duplicate form stating how much currency you are taking out of the country, and submit both for comparison to a customs official – but since you can now take out up to $500 without any declaration, it isn't necessarily a major problem if you lose the original form.

Changing money

As the black market is now a thing of the past and the exchange rate (*kurs*) is determined by market forces, there's no reason to change money anywhere other than in an official **bank** or a **currency exchange bureau** (*obmen valuty*). These can be found all over St Petersburg, including inside shops and restaurants (they're usually open for the same hours as the host establishment). Most banks set fairly similar rates, but it's worth seeking out the best one if you're changing a lot of money at once. The various rates are listed in the financial section of the *St Petersburg Times*. Commission should be negligible. You'll need to produce your passport.

Since the majority of banks and exchange bureaux only want US dollars, Deutschmarks, Finnish markka and maybe French francs, bringing any other currency will limit your options as to where you can change money. Moreover, due to widespread counterfeiting many places insist on new-style US dollars in good condition – notes in other currencies may also be refused if they're in a dodgy condition. Likewise, guard against receiving any ripped ruble notes in return. **Surplus rubles** can be converted back into the aforementioned hard currencies at most banks – you'll need your passport and currency declaration form.

Should you desperately need a cash top-up late at night, the box below details a few places that can oblige. The only time you should ever change money unofficially is with friends, having

currency exchange	обмен валюты
convertible currency	СКВ
standard units	УЕ
buying rate	покупка
selling rate	продажа
exchange rate	курс

first checked the rate in a bank and making sure that you are both happy with the deal. Otherwise stick to official changing points.

Travellers' cheques, credit cards and ATMs

Although cash is far easier to exchange, it's wise to carry some of your funds in **travellers' cheques**. In those banks and hotels that cash them, US dollar cheques are universally acceptable, and you should encounter few problems with Deutschmarks or Finnish markka. That said, the only brand that can be replaced if lost or stolen in St Petersburg is **American Express**, represented at the *Grand Hotel Europe* (Mon–Fri 9am–5pm; ☎329 60 60). American Express cheque or card holders needing help will probably find it easiest to phone the 24-hour emergency numbers in the UK – call ☎8 10 44 1273/571600 for lost cheques, ☎8 10 44 1273/696933 for lost credit cards, though replacing either will take up to a week. Amex will give you dollars for your travellers' cheques or as an advance on your credit card, but you'll have to exchange these for rubles at a bureau de change (there's one inside the Amex office, but it gives a poor rate).

The use of **credit cards** is spreading, but Russia is still a long way from being a plastic-friendly economy, so never take it for granted that you can pay by card and always check that your particular card is accepted. You'll usually need to show your passport or some other form of identification when paying by credit card. Always make sure that the transaction is properly recorded and keep the receipt.

Visa and Eurocard holders will find it relatively easy to get **cash advances** (in rubles); even small bureaux de change tend to offer this service (you'll need your passport). Mastercard and other major credit cards are generally accepted only at the larger banks. Commission fees vary from bank to bank.

24-hour exchanges

AnimaBank, Nevskiy pr. 44

Inkasbank, Botkinskaya ul. 6

Nevsky Palace Hotel, Nevskiy pr. 57

Ogni Moskvy, nab. reki Fontanki 67/69

Sberbank, *Moskva Hotel*, pl. Aleksandra Nevskovo 2

ATMs are now fairly common in the city centre, but take only a limited selection of cards. All Mostbank branches accept Visa, Eurocard, Mastercard, American Express, Union Card, Cirrus and Plus C; the *Nevsky Palace* and *Grand Hotel Europe* have ATMs that pay out in dollars as well as rubles; and AlfaBank ATMs don't level any charge on Visa withdrawals. You can find a complete list of ATMs that accept Visa cards on *www.visa.com*. A warning is in order, however: banks' security systems have been penetrated and clients' accounts cleaned out as recently as 1999, so it's prudent to use a debit or credit card with a relatively low limit, and keep the receipts for every withdrawal you make. Russian experts in bank fraud recommend that one eschews ATMs in favour of cash advances from a bank teller – but then again, the last sting on 250 Visa and Europay users was thought to have been an inside job at Sberbank. Also beware of inadvertently getting your card stuck in deactivated ATMs belonging to banks that went under during the crash of 1998.

Transferring money to Russia from abroad is quite feasible, as most now have agreements with British and American banks. One of the easiest methods is to use **Western Union**, who will transfer money in your name to specific banks in St Petersburg. With all transfers you should check beforehand exactly how much it will cost you, as both the Russian and overseas bank will levy a fee.

Mail and telecommunications

Post

The Russian **postal system** is notoriously inefficient, and there's no sign of modernization yet. Incoming international mail takes up to three weeks to arrive, while the outbound service is even less reliable. As a result, most Russians entrust letters to someone travelling to the West, for safer postage there, while foreigners either emulate them, employ an international courier firm, or communicate by email instead (see p.4).

To **post a letter**, your best bet is to try the *Grand Hotel Europe* or the *Nevsky Palace Hotel*, both of which offer a service dispatching letters only, via Finland, for around $1.50 to Europe and $2 to the US. They take around four days to arrive. Various firms offer a similar so-called **fast delivery service** (see box below), which can take anything from three to five days for letters (usually via Finland). The most expensive option is to use the international courier services (see box below). With all of these services it pays to shop around for the best deal.

St Petersburg's **main post office** (*glavniy pochtamt*) is at Pochtamtskaya ulitsa 9 (Mon–Sat 9am–9pm, Sun 10am–8pm ☎312 83 05), just off St Isaac's Square. **District post offices** (*pochta*) are generally open from 9am to 2pm and 3pm to 7pm and can be identified by the blue and yellow sign depicting a postman's horn and the frigate emblem of the city. **Parcels** *must* be taken unwrapped to the main post office, where they'll be inspected and wrapped for you, though you can then send them off from any post office. If you only want stamps, it's easier to go to the postal counters in a big **hotel** like the *Astoria* or *Pulkovskaya*, rather than queue in a post office, although there's a heavy mark-up on the price.

Fast-delivery postal services

EMS Garantpost, Konnogvardeyskiy bulvar 4 ☎311 96 71

Post International, Nevskiy pr. 20 ☎219 44 72

Westpost, Nevskiy pr. 86 ☎275 07 84, 327 30 92 or 327 32 11

International courier services

DHL, Izmaylovskiy pr. 4 ☎326 64 00; *Nevskiy Palace Hotel* ☎325 61 00

Federal Express, pr. Yuriya Gagarina 34 ☎299 90 45

TNT, nab. reki Moyki 58 ☎118 33 30; *Hotel Europe* ☎329 64 67

UPS, Shpalernaya ul. 51 ☎327 85 40

Phones

Public phonecard phones have largely superseded the old-style payphones that used *zhetony* (tokens). The most common are the green-and-white **SPT phones**, which can be used for local, intercity and international calls. They sometimes take coins as well, although this is only really practical for local calls. SPT **phonecards** are sold in metro stations, post offices and banks in various denominations of units, costing from $4 upwards.

The big hotels and flashier restaurants also have **BCL card phones**, which use encrypted satellite links for international connections. These sometimes have an echo and are expensive, although still cheaper than in your **hotel room or business centre**, where the cost of an international call can be anything from $5 to $25 a minute. Another option (mainly useful for calling the US) is the so-called **country direct service**, whereby you call a toll-free number in St Petersburg, Moscow or the US and get connected to a US operator who can place collect calls or chargecard calls to the US, and occasionally other countries. Companies offering this service are AT&T (☎325 50 42), Sprint (☎095 61 33 or 155 61 33) and MCI (☎8 10 1-800/497-7222).

Another way to make an international call is to go to a **communications centre** (*peregovorny punkt*) – there's one in every district. The main communications centre is the **International Telephone and Telegraph Office** at Bolshaya Morskaya ul. 3–5, near Admiralty Arch (daily 9am–9pm). Card-operated international phones are on the left, at the back of the office; cards are sold from the kiosk in the centre of the hall. Alternatively, you can prepay from the international calls desk and wait for your name and booth number to be announced over the tannoy – the latter method is cheaper. If you're lucky enough to have access to a **private phone**, you'll find that local calls are still free, while rates for intercity and international calls are as low as you'll find anywhere, the latter being about the same price as calls from the West to Russia.

Mobile phones are now widely used in St Petersburg, but check if you're planning to take one to Russia that it will work there, and be certain to list it on your customs declaration (see p.40). Since access tariffs are extremely high, visitors who intend to use a mobile extensively, or over several months, will save money by renting a phone from one of the many local dealers. Tariffs appear on the Web sites of GSM (*www.nwgsm.com*) and Delta Telecom (*www.deltatelecom.com*).

Nowadays it's possible to call just about any country direct. To **make a direct international call** dial 8, wait for the tone to change and then dial 10, followed by the country code, city code (omitting the initial zero if present) and subscriber number. Calls placed through the international operator (☎079) cost twice as much as those dialled direct and may take a couple of hours to come through. The number for **international directory enquiries** in St Petersburg is ☎274 93 83. To call anywhere in Russia, or most of the former Soviet republics (except the Baltic States), dial 8 followed by the city code (with any zeros).

Under the current banding system, the **cheapest times to call** are between 10pm and 8am and at weekends; this applies equally to calls made from public phones, hotels and communications centres. However, from 10pm to 11pm it's virtually impossible to get a connection as the lines are so busy.

Always bear in mind the **time difference** when calling Russia from the West. Lines are at their busiest during UK or US office hours, but you'll have fewer problems getting through at, say, 7am in the UK – which is 10am in St Petersburg. Conversely, should you phone St Petersburg after 3pm UK time, everyone will have already left the office (it's acceptable to call people at home up until midnight, local time).

Direct dialling codes

To St Petersburg

From Britain	☎ 00 7 812
From Ireland	☎ 00 7 812
From the US and Canada	☎ 011 7 812
From Australia and New Zealand	
	☎ 0011 7 812

From St Petersburg

Australia	☎ 8 (pause) 10 61
Finland	☎ 8 (pause) 10 358
Ireland	☎ 8 (pause) 10 353
New Zealand	☎ 8 (pause) 10 64
UK	☎ 8 (pause) 10 44
US and Canada	☎ 8 (pause) 10 1

Fax, email and the Internet

Given the inadequacy of the postal system, a lot of international communications are done by fax or email, and the Internet is now widely used by firms involved in business overseas. All the main post offices and district communications centres now have **fax** facilities and charge $1–1.50 per page for international transmissions. The most central **email and Internet** facilities can be found at NevaLink in the Railway Tickets Office at nab. kanala Griboedova 24 (Mon–Fri noon–6pm; ☎ 168 67 34) and on the second floor of Moscow Station (daily 8am–11.45pm; ☎ 277 25 17), the International Telephone & Telegraph Office (see above), and the Tetris Internet Café at ul. Chernyakovskovo 33, within walking distance of Ligovskiy Prospekt metro

(Mon–Fri 10am–9pm, Sat & Sun 1–9pm; ☎ 325 48 77, www.net.cafe.spb.ru), all of which charge about $2–3 an hour. Rates are $1 lower at ul. Chapaeva 6, ten minutes' walk from Gorkovskaya metro on the Petrograd Side, or the Cyber Club at Starobelskaya ul. 23, near Staraya Derevnya metro (which has private cubicles), while far-flung VIST, at Krasnoputilovskaya ul. 31 (trolleybus #27 from Kirovskiy Zavod metro), charges only $0.70 an hour.

If you bring your own computer to Russia and need to connect to the Internet, you'll require an (American) Bell lead for your modem that can connect directly to a five-pin Russian telephone plug, or a UK/Russian adaptor. Since AOL and Compuserve closed down their Russian gateways, the field has been dominated by home grown ISPs like NevaLink (☎ 310 54 42, info@nevalink.ru), Matrix (☎ 967 81 52, support@matrix) and Tario.Net (☎ 294 89 85). Clients must open an account and choose between prepaying or buying branded Internet scratch-cards from a computer stockist, valid for a set number of hours' use. With these, you call up the ISP, give your account number and then the PIN number that's on the back, every time you go online. If you bring a computer into the country, make sure you write it in your customs declaration and avoid putting it through any X-ray machines (insist on a hand examination). When using a computer in Russia be wary of the fluctuations in the electricity current. If you need help, there are computer dealers all over St Petersburg.

CYRILLIC SCRIPT AND THE INTERNET

One difficulty with accessing Web sites and receiving emails from Russia is that there are two different systems for representing Cyrillic letters. One is the so-called **WIN encoding** (officially CP-1251), the other is the **KOI-8** system, favoured by Russians among themselves. PCs with Windows 98 or later have everything needed to handle either system, providing you activate your machine by following the simple instructions on Paul Gorodyansky's free site http://ourworld.compuserve.com/homepages/PaulGor/. This enables Outlook Express users to set up both their browser and email for Cyrillic, and Hotmail and Yahoo! users to read and write emails in Cyrillic. For those with Macs or PCs with Windows 95 or earlier, you need to install Cyrillic fonts from http://funet.fi/pub/culture/russian/comp/fonts/fonts.html or http://babel.uoregon.edu/yamada/fonts/russian.html, by changing the default font in your email programme. For Web page access, PC users with Windows 98 and Internet Explorer version 5.0 or later should follow Gorodyansky's instructions. With other browsers – including Netscape or any Mac software – you need to replace the existing default font by KOI-8 or WIN Cyrillic. If you receive a document composed of question marks you've been sent it in an unreadable "ornamental" Cyrillic font, and need to ask for it to be re-sent in Arial, Courier or some other standard font.

If you don't mind paying for the extra convenience of having all communication links, as well as photocopying and the use of computers and printers, under one roof – plus the likelihood of having English-speaking staff on hand – the main **business centres** are the American Business Center at Bolshaya Morskaya ul. 7 (Mon–Fri 9am–5pm; ☎110 60 42, fax 311 07 94) and at the back of the lobby in the *Nevsky Palace Hotel*; the Helsinki Center at Nevskiy pr. 1 (Mon–Fri 9am–6pm; ☎312 35 81, fax 312 51 22); and the centres in the *Astoria*, *Grand Hotel Europe*, *Pribaltiyskaya*, *Pulkovskaya* and other, less grand hotels.

The media

Though the media is now freer from state control than it ever was in Soviet or Tsarist times, it is overwhelmingly beholden to financial oligarchs who have an interest in manipulating Russia's newspapers and TV stations to their advantage, and state control is creeping back. Unless you read Russian or have access to the Internet, local English-language papers will be your chief source of information.

Much of Russia's media is controlled by the same oligarchs who own the country's banks and industry, and the battles fought by their media proxies are carried out with blatant disregard for journalistic ethics. The main players are Boris Berezovsky, who controls ORT, TV6, *Kommersant* and *Nezavisimaya Gazeta*; Vladimir Gusinsky, whose MediaMOST group owns *Sevodnya*, *Igoti* and NTV; Uneximbank's Vladimir Potanin, who owns *Komsomolskaya Pravda*, *Izvestiya* and *Russkiy Telegraf*; and Mikhail Khodorkovsky of Bank Menatep, whose publications include the *St Petersburg Times* and the Russian *Cosmopolitan* and *Playboy*. Recently, both Gusinsky and Berezovsky have come under fire from the Kremlin, and the struggle for control of the media is one of the hottest issues in Russian politics.

The press

If you can understand the language, the **Russian press** holds some surprises for those who remember it from olden days. *Izvestiya*, once the organ of the Soviet government and later pro-Yeltsin, has seen the breakaway *Novie Izvestiya* – Russia's first colour daily – take its best journalists and most of its readers away, despite financial backing from the oil giant LUKoil. *Pravda*, the old Party daily, has also split, with the original – and still Communist – paper suing the new, Greek-owned *Pravda-5* for the right to the name, while the erstwhile Young Communists' daily, *Komsomolskaya Pravda*, has become a popular tabloid backed by Uneximbank and the gas monopoly Gazprom. The elite themselves peruse *Kommersant*, the most sober and insightful paper since *Nezavisimaya Gazeta*'s reputation for integrity succumbed to Berezovsky's patronage – while Russia's angry dispossessed buy *Sovetskaya Rossiya* or *Zavtra*, both unashamedly far right, xenophobic hate-sheets.

The best-selling **local papers** in St Petersburg are *Smena*, *Sankt-Peterburgskie Vedomosti* and *Chas Pik*, the last having strong connections with the security forces and Governor Yakovlev, and the best listings of what's on (augmented on Fridays by a separate supplement, *Pyatnitsa*).

Foreign newspapers aren't widely available in St Petersburg, but you're sure to find the *International Herald Tribune*, *Newsweek*, *The Times* and *The Guardian* in the *Grand Hotel Europe*, *Nevsky Palace* and *Astoria* hotels, heavily marked-up and a day or two old. Many foreigners therefore prefer the **local English-language press**, which is better distributed, free and will tell you what's going on locally. The doyen of the pack is the *St Petersburg Times* (published Tues & Fri), which is good for local news and features, and has a useful listings and reviews section in the Friday edition. The monthly *Neva News* is still hanging on by the skin of its teeth and is mostly read for its sociological features.

The full-colour monthly *Pulse* is more into style than news, but carries excellent club and exhibition reviews, while the magazine *Where St Petersburg* contains tourist-related features, news and listings. All are free and available from hotels, shops and restaurants frequented by Westerners. The *St Petersburg Times* was one of the first papers in the world to go online (*www.sptimes.ru*), followed by its big sister the *Moscow Times* (*www.themoscowtimes.com*) and its rival *Pulse* (*www.pulse.spb.ru*).

TV, video and radio

Russia's three national television stations are at war over more than just ratings, as the Kremlin and media moguls Berezovsky and Gusinsky vie for the power to mould public opinion. **ORT** (Channel 1) is the nation's favourite for its soaps, game shows and classic Soviet films. Its support for Yeltsin and Putin swung their elections, making Berezovsky the kingmaker of Russian politics; but now he's at loggerheads with Putin, under the same pressure that was previously applied to Gusinsky (who spent three days in Moscow's infamous Butyurka prison) after **NTV** (Channel 4) angered the Kremlin with its reportage of the war in Chechnya and the *Kursk* disaster. It also screens slick thrillers, drama and documentaries, putting it streets ahead of the wholly state-owned **RTR** (Channel 2), whose mixture of soaps, tedious state events and servile news gives its lowest rating of the three. Its local equivalents are **Channel 5** – aka Kultura or the Petersburg Channel – whose highbrow profile has been dumbed down and pervaded by praise of Governor Yakovlev, and the abysmal **LOT** (Leningrad Regional Television) that takes over its slot after 6.30pm. Additionally, there are **TV6**, a light entertainment youth channel founded with the help of CNN's Ted Turner; four secondary channels, available only with the aid of a subsidiary aerial, which show a mixture of imported US, Brazilian and Mexican films and soaps; and several local cable TV stations delivering MTV or Sky.

It's not exactly thrilling stuff, and the big hits are imported soaps and home-grown game shows – there are also a lot of adverts. Russians enjoy more choice when it comes to **videos**. Most video shops carry both Russian and foreign movies (the latter are usually dubbed into Russian). However, West Video, Nevskiy pr. 86 (Mon–Fri 10am–8pm ☎275 07 84), hires out foreign movies in the original language for around $1.20 per video, plus a $4.20 deposit.

As far as **radio** goes, most cafés and bars tune into one of the many FM music stations. The most popular is Europa Plus, which dishes out "the best of the West" on 100.5 FM, the equally mainstream Eldorado (101.4 FM) and the hipper Radio Modern (104.0 FM). Russkoe Radio (104.4 FM) is solely devoted to Russian music of the 1960s, 1970s and 1980s, and Radio Nostalgie (105.3 FM) offers a mixture of easy listening from France and Russia. For classical music, tune in to Radio Orfey (1125 KHz AM). Should you have a short-wave radio, it is also possible to pick up the BBC World Service (at variable frequencies depending on the time of day) and the Voice of America (6866 MHz).

Opening hours, public holidays and festivals

Shops in St Petersburg are generally open **Monday to Saturday from 9am to 6pm or 7pm,** though some large stores stay open later than this and many neighbourhood shops are open 24 hours. Most shops close for an hour or two for lunch between 1pm and 4pm. Sunday opening is erratic, with an increasing number of food shops, bars and restaurants choosing to open. As for the kiosks that litter the city, many stay open every day until 10pm and some stay open until the small hours.

Opening hours for **museums and galleries** tend to be from 10am or 11am to 5pm or 6pm. They are closed one day a week, but there are no hard and fast rules as to what day that might be. In addition, one day in the month will be set aside as a *sanitarniy den* or "cleaning day". Full opening hours are detailed in the text.

The situation regarding **churches** is more fluid. During the Soviet period, many were closed down altogether or converted into museums, swimming pools, cinemas and so on. The majority have now reverted to their former religious purpose, but for fear of theft may only be open for services, the times of which will be posted outside. The times of religious services in non-Orthodox Christian, Muslim and Jewish places of worship appear in the Friday edition of the *St Petersburg Times*.

Public holidays

Official **public holidays** (*prazdnik*) have been in a state of flux for years, since so many were associated with the former Soviet regime, and their post-Soviet replacements proved just as controversial. While traditional religious holidays such as Christmas and Easter have made a comeback, Good Friday is still a working day, much to the Church's annoyance. As Easter is a moveable feast according to the Orthodox calendar, it may coincide with public holidays in May, giving rise to an extended holiday period of three to four days. It's also worth noting that if public holidays fall at the weekend, a weekday will often be given off in lieu. Some holidays or anniversaries are celebrated by fireworks at 8pm or 9pm, or by the lighting of the flames on the Rostral Columns on the Strelka.

Public holidays

January 1 New Year's Day

January 6–7 Orthodox Christmas

February 23 Defenders of the Motherland Day

March 8 International Women's Day

May 1 and 2 International Labour Day/Spring Festival

May 9 Victory Day

June 12 Russian Day

November 7 no longer celebrating the anniversary of the October Revolution, but still a public holiday

---

Festivals

The best place to find information on St Petersburg's plethora of **festivals and events** is on the Internet at *www.cityvision2000.com* or *www.300.spb.ru*. Alternatively, the *St Petersburg Times, Pulse, Where St Petersburg* and posters and banners on the streets advertise events nearer the time.

There are numerous **music festivals**, from jazz (Feb, March & June) to contemporary classical (May & Oct) or avant-garde (April) – but classical music, ballet and opera claim centre stage during the ten-day **Musical Spring** (May), and the **Stars of the White Nights and Palaces of St Petersburg** festivals. These last two may be held from the end of May to the end of June (as they were in 2000) or run through June and July (as in earlier years), but will inevitably coincide with at least part of the actual **White Nights** (*Belye nochy*). This is the time when the sun barely dips below the horizon at night and the city parties into the small hours, with revellers thronging Nevskiy prospekt and the Neva embankment, where the raising of the bridges from 1.55am onwards occasions much popping of champagne corks. You can rely on nights being short and celebratory for at least two weeks on either side of the "official" White Nights between June 11 and July 2, with a day-long carnival during that period. There's also the **Festival of Festivals** film bash around this time – a rare chance to see something other than Hollywood or Euro pap – and a two-day **beer festival** on Palace Square (first weekend in June).

St Petersburg celebrates its own foundation on **City Day** (May 27) with brass bands and jolly games at various locales, especially the Peter and Paul Fortress, from which the traditional fireworks display is launched. **May Day** parades went out of fashion during the 1990s but may be on the verge of a comeback, while **Victory Day** (May 9), commemorating the surrender of the Nazis in 1945, is still fervently marked by the older generation, with a parade of war veterans down Nevskiy prospekt and wreath-laying ceremonies at the Piskarov Cemetery. The **Siege of Leningrad Day** (Sept 8) and the **anniversary of the breaking of the Blockade** (Jan 27) are also big days for veterans, but not public holidays, while the approach of **Navy Day** (last Sun in July), is heralded by the appearance of warships and subs in the Neva basin. On the day itself, motorboats ferry families out to open days on the warships, while the ships' crews drink and brawl

ashore (not a time to wander the streets), and the Rostral Columns are lit at night, augmented by a fireworks display. Thankfully, **Defenders of the Motherland Day** (Feb 23) is limited to wreath-laying ceremonies at selected sites.

Despite all the Christmas trees and bunting, Russians largely ignore the Western Christmas in the rush to prepare for **New Year** (*Noviy God*). This remains a family occasion until midnight, when a frenzied round of house-calling commences, getting steadily more drunken and continuing until dawn. As you cross the Neva, watch out for the blazing torches atop the Rostral Columns. In residential areas, you may see people dressed as *Dyed Moroz* (Grandfather Frost, the Russian equivalent of Father Christmas) and his female sidekick, Snegurochka (Snow Maiden), who do the rounds wishing neighbours a Happy New Year (*s Novim Godom!*).

The **Russian Orthodox Christmas** (*Rozhdestvo*) starts at midnight on January 6 and goes on until dawn the following day. The choir, the liturgy, the candles and the incense combine to produce a hypnotic sense of togetherness, which Russians call *sobornost*. Despite their emotional charge and Byzantine splendour, Orthodox services are come-and-go as you please, allowing non-believers to attend without embarrassment, but women should cover their heads and wear a skirt. The high point of the Orthodox calendar, though, is **Easter** (*Paskha*), when all the churches are packed with worshippers who exchange triple kisses and the salutation "Christ is Risen!" – "Verily He is Risen!" For both Easter and Christmas celebrations, the principal churches and the Alexander Nevsky Monastery are packed to the gills.

Less obviously, there are also the **religious festivals of other faiths**, celebrated in their places of worship. The synagogue on Lermontovskiy prospekt comes alive at Rosh HaShana, Yom Kippur, Hannuka and other Jewish festivals; the mosque on the Petrograd Side is the focus for Ramadan celebrations among the city's Muslim community; and the Buddhist temple across the river from Yelagin Island is at the heart of events during the sixteen-day Tibetan Buddhist New Year festival (*Tsagaalgan*; late Feb/early March).

Popular culture: sport, music and the arts

The ending of censorship and the economic crisis of the 1990s brought mixed blessings to sport, music and the arts, all of which enjoyed considerable state backing under the Soviet system. Many of the best artists, musicians and sporting figures have been lured to the West by the prospect of large earnings, leaving big gaps in the domestic scene, while imported films and sounds have reduced the demand for native offerings. On the other hand, players, directors and artists enjoy new possibilities to develop their careers and reach a wider audience.

Sport

There were very few sports at which the former Soviet Union didn't excel, such was the money poured into the system, and the rewards of foreign travel available to successful athletes. In St Petersburg, however, there are only a couple of sports events that command a mass popular following: soccer and ice hockey.

Despite a population of over five million, St Petersburg has traditionally lagged far behind Moscow in **soccer** – and many other cities too during Soviet times, when Leningrad's lacklustre premier team had its name changed from Stalinets to Zenit to avoid embarrassing the Great Leader. In recent years, however, Zenit has not only broken into the premier division but also won the Russian cup in 1999, beating Spartak Moscow in the process. Zenit now play at the Petrovskiy Stadium on the Petrograd Side, a vast improvement on their old home ground, the windswept Kirov Stadium. For more details, see p.318.

Ice hockey runs soccer a close second as Russia's most popular sport and SKA St Petersburg is one of Russia's strongest teams, though again not as successful as its Moscow rivals. Games are played at the Yubileyniy Sports Palace on the Petrograd Side or the larger Ice Palace in Malaya Okhta. Matches are fast and physical, cold but compelling viewing – the season starts in September and culminates in the annual world championships the following summer, when the Russians try their best to defeat Sweden, Canada and the US.

Music

Russia is one of the great musical nations of Europe, and Russians are justifiably proud of their **classical music** tradition. Tchaikovsky, Rimsky-Korsakov, Mussorgsky, Glinka, Stravinsky and Shostakovich are just some of the more famous figures associated with St Petersburg, and their music can still be heard regularly in concert halls across the city. Perhaps even more famous is the city's Mariinskiy company (still better known abroad by its previous name, the Kirov). Long renowned for its **ballet** troupe, the Mariinsky has now also established itself as one of the world's best **opera** companies under its flamboyant maestro Valery Gergiev. Venues and festivals are detailed in Chapter 12, "The Arts".

You can hear **folk music** on the city's main streets throughout the year, as once state-sponsored folk groups now busk for a living. The accordion and the balalaika are the mainstays of Russian folk music, but you'll see brass ensembles and manic fiddlers too – there's even a guy who plays tunes on a carpenter's saw, near the Church of the Saviour on the Blood. A stroll along Nevskiy prospekt usually unearths a group or two, and the Peter and Paul Fortress is another likely locality. Travesties of folk songs and romances are often performed in restaurant floorshows, but a few of the ensembles are worth listening to – look out for Lydia Smolyaninova, whose thin, high voice is well suited to the romances she sings.

Popular music

In a curious exception to their brilliance in other cultural fields, Russian pop music is usually regarded by foreigners as dire – and even that's too polite a word to describe the depths of bad taste plumbed by the giants of the scene, **Alla Pugachova** and **Filippe Kirkorov**. Alla gained national fame in the early 1980s and resembles a hybrid of Janis Joplin and Liberace, while Filippe is a six-foot-four, bug-eyed Adonis who sings and dresses like Elton John. They first met when he was an adoring schoolboy fan; their wedding in 1994 was like a coronation. Otherwise, the airwaves are dominated by girl and boy bands doing ultra-bland Europop, with the Pulp-like exception of **Mummi Troll** from Vladivostok and the multi-instrumental **Chiz**, whose fusion of Celtic, Russian and Soviet Roots music and imagery fits the prevailing mood of retro-patriotism. In Petersburg, you'll still hear recordings or imitators of the classic underground **rock bands** of the 1970s and '80s: **Akvarium**, fronted by Boris Grebenshikov, who are still in business; and **Kino**, who disbanded after their lead singer, Viktor Tsoy, died in a car crash in 1990. Petersburgers also remember **Sergei Kuryokhin**, who died in 1996, for his vast multimedia shows incorporating rock and classical musicians, artists and actors. There's even a festival named after him, whose Russian acronym is SKIF, which brings together DJs, performance artists and bands from Russia and afar, for three days in April. On the **club scene**, look out for local bands Dva Samolota (Two Planes), who mix reggae and dance music with bird noises, the art-dance quartet Kalibri, funk-oriented Pepinaki and visiting rappers Bogdan Titomir and Delphin.

Theatre and cinema

Theatre (*teatr*) has come to terms with the free market by playing it safe. Repertoires still rely heavily on the classics, leavened by farces, and productions at the larger theatres tend to be conservative. However, some of the smaller places are genuinely exciting – the Theatre on Liteyniy

won the Critics' Prize in 1998 and the Maliy Dramatic Theatre scooped an Olivier Award and many other prizes with Lev Dodin's productions of *The Cherry Orchard* and *The Possessed*. In April and October, the Baltiyskiy dom hosts international theatre festivals.

Puppet theatre (*Kukolniy teatr*) has a long tradition in Russia, and there are a handful of theatres devoted to the art form in St Petersburg alone. Russians also love **slapstick comedy and mime**; keep your eye open for performances by Litsedei or Mimigranty. More avant-garde **performance art** is represented by the renowned Derevo and DaNet, and at the international SKIF festival (see above).

Russian **cinema** (*kino*) has began its fight back against the deluge of Hollywood action movies and Euro soft porn by providing violence and sex in a Russian setting that's raw and contemporary or lushly historical. The St Petersburg director Andrei Balabanov has done both, with box-office hits *Brother* and *Brother 2* – tales of sibling love and contract killing – and two critically acclaimed Grand Guignol dramas, *Of Beasts and Men* and Kafka's *The Castle*. However the big money and patronage are in Moscow, where Nikita Mikhalkov, the Kremlin's favourite director, blows millions on dozy epics like *The Barber of Siberia* (in which his cameo role as Alexander III was about the only riveting moment). Other Russian films are best seen along with foreign art films, at one of the city's international film festivals, the biggest being the June Festival of Festivals.

For details of theatres, cinemas and performing arts **venues**, see Chapter 12, "The Arts".

Security, police and the Mafia

It's a measure of the new Russia that tourists no longer worry about hidden microphones or KGB agents, but muggers and mobsters. The Western media portray St Petersburg as a gangster-ridden city with shootings on every corner – an exaggeration of the situation even when it was at its worst in the early 1990s. However, visitors should certainly observe the usual precautions such as not flashing money or cameras around, and not going off with strangers. Try to blend in wherever possible – the less you look like a tourist, the smaller the risk of being targeted by petty criminals.

Personal security in St Petersburg is generally in inverse proportion to personal wealth. The main targets of crime (both Mafia-related and petty) are rich Russian businessmen or local politicians, next to whom tourists are considered small fry. While Russian financiers are in danger of assassination, the average citizen – or visitor – is no more likely to be a victim of crime than in any other large European city.

The police

The Ministry of the Interior (MVD) maintains several law-and-order forces, all of them armed and with a high profile on the streets. Foremost are the regular police, or **Militia** (*Militsiya*), which has largely replaced its old Ladas with imported patrol cars and adopted a new style of uniform based on that of US highway cops, with sartorial variations (jumpsuits, parkas, leather jackets) in shades of grey. Militiamen are much in evidence around metro stations, but are otherwise fairly unobtrusive.

The other main branch of the Militia is the **GIBDD**, or traffic police – still universally known by its former title, the GAI – who you're only likely to run into if you're driving or happen to be involved in an accident (see p.33). They wear Militia uniforms emblazoned with a badge, armband or large white letters reading ДПС (standing for *Dorozhno Patrulnaya Sluzhba*, or Highway Patrol Service).

Some checkpoints are also manned by the **OMON**, a paramilitary force charged with the responsibility of everything from riot control to counter-insurgency. In St Petersburg, they guard important state buildings, patrol crowds and lend muscle to Militia crackdowns on Mafia gangs. Dressed in green or grey camouflage and toting Kalasnikovs or pump-action shotguns, they look fearsome but are unlikely to bother tourists unless they get caught up in a raid of some kind. Should you be so unlucky, don't resist in any way – even verbally. The same goes for operations involving **RUOP**, the smaller Regional Force Against Organized Crime, whose teams wear civilian clothes or paramilitary uniforms like the OMON's, only the patch on the back reads РУОП instead of ОМОН.

Aside from having your passport scrutinized by a plainclothes agent at Pulkovo airport, you shouldn't have any contact with the once-feared KGB in its post-Soviet incarnation as the **Federal Security Service** (FSB) unless you get involved in environmental activism or high-tech acquisitions. While it remains to be seen if the FSB will become more intrusive now that one of its own former chiefs has become president of Russia, for the time being, its self-publicized counter-espionage coups are so remote from everyday life that Russians are happy to ignore it. Visitors are free to do likewise, or saunter past the Bolshoy dom (see p.221) out of curiosity (though taking photos is not advised).

You're far more likely to encounter **private security guards** in banks, stores, clubs or restaurants. Many are ex-KGB or OMON goons who can be brusque with customers at the door, especially if there's a house policy of excluding people who don't fit the bill.

The Mafia

Throughout the former USSR, the term **Mafia** is loosely applied to all kinds of rackets and crimes, whether they involve a handful of perpetrators or gangs with hundreds of members in different cities. The catch-all usage reflects the fact that so many of them originated in the nexus between black marketeering and political power in Soviet times, when the vastness of the USSR and the vagaries of central planning fostered widespread corruption during the Era of Stagnation. With the transition to capitalism the whole economy came up for grabs, as ex-Party bureaucrats acquired vast assets through privatization and black marketeers became merchant-bankers. Legitimate entrepreneurs and foreign investors were forced to pay protection money to one gang or another, while in turn leading Mafiosi found their own protectors among the political elite, police and judiciary – resulting in everyone being covered by what Russians call a *krysha* (roof).

Given its manifold links with business and politics, organized crime seems set to remain a feature of society, and its influence in St Petersburg shows no sign of abating. The assassination of the city's Deputy Governor in 1997 and the liberal politician Galina Starovoitova a year later have been followed by a spate of killings of bankers and businessmen, rivalling the most lawless period of the early 1990s – but the impact on ordinary citizens and tourists has been negligible.

Personal security

As a tourist, you're likely to encounter only **petty crime** such as thefts from cars and hotel rooms.

Sensible precautions include making photocopies of your passport and visa, leaving passports and tickets in the hotel safe, and noting down travellers' cheque and credit card numbers. If you have a car, don't leave anything in view when you park it. Vehicles without an alarm are regularly stolen and luggage and valuables make a tempting target, particularly from easily recognizable foreign and rental cars.

Though there's less risk of **being mugged** in St Petersburg than in, say, Miami, it's equally dangerous to resist, given the availability of firearms. Thankfully, most crimes of this type are faced only by drunken tourists who follow prostitutes back to strange rooms or into a taxi late at night. You're far more likely to be at risk from pickpockets – particularly groups of streetkids or gypsies, who dance around you while they rifle your pockets, but rarely injure anyone. Don't take pity on the children or give in to hassle from groups of women – they often simply note where you keep your money and somebody else gets you further down the street.

If you are unlucky enough to have something stolen, you'll need to **report it to the police**, if only to get a letter for your insurance company to claim for losses. In theory, there is a 24-hour hotline staffed by officers speaking foreign languages at the GUVD (police headquarters) in the Bolshoy dom (☎278 30 14), but in practice it often doesn't function as advertised, and may simply ask the local Militia station to call you back. If obliged to deal with a Militia man who understands only Russian, try the phrase *Menya obokrali* – "I've been robbed".

In theory, you're supposed to carry some form of **identification** at all times, and the Militia can stop you in the street and demand it. In practice, they're rarely bothered if you're clearly a foreigner (unless you're driving) and tend to confine themselves to harassing Gypsies.

Women's St Petersburg

The emancipation of women under Communism always had more to do with increasing the available workforce than with promoting equality or encouraging women to pursue their own goals. Although equal wages, maternity benefits and subsidized crèches were all prescribed by law, their provision fell far short of the ideal, saddling women with a double burden of childcare and full-time work.

As a result, feminism is something of a dirty word in Russia, and self-proclaimed feminists will get short shrift from both sexes here.

Female visitors to St Petersburg will find that Russian men veer between extreme gallantry and crude chauvinism. Sexual harassment is marginally less of a problem than in Western Europe – and nowhere near as bad as in Mediterranean countries – but without the familiar linguistic and cultural signs, it's easy to misinterpret situations. Attitudes in St Petersburg are much more liberal than in the countryside, where women travelling alone can still expect to encounter stares and comments. Single women should nonetheless avoid going to certain nightclubs and bars, where their presence may be misconstrued by the local pimps and prostitutes. Although you'll see plenty of Russian women flagging down cars as potential taxis, unaccompanied foreign women would be ill-advised to do likewise.

The main feminist contact in St Petersburg is the Centre for Gender Issues, founded by Olga Lipovskaya (☎ 455 12 48), which runs assertiveness courses, an advice line and a women's refuge, and publishes a journal called *Zhenskaya Chitenie* (Women's Reading).

Directory

BRING In summer bring a waterproof jacket or compact umbrella for occasional showers. You'll also need some protection against mosquitoes; barrier or treatment cream is advisable and you can buy anti-mosquito plugs in St Petersburg. In winter, late autumn and early spring, gloves, a hat or scarf that covers your face, and thick socks are essential. Thermal underwear goes a long way to keeping your legs warm and a pair of boots with non-slip soles is recommended for the snow and ice. A pocket torch for dark stairwells also comes in handy.

CHILDREN Although children and babies are doted on by Russians, public facilities for younger children are thin on the ground. Most supermarkets stock baby food and disposable nappies, though you may wish to bring a small supply to tide you over. Note that breastfeeding in public is totally unacceptable. Children up to the age of 7 ride free on all public transport. For a list of specific places in St Petersburg that might appeal to children, see p.312.

CIGARETTES Nearly all Western brands are available, though many of the packets sold from kiosks are made under licence (or counterfeited) in Russia or Turkey; Marlboro kiosks and hotel shops are likelier to stock the genuine article. Traditional Soviet brands like Belomor and TU-144 are truly revolting. It is normal to be approached by strangers asking for a light

(*Mozhno pokurit?*) or a cigarette. While museums and public transport are no-smoking (*ne kurit*) zones, Russians puff away everywhere else, and see nothing wrong with it. However, many fast-food chains have a no-smoking policy.

CONTRACEPTIVES Turkish-made condoms (*prezervativiy*) are available in all pharmacies and many 24-hour shops and kiosks, but are generally untrustworthy, so bring your own.

CULTURAL CENTRES AND LIBRARIES The British Council (☎325 22 77, www.britishcouncil.ru) has a small library and information centre in the courtyard of nab. reki Fontanki 46, near the Anichkov Bridge. In the same building is the Prince George Galitzine Memorial Library (Mon–Fri noon–8pm, Sat noon–4pm), which contains an extensive collection of books about Russia in English. It is not yet a lending library, but tourists are welcome to use the reading room.

DRUGS Grass (*travka*) and cannabis resin (*plastilin*) from the Altay Mountains are now commonplace on the club scene, as are acid, heroin and Ecstasy. At some clubs, the merest whiff will draw the bouncers; at others, dope-smokers are stolidly ignored. While simple possession of dope may incur only a caution, hard drugs – and smuggling – are still punishable, in theory at least, by the death penalty. The safest policy is to avoid all drugs entirely.

ELECTRICITY A standard Continental 220 volts AC; most European appliances should work as long as you have an adaptor for European-style, two-pin round plugs. North Americans will need this plus a transformer.

FILM AND PHOTOS Outlets for imported film and one-hour processing services can be found all over the city centre, Agfa, Fuji and Kodak Express all being represented. Do not take photos of foreign consulates – you might have your film confiscated. When leaving the country put films in your pocket, as Russian filmsafe X-rays do not always live up to the name.

GAY AND LESBIAN LIFE Despite more enlightened recent social policies, Russian society remains quite strongly homophobic. Male homosexuality is no longer a criminal offence and there are a number of homosexual singers and artists, but private individuals are unlikely to be open about their sexuality. A number of gay and lesbian groups are active in St Petersburg and in Moscow, and there is a small but thriving club scene in both cities. For contacts in St Petersburg, try the Gay and Lesbian Association "Kriliya" ("Wings"; ☎312 31 80, *Krilija@ilga.org*), the Tchaikovsky Fund (☎395 02 96), or check out the Web site *www.gay.ru*. For more on gay and lesbian life in St Petersburg, see p.297.

GUIDED TOURS Some museums oblige visitors to take a guided tour, while others include it as an option. You should assume it will be in Russian unless you take the trouble to arrange an English-speaking guide by phoning ahead, and even then it may depend on the museum's staffing roster as to whether there's anyone available.

LANGUAGE Russian-language tuition can be arranged in the UK through companies such as City College Manchester, Wythenshawe Park Centre, Moor Rd, Manchester M23 9BQ (2–8-week courses; ☎0161/957 1500). Alternatively, you can book a course at the Swiss-run Liden & Denz Language School in St Petersburg, Transportniy per. 11, 5th floor (☎325 22 41, *www.lidenz.ru*); a two-week course costs $720–850.

LAUNDRIES You can have your clothes washed and ironed in three days by Stirka-Servis at Liteyniy pr. 16 (☎275 65 60) and Udelniy pr. 51 (☎553 53 00; both Mon–Sat 10am–9pm) for about $0.70 per kilo, plus $1 for delivery.

LEFT LUGGAGE Most bus and train stations have lockers and/or a 24-hour left-luggage office, but you would be tempting fate to use them.

LOST PROPERTY Anything you might lose is unlikely to end up at the lost property depots (*stol nakhodok*) at Sredniy pr. 70 and ul. Zakharyevskaya 19, though there's slightly more chance of lost property being recovered at Pulkovo-2 II airport (☎324 37 87).

MARRIAGE AGENCIES The foreign-language press is full of advertisements by agencies offering to supply Russian brides for foreign males. Questions of morality and taste aside, a lot of them are purely aimed at extracting money from

hapless Westerners, and even where "genuine", many of the women are simply planning to divorce their spouses as soon as they gain a foreign residency permit or passport. For a real relationship, find someone yourself.

PATRONYMICS AND DIMINUTIVES Besides their first name and surname, every Russian has a patronymic derived from their father's name, such as Konstantinovich (son of Konstantin) or Ivanova (daughter of Ivan), which follows the first name as a polite form of address. While many older Russians abide by its use and find Western informality rather crass, the patronymic is falling out of use in society at large. Once genuine intimacy has been established Russians love to use affectionate diminutives like Sasha or Shura (for Alexander), Anya or Anichka (for Anna) and may try to make one out of your name.

PROSTITUTION Prostitution is not illegal under Russian law, and most upmarket hotels, bars and nightclubs have their quota of prostitutes. Business is fairly blatant and strictly in hard currency; the risks are the same as anywhere else in the world. In nightclubs, foreign men often don't realize that talking to or dancing with a woman can create expectations that a deal will follow; three dances constitute an unwritten contract, after which pimps may try to extract money, regardless of whether things go any further. Less obviously, it causes problems for Russian women *not* involved in prostitution, who fear to enter such places alone lest they be mistaken for a freelance prostitute and get beaten up by the mob. If you arrange to meet a Russian woman, respect any doubts she might express about the venue, and rendezvous outside so that you can go in together.

RACISM It is a sad fact that racism in Russia is a casual and common phenomenon, although it is less common for it to be expressed with violence. Mostly directed against other ethnic groups of the old Soviet Union, such as Gypsies, Chechens, Azerbaijanis and Central Asians, it also extends to Africans, Arabs, Vietnamese and Jews (the last being an old enmity, exploited by tsars and Communists alike). Anyone dark-skinned can expect to be stopped by the police on a regular basis.

STUDENT CARDS ISIC card holders get a fifty percent reduction on museum and palace admission charges, which can quickly add up to quite a saving. The card also entitles you to discounts at some cafes and nightclubs, as listed on the Sindbad Travel Web site (*www.sindbad.ru*). If you have proof that you're a student, it's possible to obtain an ISIC card at the *St Petersburg International Hostel* (see p.274), where Sindbad Travel also offers a range of discount air tickets.

SUPERSTITIONS Russians consider it bad luck to kiss or shake hands across a threshold, or return home to pick up something that's been forgotten. Before departing on a long journey, Russians gather all their luggage by the door and sit on it for a minute or two, to bring themselves luck for the journey. When buying flowers for your hostess, make certain that there's an odd number of blooms; even-numbered bouquets are for funerals. It's also considered unlucky to whistle indoors, or put a handbag on the floor.

TAMPONS These are widely available all over town. Local chemists sell Ukrainian-made Tampax, while imported ones can be found in large supermarkets.

TAPOCHKI Visiting a Russian home, you'll be invited to slip off your shoes and ease into *tapochki* (slippers), thus preventing dirt from being traipsed into the flat, and drawing you into the cosy ambience of domestic life. Their institution-al equivalent (such as visitors to many of the museums are obliged to wear) bear the same name but take the form of felt overshoes with tapes to tie around the ankles.

TIME St Petersburg uses Moscow Time, which is generally three hours ahead of Britain and eight hours ahead of US Eastern Standard Time, with the clocks going forward on the last Saturday of March and back again on the last Saturday of October.

TIPPING In taxis, the fare will usually be agreed in advance so there's no need to tip; in restaurants, no one will object if you leave an extra ten percent or so, but in most places it's not compulsory. Check, too, that it hasn't already been included. In those places where a service charge is compulsory, it ranges from ten to fifteen percent; the exact figure will be stated on the menu.

TOILETS It's generally acceptable for non-customers to use the toilets in restaurants and hotels, since public toilets (*tualet* or *WC*) are few and far between – despite efforts to boost numbers by locating Portaloo-type cabins in public parks and squares. There is a small charge, which includes a wad of toilet paper given out by the attendant. Otherwise, make for the nearest *McDonald's*. You can buy toilet paper (*tualetenaya bumaga*) in any supermarket or pharmacy.

The City

Chapter 1

Introducing the City

S t Petersburg is built on a grand scale, which makes mastering the public transport system a top priority. The city is split by the **River Neva** and its tributaries, with further sections delineated by the course of the (canalized) rivers Moyka and Fontanka, all of which conveniently divide St Petersburg into a series of islands, making it fairly easy to get your bearings.

The city centre lies on the south bank of the Neva, with the curving River Fontanka marking its southern boundary. The area **Within the Fontanka** (Chapter 2) is traversed by a series of wide avenues fanning out from the Admiralty, whose golden spire is an obvious landmark. **Nevskiy prospekt**, the easternmost of these avenues, has been the backbone of the city for the last two centuries, and passes close by many of St Petersburg's main sights, including the Winter

---

Cyrillic script, street names and abbreviations

Throughout the text, we've transliterated the names of all streets and squares, and translated those of the sights, which means that no Cyrillic appears in the main text. On the ground, however, **street signs** outside the city centre are in Cyrillic only (most of those in the city centre are now in both Cyrillic and Latin alphabets). To help you find your way around, we've included a list of the main streets, squares and museums in Cyrillic at the end of each chapter. For details of the transliteration system we've used, see p.441.

Many **streets** have officially reverted to their former (mostly pre-revolutionary) titles, though some people still use the old Soviet names. In the following chapters, streets are referred to by their "correct" name at the time of writing, but as some further changes are still possible, don't be surprised at the occasional difference between the names given in this book and those on the ground. The main **abbreviations** used in the text are: ul. (for *ulitsa*, street); nab. (for *naberezhnaya*, embankment); pr. (for *prospekt*, avenue); per. (for *pereulok*, lane); and pl. (for *ploshchad*, square). Other terms include *most* (bridge), *bulvar* (boulevard), *shosse* (highway), *alleya* (alley) and *sad* (garden). See the Glossary on p.39 for a fuller list of Russian terms.

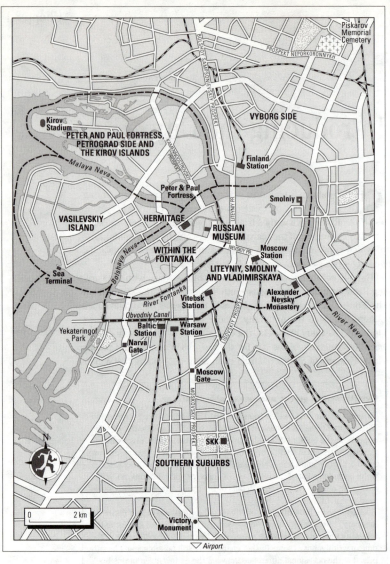

Palace, the Bronze Horseman, the city's three major cathedrals and the Summer Palace and Garden. Within the Fontanka, too, you'll find the **Hermitage** and the **Russian Museum**, galleries whose artistic wealth is covered in Chapter 3.

The largest of the city's islands, **Vasilevskiy Island** (Chapter 4) – where the founder of the city, Peter the Great, originally planned to create his new capital – still contains some of St Petersburg's oldest institutions: the university, the former Stock Exchange and the Menshikov Palace. These are all found at the island's easternmost point, known as the **Strelka**, distinguished by its triumphal, terra-cotta-coloured Rostral Columns. The rest of Vasilevskiy Island is composed of a regular grid plan of streets, which change in character from residential to industrial as you travel west.

On the north side of the Neva, opposite the Winter Palace, is a small island taken up by the **Peter and Paul Fortress** (Chapter 5). The fortress's construction anticipated the foundation of the city itself and, in addition to its strategic and military purpose, it also housed St Petersburg's first prison and its first cathedral, where the leading members of the Romanov dynasty are buried. Beyond the fortress is the residential inland district called the **Petrograd Side**, backed by a trio of islands to the north, known as the **Kirov Islands**. These have long been a popular place for the privileged to have their *dachas* (holiday cottages), and continue to provide a leafy respite for Petersburgers.

Back on the mainland, beyond the River Fontanka, the conventional sights are more dispersed and the distances between them that much greater. The area designated **Liteyniy, Smolniy and Vladimirskaya** (Chapter 6) was largely developed in the latter half of the nineteenth century and is rich in historical associations. Its finest sights are the Smolniy Cathedral, near the Institute from where the Bolsheviks orchestrated the October Revolution, and the Alexander Nevsky Monastery, in whose cemeteries many of the city's most famous personages are buried. However, don't neglect the atmospheric Vladimirskaya district, where Dostoyevsky's apartment and the Pushkinskaya 10 artists' colony are located, along with an assortment of odd museums.

The **Southern Suburbs** (Chapter 7), south of the Obvodniy Canal and characterized by sprawling factories and Soviet-era housing estates, are not included in the average visitor's itinerary. However, there are a few scattered monuments of note, one of which – the Victory Monument – you'll see en route from the airport to the city. The Chesma Church is one of the most unusual in St Petersburg and holds universal appeal; other sights are of more specialized interest, such as the 1930s architecture of the Narva District and the far-flung cemeteries to the southeast. On the north side of the Neva, the **Vyborg Side** (Chapter 8) is also largely composed of factories and tenement buildings. The Finland Station, scene of Lenin's tumultuous reception on his return from exile in 1917, is the main focus of the district, while the Piskarov Cemetery is a place of pilgrimage for those wishing to honour the city's huge sacrifice during World War II.

Chapter 2

Within the Fontanka

The heart of St Petersburg is circumscribed by the seven-kilometre-long River Fontanka and the broader River Neva, which separates it from Vasilevskiy Island and the Petrograd Side. Concentrated on this oval of land **within the Fontanka** are some of the city's greatest monuments – the Winter Palace, the Admiralty and the Bronze Horseman, the Engineers' Castle, the Summer Palace and Garden, and the cathedrals of St Isaac and Our Lady of Kazan – as well as the art collections of the Hermitage and the Russian Museum; the Mariinskiy Theatre (better known as the Kirov); the Gostiniy and Apraksin bazaars; and a whole host of former palaces associated with the good, the bad and the downright weird.

The area is defined by a fan of avenues, chief among them Nevskiy prospekt, which radiate from the Admiralty, interwoven with canals spanned by elegant bridges. The area's historical associations practically peel off the walls: here, unbridled rulers and profligate aristocrats once held sway, poets were driven to suicide, murderers wept in remorse and revolutionaries plotted assassinations. Nowadays, fronds of algae floating beneath the surface of the jet-black or mildew-green water enhance the general air of dereliction, confirmed in the backstreets by stray cats, scrawny crows and gaggles of drunks.

Canals and bridges

All the waterways in the centre of St Petersburg resemble **canals** whether they're man-made or not, having been lined with granite **embankments** (*naberezhnaya*) during the reign of Catherine the Great. Their beauty is enhanced by **bridges** whose charms are conveyed by names such as the "Bridge of Kisses" (Potseluev most) and the "Singer's Bridge" (Pevcheskiy most): for a view at water-level, take one of the **cruises** from Anichkov most on the Fontanka, Kazanskiy most on the Griboedov Canal, or Politseyskiy most on the Moyka. As for **addresses**, remember that even numbers are always on the south side of the canal or river, odd numbers on the opposite (north) embankment.

There are enough sights within the Fontanka to keep you busy for days – as well as most of the city's restaurants, theatres, concert halls, banks, airline offices and swankiest hotels. All in all, you're likely to spend much of your time in this area, and largely judge St Petersburg on the strength of it.

Nevskiy prospekt

Nevskiy prospekt is St Petersburg's equivalent of the Champs Elysées or Unter den Linden – an Imperial thoroughfare whose name is virtually synonymous with that of the city. Like St Petersburg, the avenue is on an epic scale, running all the way from the Admiralty on the banks of the Neva to the Alexander Nevsky Monastery beyond the Fontanka – a distance of 4.5km – and measuring up to 60m wide in places. Yet, at the same time, it is intensely human in its foibles and failings, juxtaposing palaces and potholes, ballerinas and beggars – as Gogol wrote in *Tales of Good and Evil*, "What a rapid phantas-magoria passes over it in a single day!"

The lower end of Nevskiy prospekt, beyond the Fontanka, is described in Chapter 6.

The prospekt manifests every style of **architecture** from eigh-teenth-century Baroque to *fin-de-siècle* Style Moderne (Russia's own version of Art Nouveau), its skyline culminating in the golden spire of the Admiralty. Nevskiy's **streetlife** reflects the New Russia: bemedalled war veterans promenading alongside teenagers in the lat-est fashions; cadets linking arms in beery camaraderie; barefoot gyp-sies and wild-eyed drunks like *muzhiks* (peasants) from the pages of Dostoyevsky; and stalls selling everything from books to ice cream. During the midsummer "White Nights", when darkness barely falls, the avenue is busy with people, even at two o'clock in the morning.

Nevskiy prospekt can really only be appreciated on foot. The least-demanding approach involves taking the **metro** to Gostiniy dvor or Nevskiy prospekt station, and **walking** the 1.5km to Palace Square (Dvortsovaya ploshchad) – an itinerary with Kazan Cathedral and two stunning canal vistas as its highlights. A longer (2.4km) but even more rewarding option is to start from Mayakovskaya metro station, 600m beyond the River Fontanka, then catch a **bus** (#7 or #22), **trolleybus** (#1, #5, #7, #10 or #22) or **minibus** #T-8 (all run along Nevskiy), or walk up to Anichkov most and proceed from there. Whichever approach you choose, the chief **landmarks** are the red-and-white tower of the City Duma; the glass cupola and globe of Dom knigi; the green dome of Kazan Cathedral; and the gilded spire of the Admiralty.

Our account progresses from Anichkov most on the Fontanka northwest towards the Winter Palace and the Admiralty. To describe Nevskiy prospekt's sights roughly in the order in which they appear, the account switches from one side of the road to the other more often than you're likely to do in practice, and merely alludes to vari-ous **turn-offs** which receive fuller coverage later in the text.

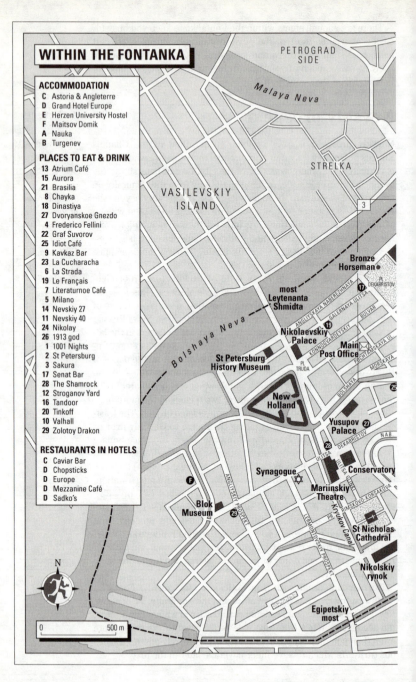

WITHIN THE FONTANKA

ACCOMMODATION
- **C** Astoria & Angleterre
- **D** Grand Hotel Europe
- **E** Herzen University Hostel
- **F** Maitsov Domik
- **A** Nauka
- **B** Turgenev

PLACES TO EAT & DRINK
- **13** Atrium Café
- **15** Aurora
- **21** Brasilia
- **8** Chayka
- **18** Dinastiya
- **27** Dvoryanskoe Gnezdo
- **4** Frederico Fellini
- **22** Graf Suvorov
- **25** Idiot Café
- **9** Kavkaz Bar
- **23** La Cucharacha
- **6** La Strada
- **19** Le Français
- **7** Literaturnoe Café
- **5** Milano
- **14** Nevskiy 27
- **11** Nevskiy 40
- **24** Nikolay
- **26** 1913 god
- **1** 1001 Nights
- **2** St Petersburg
- **3** Sakura
- **17** Senat Bar
- **28** The Shamrock
- **12** Stroganov Yard
- **16** Tandoor
- **20** Tinkoff
- **10** Valhall
- **29** Zolotoy Drakon

RESTAURANTS IN HOTELS
- **C** Caviar Bar
- **D** Chopsticks
- **D** Europe
- **D** Mezzanine Café
- **D** Sadko's

PETROGRAD SIDE

Malaya Neva

STRELKA

VASILEVSKIY ISLAND

3

Bronze Horseman

PL DEKABRISTOV

most Leytenanta Shmidta

17

Bolshaya Neva

Nikolaevskiy Palace

19

Main Post Office

St Petersburg History Museum

PL TRUDA

BOLSHAYA

25

New Holland

Yusupov Palace

27

NAB

28

DEKABRISTOV

ULITSA

Synagogue

Conservatory

F

Mariinskiy Theatre

Blok Museum

29

RIMSKOVO-KORSAKOVA

St Nicholas Cathedral

Kryukov Canal

Nikolskiy rynok

Egipetskiy most

N

0   500 m

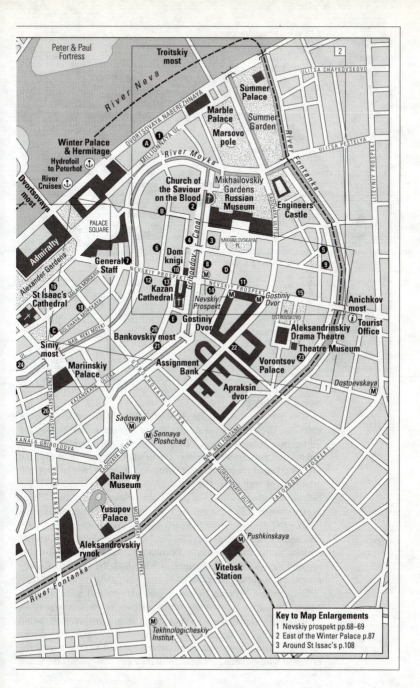

Peter & Paul
Fortress

Troitskiy
most

River Neva

Summer
Palace

Summer
Garden

Winter Palace
& Hermitage

Hydrofoil
to Peterhof

River
Cruises

Dvortsovaya NABEREZHNAYA

MILLIONNAYA UL.

A 1

River Moyka

Marble
Palace

Marsovo
pole

River Fontanka

ULITSA PESTELYA

ULITSA CHAYKOVSKOVO

2

LITEYNIY PROSPEKT

Dvortsovaya
most

PALACE
SQUARE

Admiralty

Alexander Gardens

Church of
the Saviour
on the Blood

B

Canal

2

Mikhailovskiy
Gardens
Russian
Museum

SADOVAYA ULITSA

Engineers
Castle

4

Griboedov

MIKHAILOVSKAYA P.

5

9

General
Staff

7

6

Dom
knigi

10

NEVSKIY PROSPEKT

8

M

D

NEVSKIY PROSPEKT

11

St Isaac's
Cathedral

16

18

Kazan
Cathedral

12 **13**

MALAYA MORSKAYA

BOLSHAYA MORSKAYA

14

M

Nevskiy
Prospekt

M

M

Gostiniy
Dvor

PL.
OSTROVSKOVO

15

Anichkov
most

Tourist
Office

Siniy
most

C

NAB. REKI MOYKI

E

Gostiniy
Dvor

Aleksandrinskiy
Drama Theatre

Theatre Museum

29

Mariinskiy
Palace

KAZANSKAYA ULITSA

Bankovskiy most

20

21

Assignment
Bank

22

Apraksin
dvor

Vorontsov
Palace

23

Dostoevskaya

M

1

26

VOZNESENSKIY PROSPEKT

KANALA GRIBOEDOVA

SADOVAYA ULITSA

Sadovaya

M

Sennaya
Ploshchad

M

GOROHOVAYA ULITSA

NAB. REKI FONTANKI

ZAGORODNY PROSPEKT

Railway
Museum

Yusupov
Palace

MOSKOVSKIY PROSPEKT

Aleksandrovskiy
rynok

River Fontanka

Pushkinskaya

M

Vitebsk
Station

Tekhnologicheskiy
Institut

M

Key to Map Enlargements
1 Nevskiy prospekt pp.68–69
2 East of the Winter Palace p.87
3 Around St Issac's p.108

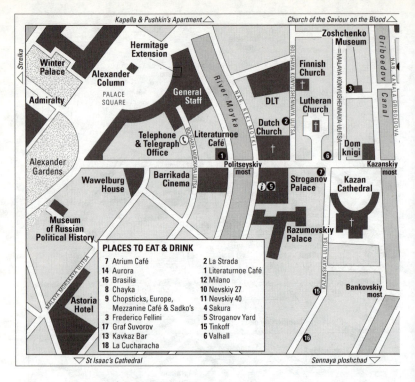

Zoshchenko Museum

Hermitage Extension

Winter Palace

Alexander Column

PALACE SQUARE

Admiralty

General Staff

River Moyka

Finnish Church †

DLT

Lutheran Church †

Dutch Church †

Dom knigi

Telephone & Telegraph Office ©

Literaturnoe Café ❶

Alexander Gardens

Politseyskiy most

Wawelburg House

Barrikada Cinema

ℹ️ ❺

Stroganov Palace ❼

Kazan Cathedral †

Kazanskiy most

Museum of Russian Political History

Razumovskiy Palace

Bankovskiy most

Astoria Hotel

PLACES TO EAT & DRINK

7 Atrium Café	2 La Strada
14 Aurora	1 Literaturnoe Café
16 Brasilia	12 Milano
8 Chayka	10 Nevskiy 27
9 Chopsticks, Europe,	11 Nevskiy 40
Mezzanine Café & Sadko's	4 Sakura
3 Frederico Fellini	5 Stroganov Yard
17 Graf Suvorov	15 Tinkoff
13 Kavkaz Bar	6 Valhall
18 La Cucharacha	

▽ St Isaac's Cathedral   Sennaya ploshchad ▽

Some history

Like so much in the city, the prospekt was built during the reign of Peter the Great under the direction of a foreigner, in this case the Frenchman Jean-Baptiste Le Blond, who ploughed through 4km of forests and meadows to connect the newly built Admiralty with the Novgorod road (now Ligovskiy prospekt). Constructed by Swedish prisoners of war (who then had to clean it every Saturday), the prospekt's grand view suggested its original title, the "Great Perspective Road", changed in 1738 to Nevskaya perspektivnaya ulitsa, after the River Neva to which it leads, and shortened to its present name twenty years later. The Bolsheviks renamed it "25 October Avenue" (after the date of the Revolution), but this was effectively ignored by the city's inhabitants, and in 1944 the avenue officially reverted to its previous name.

The contrast between Nevskiy's past and present state is illuminating. During the nineteenth century, its pavements were kept clean by the simple expedient of forcing all the prostitutes arrested during the night to sweep the street at 4am. On every corner stood a wooden box housing three policemen, who slept and ate there, and the prospekt's length was festooned with pictorial store signs, depicting

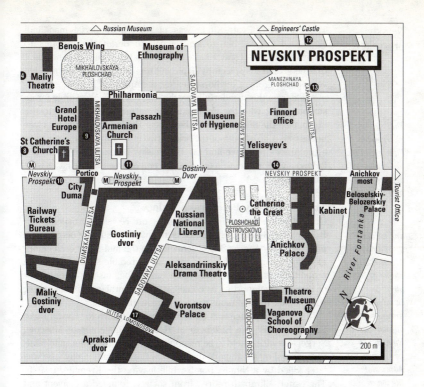

NEVSKIY PROSPEKT

Benois Wing   Museum of Ethnography

Maliy Theatre

MIKHAILOVSKAYA PLOSHCHAD

MANEZHNAYA PLOSHCHAD

Philharmonia

Grand Hotel Europe

Passazh

Museum of Hygiene

Finnord office

Armenian Church

St Catherine's Church

Yeliseyev's

Nevskiy Prospekt

Portico

Nevskiy Prospekt

Gostiniy Dvor

NEVSKIY PROSPEKT

Anichkov most

City Duma

Beloselskiy-Belozerskiy Palace

Railway Tickets Bureau

Catherine the Great

Kabinet

Gostiniy dvor

Russian National Library

PLOSHCHAD OSTROVSKOVO

Anichkov Palace

Aleksandriinskiy Drama Theatre

Maliy Gostiniy dvor

Theatre Museum

Vorontsov Palace

Vaganova School of Choreography

Apraksin dvor

Tourist Office

River Fontanka

SADOVAYA ULITSA
MIKHAILOVSKAYA ULITSA
MALAYA SADOVAYA
KARAVANNAYA ULITSA
DUMSKAYA ULITSA
SADOVAYA ULITSA
UL. ZODCHEVO ROSSI
ULITSA LOMONOSOVA

0   200 m

the merchandise for the benefit of illiterate passers-by. All traffic was horse-drawn, a "wild, bounding sea of carriages" which sped silently over the snow in winter. The impact of war and revolution was brought home to British agent Sidney Reilly when, returning after the tsar's overthrow, he found the Nevskiy almost deserted, unswept for weeks and strewn with the bodies of horses that had starved to death. Today, Nevskiy looks as prosperous and thriving as it did in Russia's so-called "best year" – 1913 – when the Empire celebrated the tercentenary of the Romanov dynasty, blissfully unaware of the disasters to come.

From Anichkov most to Passazh

Nevskiy prospekt crosses the Fontanka by way of the 54-metre-long **Anichkov most**, built in the mid-nineteenth century to replace a narrow drawbridge with wooden towers erected in the early 1700s by Colonel Anichkov. On each corner rears a dramatic bronze statue of a supple youth trying to tame a fiery steed – these are among the best-loved sculptures in St Petersburg, and were buried in the grounds of the Anichkov Palace during World War II to protect them from harm.

Their sculptor, Pyotr Klodt, was plagued by Imperial meddling: Nicholas I ordered him to send a pair to Berlin, then another to Naples. Finally, in 1850, Klodt completed a third pair – legend has it that he vented his spleen by depicting the tsar's face in the swollen veins of the groin of the horse nearest the Anichkov Palace.

Aside from this wonderfully sly dig, the bridge is irresistible for its surroundings, with the Fontanka curving majestically away to the north, past the **Sheremetev Palace**, near the landing-stage for **river boats** (see p.35). South of the bridge two more former princely piles – the Anichkov Palace and the Beloselskiy-Belozerskiy Palace (see below) – vie for attention on opposite embankments. The latter wins hands down.

*The
Sheremetev
Palace and its
museums are
described on
p.218.*

The Beloselskiy-Belozerskiy Palace

One of the most striking buildings on Nevskiy prospekt, the **Beloselskiy-Belozerskiy Palace** is an anachronistic Rococo masterpiece, built by Andrey Stakenschneider in the mid-nineteenth century, whose glorious red facade turns an incredible shade of crimson around sunset. Bearded, muscled atlantes (the masculine equivalent of caryatids) support its balconies, while Corinthian pilasters impart some rigour to its sinuous window surrounds.

*The palace is
open daily
11am–6.30pm;
phone ☎312
36 44 one day
in advance to
arrange a
guided tour in
English ($5
per group).
Admission to
the waxworks
exhibitions
costs $0.75 per
person.*

In 1884 the palace was purchased by the crown for Grand Duke Sergei and his wife Elizabeth of Hesse. As governor of Moscow, Sergei was widely held to be responsible for the three thousand fatalities caused by a stampede on Nicholas II's coronation day – he was later killed by a Nihilist bomb while leaving the Kremlin in 1905. Thereafter, Elizabeth retired from society, founded a convent and became its abbess, but suffered the same fate as several other nobles during the Revolution, when she was imprisoned at Perm and then thrown down a mineshaft. Subsequently canonized as a saint of the Russian Orthodox Church, her body now rests in Jerusalem.

On the first floor are two exhibitions of **wax figures**, spanning a thousand years of Russian history. The figures are unusually lifelike; some of the faces were modelled on the actual skulls or death masks of the historical personages that they represent. Two surprising inclusions are Casanova and Baron Münchhausen, both of whom visited St Petersburg.

Ascending the grand staircase to the second floor, note the strategically placed mirror that enabled Elizabeth to observe guests arriving and prepare to greet her favourites. A series of reception rooms culminates in an audience hall and a ballroom (now used for concerts of folk music). The palace's original concert hall has splendid oak panelling, filigree work and a ceiling with pendentive flowers and stucco traceries in the Eclectic style of the late nineteenth century.

The Anichkov Palace

Across the Fontanka lies the larger and less flamboyant Neoclassical ensemble comprising the **Kabinet**, or Chancellory, established by

Alexander I, and the cream-coloured **Anichkov Palace**, named after the colonel who established an encampment here when the city was founded. In 1741, the site was purchased by Empress Elizabeth to build a palace for her lover, Alexei Razumovsky, a Ukrainian chorister whom she may have secretly married (his nickname was "the night-time Emperor"), while Catherine the Great subsequently presented the palace to her own favourite, Potemkin. In 1817, the future Nicholas I moved in, setting a precedent for the rest of the century, during which the palace served as a home for heirs to the throne – Alexander III's wife, Maria Fyodorovna, used to host glittering balls here wearing a tiara of sapphires so large that they resembled "enormous eyes". In Soviet times the building became the Palace of Pioneers and Youth, now renamed the **Palace of Youth Creativity**. The palace is usually only open for concerts and other special events; the entrance is through the wrought-iron gates on Nevskiy prospekt.

Ploshchad Ostrovskovo

A little further up Nevskiy comes the first of the set-piece squares opening off the prospekt. Laid out by Carlo Rossi in 1828–34, the square is now called **ploshchad Ostrovskovo** after the dramatist Nikolai Ostrovsky, but some still refer to it by its pre-revolutionary name of Aleksandrinskaya ploshchad (after Tsar Nicholas I's wife, Alexandra). Locals, however, have always called it "Katkin sad" ("Katya's Garden"), after the **statue of Catherine the Great** that was erected here in 1873. Matvey Chizhov and Alexander Opekushin sculpted the ermine-robed empress almost twice as large as the figures of her favourites and advisors clustered around the pedestal, including Prince Potemkin – who grinds a Turkish turban underfoot as he chats to Marshal Suvorov – and Princess Dashkova, the first female president of the Russian Academy of Sciences. Somewhat surprisingly, this is the only statue of Catherine in St Petersburg.

Along the right-hand side of the square is the Ionic facade of the **Russian National Library**, crowned with a figure of Minerva, goddess of wisdom, and garnished with statues of philosophers. This Rossi-built extension of Petersburg's first public library, opened in 1814, now holds nearly 32 million items. Its collection of rare books includes Voltaire's library (purchased by Catherine the Great) and a postage stamp-sized edition of *Krylov's Fables*, so clearly printed that it can be read with the naked eye. A plaque on the Nevskiy side of the library attests that Lenin was a regular visitor between 1893 and 1895. His predilection for its weighty tomes is commemorated by a joke involving his wife, Krupskaya, and his lover, Inessa, in which he tells each that he will be seeing the other so that he can slope off to read in the library.

The library is open July & Aug Mon & Wed 1–9pm, Tues & Thurs–Sun 9am–5pm; Sept–June daily 9am–9pm.

Behind the statue of Catherine stands Rossi's tour de force, the **Aleksandriinskiy Drama Theatre**, its straw-coloured facade decorated with a columned loggia topped by a statue of Apollo in his char-

Catherine the Great

Catherine the Great of Russia (1729–96) always disclaimed that sobriquet,
insisting that she was merely Catherine II, but posterity has insisted upon it.
She was born Princess Sophie of Anhalt-Zerbst, in northern Germany, on
May 2, 1729, and married at the age of 15 to the 16-year-old Russian heir
apparent, Peter. The marriage was a dismal failure, and the belated birth of
a son and heir, Paul, probably owed more to the first of Catherine's lovers
than to her husband, the future Tsar **Peter III**. Notwithstanding this,
Catherine strove to make herself acceptable to the Russian court and people, unlike her husband, who made his contempt for both – and her – obvious, until their worsening relations made conflict inevitable. On July 28,
1762, with the assistance of the Orlov brothers and the support of the
Guards, Catherine staged a coup, forced Peter to abdicate, and proclaimed
herself ruler; Peter was murdered by the Orlovs a few days later.

Her reign was initially characterized by enlightened absolutism: under
Catherine's patronage, works of philosophy, literature and science were
translated into Russian; hospitals, orphanages, journals and academies
founded; roads, canals and palaces built. The Crimea was annexed to
Russia, in which quest she was greatly assisted by Prince Potemkin, who
planted the Tsarist flag on the shores of the Black Sea, having beaten back
the forces of the Ottoman Empire.

Later, however, Catherine's reactionary instincts surfaced, as the
French Revolution turned her against any hint of egalitarianism and
towards the Orthodox Church. Meanwhile, she gradually lost her taste for
older, masterful lovers such as Orlov and Potemkin, opting for ever
younger, more pliable "favourites". Estimates of their number range from
12 to 54, and although Catherine was probably no more promiscuous than
the average male European sovereign, she was judged by the standards set
by the self-righteous Habsburg Empress Maria Theresa, the so-called
"Virgin of Europe". For more about Catherine's life, see the accounts of
the Winter Palace (p.84), Peterhof (p.383), Tsarskoe Selo (p.356) and
Oranienbaum (p.347).

iot, and flanked by niche-bound statues of the muses Terpsichore
and Melpomene. Renamed the Pushkin Theatre on the centenary of
the poet Alexander Pushkin's death in 1937, the theatre once again
bears its original title, though the facade has two plaques, one with
each name. The theatre company here can trace its history back to
1756, making it the oldest in Russia, and staged the first production
of Gogol's *The Government Inspector* (1836).

The Theatre Museum and Vaganova School of Choreography

Just around the corner from the theatre, at ploshchad Ostrovskovo
6, the small but enjoyable **Theatre Museum** displays several items
belonging to the opera singer Fyodor Chaliapin, including the jewelled robe that he wore in the title role of *Boris Godunov* and the
famous portrait of him by Boris Kustodiev. It also exhibits a half-life-

sized replica of one of the Constructivist stage sets designed for the Moscow Theatre in the early 1920s. Ask an attendant to open the **ballet room**, which holds costumes from the first production of *Sleeping Beauty*. From September to May, weekly **concerts** are held in the museum.

Next door stands the **Vaganova School of Choreography**, probably the world's finest classical ballet school, which has produced dancers such as Anna Pavlova, Tamara Karsavina, Vaslav Nijinsky, Galina Ulanova, Rudolf Nureyev and Mikhail Baryshnikov. Its origins go back to 1738, when J.B. Landé began to train the children of palace servants to take part in court entertainments, though it wasn't until 1934 that a modern curriculum was implemented by the Russian choreographer Agrippina Vaganova. Over two thousand young hopefuls apply to the school every year, of which only ninety are chosen to undergo its gruelling regime. Before the Revolution, as recalled in Karsavina's memoirs, *Theatre Street*, each ballerina received a box of chocolates and a ticket for a special matinee where they would be partnered by officer cadets, to mark the tsar's name day.

The school is located on **ulitsa Zodchevo Rossi** (Master-builder Rossi Street). Of all the architect's creations, this street is the most perfectly proportioned: exactly as wide as the height of its buildings (22m) and ten times as long, with every facade, paving stone and lamppost exactly mirroring those on the opposite side of the street.

Yeliseyev's and Passazh

On the other side of Nevskiy prospekt from ploshchad Ostrovskovo is the St Petersburg branch of the famous pre-revolutionary food store, **Yeliseyev's**, baldly designated "Gastronom No. 1" during the Soviet period. Designed by Yuri Baranovsky in 1902–3, it's one of the most stunning Style Moderne buildings in the city. The interior, at its best in the delicatessen to the left of the entrance passage, has been preserved more or less intact. Intricate gold filigree work adorns the high ceiling, which is festooned with crystal fairy lights, while from the walls wrought-iron flowers burst forth, culminating in a gracefully drooping chandelier.

The best way to cross Sadovaya ulitsa is via the **underpass**, which is not only safer than braving the road but also plays host to some of the most original buskers in town. Turn right in the underpass to emerge on the northern side of Nevskiy, then head through one of the doors at no. 48 Nevskiy prospekt into **Passazh**, a 180-metre-long, galleried shopping arcade built in the mid-nineteenth century. Originally lined with expensive shops for the St Petersburg upper classes, it's now considerably more downmarket, despite the preponderance of stores selling imported goods, but the architecture still makes a favourable impression: canary-yellow walls, offset by maroon marble surrounds, topped by a glass canopied roof.

The museum is open Wed 1–7pm, Thurs–Sun 11am–6pm, closed the last Fri of the month; $1.70.

Yeliseyev's is open Mon–Sat 9am–1pm & 2–9pm.

Passazh is open Mon–Sat 10am–9pm & Sun 11am– 9pm. It runs through to Italyanskaya ulitsa, off Mikhailovskaya ploshchad, making it a useful short cut to the Russian Museum (p.153).

Go back into the underpass and turn right to emerge on the southern side of Nevskiy for a close encounter with the bustling Gostiniy dvor.

Gostiniy dvor to the Griboedov Canal

*Emerging
from Gostiniy
dvor metro
station or the
Sadovaya
underpass,
you may
encounter
people touting
coach
excursions
around the
city – for more
information
on these, ask
at the kiosks
up the road
near the
corner of
Dumskaya
ulitsa.*

The eighteenth-century **Gostiniy dvor** is a central point of reference, its columned arcades dominating the junction of Nevskiy and Sadovaya, and extending for 230 metres along the prospekt. It took over sixty years to complete, and derived its name and inspiration from the *gostiniy dvory*, or "merchants' hostels", of Old Russia, offering lodgings and storage space, besides serving as a bazaar where each product was allocated a specific area – there was even one for the sale of stolen goods, which buyers entered at their peril. Nineteenth-century visitors were also warned that the average merchant reckoned that "the worse his wares, the sooner will his customers want to renew their stock", while the doormen were "by no means content with verbally inviting the stranger to walk in", but grabbed their "arm, or coat-tails, without ceremony". The **interior** is nearly a kilometre in circumference and its upper level nowadays mostly contains boutiques selling furs and designer clothes, while the balcony around the outside offers fine views of the area and features several cafés.

The Portico and City Duma

To the northwest of the *dvor* is an elegant Neoclassical **Portico** by Luigi Rosca, now home to a theatre booking office – the simple 24-hour street **café** in front of it is a well-known meeting spot and a good place for a drink. Nearby is the entrance to an underpass leading to Nevskiy prospekt metro station – look out for the excellent blind accordionist and the groups of old ladies singing Russian folk songs in the traditional harsh *gortan* style.

The street behind the portico is known as Dumskaya ulitsa after the former seat of the **City Duma**, or pre-revolutionary municipal government, a building whose arched windows overlook the *dvor's* arcade. The Duma's triple-tiered red-and-white **tower** was erected in 1804 to give warning of fires, but later adapted for signalling between St Petersburg and the Imperial palaces outside the city. A plaque at the top of the steps commemorates the capture of the Duma by the Bolshevik Mikhail Kalinin in October 1918, which brought to an end one of the few elected institutions in Petrograd.

From the Armenian Church to St Catherine's

In Tsarist times Nevskiy prospekt was dubbed the "Street of Tolerance", due to the variety of non-Orthodox denominations which were allowed to build their churches here. Across the road from Gostiniy dvor stands the **Armenian Church** (Armyanskaya tserkov), an azure Neoclassical edifice, built in the 1770s by the German-born architect Felten, and set back from the street in its own courtyard. Converted into a workshop during Soviet times, it has now been restored as a place of worship, with a simple yet elegant decor of pastel colours and fake marble.

Next to the church, the broad, tree-lined **Mikhailovskaya ulitsa** forms a grand approach to Mikhailovskaya ploshchad and the Mikhailovskiy Palace (which contains the Russian Museum) beyond. The whole of the western side of the street is occupied by the de luxe **Grand Hotel Europe** (Yevropeyskaya), built in 1873–75 but greatly altered by the Art Nouveau architect Fyodor Lidval, and refurbished during the late 1980s by a Swedish–Russian joint venture. The hotel's bar-restaurant, *Sadko*, is a comfortable place to sit and watch the world go by on Nevskiy.

Mikhailovskaya ploshchad, at the end of Mikhailovskaya ulitsa, is described on p.101.

Continuing down the prospekt, in the middle of the next block and set back slightly from the street, **St Catherine's Church** (Kostyol Svyatoy Yekateriny) was St Petersburg's main Roman Catholic church. Its steps have now been taken over by street artists, and inside it harbours the tombs of **General Moreau**, a Frenchman who fought on the Russian side against Napoleon and died after losing his leg in the Battle of Dresden (1813), and **Stanislaw Poniatowski**, the last king of Poland. Enthroned by his erstwhile lover, Catherine the Great, Poniatowski subsequently died fighting the Russians near Leipzig, but was buried in St Petersburg. In 1938, his remains were repatriated and secretly interred in eastern Poland, before being dug up yet again and transferred to Warsaw's Royal Castle, where they remain to this day, stashed away in a coffin out of sight and still denied a decent burial, since many Poles regard him as a traitor.

The eighteenth-century church is currently under restoration, but on Christmas Day 1992 it was used for the first public Christmas service since the Revolution and now holds regular services. During the week these are in the chapel, but on Sunday, services in Russian, English and Polish are held in the church itself, in a surreal pure-white box inserted into the ruined interior. The church's exterior is flanked by two huge arches designed by Vallin de la Mothe (who also completed Gostiniy dvor).

At the end of the block, on the corner of the Griboedov embankment, **Nevskiy prospekt metro station** is a focal point for teenagers, old women selling cigarettes, and boozers, who dub it "the climate" (*klimat*), because of the warm air blowing from its vestibule – a blessing during the Russian winter.

Crossing the Griboedov Canal: Dom knigi

The wide expanse of **Kazanskiy most** (Kazan Bridge) carries Nevskiy prospekt across the **Griboedov Canal** (kanal Griboedova). Originally called the "Krivushchy" ("twisting river"), it was canalized and embanked under Catherine the Great and henceforth nicknamed the "Katinka Kanavka", or "Catherine's Gutter", flowing as it did

*The Church of
the Saviour on
the Blood is
covered on
p.91; for
details of
Bankovskiy
most and
beyond, see
p.114.*

through the heart of the notorious Haymarket district, until the Soviets renamed it after the writer Alexander Griboedov (see p.238). It's worth lingering to admire the superb views from the bridge along the canal. To the left, beyond the colonnades of Kazan Cathedral, you might be able to glimpse **Bankovskiy most** (Bank Bridge), with its gilded griffons, while to the right are the multicoloured onion domes of the **Church of the Saviour on the Blood**. If the view tempts you onto the water, small private **motorboats** can be rented from the northeastern embankment in summer for trips along the canals (see p.35 for details).

Looming above the northwestern corner of Kazanskiy most is the former emporium of the American sewing-machine company, Singer. The building is better known today as **Dom knigi** (House of Books), the largest bookstore in the city. Designed by Pavel Syusor and completed in 1904, its Style Moderne exterior is distinguished by a conical tower topped by the Singer trademark: a giant glass globe, which used to light up at night. Now an established and well-loved landmark, it was thought to be in bad taste at the time – an Imperial decree stating that all secular buildings had to be two metres lower than the Winter Palace thwarted Singer's plan for an eleven-storey structure, but failed to scotch the entire project. Before the Revolution, women used to work at sewing machines in the windows to pull in the crowds. Although the interior has been greatly altered since then, some of the original ornamentation survives, notably the brass ivy entwined around the wrought-iron banisters.

Kazan Cathedral

Kazan Cathedral (Kazanskiy sobor) is one of the grandest churches in the city, its curvaceous colonnades embracing Nevskiy prospekt like the outstretched wings of a gigantic eagle. The cathedral was built between 1801 and 1811 to house a venerated icon, Our Lady of Kazan, reputed to have appeared miraculously overnight in Kazan in 1579, and brought by Peter the Great to St Petersburg, where it resided until its miraculous disappearance in 1904. Although the cathedral was erected during the reign of Alexander I, its inspiration came from his father, the militarily obsessed Paul, and it was his idea that the cathedral should be designed and executed by Russian artists, despite being modelled on St Peter's in the Vatican.

During the Soviet period, the cathedral housed the infamous **Museum of Atheism**, whose foundation in 1932 coincided with a period of antireligious repression in Leningrad, when scores of churches were closed and clergy arrested. Containing over 150,000 exhibits, from Egyptian mummies to pictures of monks and nuns copulating, it was used to prove Marx's famous maxim that "religion is the opium of the people". Renamed the Museum of Religion during perestroika, it was moved out in 1999 and is now located on Pochtamtskaya ulitsa, near St Isaac's Cathedral. There are daily **ser-**

vices in the cathedral, which at **Easter** overflows with believers greeting each other with the salutation *Kristos voskres!* (Christ is risen!); the traditional answer is *Voistine voskres!* (Verily, He is risen!)

The exterior

The semicircular **colonnade** is made up of 96 Corinthian columns hewn from Karelian granite, but unlike in the city's other great nineteenth-century cathedral, St Isaac's, sculptural decoration was kept to a minimum: it's easy to miss the **bas-reliefs** at either end of the colonnade – depicting *Moses Striking the Rock* and *The Adoration of the Brazen Serpent* – and the bronze **statues** hidden in the porticoes of (from left to right) St Vladimir, John the Baptist, Alexander Nevsky and St Andrew. The bronze **doors** facing the prospekt are worth inspecting at close quarters: an exact copy of Ghiberti's doors for the Florentine Baptistery, which Michelangelo allegedly described as "splendid enough to serve as the gates of paradise".

In 1837, two **statues** by Boris Orlovsky were erected at either end of the colonnade: to the west, **Michael Barclay de Tolly**; to the east, **Mikhail Kutuzov**, the hero of Tolstoy's *War and Peace*. The Scottish-born General de Tolly's contentious policy of strategic retreat before Napoleon's armies prompted his replacement by the one-eyed Field Marshal Kutuzov, who used to close his good eye and pretend to sleep so that his aides could express their opinions freely. Public opinion forced Kutuzov to engage the vastly superior French troops at the Battle of Borodino (1812), which produced no clear winner despite horrendous casualties on both sides.

The interior

It's hard to predict exactly which of the various entrances will be used while the square outside is fenced off and the cathedral's interior is being refurbished – try beneath the colonnades facing Nevskiy prospekt first, and only then around the sides. Entering from Nevskiy, notice the chapel to the right, where the **tomb of Marshal Kutuzov** is overhung with captured Napolenic banners. He was buried here with full honours, on the spot where he had prayed before setting off to war.

The cathedral is open to sightseers Mon, Tues, Thurs & Fri 11am–5pm; Sat & Sun noon–5pm; free.

The object of his prayers was the icon **Our Lady of Kazan**, or *Derzhavnaya* (Sovereign), which reputedly disappeared in 1904, only to reappear miraculously in Moscow on the day of Nicholas II's abdication, where the woman who found it dreamt of being told that the divine power vested in the tsars had now returned to the Mother of God. In the latest chapter of this long-running mystery, Our Lady of Kazan is now thought to be one and the same as an icon currently in the possession of the Prince Vladimir Cathedral on the Petrograd Side. The Kazan Cathedral's own iconostases were ripped out in the 1930s, so makeshift versions now serve until new ones can be carved, in contrast to the solemnity of its granite columns and the grisaille frescos around its central cupola and barrel-vaulted wings.

On towards the Moyka

A number of lesser sights are distributed on either side of Nevskiy prospekt as it heads to the River Moyka, 250m to the northwest. Diagonally opposite the cathedral, set back behind a summer beer garden, is the mid-nineteenth-century **Lutheran Church** (Lyuteranskaya tserkov), built in a vaguely neo-Romanesque style unusual for St Petersburg. After being converted into a swimming pool (complete with diving boards and spectators' stands) in the late 1950s, it has now been returned to the Lutherans, who are slowly restoring it, as related by an exhibition in the lobby (Mon–Fri 10am–2pm & 3–6pm). During the late 1840s, Mussorgsky was a pupil at the eighteenth-century **Peterschule** (officially School No. 222) next door.

At no. 20, further on past Bolshaya Konyushennaya ulitsa, the former **Dutch Church** occupies a much larger building, but is unlikely to revert to its original function, of which the only hint is a small dome peeping over the portico, and two sculpted angels holding open the Book of Enlightenment. The House of Chess (the city's main chess club) and various shops are now ensconced here.

The restored rooms of the Stroganov Palace are open Wed–Sun 10am–6pm; $2.50. The waxworks collection is open Mon–Fri 11am–7pm, Sat & Sun noon–8pm; $0.75.

Across the prospekt, the green-and-white facade of the **Stroganov Palace** (Stroganovskiy dvorets) overlooks the intersection of Nevskiy and the River Moyka. Built by Rastrelli in 1753, it's a fine example of Russian Baroque, paying homage to the carved window-frames of traditional peasant cottages, whilst flaunting its owner's status with Doric columns and pediments emblazoned with the Stroganov coat of arms. Although from street level it's hard to make it out, this features a bear's head flanked by sables – the Stroganovs owned vast tracts of Siberia, and earned a fortune from salt trading (their chef also invented the dish known as beef stroganoff). The palace now belongs to the Russian Museum and is undergoing restoration, although most of the objects that once filled it are in the possession of the Hermitage. Only three rooms and the staircase have been completed so far, but the long-term aim is to re-create the whole interior as it was in the late eighteenth century. **Temporary exhibitions** of objects from the Russian Museum's collections are held in the completed rooms, while another section houses a **waxworks exhibition** of figures from Russian history, though it's inferior to the waxworks in the Berloselskiy-Berlozerskiy Palace. The courtyard contains a glassed-in **restaurant** with phones at every table, while another entrance farther from the bridge leads into the City Tourist Information Bureau (see p.36).

The Moyka embankment beyond the Stroganov Palace is described on p.114.

The adjacent bridge, **Politseyskiy most** (Police Bridge), spanning the River Moyka, was the first iron bridge in St Petersburg, constructed in 1806–8 to the design of Scotsman William Hastie.

Originally called the "Green Bridge" after the colour of its outer walls, it was subsequently renamed the "Police Bridge" and then, after the Revolution, "The People's Bridge", before reverting to its second name. Moored beside the northeast embankment are small private motorboats which can be rented for **canal trips** (p.35).

Beyond the Moyka

Immediately across the river stand two buildings ripe with faded good looks and historical significance. On the left-hand side, occupying the entire block between the embankment and Bolshaya Morskaya ulitsa, is a salmon-pink edifice nicknamed the "House with Columns" which now contains the **Barrikada Cinema**. The site was originally occupied by a wooden palace belonging to Empress Elizabeth, which was replaced in the late eighteenth century by a mansion for St Petersburg's chief of police. The nineteenth-century Italian architect Giacomo Quarenghi, who designed several buildings in and around St Petersburg including the Hermitage Theatre, lived on the second floor when he arrived in Russia.

Across the prospekt stands the yellow-and-white building with colonnaded arcades at either corner which formerly housed the fashionable *Café Wulf et Béranger*, frequented by the poet Pushkin, who met his second here en route to his fatal duel with D'Anthès in 1837. It later became the *Restaurant Leiner*, where Tchaikovsky is supposed to have caught cholera. Today, it contains the shamelessly touristic **Literaturnoe Café** (see p.285) and an excellent antique book shop.

At this point, you'll probably be lured off Nevskiy towards the Winter Palace by the great arch of the General Staff building (see p.80), leaving behind the **Wawelburg House** – now the headquarters of Aeroflot – which dominates the corner of Nevskiy and Malaya Morskaya ulitsa. This massive greystone pile evinces virtually every style of masonry, with an abundance of armorial reliefs, floral swags and Aztec heads. Its architect, Peretyatkovich, designed it to resemble both the Doge's Palace in Venice and the Palazzo Medici-Riccardi in Florence; the stone was imported from Sweden by the banker Wawelburg, whose initials appear on the shield crowning the pediment and above the service entrance on Malaya Morskaya ulitsa.

Malaya Morskaya ulitsa is described on p.112.

If you stick with the prospekt all the way to the needle-spired Admiralty (see p.103), it's worth watching out for a couple of buildings on the right-hand side as you go. Outside the 1930s secondary school at no. 14 is a **warning sign**, in blue and white, which reads: "Citizens! In the event of artillery fire, this side of the street is the most dangerous!" During the siege of Leningrad (1941–44), such signs were posted on the northwestern sides of the city's main thoroughfares after ballistic analysis determined that they were most at risk from Nazi shellfire. A little further on, at nos. 8 and 10, stand the oldest houses on the prospekt, dating from the early 1760s and adorned with decorative griffons and medallions.

To the Winter Palace

The best way of **approaching the Winter Palace** (which houses the Hermitage – see chapter 3) is to turn right off Nevskiy prospekt at Bolshaya Morskaya ulitsa, and head north past the Telephone and Telegraph Office. Carlo Rossi designed the northern end of Bolshaya Morskaya ulitsa to lie along the Pulkovo meridian (the Tsarist equivalent of the Greenwich meridian), so even without the giant clock which juts out from the east side of the street, you can tell it's midday when the houses cast no shadow. The beauty of this approach becomes obvious as the street curves beneath the triple arch, also designed by Rossi, of the General Staff building, and you first glimpse Palace Square, its towering Alexander Column set against the facade of the Winter Palace – it's been called "the greatest compliment ever paid by one architect to another", so eloquently does Rossi's design introduce and frame the open space and buildings of Palace Square beyond.

Bolshaya Morskaya ulitsa is described in more detail on p.114 and p.117.

Palace Square

The Admiralty and other places west of Palace Square are covered on pp.103–111.

The stark expanse of **Palace Square** (Dvortsovaya ploshchad) is inseparable from the city's turbulent past. Here, the Guards hailed Catherine as empress on the day of her coup against her husband Peter III, while later rulers revelled in showy parades. Fittingly perhaps, it was also the epicentre of the mass demonstration on what became known as "**Bloody Sunday**", which marked the beginning of the 1905 Revolution. On January 9, 1905, Father Gapon, head of a workers' society sponsored by the secret police, led thousands of strikers and their families to the square. Unarmed and bearing religious banners and portraits of the tsar and the tsaritsa, they sought to present a petition to Nicholas II, relating their hardships and begging for his help. Several thousand troops were positioned nearby, including the dreaded Preobrazhenskiy Guards, who opened fire on the crowd without warning, killing hundreds (the police figure was "more than thirty"). Gapon himself was later accused of being a traitor, and hanged by revolutionaries in a Finnish lake resort in 1906. At the outbreak of World War I, however, much of the hostility felt towards "Bloody Nicholas" after the massacre was submerged in a wave of patriotic fervour, and hundreds of thousands of people sank to their knees and bellowed "God save the tsar" as he emerged from the Winter Palace.

Despite this, within three years Tsarism had been swept away in the **February Revolution** of 1917. The determination of Kerensky's Provisional Government to continue the war enabled the Bolsheviks to mobilize support by promising "Peace, Bread, Land" and launch a second revolution. On October 25, 1917, Palace Square witnessed the famous **storming of the Winter Palace**, immortalized (and largely invented) in Eisenstein's film *October* – ironically, more people were injured during the making of the film than in the event itself. Having taken over all the key installations, Lenin (rather prematurely) announced the resignation of the Provisional Government at 10am. In fact, the first real exchange of fire didn't take place until 9.40pm, followed by blank shots from the cruiser *Aurora*, anchored down-river. Sporadic gunfire continued until around 10pm, when the three hundred-odd Cossacks defending the palace deserted en masse, leaving only a few-score officer cadets and members of the shaven-headed Women's Battalion to continue resistance. They were persuaded to lay down their arms and, in the early hours of the morning, a delegation of three to four hundred Bolsheviks entered by a side entrance and made their way through the palace's interminable rooms to arrest the Provisional Government.

Eisenstein's version of events was filmed in 1928, but by then the myth of the dramatic mass charge across the square was already part of Soviet folklore, thanks to the spectacles staged in honour of the **first anniversary of the October Revolution**. In 1918, a group of artists including Nathan Altman and Marc Chagall transformed Palace Square by covering the Alexander Column, the facades of the Winter Palace, and the General Staff building with sculptures and more than 5000 square metres of canvas plastered with avant-garde art. For the **third anniversary** (1920), under the glare of giant arc lights, a battalion of Red Army troops and thousands of citizens pretended to storm the palace, while fifty actors dressed as Kerensky (who was, in fact, absent at the time of the assault) made identical speeches and gestures, on a stage backed by Futurist designs.

In 1991, the square was at the centre of events during the referendum on the city's name, when large groups of people congregated to argue the merits of Leningrad or Petersburg. During the attempted **putsch** in August of the same year, Mayor Sobchak addressed some 150,000 citizens who assembled here in support of Boris Yeltsin and to protest against the coup. Even now, the square continues to attract political rallies, particularly of extreme Nationalists and die-hard Communists – notably during the close-run presidential elections of 1996 – but these days it is more the preserve of buskers, skateboarders and people offering horse-and-carriage rides or coach excursions to the Imperial palaces outside the city – plus the occasional beer or music festival.

The Alexander Column

Napoleon had hardly begun his 1812 retreat from Moscow when it was decided that a triumphal column should be erected in the middle of Palace Square. However, work on the **Alexander Column** (Aleksandrovskaya kolonna) didn't begin until 1830, when Auguste de Montferrand, the inexperienced architect in charge of building St Isaac's Cathedral, landed the job. Crowned by an angel, whose face is supposedly modelled on Alexander I's, the monument is 47.5m high, one of the tallest of its kind in the world. The **bas-relief** facing the Winter Palace depicts two figures representing the Niemen and Vistula, the two great rivers which Napoleon crossed on his march to Moscow, together with the simple inscription, "To Alexander I from a grateful Russia".

Its construction entailed Herculean efforts, rewarded by a faultless climax. After two years spent hewing the 600-tonne granite monolith from a Karelian rock face, and a year transporting it to St Petersburg, the column was erected in just forty minutes using a system of ramps, pulleys and ropes, pulled by two thousand war veterans. More than a thousand wooden piles had to be driven into the swampy ground to strengthen the foundations and, so the story goes, Montferrand insisted the mortar be mixed with vodka to prevent it from freezing. But the most disconcerting aspect of its construction is that the column isn't attached to the pedestal at all, but stays there simply by virtue of its immense weight.

The General Staff building

To complete the architectural ensemble around Palace Square, Alexander I purchased (and demolished) all the private houses which faced the Winter Palace, and in 1819 commissioned Carlo Rossi to design a new headquarters for the Russian Army **General Staff** (Generalniy shtab) building. The edifice frames one side of the square in a gigantic yellow arc, its sweeping facade interrupted by a colossal **arch** commemorating the Patriotic War against Napoleon. The underside is covered in armorial bas-reliefs; above the arch, Victory rides her six-horsed chariot, while two Roman soldiers restrain the horses from leaping over the edge. The whole structure was so large, rumours spread that it would collapse, prompting Rossi to declare, "If it falls, I fall with it" – he proved his point by standing on top of the arch as the scaffolding was removed. At one time the General Staff building also served as a prison: Griboedov spent four months here in 1826 as a suspected Decembrist, and Lermontov was held for five days before being exiled to the Caucasus for having written his *On the Death of a Poet* about Pushkin.

The exhibitions in the General Staff building are open Tues–Sat 10.30am–6pm, Sun 10.30am–5pm; $5. Tickets are sold in the foyer of the Hermitage.

As Samuel Hoare observed, "true to Russian type, the facade was the best part of the building", concealing "a network of smelly yards and muddy passages that made entrance difficult and health precarious". More seriously, at the outbreak of World War I, work often came to a standstill "owing to a perfect covey of saint's days and national anniversaries", while the quartermaster general "made a common habit of arriving in his office about eleven at night, and of working until seven or eight the next morning". Confusion also prevailed at the Foreign Ministry, housed in the eastern wing of the building, where, following the Bolshevik seizure of power, the head of the Petrograd Cheka (forerunners of the KGB), Moses Uritskiy, was assassinated in August 1918.

The building has now been given to the **Hermitage Museum**, and is ultimately intended to house its Impressionist and Post-Impressionist collections, and postwar art including multimedia installations, though so far only two exhibitions are in place. One is devoted to paintings by **Pierre Bonnard**, while the other, entitled **"Realms of the Eagle"**, features over six hundred works of Russian and European decorative art from the Napoleonic era, displayed in a series of rooms dating from that period and restored to Rossi's original decor.

The Winter Palace

The **Winter Palace** (Zimniy dvorets) is the finest example of Russian Baroque in St Petersburg, and at the time of its completion was the largest and most opulent palace in the city. Its 200-metre-long facade features a riot of ornamentation in the fifty bays facing the square, including two tiers of pilasters, a balustrade peppered with urns and statuary, and the prominent vertical drains so characteristic of the city. From this ultimate symbol of power, the autocrat could survey the expanse of Palace Square or gaze across the Neva to the Peter and Paul Fortress. As the journalist Alexander Herzen wrote of the palace, "Like a ship floating on the surface of the ocean, it had no real connection with the inhabitants of the deep, beyond that of eating them."

The existing Winter Palace is the **fourth structure** of that name, all of them built within half a century of each other. The first two, created for Peter the Great on the site of the present Hermitage Theatre, reflected his penchant for Dutch architecture; their remains were discovered during recent restoration and are now open to the public. In 1730, Empress Anna commissioned a third version (on the site of today's west wing) by Bartolomeo Rastrelli, but her successor Elizabeth was dissatisfied with the result and ordered him to start work on a replacement, This was intended to take two years to build and cost 859,555 rubles, though in the event it took eight years and cost 2.5 million, obliging Elizabeth to open a network of beer halls to

---

The Winter Palace and the Hermitage

Although begun as separate buildings, the **Winter Palace** and the **Hermitage** are now effectively one and the same thing. Catherine the Great created the first Hermitage and its embryonic art collection, and though "respectable" citizens were admitted after 1852, it became fully accessible only following the October Revolution – its collection swollen with Old Masters, precious objects and dozens of Impressionist master-pieces confiscated from private owners. Originally occupying only the eastern annexe, today the Hermitage's paintings take up most of the rooms in the Winter Palace. For a full account of the Hermitage collection and the state rooms, see Chapter 3.

The palace in history

The Winter Palace is as loaded with history as it is with gilt and stucco, having been a winter residence for every tsar and tsaritsa since **Peter the Great** (not to mention the court and 1500 servants). Though Peter always preferred to live at Monplaisir, he died in the second Winter Palace – the first of several Imperial demises of note associated with the building.

The first tsar to inhabit the present structure was **Peter III**, who lived with his mistress, Countess Vorontsova, in the southeastern corner of the second floor, while his wife, the future **Catherine the Great**, resided on the other side of the courtyard. On assuming the throne, Catherine redecorated and took over Peter's quarters, giving her lover, Count Orlov, the rooms directly beneath her own. Decades later, following a visit by the last of her paramours, Platon Zubov, she was found unconscious on the floor in her bedroom and later died. Given that she was then 67, it's difficult to believe the scurrilous legend that she died whilst attempting to copulate with a stallion (which supposedly crushed her when the harness suspending it from the ceiling broke).

Despite the choice of luxurious apartments available, **Nicholas I** picked himself one "no larger than a Bloomsbury dining room", furnished with barrack-like simplicity, where he worked, ate, slept and entertained his mistresses – and eventually died of influenza in the middle of the Crimean War. In contrast, his wife Alexandra ensured that no expense was spared in the adornment of her state room – the emerald green and gold Malachite Room.

Alexander II also chose to reside in a remote corner of the palace, furnished not with the Rembrandts or Rubens at his disposal, but in the simple, tasteless, bourgeois fashion of the day. In 1880 a bomb was planted below the Imperial Dining Hall by a member of the revolutionary Narodnaya Volya; eleven soldiers died, but the tsar – who had taken a break between courses – survived. A year later, however, another attempt on his life succeeded, and he died of his wounds in his apartment in the southwestern corner of the palace.

Nicholas II lived in the apartments above the Malachite Room until 1904, when increasing unrest forced the Imperial family to retreat to Tsarskoe Selo, only returning to the capital for state functions. At the outbreak of World War I, he pledged before five thousand people in the palace's St George's Hall that he would "never make peace so long as the enemy is on the soil of the fatherland", just as Alexander I had when Napoleon invaded the country in 1812. For much of the war, the great state rooms on the second floor were occupied by a hospital for invalids established by the tsaritsa, and during the February Revolution, loyalist troops made a brief last-ditch stand there.

In July 1917, the **Provisional Government** made its fateful move from the Mariinskiy Palace (see p.111) to the Winter Palace. Kerensky took over the tsaritsa's old rooms, and even slept in her four-poster bed. His ministers conferred in the Malachite Room and were arrested by the Bolsheviks in an adjacent dining room in the early hours of October 26. Party activists quickly put a stop to looting, except in the Imperial wine cellars, where every unit on guard soon got roaring drunk – and twelve people drowned. By 1922, most of the palace had been given over to the Hermitage art collection, while another part housed the Museum of the Great October Socialist Revolution (p.200) between the wars.

finance the excess. What you see now is not entirely what Rastrelli had in mind. Originally the **facade** was painted an icy turquoise blue with white trimmings; this was given a uniform coat of Venetian red in the nineteenth century, but is now sage-green and white. A fire in 1837 caused enormous damage but, in typically Russian fashion, "neither money, life nor health was spared" to restore it completely – the court was re-established there within fifteen months.

The Small and Large Hermitages and the Hermitage Theatre

Once Rastrelli had completed the Winter Palace, new buildings were gradually added to the east wing, becoming ever more austerely Neoclassical in style. The first addition was the long, thin annexe known as the **Small Hermitage** (Maliy Ermitazh). Directly inspired by Peter the Great's Hermitage at Peterhof, it was given the same, somewhat ironic, name – anything less "hermitic" would be difficult to imagine. It was built as a private retreat for Catherine the Great and it was here that she began the Imperial art collection that would eventually become the world's largest art gallery.

The **Large Hermitage** (Bolshoy Ermitazh), to the east, is made up of two separate buildings: the "Old Hermitage", facing the River Neva, was built to house the rapidly expanding Imperial art collection, and in the mid-nineteenth century this was augmented by the "New Hermitage", designed as Petersburg's first purpose-built public art gallery. Its best exterior features are the ten giant granite atlantes who hold up the porch on the south facade, their rippling, polished muscles glistening in the sunlight.

Beyond stands the **Hermitage Theatre** (Ermitazhniy teatr), built in 1775–84 by Quarenghi as a private theatre for Catherine the Great. Once a fortnight she would fill it with the capital's diplomats; the rest of the time, the average audience of private guests rarely reached double figures. The theatre's stage overlies the **remains of Peter the Great's Winter Palace** (see below), which was unearthed in the 1980s. The Hermitage Theatre is joined to the rest of the palace complex by a covered passageway which passes over the **Winter Moat** (Zimnaya kanavka), originally dug to surround Peter's palace. The views, as you look beneath the overhead passageway to the Neva beyond, and inland across the canal, are some of the loveliest in the city.

The Winter Palace of Peter the Great and Preobrazhenskiy Barracks

A sizeable remnant of the original **Winter Palace of Peter the Great**, sometimes known as "Peter's Hermitage", thought to have been levelled during the construction of the Hermitage Theatre, was rediscovered and unearthed between 1976 and 1986. The remains, only accessible on guided tours, are reached by a separate entrance at

The palace is
open Sat &
Sun
11am–3.30pm.
Tours (in
Russian only)
run every
30min. Tickets
are sold in the
lobby of the
Winter Palace;
$4.50.

To the Winter Palace

Dvortsovaya nabereznaya 32 (just beyond the Winter Moat) and consist of part of the former state courtyard flanked on two sides by arcaded galleries and small private apartments used by Peter and Catherine I. Though the flagstones and stucco look rather new, you can't help being charmed by the eagle-shaped gala sledge and open carriage used for masquerades, or by the reconstruction of Peter's turnery and other rooms, hung with Dutch still lifes and French landscapes purchased on his grand tour – not to mention a life-size wax figure of the tsar by Carlo Rastrelli, commissioned in 1725 by Peter himself.

Beyond the Winter Moat, on the south side of the Hermitage Theatre, are the former **Preobrazhenskiy Barracks**. As the first regiment of the Imperial Guard, whose colonel was always the tsar himself, the Preobrazhenskiy was the most powerful of the regiments established by Peter the Great – taking its name from Preobrazhenskoe, the summer estate where Peter had lived as a young man. During the uncertain decades following his death, the Guards became de facto kingmakers, whose allegiance was essential for any prospective ruler. This could be alienated by seemingly trivial matters – such as a change of uniform – as Peter III discovered when the Preobrazhenskiy cast off the Prussian-style garb introduced by him, and donned its old uniform of bottle-green and scarlet to salute Catherine's coup.

The view from Palace Embankment

There are more magnificent views from **Palace Embankment** (Dvortsovaya naberezhnaya) across the widest part of the River Neva. To the north, the gilded spire of the Peter and Paul Cathedral soars above its island fortress; to the west, the rust-red Rostral Columns stand proudly on the Strelka; while to the east, the river curves around past the Summer Garden and runs beneath bridges to the Petrograd and Vyborg sides. In summer, this is also the spot from which to catch **hydrofoils to Peterhof**, the great Imperial palace which stands beside the Gulf of Finland

For details of
hydrofoil
services along
the Neva to
Peterhof, see
p.332.

In Tsarist times this section of the river was the scene of the **Blessing of the Waters** on January 6, also known as the "Jordan Feast". The ceremony took place in a richly decorated wooden chapel erected for the occasion on the frozen Neva, and despite sub-zero temperatures, tradition required the entire Court to appear in silk stockings and shoes, and without winter coats: at one such event, Alexander I contracted frostbite in three of his fingers. As for ordinary folk, the most devout had their newborn babies baptized through holes in the ice. It wasn't unknown for the priest accidentally to lose his grip, or for the infant to catch pneumonia, but in such cases the parents were generally ecstatic, believing that the child had gone straight to heaven. Most bizarre of all, however, is the story of the Ice Palace on the Neva (see box on p.88).

East to the Summer Garden and Palace

There are several possible routes from the Winter Palace to Peter the Great's Summer Garden, the most direct being along either Millionnaya or the Neva embankment. Alternatively, you could follow the curve of the Moyka, taking in **Pushkin's Apartment** and the nearby church where he lay in state. Either way, you can't avoid **Marsovo pole**, where the Imperial troops used to parade. On the far side of this, surrounded by water, is the **Summer Garden**, the

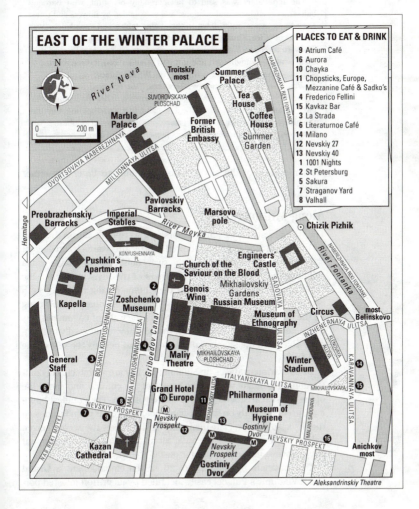

EAST OF THE WINTER PALACE

River Neva

Troitskiy most

SUVOROVSKAYA PLOSCHAD

Summer Palace

Tea House

Marble Palace

Former British Embassy

Coffee House

Summer Garden

0   200 m

DVORTSOVAYA NABEREZHNAYA

MILLIONNAYA ULITSA

Hermitage

Preobrazhenskiy Barracks

Imperial Stables

Pavlovskiy Barracks

River Moyka

Marsovo pole

Chizik Pizhik

Pushkin's Apartment

KONYUSHENNAYA PL.

Church of the Saviour on the Blood

Engineers' Castle

Kapella

Zoshchenko Museum

BOLSHAYA KONYUSHENNAYA ULITSA

MALAYA KONYUSHENNAYA ULITSA

Griboedov Canal

Benois Wing

Mikhailovskiy Gardens

Russian Museum

Museum of Ethnography

SADOVAYA ULITSA

Circus

most Belinskovo

INZHENERNAYA ULITSA

General Staff

Maliy Theatre

MIKHAILOVSKAYA PLOSHCHAD

Winter Stadium

NAB. REKI MOYKI

NEVSKIY PROSPEKT

Grand Hotel Europe

Philharmonia

ITALYANSKAYA ULITSA

MIKHAILOVSKAYA ULITSA

Museum of Hygiene

Nevskiy Prospekt

MIKHAILOVSKAYA PL.

KARAVANNAYA ULITSA

MALAYA SADOVAYA

Kazan Cathedral

Nevskiy Prospekt

Gostiniy Dvor

NEVSKIY PROSPEKT

Gostiniy Dvor

Anichkov most

▽ Aleksandrinskiy Theatre

River Fontanka

NABEREZHNAYA REKI FONTANKI

NABEREZHNAYA REKI FONTANKI

PLACES TO EAT & DRINK

- 9 Atrium Café
- 16 Aurora
- 10 Chayka
- 11 Chopsticks, Europe, Mezzanine Café & Sadko's
- 4 Frederico Fellini
- 15 Kavkaz Bar
- 3 La Strada
- 6 Literaturnoe Café
- 14 Milano
- 12 Nevskiy 27
- 13 Nevskiy 40
- 1 1001 Nights
- 2 St Petersburg
- 5 Sakura
- 7 Straganov Yard
- 8 Valhall

Empress Anna and the Ice Palace on the Neva

Like many of the early Romanovs, **Empress Anna** was extremely fond of
practical jokes. In the winter of 1739–40, she press-ganged the middle-
aged widower, Prince Golitsyn, into marrying an "extremely ugly" Mongol
lady. Anna organized the whole event, beginning with a procession of
goats, pigs, cows, camels, dogs and reindeer, pulling couples in national
dress from each of the "Barbarous Races" of the empire. Bringing up the
rear was an elephant with a cage on its back, containing Golitsyn and his
bride. After a grotesque wedding feast the newlyweds were transported to
Anne's *coup de théâtre*: a palace made entirely out of ice, erected on the
frozen Neva.

The **Ice Palace** was said to be incredibly beautiful, with Baroque
balustrades, cornices and columns, and surrounded by flowers and trees.
Everything inside, right down to the chairs, tables and chandeliers, was
carved out of ice. Finally, there was a four-poster bed upon which the couple were forced to consummate their marriage. The empress stayed with
them while they undressed and got into their icy bed, before retiring to
watch their antics from the warmth of the Winter Palace.

While Golitsyn died shortly afterwards, fate reserved an odd come-
uppance for Anna, who grew morbidly depressed under the malign influence of her lover, Count Biron. Legend has it that walking one evening in
the blue twilight of her mirrored palace, she encountered an obese figure
in full regalia, and – recognizing it as herself – died of apoplexy.

most romantic of the city's parks and home to Peter's **Summer
Palace**.

Along Millionnaya

The first private houses in St Petersburg were built across the Neva
on Petrograd Side in 1704, followed shortly afterwards by an elegant
street of houses on this side of the river, dubbed **Millionnaya ulitsa**
(Millionaires' Street) after the members of the royal family and the
wealthy aristocracy who made it their home during the nineteenth
century. Today, a new generation of Russian millionaires are buying
up the old palaces and knocking through the walls of communal flats
to create huge luxury apartments, though they're outwardly indistin-
guishable from the shabby *kommunalki* that occupy the rest of the
buildings.

Of the various **palaces** on Millionnaya, few are architecturally outstanding, but many were at the centre of the cultural and social life
of the Russian aristocracy before the Revolution. The grandest buildings, predominantly on the left-hand side, have their main facades on
the Neva, so to appreciate them fully (and to follow the account given
below) you will need to walk along the Palace embankment
(Dvortsovaya naberezhnaya) for part of the way.

The Italianate building at no. 26 on the embankment is **Grand
Duke Vladimir's Palace**, easily identified by its griffon-infested por-

tal. A notorious rake and hedonist, Vladimir was one of the most powerful public figures during the reign of his nephew, Nicholas II, but it was Vladimir's wife, Maria Pavlovna, who really set Petersburg talking. One of the tsar's most outspoken aristocratic critics, she hosted a popular salon, but left the city in the winter of 1916–17 vowing, "I'll not return until all is finished here" – and never did. It's worth trying to get inside the palace – now owned by the Academy of Sciences – to see its sumptuously gilded stairway, flanked by huge Chinese vases.

East to the Summer Garden and Palace

Further along is **Grand Duke Michael's Palace** (no. 18), an over-wrought neo-Baroque building that is so big that one of Michael's sons used a bicycle to visit his sister-in-law in another part of the palace. At **Putyatin's House**, Millionnaya no. 12, on March 3, 1917, another Grand Duke Michael – Nicholas II's brother and named successor following his abdication the previous day – renounced his right to the throne, formally ending the Romanov dynasty.

Next door at no. 10, the architect Stakenschneider took the opportunity to build himself a suitably majestic home, which hosted another popular salon in the mid-nineteenth century. The French writer **Balzac** stayed here in 1843 and met a Polish countess, Éveline Hanska, whom he had promised to marry back in 1832, once her husband died. Although the count had passed away in 1841, Balzac – a confirmed womanizer – managed to delay the marriage until 1850, just five months before he himself pegged out.

Along the Moyka

An alternative route east from the Winter Palace is to follow the **River Moyka**, which describes a graceful arc before joining the River Fontanka. Both rivers resemble canals, being embanked and adorned with handsome railings and flights of steps. East of Palace Square is the Pevcheskiy most, or "Singer's Bridge", named for the nearby **Kapella** building, home of the Imperial Court Choir (now the Glinka Choir) established by Peter the Great. Various famous Russian musicians, including Rimsky-Korsakov and, of course, Glinka, worked here, and the Kapella concert hall boasts some of the best acoustics in the city.

For more on the Kapella's concerts, see p.301.

Pushkin's apartment

Just up from the Kapella, a little wooden doorway at no. 12 leads to the garden-courtyard of **Pushkin's apartment** (the *kassa* is on the left as you enter the courtyard). Pushkin leased – though rarely managed to keep up the payments for – this relatively opulent apartment for his wife, their four children and her two sisters in the last unhappy year of his life (1836–37). The second-floor apartment consists of eleven rooms, the most evocative of which is the poet's **study**, which contains a replica of his library of over 4500 books in fourteen languages. A portrait of his teacher and fellow poet, Vasily Zhukovsky,

East to the Summer Garden and Palace

Pushkin's apartment is open Mon & Wed–Sun 11am–5pm, closed the last Fri of the month; $1, guided tour (usually in Russian) $1.50; English audio guides can be rented for $2.

Alexander Pushkin

Among Russians, **Alexander Pushkin** (1799–1837) is probably the most universally popular of all the great writers: "In him, as if in a lexicon, have been included all of the wealth, strength, and flexibility of our language," wrote Gogol, shortly after the poet's death. However, the enormous difficulties of translating Pushkin's subtle "poetry of grammar" means that he is rarely lauded with such extreme passion outside Russia. Here, though, not only is he seen as the nation's greatest poet and the father of Russian literature, but his tragic death assured him the status of a national martyr.

Born in Moscow, Pushkin was educated at the Imperial Lycée in Tsarskoe Selo (see p.358), though he was an indifferent pupil, excelling only in fencing, French and dancing. His first major poem, *Ruslan and Lyudmila*, caused an enormous stir in 1820, as did his subsequent political poems, for which he was exiled to the southern provinces of the empire. Hard drinking, gambling and sex characterized his periods of exile, during which Pushkin wrote his romantic "southern cycle" of poems, which, as he himself admitted, "smack of Byron", to whom he is often compared. In 1826, the new tsar, Nicholas I, allowed Pushkin to return to St Petersburg and met him personally, appointing himself as the poet's censor. In 1831, Pushkin married **Natalya Goncharova**, reputedly one of the most beautiful women in St Petersburg. The tsar made him a *junker* (officer cadet) so that Natalya could have an entrée into court life, which she enjoyed enormously, unlike Pushkin, who preferred a more solitary existence.

Pushkin's untimely death came at the age of 38, in a **duel** against a French officer called **D'Anthès**, the adopted son of the Dutch ambassador. The darling of the city's salons, D'Anthès set tongues wagging with his blatant advances towards Natalya, which she hardly discouraged. Eventually, Pushkin felt obliged to challenge him to a duel (January 27, 1837) – not the first time that he had fought one. D'Anthès was shot in the hand, but Pushkin received a fatal wound. The doctor posted notices outside the door of his apartment to keep his admirers informed about their hero's condition, but Pushkin died from his wounds after several days' lingering in extreme agony.

Pushkin's second in the duel was an equerry, so his **funeral** took place around the corner in the Equerries' Church on February 1, 1837. Since Pushkin was persona non grata with the regime at the time, a decree was issued forbidding university professors and students from attending. Nevertheless, the city's educated elite turned out in force, as did the diplomatic corps. Three days after the funeral, Pushkin's body was removed in secret and laid to rest at his country estate.

given to Pushkin on the publication of his first romantic poem, *Ruslan and Lyudmila*, adorns the wall, with the dedication "To the victorious pupil from the vanquished master". Pushkin kept a "blackamoor" figure on his desk to remind him of his great-grandfather, Abram Hannibal, an Abyssinian prince who served under Peter the Great, and whom he immortalized in his last, unfinished novel, *The Negro of Peter the Great*. In the Russian tradition, the clock in the study was stopped at the moment of Pushkin's death (2.45am), while in the nursery you can see the waistcoat that he wore at the duel (complete with bullet hole) and a candle from his funeral service.

Konyushennaya ploshchad and the Church of the Saviour on the Blood

East to the Summer Garden and Palace

Pushkin's funeral service in the Equerries' Church at the Imperial Stables on **Konyushennaya ploshchad** drew such crowds that cab drivers needed no other directions than "To Pushkin!" – inside the church, souvenir hunters tore his frock coat to shreds and snipped curls from his hair and sidewhiskers. Under Communism, the stables were taken over by the state removals company and the square became little more than a turnaround point for trams; now the church has been restored and the trams banished, while a stream of coaches brings tourists to admire the square's chief landmark: the **Church of the Saviour on the Blood** (Khram "Spas na krovi"; also known as the Church on Spilled Blood or the Church of the Resurrection). The city's most exotic edifice, the church is built in the neo-Russian style to resemble St Basil's in Moscow, its onion domes gilded or faceted like psychedelic pineapples, and its facade inlaid with hundreds of mosaics and ceramic panels. The church was begun in 1882 on the orders of Alexander III to commemorate his father, Alexander II, who had been assassinated on the site the year before. It was decreed that the church's tabernacle should be built on the very spot where his blood had stained the cobblestones – hence the church's unusual name and the fact that it juts out slightly into the Griboedov Canal.

The Church of the Saviour on the Blood is open 11am–7pm, closed Wed; $8.50.

Like so many churches, it was closed in the 1930s and turned into a storeroom, gravely damaging the interior; in 1970 it became a

---

The assassination of Alexander II

The **assassination of Alexander II** (March 1, 1881) followed numerous previous attempts on the tsar's life by the revolutionary Nihilist organization, Narodnaya Volya (People's Will). Their original plan involved digging a tunnel from below what is now Yeliseyev's food store and packing explosives beneath Malaya Sadovaya ulitsa, along which the tsar was expected to drive to a review at the Imperial Riding School. Although he unintentionally avoided this attempt by taking a different route, the revolutionaries had learned from previous failures, and had posted a backup team of bombers. As the Imperial party returned along the Griboedov embankment, **Nikolai Rysakov** hurled his bomb, killing a Cossack and mortally wounding himself and a child, but only denting the axle of the tsar's carriage. Ignoring the coachman's urgings to drive on, Alexander began berating his would-be assassin, who – in response to the tsar's assurance that "I am safe, thank God" – groaned, "Do not thank God yet!" As Alexander turned back towards his carriage, another terrorist, **Ignaty Grinevitsky**, threw a second bomb, which found its target. The tsar was carried off bleeding to the Winter Palace, where he expired shortly afterwards; Grinevitsky himself died of his wounds a few hours later. Legend has it that Alexander had a plan for constitutional reforms in his pocket at the time of his murder; if it's true, the Nihilists scored a spectacular own goal, since his successors were utterly opposed to any change whatsoever.

museum of mosaics, before being closed once again for over two decades. Since being reopened and reconsecrated in 1997, the church has become one of the city's foremost tourist attractions, owing to its magnificent **interior**, which is entirely covered in mosaics based on paintings by Nesterov, Vasnetsov, and other religious artists of the late nineteenth century. From Christ and the Apostles within the cupola to the images of saints and Biblical scenes on the walls and pillars, framed by wide decorative borders, the total area covered amounts to over seven thousand square metres. Despite the steep entrance charge for foreigners (buy tickets inside), it would be a shame to leave St Petersburg without seeing it.

The site's visual drama is enhanced by the magnificent **Art Nouveau railings** of the nearby Mikhailovskiy Gardens, cast from aluminium, which at that time was worth more than gold. Tourists may have themselves photographed with people in eighteenth-century costumes or enjoy a five-minute ride around Mikhailovskaya ploshchad in a horse-drawn carriage. Among the **buskers** in the vicinity, look out for the guy who plays a carpenter's saw with a violin bow; for those who want **souvenirs**, there's a host of stalls on the square between the church and the River Moyka.

Malaya Konnyushennaya and the Zoshchenko Museum

Though something of a detour, it's worth sidetracking to **Malaya Konyushennaya ulitsa**, an attractive street between Konyushennaya ploshchad and Nevskiy prospekt which has been pedestrianized and adorned with contemporary sculptures. If nothing else, it provides an excuse to cross the Griboedov Canal by a footbridge from where there's an excellent – and photogenic – view of the Church of the Saviour on the Blood.

*The
Zoshchenko
Museum is
open
Tues–Sun
10.30am–6pm,
closed the last
Wed of the
month; $0.75.*

Also on Malaya Konyushennaya ulitsa is the **Zoshchenko Museum**, reached by entering the courtyard of no. 4/2, passing through a door on the left and up a grim stairway to the third floor, to find flat #119. This tiny two-room apartment was the last residence of the satirist Mikhail Zoshchenko (1894–1958), whose life mirrored the fortunes of many writers of that era. Born into an academic Petersburg family, he volunteered for the army in 1914 and was gassed at the front. Returning home after the February Revolution he tried many professions before starting to write in 1921, and won a wide following with his short stories, whose style was copied by generations of Soviet stand-up comedians and movie actors. His novel *Before the Sunrise* was an attempt to exorcise his depression through psychoanalysis – an interest shared by Trotsky, whose downfall spelt the end of Freudianism in Russia. Although unscathed by the purges of the 1930s, Zoshchenko fell victim to the postwar *Zhdanovshchina* (see p.427); expelled from the Writers' Union for "hooligan representations", he was reduced to dire poverty. The museum contains a collage of humble personal effects and period artefacts, and preserves his bedroom, where his widow lived until 1981.

Around Marsovo pole

Back on the River Moyka, just beyond Konyushennaya ploshchad, the **Marsovo pole** (Field of Mars), once a marshy and sterile expanse, is now laid out as a pleasant park dotted with a few lilac trees – though it looks rather bare now compared to how it used to be before many of its bushes were dug up. It was used as the parade ground for the Imperial Guards early in the eighteenth century, but didn't acquire its present name until the great military reviews of the following century. Occupying the greater part of the western side are the **Pavlovskiy Barracks**, sporting an incredibly long, yellow facade broken up by three Doric porticoes. Founded by Paul I in 1796, the first recruits of the Pavlovskiy Guards were specifically chosen for their snub noses – Paul being so ashamed of his own pug nose that his face never appeared on coins ("My Ministers hope to lead me by the nose, but I haven't got one," he once remarked). Nor was the selection of guards on the basis of physical appearance so unusual – all the Preobrazhenskiy and Semyonovskiy Guards were respectively blond and brunette.

Following the overthrow of Tsarism, Marsovo pole changed character completely. Russia's first **May Day celebrations** took place here in 1917, with more than 150 platforms set up on trucks and carts representing each of the myriad political parties, including of course the Bolsheviks, from whose truck Lenin gave a speech. On March 23, 1917, the 180 people who had died in the February Revolution were buried in a common grave in the centre of the field, which was marked two years later by the erection of a low-lying granite **Monument to Revolutionary Fighters**, one of the first such works of the Soviet era. Lofty epitaphs by Commissar Lunacharsky adorn the gravestones, and **the Eternal Flame**, lit in 1957 on the fortieth anniversary of the Revolution, flickers at the centre – it's now a popular place for newlyweds to have their photo taken. Heroes of the October Revolution and the Civil War were buried here too, including the head of the Petrograd Cheka and the editor of *Krasnaya Gazeta*, both of whom were assassinated in 1918 by Socialist Revolutionaries. Finally, in 1920, sixteen thousand workers took part in a *subbotnik* (day of voluntary labour), transforming the dusty parade ground – dubbed the "Petersburg Sahara" – into the manicured park that exists today.

The Marble Palace

As thanks for orchestrating her seizure of power, Catherine the Great built her lover, Count Grigori Orlov, the costliest palace in the city, in the northwestern corner of the park. Designed by Antonio Rinaldi, and faced with green and grey marble, which had recently been dis-

East to the Summer Garden and Palace

The Marble Palace is open 10am–5pm, closed Tues, last ticket on sale an hour before closing; $5. To arrange a tour in English, call ☎315 34 48. The entrance is on Millionnaya ulitsa

covered in enormous quantities in the Urals, it quickly became known as the **Marble Palace** (Mramorniy dvorets). Catherine was a frequent visitor while the romance lasted, but as their intimacy began to wane, Orlov tried to win back her favours with gifts, the most famous of which was the 190-carat Orlov Diamond (as it came to be known). Smuggled out of India by a renegade French soldier, it was bought by an Armenian merchant who tried to sell it to Catherine. She refused to pay the asking price, at which point Orlov bought the diamond and presented it to Catherine, who never actually wore it, but had it set into the Imperial Sceptre (now in Moscow's Kremlin Armoury).

By the mid-nineteenth century the palace was in ruins, but was restored and refurbished in the late nineteenth century by Grand Duke Konstantin – a poet and playwright "when he felt like it". After the Revolution it was turned into the city's main Lenin Museum (there were seven others); the courtyard in front of the building became home to the famous armoured car from which Lenin spoke outside the Finland Station on his return from exile in 1917 – it was later removed when the museum was closed after the 1991 coup.

Rinaldi's design represents the link between Catherine's Baroque city and Alexander I's Neoclassicism, and there are elements of both at work on the **exterior** of the building. All that remains of Rinaldi's original **interior** are the main staircase and the Marble Hall, at the end of the east wing, whose walls show the wide variety of marble available from the Urals at the time. The courtyard is now occupied by the eight-tonne **statue of Alexander III** which formerly stood on the square by the Moscow Station until it was pulled down in 1937 (see p.232) – it was finally brought here in 1994 after 57 years in storage.

Lenin's armoured car is now in the Artillery Museum (p.198). See p.254 for more on Lenin's return from exile.

The palace is now a branch of the Russian Museum and is used to display part of the museum's large collection of paintings by foreign artists working in Russia in the eighteenth and nineteenth centuries, which together give an idea of the scale of European involvement in the Russian art scene. On the top floor are temporary displays of works by contemporary Russian and foreign artists plus a changing selection of modern international works donated by the German chocolate king, Peter Ludwig, and his wife, with paintings by Beuys, Warhol and the Muscovites Ilya Kabakov and Erik Bulatov.

Suvorovoskaya ploshchad

At the northern end of the park, forming the entrance to Troitskiy most (Trinity Bridge), **Suvorovskaya ploshchad** is named for the Russian general Alexander Suvorov (1730–1800), whose **bronze statue** stands on a granite plinth at the centre of the square. Suvorov, a veteran of the Italian campaigns against Napoleon, was a portly man, though he is portrayed here as a slim youth in Roman garb, representing Mars, the god of war.

On the east side, by the embankment, the late eighteenth-century building where the Russian satirical writer Ivan Krylov once lived stands beside the green mansion which housed first the Austrian and later (1863) the **British Embassy**. In March 1918 the British diplomatic corps followed the Soviet government to Moscow, leaving only a small contingent in Petrograd. Shortly after the attempt on Lenin's life in August 1918, there was a shoot-out between the British naval attaché, Captain Cromie, and the Petrograd Cheka, who stormed the building looking for counter-revolutionaries. Cromie killed a commissar before being shot dead at the top of the staircase. The remaining British officials were arrested but the ambassador was already ensconced in Vologda, and actively courting the White generals.

East to the Summer Garden and Palace

The Summer Garden

The **Summer Garden** (Letniy sad) is the city's most treasured public garden. Less than a year after founding the city in 1704, Peter the Great employed a Frenchman, Le Blond, to design a formal garden in the style of Versailles, with intricate parterres of flowers, shrubs and gravel, a glass conservatory, and orange and lemon trees. Sixty white marble statues of scenes from Aesop's *Fables* adorned the numerous fountains, their water drawn from the Fontanka. Unfortunately, a disastrous flood in 1777 wrecked the garden, uprooting trees and destroying the fountains. Reconstruction took place under Catherine the Great, who preferred the less formal, less spectacular, English-style garden that survives today.

The Summer Garden is open daily: May–Sept 9am–10pm; Oct–April 10am–7pm; closed for two weeks during April; $0.25.

Notwithstanding this – and the dress restrictions introduced during the reign of Nicholas I, which remained in force until the Revolution – the Summer Garden has always been popular with Petersburgers. Amongst the Romantics drawn here were Pushkin, Gogol, Tchaikovsky and the Ukrainian poet Shevchenko, while the novelist Ivan Goncharov used the garden as a setting for a meeting between the ill-starred couple, Oblomov and Olga, in his book *Oblomov*. The garden's popularity with lovers dates back to the early nineteenth century, when **marriage fairs** took place here on Whit Monday. The participants were mostly from the lower classes, "dressed in a great deal of finery badly put on, and a great many colours ill-assorted," as one English traveller observed. The young hopefuls would line up facing each other, men on one side, women on the other, and behind them their parents, who would enter into negotiations once a mutual preference had been expressed.

Around the garden

Surrounded on all sides by water – the Neva to the north, the Fontanka to the east, the Moyka to the south and the Swan Moat to the west – the garden is best approached from the Neva embankment, through the tall, slender wrought-iron grille, designed in 1770–84 by Yuri Felten, whose father had come to St Petersburg from Danzig in 1703 as a master cook for Peter the Great. All traces of Le Blond's fountains have disappeared, but more than eighty **Baroque statues** still punctuate the northern half of the garden (there were originally over two hundred). Few are of any great artistic merit, but together they evoke the romantic charm of eighteenth-century court life. In winter, they make a bizarre sight, enclosed in wooden boxes to protect them from the frost.

One of the most distinguished statues is that of **Cupid and Psyche**, on a platform which juts out into the Swan Moat, depicting the moment at which Psyche falls in love with Cupid, as she leans over his sleeping figure, holding a lamp to his face to catch her first glimpse. Alongside numerous other allegorical and mythological figures are several interesting historical statues, including a flattering bust of **Queen Christina of Sweden** (the fifth statue on the right as you walk straight ahead from the main gates): Christina ruled Sweden for just ten years (1632–42) before her secret conversion to Catholicism (which was proscribed in her homeland) was discovered, forcing her to abdicate. In the centre of the park is a large memorial to the popular satirical writer **Ivan Krylov** (1769–1844), paid for by public subscription. Like Aesop, Krylov used animals in his fables to illustrate human foibles, and many of his characters decorate the statue's pedestal, some of them playing musical instruments.

The Summer Palace

The palace is open May–Oct noon–5pm; Nov–April 11am–6.30pm; closed Tues & the last Mon of the month; $1.75.

In 1710, in the northeastern corner of the Summer Garden, Domenico Trezzini began working on a **Summer Palace** (Letniy dvorets) for Peter the Great. A modest two-storey building of bricks and stucco – one of the first such structures in the city – the new palace was really only a small step up from the wooden cottage in which Peter had previously lived on the other side of the river. Its position, at the point where the Fontanka joins the Neva, suited Peter's maritime bent; the seating area with benches, now laid out to the south side of the palace, was originally a small harbour.

The **palace rooms** were divided equally between husband and wife: Peter occupied the first floor, while Catherine took over the top floor. Information on each room is posted in English and Russian and the decor, though not original, has been faithfully reproduced. The tsar's **bedroom** is typically modest; his four-poster bed is significantly shorter than he was, since in those days the aristocracy slept propped half upright on pillows. Next door is Peter's **turnery**, where he would don a leather apron and spend hours bent over his mechanical lathes, presses and instruments; he also liked to receive important guests here. The room is dominated by a huge metereological device, which is connected to the palace weather vane and measures the strength and direction of the wind.

Tools from Peter's turnery and some of the objects that he made there can be seen in the Hermitage, see p.141.

In Petrine times, major banquets were held at the Menshikov Palace on Vasilevskiy Island (see p.179); the **dining room** here was

Court life in Petrine times

Along with Monplaisir at Peterhof, the Summer Palace is still faintly redolent of court life in Petrine times. Peter lived here with little pomp, preferring to lounge around in old clothes, attended only by a couple of servants
and two valets (whose stomachs he used as pillows on long journeys). This
informality nearly cost him dearly, as an attempt was made on his life by
an Old Believer (religious dissident) during a meeting in the palace reception room. Peter's hospitality was legendary – and feared. The most important summer celebration was the anniversary of the Battle of Poltava (June
28), when Peter himself served wine and beer to his veterans. Sentries
were posted at the gates to prevent guests from fleeing when the huge
buckets of corn brandy were brought on for compulsory toasting, which
wouldn't stop until all the guests were blind drunk – something the foreign
ambassadors were particularly wary of. The only willing participants were
the clergy, who "sat at their tables, smelling of radishes and onions, their
faces wreathed in smiles, drinking toast after toast". Dancing and drinking
would continue until dawn, though "many simply sank down where they
were in the garden and drifted into sleep".

used for less formal gatherings. Having taken his seat, Peter would
blithely tell his guests, "Those of you who can find places may sit
where you want. The rest of you can go home and dine with your
wives" – prompting much "cuffing and boxing" which he enjoyed
immensely. He also loved practical jokes, such as concealing dead
mice in the soup, or having dwarves burst forth from mounds of pâté.
Another source of pride, along with the turnery, was the palace's
kitchen, which was unusually modern for its day, plumbed with running water from the nearby fountains, and – most importantly –
opening directly onto the dining room: Peter liked his food hot, and
in large palaces dishes would usually be lukewarm by the time they
reached the table.

The **top floor** was the domain of Peter's wife, who became
Empress Catherine I upon his death. She was one of the most unlikely people to end up ruling Russia, having started life as a Lithuanian
peasant girl, but had a good influence on Peter – insisting that
women be present (and remain sober) during his notorious drinking
parties, and that the men could get drunk only after nine o'clock. She
was also one of the few people unmoved by his violent temper. On
one occasion, Peter smashed a Venetian mirror, shouting, "See, I can
break the most beautiful object in my house," to which she replied,
"And by doing so, have you made your palace more beautiful?"

The Tea House, Coffee House and Swan Lake

South of the Summer Palace stands the **Tea House** (Chayniy domik),
a simple Neoclassical pavilion built in 1827. Damaged by fire in
1981, it has since been restored and is now an exhibition hall. Carlo
Rossi's nearby **Coffee House** (Kofeyniy domik), on the site of an old

*The Tea House
is open only
during
exhibitions.*

grotto from Petrine times, is currently a souvenir shop. At the southern end of the garden is the **Swan Lake**, enlivened by said birds, and on its far side, at the southern entrance/exit to the gardens, stands a giant red porphyry **vase**, a gift from the Swedish King Karl Johan to Nicholas I.

The area covered in this heading is shown in detail on the map on p.87.

South of the Moyka

To the south of the Summer Garden, across the Moyka, is the idiosyncratic **Engineers' Castle**, part of it now open as a branch of the Russian Museum. There are several minor sights further south, but most people simply head for Mikhailovskaya ploshchad, dominated by the Mikhailovskiy Palace housing the main part of the **Russian Museum**, with its vast collection of Russian art. The route described below is also as good a way as any of returning to Nevskiy prospekt.

En route from the Summer Garden to the Engineers' Castle, where the Moyka joins the Fontanka, you'll notice people peering over the embankment at a small statue of a bird just above water-level, representing **Chizhik Pizhik**, the subject of a Soviet ditty derived from the nickname for an officer cadet, which runs: "Chizhik Pizhik, gde ty bil? Na Fontanke vodku pil" ("Chizhik Pizhik, where have you been? On the Fontanka drinking vodka"). The first monument of the glasnost era, it has since become a kind of good-luck talisman, and you may see boatloads of Russians throwing coins at it.

The Engineers' Castle

*The pensive poet casts a glance
At the palace buried in oblivion,
A tyrant's menacing memorial
Deserted in the mists of sleep.*
        Alexander Pushkin, *Freedom*

The Engineers' Castle is open Mon 10am–5pm, Wed–Sun 10am–6pm; $5. Guided tours in English for groups of five or more cost $8, plus $5 per person.

The heavily fortified **Engineers' Castle** (Inzhenerniy zamok), an extraordinary hybrid brick-red structure, was begun by Paul I shortly after he assumed the throne, in an attempt to allay his fear of being assassinated. To make way for it he had the wooden palace that Rastrelli had built for Empress Elizabeth – and in which he himself had been born – burnt to the ground: an act pregnant with significance for a man plagued by rumours of illegitimacy, and who wanted nothing more than to erase the memory of his mother, Catherine the Great.

Paul employed Vasily Bazhenov to design the building (first known as the Mikhailovskiy Castle after the Archangel Michael appeared in a vision to one of Paul's guards) and, in a deliberate snub to Catherine the Great's taste for a unified aesthetic, specified a different style for each of its facades. In his haste to complete the project,

Paul happily plundered much of the building material (and most of the furniture) from the various palaces his mother had built. He also insisted that his monogram appear throughout the palace – more than eight thousand times, according to one account.

In an atmosphere of almost pathological fear, Paul moved into the castle in February 1801, even before the paint was dry. He had insisted that it be surrounded by a moat (now filled in), which made the palace so damp that a thick mist filled the rooms. A trap door, which allowed access to the Pavlovskiy Barracks via a **secret passage**, was fitted close to his bedroom so that he could escape in emergencies. In the event, he spent only three weeks at the castle before his worst fears were realized and he was murdered in his bedroom (see box below) – he never made it as far as the passage.

As the scene of a regicide the castle was shunned by the Imperial family and later handed over to the Nicholas Engineering Academy (hence its present name). After the Revolution, it was used to house various libraries, institutes and record offices. Although the **interiors**

South of the Moyka

For details of Paul's early life, see p.367.

The assassination of Paul I

During the last months of **Paul I**'s life, his **mental state** deteriorated considerably. He suffered from hallucinations and lost his appetite; "the fact is," wrote the English ambassador, "and I speak it with regret, that the Emperor is literally not in his senses." Paul was already deeply unpopular with the Guards and the rest of the Romanov clan for sacking Chancellor Rostopchin – regarded as the font of Russian policy – and sending a force of Cossacks to expel the British from India without consulting anyone. Even more embarrassingly, he invited the sovereigns of Europe to settle their differences by hand-to-hand combat.

With the prospect of European conflict looming, Paul's own military leaders resolved to act to remove him from power, covertly encouraged by England's ambassador. Count Pahlen, head of foreign affairs and the police (and, ironically, Rostopchin's replacement), masterminded the plot from the sidelines, having gained the consent of the heir apparent, the future Alexander I, whose only proviso was that his father's life be spared. At midnight, March 11–12, 1801, the sixty-odd conspirators set off in the rain for the castle. En route they quenched their thirst with champagne, but were almost scared off by a flock of crows which they startled while creeping through the Summer Garden.

Paul's false sense of security in the palace had led him to replace the guard of thirty well-armed men with just two unarmed hussars, a valet and a sentry. One of the hussars put up a fight, but was quickly dealt with; the tsar, having vainly tried to conceal himself, was arrested in his nightshirt and cap. At this point, several soldiers who had got lost en route burst into the room and lunged at him, upsetting the night-light and plunging the room into darkness. In the confusion, Paul was knocked unconscious and strangled to death with his own sash. This nocturnal coup marked the end of an era: henceforth, Imperial assassinations would occur on the streets, no longer mounted by palace cliques and officers of the Guards, but by revolutionary organizations.

are currently being restored to their appearance at the time of Paul's brief residence, there is no furniture and many of the rooms are used to display paintings belonging to the Russian Museum, which now occupies most of the building. Official portraits from the eighteenth to early twentieth century dominate, among them paintings of the tsars and their families, artists and political figures, which together create an amazing record of Russian history. Other objects, previously hidden away in the museum's stores, are now granted displays in a variety of temporary shows. The charming **church** with its artificial marble columns is also occasionally open to the public. Access is via the main entrance which, contrary to appearances, is on the south side, through a gate bearing an incongruous stone inscription stolen from St Isaac's Cathedral. Take a look at the central octagonal **courtyard**, one of the castle's more successful features, before climbing the stairs immediately to the left of the main gateway.

South of the Engineers' Castle

To the south of the castle, Rossi laid out the triumphal **Klenovaya alleya** (Maple Alley) on the site of yet another of Paul's former parade grounds. At the top of the avenue is an equestrian statue of Peter the Great, erected by Paul and sporting the pithy inscription *Pradyedu pravnuk* (To grandfather from grandson), intended to quell persistent rumours of his illegitimacy.

The circus is closed from the end of July to mid-Sept; for further details, see p.304.

To the east, on Belinskovo ploshchad, St Petersburg's **State Circus** (Tsirk) occupies the late nineteenth-century premises of the Cinizelli Circus, whose traditions it maintains. To the south stand two **pavilions** designed by Rossi to house those members of Paul's *corps de gardes* who were on duty guarding the approach to the castle.

Across Inzhenernaya ulitsa, along the western side of Klenovaya alleya, is the **Winter Stadium** (Zimniy stadion), originally the Mikhailovskiy Manège – an Imperial riding school built by Rossi in the 1820s. During the Revolution, the Manège served as the headquarters of the Armoured Car Detachment, a die-hard Bolshevik unit that sped around in Austin armoured cars, attired in black leather. In 1948, the building was converted into a stadium for winter sports.

From the triangular Manezhnaya ploshchad, in front of the Winter Stadium, **Italyanskaya ulitsa** leads west to Mikhailovskaya ploshchad. The ice-blue palace on the left-hand side (no. 25) contains the **Museum of Hygiene**, which must vie with Peter the Great's Kunstkammer (see p.175) for stomach-churning potential. Gibbon brains and human organs are preserved in jars, and the effects of alcoholism on foetuses and VD on genitalia are graphically spelled out by means of rubber models. A nineteenth-century dentist's chair and one of Pavlov's dogs are among the other curiosities on show. Tourists seldom come here, but there's a steady flow of medical students throughout the week.

The Museum of Hygiene is open Mon–Fri 10am–6pm by guided tour in Russian only; $0.20.

Mikhailovskaya ploshchad and the Mikhailovskiy Gardens

South of the Moyka

All the buildings surrounding **Mikhailovskaya ploshchad** and **Mikhailovskaya ulitsa** (the road leading south to Nevskiy prospekt) were designed by Carlo Rossi in the early nineteenth century, each facade conforming to Rossi's overall Neoclassical plan. Both are named after the Mikhailovskiy Palace – the square's dominant feature – though in Soviet times Mikhailovskaya ploshchad was known as the "Square of the Arts" due to the numerous artistic institutions located here, and a **statue of Pushkin** reciting his poetry, by the city's leading postwar sculptor, Mikhail Anikushin, was erected in its centre in 1957.

The Mikhailovskiy Palace: the Russian Museum and Museum of Ethnography

Situated on the northern side of the square, the **Mikhailovskiy Palace** (Mikhailovskiy dvorets) – now the **Russian Museum** – is one of the largest palaces in the city. Another Rossi creation, its facade presents a relentless parade of Corinthian columns, epitomizing the Roman Neoclassicist architecture of Alexander I's reign. The tsar commissioned it for his brother, Grand Duke Michael, but little remains of Rossi's original interior, save the main staircase and the austere "White Room".

For a detailed account of the art collection of the Russian Museum, see Chapter 3.

At the turn of this century, the east wing, stables and laundry of the palace were replaced by a Neoclassical annexe, built to house the ethnographic collections of the Russian Museum. In 1934, this became a separate **Museum of Ethnography**, with displays of folk art, costumes, tools, reconstructed cottage and hut interiors and photographs of more than sixty nationalities, providing a fascinating insight into the peoples and cultures of the old Soviet Union.

The Museum of Ethnography is open 10am–6pm; closed Mon and the last Sun of the month; $4.

The **main hall** is lined with pink marble columns and decorated with a giant Socialist Realist frieze of peasants and workers from every nation of the former USSR. The museum proper kicks off in the west wing with the **Russian** people, tracing their peasant life, which was the norm for ninety percent of the population until early last century. On the **second-floor** north balcony you'll find exhibits on the **Ingush** and **Ossetian** peoples of the North Caucasus – though while the war in Chechnya continues, the section on the **Chechens** has been turned to face the wall.

An adjoining room covers the numerous ethnic groups who live in the melancholy landscape of the Volga basin and the Ural mountains: the largest of these are the **Tatars**, followed by the **Bashkirs** and **Chuvash**, the last one of the few non-Muslim Turkic peoples. The **Mordvinians**, **Udmurty**, **Mari** and **Komi** are also present here, Finno-Ugric peoples whose language is related to Estonian, Hungarian and Finnish. The south balcony covers the few remaining nomadic Siberian Lapps, such as the **Evenki** and **Nanaytsy**, whose movements are still dictated by the need to find pastures for their reindeer. The more numerous **Buryat** people remained nomads until after the Revolution, and traditionally practised shamanism, but have since settled more or less permanently around Lake Baikal and are now mostly practising Buddhists. The other main group represented here are the **Yakuts**, pastoralists whose language and culture continue to thrive.

The first floor of the **east wing** covers the more familiar Slav peoples, beginning with the two largest groups, the **Ukrainians** and **Belarussians**, and the Russians themselves. Both balconies on the upper floor are filled with examples of contemporary folk art, such as *matryoshka* dolls, Zhostovo trays and Palekh boxes. The southern rooms cover the **Kazakhs** and **Turkmenians**, and have a display of traditional Kazakh felt tents. There's also a **Children's Centre** (Sat & Sun 11am–5pm), where instructors teach handicrafts such as weaving, printmaking and pottery.

Just behind the palace are the **Mikhailovskiy Gardens**, whose broad lawns and deep pools of shade are especially appreciated during the hot summer months, when the White Nights find people playing badminton here at three o'clock in the morning, and there are outdoor **concerts** during the day (as advertised by the entrance gates).

The Maliy and the Philharmonia

*For details of
performances
at the Maliy
and
Philharmonia,
see pp.301–302.*

On the western side of Mikhailovskaya ploshchad stands the **Maliy Opera and Ballet Theatre** (Maliy operniy teatr) – previously known as the Mikhailovskiy – the city's main opera house after the Mariinskiy. While the building appears to be part of Rossi's masterplan, it was actually designed by the architect Bryullov – although Rossi was responsible for the square's other great musical institution, the **St Petersburg Philharmonia**, on the corner of Mikhailovskaya ulitsa, which was originally the concert hall of the Salle des Nobles.

Of all the figures associated with these institutions, the one closest to the hearts of the city's intelligentsia is **Dmitri Shostakovich** (1906–75), whose opera, *Lady Macbeth of Mtsensk*, was premiered at the Maliy in 1934 to great critical acclaim, only to be denounced by *Pravda* as "Chaos instead of Music" less than two years later. After years during which his music swung in and out of official favour, Shostakovich scored his greatest public success with his Seventh Symphony – the "Leningrad Symphony" – during the Blockade of the city in World War II. He wrote the first three movements whilst serving as an air warden (breaking off composing whenever the sirens sounded), before being evacuated to Kuybyshev, where he completed the work, which was broadcast across the Soviet Union to tremendous effect on August 13, 1942. Yet despite his obvious commitment to the war effort, he was one of the first victims of the postwar cultural purge known as the *Zhdanovshchina*, being accused of "formalist perversions and anti-democratic tendencies" in his art, and his relations with the Soviet authorities continued to be uneasy right up to his death in 1975.

Other notable events at the Philharmonia have included the premieres of Beethoven's *Missa solemnis* (1824) and Tchaikovsky's Sixth Symphony – the latter conducted by the composer just a few days before his death in 1893. It was here too that the American dancer Isadora Duncan made her Russian debut a few days after "Bloody Sunday" in 1905.

South of the Moyka

The Admiralty and the Bronze Horseman

The whimsical medusas cling angrily,
anchors rust like discarded ploughs –
and, lo, the bonds of three dimensions are all sundered
and opened are the seas of all the world.
                    Osip Mandelstam, *The Admiralty*

Standing at the western end of Nevskiy prospekt is the **Admiralty** building (Admiralteystvo), one of the world's most magnificent expressions of naval triumphalism, extending 407m along the waterfront from Palace Square to ploshchad Dekabristov. Marking the convergence of three great avenues that radiate across the city centre – Nevskiy prospekt, Gorokhovaya ulitsa and Voznesenskiy prospekt – its golden spire draws you naturally towards it on any walk along Nevskiy. Once there, you'll want to take the time to stroll in the **Alexander Garden** and explore the neighbouring ploshchad Dekabristov, which is dominated by the **Bronze Horseman**, the city's renowned statue of Peter the Great.

The area around the Admiralty is shown on the map on p.108.

The Admiralty

The **Admiralty** was originally founded by Peter the Great in 1704 as a fortified shipyard, with a primitive wooden tower and spire. A ban was placed on building in the vicinity to maintain a clear field of fire – hence the open spaces which still surround the edifice. As the shipyards moved elsewhere, and the Admiralty became purely administrative in function, Andreyan Zakharov was commissioned to design a suitable replacement.

Built in the early 1820s, the key feature of the existing building is a central **tower** rising through tiers and columns and culminating in a slender **spire** sheathed in gold. Like the spire of the Peter and Paul Cathedral, it asserted the city's European identity – differentiating its skyline from the traditional Russian medley of onion domes. It also enabled the tsar to scan the streets for miles around, using a telescope, to check whether they were being laid out according to plan. Topping the spire is a gilded **weather vane** shaped like a frigate, which has become the emblem of St Petersburg, appearing on everything from medals to shopping bags. Another piece of symbolism is encoded in the building itself, whose plan corresponds to the Greek and Cyrillic initial letter of Peter's name – Π – as does the form of the arched tower facing the Admiralty Garden.

The Admiralty's **facade** swarms with Neoclassical sculptures and reliefs, glorifying Russia's maritime potency. The archway of the main entrance is flanked by trios of nymphs bearing globes, representing the triple aspects of the goddess Hecate. A frieze below the entablature shows Neptune bequeathing his trident to Tsar Peter, while statues of Achilles and other heroes embellish the ledge below the colonnade. This in turn is topped by statues of the four seasons, winds and elements, and the mythological patrons of shipbuilding and astronomy, Isis and Urania.

The **porticoes** of the 163-metre-long side wings are similarly adorned, with reliefs of deities rewarding Russian bravery or artistry with laurel wreaths. Two lesser archways on the **embankment** side feature the Genii of Glory, a pair of angelic figures blowing trumpets (a symbol of St Petersburg); sadly, the river-front facade is marred by a row of late nineteenth-century apartment buildings. The Admiralty building has been occupied by a naval college since 1925 and the only part that is open to the public is the rather expensive restaurant in the east wing, opposite the Winter Palace. North along the embankment towards Dvortsoviy most (Palace Bridge) you'll notice a statue of **Peter the Shipbuilder**, a gift from the city of Amsterdam, where Peter worked as a common shipwright to learn the skills needed to build a Russian navy.

The Alexander Garden and prospekt

Largely obscuring the Admiralty, the wooded **Alexander Garden** (Aleksandrovskiy sad) leads towards ploshchad Dekabristov, toddlers and lovers mingling with officers from the naval college. On Sunday afternoons in summer, a Navy **brass band** plays near the Zhukovsky statue. Other Russians honoured with monuments here include Glinka, Lermontov and Gogol (near the fountain), but the nicest of the statues commemorates Colonel Przhevalsky (1839–88), whose intrepid journeys in Central Asia are commemorated by a saddled camel.

Admiralteyskiy prospekt, alongside the park, rates a mention for two buildings. The grey-and-white Neoclassical pile at no. 6 was the headquarters of the Imperial secret police for over fifty years before the Revolution and, from December 1917 until March 1918, the headquarters of the Cheka, ruled over by its boss "Iron" Felix Dzerzhinsky. Since 1995 the building has housed a small branch of the **Museum of Russian Political History**, covering the history of the secret police in three rooms on the second floor. The first room recreates the interior as it was during the reign of Alexander III, com-

The museum is open Mon–Fri 11am–6pm; $7.

plete with the curtained-off door through which agents could enter in
secret to report to their chief. The others contain photographs of
leading *Chekisti* and famous foreign spies like Reilly, plus memorabilia such as bulletproof vests and KGB medals – but unless you
understand Russian, it will only interest hardcore espionage buffs.
The entrance is beneath the iron canopy at Admiralteyskiy prospekt
6; head upstairs through the door with the IBM logo.

Two blocks further along Admiralteyskiy prospekt is the **Lobanov-
Rostovskiy House**, a massive wedge-shaped mansion built in
1817–20. The columned portico facing the prospekt is guarded by
two stone **lions** immortalized in Pushkin's poem *The Bronze
Horseman* (see below).

Ploshchad Dekabristov

Ploshchad Dekabristov – an expanse of fir trees and rose beds merg-
ing into the Alexander Garden – is largely defined by the monuments
that surround it, and known for the event recalled by its name,
"Decembrists' Square". The **Decembrists' revolt** began on the morning of December 14, 1825, when a group of reformist officers
marched three thousand soldiers into the square in an attempt to
force the Senate to veto the accession of Nicholas I and proclaim a
constitutional monarchy. Alas, the senators had already sworn allegiance to Nicholas and gone home, while the officers' leader, Prince
Trubetskoy, never showed up. The revolt turned from farce to tragedy
as the tsar surrounded the square with loyalist troops. When labourers on St Isaac's Cathedral started pelting them with bricks, Nicholas
feared that the revolt could spread and ordered his troops to attack.
By nightfall the rebellion had been crushed and interrogations were
under way, with Nicholas attending the trials and personally dictating
the sentences. Five ringleaders were hanged and 130 officers stripped
of their rank and exiled in fetters to Siberia. Although the soldiers had
only been obeying orders, with little or no idea of the revolt's aims,
dozens were forced to "run the gauntlet" of a thousand men twelve
times – that is, to be clubbed twelve thousand times.

The Bronze Horseman

Once on the square, your eyes are inevitably drawn to the famous
equestrian statue of Peter the Great, known as the **Bronze
Horseman** (Medny vsadnik), which rears up towards the waterfront.
Of all the city's monuments, none has been invested with such poet-
ic significance: a symbol of indomitable will and ruthless vision. The
statue made its literary debut in Pushkin's epic *The Bronze
Horseman* (1833), an evocation of the Great Flood of 1824. In the
poem, the only survivors are a poor clerk, Yevgeny, who climbs on
top of one of the lions outside the Lobanov-Rostovskiy House to
escape the flood waters, and the statue of the Horseman itself, which
comes to life and pursues him through the city. The radical journal-

**The
Admiralty
and the
Bronze
Horseman**

ist Herzen regarded the statue as a symbol of tyranny, whereas Andrei Bely likened it to Russia on the verge of the apocalypse: "Your two front hooves have leaped far off into the darkness, into the void, while your two rear hooves are firmly implanted in the granite soil."

The statue was commissioned by Catherine the Great to glorify "enlightened absolutism" – an ideal that she shared with Peter the Great (see box below), and which served to stress her place as his true political heir (she had, after all, no legitimate claim to the throne). Hence, the canny inscription, "To Peter I from Catherine II", which appears on the sides in Latin and Russian. The French sculptor, Etienne Falconet, was allocated the finest horses and riders in the

---

Peter the Great

Peter the Great (1672–1725) was responsible for irrevocably changing Russia's character, turning it from an ultra-parochial, backward country to an imperial power to be reckoned with. In childhood, he had experienced at first hand the savagery of Old Muscovy, when several of his family were butchered by the Kremlin Guards during a power struggle between the Naryshkin and Miloslavskiy clans. Secluded in Preobrazhenskoe, outside Moscow, he began to form his own "toy" regiments and mingle with the isolated foreign community: unlike most Russians, he was anything but xenophobic (styling himself "Peter" rather than "Pyotr"). He also taught himself to sail, and his enthusiasm for maritime affairs and Western ways was given full rein after the death of his elder brother and co-tsar, the feeble-minded Ivan V.

In 1697–98, Peter embarked on a **grand tour** of Europe, travelling incognito to be free of the burdens of protocol, so that he might concentrate on studying shipbuilding in Holland and England, where he worked on the docks as an apprentice. His aim was to create a Russian navy in order to drive back Charles XII of Sweden and secure a Baltic "Window on the West" – the genesis of **St Petersburg** itself. Yet when he wasn't poring over plans, inspecting the navy, founding institutions or leading his armies into battle, Peter enjoyed a riotous lifestyle with cronies like Menshikov (p.179) and Lefort. Together they formed the "Drunken Synod", whose parties parodied the rituals of the Orthodox Church, reflecting his crude sense of humour and his dislike of Old Russia – though the former was somewhat mitigated by his astute second wife, **Catherine I** (p.97).

Amongst Peter's innovations were the Kunstkammer, or "chamber of curiosities", Russia's first public museum (p.175), and the imposition of a tax on those who wore beards and caftans, after Peter proclaimed them backward and impractical. His westernizing reforms and lukewarm devotion to Orthodoxy alienated nobles and commoners alike – but the beheading of the Kremlin guard (1698) and the execution of his own son, **Tsarevich Alexei** (p.192), dissuaded further rebellions. Opinion remains divided over Peter's achievements. Whereas most Russians see him as a great ruler who advanced the nation, others blame him for perverting its true, Slavic destiny, or setting an autocratic precedent for Lenin and Stalin. Unlike them, however, Peter's sheer *joie de vivre* makes him hard to dislike, for all his brutality.

Imperial stables, so that he could study their movements. Later, he sketched them held motionless on a special platform, while a cavalry general of similar build to Peter sat in the saddle. The statue wasn't completed until 1782 (Falconet complaining of arrears in his salary), with disaster narrowly averted during the casting stage, when a foundry man tore off his clothes to block a crack in the mould, preventing the molten metal from escaping. Its huge **pedestal** rock was brought from the village of Lakhta, 10km outside Petersburg; Peter had supposedly surveyed the city's environs from this 1600-tonne "Thunder Rock", sculpted by the waves over millennia. A trampled serpent (symbolizing evil) wriggles limply down the back of the pedestal.

As a visit on any sunny day will confirm, the statue is a customary spot for newlyweds to be photographed, before drinking a toast on the Strelka to celebrate their nuptials (p.172). Don't even think of emulating the drunken foreigner who once climbed up onto the statue to sit behind Peter in the saddle, and was swiftly arrested and heavily fined. When he protested at the high cost of the fine, the police replied, "If you will ride with great people, you must pay great people's prices."

The Admiralty and the Bronze Horseman

The Senate and Horseguards' Manège

The colossal ochre-and-white **Senate and Synod** building on the far side of ploshchad Dekabristov was constructed in the mid-nineteenth century to replace an old mansion that had formerly housed both institutions. Peter established the Senate (1711) to run Russia in his absence, and the Holy Synod (1721) to control the Orthodox Church, and both had assumed a more permanent role by the time that Rossi designed these new premises. Echoing the General Staff, a resplendent arch unites the twin buildings, which now contain historical archives.

Further south stands the former **Horseguards' Manège** (Konnogvardeyskiy manezh), which was built as an indoor riding school at the beginning of the nineteenth century. The architect Quarenghi felt that its prime location called for a temple-like portico fronted by the Sons of Zeus reining in wild horses, which was copied from a similar arrangement outside the Quirinale Palace in Rome. In 1840 the naked youths were removed after the Holy Synod objected to their presence within sight of St Isaac's Cathedral, and they were only reinstated in 1954. The Manège was used for concerts in Tsarist times (Johann Strauss conducted here), but is now the **Central Exhibition Hall**, used for both modern art and trade exhibitions.

St Isaac's Cathedral and around

Looming majestically above the rooftops to the southeast of ploshchad Dekabristov, **St Isaac's Cathedral** (Isaakievsky sobor) – one of the city's premier tourist attractions – is visible from way out in the Gulf of Finland, but is too massive to grasp at close quarters. It stands on its own square, **Isaakievskaya ploshchad** (St Isaac's Square), and it's

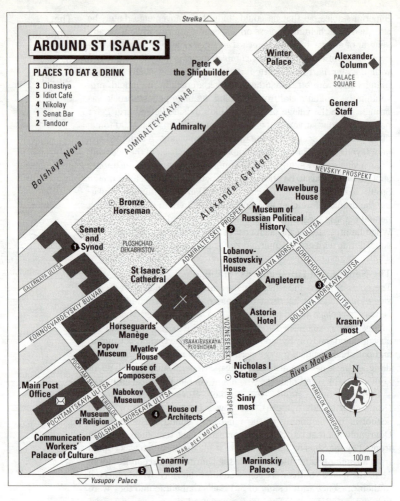

AROUND ST ISAAC'S

PLACES TO EAT & DRINK

3 Dinastiya
5 Idiot Café
4 Nikolay
1 Senat Bar
2 Tandoor

△ Strelka

Peter the Shipbuilder

Winter Palace

Alexander Column

PALACE SQUARE

General Staff

Admiralty

ADMIRALTEYSKAYA NAB.

Bolshaya Neva

Alexander Garden

NEVSKIY PROSPEKT

Bronze Horseman

Wawelburg House

Museum of Russian Political History

ADMIRALTEYSKIY PROSPEKT

Senate and Synod

PLOSHCHAD DEKABRISTOV

Lobanov-Rostovskiy House

GALERNAYA ULITSA

St Isaac's Cathedral

Angleterre

MALAYA MORSKAYA ULITSA

GOROKHOVAYA ULITSA

Astoria Hotel

BOLSHAYA MORSKAYA ULITSA

KONNOGVARDEYSKIY BULVAR

Horseguards' Manège

ISAAKIEVSKAYA PLOSHCHAD

Krasniy most

Popov Museum

Myatlev House

VOZNESENSKIY

House of Composers

POCHTAMTSKIY PEREULOK

Main Post Office

Nabokov Museum

PROSPEKT

River Moyka

N

Nicholas I Statue

POCHTAMTSKAYA ULITSA

Museum of Religion

BOLSHAYA MORSKAYA ULITSA

House of Architects

Siniy most

PEREULOK GRIBOEDOVA

Communication Workers' Palace of Culture

NAB. REKI MOYKI

Fonarniy most

Mariinskiy Palace

0   100 m

▽ Yusupov Palace

from the centre of this that you'll get the best view of the cathedral. By day, its gilded dome is one of the glories of St Petersburg's skyline; at night, its gigantic porticoes and statues seem almost menacing, like something dredged up from the sea bed. Its opulent interior is equally impressive, as is the wonderful view from its colonnade.

During World War II, the cathedral appeared on Luftwaffe bombing maps as "reference point no. 1", and the park to the south was dug up and planted with cabbages to help feed the famished city. Today, the only hazard to be encountered on Isaakievskaya ploshchad is the traffic, zooming across from all sides, but worth braving for a bevy of interesting buildings around its edges.

The Cathedral

The **Cathedral** is the fourth church in St Petersburg to have been dedicated to St Isaac of Dalmatia, a Byzantine monk whose feast day fell on Peter the Great's birthday (May 30). The previous one on this site was judged too small even before its completion, so a competition to design a replacement was announced after Russia's victory over Napoleon in 1812. By submitting no fewer than 24 designs in various styles, a young unknown architect, Auguste de Montferrand, impressed Alexander I into giving him the commission, though he soon required help from more experienced architects. The tsar insisted that the walls of the previous church be preserved, causing huge problems until he relented three years later, at which point everything was demolished and work began again from scratch. Many reckoned that construction (1818–42) and decoration (1842–58) were deliberately prolonged, owing to the popular superstition that the Romanov dynasty would end with the cathedral's completion – a more likely explanation is that the delays were caused by Montferrand's incompetence.

Throughout the Soviet period, the cathedral was turned into a Museum of Atheism, where visitors could admire an enormous Foucault's pendulum, installed beneath the dome – it supposedly proved the falsity of religion by demonstrating the earth's rotation. St Isaac's is not likely to be handed back to the Church and, although it has been reconsecrated, it is still classified as a museum. Beyond the railings on the southern side of the cathedral, two doors lead to the interior (left) and the *kolonnada* (right), each of which has a separate exit, so that you have to go back round again to see the other one. **Photography** is not permitted inside, nor from the colonnade (though Russians ignore the rule).

The interior

The cathedral's vast **interior** is decorated with fourteen kinds of marble, as well as jasper, malachite, gilded stucco, frescoes and mosaics. An 800-square-metre painting by Karl Bryullov of the Virgin surrounded by saints and angels covers the inside of the cupola, while biblical scenes by Ivan Vitali appear in bas-relief on the huge bronze **doors** and as murals and mosaics elsewhere (all labelled in English). Malachite and lazurite columns frame a white marble **iconostasis**, decorated by Neff, Bryullov and Zhivago, its wings flanking the gilded bronze doors into the **sanctuary**. Only the monarch and the patriarch were admitted to the sanctuary, whose stained-glass window is contrary to Orthodox tradition (though perfectly acceptable elsewhere in an Orthodox church). At the back of the nave are vintage scale-models of the cathedral and its dome, and a bust and cast-iron relief of Montferrand. When the architect died after forty years' working on the project, his widow begged that he be interred in St Isaac's crypt, but the tsar refused to sully it with the

Tickets for the interior (11am–6pm, closed Wed; $8) and colonnade (11am–5pm, closed Wed; $3) are sold from kiosks opposite the Lobanov-Rostovskiy House.

tomb of a non-Orthodox believer and sent his coffin home to France. However, Montferrand was accorded an image on the extreme left of the western portico (the cast-iron relief is a scaled-down copy of this figure).

The dome and colonnade
The cathedral's height (101.5m) and rooftop statues are best appreciated by climbing the 262 steps up to its **dome** – the third largest cathedral dome in Europe. This consists of three hemispherical shells mounted one inside the other, with 100,000 clay pots fixed between the outer and middle layers to form a lightweight vault and enhance the acoustics. Nearly 100kg of gold leaf was used to cover the exterior of the dome, helping push the total cost of the cathedral to 23,256,000 roubles (six times that of the Winter Palace). The sixty men who died from inhaling mercury fumes during the gilding process were not the only fatalities amongst the serf-labourers, who worked fifteen hours a day without any holidays, since Nicholas believed that "idleness can only do them harm". Dwarfed by a great **colonnade** topped with 24 statues, the dome's windswept iron gallery offers a stunning panoramic view of central St Petersburg.

Around Isaakievskaya ploshchad
On the eastern side of Isaakievskaya ploshchad, the pinkish-grey **Astoria Hotel** is famous for those who have – and haven't – stayed there. Built in the early 1900s, its former guests include the American Communists John Reed and Louise Bryant, and the Russian-born Anarchists Emma Goldman and Alexander Berkman. It's said that Hitler planned to hold a victory banquet here once Leningrad had fallen, and sent out invitations specifying the month and hour, but leaving out the exact date. Adjacent to the Astoria is a smaller, butterscotch annex named the *Angleterre*, where the poet Sergei Yesenin apparently slashed his wrists and hanged himself in 1925, leaving a verse written in his own blood:

> *See you again, my friend, I'll see you*
> *Good friend, you're here inside me*
> *The foretold parting is a promise to*
> *Be, one day, once more, beside me.*
> *See you again, my friend, no words, no hand*
> *Don't grieve, don't let your brow betray you*
> *In life there's nothing new in a dying man.*

In 1998, however, Yesenin's niece pressed the authorities to reopen the investigation into his death, following allegations that Yesenin was killed by the secret police. The theory is that Trotsky ordered him to be beaten up, to dissuade Yesenin from planning to emigrate, but the *chekisti* entrusted with the job killed him by accident, and faked a suicide to cover it up – the poem being written by the *chekist* commander Yakov Blumkin.

At the centre of the square prances a haughty, bronze equestrian **statue of Nicholas I**, known to his subjects as "the Stick" (*Palkin*) and abroad as the "Gendarme of Europe". Its granite, porphyry and marble pedestal is adorned with figures representing Faith, Wisdom, Justice and Might – modelled, it's said, on Nicholas's daughters; bas-reliefs depict the achievements of his reign, and four lamp stands flaunt screaming eagles.

Along the west side

Across the square from the Astoria and the tsar's statue are a trio of buildings with diverse antecedents. The **Myatlev House** (no. 9) is the oldest on the square, dating from the 1760s, its medallioned facade bearing a plaque attesting to the fact that the French encyclopedist Denis Diderot stayed here (Oct 1773 to March 1774) at the invitation of Catherine the Great. When Diderot fell on hard times, she bought his library but allowed him to keep the books and be paid for "cura-torship" until his death. The house is named after a later owner, the poet Ivan Myatlev. Alongside stands a brown granite building that served as the German Embassy until the outbreak of World War I, when a mob tore down its statues, flung them in the Moyka and loot-ed the building in an orgy of hysterical patriotism. It now houses the Dresdener Bank.

Further south stands a pilastered Doric building, which since Soviet times has housed the renowned **Vavilov Institute of Plant Breeding** (a French wine shop is also now ensconced in the lobby). The institute is proud to have preserved its collection of 56,000 edi-ble specimens throughout the Blockade – when 29 of its staff died of malnutrition – and equally proud of its founder, Nikolai Vavilov (1887–1943), Russia's greatest geneticist. The Brezhnev-era memo-rial plaque fails to mention that he was arrested, tortured, accused of heading a non-existent underground opposition party, and died in prison during Stalin's time. Around the side of the building, on the Moyka embankment, a tetrahedral granite **obelisk** marks the level of the worst floods in the city's history – the five-metre watermark is at chest height, and a mark well above head level can also be seen.

The Siniy most and the Mariinskiy Palace

Isaakievskaya ploshchad's southern end continues across the **Siniy most**, or Blue Bridge, which is so wide that you hardly realize the Moyka is flowing beneath it. Like the Red and Green bridges further along the Moyka, the Siniy gets its name from the colour of its river-facing sides. Until Alexander II abolished serfdom in 1861, serfs were bought and sold here in what amounted to a slave market.

Beyond the bridge, the **Mariinskiy Palace** (Mariinskiy dvorets) now flies the tricolour and crest of the Russian Federation, but the

Guided tours of the Mariinskiy Palace are currently suspended for security reasons; call ☎319 94 18 for the latest info.

*The area
beyond the
Mariinsky
Palace is
covered under
"West of St
Isaac's"
(p.117) and
"Between the
Yusupov
Palace and the
Blok Museum"
(p.120).*

palace's pediment still sports the five awards bestowed on Leningrad during the Soviet era – a schizoid heraldry which reflects the palace's colourful history. Built for Maria, the favourite daughter of Nicholas I, it later became the seat of the State Council; the Council of Ministers met here while Tsarism was falling, as did the Provisional Government before it moved into the Winter Palace. After 1948, the palace housed the Executive Committee of the City Council, which was effectively run by the Communist Party until the setting up of a mayoralty in 1991. During the putsch that year, thousands of citizens turned out to defend the democratically elected council and mayoralty, but the latter then transferred to the Smolniy Institute, leaving the palace to the City Legislative Council, which Yeltsin dissolved in 1993. The Council was eventually reconstituted in 1995, but still has an uneasy relationship with the City Executive (now the Governor's office) at the Smolniy, which has far more power.

The interior of the palace boasts a monumental staircase and colonnaded **Rotunda Hall** (depicted in a huge painting by Ilya Repin, now in the Russian Museum). The **Red Drawing Room** has mahogany doors inlaid with ivory, mother-of-pearl and precious metals, while the attic contains a private chapel, decorated with pseudo-Byzantine frescoes.

Between Nevskiy and Voznesenskiy prospekts

If you don't reach St Isaac's Cathedral by way of the Admiralty and ploshchad Dekabristov, you'll probably approach it along one of the streets or canals **between Nevskiy and Voznesenskiy prospekts**. These two avenues delineate a central wedge full of contrasts and vitality, encompassing the old financial district along Bolshaya and Malaya Morskaya, the faded beauty of the Moyka and Griboedov embankments, and the bustling lowlife of Sadovaya ulitsa and Sennaya ploshchad.

Malaya and Bolshaya Morskaya

Before the Revolution, financiers and aristocrats congregated in the banks and clubs of **Bolshaya Morskaya** and **Malaya Morskaya** (Great and Little Morskaya), a pair of streets dubbed "the City". In 1918, these were taken over or shut down, leaving only imposing facades as a reminder of their heyday – until an influx of foreign companies revitalized their prospects and sent property values soaring in the 1990s. As these streets are the nexus of downtown St Petersburg, you're bound to pass this way often.

Malaya Morskaya

Turning off Nevskiy prospekt at the Wawelburg House (see p.79), you find yourself on **Malaya Morskaya ulitsa**, with its many literary and artistic associations. Number 10, on the left-hand side, is known as the "**Queen of Spades' House**", having once been the residence of Princess N.P. Golitsyna, who is thought to have been the model for the countess in Pushkin's short story *The Queen of Spades*. A former society beauty, she was an old woman in Pushkin's day, when she was nicknamed "Princess Moustache". By a neat coincidence, *The Queen of Spades* was later turned into an opera by **Pyotr Tchaikovsky**, who occupied the Empire-style block diagonally across the street at no. 13, on the corner of Gorokhovaya ulitsa. It was here that he died on October 25, 1893, most likely from cholera contracted from a glass of unboiled water that he consumed in the Restaurant Leiner on Nevskiy prospekt (the theory that he committed suicide to avoid a scandal over his love affair with his nephew is now discredited, following research showing that homosexuality was generally tolerated in Russian high society at that time).

A block further on, a plaque at no. 17 remembers **Nikolai Gogol**, who lived there from 1833 to 1836, during which time he wrote such short stories as *The Nose*, *Nevskiy Prospekt* and *Diary of a Madman* – set in a St Petersburg where "everything breathes falsehood" – and his satirical drama *The Government Inspector*. Despite the play's success, Gogol felt misunderstood and victimized, and left the city two months after its premiere. His last years were marked by religious mania and despair: lapsing into melancholia, he ate only pickled cabbage and, suffering from cataleptic fits, died after being mistakenly buried alive in a Moscow cemetery in 1852 – as was discovered years later when his body was exhumed, and claw marks were found inside the coffin.

Fabergé

Carl Fabergé (1846–1920) turned a small family jewellers in St Petersburg into a world-famous company with branches in Moscow, Kiev, Odessa and London. In 1884, Alexander III commissioned him to design a jewelled Easter egg for the empress – the first in a series of **Imperial Eggs** exchanged by the tsar and tsaritsa every year until the fall of the Romanovs. Although most reference books state that there were 56 eggs in total, the art historian Valentin Skurlov believes that only 50 were made expressly for the Imperial family. Even more intricate was the **Grand Siberian Railway Egg**, produced to mark the completion of the line to Vladivostok. Its enamelled gold shell is engraved in silver with a map of the route, each station marked by a gem; inside is a tiny gold-and-platinum replica of the Trans-Siberian Express, which runs when the clockwork locomotive is wound up. After the Bolsheviks closed down his Russian branches in 1918, Carl fled the country, while many of his *objets d'art* were smuggled out or sold off by the state. The first Imperial Egg sold at Christie's in London fetched £85/$136 (in 1934); a recent sale in Geneva notched up £2.25 million/$3.6 million. The largest collection is owned by the Kremlin Armoury in Moscow, though you might find some Imperial Eggs or other Fabergé objects on display in the Hermitage.

Bolshaya Morskaya

Running parallel to Malaya Morskaya a block to the northwest, the longer **Bolshaya Morskaya ulitsa** features a succession of grandiose facades interspersed with airline offices. At no. 15, on the right, stands the former **Russian Commercial and Industrial Bank**, sporting ornate bronze doors; across the road, the old **Fabergé** emporium (see box on p.113) at no. 24 is recognizable by its curvaceous pillars. Diagonally opposite at no. 29 is a Baroque mansion reminiscent of a miniature Winter Palace, containing the **Bank for Foreign Economic Affairs**. Beyond Gorokhovaya ulitsa, a statue of Mother Russia succouring a widow, child and pensioner crowns the former **Rossiya Insurance Company**.

Along the Moyka embankment

Walking along the **River Moyka embankment** (naberezhnaya Reki Moyki) from Nevskiy prospekt to Isaakievskaya ploshchad takes longer, but its melancholy charm is hard to resist – the sooty tan, beige and grey facades like a Canaletto canal vista painted by L.S. Lowry.

Turning off Nevskiy prospekt by the Stroganov Palace (see p.78) brings you to the eighteenth-century **Razumovskiy Palace**, while further along is the old **Foundling House** (Vospitatelniy dom) for abandoned babies, which by 1837 was taking in 25,000 children a year, before farming them out to peasant familes for "nursing". Today, both buildings belong to the Herzen Pedagogical Institute.

Immediately beyond, the Moyka is spanned by **Krasniy most**, or Red Bridge, carrying Gorokhovaya ulitsa across the river. Of the four similar wrought-iron bridges built across the Moyka in the early nineteenth century, it alone retains its original form, featuring four granite obelisks topped with gilded spheres. On the northern side of the river is a multi-storey workshop with a striking Art Nouveau facade. From Krasniy most, it's 400m along the embankment to Siniy most at the bottom of Isaakievskaya ploshchad (see p.11).

Along the Griboedov Canal

*For a
description of
Lviniy most
and other
sights beyond
Voznesenskiy
prospekt, see
p.121.*

The winding **Griboedov Canal** (Kanal Griboedova) makes a fairly indirect approach to St Isaac's, but the views are so lovely you hardly notice the distance. At the very least, you should walk as far as Bankovskiy most, the first footbridge you come to off Nevskiy prospekt.

Immediately off Nevskiy, the south bank of the canal is thronged with people visiting the **Railway Tickets Bureau** (no. 18). At the end of this block stands the **Maliy Gostiniy dvor**, a smaller, now defunct offshoot of the great bazaar further east, while a little further on are the wrought-iron railings and curved rear wings (now the main entrance) of the former **Assignment Bank**. The bank lent its name to the picturesque **Bankovskiy most**, or Bank Bridge, whose suspension cables issue from the mouths of four griffons with gilded wings – in ancient Greece, these mythical creatures were thought to be the guardians of gold. Its designer, Walter Traitteur, also built Lviniy most (Lion Bridge), further along the canal.

Beyond this point the canal runs beneath **Muchnoy most** – a wrought-iron footbridge – and the humped **Kamenniy most** (Stone Bridge), which carries Gorokhovaya ulitsa across the canal. Looking north up the avenue from the bridge you can see the Admiralty spire; in the other direction, the Theatre of Young Spectators. In 1880, the Narodnaya Volya planted dynamite beneath the bridge in an attempt to kill Alexander II as he rode across, but the plan failed.

Soon after Kamenniy most the canal becomes tree-lined and veers left, passing beneath the arched, wrought-iron **Demidov most**. South of here the embankment opens on to **Sennaya ploshchad**, which was the setting for much of *Crime and Punishment* (see p.116), and still reeks of abandonment. Thereafter, the canal switchbacks through a residential area, spanned by a pair of bridges with gilt finials, and under **Voznesenskiy most**, decorated with bundles of spears and gilded rosettes, which carries Voznesenskiy prospekt across the Griboedov Canal.

Sadovaya ulitsa

The longest of the routes between Nevskiy and Voznesenskiy prospekts is quite unlike the others. Thronged with people and traffic, the two-kilometre length of **Sadovaya ulitsa** is sometimes shocking in its poverty, its pavements home to an arresting **streetlife** and lined with palatial edifices which are crammed with some of the city's most crowded communal apartments. If you're aiming straight for St Nicholas Cathedral (p.125), catch one of the **trams** that rattle along Sadovaya, alighting at the Voznesenskiy prospekt turn-off (#2) or nearer the cathedral (#14 or #54).

Originally bordered by country estates (hence its name, "Garden Street"), Sadovaya became a centre for trade and vice in the nineteenth century, when its markets and slums rubbed shoulders with prestigious institutions – much as they do today. The initial stretch is flanked by the Gostiniy dvor (p.74) and, further on, by the old **Vorontsov Palace**, set back from the south side of the street behind ornate railings. Built between 1749 and 1757 by Rastrelli, this later housed the elite *corps des pages* (Pazheskiy korpus), an academy for boys from the highest ranks of the nobility, whose students included Rasputin's assassin Yusupov, the anarchist Prince Kropotkin, and several of the Decembrists. Today it serves as the Suvorov Military Academy, whose cadets cut a dash in their black-and-red uniforms.

On the next block stands the **Apraksin dvor**, a labyrinthine complex of shops and *ateliers* fronting seedy cul-de-sacs full of lockups.

Built by Corsini in the 1860s, it took its name from an earlier warren
dedicated to Peter the Great's admiral, Fyodor Apraksin, which
Murray's Handbook described in the 1870s as crowded with "a
motley populace", all "bearded and furred and thoroughly un-
European". The *dvor* is slowly being gentrified, with antique shops
and cafes rubbing shoulders with the vestiges of a flea-market in the
yard.

Sennaya ploshchad and beyond

At the point where Sadovaya ulitsa nears the Griboedov Canal there's
a large open space, partitioned by tramlines and sporting a crane
looming above a skeletal bus terminal. **Sennaya ploshchad** (Hay
Square) is far from elegant – but nowhere near as bad as when it was
known, and functioned, as the **Haymarket**. Like its namesake in
nineteenth-century London, this embodied squalor, vice and degradation on an awesome scale. Here, infants were sold to be mutilated
by professional beggars, and ten-year-old prostitutes were rented out
for fifty kopeks a night. Thousands of people slept outdoors, huddled
around fires, trading their shirt for a bite to eat or a gulp of vodka.

The Haymarket was the setting for *Crime and Punishment*,
whose feverish protagonist, Raskolnikov, mingled with the "different sorts of tradespeople and rag-and-bone men" and finally knelt in
the middle of the square in atonement for the murder of the old
money-lender. Just across the canal from the Haymarket lay
Joiners' Lane (now ulitsa Przhevalskovo), where every house har-
boured a grog store. While writing his masterpiece between 1864
and 1867, **Dostoyevsky** lived on the right-hand side of the second
block, at Kaznechskaya ulitsa 7, which may have been the model for
Raskolnikov's rooming house (another possibility is the building at
Grazhdanskaya ulitsa 19, further along on the other side of the
road), whilst it's thought that the novel's detailed description of
Sonya Marmeladov's lodgings could have been based on no. 63 or
no.73 on the Griboedov embankment, just around the bend in the
canal.

In Soviet times Sennaya ploshchad was paved over and optimisti-
cally renamed ploshchad Mira (Peace Square); it now features two
metro stations – Sennaya ploshchad and Sadovaya (entered by an
underpass). Numerous **kiosks** sell the cheapest food in town and the
square bustles with life day and night. Pickpockets are rife, however,
and the area is best avoided after dark.

Beyond Sennaya ploshchad

*The Railway
Museum is
open Mon–
Thurs & Sun
11am–5pm,
closed the last
Thurs of the
month; $0.50.*

A couple of minor sights might tempt you further along Sadovaya
ulitsa beyond Sennaya ploshchad. Roughly 100m along on the left, a
small **Railway Museum** (Muzey Zheleznodorozhnovo Transporta) at
no. 50 retains a statue of Lenin hailing the railway workers and a

model of an armoured train used in the Civil War. The rooms also contain intricate scale models of bridges and locomotives (including some futuristic bullet trains that were never built), and a walk-through section of an old "soft class" sleeping carriage, with velvet upholstery and Art Nouveau fixtures.

Between Nevskiy and Voznesenskiy prospekts

During summer, the **park** beside the museum is perfumed with the smell of lilac trees and at weekends thronged with sunbathers. Still known as the Yusupovskiy sad, it originally formed the grounds of the **Yusupov Palace** on the Fontanka, which dated back to the 1720s. The existing palace – built in the 1790s – subsequently became an engineering institute, while the Yusupovs bought another palace beside the Moyka, where the last of the dynasty murdered Rasputin (see p.121).

For the further reaches of Sadovaya ulitsa, see p.126.

Further on, the junction with Voznesenskiy prospekt is flanked by the arcades of the former **Aleksandrovskiy rynok** (Alexander Market), a huge polygonal structure stretching from Sadovaya ulitsa to the Fontanka embankment. From here, you can ride a #2 tram down the prospekt and across the Fontanka to the Trinity Cathedral (p.241), or head westwards across the Griboedov Canal to the St Nicholas Cathedral (p.125). Both buildings are easily recognizable from afar, the former by its ink-blue cupolas, the latter by its gilded onion domes and belfry.

West of St Isaac's

The area **west of St Isaac's** has fewer obvious sights than the quarter between the Moyka and the Fontanka, so it pays to be selective in your visits. Apart from the mansions on Bolshaya Morskaya ulitsa and the Main Post Office on Pochtamtskaya ulitsa, there's not much to see until you hit ploshchad Truda and New Holland, or the further reaches of the Neva embankment, roughly 800m beyond Isaakievskaya ploshchad. However, there is a nice feel to the area, whose leafy embankments and residential character give it a genteel atmosphere and make for pleasant evening walks during the summer.

The area covered by this heading is shown in detail on the map on p.108.

Along Bolshaya Morskaya ulitsa

Such attractions as there are in the immediate vicinity present a discreet face to the world, particularly along **Bolshaya Morskaya ulitsa**. Several big names in pre-revolutionary Petersburg lived on the northern side of the road, where Montferrand built mansions for the industrialist Pyotr Demidov (no. 43) and the socialite Princess Gagarina (no. 45). The latter is now the **House of Composers** (Dom kompozitorov), whose picturesque coffered hall can be admired under the pretext of visiting the restaurant in the building.

The Nabokov Museum

The Nabokov
Museum is
open Mon–Fri
10am–5pm;
$0.50. Guided
tours in
English can be
booked on
☎315 47 13
for a fee
depending on
the size of the
group.

Next door to the House of Composers, at no.47, the **Nabokov
Museum** occupies the birthplace and childhood home of the great
Russian writer, best known abroad for his novel *Lolita*. Opened in
1997, it is the foremost centre for Nabokov studies in Russia and
hosts cultural events ranging from jazz concerts and exhibitions of
contemporary art to an annual Bloomsday (June 16) honouring
Joyce's *Ulysses* (the two writers admired each other's work).
Besides some of Nabokov's personal effects and first editions, visitors can see the oak-panelled library and walnut-ceilinged dining
room which he lovingly described in *Speak, Memory*. The Nabokov
family was immensely wealthy and epitomized the cosmopolitan St
Petersburg intelligentsia: the children all spoke three languages and
their father helped draft the constitution of the Provisional
Government, only to be killed in Berlin in 1922 in the act of shield-
ing the Kadet leader, Milyukov, from an assassin.

On the anniversary of Nabokov's birth (April 23 by the New
Calendar), the museum organizes an excursion to the family's **country estate at Rozhdestveno**, 70km from St Petersburg, whose mansion is being reconstructed following a fire in 1995 – for details, visit
www.nabokovhouse.spb.ru.

The House of Architects and around

Across the road at no. 52, the **House of Architects** (Dom arkhitek-
torov) boasts a splendid interior – its original owner entertained the
tsar in the Bronze Hall, whose malachite panels and gilded stucco
work make the panelled dining room downstairs seem drab by comparison. This is now the *Nikolay* restaurant (see p.291), whose man-
agement will give guests a twenty-minute tour ($2) of the upstairs
rooms if asked.

A little further along, the **Communications Workers' Palace of
Culture**, alongside the River Moyka, is as far removed as you could
imagine from the German Reformed Church that stood here before the
Revolution, from which the existing building was created in the 1930s
by removing the spire and other projections. From here you can walk
across **Fonarniy most** (Lamp Bridge) – whose lampposts are shaped
like treble clefs – to visit the Yusupov Palace (p.121) on the Moyka, or
head up towards the Post Office and Konnogvardeyskiy bulvar.

The Main Post Office and Popov Museum

The post office
is open Mon–
Sat 9am–
7.30pm, Sun
10am–5.30pm.

Heading up Pochtamtskiy pereulok, you'll soon catch sight of the
Main Post Office (Glavniy pochtamt), with its distinctive overhead
gallery spanning Pochtamtskaya ulitsa. Designed by Nikolai Lvov in
the 1780s, the post office originally centred on a courtyard occupied
by stables and farriers; the gallery leading to the Postmaster
General's house across the street was added in 1859. It's worth popping inside to see the Art Nouveau hall, with its ornate ironwork and

glass ceiling, created by the conversion of the original courtyard early last century.

West of St Isaac's

Outside, the overhead gallery displays a **Clock of the World**, whose square outer face shows Moscow time, the standard against which all Russian time-zones are measured, while the round, inner face gives the hour in major cities across the world – it made a brief appearance during the high-speed tank and car chase in the James Bond film *Goldeneye*.

Continuing north along Pochtamtskiy pereulok, it's not far to the **Popov Museum of Communications**. Russians regard **Alexander Popov** (1859–1906) rather than Marconi as the inventor of the radio. Popov transmitted a signal in the laboratories of Petersburg University on March 24, 1896, almost a year before Marconi, but news of his achievement was slow to leave Russia, whereas Marconi was a skilled self-publicist. Ironically, some historians now believe that both were beaten by a Welshman, David Hughes, who may have transmitted the world's first radio signal at Portland Place, London, in 1879.

The Museum of Communications is currently closed, but some of its exhibits can be seen in Popov's former apartment on the Petrograd Side (see p.205).

From Konnogvardeyskiy bulvar to the Nikolaevskiy Palace

Just around the corner from the Popov Museum, the broad, tree-lined **Konnogvardeyskiy bulvar** runs from the Triumphal Columns near the Horseguards' Manège to ploshchad Truda, 650m southwest. Laid out in 1842 along the course of an old canal, Konnogvardeyskiy bulvar (Horseguards' Boulevard) got its name from the regimental barracks that stood at no. 4. At the far end of the boulevard on ploshchad Truda (Labour Square) stands the huge Italianate **Nikolaevskiy Palace**, built by Stakenschneider for Grand Duke Nicholas, but used as a boarding school for young noblewomen until after the Revolution, when it was allocated to the city's Trade Union Council as a Palace of Labour. Nowadays, its grand **ballroom** is used for nightly "folklore" concerts, accompanied by a champagne, vodka and caviar buffet. At the very least you should nip inside the lobby to see the vast double staircase, while a visit to room 44 on the first floor will reward you with the sight of the ornately panelled **Moorish Smoking Room**. From ploshchad Truda you can head south to New Holland, or north to the Neva embankment.

For details of the folklore show, see p.300.

New Holland and around

Early in the eighteenth century, a canal was built between the Moyka and the Neva, creating a triangular islet later known as **New Holland** (Novaya Gollandiya). Surrounded by water, it offered an ideal storage place for inflammable materials, such as timber, which could then be transported by barge to the shipyards. In 1763, the wooden sheds were replaced by red-brick structures of different heights, enabling the timber to be stored vertically. The most distinctive feature of the design is the great **arch** facing the Moyka, which spans a canal leading to the centre of New Holland. Though you can't get inside, the complex appears romantic in its overgrown isolation, with a row of Dutch-looking houses to the east.

Along the embankment

The **Neva embankment** two blocks north of New Holland is lined with mansions from the eighteenth century, when it was first called the **Angliyskaya naberezhnaya** (English Quay), as it is again now. This fashionable promenade was the centre of St Petersburg's flourishing British community in the nineteenth century. Its Soviet name – naberezhnaya Krasnovo Flota (Red Fleet Embankment) – alluded to the bombardment of the Winter Palace by the cruiser *Aurora* at the outset of the Bolshevik Revolution. On the night of October 25,

The Aurora *is
now moored
off Petrograd
Side, as
described on
p.201.*

1917, the *Aurora* steamed into the Neva and dropped anchor near the middle span of what is now Leytenanta Shmidta most (Lieutenant Schmidt Bridge), trained its guns over the roof of the Winter Palace and at 9.40pm fired the (blank) shots that "reverberated around the world". The event is commemorated by a granite **stela** inscribed with a hammer and sickle, near the bridge.

*The museum is
open
11am–5pm;
closed Wed and
the last Thurs
of the month;
$1. Guided
tours in
English by
arrangement
on ☎ 311 75
44.*

The main reason to poke around this end of the embankment is to visit the **St Petersburg History Museum**, which occupies the eighteenth-century Rumyantsev Palace at Angliyskaya naberezhnaya 44. While much of the exhibition is being reworked to reveal the palace interior and to take account of post-Soviet historical thinking, the section on **the city during the Blockade** (for more on which, see p.221 and p.259) remains in place. Displays cover the defence of the city, with a model of an anti-aircraft position and a life-sized bomb shelter. Next come dioramas depicting the efforts necessary to survive during winter, when water had to be drawn through holes in the ice and firewood scavenged from snowdrifts to feed the tiny makeshift stoves known as *burzhuiki*. Supplies arrived by the "Road of Life" across Lake Ladoga, enabling Leningrad to maintain a basic existence until the Blockade was broken in January 1944 and the Red Army went on to the offensive. A copy of the diary of 11-year-old Tanya Savicheva, recording the deaths of members of her family, is also on display here.

Between the Yusupov Palace and the Blok Museum

The area between the Yusupov Palace and the Blok Museum knits together several strands in the city's cultural history, being the site of the **Conservatory** and the **Mariinskiy Theatre** (home of the Kirov Ballet); the **synagogue** and the much-loved **St Nicholas Cathedral**;

the fabulous **Yusupov Palace**, where Rasputin was murdered; and the former **residence of the poet Blok**. It's a ten- to fifteen-minute walk from St Isaac's to the Yusupov Palace, and not much further to the Mariinskiy, from where it's just a few blocks to the cathedral or the synagogue. From here, it's a further fifteen-minute walk or a short tram ride to the Blok Museum, set somewhat apart on the western edge of the district. The Mariinskiy and St Nicholas Cathedral can also be reached by following the Griboedov Canal as it bends around beyond Voznesenskiy prospekt. This route takes you past the beautiful **Lviniy most**, or Lion Bridge, whose suspension cables emerge from the jaws of four stone lions with wavy manes.

The Yusupov Palace on the Moyka

The **Yusupov Palace** (Yusupovskiy dvorets) on the Moyka embankment (not to be confused with the palace of the same name on the Fontanka – see p.117) is famed as the scene of Rasputin's murder by Prince Yusupov, but really deserves a visit in its own right as the finest palace in St Petersburg, embodying the tastes of four generations of nobles and rivalling the residences of the tsars, but on a more intimate scale. Situated at naberezhnaya reki Moyki 94, between the Pochtamtskiy and Potseluev bridges, the building still belongs to the Union of Educational Workers, which used it as a headquarters and clubhouse during Soviet times, but now functions as a museum and may even be rented for private parties, with ballet dancers, musicians and liveried servants – if you have $5000 to spare.

The museum offers two **guided tours** on a regular basis. The general tour ($4.50) runs every hour from 11am to 3pm and covers the family living quarters and ceremonial rooms, but *not* the cellar where Rasputin was murdered, which is the focus of another tour (every hour from 1.30pm; $2), nor the private quarters of Princess Zinaida and Irina (only viewable by prior arrangement on ☎314 88 93). On both tours the commentary is in Russian, but you can rent an English-language audio-guide ($1.60) for the general tour. For tours in English or for groups, ring beforehand on ☎314 88 93 (cost varies according to size of group).

The ceremonial rooms

The magnificent **ceremonial rooms** were created or reworked by each successive Yusupov as they came into their inheritance, so the diversity of styles is matched by the personalities behind them, from Boris – who started the ball rolling in the 1830s – down to his great-grandson Felix in the 1900s. Tours begin with a suite of rooms designed in the 1860s by the Italian Ippolito Monighetti for Boris's son Nikolai, featuring an embossed **Turkish study** and an extravagant **Moorish dining hall** with gold filigree arabesques and "blackamoor" figures holding incense vases. After his wife died, Nikolai slept in a small study-bedroom linked by a private staircase to the apartments of his daughter, Zinaida, whose portrait by Serov hangs downstairs. There is also a **buffet room** with embossed leather walls and ceramics standing in for the pilfered family silver; notice the crane-headed walking sticks in the corner.

Ascending the voluptuous marble **State Staircase**, flanked by allegorical statues of Asia, Africa, Europe and the Americas symbolizing hospitality beneath a chandelier holding 130 candles, you reach the classical rooms designed by Andrei Mikhailov for Prince Boris in the 1830s, with green, blue and red **drawing rooms** preceding a **large rotunda**, a white colonnaded **concert hall** and a **ballroom** with a barrel-vaulted ceiling that's really a *trompe l'oeil* canvas hung from chains. After these were completed, Boris had an entire wing built to house the **art collection** amassed by his own father, Nikolai, at Arkhangelskoe outside Moscow, including the **Canova Rotunda** – which contains the celebrated *Cupid and Psyche* and *Cupid with a Bow and Quiver* by the sculptor after whom it is named – and a lovely private **theatre** where Glinka's opera *Ivan Susanin* was premiered in 1836 by the Yusopov troupe of freed-serf actors, who also served as oarsmen on the Moyka and the Neva. The Renaissance-style **Tapestry Hall** that Boris added in the 1840s and the coffered **Oak Dining Room**, commissioned by Zinaida in the 1890s, fit harmoniously into the ensemble.

The cellar

Although small and plain compared to the rest of the palace, few visitors can resist visiting the site of **Rasputin's murder**, where a waxworks tableau portrays the events of December 16, 1916. The deed was planned by Prince Felix Yusupov, the ultra-monarchist Vladimir Purishkevich, the tsar's cousin, Grand Duke Dmitri Pavlovich, Dr Lazovert (who obtained the cyanide) and Guards' Captain Sukhotin. The last four waited in Yusupov's apartments while the Prince led Rasputin – who had been lured to the palace on the pretext of an assignation with Yusupov's wife Irina – to the cellar, where two rooms had been furnished and a table laid with cakes and bottles of sweet wine, laced with cyanide. The poison, however, failed to have any effect, and so Yusupov hurried upstairs, fetched his revolver and shot Rasputin from behind. Yusupov relates how he left Rasputin for dead, but when he returned later, Rasputin leapt up and tried to strangle him, before escaping into the courtyard, where Purishkevich finished him off with four shots. When the coast was clear, the body was driven across the city and dumped, bound but unweighted, into the Malaya Nevka – but instead of being carried out to sea, the corpse was washed ashore downstream and found on January 1, 1917.

The results of the autopsy remained unknown until the recent publication of Edvard Radzinsky's *Rasputin: The Last Word*, which used hitherto secret documents to argue that Yusupov invented the tale of Rasputin's supernatural vitality to make his own role seem more heroic, and conceal the fact that he bungled by over-diluting the poisoned wine – though another theory states that Dr Lazovert substituted a harmless chemical for the cyanide (as he swore on his deathbed) or that Rasputin's alcoholic gastritis made him immune. Whatever the truth, the conspirators escaped remarkably lightly, the Grand Duke being exiled to Persia and Yusupov to his estates in the Crimea, while the others weren't punished at all.

Between the Yusupov Palace and the Blok Museum

The private apartments
By prior arrangement you can also tour the **private apartments**, which are as grand as the ceremonial rooms, but smaller. **Princess Zinaida's suite** was designed by Monighetti and redone by Alexander Stepanov after she inherited the palace in 1890. Her Rococo **Porcelain Boudoir** and **White Drawing Room** are perhaps the finest rooms in the palace, with an intimacy also characteristic of the **Henri**

You can also see the house where Rasputin lived (p.239), the bridge where his body was dumped (p.214) and the palace where it lay in state (p.247). Rasputin was buried near Tsarskoe Selo (p.360), but was later exhumed and laid to rest at Pargolovo, north of St Petersburg.

Rasputin

Born in the Siberian village of Povroskoye in 1869, Grigori Efimovich **Rasputin** supposedly acquired his surname – meaning "dissolute"* – by virtue of his sexual vitality: his wife (by whom he had four children) said of his philandering, "it makes no difference, he has enough for all". Wanted for horse-rustling, Rasputin sought refuge in a monastery, emerging as a wandering holy man (*starets*). After a two-year pilgrimage to Mount Athos in Greece he returned home to preach, attracting a wide following. An entrée into provincial Kazan society led to the salons of St Petersburg via a chain of female admirers, who introduced Rasputin to the tsar and tsaritsa in November 1905. He proved a godsend to the royal family on account of his apparent ability to control through hypnotism the wellbeing of their haemophiliac son, Alexei, whom conventional physicians had been unable to help. In 1907, Alexei had a severe attack of internal bleeding while Rasputin was in Siberia. Alerted by telegram, he replied, "the illness is not as serious as it seems. Don't let the doctors worry him" – and from that moment on Alexei began to recover.

As Rasputin's influence at court increased, his enemies multiplied. Although he was against Russia entering World War I (and crucially absent when the decision was taken), he was blamed for the mistakes of the corrupt ministers appointed on his recommendation. His orgies in Moscow and Petersburg were a public scandal; worse still, it was whispered that he kept the tsar doped and slept with the empress (or her daughters). Aristocratic and bourgeois society rejoiced at his murder, but the peasants were bitter, believing that Rasputin was killed by the courtiers because he let the tsar hear the voice of the people. Rasputin himself prophesized that should he be killed by the nobility, the monarchy would not survive – true to his words, the February Revolution occurred less than three months after his death.

*Colin Wilson dissents, asserting that it was a common local surname, derived from the word *rasput* (crossroads).

II Drawing Room – none of which bear any trace of her estranged husband, but bespeak an enjoyable widowhood. She eventually moved out after her son, Felix, married the tsar's niece, Princess Irina, and the couple commissioned their own apartments, designed in the Neoclassical style by Andrei Vaitens and Andrei Beloborodov. Having delighted in transvestitism and homosexuality while at Oxford, Felix asked Rasputin to "cure" his "illness", only to be enraged when the latter tried to seduce him instead. **Irina's suite** is notable for its **Silver Bathroom**, and may soon feature a replica of her armoured-glass safe, which allowed her to select pieces of jewellery at the touch of a button. A **ballroom** and a delightful **winter garden** complete the tour, as **Felix's suite** has yet to be fully restored and opened to visitors.

The Mariinskiy Theatre and Conservatory

Southwest from the Yusupov Palace, Teatralnaya ploshchad (Theatre Square) is dominated by the hulking premises of two of the most renowned cultural institutions in St Petersburg: the Mariinskiy Theatre and the Conservatory. Externally graceless, the interior of the **Mariinskiy Theatre** is wonderful, its dull sea-green facade concealing a vast auditorium decorated in blue velvet, ablaze with lamps and chandeliers.

Established in 1860 (though ballet performances didn't start until twenty years later), the Mariinksiy's golden era was at the turn of the last century, when audiences watched Anna Pavlova, Mathilde Kshesinkaya and Vaclav Nijinsky dance, and heard Fyodor Chaliapin sing. Most of the company's stars left shortly before or after the Revolution but, following a lean period, it gained new popularity in the Soviet era thanks to composers Prokofiev and Khachaturian, and dancers such as Galina Ulanova. The company remains best known abroad as the **Kirov**, a title bestowed on it in 1935, when numerous institutions were renamed in honour of this Bolshevik "martyr" (p.204); but natives of the city have always called it by its affectionate diminutive, "Mariinka".

Opposite stands the **Conservatory**, the premier institution of higher musical education in Russia, founded in 1862 by the pianist and composer Anton Rubinstein – though the building wasn't completed until the 1880s. Rubinstein hated Russian music and ran the institution on conservative, European lines, though his regime relaxed sufficiently to allow the premieres here of Mussorgsky's *Boris Godunov* (1874), Borodin's *Prince Igor* (1890) and Tchaikovsky's *Sleeping Beauty* (1890). Tchaikovsky was one of the Conservatory's first graduates, while another, Shostakovich, taught here in the 1930s. Since 1944 it has been named after the composer Rimsky-Korsakov, whose **statue** stands near the building (as does one of Glinka).

Leading figures in the world of music and drama once lived close to the Conservatory. The choreographer **Michel Fokine**

(1880–1942) had an apartment at naberezhnaya Kanala Griboedova 109, to the southeast; ballerina **Tamara Karsavina** owned a house (no. 8) on the Kryukov Canal, northwest of the Mariinskiy; while ulitsa Glinki 3–5 was the family home of **Igor Stravinsky** (1882–1971), until he married his first cousin – contrary to Orthodox custom – and had to leave home to spare his family the shame.

Between the Yusupov Palace and the Blok Museum

St Nicholas Cathedral and beyond

Few tourists can resist the **St Nicholas Cathedral** (Nikolskiy sobor), to the south of Teatralnaya ploshchad. Traditionally known as the "Sailors' Church" after the naval officers who once prayed here, the cathedral is a lovely example of eighteenth-century Russian Baroque. The exterior (by Savva Chevakinsky) is painted ice blue, with white Corinthian pilasters and aedicules (window surrounds), crowned by five gilded cupolas and onion domes. Its low, vaulted interior is festooned with icons and – as at other working cathedrals – you might find a funeral in one part of the nave and a baptism in another going on simultaneously. During **services**, which start at 6pm, the cathedral resounds with the sonorous Orthodox liturgy, chanted and sung amid clouds of incense. In Tsarist times, the lofty freestanding **bell tower** used to harbour a flock of pigeons, fed "with the rice which the pious place there for the dead".

Legend has it that the bells of St Petersburg ring whenever someone makes an offering pleasing to God. A fairy tale relates how two waifs intended to donate a crust of bread and a one-kopek coin, but the boy gave the bread to a sick beggar and stayed to nurse him, telling his sister to go on alone. When she arrived at St Nicholas just before closing time, the offering tables were laden with gold coins and gifts, but – as she put her kopek down – the bells tolled across the city.

Beyond the cathedral

Approaching the cathedral from the north, you'll have already seen two of the finest sights in this part of town. Looking down ulitsa Glinki, the golden onion domes of St Nicholas are superimposed against the massive blue cupolas of the Trinity Cathedral, south of the Fontanka. Another lovely view unfolds to the northwest of St Nicholas where, from the junction of the River Moyka and the Kryukov Canal, you can see half a dozen curvaceous bridges at once.

See p.241 for details of Trinity Cathedral.

By heading east from the cathedral, along prospekt Rimskovo-Korsakova and across the Griboedov Canal, you'll find yourself near no. 104 on the Griboedov embankment, which is reckoned to have been the model for the **house of Alyona Ivanovna**, the old money-lender murdered by Raskolnikov in *Crime and Punishment*. Using an axe stolen from a basement near his lodgings, he struck repeatedly at her "thin, fair, greying hair," until "blood gushed out as from an overturned tumbler". The "site" of the crime is reckoned to have been flat 74, on the third floor, reached by entrance no. 5 – the stairwell of which is covered in graffiti related to the murder. Another curious literary monument in this part of town is **Major Kovalyov's Nose** – a bronze nose sticking from the wall of Voznesenskiy prospekt 36, in tribute to Gogol's classic story *The Nose*.

Whilst in a Dostoyevskian mood, the area to the south of St Nicholas also rates a mention. Immediately across the Griboedov Canal lies the erstwhile **Nikolskiy rynok** (Nicholas Market), an arcaded structure built in 1788–89 which served as an informal labour exchange in the nineteenth century. Further along Sadovaya, beyond what is now ploshchad Turgeneva, the **Petrashevsky Circle** of utopian socialists used to meet at the home of Mikhail Butashevich-Petrashevsky until their arrest in 1849. Amongst those imprisoned in the Peter and Paul Fortress was the young **Dostoyevsky**, who, like twenty of his comrades, was condemned to death by firing squad, but then reprieved at the last moment.

*Dostoyevsky's
mock
execution is
described on
p.238.*

Finally, it would be churlish not to mention the **Egipetskiy most** (Egyptian Bridge), flanked with cast-iron obelisks and sphinxes with gilded headgear, which carries Lermontovskiy prospekt across the Fontanka. Beyond here you can see the *Sovetskaya* hotel and the Trinity Cathedral.

West to the Synagogue and Blok Museum

West of Teatralnaya ploshchad, **ulitsa Dekabristov** runs off towards the docks, a thicket of cranes looming at the far end of the avenue. Immediately beyond the Kryukov Canal stands the **First Five-Year Plan Palace of Culture**, a 1930s monolith built on the site of the former Lithuanian Market. From here, it's a short walk to St Petersburg's main **synagogue**, or a tram ride (#31 or #90) from Teatralnaya ploshchad down the length of ulitsa Dekabristov to the Blok Museum, commemorating one of the greatest Russian poets of the twentieth century.

The Synagogue

St Petersburg's **Synagogue** stands discreetly just off ulitsa Dekabristov, its corkscrew-ribbed cupola poking above the rooftops on the corner of Lermontovskiy prospekt, and wrought-iron gates leading into a shady compound where elders gossip and children play hopscotch. Visitors are first taken to the gift shop to obtain a skullcap, and then into the **Small Synagogue** (Malaya sinagoga), whose coffered prayer hall is used for everyday worship; Torah and Hebrew lessons occur in the adjacent *Yeshiva*, which also dispenses cheap meals to Jewish pensioners. Although the **Great Synagogue** (Bolshaya sinagoga) is reserved for festivals, you can peer through the doors of its main hall, decorated in yellow and white, with a mass of stucco squinches and stalactite mouldings – a combination of local colour and Moorish motifs that characterizes synagogues throughout Eastern Europe.

What makes it different is that Leningrad's Jewish community escaped Nazi genocide, so the synagogue lacks the haunting emptiness of its counterparts in, say, Poland or Hungary. That said, Jewish cultural life was repressed for most of the Soviet era, and several of the purges were anti-Semitic in character. Paradoxically, perestroika both strengthened and diminished the community, inaugurating religious and cultural freedom whilst opening the floodgates of emigration to Israel. Sadly, it is often **anti-Semitism** – no longer fostered by the state, but openly expressed by extreme nationalists and not a few ordinary Russians – that impels many to leave.

Between the Yusupov Palace and the Blok Museum

There is also a funerary synagogue by the old Jewish Cemetery, way out in the suburbs (p.250).

The Blok Museum

The Symbolist poet **Alexander Blok** (1880–1921) belonged to the so-called "Silver Age" of Russian poetry, which lasted from the beginning of the century to the mid-1920s, by which time many of its greatest talents had died, killed themselves, or been forced into internal exile by official hostility. Blok's first poems expressed his passion for Lyubov Mendeleyeva, the actress daughter of the scientist Mendeleyev, whom he married in 1903. Later, Blok told Stanislavsky, "Russia is the theme of my life", a theme that reached its apotheosis in the winter of 1918 with *The Twelve* (*Dvenadtsat*), Blok's fusion of religious imagery, slang, revolutionary slogans and songs. Watched over by Jesus Christ, a dozen Red Guards march through a blizzard and the maelstrom of the Revolution, whose imperative Blok voiced as:

Comrades, take aim and don't be scared,
Let's blast away at Holy Russia.

The Twelve caused a sensation amongst his fellow poets, yet the Bolsheviks barely acknowledged it, perhaps because, as Kamenev admitted, "it celebrates what we, old Socialists, fear most of all". For the last two years of his life, Blok suffered from scurvy, asthma, delirium and depression. Sensing his end, he wrote bitterly, "Dirty rotten Mother Russia has devoured me as a sow gobbles up her sucking pig". Gorky tried to get him into a Finnish sanatorium, but he died on August 20, 1921.

In 1980, his former apartment at ulitsa Dekabristov 57, overlooking the Pryazhka Canal, was turned into the **Blok Museum**. Having collected a pair of slippers from the downstairs lobby, you can visit an exhibition of Blok's childhood drawings, photos of the poet and first editions of his work on the floor above. Two floors up, Blok and Lyubov's **apartment** is preserved much as it was when they lived there, with their brass nameplate on the door, and an antique telephone and hat stand in the hall. The *babushka* keeps the house plants and flowers (which Blok loved) well watered, and can point out the display of first drafts of *The Twelve*. Finally, after going back

The Blok Museum is open 11am–5pm; closed Wed and the last Tues of the month; $1. Take minibus #T-1 or tram #31 or #90 from ulitsa Dekabristov to the corner of Angliyskiy prospekt.

Streets and squares

Admiralteyskaya naberezhnaya	Адмиралтейская набережная
ploshchad Belinskovo	площадь Белинского
Bolshaya Konyushennaya ulitsa	Большая Конюшенная улица
Bolshaya Morskaya ulitsa	Большая Морская улица
ploshchad Dekabristov	площадь Декабристов
Dvortsovaya naberezhnaya	Дворцовая набережная
Dvortsovaya ploshchad	Дворцовая площадь
naberezhnaya reki Fontanki	набережная реки Фонтанки
Gorokhovaya ulitsa	Гороховая улица
kanal Griboedova	канал Грибоедова
Italyanskaya ulitsa	Итальянская улица
Isaakievskaya ploshchad	Исаакиевская площадь
Konnogvardeyskiy bulvar	Конногвардейский бульвар
Konyushennaya ploshchad	Конюшенная площадь
Malaya Konyushennaya ulitsa	Малая Конюшенная улица
Malaya Morskaya ulitsa	Малая Морская улица
Marsovo pole	Марсово поле
Mikhailovskaya ulitsa	Михайловская улица
Mikhailovskaya ploshchad	Михайловскаяулица площаь
Millionnaya ulitsa	Миллионная улица
naberezhnaya reki Moyki	набережная реки Мойки
Nevskiy prospekt	Невский проспект
ploshchad Ostrovskovo	площадь Островского
Sadovaya ulitsa	Садовая улица
Sennaya ploshchad	Сенная площадь
Teatralnaya ploshchad	Театральная площадь
ploshchad Truda	площадь Труда
Voznesenskiy prospekt	Вознесенский проспект

Metro stations

Gostiniy dvor	Гостиный двор
Nevskiy prospekt	Невский проспект
Sadovaya	Садовая
Sennaya ploshchad	Сенная площадь

Museums

Blok Museum	музей-квартира А.А. Блока
Ethnographical Museum	Этнографический музей
Hermitage	Эрмитаж
Museum of Hygiene	музей Гигиены
St Petersburg History Museum	музей истории Санкт Петербурга
Museum of Russian Political History	музей политической истории России
Nabokov Museum	музей Набокова
Popov Museum of Communications	музей Связи им. А.С. Попова
Pushkin Museum	музей-квартира А.С. Пушкина
Railway Museum	музей Железнодорожного транспорта
Russian Museum	Русский музей
Theatre Museum	Театральный музей
Zoshchenko Museum	музей М.М. Зощенко

down to the first floor, you'll be admitted to a room containing Blok's stubbled **death mask**.

Across the road, the ballerina **Anna Pavlova** (1881–1931) lived in the apartment building on the southwestern corner of ulitsa Dekabristov and Angliyskiy prospekt (formerly named Maklina prospekt after John Maclean, one of the leaders of Scotland's "Red Clydeside", as a mark of international solidarity in 1918).

Chapter 3

The Hermitage and the Russian Museum

I**n a city full of museums, there are two which stand head and shoulders above the rest. The **Hermitage** is one of the world's great art museums, embracing everything from ancient Scythian goldwork to Impressionism and Cubism. As it's partly housed in the Winter Palace, visitors also get to see the opulent state rooms with their magnificent furnishings. The **Russian Museum** is less ostentatious and quite different in spirit. Devoted to native artists, it conveys the history of Russian art from icon-painting to Symbolism, continuing through Futurism to Socialist Realism.

While the Hermitage requires two or three **visits** to do it any kind of justice, the Russian Museum's main building – the Mikhailovskiy Palace – can be covered fairly easily in a day. In both museums, visitors must store coats and bags in the cloakroom and purchase permits to **photograph** or film the artworks; flash photography is forbidden. Both museums are the subject of numerous glossy **art books**, on sale in the museums themselves and on the streets outside.

The Hermitage

Many tourists come to St Petersburg simply to visit the **Hermitage** (Ermitazh), a museum of awesome size and diversity. To visit all 350 exhibition rooms would entail walking a distance of about 10km and, at the last count, the collection contained over three million items – it was calculated that merely to glance at each one would take nine years. The museum contains more than 12,000 sculptures, 16,000 paintings, 600,000 drawings and prints, and 266,000 works of applied art, plus more than a million coins and medals, and although only a small percentage of these is on show, it's still more than enough to keep you captivated.

The Hermitage has excellent examples of Italian High Renaissance art, as well as unparalleled groups of paintings by

Rembrandt, the French Impressionists, Picasso and Matisse – not to mention fabulous treasures from Siberia and Central Asia, Egyptian and Classical antiquities, and Persian and Chinese artworks, among others. Last but certainly not least, there is the interior of the **Winter Palace** itself, with its magnificent **state rooms**, where the tsars once held court and the Provisional Government was arrested by the Bolsheviks.

For the history of the Winter Palace, see p.84.

The **origins of the Hermitage** collection date back to Peter the Great's purchase of two dozen maritime scenes during his visit to Holland in 1697, which were hung in the palace of Monplaisir at Peterhof. As his collection grew, Peter installed works in the Winter Palace, setting a precedent for Catherine the Great, who had the Hermitage built specifically to house her burgeoning art collection. She bought 225 paintings from the Prussian merchant Gotzkowski (probably to annoy her rival Frederick the Great, who had had to turn them down due to a shortage of cash), as well as 600 belonging to Count Brühl of Saxony and the extensive Crozat and Walpole collections. Having started amassing art later than other European monarchs, she – and her successors – spared no expense: Alexander I bought 98 pictures from the collection of Napoleon's wife Josephine, and Nicholas I purchased the collection of Napoleon's stepdaughter. By the mid-nineteenth century, the Russian monarchy owned the finest art collection in Europe.

Until 1852, only royalty and court guests could enter the Hermitage; thereafter "decent citizens" were admitted on certain days and professional curators were appointed, making it a public museum in all but name. After the October Revolution the Hermitage became the home of private collections expropriated by the Bolsheviks – most notably Impressionist paintings and works by Picasso and Matisse. During World War II, 45 carriage-loads of treasures were evacuated to Sverdlovsk, but tours of the Hermitage continued, with guides describing the works that normally hung there for the benefit of troops on leave from the front, while its huge cellars served as a bomb shelter for two thousand people.

Despite its prestige, the Hermitage suffered grave neglect during the Brezhnev era, and pictures from its collection were often presented to "friends" of the Soviet Union. This led to the widely believed (but false) rumour that the local Party boss borrowed an Imperial dinner service for his daughter's wedding party, and that several pieces were broken. Belated repair work on the building began in 1985, helped further by major support in the 1990s from UNESCO, the Dutch government and French sponsors. It is hoped that the museum's facilities can be brought up to world-class standard by 2003 – the tercentenary of the founding of St Petersburg.

The Hermitage's **modernization** strategy includes replacing the old cataloguing system with an online database, and using the General

The Hermitage

The Hermitage

Staff building (see p.82) on Palace Square to exhibit many items that have hitherto languished in storerooms for lack of space, while displaying more postwar and contemporary art. Among the changes likely to affect visitors in the near future are the relocation of the **main entrance** from the Neva embankment to Palace Square, via the courtyard of the Winter Palace (scheduled to occur in late June, 2001), and the transferral of some collections to the General Staff building – these will ultimately include the **Impressionist and Post-Impressionist paintings** that are currently on the third floor of the Winter Palace (this is a long-term project that may not happen until 2003 or even later, though works might be removed for crating at an earlier date – check at the Hermitage for further information if you're hoping to see particular pieces). Note that the existing exhibits in the **General Staff building** are covered in the previous chapter (see p.83), though tickets should be purchased in the Hermitage if you wish to see them.

Visiting the Hermitage

It's impossible to see all the finest works in the Hermitage during a single visit, so concentrate on what interests you rather than just wandering aimlessly from room to room. To help you plan your visit and for ease of reference our account is arranged according to subject. Bear in mind that some rooms may be closed for restoration, while others may be open erratically owing to lack of staff (especially in summer, when many of the room attendants take their holidays), so if you want to see a particular section it's worth checking opening times in advance with staff in the excursion bureau by the cloakrooms. Once inside, it's hard to know where one building ends and another begins, and the direction signs are often misleading. However, almost all rooms are numbered, usually on a plaque above the inside of the doorway. While many paintings are now captioned in English as well as Russian, the ongoing process of relabelling has yet to reach less-visited sections, which are also unlikely to be covered by the museum's audio-guides.

There are currently four different **audio-guides** to the Hermitage: a general tour (90min; $4.25), and individual tapes entitled "French and Dutch paintings of the seventeenth century", "From the Impressionists to Picasso", and "Unknown masterpieces" (the "Hidden treasures") – costing $3.50 each. Alternatively, it's often possible to tag onto a tour group for some free commentary, or use the **interactive facilities** (near the café and elsewhere) to access the Hermitage **Web site** (*www.hermitage.ru*), featuring virtual tours of the state rooms and some 2000 exhibits (it's planned to include them all, eventually).

Tickets are on sale at the back of the entrance hall (queues are usually short except from June to Aug) and are valid for everything except the Golden Rooms (see p.135) and Peter the Great's Winter Palace. Separate tickets for timed entry to these exhibitions should be purchased here before you go in. The cloakrooms and excursion bureau are off to the right, while a doorway on the left leads into the Rastrelli

The Hermitage is open Tues–Sat 10.30am–6pm, Sun 10.30am–5pm; $9, free for under-17s, students, disabled people, and families with three or more children. Last tickets go on sale 1hr before closing. Separate tickets are required for the Golden Rooms (see p.135) and the Winter Palace of Peter the Great (see p.85).

Where to find what in the Hermitage

This checklist gives the floor and room numbers of the **main permanent exhibitions**. Those marked by asterisks may be open at irregular times as staff numbers allow; the ones in bold type are especially recommended.

Archeology and Siberian artefacts	*First floor 11–27*
Central Asian artefacts	*First floor 55–66**
Classical antiquities	*First floor 101–131*
Dutch, Flemish and Netherlandish	
art: 15th–18th century	*Second floor 245–254,*
	258, 261 & 262
Egyptian antiquities	*First floor 100*
English art: 17th–19th century	*Second floor 298–300*
Fabergé jewellery	*Second floor 307*
French art: 15th–18th century	*Second floor 272–289*
Hidden Treasures (trophy art)	*Second floor, off rooms 200 & 202*
Golden Rooms	*First floor 42 and off room 121*
German art: 15th–18th century	*Second floor 263–268**
Italian art: 13th–16th century	*Second floor 207–230*
Italian art: 16th–18th century	*Second floor 231–238*
Modern European art	*Third floor 314–350*
Numismatic collection	*Third floor 398–400**
Oriental art and culture	*Third floor 351–397**
Russian art and culture	*Second floor 151–173*
Russian palace interiors	*Second floor 175–187*
Spanish art: 16th–18th century	*Second floor 239 & 240*
State Rooms	*Second floor 155, 156, 188–198,*
	204, 271, 282, 289 & 304–307

Gallery, where there's a sales desk selling plans of the museum. At the far end of the gallery is the Jordan Staircase, a doorway to the right of which leads into a long corridor containing the **café** and excellent museum **shop**. You can either go along the corridor and start exploring the Antiquities on the first floor, or head up the Jordan Staircase to the state rooms and collections on the second floor. We have numbered **floors** in the Russian and US fashion; what the British call the ground floor we have called the first (note, however, that the Hermitage's own English-language floor plans adhere to the British convention, and are also printed the other way up from the plans in this book).

*The nearest
metro station
is Nevskiy
prospekt.*

Archeology and Siberian artefacts

The Hermitage's collection of **Archeology and Siberian artefacts** is undeservedly one of the least visited sections of the museum. It requires a detour into the dingy west wing of the Winter Palace, but in return you'll be rewarded with some weird and wonderful arte-

*First floor,
rooms 11–27 &
55–66.*

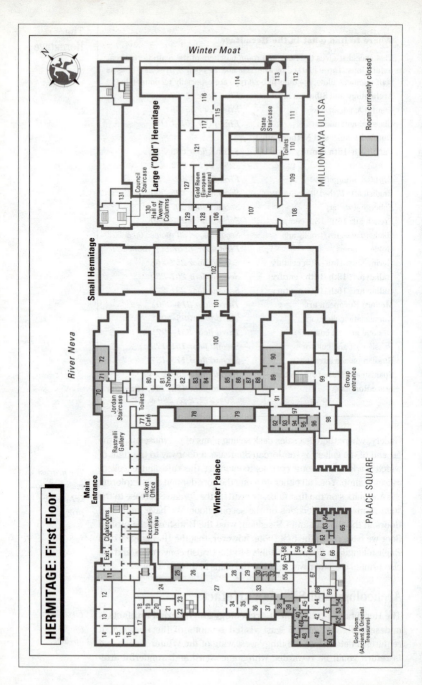

HERMITAGE: First Floor

Winter Moat

Large ("Old") Hermitage

Small Hermitage

River Neva

Winter Palace

Council Staircase

Gold Room (European Treasures)

Hall of Twenty Columns

State Staircase

Toilets

MILLIONNAYA ULITSA

Room currently closed

Jordan Staircase

Rastrelli Gallery

Café

Toilets

Shop

Group entrance

Main Entrance

Exit

Cloakrooms

Ticket Office

Excursion bureau

Gold Room (Ancient & Oriental Treasures)

PALACE SQUARE

facts, the most exciting of which are provided by the nomadic tribes of the fifth and fourth centuries BC, who buried their chiefs deep under the earth with all the paraphernalia required for the afterlife. Between 1929 and 1949, archeologists excavated five burial mounds at **Pazyryk** in the Altay highlands, uncovering a huge log chamber and sarcophagus containing the body of a chief, a felt rug as large as half a tennis court, draped over poles to form a tent, and a funerary chariot and the carcass of a horse (all in room 26). Other objects uncovered included a human head and a tatooed shoulder, appliqué saddles and reindeer horns that were affixed to horses' heads for ceremonial burials, and a brazier and tent used for smoking hashish (room 22), all of them preserved by the permafrost.

Also remarkable are the numerous **Scythian artefacts** in rooms 16–20, including military and domestic items decorated with stylized bears, elks, horses, lions and birds – the gilded objects here are copies of originals now in the Golden Rooms (see below). Finally, if room 12 is open, don't miss the huge slab of granite covered with zoomorphic petroglyphs from the shore of Lake Onega, dating from the second or third millennium BC.

One of the Golden Rooms (room 42) lies further down the corridor, while rooms 55–66 exhibit an ever-changing array of artefacts from **Central Asia**, the Mongol-Tatar **Golden Horde** and the mysterious civilization of **Uratu**, in the highlands of eastern Turkey.

The Golden Rooms

The **Golden Rooms** (Dragotsenosti Galleryii) contain some of the Hermitage's smallest and most valuable treasures, displayed under strict security to visitors on **guided tours** ($9). Since these are often block-booked by tour groups, you should enquire as far ahead as possible at the excursion bureau off the main lobby in the Winter Palace, from where tours begin (in English at 12.15 and 2.15pm). Bear in mind, moreover, that there are two separate Golden Rooms in different parts of the Hermitage, though at the time of writing only one of them – room 42 of the Winter Palace – was open.

First floor, room 42, and off room 121.

Room 42 exhibits ancient goldwork by the nomadic peoples of the northern Caucasus and Black Sea littoral, such as the Scythians and Sarmatians, and the Greek colonists who traded with them for a millennium. **Scythian** art is characterized by the Animal Style, which the **Sarmatian** tribes on the northern shores of the Caspian Sea embellished with gems (as in the diadem inset with garnets, turquoises, pearls and an amethyst cameo of a Greek goddess). The **Black Sea Greeks** also produced objects in this style for Scythian clients, such as the electrum goblet discovered in a tumulus near Kerch – and it could also be found in western Siberia, as evinced by belt buckles depicting a boar hunt and dragons beside the Tree of Life.

This room also contains the Hermitage's unrivalled collection of ancient Persian or **Sassanid silver**, found in the Urals and Kama region, where it was probably traded for furs. Of particular note are two shallow bowls used for drinking wine, one depicting King Shapur II hunting and the other an episode from Firdausi's poem *Shah Náma*. Additionally, there is a large and ever-changing selection of items from the Hermitage's **Byzantine**, **Turkish**, **Indian**, **Chinese and Mongolian jewellery** collections, and even some **Pre-Columbian** items from Latin America, such as the Mexican gold pectoral in the shape of a warrior bedecked in eagle feathers.

The **other Golden Room**, situated near room 121 in the Large Hermitage, was closed at the time of writing – when open, it's planned to display European treasures from the Middle Ages onwards, concluding with jewellery by Fabergé and other Russian goldsmiths of the time.

The antiquities

First floor,
rooms
100–131.

Even if your interest in this collection is limited, a stroll through the **antiquities** rooms is highly recommended. One of the least crowded parts of the Hermitage, the rooms are perfectly in keeping with their contents, marvellously decorated with a variety of Antique features and motifs, one of the best examples being the Hall of Twenty Columns.

The trail begins in the Egyptian Hall (room 100), which houses the Hermitage's modest collection of **Egyptian antiquities**, consisting mainly of funerary artefacts taken from the Middle Kingdom tombs of four Pharaonic officials, whose painted sarcophagi and shrivelled mummies occupy centre stage. In the hall's display cases are amulets and heart scarabs intended to ensure the officials' safe passage into the afterlife, *shabti* (funerary) figures to perform menial tasks on their behalf, and texts from the *Book of the Dead* showing the judgement of Osiris.

Classical antiquities

The more extensive **Classical antiquities** (Greek and Roman) section begins with displays of Roman bas-reliefs in the corridor (room 102). From room 106 you can go either left or right, but you'll have to retrace your steps at some point if you want to see the whole section.

Heading left, into room 128, you're confronted by the colossal **Kolyvan Vase**, whose elliptical bowl is over 5m long and 3m wide. Carved from Altay jasper over eleven years, it required 154 horses to drag it to Barnaul, whence it was hauled across frozen rivers to St Petersburg, to be kept in a shed while the walls of the New Hermitage were built around it. In room 129 you'll find a gold funerary wreath inset with carnelian and some amusing little bronze mice nibbling nuts. Next door is the **Hall of Twenty Columns** (room 130), painted with Greco-Egyptian motifs and filled with Apulian amphorae and breastplates, Campanian vases and Etruscan bronzes from the third or fourth century BC. Room 131 displays busts of the emperors Titus and Vespasian, and exits near the **Council Staircase**, whose orange and pink marble walls and wine-red pillars presage the European art on the floor above.

Alternatively, head right from room 106 into the green marble **Jupiter Hall** (room 107), devoted to Classical statues, of which Venus disrobing, a vast seated Jupiter, and a club-wielding Muse of Tragedy are the most eye-catching. There are more fine statues in the rooms beyond, particularly in 109, where Dionysus – grapes and artichoke in hand – gazes at a savage panther in the central aisle and at the Muse of Dance with her lyre. The muses also feature in room 110, which overlooks the muscular atlantes supporting the Hermitage facade on Millionnaya ulitsa. From this room you can reach the second floor via the **State Staircase**, its three flights flanked by tawny marble walls and grey columns.

Staying on the first floor, rooms 111–114 contain superb Attic vases decorated with fine red-and-black figurative designs, and some rather dry Roman copies of Greek sculptures. However, the real incentive to carry on is to see Catherine the Great's collection of antique cameos and intaglios (room 121). The lapidary **Gonzaga Cameo** is one of the largest in the world – a triple-layered sardonyx bearing the profiles of Ptolemy Philadelphus and Queen Arsinoe, carved in Alexandria during the third century BC.

The State Rooms

The **State Rooms** of the Winter Palace are as memorable as anything on display in the Hermitage, and best seen while you've still got plenty of energy. Glittering with gold leaf and crystal chandeliers, and boasting acres of marble (mostly artificial), parquet, frescoes and mouldings, they attest to the opulence of the Imperial court. Having witnessed gala balls and thanksgiving services, investitures and declarations of war, the State Rooms then provided a stage for the posturings of the Provisional Government.

The most direct approach from the first floor is via the **Jordan Staircase**, whose twin flights are overlooked by caryatids, *trompe l'oeil* atlantes and a fresco of the gods on Mount Olympus by Gaspar Diziani. The walls and balustrades drip with decoration – a typically effusive design by Bartolomeo Rastrelli, who created similar stairways for the Imperial summer palaces at Peterhof and Tsarskoe Selo. What you see, however, owes as much to Vasily Stasov, who restored the State Rooms after a devastating fire in 1837 and toned down some of the wilder excesses of his predecessors.

From the top of the staircase, you can strike out on two separate excursions into the State Rooms, one culminating in the Alexander Hall, the other leading to the Malachite Room. We've described the former route first – the amount of backtracking involved to cover both is about the same.

The Hermitage

Head up the Council Staircase to reach the second floor.

Second floor, rooms 155, 156, 188–198, 271 & 282. The other State Rooms (nos. 204, 289 & 304–307) are covered on p.142.

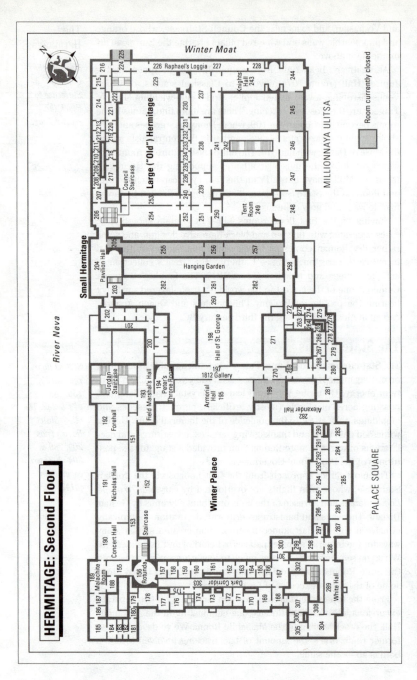

HERMITAGE: Second Floor

River Neva

Winter Moat

226 Raphael's Loggia 227

Knights Hall 243

Large ("Old") Hermitage

Council Staircase

Small Hermitage

204 Pavilion Hall

Hanging Garden

Jordan Staircase

Field Marshal's Hall

Peter's Throne Room

197 1812 Gallery

198 Hall of St. George

194

Armorial Hall 195

282 Alexander Hall

196

Forehall

Nicholas Hall

Concert Hall

189 Malachite Room

156 Rotunda

Dark Corridor 303

White Hall

Winter Palace

Staircase

Tent Room 249

Room currently closed

MILLIONNAYA ULITSA

PALACE SQUARE

To the Alexander Hall

Passing through the door on the left of the landing, you enter the
Field Marshals' Hall (room 193), so called because of the portraits
of Russian military leaders that hung here before the Revolution; one
has now been returned and others may follow. The hall was originally designed by Montferrand, whose careless juxtaposition of heating
flues and flammable materials may have caused the great fire of
1837, which started in this room. Its current form reflects Stasov's
Neoclassicism: pearly white, festooned with outsized vases and statuary, and dominated by a massive bronze chandelier. In the corner
stands a **coronation carriage**, ordered by Peter the Great while he
was in Paris.

The next stop is **Peter's Throne Room** (room 194). Its title is
purely honorific, since Peter the Great died over a century before
Montferrand designed the room, but the atmosphere is nevertheless
palpably reverential. The walls are covered with burgundy velvet
embroidered with Romanov eagles, while an oak and silver throne
which actually belonged to Peter occupies a dais below scores of
gilded birds converging on the chamber's vault.

Stasov's Neoclassical decoration ran riot in the adjacent **Armorial
Hall** (room 195). Stucco warriors and battle standards flank the
doors at either end, while gilded columns, giant lampstands and
cases full of silverware vie for your attention. Also in this room is a
restored late eighteenth-century Imperial carriage, of which Fabergé
made a tiny copy only 6cm long to go inside one of the eggs commissioned by the Imperial family. The **1812 Gallery** (room 197) was
modelled by Rossi on the Waterloo Chamber at Windsor Castle (also
built to commemorate the victory over Napoleon). An Englishman,
George Dawe, was commissioned to paint the portraits of Russian
military leaders that line the barrel-vaulted gallery (some died before
the portraits were completed and the gaps remain unfilled).
Alexander I and his ally, Franz I of Austria, merit life-sized equestrian portraits at the northern end.

Alongside the 1812 Gallery lies the enormous **Hall of St George**
(room 198) – the main throne room. Built by Quarenghi, with lavish
use of Carrara marble, the hall was inaugurated on St George's day
in 1795 and became associated with solemn acts of state. Here,
Alexander I swore that he would never make peace until Napoleon
had been driven from Russia, and Nicholas II similarly vowed to
defeat Germany at the outbreak of World War I.

To the left of room 270 is the **Cathedral** (room 271); used originally as the private court chapel and not as large as its name suggests. Rastrelli's gilded Baroque interior was hardly touched by the
fire of 1837, and the proportions are such that the ceiling seems to
soar up into the heavens, despite the small scale. Walk back through
room 270, left into 280 and then turn right through 281 to emerge in
the magnificent **Alexander Hall** (room 282), designed by Alexander

Bryullov in 1837 to commemorate the Napoleonic Wars. The military theme is reflected in the sky-blue and white bas-reliefs that cover the walls. Also notable are the stucco palm "umbrellas" that sprout from the vaulting and the intricate parquet floor. The hall is used for temporary exhibitions and interrupts a series of rooms devoted to French art (see p.147). At this point, you'll need to retrace your steps to the Jordan Staircase to see the rest of the state rooms.

To the Malachite Room and beyond

The northern wing harbours some of the most famous rooms in the Winter Palace, chiefly associated with Nicholas II and the Provisional Government. Immediately ahead of the Jordan Staircase is a **Forehall** (room 192), centred on a malachite and bronze pavilion which was used for champagne buffets whenever balls took place in the adjacent **Nicholas Hall** (room 191). Named after the portrait of Nicholas I installed here in 1856, the hall can accommodate five thousand people and is used, along with the Forehall and the Concert Hall, to stage prestigious temporary exhibitions.

At this point, it's worth a detour into the corridor (rooms 151 & 153), recently designated the **Gallery of Russian Tsars**, hung with portraits of the same. Of particular interest are two of Catherine the Great, painted fourteen years apart; her luckless son Paul, his snub nose flatteringly filled out; and Nicholas II, in a humble pose suited to his posthumous canonization as an Orthodox martyr. The adjoining **Concert Hall** (room 190) affords a fine view of the Rostral Columns, and by the far wall stands the enormous Baroque silver sarcophagus of St Alexander Nevsky, resembling a giant pen-and-ink stand.

The **Malachite Room** (room 189), beyond the Concert Hall, was created in 1837 for Nicholas I's wife, Alexandra Fyodorovna, its pilasters, fireplace, tables and knick-knacks all fashioned from the lustrous green stone (mined in the Urals) that gives the room its name. Kerensky's Provisional Government met here from July 1917 until their arrest by the Bolsheviks three months later, and it's easy to imagine the despondent ministers slumping on the divan before adjourning to the adjacent **White Dining Room** (room 188), hung with allegorical tapestries of Africa, Asia and America. Here they were arrested (Kerensky had already fled) and obliged to sign a protocol dissolving the Provisional Government – the mantelpiece clock was stopped at that moment (2am).

From here you enter the barrel-vaulted **Moorish Dining Room** (room 155), named after the black ceremonial guards costumed as Moors, who stood outside in the Tsarist times. Beyond lies the **Rotunda** (room 156), a lofty circular room with a coffered dome encircled by a balcony. In the centre stands a model of a triumphal column topped with a statue of Peter, which he planned to erect on Palace Square, but which was never built.

From the Rotunda, you can continue southwards into the section on Russian art and culture (see below), or go back through the Malachite Room to visit the exhibition of Russian palace interiors.

Russian palace interiors

Opened in the 1980s as a temporary exhibition, the **nineteenth-century Russian palace interiors** proved so popular that they have remained in place ever since. The exhibition consists of a series of rooms, each arranged with furniture and objects of applied art recreating the interior styles of each decade from the early 1800s to the Revolution. From the Empire-style Music Room, with its exquisite instruments by Hambs, you progress to the late nineteenth-century Oriental Smoking Room, Nicholas II's Gothic Library, the Art Nouveau nursery with its luxurious child-sized furniture (used by Nicholas and Alexandra's children), and finally the bourgeois Russian Revival-style sitting room by Malyutin. Much of the furniture was designed by the architects who were working on the building at the time; in the Gothic Study, which represents the 1830s, even the waste bin forms an integral part of the ensemble.

Second floor, rooms 175–187.

This exhibition closes for lunch from 12.30pm to 1.30pm.

Russian art and culture

The section on **Russian art and culture** nominally starts with the Gallery of Russian Tsars (see p.140), and the adjacent room 152, containing a copy of Kneller's famous portrait of the young Peter the Great. It then resumes in room 157, beyond the Rotunda, and includes rooms on both sides of the Dark Corridor (though not all of them are open) containing a miscellany of objects including sundials, a universal clock, equipment for extracting teeth and engravings showing the rapid growth of St Petersburg. You'll also find busts of Peter and Menshikov and some of the many objects that Peter created in his private turnery, including an impressive multi-tiered ivory chandelier.

Second floor, rooms 151–173.

Rooms 168–173 exhibit an array of more familiar items, the result of Peter's bringing in foreign craftsmen and the subsequent boom in painting and the applied arts during Catherine the Great's reign. Look out for the lizard-armed chair designed by Catherine's favourite architect, the Scotsman Charles Cameron, in room 171. Paul's throne as Grand Master of the Knights of Malta (other European sovereigns had turned the post down, considering it too much bother and expense) is in room 172, followed by incredible filigree ivory vases and the uniquely Russian steel dressing-table and desk sets in room 173.

From here you can continue on to the White Hall and Gold Drawing Room (see p.142) or return to the Field Marshals' Hall (see p.139) and head for the Western European art section in the Large Hermitage (see p.139).

*Second floor,
rooms 289 &
304–307.*

The White Hall and Gold Drawing Room

Running round the southwest corner of the Winter Palace are several further state rooms which were revamped after the fire of 1837 for the wedding of the future Alexander II and Maria of Hessen-Darmstadt. The only significant interior to survive in its original restored state, however, is Alexander Bryullov's **White Hall** (room 289), its lightness and airiness in striking contrast to the surrounding apartments. It now houses some skilfully made furniture along with eight large landscapes and many smaller works by Hubert Robert, a French artist who found fame in Russia while remaining largely unknown in Western Europe.

From here you emerge into one of the palace's most vulgar state rooms, the **Gold Drawing Room** (room 304). Reworked in the 1850s, the walls and ceiling are completely gilded and the room contains French and Italian cameos displayed in hexagonal cases.

The next room along, the **State Corner Study** (room 305), contains Sèvres porcelain and pieces from the Josiah Wedgwood "Green Frog Service" made for Catherine the Great – the frog being the whimsical coat of arms that she chose for her Chesma Palace. Beyond lies the 1850s **Raspberry Boudoir** (room 306) – the former private room of Alexander II's wife, Maria Alexandrovna – decorated in "Second Baroque" style, with rich crimson hangings plus gold and mirrors galore.

Bringing this sequence of rooms to an end with a flourish, room 307 displays **jewellery by Fabergé** from the collections of the Hermitage, other museums in St Petersburg and the Imperial palaces. Among the array of tiaras, bracelets and cigarette cases, look out for the exquisitely delicate *Cornflower* and *Daisy*, carved from rock crystal.

Hidden Treasures

*Second floor,
rooms
200–202.
Closes 5pm,
4pm on Sun.*

In 1993, the Hermitage was the first museum in Russia to admit possession of stores of "**trophy art**", appropriated from Germany at the end of World War II – some of it had previously been stolen by the Nazis in occupied Europe. As Russian legislators are at one with public opinion in opposing the return of any artworks until Russian claims for treasures despoiled by the Nazis are settled, the exhibition entitled "Hidden Treasures Revealed" is likely to remain for some time yet – although its curator has so far resisted orders that the paintings should be integrated into the main catalogue of the Hermitage, in case they end up being repatriated after all.

The exhibition includes ten **Renoirs**, ranging from *Woman Brushing her Hair* to the light-filled *Low Tide at Yport*; four **Van Goghs**, notably the *White House at Night*; **Monet**'s lush *Garden in Bordighera*; **Gauguin**'s *Late Afternoon* and *Two Sisters* from his Tahitian period; and six **Cezannes**, including a *Mont Sainte-*

Victoire and *Bathers*. Also look out for the *Road to Castel Gondolfo*, by **Derain**, the *Place de la Concorde* by **Degas**, and **Manet**'s *Portrait of Mme Isabelle Lemonnier*. **Daumier**'s *The Burden*, with its toiling laundress and child, is a rare exception to the prevailing mood of sunny optimism.

The Hermitage

Italian art: thirteenth to eighteenth century

Spread through a series of small rooms in the Large Hermitage, **Italian art** is well represented, with works by Leonardo, Botticelli, Michelangelo, Raphael and Titian, although there is a poor showing of works by the stars of the early Renaissance.

Second floor, rooms 207–238.

The most direct approach is via the Council Staircase (from Antiquities on the first floor), which emerges at the start of the section. Alternatively, if you are coming from the Field Marshals' Hall (room 193), head along the corridor (rooms 200 and 201) and over the covered bridge into another state room, the **Pavilion Hall** (room 204). Built by Stackenschneider in 1856, this dazzlingly light room combines elements of Classical, Islamic and Renaissance architecture, and contains a gilded balcony overlooking a mosaic based on one discovered in a Roman bathhouse. Taking centre stage is the **Peacock Clock**, a miracle of English craftsmanship, which once belonged to Catherine's lover Potemkin. Check with the excursion office as to which days the peacock "performs" – spreading its tail as the cockerel crows on the hour, while a mushroom rotates in surreal accompaniment.

Simone Martini to Leonardo da Vinci

Room 207 boasts a typically graceful and colourful *Madonna* by the thirteenth-century Sienese painter **Simone Martini**, and an equally opulent *Five Apostles* by **Gentile da Fabriano** (one of his relatively few surviving compositions). A tiny polygonal chamber leads to room 209, which contains the radiant *St Augustus's Vision* by **Fra Filippo Lippi**, and work by the Dominican **Fra Angelico**, whose fresco *Madonna and Child, St Dominic and St Thomas Aquinas* is the largest painting in the room. Della Robbia terracottas and superb bas-reliefs by Rossellino fill the next few rooms. Room 213 holds two small paintings by the distinctive hand of **Botticelli**, two serene canvases by **Pietro Perugino**, an Umbrian painter who worked on the Sistine Chapel and is best known as Raphael's teacher, and some gentle works by **Filippino Lippi**.

The high coffered ceiling and ornate decor of room 214 rather upstage the only two works by **Leonardo da Vinci** in Russia, both of which stand in isolation near the centre of the room. The earlier one – a lively piece with a youthful Mary dandling Jesus on her knee – is known as the *Benois Madonna*, after the family who sold it to Nicholas II in 1914. The other is the *Madonna Litta*, a later and more accomplished work, depicting the Virgin suckling the infant Jesus.

The following room concentrates on Leonardo's immediate successors: *Portrait of a Woman* (also known as *Colombine* or *Flora*) is by his most faithful pupil, **Francesco Melzi**, in whose arms he died.

The Raphael Loggia, Michelangelo and Caravaggio

Continue through room 216 with its few examples of Mannerist works into the **Raphael Loggia**, a magnificently long and high gallery, lit by large windows looking out over the Winter Moat and the Hermitage Theatre. Commissioned by Catherine the Great, the loggia was created between 1783 and 1792 by Quarenghi as a copy of Raphael's famous gallery in the Vatican Palace. Every surface, wall and vault is covered with paintings – copies on canvas of Raphael's frescoes.

To the right as you enter the Raphael Loggia is room 229, whose highlights include Raphael's early *Madonna Conestabile*, completed at the age of 17. Raphael's slightly later *Holy Family* depicts a beardless, though still fairly aged, Joseph, and an uncertain Madonna and Child. Straight ahead in the Small Skylight Room (237) are vast canvases by **Tintoretto**, **Veronese** and other High Renaissance luminaries, while to the right in room 230 you'll find frescoes by the School of Raphael and a sculpture by **Michelangelo** – the spiritually anguished *Crouching Youth* – whose taut musculature bears the sculptor's chisel marks. The famous *Lute Player* by **Caravaggio** can be found in room 232 and **Alessandro Magnasco's** *Banditti at Rest* in room 233.

To view the rest of the Italian art collection you'll need to retrace your steps to room 216. On the way back, if you have time for a small detour, turn right through room 237 (instead of left into room 229) into the **Gallery of Ancient Painting** (room 241), which, despite its name, displays eighteenth-century European sculpture, including Canova's *Three Graces* and *Repentant Magdalene*. The **Knights' Hall** (room 243) beyond has exhibitions from the vast stores of highly decorated European weapons and armour in the Imperial arsenal; the horses here were stuffed by Klodt, who sculpted the ones on Anichkov most. In the adjacent **Twelve-Column Hall** (room 244) are temporary exhibitions of delicate artworks such as textiles, icons or watercolours.

Rooms 239–240 display the Spanish art collection (see p.145).

From room 217, you can go back past the Council Staircase to room 254 to see the Hermitage's stunning collection of Rembrandts.

Veronese and Titian

Once back in room 216, turn left along a corridor to room 222, which contains a few paintings by **Veronese**, including a confident *Self-portrait*. This room leads on to a fine collection of works by **Titian**, the most famous being the *Danaë* (room 221) – one of five versions of the same subject which Titian made (the best known is in the Prado) – in which a Michelangelesque nude languishes on a bed while Zeus appears as a shower of golden coins, though some regard the powerful *Saint Sebastian* and sensuous *Penitent Magdalene* of his final years as finer works. His *Portrait of a Young Woman* wearing a man's cloak, with one arm drawn across her breast, hangs in room 219.

Room 218 contains the **Embriachi ivories** – pieces of carved walrus tusk used to make altars in the sixteenth century. The *Judith* by **Giorgione** in room 217 is one of only a few paintings in the world more or less firmly attributed to him.

Spanish art: sixteenth to eighteenth century

The Hermitage's collection of **Spanish art** is the largest in the world outside Spain. Among the earlier works in room 240 are a superb late fifteenth-century *Entombment of Christ* by an unknown master, and **El Greco**'s painterly depiction of *SS Peter and Paul* – according to legend, it was St Paul who converted the painter's native Greek island of Crete to Christianity.

Second floor, rooms 239 & 240.

Room 239, the Skylight Room, displays examples of the flowering of Spanish art during the seventeenth century – large religious works created for churches and monasteries, as well as more intimate pieces. Among the monumental compositions are *St Jerome Listening to the Sound of the Trumpet* by **Ribera**, and **Zurbarán**'s *St Laurentio* altarpiece, painted for the Monastery of St Joseph in Seville. **Murillo**'s *Immaculate Conception* differs from the usual presentation of the Virgin with her feet on the moon and stars overhead by taking the Assumption as its leitmotif – hence the picture's other title, *The Assumption of the Madonna*. His sugary *Adoration of Christ* is accompanied by the cheeky *Boy with a Dog*, equally typical of his sentimental style.

While religious themes were esteemed, **Velázquez** was equally willing to paint what were scornfully called *bodegón* (tavern) scenes, such as *Luncheon* – the figure on the right is supposedly Velázquez himself, who was only 18 at the time. In later life he concentrated largely on portrayals of the Spanish royal family: his *Portrait of Count Olivarez* depicts the *éminence grise* and power behind the throne, who was also a friend of the artist. Another penetrating work is **Goya**'s portrait of the actress Antonia Zaráte, who died of consumption shortly after the completion of this picture, which betrays her inner anxiety.

Dutch, Flemish and Netherlandish art: fifteenth to eighteenth century

One of the Hermitage's great glories is its **Dutch, Flemish and Netherlandish art** collection. As well as one of the largest gatherings of works by Rembrandt outside the Netherlands, you'll also find one of the world's finest collections of paintings by Rubens and Van Dyck, many of which came from the Walpole Collection of Houghton

Hall in Norfolk, bought by Catherine the Great in 1779 (see English art, p.149). If you've come from the Italian art section, you'll start with the Rembrandts in room 254. Be warned that these are amongst the most crowded rooms in the Hermitage.

Rembrandt

Second floor,
rooms
245–254, 258,
261 & 262.

The twenty or so paintings attributed to **Rembrandt** (room 254) comprise some of the finest works from his early period of success in the 1630s, including light, optimistic canvases such as *Flora*, which is actually a portrait of his wife Saskia, completed shortly after their marriage. *Abraham Sacrificing Isaac* is from the same period, though more serious in content, while the *Descent from the Cross* is set at night to allow a dramatic use of light which focuses attention on the body of Christ and the grief-stricken Mary, prematurely aged and on the verge of collapse.

Rembrandt's *Danaë*, slashed by a deranged visitor in 1985, is back on show after years of restoration, accompanied by an exhibition on the dilemmas and technicalities of restoring such damaged canvases. The picture was one of Rembrandt's personal favourites, and he parted with it only when he was forced to declare himself bankrupt in 1656.

Bankruptcy was not the only misfortune that Rembrandt suffered in later life: Saskia had died in 1642, shortly after giving birth to their fourth child, but Rembrandt married again in 1645, the same year he painted the calm domestic scene in *The Holy Family*, set in a Dutch carpenter's shop. The heavenly reward of the penitent is the theme of *The Return of the Prodigal Son*, bathed in scarlet and gold, one of Rembrandt's last big canvases.

To the Tent Room and beyond

The vast **Tent Room** (249), so called because of its unusual pitched roof and beautiful coffered ceiling painted in pastel shades, is stuffed with seventeenth-century Dutch genre paintings by Frans Hals, Jan Steen, Salomon van Ruisdael, and others. Beyond, room 248 is also lavishly decorated, with artificial marble columns supporting a finely patterned ceiling, hung with an octagonal chandelier resembling miniature organ pipes. Among the many paintings here are several small canvases by **Jan Brueghel**, son of the great Pieter Brueghel the Elder (none of whose works appear in the Hermitage). Jan was an accomplished artist in his own right, a specialist in landscapes and still lifes, which are on display by the window.

Rubens and Van Dyck

Works by **Rubens** at the height of his career (1610–20) fill room 247, including *Descent from the Cross*, a famous altarpiece painted for the Capuchin monastery at Lierre, near Antwerp. In Rembrandt's version (see above), the reality of human suffering and the use of light were paramount; with Rubens on the other hand, what is important is the contrast between the clothes of the figures and the pallid body of Christ. The one late work by Rubens, painted in the last year of his life, rejects the traditional portrayal of *Bacchus* as a youthful party-goer and depicts him instead as a jovial slob, enveloped in folds of fat.

As was usual when commissions poured in, students in Rubens' studio worked on the master's paintings. Among his assistants was the young Van Dyck, who worked on the monumental *Feast at the House of Simon the Pharisee*, a resolutely secular treatment of a biblical theme. Room 246 features paintings by **Van Dyck** himself, who was court painter to (and knighted by) Charles I of England from 1632 until his death in 1641. His finest works date from this last period, when he concentrated largely on portraits, including those of the English architect Inigo Jones, Thomas Wharton, Charles I and Queen Henrietta Maria, all of which are on display here. Among his earlier works, there's a wonderful self-portrait revealing a ginger-haired young sophisticate.

Retracing your steps through room 248 brings you to a corridor (room 258) lined with Flemish landscapes and winter scenes by Leytens and Savery. **Room 262**, which runs alongside Catherine's Hanging Garden, is one of the least visited rooms on this floor, but well worth a look for its selection of Netherlandish art. Look out for **Roger van der Weyden**'s *St Luke and the Virgin*, the two halves of which were purchased separately by the Hermitage before it was realized that they belonged together. Other gems are Robert Campen's diptych *Trinity, Virgin and Child*, Lucas van Leyden's *Healing of the Blind Man*, and Dirk Jacobsz's brilliant group por-traits of the Amsterdam Shooting Corporation.

Room 258 leads through to the collection of German art in rooms 263–268.

German art: fifteenth to eighteenth century

The Hermitage's small collection of **German art** from the fifteenth to eighteenth century is conveniently approached from the Dutch, Flemish and Netherlandish art section by continuing along the corri-dor (room 258) through to room 263. Unfortunately, this section is usually closed in summer, but if you are here at the right time of year, you'll be able to see a few paintings by well-known names, including Lucas **Cranach**'s *Portrait of a Woman* and the first of his series of *Venus and Cupid* paintings, which dates from 1509. Ambrosius **Holbein**, older brother of Hans, lived a short life – his *Portrait of a Young Man* was completed at the age of 23, shortly before he died.

Second floor, rooms 263–268.

French art: fifteenth to eighteenth century

Thanks to an obsession with all things French during the reigns of Catherine and Elizabeth, the Hermitage features an impressive col-lection of **French art**, particularly from the seventeenth and eigh-teenth centuries. Numerous French artists were employed by the

Second floor, rooms 272–281 & 283–288.

Romanovs, starting with Caravaque, who was engaged by Peter the Great and remained in Russia until his death. Nevertheless, the art has lost its appeal for many, bound up as it is with the cloyingly frivolous tastes of the French and Russian aristocracy, and these rooms are among the least visited in the Hermitage.

The collection begins in room 272 with French fifteenth- and sixteenth-century metalwork, blue Limoges enamel tiles and carved furniture. The earliest French paintings, from the fifteenth and sixteenth centuries, are in room 274, while room 275 displays **Simon Vouet**'s allegorical portraits. The next two rooms contain fairly minor works, but for those not enamoured of cherubs, there's the happy sight of them being slaughtered en masse by Roman soldiers in Bourdon's *Massacre of the Innocents*.

From Poussin to Greuze

The Hermitage is particularly renowned for its collection of paintings by **Nicolas Poussin**, the founder of French Neoclassicism, whose artistic philosophy of order, reason and design was the antithesis of Rubens' more painterly style – the few drops of blood visible on Poussin's unusually frenetic *Battle of the Israelites with the Amalekites* (room 279) are purely symbolic. Also in room 279 is his best-known work in the Hermitage, the colourful *Landscape with Polythemus*, whose orderly symbolism encapsulates Poussin's rational philosophy of painting.

The other great French artist of the day was **Claude Lorrain** (real name, Claude Gelée), who began his career as a pastry cook to an Italian painter. Room 280 exhibits tranquil pastoral scenes depicting the lost Golden Age of Antiquity, and his use of light – as in *The Four Times of Day* – greatly influenced English artists such as Turner. But the primary role of art during the Golden Age of the "Sun King" was the glorification of absolute monarchy, as depicted in Pierre Mignard's gigantic *Magnanimity of Alexander the Great* in room 281.

Passing through the Alexander Hall, one of the Winter Palace's state rooms (see p.139), you soon come to room 284, with its works by **Antoine Watteau**. Best known for his cameos of socialites frozen in attitudes of pleasure – *The Embarrassing Proposal* is a good example – Watteau's paintings seem frivolous and insincere to contemporary eyes, but his technique of "divisionism" (juxtaposing pure colours on the canvas, rather than mixing them on the palette) was a major influence on Seurat and the Pointillist school.

Room 285 has a few works by Watteau's followers **Nicolas Lancret** and **Jean-Baptiste Pater**, but the most powerful piece is **François Lemoyne**'s voluptuous and wicked *Jupiter and Io* – thought to be a copy of a lost painting by Correggio – in which Jupiter disguises himself as a cloud in order to seduce the young maid. The room also contains a selection of paintings by **François**

Boucher, whose talents were considered by many to be wasted on the production of profitable pictures of naked gods and goddesses frolicking.

The
Hermitage

The intellectual atmosphere of Enlightenment France seen in the paintings in room 287 contrasts with the more corporeal works in previous rooms. The major piece, **Chardin**'s marvellous *Still Life with the Attributes of the Arts*, commissioned by the St Petersburg Academy of Art, was sold by the Hermitage in 1849 under orders from Nicholas I, and only re-acquired by the museum during the Soviet period. The statue of the aged Voltaire by **Houdon** escaped a similar fate when, instead of following Nicholas's order to "get rid of this old monkey", a far-sighted museum curator simply locked it out of sight.

Critics have accused **Jean-Baptiste Greuze**, whom Catherine the Great greatly admired, of "insincerity, artificiality and misplaced voluptuousness". Judging by the works in room 288, it's difficult to disagree, yet he was originally popular precisely because "morality paintings" like *Spoilt Child* and *Paralytic Helped By His Children* represented a move away from the frivolity of Rococo.

English art: seventeenth to nineteenth century

When the Hermitage opened to the public in 1852, it was the only gallery in Europe with a collection of **English art**. Its core consists of the famous **Houghton Hall Collection** of Sir Robert Walpole, which Catherine the Great purchased from his dissolute grandson for a paltry £40,000 – thereby achieving posthumous revenge on Walpole, who had called her the "philosophizing tyrant". To rub it in, her buyer left a portrait of the empress on the bare walls of Houghton Hall.

Second floor, rooms 298–300.

The cream of the Hermitage's collection is the series of works by **Joshua Reynolds**, particularly *The Infant Hercules Strangling Serpents*, one of the last paintings he completed before he went blind. Commissioned by Catherine, it is supposed to symbolize Russia besting her foes, but also features several of Reynolds' English contemporaries (including Dr Johnson as Tiresias). The other great masterpiece is **Thomas Gainsborough**'s wonderful *Portrait of a Lady in a Blue Shawl*. Also in the collection is part of the unique 944-piece "Green Frog Service" made by **Josiah Wedgwood** for Catherine's Chesma Palace (another part of which is on display in room 305; see p.142).

Modern European art

After the State Rooms and the Special Collection, the third floor of the Winter Palace is the most popular section of the Hermitage, covering **modern European art** in the nineteenth and twentieth centuries. To get there, take the staircase leading off from room 269 on the second floor, which brings you out at the beginning of the col-

Third floor, rooms 314–350.

HERMITAGE: Third Floor

Room currently closed

River Neva

391 392 393 394 395 396
390
389
388
387 386 385 384
397
383
382
381a 381
367 351a
366 351 352
365
364 359 353
363 354
362 355
361 356
360 357
370 369 368 358
371 375 376
333 334 335 336 337 338 339 340 341 342
350
349 348 347 346 345 344 343

398 399 400

Winter Palace

327
326
328 325
329 324
315 314 332 331 330 323
320 321 322
316 317 318 319

N

PALACE SQUARE

lection. The range of work is impressively wide, but the highlight is undoubtedly the unique collection of works by **Matisse** and **Picasso**, which was assembled largely by two Moscow philanthropists, Sergei Shchukin and Ivan Morozov. Between them, they bought nearly fifty paintings by each artist in the five years before World War I, and they were also largely responsible for collecting the fine spread of Impressionist paintings also on display in this section.

In few other places in the world did such brilliant collections exist, and the works influenced a whole generation of Russian artists. Following the October Revolution, both collections were confiscated by the state, and in 1948 were divided between the Pushkin Museum of Fine Arts in Moscow and the Hermitage. However, whereas Morozov was coerced into assigning his pictures to the state, Shchukin never did, and when one of the Matisses was sent to Italy in 2000, his grandson filed a lawsuit for its recovery, obliging the Hermitage to order its immediate return to Russia.

As it's intended eventually to move the Hermitage's Impressionist and Post-Impressionist art into the General Staff building, you should expect to find major changes in this section from 2002 onwards (if not earlier), as pictures are taken down to be packed up for the short journey across Palace Square to their new home.

The
Hermitage

From Gros to Gauguin

The earliest works currently on show in this section are in room 314, which features early nineteenth-century portraits by **Roland Lefevre** and a swashbuckling picture of Napoleon by **Antoine-Jean Gros**, a pupil of David, but one whose fiery palette displays his admiration for Rubens. Next door in room 332 you'll find some early nineteenth-century paintings by **Prud'hon** and **Guerin**; beyond here, in room 331, **Ingres'** portrait of *N.D. Guryev* provides a marvellous contrast to the Romanticism epitomized by two small canvases by **Eugene Delacroix**, *Moroccan Arab Saddling a Horse* and *Lion Hunt in Morocco*.

At the far end of this section, it's worth a detour to see the pastels by **Degas**, **Picasso** and others in room 327, before retracing your steps and turning the corner into rooms 321–322, which are devoted to the forerunners of Impressionism: the artists of the Barbizon School. Small and shimmering pearly landscapes by **Camille Corot** and gentle works by **Charles-François Daubigny** contrast with **Constant Troyon's** large *Going to Market*, filled with early morning light.

From here, the adjacent room 320 takes you straight into the world of the Impressionists with **Renoir's** full-length, richly clothed portrait of Jeanne Samary. Aside from a couple of simple landscapes by **Alfred Sisley**, room 319 is dominated by **Monet**, ranging from early works such as the bright, direct *Woman in a Garden* (1867) to the atmospheric, fog-bound *Waterloo Bridge* (1902). Room 318 contains a good sample of **Cézanne's** work, including a typically contemplative portrait, *The Smoker*, and one of the *Mont Sainte-Victoire* series, whose chromatic blocks provided a point of departure for Cubism. The only one of the older generation of Impressionists to appreciate Cézanne in his lifetime was **Pissarro**, represented here by *Boulevard Montmartre* and *French Theatre Square*.

Arles Women, an unusual canvas painted by **Van Gogh** whilst under Gauguin's influence, dominates room 317, which also contains a couple of Van Gogh landscapes and the little-known *Arena at Arles*. Alongside these are a couple of small canvases by the self-taught **Henri Rousseau** and Pointillist works by **Paul Signac** and **Henri-Edmond Cross**. Room 316 is entirely devoted to paintings by **Gauguin** dating from his soujourn in Tahiti.

For the rest of the collection, head across the balcony above the Alexander Hall to room 343, which marks the beginning of the later, mostly twentieth-century collection, with its landscapes, interiors and Parisian street scenes by **Jean Édouard Vuillard** – works by his contemporaries Bonnard and Denis have already been transferred to the General Staff building (see p.83).

The Picasso and Matisse collections

The **Picasso** collection begins in room 344 and covers his best-loved early periods. The earliest painting on show is *The Absinthe Drinker* of 1901, and there are also two paintings from his Blue Period (1901–04) – the larger, *Sisters*, features gaunt, emaciated figures typical of his style at the time. There are several early Cubist works, such as the discernibly figurative *Woman with a Fan* (1908), while room 345 concentrates on later Cubist pieces, such as his *Still Life* of 1913, along with some of his ceramics.

The precise content of these rooms changes frequently, as works are often out on loan.

Some of **Matisse**'s most important works were commissioned by his patron, Shchukin, whom he visited in St Petersburg on a number of occasions between 1908 and 1913, though the earliest works on display are a series of Neo-Impressionist still lifes (room 346) dating from 1898–1901. Later works include the heavily outlined, Fauvist *Nude, Black and Gold* (1908), while colour and decoration are more important than subject matter and perspective in the profusely ornate *The Red Room* of 1908 (room 347), which was designed for Shchukin's dining room, thus fulfilling Matisse's stated objective to create art "as relaxing as a comfortable armchair".

The focal points of room 347, however, are Matisse's two paintings commissioned by Shchukin for his staircase – *Music* and *Dance* – which marked a turning point in the artist's career, the pink flesh of his earlier versions being replaced with red-hot primitive figures on a deep green-and-blue background. When first exhibited in October 1910 at the Salon d'Automne in Paris, the pictures were panned by both French and Russian critics. Shchukin took fright at their reaction and cancelled the commission, but changed his mind on the train back to Russia. After the pictures were hung in his mansion, Shchukin feared that the nude flautist would disturb his female guests, and personally painted out the musician's genitals.

One of Matisse's portraits of his mistress and model Lydia Delektorskaya can be seen next door in room 348. The other works in this room, such as *Arab Coffee House* and *Sur La Terrasse*, are on Spanish and Moroccan themes, but display many of the pictorial qualities associated with Russian folk art and icons, reflecting the lasting impact on Matisse of his visits to Russia.

Vlaminck to Kandinsky

Fauvism – characterized by the use of bright colours and simplified forms – links the painters whose works are exhibited in room 349, though few of the paintings here are representative of that style. The startling and deliberately provocative portraits of fashionable Parisians are by the Dutch artist **Kees van Dongen**, who hovered on the edge of Berlin's *Die Brücke* group and the Fauvist circle. **Maurice de Vlaminck**, a racing cyclist and violinist who boasted he had never set foot inside the Louvre, is represented by several atypical early Cézanne-type landscapes. **Albert Marquet**, though associated with the Fauvists, is actually better known for his rather dour port scenes, some of which are on display here. The childlike paintings by **André Derain** in room 350 are better examples of Fauvism, though here too you'll find some unusually dark early landscapes and a thoroughly Cubist *Man Reading Newspaper*. There are also several figurative works by the card-carrying Communist **Fernand Léger**, dating from 1932 to 1948.

Room 333 is the only one in the Hermitage to feature a modern Russian artist, containing four paintings by **Vasily Kandinsky**, who spent much of his life abroad. Rooms 334–336 are used to display a bequest of modern Italian sculpture, but the modern European art section continues in room 338 with landscapes by **Rockwell Kent**, hero of Spanish painters right up to the 1980s. His ideal of manliness in the face of nature is exemplified in his *Seal Hunt in North Greenland*. Rooms 339–341 have a higgledy-piggledy selection of late nineteenth- and early twentieth-century Spanish, Dutch and German works, plus several paintings by **Caspar David Friedrich**.

Oriental art and culture and the Numismatic Collection

The western wing of the third floor is devoted to **Oriental art and culture**, from Mameluke glassware to Japanese woodcuts – but it's hard to give specific directions, as many sections are being reorganized. One fixed point is the **Byzantine collection** (rooms 381, 381a & 382), with its magnificent silverware and carved ivory, including a superb diptych depicting gladiatorial battles between men and beasts. Another is the exhibition of **Indian miniatures** in room 369, including depictions of a Bodhisattva and a monk from the Cave of a Thousand Buddhas monastery. Room 359 was the Corridor of the Maids of Honour where Alexander II installed his mistress, Princess Yurevskaya, while the corner suite of rooms (389–393) once used by Nicholas I and Empress Maria Fyodorovna and occupied by Kerensky in June 1917 now houses **Sassanid silverware**.

Third floor, 351–397.

The **northern wing** of the third floor is accessible via a staircase from the Rotunda (room 156) on the second floor and harbours a **Numismatic Collection** (398–400), including Russian medals and Classical intaglios in gold mounts; only a selection is on view at any one time in temporary exhibitions.

The temporary exhibitions of the Numismatic Collection are open Tues & Thurs.

The Russian Museum

The origins of the **Russian Museum** (Russkiy muzey) date back to the reign of Alexander III, who began to buy Russian art at the end of the nineteenth century with a view to establishing a national museum. His plans were realized by Nicholas II, who purchased the Mikhailovskiy Palace and opened it in 1898 as the country's first public museum of Russian art. During the 1930s, the museum expanded into the palace's Rossi Wing and, later, into the Benois Wing beside the Griboedov Canal.

Along with the Tretyakov Gallery in Moscow, the museum contains the finest collection of **Russian art** in the world – some 400,000 works in total – ranging from medieval icons to the latest in conceptual art. The works neatly mirror Russia's history, tracing the development of the nation's art from Peter the Great's insistence on a break with old Muscovite traditions to the officially approved style of the latter-day Romanovs; from the soul-searching of the Wanderers and the explosion of Symbolism and Futurism to the Stalinist art form known as Socialist Realism and, most recently, Western-inspired multimedia.

Although nearly everything kept locked away during the Soviet years has long since been opened up, the cash-strapped museum earns money by sending many of its most popular works (from the Russian avant-garde collection) for exhibition abroad, so Russians are still unable to see a major part of their heritage. However, some avant-garde works are on show and others are included in **temporary exhibitions** in the Benois Wing.

On a more positive note, in recent years the Russian Museum has acquired three new buildings: the **Marble Palace** (see p.98), the **Engineers' Castle** (see p.98) and the **Stroganov Palace** (see p.78), enabling it to show more of its eighteenth-century art collection and some of the thousands of works of Russian applied art formerly relegated to the stores for lack of space. The museum's **Web site** (*www.rusmuseum.ru*) features some highlights of the collection, though it's less informative and up-to-date than the Hermitage's site.

Visiting the Russian Museum

The Russian Museum is open Mon 10am–5pm, Wed–Sun 10am–6pm; $8. English-language guided tours ($10) for up to ten people can be arranged by calling ☎314 34 48. The nearest metros are Nevskiy prospekt and Gostiniy dvor.

The museum is situated on Mikhailovskaya ploshchad, off Nevskiy prospekt. After making your way through the main gates, head right across the courtyard to the eastern side of the main portico; the **ticket office** is down a few steps in the basement. From the ticket office, go upstairs to the **main entrance hall**, which now houses part of the **gallery shop**.

The **collection** is arranged more or less chronologically, but from top to bottom, so that starting in the east wing of the second floor and finishing on the first floor of the Rossi Wing, you'll have gone from icons to the Wanderers. Then you move across to the Benois Wing, which covers Symbolism and the leftovers from the loans of avant-garde art, and also houses temporary exhibitions. Painting titles are generally in both Russian and English. Due to major reconstruction in the main building and the ongoing relocation of some of the paintings to the other branches of the museum, there may be some differences between our account and works on view at the time of your visit.

The second floor

To view the works on the **second floor** chronologically, start in room
1 and walk anticlockwise round the building – an approach that
emphasizes the giant leap from early icon painting to the art of the
eighteenth and nineteenth centuries. If you're here solely for the
modern stuff, you could skip this floor entirely, but it would be a
shame to miss out on the icons in rooms 1–4, or such extravaganzas
as *The Last Day of Pompeii* or *The Ninth Wave*.

Russian icons

For many centuries Russian art was exclusively religious in theme,
and limited to mosaics, frescoes and **icons**, the holy images venerated in Orthodox churches and households. The early icon painters
were medieval monks for whom painting was a spiritual devotion, to
be accompanied by fasting and prayer. Icons were repainted when
their colours dulled and were often overlaid with golden, gem-
encrusted frames. Their style and content were dictated by the
canons of Byzantine art, faithfully preserved by the schools of
Vladimir and Suzdal. However, a bolder and brighter Russian style
emerged at Novgorod from the twelfth century onwards, which was
to influence the development of Russian art as a whole strongly, and
even the work of such "foreign" artists as Theophanes the Greek.

Icon painting reached a crossroads in the seventeenth century,
when the Russian Orthodox Church was split between supporters of
Patriarch Nikon and the arch-conservative Avvakum, both of whom
opposed any innovations in painting. Nikon poked out the eyes of

Rooms 1–4.

icons that offended him, while Avvakum fulminated against those
who depicted Immanuel the Saviour "like a German, fat-bellied and
corpulent". Ironically, the result was a gradual secularization of art,
as Tsar Mikhail Romanov (1613–45) encouraged a new form known
as the *parsuna*, or the representation of an ordinary human being –
in fact, somewhere between an icon and realistic portraiture. Artists
also began to paint on canvas as well as the traditional wooden panel,
and although icon painting continued right up to the 1917
Revolution, its glory days had long passed, as Russia's leading
painters concentrated on secular art.

One of the oldest works in room 1 is the small, early twelfth-century icon, *The Angel with the Golden Hair*, originally part of a
deesis – the third and most important tier of an iconostasis, with
Christ in Majesty occupying the central position. Historical events
inspired the fourteenth-century icon *Boris and Gleb*, depicting the
young princes of Kiev who were murdered by their elder brother
Svyatopolk; and the fifteenth-century *Battle Between the Men of
Suzdal and Novgorod* in room 2. Room 3 contains several works
attributed to Russia's greatest icon painter, the monk **Andrey Rublev**
(c.1340–c.1430), including the two-metre-high *Apostle Peter* and
Apostle Paul, both of which originally formed part of the iconostasis
of the Assumption Cathedral in Vladimir. The icons in room 4 are
largely from the monasteries of the Russian north, with some examples of the heavy, seventeenth-century Moscow style, such as
Trinity (1671), of which the leading exponent was Simon Ushakov.

Petrine art

Since many of the paintings of eighteenth-century Russia compare
poorly with those of the West, the reasons for viewing them are as
much historical as artistic. The reign of **Peter the Great** marked a
turning point in Russian art. On his famous grand tour of Europe in
1697, the tsar began avidly buying pictures, initiating an activity that
was to become an obsession with the later Romanovs. Then, in his
determination to establish St Petersburg as the new artistic centre of
Russia, Peter transferred the state icon workshop here from the
Kremlin Armoury in Moscow, although he had no intention of building on that tradition, being intent instead on introducing Western art
forms to Russia.

Encouraged by Peter, many foreign artists settled permanently in
St Petersburg. Among the first generation was the German painter
Gottfried Tannhauer (c.1680–c.1733), several of whose portraits of
the tsar can be found in room 5; the most memorable is *Peter the
Great on his Death-bed* (although here it is attributed to Ivan
Nikitin). Peter's other great contribution to Russian art was his
enlightened policy of sending the best young artists abroad to be
trained – a long-term investment which meant that Peter saw little of
their work in his lifetime. The promising **Andrey Matveev**

(1701–39) went to Holland, and the unfinished *Self-portrait of the Artist and his Wife* is one of only a few of his canvases to have survived. The Nikitin brothers (Ivan and Roman) were sent to Italy, and **Ivan Nikitin**'s *Portrait of a Hetman* shows his command of Western techniques, particularly those of the Dutch school.

Art under Elizabeth and Catherine

Rooms 6–11.

It wasn't until Elizabeth ascended the throne that Peter's plans to found a Russian **Academy of Arts** came to fruition. In 1757, an edict by the Senate established an academy in St Petersburg, although in its early years it remained an administrative department of Moscow University. Elizabeth's court artist was **Ivan Vishnyakov** (1699–1761), whose portraits in room 6 of, among others, William and Sarah Fermor, are not that far from the *parsuna* style (see p.156). Vishnyakov's successor, **Alexei Antropov** (1716–95), served under Catherine the Great – who established the Academy as an independent body – and his portraiture shows a further move towards individual characterization. Ironically, Antropov's most famous (though by no means best) painting is a *Portrait of Peter III*, Catherine's detested husband, whose elongated body and minuscule head are overwhelmed by an excess of background detail. Room 6 also contains mosaic portraits of Peter the Great and Catherine the Great produced by the Imperial Glass Factory.

The main reason to pause in the tapestry-laden room 7 is to admire the matronly bronze statue of Empress Anna, known as *Anna Ivanovna and an Arab Boy*, by the Italian sculptor Carlo Rastrelli, father of the famous architect. Room 8 is largely given over to the talented portraitist **Fyodor Rokotov** (1736–1808), whose lively bust-length portraits put the emphasis firmly on the characters of the sitters.

Room 9 concentrates on the work of the Ukrainian artist **Anton Losenko** (1737–73), whose rather awkward *St Vladimir and Rogneda* was the first attempt by a native painter to depict a national historical subject on a large scale. Losenko's other canvases cover themes on a similarly grand scale, but concern more traditional biblical subjects, such as the (comically translated) *Wonderful Catch*, depicting Jesus doing a bit of proxy fishing, and a typically academic portrait of *Cain*.

The centrepiece of the next room is the life-sized statue, *Catherine, the Legislator*, a relaxed work by **Fedot Shubin** (1740–1805), Russia's first great sculptor – Catherine and Potemkin were virtually the only enthusiastic patrons of his flowing Rococo style. On the walls hang paintings by **Dmitri Levitsky** (1735–1822), a Ukrainian Pole who, having never travelled abroad, could justifiably claim to be Russia's first truly homegrown talent. In 1770 he took the Academy by storm, exhibiting over twenty canvases including a portrait of the Academy's director, Kokorinov, in a lilac satin suit. His best-known works, however, are the series of light-hearted

The Russian Museum

portraits of Catherine's favourite pupils from the Smolniy Institute for Young Noblewomen.

Apart from the main staircase, room 11, known as the **White Hall** (Bely zal), is the finest example of the original white, gold and blue Neoclassical decor, designed – right down to the furniture – by the palace's architect, Carlo Rossi. Working with Rossi on the decor was **Vladimir Borovikovsky** (1757–1825), whose sickly sentimental paintings of the Russian aristocracy quickly made him the most sought-after portraitist of the late eighteenth century. The most striking exception (in room 12) is his *Portrait of Catherine the Great in the Park at Tsarskoe Selo*, a remarkably frank portrayal of the elderly empress, exercising one of her dogs.

The nineteenth-century academy style

Rooms 12–17.

The French Revolution and the rise of Napoleon resulted in a marked shift in the official academy style, away from Paris and towards Rome. Large paintings devoted to patriotic themes became extremely popular, exemplified by Luchaninov's *Blessing of a Volunteer of 1812* in room 14. Neoclassicism became the order of the day: *The Siege of Kazan* and *Coronation of Mikhail Fyodorovich* by **Grigori Ugryumov** (1764–1823) were commissioned specifically for the Mikhailovskiy Palace. Also worth examining are the works of **Fyodor Alekseev** (1753–1824), whose views of various Russian cities, including St Petersburg, owe much to Canaletto.

Room 15 is filled with monumental canvases in wildly ornate gilded frames, though few of the pictures can match the sheer theatricality of *The Last Day of Pompeii*, painted by **Karl Bryullov** (1799–1852) while he was living in Rome. With this work, he became the first academy painter to enjoy an international reputation: it was hailed as a masterpiece by the Italian critics and won the Grand Prix at the Paris Salon in 1834. Sir Walter Scott reportedly sat for an hour in front of it before pronouncing that it was "not a painting but an epic" (though unkind commentators claim Scott's apparent devotion was due more to his great age and immobility). Other works by Bryullov include a couple of self-portraits: one as a swaggering ginger-haired youth; the later one clearly portraying the debilitating effects of the tuberculosis which cost him his life.

Another painter of international repute was **Ivan Aivazovsky** (1817–1900), who produced a staggering four to five thousand pictures during his lifetime. Several of his gargantuan seascapes can also be seen in room 15, including *The Ninth Wave* (1859), inspired by the Book of Revelations, which was said to prophesy the downfall of the Romanovs.

As a reaction to the repressive artistic policies of Alexander I and Nicholas I, many Russian artists made the decision to live abroad, mostly in Italy, where they could paint more freely. Rome was the favoured destination and from 1820 onwards there was a semi-permanent Russian artists' colony there, which included the likes of Matveev, Bryullov, Vorobyov and **Silvestr Shchedrin** (1791–1830), whose Italian landscapes line the small corridor which forms room 16.

The final chamber on the second floor, room 17, is devoted mostly to the Romantic portraitist **Orest Kiprensky** (1782–1836), who also lived in Rome for much of his life. His tragic romances and his capacity for drink were legendary, and, like a true Romantic, he died of tuberculosis in wretched circumstances. The finest of his early portraits is of E.V. Davidov, a beefy young Hussar officer who lost an arm and a leg in battle shortly after the picture was completed.

The first floor

On the **first floor** it's possible to see how Russian art gradually escaped from its academic confines and came of age in the late nineteenth century. A new generation of artists refused to become émigrés, ape Western schools or obey the dictates of the Academy – they became known as the **Wanderers** (*peredvizhniki*) because they were forced to display their paintings at travelling or "wandering" exhibitions. Most of them were in sympathy with the Populist movement and abided by Chernyshevsky's dictum that "Only content is able to refute the accusation that art is an empty diversion". But by 1900, although they had become the new orthodoxy, the Wanderers were a spent artistic force: all the running was being made by Mir iskusstva, Jack of Diamonds and other movements, while an explosion of Futurism was imminent.

The Rossi Wing, however, only traces this development as far as the works of Repin and Kuindzhi – to continue the story you'll need

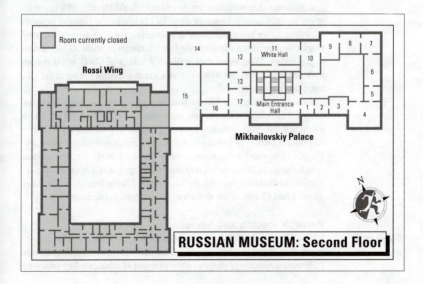

to go on to the Benois Wing (see p.164). If you wish to skip the lead up to Repin, you can go straight into room 38 at the bottom of the stairs instead of turning left into room 18, where the first-floor exhibition actually begins.

Genre painting

Rooms 18–20.

While state commissions usually went to artists who produced safe, monumental academic works, the late eighteenth- and nineteenth-century nobility and merchant class developed a taste for **genre painting** – idealized scenes of rural life in particular. An early exponent was **Alexei Venetsianov** (1780–1847), whose merits (and failings) are evident from works in room 19 such as *Cleaning the Sugar-beet*, with its authentic note of misery, or *In The Threshing Barn*, a stage-set for figures in dreamlike poses. The river scenes by serf-turned-painter **Grigori Soroka** (1823–64) – who was Venetsianov's pupil and later hanged himself to avoid a sentence of flogging – carry more conviction. Amongst the genre scenes of artisans and bourgeois life is Pavel Fedotov's *The Major's Courtship*, in which a self-satisfied officer comes to inspect his plump young bride. Room 20 contains portraits by **Vasily Tropinin** (1770–1857), whose sitters are depicted in a sketchy but precise style vaguely reminiscent of Ingres.

The Ivanov rooms

Rooms 21 & 22.

Aside from Bryullov, the greatest painter to emerge from the Academy in the early nineteenth century was **Alexander Ivanov** (1806–58). Trained by his father, an academician, Ivanov's superb draughtsmanship won him the Academy's Gold Medal and a grant to study in Italy, where he spent most of his life in the Russian colony. However, after being made an academician for *The Appearance of Christ before Mary Magdalene* (which hangs in room 21) he wrote to his father, "You think that a lifelong salary of 6000–8000 rubles and a safe place in the Academy is a great blessing for an artist . . . but I think it is a curse."

The Appearance of Christ was one of a series of huge pictures inspired by religious mysticism, culminating in the work for which he made six hundred sketches (some of which are on display in room 22) over a period of twenty years: *Christ's Appearance before the People*. The version on display here is a final study for the version which hangs in Moscow's Tretyakov Gallery, but it's finished to perfection, brilliantly coloured, with a crowd of half-clad folk in the foreground and Christ in the distance, almost lost in the haze.

Perov, Korzukin and Savrasov

Rooms 23 & 24.

Room 23, a vaulted hall decorated with frescoes, musters an assortment of genre painting, ranging from the sentimental Solomatkin's *Policemen Singing Praises* to the pointed *Monastery Refectory* by

Vasily Perov (1834–82), which shows the monks boozing and guzzling while the poor get short shrift. The son of a baron exiled to Siberia, Perov began his career with satires against corrupt officialdom and had several works banned by the authorities, but later made his peace with the establishment. Another dissident painter who drifted back to the shelter of the Academy was **Alexei Korzukin** (1835–94), whose striking *Funeral Repast at the Cemetery* hangs diagonally opposite the *Palm Sunday in Moscow Under Tsar Alexei Mikhailovich* by **Vyacheslav Shvarts** (1838–69), depicting a magnificent procession outside the Kremlin, beneath a stormy sky.

The next room (24) is largely devoted to landscapes by **Alexei Savrasov** (1830–97), generally reckoned to be the "father of Russian landscape painting" and renowned as the teacher of Levitan, who was to surpass his achievements. Though best known for *The Rooks Have Returned* in the Tretyakov Gallery, Savrasov is well represented here by *The Thaw at Yaroslavl* and *Sunset over the Marshes*.

Kramskoy and Ge

In room 25, you'll find several portraits by **Ivan Kramskoy** (1837–87), the leader of the Wanderers, who marched out of the Academy in 1863 vowing to create a truly Russian school of art. Though little different in style from those of his contemporaries in the West, Kramskoy's portraits are notable for their challenging stares, as in the one of the artist Shishkin, or in *Mina Moiseev* and *Inconsolable Grief*.

Rooms 25 & 26.

Room 26 is devoted to the work of **Nicholas Ge** (1831–94), whose name is pronounced – and often spelled – "Gay". The grandson of a French émigré, Ge was torn between mathematics and painting until the award of the Academy's Gold Medal and a travel bursary decided the issue. As one of the founder members of the Wanderers, he soon turned from landscapes to religious themes under the influence of Ivanov. Two of Ge's most striking works are *Christ and His Disciples in the Garden of Gethsemane* and *The Last Supper* – the latter's departure from traditional iconography horrifed the critics. But the painting for which he is best known to most Russians is *Peter I Interrogating his Son Alexei at Peterhof* – Peter later had his son killed.

Landscapists and social commentators

During the Wanderers' meanderings, landscape painters were forging ahead on the path beaten by Savrasov. Room 27 exhibits work by **Ivan Shishkin** (1832–98), who was offered a travelling scholarship to Prague, Munich, Düsseldorf and Zurich. *In the Thicket*, *Mast Pine Grove* and *Oak Trees* are meticulously detailed, but some critics feel that they lack a sense of place. The accusation certainly can't be levelled at the wintry Russian landscapes of **Fyodor Vasiliev** (1850–73),

Rooms 27–32.

The Russian Museum

in room 28. His desolate *The Thaw* was painted in the year that he became seriously ill with tuberculosis, but *View of the Volga with Barques*, which dates from the year before, exudes freshness.

In room 29, at the back of the main staircase, is a store selling expensive souvenirs and reproductions of Russian art: Fabergé picture frames, Suprematist plates and jewellery.

Subsequent rooms are the domain of **Populist art**, characterized by its strong social commentary. Titles like *Dividing the Family Property* by **Vasily Maximov** and *The Convicted Person* and *Doss House*, both by **Vladimir Makovsky** (1846–1920), tell their own tale. Also notice *Before the Wedding*, by **Fyodor Zhuravlyov** (1836–1901), whose weeping bride and baffled parents invite speculation about a loveless match or shameful secret.

Other concerns are evident in room 31, which is dominated by *To the War* by **Karl Savitsky**, where conscripts are bid a tearful farewell at the station. Here too hangs *Harvesting* by **Grigori Myasoyedov** (1834–1911), the so-called "father" of the Wanderers.

A mournful *Peasant in Trouble*, carved by Chizhov, foreshadows three forceful statues by **Mikhail Antokolsky** (1842–1902) in room 32. Beyond his vulpine white-marble Mephistopheles, statues of Spinoza and Nestor the Annalist flank the vast canvas *Christ and the Adulteress*, by **Vasily Polenov** (1844–1927), in which Christ's humility is contrasted with the vicious piety of the priests, who incite the mob to stone a woman to death.

The Repin rooms

Rooms 33–35.

Ilya Repin (1844–1930) was a late recruit to the Wanderers who subsequently became the foremost realist painter of his generation. Apprenticed at an early age to an icon workshop, he was later trained at the Academy, where he produced prize-winning student works such as the Russian Museum's *Christ Raising the Daughter of Jairus*, *The Negro Woman* and *Leave-taking of a Recruit*. However, the painting that made him famous was *Barge-haulers on the Volga*, a study in human drudgery and degradation that became an icon for the Populist movement and was later praised by Lenin as brilliant propaganda.

From room 35 a doorway leads into the annexe described on p.163.

Repin's portraits of the composers Glazunov and Rimsky-Korsakov are worthy of note, and the political changes in Russia have made it possible at last to display the full-length portrait of Nicholas II, albeit a laughably bad painting. However, Repin's reputation is quickly restored by his lively historical work, *The Zaporozhe Cossacks Writing a Mocking Letter to the Sultan*, in which swarthy warriors compose a reply to Sultan Mohammed IV's ultimatum – a lavishly detailed painting that took over twelve years to complete.

After the Revolution, Repin retired to his house in Karelia, now a delightful museum (see p.384).

Lastly, in room 54 (off the Surikov section – see below) hangs Repin's *Ceremonial Meeting of the State Council, 7 May 1901*, a vast work that required scores of preliminary studies. The councillors are painted like a still life, while Nicholas II is reduced to insignificance in the Grand Hall of the Mariinskiy Palace.

Surikov and Kuindzhi

During the 1880s, Russian historical painting adopted a form of Slavic mysticism, the leading exponent of which was Siberian-born **Vasily Surikov** (1846–1916), who studied at the Academy and was influenced by Alexander Ivanov. After his *Morning of the Execution of the Streltsy* (in the Tretyakov Gallery), Surikov is best known for the huge canvases here (room 36), particularly *Yermak's Conquest of Siberia*, which depicts the Cossacks storming across the Irtysh to smash the Tatar hordes in 1595. After the death of his wife, Surikov retreated to Siberia, but in 1891 resumed his career with *Taking the Snow Fortress by Storm*. Take a look also at *Suvorov Crossing the Alps*, in which the army seems to be tobogganing down the mountain like a group of excited schoolboys.

Rooms 37 and 38 are mainly devoted to the works of **Arkhip Kuindzhi** (1841–1910), originally part of the Wanderers group but increasingly distant from them as his works made ever greater use of colour as a symbolic element, as in *Moonlight on the River Dnieper* – a tendency taken to its extreme in the works of his pupil Nikolai Roerich (see p.166).

The Rossi Wing

Returning to room 35, you can branch off into a part of the Rossi Wing whose exhibits offer a rapid survey of the different trends in late nineteenth-century Russian art. **Room 49** (access via rooms 41 & 47), a long corridor running parallel to the annexe rooms, holds a changing display of watercolours and drawings from the second half of the nineteenth century.

Starting in room 39 you'll find a display of works by **Vasily Vereshchagin**. Like many artists in Europe at the time, Vereshchagin was drawn by the Orient and its mysticism, a fascination that's clearly felt in large canvases such as *Imperial Tombs at Jerusalem*.

Other artists, such as **Nikolai Kasalkin,** continued their subdued social protest. The gentle pity of his *Gleaning Coal in an Abandoned Pit* (room 40) contrasts strongly with the raucousness of **Konstantin Melarsky**'s *Booths on Admiralty Square* (further on in room 42), in which the element of social satire takes a back seat to the pleasure of simply depicting the hustle and bustle of a nineteenth-century fair. The Slavic fantasies of **Viktor Vasnetsov** (1846–1926), a priest's son who quit the seminary to apprentice himself to a lithographer and later won a place at the Academy, are superbly represented in room 41 by *Scythians and Slavs Fighting* and *A Russian Knight at the Crossway*.

Renewed interest in "old" Russia, before the westernizing – and, as many saw it, corrupting – influence of Peter the Great, inspired artists like **Apollinary Vasnetsov** (room 43) to produce paintings on the theme of seventeenth-century Moscow. **Andrey Ryabushkin** (1861–1904) even echoed the characteristics of *parsuna* painting (see p.156) in his depictions of a *Seventeenth-century Merchant Family*, and in showing the mud and filth of *Seventeenth-century Moscow on a Festival Day* (room 45).

Room 47 is devoted entirely to **Filip Malyavin** (1869–1940), a lay brother at the Russian monastery on Mount Athos in Greece before he began painting compositions of peasant women with billowing scarves and skirts, their faces and limbs emerging from flat, brilliantly coloured planes, more suggestive of Gauguin or Klimt than anything else. Also on show are some of his more traditional portraits, such as those of the artist Anna Ostroumova and the critic Ilya Grabar.

Room 48 contains a small **shop**, from where you can continue straight ahead into the Benois Wing or turn to the left for the exhibition of Russian folk art on the west side of the Rossi Wing.

Folk art

Rooms I–X.

Traditional **Russian folk art** occupies ten rooms in the Rossi Wing. The objects on display here were part of everyday life in Russian villages and many had a mystical significance.

Room I contains traditional *naboyki*, or block-printed indigo textiles and glazed tiles of the type often used on seventeenth- and eighteenth-century buildings. Rooms II and III contain carved wooden objects, the latter room being dominated by the huge carved pediment of a peasant *izba* or cottage (1888). The rooms that follow are filled with the sort of things still produced by contemporary craftsmen, such as toys, lace, ceramics and lacquerware, plus a huge display of *Khokloma* painted wooden cups and plates.

The Benois Wing

The Benois Wing has the same official opening hours as the main building, but doesn't always keep to them.

The **Benois Wing** holds the museum's collection of late nineteenth- and twentieth-century Russian art – the permanent collection is housed on the second floor, while the first floor is given over entirely to temporary exhibitions of contemporary Russian and world art. Bear in mind that some of the better-known avant-garde works in the permanent collection are often out on loan to museums around the world and may not be on show when you visit.

To reach the second floor of the Benois Wing from the main building, head along the corridor from the shop (room 48) on the first floor and up the staircase; to reach the first floor, you need to go outside and enter the Benois Wing's own entrance on the Griboedov embankment. Temporary exhibitions on the first floor require separate tickets, available from the *kassa* at the Griboedov embankment entrance, where you can also buy tickets to all other exhibitions in the Russian Museum.

Abramtsevo artists and the World of Art

The Russian Museum

Rooms 66–71.

Entering the Benois Wing galleries on the second floor throws you straight into the world of **Mikhail Vrubel** (1856–1910), whose impact on Russian art was comparable to that of Cézanne in the West. He was a regular at Abramtsevo, the Moscow country estate of wealthy merchant Savva Mamontov and home to a colony of Russian revival artists.

Vrubel suffered from instability and intense introspection, as reflected in his cabalistic and erotic works, such as *Demon in Flight* (room 66) from his series of "Demon" paintings. The next room (67) is dominated by the religious member of the Wanderers, **Mikhail Nesterov** (1862–1942), whose quiet, mystical paintings, such as *Holy Russia*, contrast with Vrubel's passionate and swirling colours. During the Soviet period, Nesterov's religious paintings were not appreciated and he directed his energies and spiritual interest to portraiture.

In room 68, the Symbolist atmosphere is interrupted by works from the so-called **Silver Age** – the period of early twentieth-century Russian art associated with followers of the World of Art movement (see p.219) and Serge Diaghilev, the editor of the *World of Art* magazine who later became better known for his Ballets Russes. **Léon Bakst** (1866–1924), who designed many of Nijinsky's costumes for the Ballets Russes, is represented here by a startling portrait of Diaghilev. The **World of Art** movement supported "art for art's sake" and produced highly decorative works which often recalled the lightness and daintiness of painters such as Watteau; the most obvious examples are Konstantin Somov's eighteenth-century fancies, or Alexandre Benois' *Commedia dell'arte*.

The work of **Viktor Borisov-Musatov** (1870–1905) exemplified the Symbolist movement, although most of his paintings on display here (room 69), such as *Self-portrait with his Sister*, are more Impressionistic – his moodier, Symbolist paintings can be seen at the Tretyakov Gallery in Moscow. Also in room 69 are several works by **Alexander Golovin** (1863–1930), a theatrical designer who worked at Abramtsevo and with Diaghilev – note particularly his theatrical portrait of Fyodor Chaliapin as Boris Godunov.

Valentin Serov (1865–1911) was largely brought up at Abramtsevo and was one of the most technically accomplished artists of his time. He painted many society portraits, including one in room 70 of Princess Zinaida Yusupova, mother of Felix Yusupov, Rasputin's murderer. Serov's later portraits, such as that of *Ida Rubenstein* in room 71, were more affected by contemporary artistic developments.

Roerich, Petrov-Vodkin and others

Rooms 72–77.

Rooms 72–77 of the Benois Wing contain a hotchpotch of works left over from various exhibitions. In rooms 72 and 73 you can see the pre-revolutionary work of several artists who were somewhat unlikely darlings of the Soviet period. These include **Boris Kustodiev** (1878–1927), who painted fleshy merchants' wives and bourgeois holidays (he turned to producing revolutionary celebrations after 1917), and **Zinaida Serebriakova** (1884–1967), whose work has an independent, brash feel to it that was to influence Soviet art through to the 1970s and mark her out as a proto-feminist.

Nikolai Roerich (1874–1947) was passionately interested in archeology and the Orient. His Symbolist use of saturated colour was first applied to subjects from Russian history, such as *Prince Igor's Campaign* (room 74), and later to Oriental mysticism, particularly after he went to live in India. The works of the **Blue Rose** group in the next room seem pale in comparison, dominated by soft blues and greens, as exemplified by Pavel Kuznetsov's *In the Steppes*, and favouring limpidity of colour over intensity, as in *Sheep Shearing* by Martiros Saryan (1880–1972).

A changing selection of works from the Russian avant-garde is displayed in rooms 78–80.

Room 76 includes the work of **Kuzma Petrov-Vodkin** (1878–1939), an artist who remained independent of many of the groups which came and went during the first decade of the century. His theories on composition and spatial construction of the picture surface were highly influential on Soviet painters well into the 1970s, while his pre-revolutionary paintings made him popular with the authorities, at least until the rise of Socialist Realism.

Nathan Altman (1889–1970) is best known for his portrait of the poetess Anna Akhmatova which hangs in room 77. Also notable in this room is the Expressionist portrait of the stage director Vsevolod Meyerhold by V. Grigoriev.

Kandinsky

Vasily Kandinsky (1866–1944) spent much of his artistic career in Munich, where with Franz Marc he launched the *Blaue Reiter* (Blue Rider) group, which dealt a deathblow to European naturalism. Kandinsky believed in abstraction from nature and the spiritualization of art; each colour was thought to have a "corresponding vibration of the human soul". Although his theories greatly influenced many artists, in 1920 the Institute of Artistic Culture rejected them as too "subjective" and Kandinsky left Russia to take up a post at the Weimar Bauhaus. Happily, the Russian Museum retains many of his *Impressions* and *Improvisations* – two series of works expressing Kandinsky's inner spiritual feelings – although they are not on display at the time of writing.

Primitivism and Rayonism

In the years before the outbreak of war in 1914, Russian art was in ferment. Moscow led the way with movements akin to the *Blaue Reiter* and Cubism. The leading exponents of what became known as Primitivism were **Natalya Goncharova** (1881–1962) and **Mikhail Larionov** (1881–1964), both of whom quit the Jack of Diamonds movement in 1911 to form a new group, the Donkey's Tail. Goncharova asserted that all art was dead or decadent, except in Russia; that Picasso was a fraud and Cubism was old hat. Larionov took to Italian Futurism and launched a new style called **Rayonism**, whose manifesto declared that the genius of the age consisted of "trousers, jackets, shoes, tramways, buses, aeroplanes, railways, magnificent ships . . ." In Rayonist pictures rays of light break the object up, scatter it across the picture surface, creating a sense of movement, progression and absence of artificial stillness. The Russian Museum owns Goncharova's *Sunflowers and Peasants* and *The Cyclist*, and Larionov's *Rayonist Landscape* and *A Corner of the Garden*.

The Russian Museum

Futurism, Suprematism and Constructivism
Futurism is a catch-all term for the explosion of artistic styles and theories between 1910 and 1920. Early Futurists, such as the Burlyuk brothers and Mayakovsky, were out to shock – the Futurist manifesto was entitled *A Slap in the Face of Public Taste*. More cerebral was **Kazimir Malevich** (1878–1935), whose Cubo-Futurism – influenced by the bold lines of Russian icons and peasant woodcuts – evolved into what he termed **Suprematism**, the "art of pure sensation". The Russian Museum has 136 works by Malevich, ranging from geometric canvases like *Black Circle* and *Suprematism: Yellow and Black* to the figurative *Red Cavalry*. Also look out for *Abstract Compositions* by **Olga Rozanova** (1886–1918), whose minimalism was later applied to ceramics and fabrics for the masses (now, ironically, collectors' items).

Malevich's rival for ascendancy over the avant-garde movement was **Vladimir Tatlin** (1885–1953), whose early paintings, such as *The Sailor* (probably a self-portrait), gave little hint of what was to come. Having anticipated Dadaism with his junk collages, Tatlin experimented with theatre design and the "Culture of Materials". What came to be called **Constructivism** owed much to his collaboration with the director Meyerhold and the painters **Lyubov Popova** (1889–1924) and **Nadezhda Udaltsova** (1885–1961). Much of their conceptual work was never realized: Tatlin's glider, *Letatlin*, never left the ground, while his *Monument to the Third International* – intended to be over 396m high and revolve on its axis – got a dusty response from Lenin. The Russian Museum has the remains of Tatlin's model of the monument and Popova's *Seated Figure*.

Agitprop and Socialist Realism
Many artists threw themselves into the Revolution and produced what became known as **agitprop**, or "agitational propaganda". Posters became the new medium, brilliantly exploited by **Vladimir Lebedev** (1891–1967), **Alexander Rodchenko** (1891–1956) and the proto-punk poet **Mayakovsky** (see p.234), much of whose work

promoted subjects such as public health, literacy and recruitment for the Red Army. The best-known example of agitprop is *Beat the Whites with the Red Wedge* by **El Lissitzky** (1890–1941); less ephemeral were paintings like *Formula of the Petrograd Proletariat* – a masterpiece by **Pavel Filonov** (1883–1941), whose complex theories inspired generations of followers – and the work of Kuzma Petrov-Vodkin (see p.166).

By the 1920s the avant-garde movement was divided between those who saw art as a spiritual activity which, by becoming useful, ceased to exist, and those who insisted that artists must become technicians to bring "art into life" for the benefit of the masses. The debate raged on until Stalin put an end to it all by making **Socialist Realism** obligatory in 1932. Its principles, as articulated by Stalin's mouthpiece Andrey Zhdanov, were *partiinost*, *ideinost* and *narodnost* (Party character, socialist content and national roots); its chief exponents were **Isaak Brodsky** (1884–1939), responsible for such works as *Lenin in the Smolniy*, and **Alexander Gerasimov** (1881–1963), to whom the world is indebted for *Stalin at the XVIth Congress of the Communist Party.*

Hermitage	Эрмитаж
Russian Museum	Русский музей

Chapter 4

Vasilevskiy Island

Buffeted by storms from the Gulf of Finland, **Vasilevskiy Island** (Vasilevskiy ostrov) cleaves the River Neva into its Bolshaya and Malaya branches, forming a strategic wedge whose eastern tip – or **Strelka** – is as much a part of St Petersburg's waterfront as the Winter Palace or Admiralty. The Strelka's Rostral Columns and former stock exchange (now the Naval Museum) are vivid reminders that the city's port and commercial centre were once located here, while another, more enduring aspect of Vasilevskiy's erstwhile importance is the intellectual heritage bequeathed by St Petersburg's **University**, bolstered by a clutch of **museums**, including Peter the Great's infamous Kunstkammer, or "chamber of curiosities".

Originally, Peter envisaged making the island the centre of his capital. The first governor of St Petersburg, Alexander Menshikov, was an early resident (his **Menshikov Palace** is now the oldest building on the island) and Peter compelled other rich landowners and merchants to settle here. By 1726 the island had ten streets and over a thousand inhabitants, but wilderness still predominated and wolves remained a menace for decades to come. Living on the island also entailed hazardous crossings by sailing boat, as Peter had banned the use of rowing boats in order to instil a love of sailing, but unfortunately the ex-ferrymen made poor sailors. Moreover, Vasilevskiy Island became isolated from the mainland whenever a storm blew up or the Neva was choked with ice, destroying any hope of the island becoming the centre of St Petersburg.

Although Peter's plan for a network of canals was thwarted by Menshikov, who had them built so narrow as to be useless, their layout determined the grid of **avenues** and **lines** (see box on p.172) within which subsequent development occurred. Politically, the proximity of factories and workers' slums to the university's student quarter fostered local militancy during the revolutions of 1905 and 1917. In Soviet times, the western side of the island was extensively redeveloped, starting with the **Gavan** district and the **Sea Terminal**, while the leaden gigantism of the Brezhnev era is epitomized by the **Primorskiy district** around the *Hotel Pribaltiyskaya*.

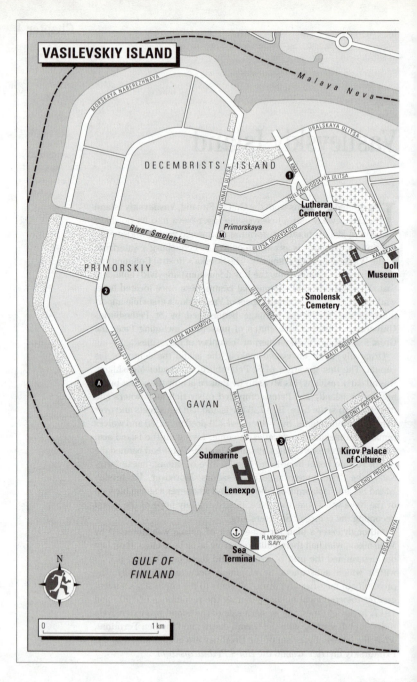

VASILEVSKIY ISLAND

Malaya Neva

MORSKAYA NABEREZHNAYA

DECEMBRISTS' ISLAND

URALSKAYA ULITSA

ZHELEZNOVODSKAYA ULITSA

NALICHNAYA ULITSA

PR. KIMA

Lutheran Cemetery

River Smolenka

Primorskaya Ⓜ

ULITSA ODOEVSKOVO

KAMSKAYA

PRIMORSKIY

Doll Museum

Smolensk Cemetery

ULITSA BERINGA

ULITSA NAKHIMOVA

ULITSA KORABLESTROITELEY

MALLY PROSPEKT

A

GAVAN

SREDNIY PROSPEKT

NALICHNAYA ULITSA

Kirov Palace of Culture

Submarine

BOLSHOY PROSPEKT

Lenexpo

KOSAYA LINIYA

⚓ Sea Terminal

PL. MORSKOY SLAVY

GULF OF FINLAND

N

0 ——————— 1 km

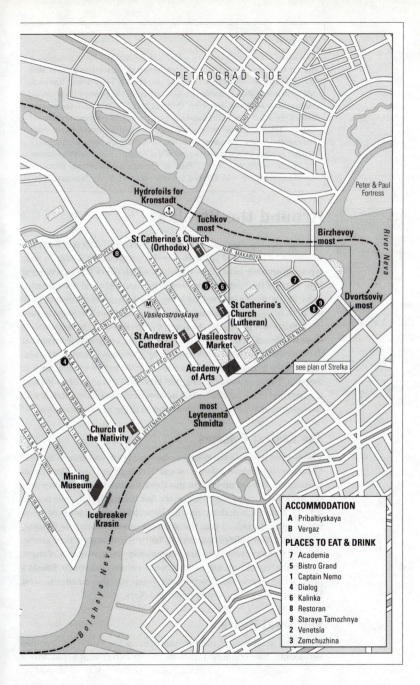

ST PETERSBURG

Around the Strelka

Although you can reach the **Strelka** by minibus (#T-129 & #T-147) or
trolleybus (#1, #7 & #10) from Nevskiy prospekt, it's better to walk
across **Dvortsoviy most** (Palace Bridge), which offers fabulous views of
both banks of the Neva. Built between 1908 and 1914 and reconstructed
in the 1970s, the 250-metre-long bridge has the largest liftable span of all
the Neva bridges – an amazing sight when it rises to allow ships to pass
through late at night. By day, however, the Strelka steals the show with its
Rostral Columns and Stock Exchange building, an ensemble created at
the beginning of the nineteenth century by Thomas de Thomon, who also
designed the granite embankments and cobbled ramps leading down to
the Neva. This area was a working port between 1733 and 1885 – it's now
the favoured place for newlyweds to come and toast their nuptials with
champagne, after having their photos taken at the Bronze Horseman.

The Rostral Columns

Designed as navigational beacons, the twin brick-and-stucco **Rostral
Columns** (Rostralnye kolonny) stand 32m high and once blazed with
burning hemp oil at night; now gas-fired, the torches are lit only during festivals, such as Navy Day on the last Sunday in July (see box on
p.174). Their form derives from the Imperial Roman custom of erecting columns decorated with the sawn-off prows, or *rostrae* (beaks),
of Carthaginian galleys captured in battle – although it is of course
Russian naval victories that are honoured by these Rostral Columns.
Crumbling figures at the base of each column personify Russia's
great trade rivers: the Dnieper and Volga (on the column nearest
Dvortsoviy most), and the Volkhov and Neva.

The Naval Museum

A sculptural tableau of Neptune harnessing the Baltic's tributaries
surmounts the columned facade of St Petersburg's old Stock

Exchange (Birzha), a monumental pile modelled on the temple of Paestum in southern Italy. Made redundant by the Bolshevik Revolution, the building was later turned into the **Naval Museum** (Voenno-Morskoy muzey). From the **entrance** around the left side of its broad stairway, head upstairs, past a ballistic missile and statues of Red sailors, to see the host of model ships in the former exchange hall. The prize exhibits here are the *botik* (boat) in which Peter learned to sail – a vessel dubbed the "Grandfather of the Russian Navy" – and Russia's oldest surviving submarine, designed by Dzhevetsky 1881. Exhibits recounting the disaster at Tsushima Bay (see box on p.174) are relegated to the back of the hall, while the surrounding rooms chart events during the Revolution and World War II (with mug shots of the *Potemkin* mutineers and Kronstadt sailors) and conclude with the navy's postwar expansion. A collection of carved figureheads from eighteenth-century vessels fills the staircase up to the top floor, which is used for temporary exhibitions.

Around the Strelka

The Naval Museum is open Wed–Sun 10.30am–5.30 pm, closed the last Thurs of the month; $2. Guided tours in English ($11 per group) can be arranged on ☎328 25 02.

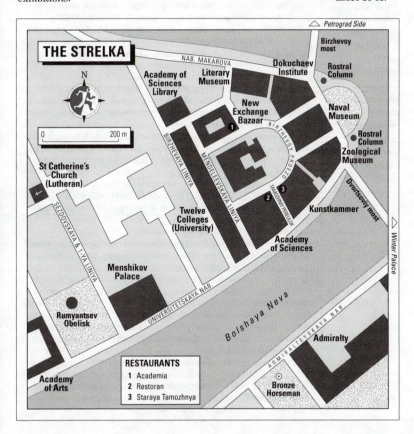

THE STRELKA

N

0   200 m

△ Petrograd Side

NAB. MAKAROVA

Academy of Sciences Library

Literary Museum

Dokuchaev Institute

Birzhevoy most

Rostral Column

New Exchange Bazaar

1

BIRZHEVOY PROEZD

Naval Museum

Rostral Column

Zoological Museum

St Catherine's Church (Lutheran)

BIRZHEVAYA LINIYA

MENDELEEVSKAYA LINIYA

3

2

TAMOZHNIY PEREULOK

Kunstkammer

Dvortsovy most

△ Winter Palace

SEZDOVSKAYA & 1-YA LINIYA

Twelve Colleges (University)

Academy of Sciences

Menshikov Palace

UNIVERSITETSKAYA NAB.

Bolshaya Neva

Rumyantsev Obelisk

ADMIRALTEYSKAYA NAB.

Admiralty

RESTAURANTS
1 Academia
2 Restoran
3 Staraya Tamozhnya

Academy of Arts

Bronze Horseman

Around the Strelka

Other maritime attractions on Vasilevskiy Island include the icebreaker Krasin (see p.181) at naberezhnaya Leytenanta Shmidta, and the D-2 Narodovolets submarine near the Sea Terminal (see p.183).

The Russian navy

Before Peter the Great founded the **Russian navy** in 1696, the country had no seafaring tradition. Initially composed of one ship and three admirals, the navy developed by trial and error using techniques imported from Holland and England, where the tsar had studied shipbuilding. At first, the emphasis was on building galleys rather than heavier men o' war – a strategy that paid off when the lighter Russian boats outmanoeuvred the Swedish fleet in the shallow waters off **Hangö** in 1714. But substandard ships and seamanship remained a problem until the reign of Catherine the Great, when in 1770 Russia won its first major sea battle at **Chesma Bay** in the Aegean.

Like its contemporary British counterpart, the Tsarist navy relied on the press gang and savage discipline, and by the end of the nineteenth century its vessels had become outmoded and its leadership incompetent. In 1904, the Pacific Fleet was decimated by a surprise Japanese attack on **Port Arthur**, on Russia's Pacific coast. Ordered to sail halfway around the world to avenge this, the Baltic Fleet almost caused a war with Britain by firing on an English fishing fleet in dense fog, believing it to be the Japanese navy. When the Russian fleet finally arrived in Japanese waters seven months later, it was annihilated in two days of fighting at **Tsushima Bay**.

Henceforth, the navy was more noted for its **mutinies**, starting with that of the crew of the battleship *Potemkin* of the Black Sea Fleet in 1905. Sailors of the Baltic Fleet played a major role in the revolutions of 1917, and in 1921 they came out against the Bolsheviks, who crushed the **Kronstadt revolt** with characteristic ruthlessness. Essentially limited to an ancillary role during **World War II**, the navy remained a poor relation of the other services until the 1970s, when it underwent a massive, hubristic expansion under **Admiral Gorshkov**, who dreamt of projecting Soviet naval power across the globe.

The demise of the USSR saw the Soviet navy carved up between Russia, the Ukraine and Azerbaijan – the Russian navy's bitter wrangles with the Ukraine over the Crimean Fleet were followed by the galling sight of Ukrainian and NATO warships on joint exercises in the Black Sea. This gave Russia's naval chiefs an ironclad excuse not to scale down their operations, something they achieved – despite the naval budget being slashed during the Yeltsin years – by not paying or feeding sailors and skimping on maintenance and technical support. The resulting decline in safety standards and morale made a tragedy inevitable.

The **Kursk disaster** happened only sixty miles from the headquarters of the Northern Fleet on the Kola Peninsula, shortly after posters had appeared in Moscow hailing the bid by the High Command of the Russian navy to take over the Strategic Rocket Forces with the slogan *A Mighty Fleet for Russia's Glory* – presenting the ironic spectacle of a navy pursuing grandiose expansionist plans at a time when it was unable even to keep its own submarines afloat. Events destroyed these illusions as surely as they condemned the *Kursk*'s crew to death and caused universal outrage in Russia, where the media did its job properly for a change.

Meanwhile, the **Baltic Fleet** remains based in St Petersburg, a city with three naval colleges and shipyards galore. In the run up to **Navy Day** (last Sun in July), battleships and submarines are anchored mid-river in the heart of the city, before the festival starts with a regatta and ends with fireworks and drunken sailors roaming Nevskiy prospekt, while the Rostral Columns blaze after dark.

Around naberezhnaya Makarova

Around the Strelka

The Strelka's two warehouses and customs building were all converted to academic use early this century, when the Northern Warehouse became the Dokuchaev Institute for Soil Sciences and the Customs House on naberezhnaya Makarova was taken over by the Institute of Russian Literature. Familiarly known as the "Pushkin House" (Pushkinskiy dom), the latter is now home to the **Literary Museum**, founded in 1905. Its four rooms contain period furniture – two of the more famous pieces being Gogol's armchair and Tolstoy's desk. There are also portraits and personal effects, including the poet Lermontov's cavalry sabre and Tolstoy's shirt and boots, but their actual manuscripts are seldom exhibited.

The Literary Museum is currently closed; call ☎ 328 05 02 for the latest information.

It's worth turning the corner to see the **New Exchange Bazaar**, a scaled-down version of the Gostiniy dvor, built by Quarenghi in the early nineteenth century. Once a bustling market, it's now a service depot belonging to the Academy of Sciences Library (Biblioteka Akademii Nauk, or BAN), which stands over the road on the corner with Birzhevaya liniya. The library itself contains around nine million volumes, including *The Apostle*, Russia's first printed book, dating from 1564, as well as Peter the Great's own library and schoolbooks belonging to the poet and scientist Mikhail Lomonosov.

The Zoological Museum

Of more popular appeal than the library is the **Zoological Museum** (Zoologicheskiy muzey), located in the Southern Warehouse on Universitetskaya naberezhnaya (University Embankment) facing Dvortsoviy most. Founded in 1832, the museum has one of the finest collections of its kind in the world, with over one hundred thousand specimens, including a set of stuffed animals that once belonged to Peter the Great (among them his dog Titan and his warhorse Lizetta). Upstairs, you're confronted by the skeleton of a blue whale, along with models of polar bears and other arctic life. The side hall traces the evolution of vertebrates and invertebrates (note the giant Kamchatka crab), as well as mammals, with realistic tableaux of stuffed animals showing each species in its habitat.

The Zoological Museum is open 11am–6pm, closed Fri; $1. Tours in English ($9 per group) by arrangement on ☎ 328 01 12.

The museum's beloved prehistoric **mammoths** are accompanied by models and photographs detailing their excavation – the most evocative display shows the discovery of a 44,000-year-old mammoth in the permafrost of Yakutsia in 1903. Other finds in 1961 and 1977 (the latter a baby mammoth) are recalled with photographs, as the actual animals themselves are in museums elsewhere. The top floor of the museum is devoted to insects.

The Kunstkammer

Even more alluring than the Zoological Museum is the **Kunstkammer** next door, instantly recognizable by its tower and entered from an alley to the west. Founded by Peter in 1714, its name (meaning "art chamber" in German) was an attempt to dignify his fascination for curiosities and freaks. Forming the centrepiece of the collection were two thousand preparations by the Dutch embalmer Frederik Ruysch and an ethnographic "chamber of wonders", also purchased in Holland. In Russia, Peter offered rewards for "human monsters" and unknown birds and animals, with a premium for especially odd ones. Dead specimens had to be preserved in vinegar or vodka (for which their original owners were reimbursed by the Imperial pharmacy), while, to attract visitors, each guest received a glass of vodka. Originally, the Kunstkammer even had live exhibits, such as a man with only two digits on each limb, and a hermaphrodite (who escaped). After the Revolution, it's said, an impoverished aristocrat found work there, and secretly drained off the spirit in which the curios were preserved to sell to unsuspecting drinkers.

The museums are open 11am–4.45pm, closed Thurs & last Wed of the month; $1.75. English-language guided tours ($9 per group) of the Museum of Anthropology and Ethnography can be booked on ☎328 14 12.

The building now unites three establishments under one roof (all have the same opening hours and are covered by one ticket). Continuing the Kunstkammer's work in a contemporary vein is the **Museum of Anthropology and Ethnography** (Muzey Antropologii i Etnografii), displaying everything from Balinese puppets to Inuit kayaks and including some lovely dioramas of native village life. Africa and the Americas are dealt with on the first floor and the section upstairs covers Southeast Asia, the Antipodes and Melanesia. Many of the exhibits are beautifully crafted, and their sheer diversity makes this a fascinating museum, despite the fact that the captions are only in Russian (note, however, that guided tours in English can be booked in advance, along with specialized tours on subjects such as tribal initiation ceremonies). The museum also plays host to contemporary art **exhibitions and events**; its **Web site** (*www.kunstkamera.ru*) has lots of historical facts but little up-to-date information.

In the round hall between the Japanese theatre and the Africa section, a selection of Peter's curios and grotesqueries is all that remains of the **Kunstkammer's original collections**, though it still manages to excite wonder and disgust. Among the pickled specimens on display are Siamese twins, a two-faced man and a two-headed calf. Although the outsized penis and the skin of Peter's favourite giant, "Bourgeois", are no longer exhibited, you can still see the giant's skeleton. Also shown are surgical and dental instruments, and teeth pulled by the tsar himself, a keen amateur dentist who kept records of his victims, among them "a person who made tablecloths" and "a fast-walking messenger".

A tiny staircase off the Bali and Micronesia gallery, which is directly above the Kunstkammer, leads to the **Lomonosov Museum**, devoted to the polymath Mikhail Lomonosov (1711–65). The son of a fisherman from Archangel, Lomonosov codified Russian grammar, wrote verses, studied minerals and the heavens, and anticipated Dalton's theory of the atomic structure of matter in his *Elementa Chymiae*

Mathematica (1741). He also helped design the **Great Academic Globe**, a kind of eighteenth-century planetarium. Spectators sat inside the globe, which rotated on its axis, causing the planets and stars painted on the inner surface to revolve. Stolen from Tsarskoe Selo during World War II, the globe was found at Lübeck in 1947 and returned to the Kunstkammer, where it now occupies a room in the tower. Unfortunately, repair work on the tower means that the Globe won't be accessible to visitors in the foreseeable future.

The Academy of Sciences

The next building along Universitetskaya naberezhnaya houses the **Academy of Sciences** (Akademiya nauk), the idea for which, like so many Russian institutions, was first mooted by Peter (who asked the German scientist and philosopher Leibnitz to devise a constitution), but only formally established after his death. In 1934, the academy's administrative functions were transferred to Moscow, leaving the Leningrad branch in charge of various institutes, the Zoological Museum and the library. Its austerely Neoclassical headquarters – built by Quarenghi between 1784 and 1787 – feature a mosaic of the Battle of Poltava by Lomonosov on the upper landing of the grand staircase, which can be glimpsed from the downstairs lobby (you probably won't be allowed any further). A **statue of Lomonosov** stands on Mendeleevskaya liniya, just beyond the academy.

The Twelve Colleges and the University

The western side of Mendeleevskaya liniya is flanked by the second-oldest building on the island, the **Twelve Colleges** (Dvenadtsat kollegii), its 400-metre-long facade now painted sienna red with white facings, as in Petrine times. Executed by Trezzini, the building was designed to epitomize Peter's idea of a modern, efficient bureaucracy: the separate doors to the dozen different departments signified their autonomy and the uniform facade their common purpose. He was later enraged to discover that Menshikov had tampered with the plans, reducing the size of the buildings so as not to intrude on his own estates.

The *kollegii* were eventually replaced by ministries across the river, and in 1819 the building was given to **St Petersburg University** (Universitet Sankt-Peterburga). A bastion of free thinking and radicalism in Tsarist times, it educated many famous names in science, literature and politics. It was here that **Dimitry Mendeleyev** (1834–1907) worked out the Periodic Table of Elements in 1869 – his study has been turned into a small **museum** preserving his laboratory equipment and personal effects. The rector's house was the childhood home of the Symbolist poet Alexander Blok (who married Mendeleyev's daughter), while Alexander Popov sent what was arguably the world's first radio signal from the university labs (see p.119). Other alumni include Nikolai Chernyshevsky, author of the

The Mendeleyev Museum is open Mon–Fri 11am–4pm; $2.

Utopian revolutionary novel *What is to be Done?*; Alexander Ulyanov, hanged for plotting to kill Alexander III; his brother Vladimir Ilyich – better known as Lenin – who graduated with honours in law in 1891; and Russia's president, Vladimir Putin, who joined the KGB after completing his law degree in 1975.

The university's students were at the forefront of nineteenth-century protests, and during the 1905 Revolution thousands of workers gathered here every evening to seek news and leadership. In Stalinist times, scores of students and staff were sent to the camps and, adding insult to injury, the university was later named after Andrei Zhdanov, former Leningrad Party boss and scourge of the intelligentsia. Having dropped Zhdanov's name in the Gorbachev era, the university considered for a while whether to adopt Peter the Great or academician and dissident Andrei Sakharov as its namesake – but finally the decision was taken to stay simply with "St Petersburg".

To the Menshikov Palace

Continuing westwards along the river-front down Universitetskaya naberezhnaya, you'll come to the former barracks of the **First Cadet Corps**, which trained the sons of the aristocracy for a military career. Cadets usually joined between the ages of 10 and 14 – a contemporary report states that "on one occasion, when formed in square and charged by cavalry, their little hearts failed them and they took to their heels in all directions". Their summer manoeuvres were observed by the tsar, who took a great interest in his "Lilliputian regiments".

In July 1917 the barracks hosted the First Congress of Workers' and Soldiers' Deputies, in which only ten percent of the deputies were Bolsheviks. When a speaker claimed that there wasn't a party willing to take control, Lenin shouted from the floor, "There is! No party has the right to refuse power and our party does not refuse it. It is ready to assume power at any time." In honour of his impudence, a nearby street is named Sezdovskaya (Congress) liniya.

The Menshikov Palace is open Tues–Sun 10.30am–4.30 pm; $4.50. There are free guided tours in Russian every 30min; free tours in English, French & German can be booked in advance on ☎323 11 12.

The Menshikov Palace

The chief reason to walk this far is to visit the **Menshikov Palace** (Menshikovskiy dvorets), a gabled yellow-and-white building beside the old First Cadet Corps. Built in the early eighteenth century, it was the first residential structure on Vasilevskiy Island and the finest one in the city, surpassing even Peter's Summer Palace – the tsar had no objections, however, preferring to entertain at the Menshikov Palace, which was furnished to suit his tastes. Though not as sumptuous as the later Imperial palaces, it sports fine Petrine-era decor. The **entrance** is below street level, past the main portico.

On the first floor is the **kitchen** and a **dining room** furnished with tapestries. Objects on display include period costumes, plus a lathe and tools belonging to Peter. The statues in the Italianate hallway were imported from Europe by Menshikov in his desire to emulate

Peter, and the stairway bears their entwined monograms. The rooms upstairs commence with the **secretary's quarters**, featuring plans of Kraków, Leyden and Utrecht, followed by two rooms faced with white and blue Dutch tiles. Family portraits and seascapes hang on red ribbons, as was the fashion at that time.

The room containing the German four-poster bed and brass foot-warmer served as a bedroom for the sister of Menshikov's wife, after which comes Menshikov's **Walnut Study**, decorated with gilded pilasters and a life-sized portrait of Peter. The study's mirrors were a bold innovation in eighteenth-century Russia, where prior to Peter's time they had been anathematized by the Orthodox Church.

The stuccoed and gilt-chandeliered **Grand Hall** once hosted a "Dwarves' Wedding" for Peter's entertainment, with little tables in the centre set with miniature cutlery. Though the dwarves' drunk-en cavorting provoked hilarity, Menshikov regretted that they couldn't fire a tiny cannon specially cast for the occasion, for fear of disturbing his only son, lying ill elsewhere in the palace. The boy expired that night (which didn't stop Menshikov from cele-brating his own name day soon afterwards) and the dwarf bride later died in childbirth – marriages between dwarves were subse-quently forbidden.

Prince Menshikov

Of all the adventurers that staked their fortunes on Peter the Great, none was closer to the tsar than **Alexander Menshikov** (1673–1729). Humbly born (it was rumoured that he sold pies on the streets of Moscow as a child), Menshikov accompanied Peter on his Grand Tour of Europe in 1697. The tsar liked his enthusiasm for shipbuilding and carousing, and his artful blend of "servility, familiarity and impertinence": soon they were inseparable.

After helping to crush the *streltsy* mutiny, Menshikov was showered with favours and responsibilities, becoming commandant of Schlüsselburg and the first governor of St Petersburg. In 1703 he acquired a mistress whom Peter subsequently took a fancy to, married in secret and later crowned as Catherine I. The tsar addressed Menshikov as *Mein Herz* (My Heart), causing speculation that their relationship went "beyond hon-ourable affection". In any event, Peter tolerated Menshikov's vanity (exemplified by the latter's palace at Oranienbaum, which was grander than the tsar's) and persistent corruption, forgiving peculations that oth-ers would have paid for with their lives.

As Peter lay dying, Menshikov engineered Catherine's succession as empress, then had all charges pending against himself annulled. He con-tinued to flourish until Catherine's demise in 1727 when – accused of trea-son and fined 500,000 rubles – he was exiled to his Ukrainian estates by the boy-tsar Peter II, but allowed to depart with sixty wagon-loads of valu-ables. Less than a year later, however, Menshikov and his family were stripped of all their possessions and exiled to a remote Siberian village, where they died in poverty.

On the **embankment** outside the palace you can see the granite abutments of the old St Isaac's Bridge of 1729 – the first bridge across the Neva. The abutments supported a wooden pontoon bridge that had to be dismantled annually before the river froze and rebuilt after it thawed; it finally burned down in 1916.

West to the Krasin

Beyond the Menshikov Palace the sights are fewer and further apart, involving quite a bit of walking. Across Sezdovskaya and 1-ya liniya you come first to a shady park centred on the **Rumyantsev Obelisk**, commemorating the victories of Marshal Rumyantsev in the Russo–Turkish wars of 1768–74. Hewn from black granite and surmounted by a gilded orb and eagle, it was erected on Marsovo pole in 1799 and transferred to its present site in 1818.

The Academy of Arts and Pavlov Museum

On the western side of the park is the **Academy of Arts** (Akademiya khudozhestv), a huge mustard-coloured edifice built between 1764 and 1788 by Vallin de la Mothe and Alexander Kokoroniv. Students joined at the age of six and graduated at 21 and, like the university, the academy boasts an impressive roll call of graduates, including the architects Zakharov and Voronikhin; Pyotr Klodt, sculptor of the horses on the Anichkov Bridge; and the painters Karl Bryullov and Ilya Repin. Most of the building is now occupied by the Academic Repin Institute of Painting, Sculpture and Architecture, but the Russian Academy of Arts maintains a museum on the second and third floors, known as the **"Academic Circle"**. Among the many paintings on display are student works by Repin and Polonev. Diploma work by contemporary students is exhibited each year at the end of June in the grandiose Parade Hall, and periodic temporary exhibitions show works from the museum's storerooms, such as Sir Charles Barry's original designs for the Houses of Parliament in London.

The Academic Circle is open Wed & Thurs 11am–5pm; $4.25. Guided tours in Russian by arrangement on ☎323 35 78 or 323 64 96.

The embankment in front of the building is ennobled by two Egyptian **sphinxes**. Carved from Aswan granite and weighing 32 tonnes apiece, they were found at Luxor in the 1820s and brought to Russia in 1832. A hieroglyphic inscription identifies them with Pharaoh Amunhotep III (1417–1379 BC), "Son of Ra, ruler of Thebes, the builder of monuments rising to the sky like four pillars holding up the vault of the heavens".

It was just around the corner from the academy, on 4–5ya liniya, that the six-thousand-strong Vasilevskiy Island contingent of the workers' march on "Bloody Sunday" (see p.80) was confronted by soldiers and mounted police, who then charged the crowd. Students and workers began to arm themselves and erect barricades, which the authorities smashed with repeated volleys of rifle and cannon fire, killing and wounding hundreds.

Continuing down the embankment, the **Academicians' House** (Dom akademikov), on the corner with 6–7ya liniya, has provided permanent accommodation for more than eighty scientists and linguists over the 250 years since it was built. The **Pavlov Memorial Museum**, housed in the apartment (no. 11) where the Nobel Prize-winning physiologist Ivan Pavlov lived until his death in 1936, contains a miscellany of books, photos of experiments and personal possessions and is only likely to appeal to real enthusiasts.

Along naberezhnaya Leytenanta Shmidta

Between 1842 and 1850, the first permanent stone bridge across the Neva was erected near the Academicians' House and named after St Nicholas. Rebuilt and widened in the 1930s, the bridge's present name, **most Leytenanta Shmidta**, honours Lieutenant Pyotr Schmidt, who led a mutiny aboard the cruiser *Ochakov* during the 1905 Revolution and signalled to the tsar, "I assume command of the Southern Fleet. Schmidt."

In 1918, his name was also bestowed upon the embankment beyond – naberezhnaya Leytenanta Shmidta – where he attended the **Higher Naval College** at no. 17. The oldest in Russia, the college boasts of having trained Rimsky-Korsakov (before he decided to study music) and several admirals. Whereas tributes are also paid to Nakhimov (the defender of Sebastopol), Lazarev (co-leader of the 1820 Antarctic expedition) and Krusenstern (who circumnavigated the globe in 1803–6), a veil is drawn over Rozhestvensky (who led the Baltic Fleet to disaster at Tsushima Bay) and Kolchak (a White Army leader during the Civil War). A plaque recalls that Lenin delivered a lecture here in May 1917 entitled "War and Revolution". Two hundred metres further west is the Byzantine-style **Church of the Nativity**, whose swirly green domes lend a touch of glamour to the waterfront.

The Krasin and the Mining Museum

Some 500m further down-river from the Church of the Nativity (take trolleybus #37 or #63 from the corner of 8–9ya liniya along naberezhnaya Leytenanta Shmidta) is the **icebreaker Krasin**, a veteran of the Soviet "Conquest of the North", now granted honourable retirement by the embankment near 20–21ya liniya. Built for the tsar's navy and launched at Newcastle-upon-Tyne in England in 1917, it was at the forefront of the international mission to rescue Nobile's polar expedition in 1928, and was the only Soviet ship in the historic convoy to Murmansk, code-named PQ-15, which ran the gauntlet of Nazi U-boats in order to deliver vital war materials to the USSR. Today, it claims the distinction of being the world's only floating icebreaker museum, and hopes to find a new role as a tourist

West to the Krasin

The Pavlov Museum can only be viewed by prior arrangement on ☎323 72 34 (visiting times Sept–June Mon–Wed & Fri 11am–5pm). For more on Pavlov and his dogs, see p.206.

The Krasin *is open Tues–Fri 11am–6pm, Sat & Sun 10am–6pm; $2.*

West to the
Krasin

*The Mining
Museum is
open
Mon–Thurs &
Sun
11am–5.30pm,
closed last
Thurs of the
month; $0.50.*

cruiser. Meanwhile, its old steam engine is still functioning, and the ship's interior is a feast of antique redwood, bronze and cut glass, maintained with loving care.

The icebreaker is moored beside the Mining Institute (Gorniy institut), founded by Peter the Great, whose columned portico is flanked by statues of Pluto raping Proserpine and Hercules struggling with Antaeus. Inside, a **Mining Museum** exhibits samples of the earth's mineral wealth, with prize exhibits including a chunk of Ukrainian malachite weighing 1054kg, a copper nugget from Kazakhstan weighing 842kg, a quartz crystal weighing 800kg, and an iron meteorite that landed in Yenisey province in Siberia.

Bolshoy prospekt and the Sea Terminal

Vasilevskiy Island's main focus is the wide and shady **Bolshoy prospekt**, running 3.5km from Sezdovskaya liniya southwest to the Sea Terminal. Lined with a mixture of Art Nouveau town houses and 1960s apartment buildings, the nicest stretch is around the Vasileostrov Market, within walking distance of Vasileostrovskaya metro station or Universitetskaya naberezhnaya. You can also reach the prospekt on #10 trolleybus from Nevskiy prospekt.

From Sezdovskaya to 6–7ya liniya

The Sezdovskaya end of the prospekt is distinguished by the former Lutheran **Church of St Catherine** (Tserkov Svyatoy Yekateriny), a porticoed Neoclassical edifice that once catered to the island's German community and is now a recording studio, although the recording company that uses it, Melodiya, sponsors services and concerts in the church on Sundays. The **apartment building** at Bolshoy prospekt 6 was the scene of a well-known tragedy of the Blockade. Between December 1941 and May 1942, 11-year-old Tanya Savicheva recorded in her diary the deaths of her sister, grandmother, brother, uncles and mother – all from starvation. Tanya herself was evacuated, but died the following year. Her diary is now in the St Petersburg History Museum (see p.120).

*The market is
open Mon–Sat
8am–8pm; the
pharmacy,
Mon–Fri
8am–9pm, Sat
10am–6pm.*

Three blocks west of the church is **Vasileostrovskiy Market**, next door to which stands its eighteenth-century forerunner, the Andreevskiy rynok bazaar. Around the corner on 6–7ya liniya the turreted building at no. 16 is the **oldest pharmacy** in St Petersburg, established by Professor de Pohl and sons over 120 years ago – it's worth popping inside to see the elegant teak cabinets and engraved glass *kassa* (cash desk).

Opposite the market stands the **Cathedral of St Andrew** (Andreevskiy sobor), whose pink-and-white facade harbours a vaulted chapel containing a Baroque iconostasis (Sunday liturgy is at

10am). Just around the corner on 6–7ya liniya is the smaller **Church of the Three Holy Men** (tserkov Tryokh Svyatiteley), completed in 1760 – the same year that work commenced on the cathedral.

Around the Sea Terminal

From 20–21ya liniya onwards, the avenue is flanked by decaying factories and municipal depots, culminating in the **Sea Terminal** on ploshchad Morskoy slavy (Marine Glory Square), a moribund area except when there's a visiting cruise liner. It was enlivened for a while by the presence of foreign hotel ships, but in 1994 these sailed for home leaving the square to the trade exhibition firm, LenExpo, and the moribund **Hotel Morskaya** that squats above the terminal.

The only thing here of interest to visitors is a mothballed **submarine** – the *D-2 Narodovolets* – surreally perched above an inlet used by yachts. The only survivor of six "Dekabrist" class diesel submarines constructed at the Leningrad Baltic shipyards in the late 1920s, it saw active service with the Northern Fleet in the Bering and White seas and with the Baltic Fleet during World War II, before its retirement in 1956. It was rescued from the scrapyard and in 1994 opened as a branch of the Naval Museum dedicated to the submarine service; **guided tours** in Russian are conducted by an affable ex-nuclear submariner who – if the Cold War had turned hot – might have been instrumental in wiping your home town off the map.

The Narodovolets is open Wed–Sun 10am–5pm (entry by tour only; last one at 3.30pm), closed the last Fri of the month; $2.

The sub is divided into seven sections by watertight doors, each with a brass plaque showing the alphabet in Morse code, so that crewmen could communicate by knocking if the internal system failed. The **interior** is cramped, but much less than it would have been for the 53-man crew, as many of the bunk beds have since been removed. You can't help marvelling (or shuddering) at the minuscule size of the captain's cabin, the cook's galley, and the toilet cubicle – not to mention the torpedo room, where crewmen slept alongside the torpedoes. One's reluctant respect for the crew (six of whom are still alive) is enhanced when you learn that, in the event of an emergency, they were obliged to escape by swimming out through the torpedo tubes, and that their diving suits were only strong enough to protect them from the pressure at one-third of the depth at which the sub might be in operation. The similarities with the conditions that led to the *Kursk* disaster are chilling.

Sredniy prospekt and Gavan

The island's "Middle Avenue", **Sredniy prospekt**, runs parallel to Bolshoy prospekt, 500m to the north. Starting from Vasileostrovskaya metro station on the corner of 6–7ya liniya, you can catch tram #11 or #40 along the length of the prospekt, past a few places worth a mention. Head northeast to the corner of 2–3ya liniya, where you'll find the Gothic **Lutheran Church of St Michael**, which until a few years ago housed a toy factory but now belongs to various Lutheran missionary organizations and holds regular services (Sun 9.30am in English, 11.30am in Russian). On Sezdovskaya liniya stands the Orthodox **Church of St Catherine**, whose lofty dome and belfry are a local landmark.

Travelling the other way, out towards Gavan, you'll pass a handsome pair of Art Nouveau apartment buildings on the corner of 10–11ya liniya. Across the road from the second one is a shabbier building (no. 64) where **Stalin** lived after returning from his Siberian exile in March 1917. Though other comrades cold-shouldered him, Stalin was welcomed by Sergei Alliluev, an old friend from the Caucasus who offered him lodgings. Here, Stalin met the Alliluevs' youngest daughter, Nadezhda, whom he later married. Her death in 1932 is ascribed either to suicide (motivated by grief and shame at the purges), or a fatal beating by her husband. Their daughter said that any trace of love or pity in Stalin's character died with her, which might explain his well-known dislike of Leningrad – though the city's cosmopolitan sophistication and Tsarist past obviously rankled too.

The Kirov Palace of Culture and Gavan

Trotsky's other works are described on p.222 and p.246. If the architect had been related to his famous namesake, he might have ended up in the Bolshoy dom instead of building it.

Further southwest along the prospekt, buses stop a block or so from the **Kirov Palace of Culture**. Intended to be the largest institution of its kind in the USSR when it was built in the 1930s, this vast prefabricated shed epitomizes the ugly side of Soviet Constructivism. It was designed by Noy Trotsky (who also designed the Bolshoy dom and the Soviet House) but today its pretensions are mocked by the crumbling slabs and sagging doors. The palace now hosts numerous small firms, the local Jewish society and occasional **discos**.

Beyond here lies the **Gavan** (Docks) district, a mixture of high-rise buildings shedding their tiles and 1950s low-rise apartments known as *Khrushchoby* (a pun on the Russian for "slum" and the name of the then Soviet leader). By a quirk of planning, one estate has a morgue and a Palace of Weddings right next to each other. Another claim to folkloric significance is the "sighting" of tanks here during the putsch of 1991, a rumour that did the rounds until someone scoffed, "Where are they coming from? The sea?"

West to the Primorskiy district

Beyond the factories north of Sredniy is **Maliy prospekt**, or "Small Avenue" – in fact it's just as long, but grimmer in parts, and the only real reason to visit is the **Doll Museum** and the **Smolensk cemeteries** on the banks of the River Smolenka.

The Doll Museum and Smolensk cemeteries

West to the Primorskiy district

From Vasileostrovskaya metro it's a fifteen-minute walk or a short ride on tram #1, which you can get from just around the corner on 8–9ya liniya. The tram terminates opposite the **Doll Museum** at Kamskaya ulitsa 8, whose delightful collection of 1500 dolls – mostly antiques – puts visitors in the mood to buy something by contemporary doll-makers, for whom the museum is a retail outlet. It also sells souvenirs and doll-making equipment. Young girls will love it, but parents could end up reaching for their credit cards.

The Doll Museum is open daily 10am–6pm; free.

The **Smolensk Orthodox Cemetery** (Smolenskoe pravoslavnoe kladbishche) takes its name from the old Smolensk Field, where the revolutionary Karakizov was hanged in 1866 for his attempt on the life of Alexander II, and another unsuccessful assassin, Solovyov, was executed in 1879. Many of the graves are smothered with vegetation, but the church inside the walls, and the chapel of Kseniya Peterburgskaya (the city's favourite saint) – where believers kiss the walls – are both carefully tended. Since the Smolensk Orthodox Cemetery was, as its name suggests, reserved strictly for Russian Orthodox believers, the dead of other religious denominations (mainly foreigners) were relegated to the smaller **Smolensk Lutheran Cemetery** (Smolenskoe lyuteranskoe kladbishche), north of the River Smolenka. The graves of a few British families are here, including those of the Scot Charles Baird, owner of a St Petersburg iron foundry, which made (to his specifications) the neo-Gothic memorials that identify the family graves. Admiral Alexis Greig, commander of the Russian Black Sea Fleet, and his son, Admiral Samuel Greig, who led the defence of Sebastopol against the British during the Crimean War, are both buried in a family plot beside the central alley. A recent addition to the roll was the yachtsman **Greg Palmer**, who helped build the *Shtandart* (p.228).

The Pribaltiyskaya and beyond

Trolleybus #12 runs the length of Maliy prospekt before heading north into an area of huge apartment blocks en route to ulitsa Korablestroiteley, where a plaza worthy of Ceaucescu's Bucharest fronts the Swedish-built **Hotel Pribaltiyskaya**. The statue outside, which looks like two men enjoying themselves in a sauna, honours the founders of the Russian fleet. Many local streets hereabouts reflect the district's maritime past, named after shipbuilders (Korablestroiteley), skippers (Shkiperskiy), bosuns (Botsmanskaya) and midshipmen (Michmanskaya).

This "New Maritime" – or **Primorskiy** – district speads as far as **Decembrists' Island** (ostrov Dekabristov) to the north, the burial place of the executed participants of the Decembrist uprising. The island's sea wall is an impressive sight from the Gulf, especially when it catches the sun around dusk.

West to the Primorskiy district

Streets and squares

Birzhevaya liniya	Биржевая линия
Bolshoy prospekt	Большой проспект
Kamskaya ul.	Камская ул.
ul. Korablestroiteley	ул. Кораблестроителей
nab. Leytenanta Shmidta	наб. Лейтенанта Шмидта
nab. Makarova	наб. Макарова
Maliy prospekt	Малый проспект
Mendeleevskaya liniya	Менделеевская линия
Nalichnaya ul.	Наличная ул.
Sezdovskaya liniya	Съездовская линия
Sredniy prospekt	Средний проспект
Universitetskaya nab.	Университетская наб.

Metro stations

Primorskaya	Приморская
Vasileostrovskaya	Василеостровская

Buildings and museums

Academy of Arts	Академия художеств
Academy of Sciences	Академия наук
Doll Museum	музей Кукол
Literary Museum	Литературный музей
Menshikov Palace	Меншиковский дворец
Mining Museum	Горный музей
Museum of Anthropology and Ethnography	музей Антропологии и тнографии
Naval Museum	Военно-Морской музей
St Petersburg University	Университет Санкт-Петербурга
Submarine *D-2 Narodovolets*	Подводная лодка Д-2 "Народоволец"
Zoological Museum	Зоологический музей

Chapter 5

The Peter and Paul Fortress, Petrograd Side and the Kirov Islands

Across the Neva from the Winter Palace, on the small Zayachiy (Hare) Island, lies the **Peter and Paul Fortress** – the historic kernel of St Petersburg, dating from 1703. This doughty fortress-cum-prison has had many of its buildings converted into museums and features a splendid cathedral containing the tombs of the Romanov monarchs. From the fortress, you can walk across to the urban mass of the **Petrograd Side** (Petrogradskaya storona), a mainly residential area crammed with Style Moderne buildings, which owes its character to a housing boom that started in the 1890s: by 1913 its population had risen from 75,000 to 250,000, after the newly completed Troitskiy most (Trinity Bridge) made the Petrograd Side accessible from the city centre. It contains a few sites of interest, those nearest to the fortress including Petersburg's **Mosque** and the **Museum of Russian Political History**, after which you can head east along the embankment to the legendary cruiser **Aurora**, which fired the opening shots of the Bolshevik Revolution. Inland, statues and memorial apartments commemorate the famous people who lived or worked on the Petrograd Side (including Shostakovich, Lenin and Pavlov), but the chief attraction is the **Botanical Gardens** on the adjacent Aptekarskiy (Apothecary's) Island.

More appealing still are the wooded **Kirov Islands**, northwest of the Petrograd Side, bounded by the Malaya, Srednaya and Bolshaya Nevka rivers. Long favoured as recreational areas, **Kamenniy** (Stone) and **Yelagin** islands feature a host of picturesque *dachas* and official residences, as well as two summer **palaces**, while **Krestovskiy** island sports the mega-sized Kirov Stadium and a yacht club.

Approaches

Many of the prime sights – including the fortress – are within five to ten minutes' walk of **Gorkovskaya metro station** (on the

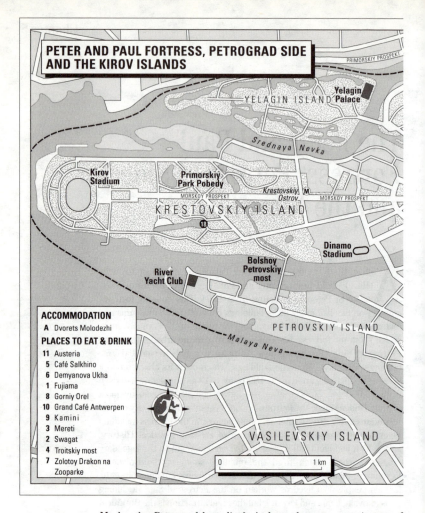

PETER AND PAUL FORTRESS, PETROGRAD SIDE AND THE KIROV ISLANDS

PRIMORSKIY PROSPEKT

Yelagin Palace

YELAGIN ISLAND

Srednaya Nevka

Kirov Stadium

Primorskiy Park Pobedy

Krestovskiy Ostrov (M)

MORSKOY PROSPEKT

MORSKOY PROSPEKT

K R E S T O V S K I Y   I S L A N D

18

Dinamo Stadium

Bolshoy Petrovskiy most

River Yacht Club

PETROVSKIY ISLAND

Malaya Neva

N

VASILEVSKIY ISLAND

0 ————— 1 km

ACCOMMODATION

A Dvorets Molodezhi

PLACES TO EAT & DRINK

11 Austeria
5 Café Salkhino
6 Demyanova Ukha
1 Fujiama
8 Gorniy Orel
10 Grand Café Antwerpen
9 Kamini
3 Mereti
2 Swagat
4 Troitskiy most
7 Zolotoy Drakon na Zooparke

Moskovsko–Petrogradskaya line). A slower but more scenic way of getting to the fortress from the city centre is **by tram** across Troitskiy most; take number #2, #34 or #54 from the northeast corner of Marsovo pole. Coming **on foot** from Vasilevskiy Island takes fifteen minutes – en route you'll cross **Birzhevoy most** (Exchange Bridge), from where there are fine views of the fortress and of the floating bars around the Kronverk Moat. Walking across the handsome, but busy, 526-metre-long **Troitskiy most** isn't especially enjoyable on account of the traffic and (in summer) the heat, although it does provide a superb view of the Strelka. For a week or so each spring, when the fish are rising, the bridge is packed with fishermen day and night.

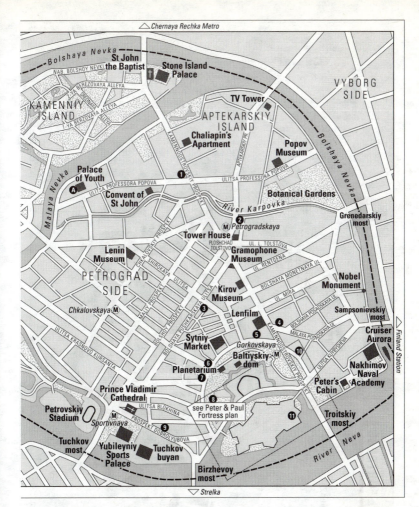

Bolshaya Nevka

St John
the Baptist

Stone Island
Palace

VYBORG
SIDE

TV Tower

KAMENNIY
ISLAND

APTEKARSKIY
ISLAND

Chaliapin's
Apartment

Popov
Museum

Palace
of Youth

Convent of
St John

Botanical Gardens

River Karpovka

Grenadarskiy
most

Petrogradskaya

Tower House

Lenin
Museum

Gramophone
Museum

Nobel
Monument

PETROGRAD
SIDE

Kirov
Museum

Chkalovskaya

Lenfilm

Sampsonievskiy
most

Cruiser
Aurora

Sytniy
Market

Gorkovskaya

Nakhimov
Naval
Academy

Baltiyskiy
dom

Planetarium

Peter's
Cabin

Prince Vladimir
Cathedral

ULITSA BLOKHINA

see Peter & Paul
Fortress plan

Petrovskiy
Stadium

Sportivnaya

Troitskiy
most

River Neva

Tuchkov
most

Yubileyniy
Sports
Palace

Tuchkov
buyan

Birzhevoy
most

▽ Strelka

The Peter and Paul Fortress

ST PETERSBURG

Built to secure Russia's hold on the Neva delta, the **Peter and Paul Fortress** (Petropavlovskaya krepost) anticipated the foundation of St Petersburg by a year – and may even have suggested to Peter the Great the idea of building a city here. During 1703, forced labourers (who perished in their thousands) toiled from dawn to dusk on Zayachiy Island, constructing the fortress in just seven months. The crude earthworks were subsequently replaced by brick walls under the direction of Trezzini and later faced with granite slabs. Work proceeded on a section-by-section basis so as not to weaken the

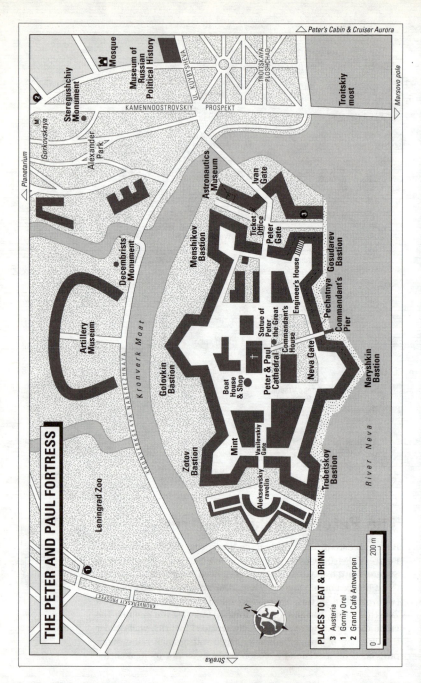

THE PETER AND PAUL FORTRESS

PLACES TO EAT & DRINK

3 Austeria
1 Gorniy Orel
2 Grand Café Antwerpen

0   200 m

△ Peter's Cabin & Cruiser Aurora

△ Marsovo pole

△ Strelka

Leningrad Zoo

Artillery Museum

Planetarium

Alexander Park

Steregushchiy Monument

Mosque

Museum of Russian Political History

UL KUYBYSHEVA

TROITSKAYA PLOSHCHAD

Troitskiy most

KAMENNOOSTROVSKIY PROSPEKT

Gorkovskaya

Decembrists' Monument

Astronautics Museum

Ivan Gate

Ticket Office

Peter Gate

Menshikov Bastion

Pechatnya

Gosudarev Bastion

Engineer's House

Commandant's Pier

Golovkin Bastion

Statue of Peter the Great

Commandant's House

Boat House & Shop

Peter & Paul Cathedral

Neva Gate

Naryshkin Bastion

Mint

Vasilevskiy Gate

Zotov Bastion

Trubetskoy Bastion

River Neva

Alekseevskiy ravelin

Kronverk Moat

KRONVERKSKAYA NABEREZHNAYA

KRONVERKSKIY PROSPEKT

N

defences, whose cannons and four-metre-thick walls were never
actually tested by an invader – though contemporary observers reckoned that the hexahedral layout would have precluded concentrated
defensive fire, making the fortress a pushover for any determined
assailant.

The fortress's role as a **prison** dates back to 1718, when Peter the
Great's son, Alexei, was tortured to death within its walls. The
"Secret House", built to contain Empress Anna's opponents, was
subsequently used by Nicholas I to hold the Decembrists; later generations of revolutionaries were incarcerated in the Trubetskoy
Bastion. The fortress was known as the "Russian Bastille", its grim
reputation only surpassed by that of the Schlüsselburg fortress on
Lake Ladoga, until the Soviet era made other prisons synonymous
with even greater terror.

Today the fortress is cherished as a historic monument – especially its **Cathedral**, which is revered by monarchists as the burial place
of the Romanovs; ongoing rumours of its return to the Orthodox
Church are, so far, unfounded. Incongruously, the island on which the
fortress is sited is a magnet for sunbathers, who pack its **beaches** in
summer, and for the hardy folk known as *morzhi* (walruses), who
break holes in the ice in winter to swim in temperatures of -20°C.

The fortress is permanently open (no admission charge), but its
cathedral and museums keep regular **opening hours** – all are covered by a single **ticket** (sold at the *kassa* in the Ioannovskiy ravelin,
near the Ivan Gate, or at the Boat House outside the Peter and Paul
Cathedral), which should be retained until you've finished sightseeing. The only attraction not covered is the Neva Panorama walkway
along the ramparts overlooking the river, tickets for which are sold
on the spot.

*The cathedral
and museums
are open Mon
& Thurs–Sun
11am–6pm,
Tues
11am–5pm,
closed the last
Tues of the
month; $3.
Guided tours
in English can
be booked on
☎ 238 45 40,
or you can
rent an audio-
guide for $3.*

The gates, ramparts and bastions

Approached by a wrought-iron footbridge on the east side of the
fortress, the yellow-and-white **Ivan Gate** (Ioannovskie vorota) pene-
trates an outlying rampart, the **Ioannovskiy ravelin**, which was
added to the fortress in 1740. It's the last place you'd associate with
space travel, but it once accommodated the research laboratory
where the first Soviet liquid-fuelled rocket was developed in
1932–33. Today, the **Astronautics Museum** – off to the right as you
come through the Ivan Gate – traces the history of the Soviet space
programme from *Sputnik* to the *Mir* orbital station, paying homage
to the visionary scientist Konstantin Tsiolkovsky. Decades before the
first satellite was put into orbit, he suggested multistage rockets to
overcome the adverse mass/fuel ratio, concluding that "Our planet is
the cradle of reason, but we cannot live in a cradle for ever". For a
small fee, visitors may photograph each other sitting inside a
cramped re-entry capsule of the kind that Soviet cosmonauts
returned to Earth in.

Straight ahead is the main entrance to the fortress proper, where balalaika players lurk in the shadows of the **Peter Gate** (Petrovskie vorota). Designed by Trezzini as a triumphal arch, the gate sports the double-headed eagle of the Romanovs and a wooden bas-relief depicting St Peter casting down the evil magus Simon. Lest anyone should miss the allegory of his defeat of Charles XII of Sweden, Tsar Peter appears among the onlookers, wearing a laurel wreath, while his martial and legislative virtues are personified by statues of Minerva (left) and Bellona (right), in niches flanking the gate.

Each of the six fortress **bastions** is named after the individual responsible for its construction, namely the *Gosudar* (Sovereign) and his cohorts Menshikov, Naryshkin, Zotov, Golovkin and Trubetskoy. The **Gosudarev Bastion** was the site of Tsarevich Alexei's death (see box below) and, on a lighter note, a blue *morzh* painted on its outer wall signifies that the "walruses" swim nearby. You can also enjoy a **panorama of the Neva basin and Winter Palace** from a walkway atop the ramparts, running from the Gosudarev to the **Naryshkin Bastion**. Beside the latter are two cannons which fire a single shot every day at noon (a custom originating in the eighteenth century, when few people had clocks), and a 24-gun salute at 8pm on January 27 to mark the anniversary of the breaking of the siege of Leningrad; a shot fired at any other time signifies a flood warning. In 1917, the Bolsheviks agreed that a red lamp hung on the bastion's flagpole would be the signal for the

*Admission to
the Neva
panorama
costs $1.*

The death of Tsarevich Alexei

The life and death of **Tsarevich Alexei** (1690–1718) is a shameful indictment of his father, Peter the Great. Since childhood, the timid Alexei took after his mother, Evdokiya, whom Peter confined to a convent when Alexei was eight. His pious temperament was the antithesis of Peter's; his hostility to foreign innovations another cause of paternal contempt and filial bitterness. Ordered to live abroad, he communicated with clerics opposed to Peter's policies, promising to repeal them once he became tsar. When Peter told him to mend his ways or be "cut off like a gangrenous growth", Alexei offered to renounce the succession and become a monk, but then claimed sanctuary in Austria. Inveigled back home, he foolishly disclosed accomplice "conspirators" who, under torture, identified others. The tsar then confined Alexei in the Gosudarev Bastion and ordered his **interrogation** to begin with 25 lashes.

Although subsequent "confessions" convinced Peter that Alexei's death was essential to preserve his own security, he tried to shift the decision on to the clergy (who equivocated) and a secular court (which endorsed the verdict). Two days later the tsarevich was dead – officially from apoplexy, though rumour suggested that Peter himself beat Alexei to death. Ironically, the demise of the tsar's younger son, Peter Petrovich, a year later left Alexei's infant (also called Peter) the only surviving male of the Romanov line.

Aurora to open fire on the Winter Palace, but when the moment arrived, the only lantern available wasn't red and couldn't be attached to the flagpole – so they had to wave it, instead.

Between these two bastions is the **Neva Gate**, whose Neoclassical arch lists the "catastrophic" floods that have befallen St Petersburg (less serious ones being too numerous to count). The glorious view of Palace Embankment across the Neva from here would have afforded little consolation to prisoners leaving from the **Commandant's Pier**, bound for the gallows at Schlüsselburg. In the passageway leading through to the fortress from the pier, you'll find the entrance to the **Pechatnya**, a museum demonstrating the art of printing with the help of half-a-dozen working vintage presses. The museum also exhibits various finds from excavations within the fortress, including the remains of an original cell.

The Engineers' House and the Commandant's House

The tree-lined path from the Neva Gate to the centre of the fortress is flanked to the southeast by the **Engineers' House** (Inzhenerniy dom). Originally occupied by military engineers, this now houses the interesting "Return to St Petersburg" exhibition, starting with eighteenth- and nineteenth-century cityscapes and progressing through to Art Nouveau crafts. Among its varied exhibits is a decree signed by Catherine the Great and a bust of the empress herself, which appears amongst a collection of bronzes, including one of Ivan the Terrible. Best of all are the vintage appliances including typewriters and sewing machines, and re-created domestic interiors, juxtaposed with some wonderful store-front signs and music boxes which you can hear being played on Mondays, Thursdays and Fridays from 3pm to 4pm.

Just along from the Engineers' House is a controversial **statue of Peter the Great**, unveiled in 1990. While some regard it as a slur on the city's founder, more people are intrigued by its (slightly) exaggerated portrayal of Peter's extraordinary physique. His spidery legs and fingers, massive torso and rounded shoulders are offset by a tiny head that uncannily resembles that of Marlon Brando as Don Corleone in *The Godfather*. Its sculptor, Mikhail Shemiakin, has lived in America since the early 1970s; the statue was a gift to the country of his birth.

Further along stands the **Commandant's House** (Ober-Komendantskiy dom), built in the 1740s and used for major political trials throughout the following century. Inside, another exhibition, "The History of St Petersburg", covers the foundation of the city up to the late nineteenth century and includes a mock-up of the room where the Decembrists and the Petrashevsky Circle were interrogated in the presence of Nicholas I, who personally dictated their sentences.

The Peter and Paul Cathedral

The golden spire of the **Peter and Paul Cathedral** (Petropavlovskiy sobor) signals defiance from the heart of the fortress. "A hundred cannon, impregnable bastions and a garrison of 3000 men defend the place, which can be desecrated only when all St Petersburg lies in ruins," asserted *Murray's Handbook* in 1849. As a token of Peter's intent, a wooden church was erected on this site as soon as the fortress had been founded, replaced by a stone cathedral once the defences were upgraded. Looking far more Protestant than Orthodox, the cathedral's soaring spire was a visible assertion of Peter's wish that the skyline of St Petersburg should be the antithesis of Moscow's.

The **belfry** was erected first and the ground was allowed time to settle beneath its weight before work commenced on the remainder of the cathedral, which was completed by Trezzini in 1733, long after Peter had died. The facade of the cathedral looks Dutch, while the gilded **spire** was deliberately made higher than the Ivan the Great Bell Tower in the Kremlin – at a height of 122m it remained the tallest structure in the city until the construction of the television tower in 1962 (see p.206). When the angel on top of the spire was blown askew in 1830, a roofer – Pyotr Telushkin – volunteered to climb up and fix it, using only a rope and hook, a feat later repeated by professional alpinists who camouflaged the spire to save it from the Luftwaffe in World War II and have restored it twice since then. During the 1997 **restoration**, the alpinists found a note in a bottle left by those who restored it forty years earlier. Addressed to "future climbers", the note complained of low pay and time pressures. Continuing the tradition, the restorers of 1997 left their own message in a bottle for the next team to scale the spire.

The **interior** is painted in tutti-frutti colours, with marbled columns ascending to a canopy of gilded acanthus leaves. Sited around the nave are the **tombs of the Romanov monarchs** from Peter the Great onwards (excluding Peter II and Ivan VI), whose coffins repose in vaults beneath the sarcophagi. All have marble slabs (designed in 1865, when the cathedral underwent major restoration) except for those of Alexander II and his wife, whose sarcophagi of Altay jasper and Urals rhodonite took seventeen years to carve and polish. The tombs of Peter (the only one sporting a bust of its occupant) and Catherine the Great are situated to the right of the iconostasis. Alexei is said to have been interred under the aisle, where "he would always be trampled on", but was actually buried in the family vault below Peter's sarcophagus.

On July 17, 1998, the remains of Russia's last royal family were finally laid to rest here, exactly eighty years after they were executed by the Bolsheviks in Yekaterinburg. Located in a separate chapel, off to the right as you enter the cathedral, the tomb officially contains the remains of Nicholas II, Alexandra and three of their five children, plus four servants who were shot with the family – although the Church remains sufficiently doubtful of their authenticity that, despite canonizing them as Orthodox martyrs, it has not declared the remains to be holy relics.

As a devout Slavophile, Nicholas would have probably preferred to end up in Moscow's Cathedral of the Archangel (where rulers before Peter the Great were buried) rather than in St Petersburg – which he detested – in a cathedral that looks more Protestant than Orthodox. The only icons to be found are on the **iconostasis,** dominated by the archangels Gabriel and Michael and framed by what look like stage curtains, with tassels and cords, all in wood. This lovely piece of work was designed by Ivan Zarudny and carved by Moscow craftsmen in the early eighteenth century. Nearby stand a pulpit (unusual in an Orthodox church) and a dais where the tsar's throne once stood.

The Grand Ducal Mausoleum

A side door leads from the nave into a corridor on the left lined with plans of the fortress and photos showing how it was protected in wartime and restored afterwards. In a room off the corridor is an exhibition on the **history of the Mint**, containing Tsarist and Soviet coins and medals. Look out for the medallion bearing Stalin's head and the replicas of the plaques that were sent to the Moon, Mars and Venus by Soviet spacecraft, all of which were manufactured in the fortress mint. You may also encounter a man dressed as Peter the Great, operating the hand-turned lathe with which he crafted many objects now exhibited in the Hermitage.

At the end of the corridor is the lofty **Grand Ducal Mausoleum** (Usypalnitsa), built for Nicholas II's cousins early this century as the cathedral itself became too crowded for the burial of any but the closest relatives. The principal tomb belongs to Archduke Vladimir, the heir to the Romanov dynasty, who was born in Belgium after the Revolution and died in Miami – his remains were returned to Russia in 1992.

The Boat House and Mint

Opposite the cathedral exit stands a **Boat House** (Botniy dom) topped by a nymph with an oar, symbolizing navigation. The Neoclassical pavilion was erected in the 1760s to preserve the small boat in which Peter made his first sailing trips on the River Yauza, outside Moscow. That original boat now reposes in the Naval Museum (see p.173), while the Boat House contains an exact replica, and a souvenir shop.

In the surrounding courtyard on January 27, 1919, the Bolsheviks shot four grand dukes and other hostages taken at the start of the Red Terror the previous year, whom they had sentenced to death in retaliation for the murders of Rosa Luxemburg and Karl Liebknicht

in Berlin. When Maxim Gorky pleaded for the life of Grand Duke –
and liberal historian – Nikolai Mikhailovich, Lenin replied: "The
Revolution does not need historians". As yet, there is no memorial to
the dozens shot here during the Civil War.

Across the courtyard looms the **Mint** (Monetniy dvor), a yellow-
and-white edifice dating from the 1790s, before which time coins
were minted in the Naryshkin and Trubetskoy bastions. The world's
first lever press for coining money was devised here in 1811 and the
Mint is still busy turning out coins and commemorative medallions,
as proclaimed by its smoking chimney. There's no admission to the
public, so it's best to carry on to the Trubetskoy Bastion.

The Trubetskoy Bastion

Converted into a jail under the supposedly liberal Alexander II, the
Trubetskoy Bastion soon became the regime's main interrogation
centre and a prison for generations of revolutionaries. First to be
confined here were members of the Zemlya i Volya (Land and
Liberty) and Narodnaya Volya (People's Will) organizations – the latter group responsible for killing Alexander himself. Next came
would-be assassins such as Lenin's brother, Alexander Ulyanov;
Socialist Revolutionary bombers like Vera Figner; and Gorky and
Trotsky in 1905. After the February Revolution, Tsarist ministers
were imprisoned here, to be followed by members of the Provisional
Government once the Bolsheviks took over. In a final turn of the
wheel of repression, radical Kronstadt sailors were kept here before
being shot or sent to the Gulag in 1921. The following year the
prison became a museum to the infamies of Tsarism, omitting any
mention of its role after the Revolution, a period which is still glossed
over by tour guides.

The Prison Museum

*See the
Bolshoy dom
(p.221) and
Kresty Prison
(p.257) for
information
on the purges
of the Soviet
era in
Leningrad.*

Selective coverage aside, the **Prison Museum** fails to convey the full
horror of conditions in Tsarist times. The accessible **cells** are stark
and gloomy, but far worse ones existed within the ramparts, where
the perpetual damp and cold made tuberculosis inevitable. Prisoners
were never allowed to see each other and rarely glimpsed their jailers. Some were denied visitors and reading material for decades;
many went mad after a few years and several committed suicide. The
corridors were carpeted to deaden sound, enabling the "Specials" to
creep up and spy through the door slits without warning. This green-
cloaked elite were the only guards allowed to see the prisoners' faces
or give them orders (conversations were forbidden), but they were
never told the prisoners' names in order to prevent word of their
identity reaching the outside world. Inmates managed to communicate amongst themselves by knocking out messages in the "prisoners' alphabet" – a kind of morse code – but anyone caught doing so
risked being confined to an unlit punishment cell (*kartser*) and fed

on bread and water. Once a fortnight, each inmate was escorted to the **bathhouse** in the courtyard for a solitary scrub and exercise, but the corridor windows were painted over so that none might see who was exercising. A monument and a quotation from the anarchist Prince Kropotkin (a former prisoner) commemorate the prisoners' sufferings.

The Alekseevskiy ravelin

Leaving the fortress by its western **Vasilevskiy Gate**, you'll notice a U-shaped outbuilding which marks the site of the now-demolished **Alekseevskiy ravelin**. Built by Empress Anna in the 1730s, this bastion contained the first long-term prison in the fortress, its maximum security "**Secret House**" reserved for those who fell foul of the intrigues of Anna's favourite, Count Biron. Here, too, Catherine the Great confined Alexander Radishchev for criticizing Russia's backwardness in his *Journey from St Petersburg to Moscow* (1780); and Alexander I imprisoned Ivan Pososhkov, author of *On Poverty and On Wealth*, who died in captivity in 1826. Under Nicholas I, the prison held many of the Decembrists and the Petrashevsky Circle (including Dostoyevsky); Bakunin (whose grovelling *Confessions* saved him from the gallows); and Chernyshevsky (who wrote *What is to be Done?* whilst in prison).

Around the Kronverk

Apart from its own ramparts and bastions, the Peter and Paul Fortress was further protected by a system of outlying ramparts called the **Kronverk** – a name later given both to the moat separating Zayachiy Island from the "mainland" Petrograd Side and to the avenue encircling a park containing the zoo and the Artillery Museum.

The zoo

Immediately northeast of the fortress over the Kronverk Moat, the **Leningrad Zoo** (as it is still named) dates back to 1865, though a recent modernization programme ran aground financially after many of its larger animals were sent to other zoos – its elephant to Tashkent and its hippopotamuses to Kiev – leaving it bereft of both funds and species. It now manages to stagger on somehow and is proud that its polar bears and giraffes have procreated in captivity, while pinning its hopes on corporate sponsorship and an adoption programme (as advertised on its Web site, *www.lenzoopark.spb.ru*). Its staff are also proud of the fact that none of the zoo's animals were eaten during the Blockade, and dismiss the legend that victims of the Red Terror were fed alive to the carnivores when food was scarce during the Civil War.

*The zoo is
open
Tues–Sun:
May–Oct
10am–6pm;
Nov–April
10am–4pm;
$1.*

The Artillery Museum

Across the Kronverk Moat from the fortress's Golovkin Bastion
stands a vast horseshoe-shaped arsenal, fronted by tanks and missile
launchers. Inside, the **Artillery Museum** (Voenno-Istoricheskiy
muzey Artillerii) has displays of artillery from medieval times until
1812, along with the pike which Peter carried as a foot soldier, an
ornate coach from which Kutuzov harangued his troops at Borodino,
and regimental banners (one depicting the Last Judgement, with foreigners writhing in hell).

*The Artillery
Museum is
open Wed–Sun
11am–5pm;
$1.75. Guided
tours in
Russian by
arrangement
on ☎233 03
82.*

Amongst the World War II exhibits upstairs are a "Katyusha" mul-
tiple-rocket launcher, a huge mural of trench warfare at Stalingrad
and a diorama of Kursk, where the biggest tank battle in history took
place. Next comes a corridor devoted to Signals, climaxing with a
model of the ruined Reichstag and a gleeful painting of Hitler committing suicide.

Back downstairs in Hall 10 you'll find **Lenin's armoured car**,
Enemy of Capital, on which he rode in triumph from Finland
Station on April 3, 1917, making speeches from its gun turret.
Nearby is a model of a dog with a mine strapped to its back; the
Soviets trained them to run underneath Nazi tanks. Also notice the
snazzy Red Army **uniforms** of the Civil War era, designed by a
Futurist artist later killed in the purges.

The Decembrists' Monument

On a grassy knoll just to the east of the arsenal, the **Decembrists'
Monument** marks the spot where five leaders of the revolt were executed in July 1826. The gallows were erected in front of the condemned officers, who were ritually degraded by having their
epaulettes torn off and their swords broken before the hoods and
nooses were slipped over their heads. The ropes broke for three of
the men, but rather than being reprieved (as was customary in such
cases), fresh ropes were brought and the hangings were repeated.
The obelisk is inscribed with a poem by Pushkin, dedicated to a
friend sentenced to a term of hard labour in Siberia for his part in the
revolt:

> *Dear friend, have faith;*
> *The wakeful skies presage a dawn of wonder,*
> *Russia shall from her age-old sleep arise,*
> *And despotism shall be crushed;*
> *Upon its ruins our names incise.*

The Alexander Park and Kronverkskiy prospekt

East of the monument the spacious and wooded **Alexander Park**,
laid out in 1845, features the **Steregushchiy Monument**, which commemorates the sailors who scuttled their torpedo boat rather than let

it be captured at Tsushima Bay in 1904. Heading north through the park you'll come to a Stalinist-era complex that has embraced capitalism with gusto: the **Planetarium** houses the largest nightclub in St Petersburg and the Komsomol Theatre, now the **Baltiyskiy dom** cultural complex, hosts gay parties, alternative arts festivals and all-night shows of performance art. The two buildings occupy the site of what was once the "Nicholas II People's House", one of the great forums of the 1917 Revolution.

A little further north, **Kronverkskiy prospekt** loops around the Alexander Park to the junction with Kamennoostrovskiy prospekt (see p.203) on its eastern side, near Gorkovskaya metro station (trams #6 and #63 run along here en route to and from Vasilevskiy Island). Until 1993 Kronverkskiy prospekt bore the name of the writer **Maxim Gorky**, who lived at no. 23 from 1914 to 1921. The dropping of his name reflects Gorky's diminished status in the post-Communist era, although Gorkovskaya metro station isn't likely to change its name. Halfway round the prospekt on its northern side is **Sytniy Market**, which sells fresh produce if you fancy a picnic in the park.

The market is open Mon–Sat 8am–7pm, Sun 8am–4pm.

Maxim Gorky

Orphaned and sent out to work as a young boy, Alexei Maximovich Peshkov (1868–1936) achieved success in his thirties under the *nom de plume* **Maxim Gorky**. A natural radical, he took a leading role in the 1905 Revolution, for which he was sentenced to prison. After protests from Western writers, his prison sentence was commuted to exile abroad, where he raised funds for the Bolsheviks from his hideaway on Capri (taking time out to play Lenin at chess). Returning home in 1913, Gorky continued to support the Bolsheviks until after the Revolution, when he began to attack Lenin for seizing power and relying on terror.

Having left Russia in 1921 – ostensibly on the grounds of ill health – Gorky was wooed back home in 1928 to become chairman of the new Union of Soviet Writers. His own novel *Mother* was advanced as a model of Socialist Realism, the literary genre promulgated by the Union in 1932. He also collaborated on a paean to the White Sea Canal – "the first book in Russian literature to glorify slave labour", according to Solzhenitsyn. As a murky finale, Gorky's mysterious death in 1936 was used by Stalin as a pretext for the arrest of Yagoda, head of the NKVD secret police. Decades of official acclaim have tarnished his reputation and nowadays Gorky's work is often scorned as trite agitprop, lacking depth and subtlety.

Towards Troitskaya ploshchad

Heading east from the fortress, you'll reach the large open space of Troitskaya ploshchad, with Kamennoostrovskiy prospekt running along its western side. To the north looms St Petersburg's **Mosque** (*Mechet*), whose ovoid cupola was copied from that of the mausoleum of Tamerlane in Samarkand. The cupola and the fluted finials of its twin minarets are faced with brilliant azure tiles, which greatly enliven the severe-looking structure; its Islamic identity is otherwise apparent only from the arabesques around its portals. Constructed between 1910 and 1914 at the behest of the last emir of Bukhara to serve the city's Sunni Muslim community, the mosque is currently being restored, but violent conflicts between differing factions surround the work, which is progressing at a snail's pace. Although the exterior can be viewed any time by entering the gate on Konniy pereulok (just around the northern corner of the building), the mosque is only **open for worship** (daily 12.30–2pm). Non-Muslims are permitted to enter if they observe the usual proprieties (such as taking off your shoes before going inside).

The Museum of Russian Political History

*The museum is
open
10am–6pm,
closed Thurs;
$2. Guided
tours (in
Russian only)
by
arrangement
on ☎233 03
82.*

Heading south and turning left onto ulitsa Kuybysheva, you'll find the former **house of Mathilda Kshesinskaya** (1872–1971), Russia's prima ballerina before the Revolution, whose affair with Crown Prince Nicholas (later Nicholas II) was the talk of late nineteenth-century St Petersburg. The house is the epitome of Style Moderne, its facade decorated with tiles and floral tracery; Gorky sniffed that she earned it "with leg-shaking and arm-swinging". In March 1917 the Bolsheviks commandeered the house as their headquarters: Lenin came here straight from the Finland Station, addressed crowds from its balcony and mapped out Party strategy here until July 1917, when a Provisional Government clampdown sent the Bolsheviks into hiding and the house was wrecked by loyalist troops.

After restoration, it was an obvious site for the Museum of the Great October Socialist Revolution, which moved here from the Winter Palace in 1957 and remained an "obligatory" sight until its sanctity was undermined by perestroika. In 1991 it was replaced by an anti-Communist but more open-minded **Museum of Russian Political History**, with exhibitions covering political movements in Russia over the last hundred years, and the life of Kshesinskaya herself. The wax tableaux of historical figures that initially attracted visitors have now been replaced by less eye-catching but more authentic exhibits, such as Red and White Guard uniforms from the Civil War, and a chunk of the Berlin Wall. By heading down to the basement and up the backstairs you can reach the second-floor quarters used by the Bolshevik Central Committee in July 1917, including the room occupied by Lenin. It was from the balcony of this room that he addressed supporters gathered outside the mansion.

Troitskaya ploshchad

Following the liquidation of the Museum of the Great October Socialist Revolution, the nearby ploshchad Revolyutsii reverted to its original name, **Troitskaya ploshchad**, derived from the Trinity Cathedral (Troitskiy sobor) that once formed the nucleus of the Petrograd Side's merchants' quarter. In 1905, the square was the scene of one of the worst massacres of "Bloody Sunday", when 48 people were killed and scores wounded after soldiers opened fire on demonstrators approaching Troitskiy most to the south. In 1917, Trotsky harangued crowds here before the October Revolution. Troitskaya ploshchad's present appearance dates from the mid-1930s, when the cathedral was demolished to make way for a gigantic Stalinist administrative building and the square was turned into a park.

East along the embankment

Walking east from Troitskaya ploshchad along the embankment, it's hard to imagine this area as the bustling port it was in Petersburg's infancy until you encounter **Peter's Cabin** (Domik Petra) in a park halfway along. Encased in a protective structure and preserved as a museum, it was built by army carpenters in May 1703 to enable the tsar to keep a close eye on the construction of the Peter and Paul Fortress over that summer. Its rough-hewn pine logs are painted to resemble bricks and there are only three rooms. Peter slept on a cot in what doubles as the hallway; the dining room and study look ready for his return. The museum includes his frock coat and pipe and a rowing boat that he made himself, as well as engravings of St Petersburg, Kronstadt and the battles of Hangö and Poltava.

Peter's Cabin is open Mon & Wed–Sun 10am–5pm, closed last Mon of the month; $1.

On the embankment opposite the cabin are two **Shih Tza** (lion) statues of the kind that flank temples in China and Mongolia, brought here in 1907 from Kirin in Manchuria, where the Tsarist Empire was contending with Japan for control of the region's mineral resources.

Further along stands the imposing **residential block** of the Nakhimov Academy, a mustard-coloured building topped by Red Guard and Sailor statues (now accompanied by neon advertising) and decorated with Futurist stucco panels featuring tractors, banners and ships' prows. Designed by Levinson and Fomin (1938–44), it was once an Intourist hotel. At the far end of the embankment the bronze figure of a veiled woman is a monument commemorating the tercentenary of the Russian navy. Close by, the **Nakhimov Naval Academy** occupies a peacock-blue, Baroque-style building completed in 1912. As a college for aspiring naval officers, its title and setting could hardly be more inspirational: named after the "hero of Sebastopol" in the Crimean War, the academy is bang opposite the warship whose cannon heralded the October Revolution.

The Aurora

The cruiser **Aurora** (kreyser *Avrora*) looks comically miscast for its dramatic role in history, resembling an outsized model battleship complete with smart paint job and gleaming brasswork. Having long been an icon of the Revolution, it is now mocked by some as "the world's deadliest weapon – with one shot, it ruined the country for 75 years". Yet few would wish to see the *Aurora* removed, or credit the rumour that the original was secretly replaced by a less decrepit sister ship some time in the 1970s. As a historical relic, it inspires affection across the political spectrum.

The 6731-tonne cruiser experienced a baptism of fire at Tsushima Bay, when it was one of the few ships in the Baltic Fleet that avoided being sunk by the Japanese. Docked in Petrograd for an overhaul just before the February Revolution, the *Aurora* was the first ship in the fleet to side with the Bolsheviks. On the night of October 25 it moved down-river and dropped anchor by what is now most Leytenanta Shmidta. At 9.40pm its forward cannon fired the historic blank shot at the Winter Palace – the first in a sporadic barrage that accompanied the "storming" of the building (see p.81). After the palace had fallen, the ship's radio was used to broadcast Lenin's address, "To the Citizens of Russia!", proclaiming the victory of the proletarian revolution.

*The aurora is
open
Tues–Thurs,
Sat & Sun
10.30am–4pm;
free. Guided
tours ($3.50)
can be booked
on ☎230 34
40.*

In the early 1920s the *Aurora* was converted into a training ship. With the advent of war in 1941, its heavy guns were removed for use on the Leningrad front, and the vessel was deliberately scuttled and sunk in shallow water near Oranienbaum for its own protection. Raised in peacetime, it was moored in its present location and declared a national monument in 1948, later opening as a **museum**. Four wardrooms on the top deck are given over to exhibits relating the warship's history; the final one contains the "fraternal gifts" from the days when international socialism meant something, including a model of the schooner *Granma* (dubbed "the little sister of the *Aurora*"), which landed Fidel Castro and his *compañeros* in Cuba. If you want to see more of the ship, you can book a guided tour of the cabins, engine rooms and ammunition magazines on the lower decks, which gives a more realistic idea of conditions aboard the vessel than the sanitized wardrooms above the waterline.

North to the Nobel monument

Two hundred metres northwards, the Bolshaya Nevka is spanned by the **Sampsonievskiy most** (Samson Bridge), which Lenin's armoured car crossed en route from Finland Station to the Kshesinskaya mansion, and which was consequently named the "Freedom Bridge" during the Communist era. A similar distance further north stands the **Nobel monument**, its fractured forms crowned by a glass wreath, an oddly appropriate memorial to the Swedish industrialist who invented dynamite and established the Nobel Prizes – his family owned several factories in St Petersburg before the Revolution.

Along Kamennoostrovskiy prospekt

Architecturally and socially, Petrograd Side takes its tone from **Kamennoostrovskiy prospekt** (Stone Island Avenue), an urban canyon that peters out as it approaches its namesake island. Many Petersburgers feel this avenue is at least as elegant as Nevskiy prospekt, with as much to offer in the way of shops, cinemas, restaurants and fine architecture – especially around Avstriyskaya ploshchad (Austrian Square), at the intersection with ulitsa Mira. The initial stretch from the Neva up to the intersection is flanked by imposing villas and apartment buildings, built early this century when the avenue suddenly became a fashionable place to live. The area beyond Petrogradskaya metro station is less notable from an architectural viewpoint, but Aptekarskiy Island, at the prospekt's northern end, and the side streets hold some appeal. Given that the avenue is 2.5km long and that the distance between metro stations is 1km, hopping on the rather infrequent #46 bus can save you a lot of footslogging between sights.

Around Gorkovskaya metro

Across the road from the Gorky statue at the lower end of the avenue stands a U-shaped **Style Moderne apartment building** (nos. 1–3) designed by Fyodor Lidval in 1902. The upper storeys are decorated with stucco shingles and fairytale beasts, while bizarre fish flank the main entrance, whose lobby contains stained-glass panels. At no. 5 is the beige-and-white former **villa of Count Sergei Witte**, the great industrialist of Tsarist Russia, who started as a railway clerk and rose through the civil service to become Finance Minister. Though highly successful in unleashing capitalist energies within Russia, his hopes for political liberalization were consistently dashed by Nicholas II, who also ignored his advice on foreign affairs: after Witte was assassinated by an ultra-right fanatic in 1915, Nicholas remarked that his death was "a great relief" and "a sign from God".

Lenfilm Studios

Another token of talent spurned lies 100m up the avenue, in a Doric-porticoed, yellow building (nos. 10–12), set back behind a garden on the left. Founded in 1918 on the site of the Akvarium Summer Theatre (where the Lumière brothers had presented the first motion picture in Russia on May 4, 1896), the **Lenfilm Studios** were once the glory of the Soviet cinema industry, producing up to fifteen movies a year. During its golden era, between the wars, most of the films, such as the Vasilev brothers' *Chapaev*, focused on ordinary people making history. In the postwar period, Lenfilm gained international kudos with Kozintsev's adaptations of the works of

Shakespeare, but many directors had their best work suppressed for years, until perestroika changed everything. The subsequent release of over two hundred banned films, followed by a new wave of *cher-nukha*, or "black" movies, dealing with Stalin and the camps, rapidly sated the public who had discovered the delights of home videos and Hollywood in the meantime.

The loss of its audience and state subsidies caused a crisis of confidence within Lenfilm, which was eventually broken up into smaller studios. These continue to produce highly acclaimed films – Aranovich's *Year of the Dog*, for instance, was a hit at the 1994 Berlin Festival, and more recent successes include Andrei Balabanov's *The Castle*, *Brother*, and *Of Freaks and Men*. Most income, however, is now generated by collaborations with foreign companies: the Bond film *Goldeneye*, the spy thriller *Midnight in St Petersburg* and the romantic drama *Onegin* were filmed using ex-Lenfilm crews.

The Kirov Museum

Of more tangible historic interest is the hulking building at nos. 26–28, built shortly before World War I by the fashionable architect Leonty Benois. After the Revolution its luxury apartments were assigned to Bolshevik officials, including the head of the Leningrad Party organization, **Sergei Kirov** (1886–1934), who lived in apartment no. 20 from 1926 until his death. The apartment is now the **Kirov Museum** (Muzey S.M. Kirova), and the dining room, library (containing over 20,000 volumes) and study (with its polar bearskin rug and telephone hotline to the Kremlin) have all been preserved. On the wall behind the desk hangs a picture of Stalin, who almost certainly organized Kirov's murder at the Smolniy (see p.227).

The Kirov Museum is open 11am–5pm, closed Wed & last Tues of the month; $1.50. Guided tours in English ($10 per group) by arrangement on ☎346 02 17.

Posthumously lauded as a Bolshevik martyr, Kirov's name was bestowed on streets and buildings across the USSR – including the avenue outside the apartment, which became Kirovskiy prospekt in 1934. The museum ignores the big questions about Kirov's demise (and his own readiness to "make short work of enemies"), preferring to dwell on his achievements as an *aktivist* and his love of skiing and fishing, but in recent years it has fished out some marvellous Socialist Realist posters and Stalin-era material for a series of temporary exhibitions.

Ploshchad Tolstovo and beyond

A couple of blocks further north, the avenue meets Bolshoy prospekt at **ploshchad Tolstovo** (Tolstoy Square), flanked by a building known as the **Tower House**, encrusted with balconies and crenellations copied from English, Scottish and Andalusian castles. Less obvious but worth seeing is the private **Gramophone Museum**, within the flat (no. 35) of former clown and bear-trainer Vladimir Deryabkin, entered via Kamennoostrovskiy prospekt 32. Since 1972, Deryabkin has collected and restored over 300 machines from around the world to working order, and welcomes visitors (he speaks a little English), settling them down in a cosy den before a partition rises with a fanfare to reveal a room full of antique beauties. The collection includes a phonograph of Edison's and a life-size ceramic sculpture of "Nipper", the canine trademark of the American RCA label.

Further north, the blue-and-white logo of the **Dom Mod** (Fashion House) overshadows the vestibule of **Petrogradskaya metro station**, opposite the **Lensoviet Palace of Culture**, which is now home to a flourishing array of slot machines, along with film screenings and jazz and pop gigs. Further on is a large house (nos. 44–46) with central arches built just before World War I for the last emir of Bukhara who, in 1920, fled from the Red Army to Afghanistan, "dropping favourite dancing boy after favourite dancing boy" to impede his pursuers. Beyond the house, the **River Karpovka** flows westwards from the Bolshaya to the Malaya Nevka, separating "mainland" Petrograd Side from Aptekarskiy Island, which is reached by the Pioneers' Bridge.

Along Kamennoost-rovskiy prospekt

The Gramophone Museum is open daily 11am–6pm; $1. Advance booking on ☎ 346 09 51 is advisable.

Aptekarskiy Island

A leafier extension of the Petrograd Side, **Aptekarskiy (Apothecary's) Island** takes its name from the medicinal kitchen gardens established beside the Karpovka in 1713. A little over a century later, these became the Imperial **Botanical Gardens** (Botanicheskiy sad), which now boast seven hundred species of trees and shrubs, as well as **greenhouses** containing 3500 plants from places as far afield as Ethiopia and Brazil. The most prized specimen of all is the "Queen of the Night Cactus", whose flowers open for one warm summer night a year and close at dawn (the gardens stay open at night for the occasion). Another attraction is the delightful Constructivist-style *Orangerie* **café** – a cosy subtropical haven during wintertime.

The Botanical Gardens are open 10am–6pm, closed Fri; free.

The entrance to the gardens lies 600m east of Kamennoostrovskiy prospekt along ulitsa Professora Popova, named after the scientist whom Russians credit with inventing the radio (see p.119). Across the road from the gardens, with its main building constructed in an odd mixture of English Gothic and Style Moderne, the **Electro-Technical Institute** is where Popov spent his final years refining his invention and exploring the electromagnetic spectrum. His abode-cum-laboratory is preserved as the **Popov Museum**, in flat #33, at ultisa Professora Popova 5. Dr Who would feel at home amongst its Edwardian jumble, but the scientific import of its contents and Popov's work will be lost on visitors who can't speak Russian or afford a guided tour in English.

The Popov Museum is open Mon–Fri 11am–4.30pm; free. Guided tours ($20) in English by arrangement on ☎ 234 59 00.

At that time, the street would have been heavily guarded due to the presence at its far end of the *dacha* of **Count Pyotr Stolypin**. Stolypin was Nicholas II's ablest minister after Witte (and Witte's bitter rival), and oversaw the suppression of the 1905 Revolution (prison trains were dubbed "Stolypin wagons"), whilst banking his hopes for future stability on the growing class of wealthy peasants. In 1906, a Socialist Revolutionary suicide squad blew up the *dacha*, killing 32 people, but not their intended target, Stolypin – he was shot dead five years later by a lone assassin at the Kiev Opera House.

*Call ☎232 97
85 to ask
whether the
observation
platform has
reopened to
sightseers.*

A couple of blocks north, up Aptekarskiy prospekt, St Petersburg's red-and-white **Television Tower**, built by an all-female construction crew in 1962, was the first in the USSR and is still the city's tallest structure, surpassing the spire of the Peter and Paul Cathedral. Originally 316m in height, it stood one metre higher than the Eiffel Tower until 1985, when a new, shorter antenna was installed, reducing its height by six metres. Until 1999, when access was suspended for security reasons, it was possible to enjoy a fabulous **view of the city** from the tower's observation platform, 191m up – although the two-minute ride in the tiny, tin-can elevator and the flimsy chain-link fence surrounding the platform meant that it was not an experience for the faint-hearted.

Chaliapin's apartment

The next street off the prospekt once resounded to the legendary *basso* of opera singer **Fyodor Chaliapin** (1873–1938), who settled at ulitsa Graftio no. 2b in 1914, having made his fortune in classic rags-to-riches fashion. Born in Kazan, Chaliapin worked as a porter and stevedore before joining a dance troupe at the age of 17. He made his operatic debut in the provinces and eventually landed a job at the Mariinskiy Theatre. However, it was in Moscow that he became famous, first at the Private Opera and then as a soloist at the Bolshoy, notably in the title roles of *Boris Godunov* and *Ivan the Terrible*. Together with Nijinsky, he was the star of Diaghilev's Ballets Russes, which took Paris by storm in 1909.

*The apartment
is open
Wed–Sun
noon–6pm,
closed last Fri
of the month;
$1.75.
Concerts are
held Sept–May
– for info and
bookings call
☎234 26 98.*

Initially enthused by the Revolution, Chaliapin later decided to move to Paris – where Diaghilev and Alexandre Benois had already settled – leaving his apartment to a friend, who preserved his belongings. The Chaliapin **memorial apartment**, filled with operatic mementoes and tortoiseshell furniture, has reopened after renovation and is still used as an occasional venue for chamber-music concerts. However, the best items (including his jewelled costume from *Boris Godunov* and a splendid portrait by Kustodiev) are now in the Theatre Museum on ploshchad Ostrovskovo (see p.72).

Pavlov and the Institute of Experimental Medicine

The name of the last street on the right – Akademika Pavlova – honours the scientist **Ivan Pavlov** (1849–1936), who worked for almost five decades at the **Institute of Experimental Medicine** at no. 12. The son of a village priest, Pavlov was educated at a seminary, then studied science at St Petersburg University and medicine at the Military Academy, before becoming director of the institute in 1891. From investigating blood circulation he turned to digestion, developing the theory of conditioned reflexes through his experiments on **dogs**. Awarded the Nobel Prize for medicine in 1904, he continued his research after the Revolution with the support of Lenin, who considered Pavlov's work a major contribution to materialist philosophy. Ironically, Pavlov was a devout Christian, but the regime turned a blind eye to his role as a church elder, awarding him a pension of twenty thousand rubles on his 85th birthday, when Pavlov had a statue of a dog erected in the institute's forecourt.

Along Kamennoost-rovskiy prospekt

The final stretch of Kamennoostro-vskiy prospekt lies across the Malaya Nevka, on Kamenniy Island (see p.210).

The west of the island

Retracing your steps down Kamennoostrovskiy prospekt, then turning right and walking for five minutes along the Karpovka embankment, brings you to the **Convent of St John** (Ioannovskiy monastir), a brown-and-white brick complex crowned by Byzantine domes and gilded crosses. Built to house the tomb of Father John of Kronstadt, a famous late nineteenth-century preacher, anti-Semite and friend of the Imperial family, the convent was an early target in the anti-religious campaigns of the 1920s, when its nuns were deported to the Solovetskiy Islands for refusing to support a quisling church movement. The convent has now been re-established and its church opened for public services.

Along Bolshoy prospekt

The rest of the Petrograd Side spreads out around **Bolshoy prospekt**, an apartment-lined thoroughfare running southwest off Kamennoostrovskiy prospekt at ploshchad Tolstovo. Public **transport** follows a one-way system – down Bolshoy prospekt towards Vasilevskiy Island and then up Bolshaya Pushkarskaya ulitsa to Kamennoostrovskiy prospekt. As Bolshoy prospekt's sights unfold more dramatically when approached from the direction of Vasilevskiy Island, you might prefer to take trams #6, #31, #40 or #63 from Vasileostrovskaya metro station, getting off the other side of Tuchkov most. Alternatively, take the metro directly to Sportivnaya station, near the northern end of the bridge. Our account proceeds in this direction, starting from Tuchkov most.

In from the waterfront

Crossing **Tuchkov most** from Vasilevskiy Island you'll see the **Tuchkov buyan** on your right, a hulking yellow-and-white warehouse built by Rinaldi in 1763 on what was once an island, separated from

Zenit

The "City of Lenin" may have reverted to St Petersburg, but its premier
soccer team certainly won't be returning to its original title. When founded
in 1931, it was called "Stalinets", but the team's lack of success reflected
badly on the Great Leader, so in 1940 it assumed the name of its sponsor
– the Zenit optical company (had this not occurred, and had Stalin's vision
of a 200,000-seater stadium in Moscow been realized, the Soviet Cup Final
might conceivably have been billed as "Stalin Leningrad v. Stalingrad, at
the Stalin Stadium").

During Soviet times, the team's poor performance was ascribed to the
fact that Zenit had to play its first matches of the season in southern resort
towns and train indoors (disparaged as "drawing-room football") while its
own pitch at the Kirov Stadium thawed and dried out – though this didn't
seem to hamper the city's traditional "second" team, Lokomotiv St
Petersburg, to whom many fans transferred their allegiance during the
early 1990s, when Zenit languished in the second division. However, since
moving to the Petrovskiy Stadium (which has undersoil heating), Zenit has
not only muscled its way back into the first division but even won the cup
from its hated rivals, Spartak Moscow, in 1999, and its fans are now legion
in the city.

the Petrograd Side by a canal. The topography of the waterfront,
with its many wharves and small islands, lends grandeur to the
Petrovskiy Stadium (formerly the Lenin Stadium) across the way, a
columned, moated arena flanked by floodlights, which was revamped
for the Goodwill Games in 1994 and is now home to St Petersburg's
premier football club, **Zenit** (see box above). On the avenue's other
side, the **Yubileyniy Sports Palace** hosts ice hockey and volleyball
matches, as well as rock concerts and discos; nearby is the
Sportivnaya metro station.

Further inland, just to the east of Bolshoy prospekt, rise the proud
belfry and onion domes of the **Prince Vladimir Cathedral** (Knyaz
Vladimirskiy sobor; open for services only), an eighteenth-century
fusion of Baroque and Classical styles by Trezzini and Rinaldi. In pre-
revolutionary times, the cathedral lent its name to the Vladimir Military
Academy, 500m up ulitsa Krasnovo Kursanta, whose cadets resisted
the Bolshevik takeover until the building was bombarded. To really get
a feel for the atmosphere of the Petrograd Side, you should also check
out one of its most characteristic thoroughfares, **Maliy prospekt**,
which runs parallel to Bolshoy prospekt for most of the way.

Lenin's stay in the backstreets

The northern backstreets of Petrograd Side consist of derelict apartment buildings and shabby *kommunalki* (communal apartments).
Always a low-rent area, it was here that Lenin stayed following his
return from Switzerland. After his death, some of the apartments
associated with him were turned into Lenin museums, a species now

fallen on hard times. Only the **Yelizarov apartment** is still open; another apartment is now used to store material.

Tram #31 from Kronverkskiy prospekt or bus #134 from Kamenniy Island or Marsovo pole will drop you near **ulitsa Lenina 52** (now renamed Shirokaya ulitsa, though most people still refer to it by its old name), where Lenin's sister Anna and her husband Mark Yelizarov lived in apartment no. 24, which has been preserved intact. Lenin and his wife, Krupskaya, arrived here at dawn after their triumphant welcome at the Kshesinskaya mansion and made the apartment their home for the next six weeks. In late July they moved to safer quarters before leaving Petrograd to escape arrest, Lenin hiding out first at Razliv and later in Finland. To muster support and dispel claims that he was out of touch, Lenin slipped back into town two weeks before a crucial meeting of the Central Committee at **naberezhnaya reki Karpovki 32**, apartment no. 31 – ironically, the apartment belonged to a political opponent whose Bolshevik wife knew that he would be out for the night. The committee arrived in disguise (Lenin had shaved off his beard and was wearing a wig), and after intense argument, everyone but Zinoviev and Kamenev was persuaded to endorse Lenin's proposal that preparations for a coup – written in pencil on squared sheets torn from a child's notebook – should begin, though no firm date was set.

Along
Bolshoy
prospekt

The Yelizarov apartment is open 10am–5pm, closed Wed & Sun; $1.50. Leonid Nalivkin (☎ 235 37 78) offers private tours in English for serious Leninists.

The Kirov Islands

The verdant archipelago lying off the northern flank of Petrograd Side is officially known as the **Kirov Islands** (Kirovskie ostrova), but everyone in St Petersburg uses the islands' traditional individual names: **Kamenniy**, **Yelagin** and **Krestovskiy**. Originally bestowed upon Imperial favourites, the islands soon became a summer residence for the wealthy and a place of enjoyment for all. This is still the case, except that most of the villas now belong to either institutions or foreigners, with telltale Mercedes parked along the quiet avenues and birch groves. Kamenniy and Yelagin islands harbour elegant palaces – one of which you can go inside – while Krestovskiy Island sports a gigantic stadium.

The only drawback is the size of the archipelago: seeing it all entails more walking around than is pleasant unless you use what limited **public transport** is available.

Approaches

The eastern end of **Kamenniy Island** is accessible by bus from Kamennoostrovskiy prospekt (#46) or the Kronverk (#134); alternatively, it's a ten-minute walk from Chernaya rechka metro on the Vyborg Side. The interior of Kamenniy Island and the eastern end of **Krestovskiy Island** are also covered by bus #134, leaving from 2ya Berezovaya alleya, which runs off Kamennoostrovskiy prospekt on

Kamenniy Island; alternatively, take the metro to Krestovskiy Ostrov station. **Yelagin Island** can be reached on foot from the western end of 2ya Berezovaya alleya, or you can walk across the bridge from Primorskiy prospekt, 2.5km west of Chernaya rechka metro (tram #2, #31 or #37 along ulitsa Savushkina, or bus #411 or #416 along the embankment), taking in the Buddhist Temple (p.262) en route.

Kamenniy Island

Reached from Aptekarskiy Island by the handsome Kamennoostrovskiy most, adorned with bronze reliefs and granite obelisks, **Kamenniy (Stone) Island** lends its name to the Petrograd Side's main avenue, as well as the palace on the island's eastern tip. Built in 1776 by Catherine the Great for her son Paul, the **Stone Island Palace** (Kamennoostrovskiy dvorets) was inherited by Alexander I, who oversaw the war against Napoleon from here. Appropriately, the palace is now a military sanatorium, so you'll have to peer through the fence to see the columned portico with steps leading down to the water, or the English-style garden, but you can get a good view of the ornate frontage from the north. Nearer the main road stands the **Church of St John the Baptist** (Tserkov Svyatovo Ioanna Predtechi), a Gothic building by Yuri Felten, who probably also supervised the construction of the palace. Turned into a sports hall after World War II, the church was re-established in 1990; services are held at weekends and on feast days.

Kamenniy Island was originally owned by Peter the Great's chancellor, Gavril Golovkin, and later passed into the hands of Alexei Bestuzhev-Ryumin, who brought thousands of serfs from Ukraine to drain the land and build embankments. By the end of the eighteenth century several aristocrats had built summer homes here, and in 1832 Russia's oldest noble family commissioned the architect Shustov to build the **Dolgorukov mansion** at no. 11 on naberezhnaya Maloy Nevki, 200m west of Kamennoostrovskiy most. A little further along the embankment are two green-and-gold Grecian **sphinxes** – the leafy area around them makes a nice spot to sit and rest a while.

Yelagin Island

Known before the Revolution as the "Garden of Joy", on account of the orgiastic revels which took place here during the White Nights, **Yelagin Island** is nowadays designated a "Central Park of Culture and Rest", with traffic banned from its roads, and access from the archipelago and the mainland limited to wooden footbridges. Though largely deserted on working days, its serpentine lakes and shady clearings attract families at weekends and hordes of revellers on public holidays, particularly during the carnivals marking the beginning and ending of the White Nights (see p.48). During the summer, you

The island is open daily: summer 10am–10pm; winter 10am–8pm.

can rent **rowing boats** on the lake to the west of the main street and use the Dinamo **tennis courts** (☎236 31 31) near the palace. There is also an island inhabited by **monkeys** who have got into the habit of stealing clothes and wallets from drunken rowers who land there. And if a two-kilometre walk doesn't faze you, there's the lure of watching the sun set over the Gulf of Finland from a spit of land at the extreme west of the island dignified by granite lions.

The Yelagin Palace

The island's chief attraction is the **Yelagin Palace** (Yelaginskiy dvorets), commissioned by Alexander I for his mother, Maria Fyodorovna, in 1817. Eyebrows must have been raised when the job was given to Carlo Rossi, as rumour had it that he was fathered by Paul I, Maria Fyodorovna's late husband, and thus was Alexander's half-brother. Whatever the truth, Rossi proved equal to his first major commission, creating an ensemble of graceful buildings, decorated with the utmost refinement.

The palace is open Wed–Sun 10am–6pm; $1.50, temporary exhibitions $3. Guided tours in Russian ($1) by arrangement on ☎430 11 31.

The Neoclassical palace has half-a-dozen exquisite **rooms** linked by bronze-inlaid mahogany doors. Moulded friezes are juxtaposed with motifs in *grisaille* – a technique using different shades of one or two colours to suggest bas-relief – while the **Grand Hall** boasts a plethora of statuary and *trompe l'oeil*. Temporary exhibitions are held on the upper floor and require a separate ticket (although they're not usually worth the extra expense).

Alexander I

Alexander I embraced his destiny with reluctance, being fated to spend his reign (1801–25) dealing with Napoleon when all he really wanted to do was live quietly in Switzerland as a private citizen. Though his armies would make Russia a major European power, Alexander learned to detest the military during childhood, when he was made to drill in all weathers by his father, Paul – accounting for his morbid horror of rain. Shy, short-sighted, and partially lame and deaf, he felt happier in the company of his grandmother, Catherine the Great, who shared his interest in free thinking.

When Alexander consented to a coup against his father, he didn't anticipate that Paul would be murdered (p.99). Upon hearing the news, Alexander burst into tears, until one of the conspirators snapped, "Stop playing the child and go rule!" As tsar, his sense of guilt possibly inclined him to propose a utopian European confederation at the Congress of Vienna, whose failure turned him towards religion. In the winter of 1825, he reportedly died whilst on holiday in the Crimea, but wild rumours of trickery impelled his mother to travel to Moscow and privately view the body in its coffin (which, against normal practice, had already been sealed). Despite a positive identification, tales persisted that she had lied and Alexander had faked his own death to become a hermit and atone for Paul's murder. Many legends identified him with a holy man called Dmitri of Siberia, and it is also said that a curious descendant opened Alexander's coffin, to find only sand and medals inside.

Admission **tickets** are sold at the kiosk beside the path to the left of the drive, which leads to the palace outbuildings. To minimize odours, the **kitchen** windows were positioned to open onto an enclosed courtyard, and the exterior facade is adorned with statues. Opposite stands the **Orangerie** (now a slot-machine arcade), and further along the path are the former **stables** (with a café at the back).

Krestovskiy Island

The 420-hectare **Krestovskiy Island** was the last of the Kirov Islands to be developed, since its swampy terrain and proximity to the slums of the Petrograd Side deterred the wealthy from building here. Before the Imperial Yacht Club based itself on the island, Krestovskiy was "peculiarly the resort of the lower classes", to where, *Murray's Handbook* observed, "flock the Muzhik and the Kupez in gay gondolas, to enjoy, in the woods, their national amusements of swings and Russian mountains". Following the Revolution, entertainments became organized and sports facilities were developed, starting in 1925 with the **Dinamo Stadium** beside the Malaya Nevka and culminating in the building of the extraordinary Kirov Stadium at the western end of the island.

Primorskiy Park Pobedy and the Kirov Stadium

The avenue leading to the Kirov Stadium bisects the **Primorskiy Park Pobedy**. The park poignantly recalls the autumn of 1945 when one hundred thousand citizens honoured the dead of the Blockade and celebrated their own survival by creating two large Victory Parks – one in the south of the city, the other on Krestovskiy Island:

> *Early in the morning, the people*
> *of Leningrad went out*
> *In huge crowds to the seashore,*
> *And each of them planted a tree*
> *Upon that strip of land, marshy, deserted*
> *In memory of that great Victory Day,*
> *Look at it now – it is a comely orchard . . .*

Anna Akhmatova

Construction of the **Kirov Stadium** (Stadion imeni S.M. Kirova), the largest stadium in Russia after the Lenin Stadium in Moscow, began in 1932, but it wasn't completed until 1950 due to the war. Its design was simple and its execution revolutionary – for the stadium was fashioned from mud. More than one million cubic metres were scooped from the Gulf bed and piped inland to build a ring-shaped mound. The "crater" bottom became the sports arena, its inner walls terraced to provide seating for 75,000 spectators, and the exterior was embellished with grand colonnades. Alas, the architects didn't take account of the weather on the Gulf, which makes the stadium

the most bracing of all the great Socialist Super Bowls and renders
the pitch unusable for six months of the year. Nowadays it's rarely
used, since the smaller Petrovskiy Stadium has better facilities,
including under-field heating. At the start of the avenue that leads to
the stadium's gigantic stairway, you'll see V.B. Pinchuk's **statue of
Kirov** in ticket-collecting mode.

The stadium can be reached from Kamenniy Island by taking bus
#134 to Krestovskiy Ostrov metro station on Morskoy prospekt, and
then catching bus #71 to the end of the line, or walking (around 15min).

Across the Malaya Nevka

On the south side of Krestovskiy Island, the Malaya Nevka is spanned
by several bridges including the **Bolshoy Petrovskiy most**, from

---

Streets and squares

ul. Akademika Pavlova	ул. Академика Павлова
Avstriyskaya ploshchad	Австрийская площадь
Bolshoy prospekt	Большой проспект
ul. Graftio	ул. Графтио
Kamennoostrovskiy prospekt	Каменноостровский проспект
Kronverkskiy prospekt	Кронверкский проспект
ul. Kuybysheva	ул. Куйбышева
Maliy prospekt	Малый проспект
ul. Professora Popova	ул. профессора Попова
nab. reki Karpovki	наб. реки Карповки
ploshchad Tolstovo	площадь Толстого
Shirokaya ulitsa	Широкая улица
Troitskaya ploshchad	Троицкая площадь

Metro stations

Chkalovskaya	Чкаловская
Gorkovskaya	Горьковская
Krestovskiy Ostrov	Крестовский Остров
Petrogradskaya	Петроградская
Sportivnaya	Спортивная

Museums

Artillery Museum	Военно-Исторический музей Артиллерии
Chaliapin memorial apartment	мемориальная квартира Ф.И. Шаляпина
Gramophone Museum	музей Граммофонов
Kirov Museum	музей С.М. Кирова
Museum of Russian Political History	музей политической истории России
Peter's Cabin	домик Петра
Popov Museum	музей Попова
Yelagin Palace	Елагинский дворец

The Kirov Islands

which **Rasputin's body** was dumped after he was shot at the Yusupov Palace. As an autopsy revealed, Rasputin was still alive, and the freezing water shocked him out of unconsciousness, for he apparently managed to free one hand and cross himself before drowning. The body was found washed up down-river after someone spotted one of his boots lying on the ice. The bridge connects with a detached sliver of the Petrograd Side known as **Petrovskiy Island**. Until the turn of this century, it was the weekend haunt of the city's German community, and though it's mostly been built over since, several small parks remain. Its western tip – Petrovskaya Kosa – harbours the **River Yacht Club**, which offers sailing trips around the Gulf; to get there, take trolleybus #7 from Sportivnaya metro to the end of the line, then walk the remaining 600m.

Chapter 6

Liteyniy, Smolniy and Vladimirskaya

The areas of **Liteyniy, Smolniy** and **Vladimirskaya** make up the remainder of central "mainland" St Petersburg and provide the main points of interest between the River Fontanka and the Obvodniy Canal. Predominantly residential, the districts largely developed in the latter half of the nineteenth century, and to natives of the city each has a specific resonance. **Liteyniy prospekt** has been a centre of the arts, shopping and – with the secret police headquarters at its northern end – repression since the middle of the last century. A couple of kilometres to the east lies the **Smolniy** district, whose focal point, Rastrelli's rocket-like **Smolniy Convent**, is a must on anyone's itinerary, as is the **Smolniy Institute**, from where the Bolsheviks launched the October Revolution.

Further south, the cemeteries at the **Alexander Nevsky Monastery** are the resting place for some of the city's most notable personalities, while back nearer the city centre is the bustling market quarter of **Vladimirskaya**, with its cluster of museums, including Dostoyevsky's apartment. Running southwest from Vladimirskaya is **Zagorodniy prospekt**, home of a musical tradition particularly associated with the Rimsky-Korsakov Museum the square known as **Tekhnologicheskiy Institut**; while further south is the blue-domed **Trinity Cathedral**.

Liteyniy prospekt

Liteyniy prospekt – running due north from Nevskiy prospekt to the Neva – is one of the oldest streets in the city, taking its name from the Liteyniy dvor, or "Smelting House", a cannon foundry established on the left bank of the Neva in 1711. It quickly became a major shopping street and the next most important avenue on the south bank after Nevskiy. While Liteyniy exhibits less of the architectural diversity of Nevskiy prospekt, there's plenty of streetlife to observe and a

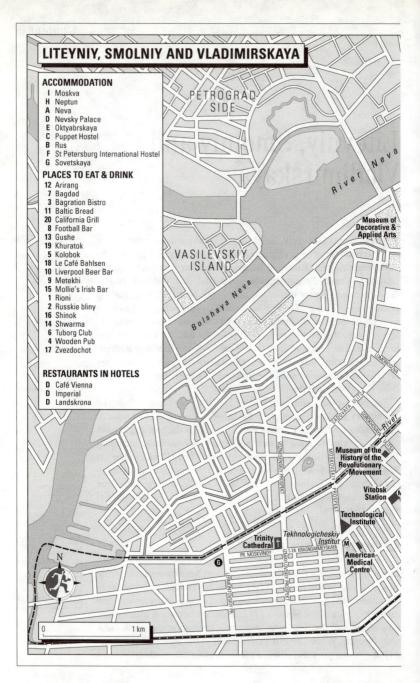

LITEYNIY, SMOLNIY AND VLADIMIRSKAYA

ACCOMMODATION
I Moskva
H Neptun
A Neva
D Nevsky Palace
E Oktyabrskaya
C Puppet Hostel
B Rus
F St Petersburg International Hostel
G Sovetskaya

PLACES TO EAT & DRINK
12 Arirang
7 Bagdad
3 Bagration Bistro
11 Baltic Bread
20 California Grill
8 Football Bar
13 Gushe
19 Khuratok
5 Kolobok
18 Le Café Bahlsen
10 Liverpool Beer Bar
9 Metekhi
15 Mollie's Irish Bar
1 Rioni
2 Russkie bliny
16 Shinok
14 Shwarma
6 Tuborg Club
4 Wooden Pub
17 Zvezdochot

RESTAURANTS IN HOTELS
D Café Vienna
D Imperial
D Landskrona

PETROGRAD SIDE

River Neva

Museum of Decorative & Applied Arts

VASILEVSKIY ISLAND

Bolshaya Neva

LOMONOSOVA

SADOVAYA ULITSA

GORKOVOY River

MOSKVOSKY

Museum of the History of the Revolutionary Movement

Vitebsk Station

Technological Institute

Trinity Cathedral

Tekhnologicheskiy Institut

PR. MOSKVINOY

1-YA KRASNOARMEYSKAYA

IZMAILOVSKY PROSPEKT

American Medical Centre

N

0   1 km

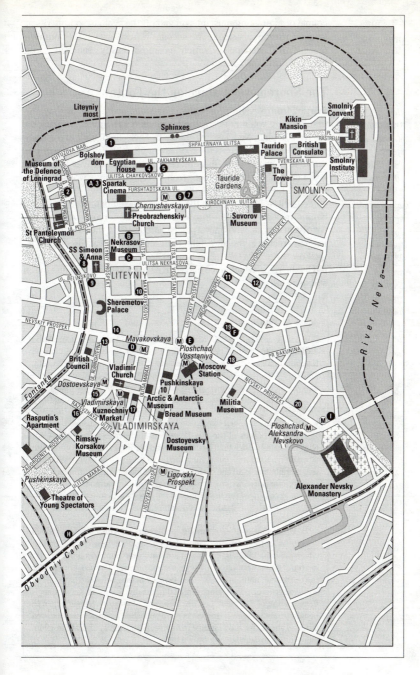

Liteyniy most

Sphinxes

Kutuzova Nab

Museum of
the Defence
of Leningrad

Bolshoy
dom

Egyptian
House

ULITSA CHAYKOVSKOVO

A 3 Spartak
Cinema

FURSHTADTSKAYA UL.

St Panteleymon
Church

Chernyshevskaya

Preobrazhenskiy
Church

Nekrasov
Museum

SS Simeon
& Anna

UL. BELINSKOVO

UL. PESTELYA

LITEYNIY

Sheremetev
Palace

NEVSKIY PROSPEKT

Fontanka

British
Council

Dostoevskaya

Vladimir
Church

Mayakovskaya

Ploshchad
Vosstaniya

Pushkinskaya

Moscow
Station

Arctic & Antarctic
Museum

Bread Museum

VLADIMIRSKAYA

Rasputin's
Apartment

Vladimirskaya

Kuznechniy
Market

Rimsky-
Korsakov
Museum

Dostoyevsky
Museum

Pushkinskaya

Ligovskiy
Prospekt

Theatre of
Young Spectators

Obvodniy Canal

SHPALERNAYA ULITSA

UL. ZAKHAREVSKAYA

Kikin
Mansion

Tauride
Palace

British
Consulate

Smolniy
Convent

PL.
RASTRELLI

Smolniy
Institute

The
Tower

TVERSKAYA UL.

Tauride
Gardens

SMOLNIY

KIROCHNAYA ULITSA

Suvorov
Museum

ULITSA NEKRASOVA

River Neva

PR BAKUNINA

NEVSKIY PROSPEKT

Militia
Museum

Ploshchad
Aleksandra
Nevskovo

Alexander Nevsky
Monastery

ULITSA MARATA

LIGOVSKIY PROSPEKT

couple of interesting museums on and off the avenue, so it merits at least an afternoon's stroll. The account below starts at the southern end of the prospekt, which is most easily reached from Mayakovskaya metro station.

The Sheremetev Palace on the Fontanka

*The
Akhmatova
Museum is
open
Tues–Sun
10.30am–
5.30pm, closed
last Wed of the
month; $1.
Tour $2
(phone ☎272
22 11 to
arrange an
English-
language
tour).*

Starting from Nevskiy prospekt and walking north along Liteyniy, the first building you'll notice is the **Mariinskaya Hospital**, set back on the right, a plain Neoclassical edifice by Quarenghi, built in the early 1800s. Diagonally across the road at no. 53, white arrows direct you through the yard to the **Sheremetev Palace on the River Fontanka** – you can only enter the palace from here, though it's worth making the circuitous trip round to the palace's river-facing side to see its golden-yellow facade, one of the glories of the embankment, set back behind majestic wrought-iron gates. Named after one of Peter the Great's marshals, who built a palace here in 1712, the existing building was erected in the mid-eighteenth century and was also known as the Fontanniy dom (Fountain House) because of the many fountains, fed by the river, which once played in its grounds – a nickname that's still used today.

Anna Akhmatova

Born in Odessa in 1889 and brought up in Tsarskoe Selo, **Anna Akhmatova** lived most of her life in St Petersburg, where she married Nikolai Gumilyov, an Assyriologist and founder of the Poets' Guild. Together with Osip Mandelstam, they made the guild the centre of the movement known as **Acmeism**, whose avowed principles were clarity and freshness. Akhmatova's marriage to Gumilyov was an unhappy one (they divorced in 1918), and after he was executed by the state in 1921 for treason, the stigma attached to Akhmatova kept her silent for the next decade.

The mass purges of the mid-1930s impelled her to write again – not least because Mandelstam, her son Lev and her lover, Nikolai Punin, were all arrested. Her *Requiem* cycle is the finest poetry to have emerged from that terrible era. With the outbreak of war, Akhmatova threw herself into the patriotic cause, writing one of the great Russian war poems, *Courage*. Having experienced the first winter of the Blockade before being evacuated to Tashkent, she gradually re-established her career and had several works published.

In 1946, shortly after returning to Leningrad, Akhmatova was vilified once more in the infamous "cultural report" by Party Secretary Zhdanov, which described her as "a nun and a whore, who combines harlotry with prayer". She was put under 24-hour surveillance and Lev was arrested for the third time, until, in 1950 – like so many before her – she gave in and wrote a series of poems glorifying Stalin. Finally, following Khrushchev's denunciation of Stalinism, Lev was freed and Akhmatova herself began to benefit from the "thaw". Her works were published again, she was allowed to travel abroad for the first time in fifty years and, until her death in 1966, enjoyed the acclaim so long denied her.

One of the greatest poets of Russia's "Silver Age", Anna Akhmatova lived on the third floor of the palace's southern wing between 1933 and 1941 and again from 1944 to 1954 – some of the worst years of her life (see box opposite). Although the palace's **Akhmatova Museum** consists of various rooms containing exhibits relating to her life, she actually lived, worked and slept in only one of them, where you'll find her desk, above which hangs a pen-portrait by Modigliani, the only surviving one of a series executed during a trip to Paris in 1911.

In another part of the palace is the newly opened **Musical Instruments Museum**, previously located near St Isaac's. Its collection runs the gamut from Polish violins to Buryat horns, beautifully crafted in diverse styles; it's worth paying for a tour in English to hear recordings of how the instruments sound.

Liteyniy prospekt

The Musical Instruments Museum is open Wed–Sun noon–5pm; closed last Wed of the month; $2. Tours $3 (group rate).

The art world on the prospekt

For many years, the cultural life of St Petersburg – and Russia as a whole – was strongly influenced by two publications based on Liteyniy prospekt. During the latter part of the nineteenth century, educated Russians imbibed new writing and ideas from **Sovremennik** (*The Contemporary*), the literary journal co-edited by **Nikolai Nekrasov** and **Ivan Panaev**, who lived in adjacent apartments at Liteyniy prospekt 32 and who both enjoyed a cosy *ménage à trois* with Ivan's wife, Avdotya Panaeva – herself a writer. All three campaigned for the emancipation of women – but it was for highlighting the plight of the peasants before and after the Emancipation Act in 1861 that Nekrasov fell foul of the censors, thus earning posthumous approval in Soviet times, when his apartment was turned into the **Nekrasov Museum**. It was an unlikely editorial office: the comfortably furnished suite even includes a ballroom. Nekrasov's bedroom is laid out as it was in the last year of his life, reconstructed from the sick-bed scene which hangs in situ.

A generation or so later, in the decades before the Revolution, the standard-bearer was the **Mir iskusstva** (World of Art) movement and magazine, whose influence long outlasted its relatively short life (1898–1904). Partly in reaction to the didactic artistic movements of the nineteenth century, the movement's philosophy was "Art for Art's sake". The magazine was produced in full colour, with elaborate woodcuts and typography and promoted Style Moderne (the native version of Art Nouveau), as well as hitherto neglected aspects of Russian culture. Artists Alexandre Benois, Léon Bakst and Nikolai Roerich provided most of its material, but the magazine owed much to **Sergei Diaghilev**, the impresario known for his Russian ballet seasons in Paris, who edited it from his apartment at Liteyniy prospekt 45, on the corner of ulitsa Belinskovo.

The Nekrasov Museum is closed until 2001; call ☎272 01 65 for further information.

The Preobrazhenskiy Church and beyond

A short way down ulitsa Pestelya, off Liteyniy, an oval wrought-iron grille enclosing captured Turkish cannon surrounds the Cathedral of the Transfiguration, better known as the **Preobrazhenskiy Church**. The original regimental church, which burnt down in 1825, was erected by **Empress Elizabeth**, the daughter of Peter the Great, as a token of gratitude to the Preobrazhenskiy Guards, whom she won over in her bid for power in 1741 with the immortal rallying cry: "Lads! You know whose daughter I am. Follow me." The present five-domed, Neoclassical structure was designed by Stasov in the late 1820s and served as an ad hoc military museum during the nineteenth century. It is now a working church again, and its **choir** is one of the best in the city (most of its members also sing in the Kapella Choir) and can be heard at weekend services.

A block north on Kirochnaya ulitsa stands another Neoclassical edifice: the sky-blue, erstwhile Lutheran Church of St Anna, whose pretty semicircular colonnade faces Furshtadtskaya ulitsa. Built by Felten in the 1770s, it was converted in 1939 into the **Spartak Cinema** – still the best art-house cinema in town – although it's now being used once more by missionary Lutherans, who hold services in a kind of annex and want the entire building returned to the church.

West of Liteyniy prospekt

West of Liteyniy prospekt, a network of leafy residential streets form what the locals call a "city within a city" – a quiet neighbourhood lined with bourgeois residences. After the Revolution its spacious apartments were subdivided into *kommunalki* (communal flats), many of which were assigned to specific groups of workers such as street cleaners or artists (for whom the upper-storey flats made superb studios), making the neighbourhood far more socially diverse than it would be in most Western cities. In recent years, however, the process has gone into reverse, as property developers persuade the poorer (often elderly or alcoholic) residents to exchange their rooms for high-rise flats in the suburbs, before removing the partition walls to recreate the original apartments, which can then be sold for upwards of $50,000 – a trend that's manifest all over the city centre.

The Museum of Decorative and Applied Arts is open daily 11am–4.30pm; free. English-language guided tours can be booked on ☎273 32 58.

Apart from being a pleasant area to stroll through, there's a smattering of sights along **Solyanoy pereulok** (Salt Lane), which runs parallel to the Fontanka embankment, starting with the early Baroque terracotta-and-white **Church of St Panteleymon** on the corner of ulitsa Pestelya – it's now a working church again after many years of service as the Museum of the History of Leningrad.

Next door, and of more interest, is the Mukhina College, which houses the **Museum of Decorative and Applied Arts**. Founded in

1876 by the banker Baron Steiglitz, the college occupies an imposing building which was designed by its first director, Max Messmacher, and modelled on St Mark's Library in Venice. Students were involved in painting its splendid neo-Renaissance interior and in restoring it after World War II. Although many of the museum's finest treasures were appropriated by the Hermitage during Soviet times, it still houses a fine collection of tiled stoves (*pechki*), Russian dolls, porcelain and furniture – most of the exhibits date from the eighteenth century. In July, student diploma exhibitions are held in the Medici Hall, whose gigantic glass mansard roof has recently been restored. On your way in, note the elaborate lampstand in front of the building whose base features four cherubs practising the decorative arts.

Further up the street, a pair of anti-aircraft cannons flank the entrance to the **Museum of the Defence of Leningrad**, devoted to "the Blockade" – the three-year siege of the city during World War II. The museum consists of one large exhibition hall on the second floor, with a fine array of wartime posters, including Todize's famous *Rodina-Mat zovyot!* (The Motherland calls!). The centrepiece is a reconstruction of a typical apartment during the Blockade, complete with boarded-up windows, smoke-blackened walls and a few pieces of furniture – the rest having been used as fuel on the tiny stove. Around the edges of the hall are exhibits on artistic life during the siege. It's a measure of the importance of the arts in the city that, despite the desperate lack of resources, several theatres and concert halls functioned throughout the Blockade, and even during the dreadful winter of 1941–42, Leningrad's starving citizens continued to attend exhibitions and concerts.

Liteyniy prospekt

The Museum of the Defence of Leningrad is open 10am–5pm, Tues till 3pm, closed Wed & last Thurs of the month; $1.50. Guided tours in Russian by prior arrangement on ☎275 72 08.

For more on the Blockade, see p.259.

The Bolshoy dom

The city's record of heroism is even more poignant given that it owed so much of its suffering not to Russia's enemies, but to its own government – above all, to the Stalinist purges following the assassination of the Leningrad Party secretary, Sergei Kirov, in 1934. This purge was implemented from the headquarters of the secret police, universally known as the **Bolshoy dom** (Big House), from whose roof – it was said – "you can see Kolyma" (a labour camp in the Arctic Circle).

With chilling consistency, the Bolshoy dom – at Liteyniy prospekt 4 – stands on the site of the old St Petersburg Regional Court, the scene of some of the most famous political trials in Tsarist times. By the late 1870s, public opinion had begun to turn in favour of the radicals who were arraigned in the mass trials of "the 50" and "the 193"; when Vera Zasulich shot a police chief who had ordered an imprisoned student to be flogged, she too was tried here, but was acquitted to popular acclaim. The Nihilist assassins of Alexander II were condemned to death here, as was Lenin's brother for his attempt on the life of Alexander III; and Trotsky and other leaders of the 1905

Revolution wound up in the court after the December clampdown.

After the court was torched in the 1917 February Revolution, a new building was custom-built for the OGPU – as the secret police were then known. Designed in 1931–32 by a trio of architects led by Noy Trotsky (no relation), it was one of the few large buildings erected in the city centre between the wars, and featured three subterranean levels plus the seven floors above ground. Ironically, during the Blockade it was one of the most comfortable places in Leningrad: heated (for the benefit of the jailers), shellproof and with a reliable supply of food – although political prisoners had to share cells with cannibals arrested for eating or selling human flesh.

The present occupants of the Bolshoy dom now style themselves the **Federal Security Service (FSB)**, the post-Soviet name for the old KGB. Though ostensibly reformed under Yeltsin, the FSB still saw fit to persecute a Russian naval officer who revealed details of radioactive pollution in the Baltic and Bering seas to Norwegian ecologists, and is believed to have smeared the procurator general after he began investigating corruption in the Kremlin. Yet its reputation (like that of its former boss, Vladimir Putin) has risen as fears of crime, terrorism and poverty have eclipsed the anxiety that the KGB once inspired. In Soviet times the street was named after the revolutionary Ivan Kalyaev, and every inhabitant of the city still knows what "to Kalyaeva" (*na Kalyaeva*) – an old euphemism for being arrested – signifies.

In a similar vein, around the corner at Shpalernaya ulitsa 25, is the old Tsarist **House of Detention**, rebuilt after it was burnt down by demonstrators in the February Revolution. Almost every notable revolutionary was interned here at some point, including Lenin, who spent fourteen months in the House of Detention before being exiled

---

The Egyptian House and the Gum Arabists

As the Bolshoy dom is by no means the only building in the vicinity housing security or law-enforcement agencies, **Zakharevskaya ulitsa** is probably the last place you'd expect to find flourishing centres of artistic bohemia. Yet in the early days of perestroika, the city's first art squat existed at no. 10, and was often visited by KGB officers out of curiosity rather than duty. Though later eclipsed by the better-known Pushkinskaya 10 (see p.233), this tradition is still upheld in the so-called **Egyptian House** at Zakharevskaya 23 – a huge decrepit 1900s apartment block decorated all over with Pharaonic statues and reliefs, whose array of businesses at street level includes a gun shop and the *Café Alibi*. With an entrée from the right person you can visit the studio-squat of the **New Seriousness Movement**, or "**Gum Arabists**", an offshoot of the New Academy of Fine Arts at Pushkinskaya 10. The movement's members are engaged in rediscovering and refining bygone techniques such as painting in wax encaustic and gum arabic photography – each of the photographs produced by the latter method, which involves exposing film to light over hours or even days, is a unique one-off.

to Siberia in 1897. According to veteran revolutionaries who experienced both Tsarist and Soviet prisons, conditions were far better in the former, which tolerated visits by prisoners' wives, gifts of food at Easter and Christmas and inspections by the Red Cross.

As a sombre finale to this aspect of the city's history, you can walk to the riverside and east along the embankment to see Mikhail Shemiakin's memorial to the victims of political repression, erected in 1996. It consists of a pair of **sphinxes**, whose serene countenances are half eaten away to reveal their skulls beneath, and a miniature cell window mounted on the embankment wall, through which you can peer across the river towards Kresty Prison, where so many victims of the purges were incarcerated (see p.257).

The Smolniy district

Tucked into a bend in the River Neva, the **Smolniy district** is a quiet, slightly remote quarter, badly served by public transport. Most tourists are drawn here by the **Smolniy Convent**, while Petersburgers come to visit the **Tauride Gardens**. In Tsarist times the district was called Rozhdestvenskiy, after the regiment which had its barracks in the area, but with the establishment of the State Duma and, later, the Petrograd Soviet in the Tauride Palace, the district evolved into the country's main centre of power. The Smolniy Institute was the Bolsheviks' principal base during and after the October Revolution; it subsequently became the Leningrad Party headquarters.

Although it's possible to walk the two kilometres from Chernyshevskaya metro, through the Tauride Gardens and on to the Smolniy complex, you may prefer to take trolleybus #15 a couple of stops down Kirochnaya ulitsa to the Suvorov Museum, near the southeastern corner of the Tauride Gardens.

Along Furshtadtskaya ulitsa

If you're intent on walking, head east down Furshtadtskaya ulitsa from Chernyshevskaya metro. This leafy avenue is lined with imposing mansions and was one of the most fashionable streets in pre-revolutionary St Petersburg. The leading Duma politicians Rodzyanko and Guchkov lived at nos. 20 and 36 respectively; at the other end of the political spectrum, Pyotr Lavrov, the nineteenth-century agrarian populist, lived at no. 12; while Dmitri Stasov, a lawyer who defended revolutionaries and hid Lenin for a time in 1917, lived in the same building as Rodzyanko. The street culminates in the pink, neo-Baroque **Palace of Weddings**, or registry office, which sports a fancy covered bridge.

The US, Austrian and German consulates are also on Furshtadtskaya ulitsa. Don't photograph them.

Around the Tauride Gardens

At the end of Furshtadtskaya ulitsa are the **Tauride Gardens** (Tavricheskiy sad), which back onto the Tauride Palace. The gardens are now primarily a children's park, boasting an antiquated **fairground** on the western side, though there's the usual panoply of ponds, sunbathers and courting couples as well.

Near the southeastern corner of the park, at the busy junction of Kirochnaya and Tavricheskaya ulitsa, stands the **Suvorov Museum**, a quasi-fortified building erected in 1902 to commemorate the eighteenth-century generalissimo Alexander Suvorov. The museum displays Suvorov's personal effects, period militaria and antique toy soldiers, while its exterior is distinguished by colourful mosaics depicting his departure for the Italian campaign of 1799, and Russian troops crossing the Alps. The former features a small fir-tree made by the writer Zoshchenko as a child; his artist father designed the mosaics. "The harder the training, the easier the battle," was one of Suvorov's favourite maxims, many of which were taught to schoolchildren in Soviet times, although Suvorov himself was so sickly as a child that he wasn't signed up for the Guards until the age of 12, unlike his contemporaries, who were "put down" for their regiments at birth.

*The Suvorov
Museum is
open Mon
10am–5pm,
Tues–Thurs
10am–6pm &
Sat
10am–7pm;
$1.*

Tavricheskaya ulitsa, on the eastern side of the park, contains some impressive turn-of-the-century buildings along its southern section, many of them now largely owned by Mafiosi from the Tambov and Solnechnoe gangs, to the despair of law-abiding residents. Overlooking the gardens, the top floor of the circular tower on the corner of Tverskaya ulitsa once hosted the salon known as "**The Tower**" (Bashnya), frequented by Akhmatova, Blok, Mandelstam, Roerich and others. The sprawling open-plan apartment belonged to the mystic and poet Vyacheslav Ivanov, who presided like a high priest over his famous "Wednesdays" – intellectual free-for-alls which often lasted for days. The salon died out after Ivanov emigrated in 1912.

*The tower is
closed to the
public.*

The Tauride Palace

Situated in the northeastern corner of the park, the **Tauride Palace** (Tavricheskiy dvorets) was built by Catherine the Great for her lover, Prince Potemkin, the brains behind the annexation of the Crimea (then known as Tauris or Tavriya, hence the palace's name). Completed by Stasov in 1789, the palace is one of the city's earliest examples of austere Neoclassicism. From Shpalernaya ulitsa, you can still admire the yellow main facade, whose six-columned portico is almost entirely devoid of decorative detail, but the original view north across the Neva is now obscured by factories, and the fabulous interior was deliberately ruined by Catherine's son, Paul, who turned it into a stables and barracks for the Horseguards. Foremost among its chambers was the **Catherine Hall**, a long gallery with rounded ends, which opened onto a Winter Garden where tropical birds flitted amidst rose and jasmine bushes under a glass canopy. Potemkin occupied the palace for just over a year before his death in 1791, and

Prince Potemkin

Born into poverty in the Smolensk region, **Grigori Potemkin** (1739–91) –
pronounced "Pot*yom*kin" – joined the army and quickly rose through the
ranks, largely due to his bottomless reserves of energy and courage.
Physically imposing, but far from beautiful (he got rid of an infected eye
by deliberately lancing it in a fit of impatience), Potemkin was soon
noticed by Catherine the Great and became her lover. Between campaigns
he would arrive unannounced at the Winter Palace, unshaven and clad
only in his dressing gown and slippers. Even after she took other lovers –
some of whom he selected – Potemkin remained her foremost friend and
courtier, demonstrating his mastery of diplomacy during her inspection
tour of the Crimea in 1787. As governor general of the newly conquered
region, he was at pains to portray it as more prosperous than it was: fake
villages were erected along Catherine's route, while local peasants were
given a fresh set of clothes and ordered to look cheerful – a trick perfect-
ed in the Soviet era, when "Potemkin tours" of factories and towns were de
rigueur for VIPs and foreign tourists.

threw the greatest New Year's Eve Ball the city had ever witnessed in
a final effort to revive Catherine's love for him. Over three thousand
guests filled the rooms, which were lit by fourteen thousand multicoloured oil lamps and twenty thousand candles. At the entrance, the
guests were met by an elephant covered in gems and ridden by a
Persian; beyond, a curtain lifted to reveal a stage on which ballets
and choral works were performed.

The palace is now in the hands of local authorities and, sadly,
closed to the public, but it retains a vital place in the city's history. In
1905, it was chosen as the venue for the **State Duma**, which – following the first parliamentary elections in Russian history – was
inaugurated in May 1906. On February 27, 1917, in the final throes
of the Tsarist autocracy, over thirty thousand mutinous troops and
countless demonstrators converged on the palace; inside a
Provisional Committee was formed, which later became the
Provisional Government. Simultaneously, in another wing of the
palace, the Petrograd Soviet was re-established, thus creating a state
of "dual power" that persisted until the October Revolution.

On January 5, 1918, the long-awaited **Constituent Assembly** met
for the first and last time in the Tauride Palace. As the first Russian
parliament elected by universal suffrage, this was meant to be "the
crowning jewel in Russian democratic life", but Lenin already privately regarded it as "an old fairytale which there is no reason to carry on
further". Having received only a quarter of the vote, the Bolsheviks
surrounded the palace the following day, preventing many delegates
from entering; Red Guards eventually dismissed those inside the
building with the words: "Push off. We want to go home."

In the 1930s the palace was home to the All-Union Communist
University and, following the war, housed the Leningrad Higher

Party School up until 1990. It is now used for prestigious conferences and meetings.

Along Shpalernaya ulitsa

The Smolniy Complex (see below) lies east of the Tauride Gardens at
the far end of **Shpalernaya ulitsa**, remarkable chiefly for its **statue
of Felix Dzerzhinsky**, the "steel-eyed, spade-bearded" Polish
founder of the Soviet secret police, the Cheka (meaning "linchpin" in
Russian). Erected in 1981, the statue was described by one Soviet
guidebook as expressing his "decisiveness and iron will", though
when slick with rain it looks more like a rubber-fetishist's dream,
clad in glistening jackboots, greatcoat and peaked cap.

Just past Dzerzhinsky, set back from the corner of Stavropolskaya
and Shpalernaya ulitsa, is the orange **Kikin Mansion**, a modest
Baroque country house. One of the oldest surviving buildings in the
city, it was erected in 1714 for Alexander Kikin, the head of the
Admiralty and one of Peter the Great's companions on his Grand Tour
of Europe. Later, however, Kikin was a prime mover in the conspira-
cy against Peter, which also involved the tsar's son, Alexei – both
Kikin and Alexei were tortured to death as a result. Damaged by shellfire in World War II, the house has since been restored to something
akin to its former glory and now serves as a children's music school.

The Smolniy complex

*The Smolniy
complex can
be reached by
minibus #T-8
and #T-125,
or by bus #22,
#46, #58,
#134 or
#136.*

From the Kikin Mansion, it's impossible to miss the glorious ice-blue
cathedral towering on the eastern horizon, which is the focal point
and architectural masterpiece of the **Smolniy Complex**. Prosaically,
its name derives from the Smolyanoy dvor, or "tar yard", sited here
in the eighteenth century to caulk Peter the Great's warships. Later,
Empress Elizabeth founded a convent on the site and Catherine the
Great also started a boarding school for the daughters of the nobility – the Smolniy Institute for Young Noblewomen – which later
became the headquarters of the Bolsheviks during the October
Revolution.

The Smolniy Convent

*The cathedral
is open
11am–4pm,
closed Thurs;
$3.50. For
information
on concerts
call ☎271 91
82.*

Rastrelli's grandiose plans for the **Smolniy Convent** (Smolniy
monastyr) were never completed, not least because Empress
Elizabeth's personal extravagance almost bankrupted the Imperial
coffers. Had the original plans been realized, the building would be
entirely different in character. Apart from the proposed Rococo
detailing, the major omission is a 140-metre-high bell tower, which
would have been the tallest structure in the city. As it turned out, the
empress ran out of money and the building was finished by Stasov
only in 1835, in a more restrained Neoclassical fashion and with a
bell tower only half of the proposed height.

Nevertheless, the view of the **exterior** from ploshchad Rastrelli is superb: the central five-domed cathedral offset by four large matching domes which rise in perfect symmetry from the surrounding outbuildings. The cathedral's austere white **interior** is disappointingly severe and suffered from neglect during the Soviet era, so it's not worth paying to go inside unless you're interested in seeing whatever temporary exhibition is showing on the first floor, or feeling energetic enough to climb up the bell tower for a splendid **view** of the Smolniy district. In addition to the services held here on weekends and religious holidays, the cathedral also hosts occasional **concerts** (early September to late June).

The Smolniy Institute

The **Smolniy Institute** – now the Governor's office – was built in 1806–08 to house the Institute for Young Noblewomen, but gained its notoriety after the Bolshevik-dominated Petrograd Soviet moved here from the Tauride Palace in August 1917. Soon, the Smolniy was "deep in autumn mud chomped from thousands of pairs of boots", with Red Guards sleeping in its dormitories and armoured cars parked in the courtyard. Here, too, the powerful **Military Revolutionary Committee** was established, which the Bolsheviks used as a legal means of arming their supporters in preparation for a coup. On the evening of October 25, the second **All-Russian Congress of Soviets** met at the Smolniy to the sound of shellfire. The Bolsheviks, who had a sizeable majority, tried to present the coup as a fait accompli, though fighting was still going on and the Provisional Government had yet to be arrested in the Winter Palace. When the Menshevik opposition called for an immediate ceasefire, Trotsky retorted: "You are miserable bankrupts, your role is played out. Go where you ought to be: into the dustbin of history." The next day, Party Chairman Kamenev announced the abolition of the death penalty and the release of all political prisoners (except those whom the Bolsheviks were rounding up), while Lenin read out the first two decrees of the Soviet government – calling for an end to the war and for the handing over of all private land to Peasant Committees and Soviets. The Smolniy served as the seat of Soviet power until March 1918, when the city's ostensible vulnerability in the Civil War impelled the government to move to Moscow.

The Smolniy Insitute is not open to the public.

Later, as the headquarters of the Leningrad Party organization, the Smolniy Institute witnessed the **assassination of Kirov**, the local Party boss, by Leonid Nikolaev on December 1, 1934. Stalin (who is thought to have masterminded the plot) immediately rushed to Leningrad and personally interrogated Nikolaev, before passing an illegal decree enabling capital sentences to be carried out immediately – whereupon Nikolaev and 37 others were promptly executed. This marked the beginning of a mass purge of Leningrad during which as many as one-quarter of the city's

The Smolniy district

The Shtandart

Until recently, the northern tip of the Smolniy area was home to the **Shtandart** – a life-sized replica of the 28-gun frigate that was Peter the Great's flagship and personal yacht, constructed by Russian and foreign volunteers during the late 1990s, in an improvised shipyard beside the Neva, north of ploshchad Rastrelli.

The original *Shtandart* was built on the River Svir in 1703, after Peter's return from Europe, using plans he had obtained from the British Admiralty. Its first role was to protect the construction of the Peter and Paul Fortress against Swedish assault, but soon after, in 1704–5, it saw active service as it sailed ahead of the Russian war galleys into the Baltic, sometimes with Peter in command. Though its guns never fired a shot in anger, Peter regarded the *Shtandart* as the "first born" of the Russian navy and ordered that it be preserved as a monument. After his death, Peter's widow, Catherine I, decreed that the rotting ship be rebuilt, but her order was never carried out.

The **recreation** of the *Shtandart* was the brainchild of Vladimir Martous, a boat-building graduate of the Marine Technical University, and naval historian Professor Krainyukov, who spent three years recreating the lost plans and dimensions of the vessel from shipyard records. A chance meeting with New Zealand-born yachtsman Greg Palmer led to international interest in the project, while a growing band of youthful enthusiasts toiled in the shipyard, shifting timbers and hewing planks. By the end, the project was patronized by Governor Yakovlev and Britain's Prince Andrew who, at the ship's launching ceremony in June 2000, bestowed on the ship the right to bear the flag of Peter the Great (a distant ancestor) before it sailed into the Neva Basin in front of a crowd of 40,000, bound for the Amsterdam and Bremerhaven Tall Ships festivals. The *Shtandart* will act as a roving ambassador for the city, and a sail-training ship for young volunteers and international crews, until it returns home when the Tall Ships race comes to St Petersburg in 2003.

For information on its progress around Europe and supporting the project, contact Ann Palmer (☎ or fax 279 86 26, *apalmer@shtandart.spb.ru*) or Vladimir Martous (☎271 19 40, *vmartous@shtandart.spb.ru*). It's possible that the ship will return permanently to St Petersburg at some point, though no one yet knows where it might be moored.

population are thought to have been arrested, the majority of them destined for the Gulag.

Nowadays, the Smolniy isn't open to visitors, though nobody minds if you stroll around the **monuments** in the gardens in front. In 1923–24 two simple commemorative propylaea were built, with the inscriptions "Workers of All Countries Unite!" and "The First Soviet of the Proletarian Dictatorship". The busts of Marx and Engels still face each other across the gravel paths, while Lenin himself stands before the porticoed entrance. The square in front of the propylaea is also the site of the **British Consulate**, which rejoices in the address 5 ploshchad Proletarskoy dikatatury (Dictatorship of the Proletariat Square).

The eastern end of Nevskiy prospekt

More than half of **Nevskiy prospekt** – some 2.5km – lies to the east of the River Fontanka, but for much of its length holds little of interest. Its chief attraction is the **Alexander Nevsky Monastery**, in the grounds of which are buried the city's most illustrious writers, artists and politicians. At some point you may also find yourself in **ploshchad Vosstaniya**, halfway along the prospekt, a major road and metro junction and home to Moscow Station. Beyond the station, the avenue is traditionally known as the **Stariy Nevskiy** – or "Old Nevskiy" – though it's not marked on maps as such.

Alexander Nevsky Monastery

At the southeastern end of the prospekt, beside the Neva, lies the **Alexander Nevsky Monastery** (Aleksandro-Nevskaya lavra), across

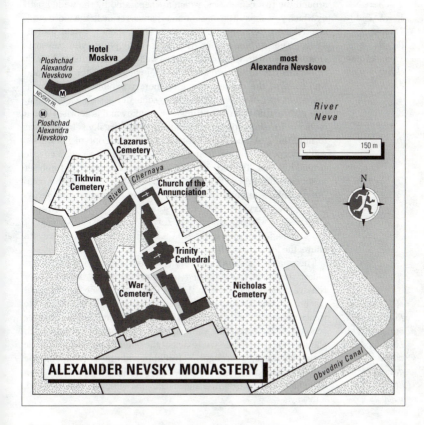

The eastern end of Nevskiy prospekt

the road from Ploshchad Aleksandra Nevskovo metro. The monastery was founded in 1713 by Peter the Great, on what was once believed to be the site of the thirteenth-century battle in which Prince Alexander of Novgorod defeated the Swedes, thus earning himself the sobriquet "Alexander Nevsky" (the name "Nevsky" being derived from the River Neva). In 1724, Peter had the recently canonized prince's remains transferred from Vladimir to the monastery, and from 1797 it became one of only four in the Russian Empire to be given the title of *lavra*, the highest rank in Orthodox monasticism.

The monastery complex includes the Tikhvin and Lazarus cemeteries and the Trinity Cathedral. A ticket is required for entry into the cemeteries, but not for the monastery itself or the cathedral, which are both open daily from dawn to dusk. The **ticket office** is just inside the main entrance.

The Tikhvin and Lazarus cemeteries

The cemeteries are open March–Sept 11am–6pm; Oct–Feb 11am–3.30pm; closed Thurs; $1.50.

Many tourists visit the monastery with the main aim of looking around the two cemeteries, which are separated by the walled path by which you enter. The most famous names reside in the more modern **Tikhvin Cemetery** (Tikhvinskoe kladbishche), established in 1823. The *babushka* at the gate will point you towards **Dostoyevsky**'s grave, which is just as well since his name is difficult to decipher from the ornate Cyrillic. Moving along the right-hand wall towards the chapel (now a temporary exhibition hall), you'll reach a cluster of graves belonging to some of Russia's leading composers. The first belongs to **Rimsky-Korsakov** and is adorned with a medieval Russian cross inset with icons; **Mussorgsky** is buried next to him, the grave decorated with a phrase from one of his works; while **Borodin**'s snippet from *Prince Igor* is set in a gilded mosaic behind his bust. **Tchaikovsky** has a grander, monumental tomb set in its own flowerbed. Other figures buried here include the composers **Rubinstein** and **Glinka**, the painters **Kustodiev** and **Serov**, the fabulist **Krylov**, the critic **Stasov** and the actor **Nikolai Cherkassov**, who played *Ivan the Terrible* in Eisenstein's trilogy of films. A map in Cyrillic in the southeastern corner of the graveyard shows the location of all the graves.

More famous Russians are buried in the Literatorskie mostki graveyard, described on p.250.

The smaller **Lazarus Cemetery** (Lazarovskoe kladbishche) is the oldest in the city, established by Peter the Great, whose sister Natalya was buried here in 1716. There are fewer international celebrities, but it's just as interesting in terms of funereal art: the tombs are strewn with death masks, skulls and crossbones and other sculptures. By consulting the map to the left of the entrance, you should be able to locate the tombs of the polymath **Lomonosov**, the architects **Rossi**, **Quarenghi**, **Voronikhin** and **Starov** (who built the Trinity Cathedral, see below), and Pushkin's wife, **Natalya Goncharova**, who is buried under the name of her second husband, Lanskaya.

The monastery and Trinity Cathedral

To reach the monastery itself, continue along the walled path, lined with alms-seekers, past Trezzini's **Church of the Annunciation**, completed in 1722. This was the original burial place of Peter III, Catherine the Great's deposed husband, but on her death their son Paul had them both buried in the traditional resting place of the Romanov rulers, the Peter and Paul Cathedral (see p.194). The raspberry-red, two-storey buildings of the monastery itself form an enclosed tree-filled quadrant, which serves as a cemetery for Communist activists and heroes of World War II. Trotsky's driver is buried in the grave behind the curious ensemble of iron chains and wheels, directly opposite the front steps of the Trinity Cathedral.

Trezzini also drew up an ambitious design for the monastery's **Trinity Cathedral** (not be confused with the Trinity Cathedral located further southwest, beyond Zagorodniy prospekt), but failed to orient it towards the east, as Orthodox custom required, so the plans were scrapped. The job was left to Ivan Starov to finish, who completed a rather more modest building in a Neoclassical style that sits awkwardly with the rest of the complex. The **interior**, however, is worth exploring, but bear in mind that this is a working church, not a museum. On Sundays it is pungent with incense and packed with worshippers genuflecting, kissing icons and lighting candles, while its choir is one of St Petersburg's best. The red agate and white marble **iconostasis** contains copies of works by Van Dyck and Rubens (among others), and a gilded canopy to the right shelters a modest copy of the silver sarcophagus of Alexander Nevsky that is now in the Hermitage.

To escape the crowds, head round the back of the cathedral to the **Nicholas Cemetery**, an overgrown graveyard where the monastery's scholars and priests are buried, as well as ordinary folk. Alas, the Soviet system made little provision for dignified burials; the bereaved had to ride in the back of a hearse resembling a delivery van, holding on to the coffin to stop it from sliding about.

The Militia Museum

The intriguing **Militia Museum** is known to few tourists or ordinary Petersburgers, being primarily intended for the Militia (police) themselves. Its discretion is matched by its location, on the right-hand side of the courtyard of Poltavskaya ultisa no. 12, running south off Nevskiy prospekt midway between the Alexander Nevsky Monastery and ploschad Vosstaniya. There's no sign as such, but Militia notices and roster-boards give the game away. All visitors to the museum are obliged to take a guided tour in Russian, which is interesting if you are able to understand the language or can bring an interpreter along.

The museum's five halls trace the **history of the Militia**, since its establishment in 1917 until the 1970s, starting with their activities during the Civil War and the NEP era, when gangsterism and fraud

The eastern end of Nevskiy prospekt

The Nicholas Cemetery is open daily: summer 9am–9pm; winter 9am–6pm.

The Militia Museum is open Mon–Fri 10am–6pm; visits by appointment only on ☎279 42 33; $8.50 group rate, individual rate negotiable.

in Russia were as rife as they are today – look out for the mug shots of notorious 1920s criminals like "Belka" (Squirrel) and the Alexandrov safe-cracking gang. During World War II, the Militia were responsible for civil defence in Leningrad and active as partisans behind enemy lines; there is also material documenting the Militia's social work amongst gangs of orphans. Further exhibits relate to some of the more macabre cases that the Militia were called upon to solve, including gruesome photos of dismembered bodies from the Rosenblat and "Head in a Bucket" **murder cases** of the 1940s – dioramas of muggings and the stuffed police tracker dog Sultan provide a light interlude. The main hall with its crimson banners is used for swearing in new recruits and another room (not open to visitors) contains mocked-up crime scenes on which trainee officers get to practise their forensic techniques.

Coincidentally, one of the most notorious crimes in the city's recent history happened only five minutes' drive from the museum, in 1997, when St Petersburg's Vice-Governor, Mikhail Manevich, was killed by a rooftop sniper as his car turned off Nevskiy prospekt on to ulitsa Marata. Nobody has ever been arrested for the crime, and even the police admit that it will probably never be solved – though it's thought that the motive was to halt his investigation of fraudulent city property deals.

Around ploshchad Vosstaniya

At the only bend in Nevskiy prospekt, the busy intersection of **ploshchad Vosstaniya** (Uprising Square) is dominated by **Moscow Station** (Moskovskiy vokzal), whose grand green-and-white facade looks more like a palace than a rail terminal; the architect built an identical one at the other end of the line in Moscow. Today, the facade is all that remains of the original station, which has been ruthlessly modernized inside. In 1993, a bust of Lenin was removed from the station hall by the city authorities, leading to protests by Communists and members of the older generation, who erected a plaque in its place reading: "On this spot, Mayor Sobchak betrayed the people of Leningrad", which remained there for several months until it was replaced by the present bust of Peter the Great.

The square itself was previously called Znamenskaya ploshchad, named after a church which was demolished in 1940 and replaced by the spired rotunda of Ploshchad Vosstaniya metro station (linked by a pedestrian subway to Mayakovskaya metro, further up Nevskiy). The square witnessed some of the bloodiest exchanges between police and demonstrators during the February Revolution, hence its current name: it was at a mass gathering on February 25 that Cossacks first turned on the police, shooting the leader of a mounted detachment. The battle for control of the square raged until the following day, when forty demonstrators were killed by police.

The central **obelisk** was erected in 1985, on the site of a much ridiculed equestrian statue of Alexander III, which workers called the

The statue of Alexander III is now in the courtyard of the Marble Palace.

"Hippopotamus" and mocked by reciting the lines: "Here stands a
chest of drawers/On the chest a hippopotamus/And on the hippopotamus sits an idiot." Initially, the Bolsheviks retained the statue
but added a sarcastic inscription by their unofficial poet laureate,
Demyan Bedny: "My son and my father were executed in their prime,
but I have attained posthumous glory: I stand here as an iron scare-
crow for the country which has forever thrown off the yoke of autocracy." A leaden joke, the statue was finally carted away in 1937, not
long after Bedny himself fell from Stalin's favour.

Pushkinskaya 10

From ploshchad Vosstaniya, turn left down Ligovskiy prospekt and
pass through the arch of no. 53 to reach the famous artists' colony
known as **Pushkinskaya 10** (Pushkinskaya desyat). One of the first
buildings in the city to be occupied by artists and dropouts,
Pushkinskaya 10 remains a vital force on St Petersburg's cultural
scene, even though the building itself has largely been refurbished
and sold off to wealthy individuals – this is why visitors can no longer
use the gated entrance on Pushkinskaya ulitsa, but must enter from
Ligovskiy prospekt, even though most of the galleries and studios
remain in the wing beside Pushkinskaya.

The **Museum of the New Academy of Fine Arts** (Sat 4–7pm; free)
on the fourth floor celebrates a decade of creative work by diverse
individuals sharing an aesthetic known as Neo-Academism, whose
"cruel naiveté" subverts both classicism and postmodernism. The
Academy's founder, Timur Novikov, is still a commanding presence
on the scene, despite going blind some years ago; many of the artists
whose work appears in the **Museum of Nonconformist Art**
(Tues–Sat 3–7pm; free) were once his protégés. Other studios worth
a visit include **FOTOimage** (Sat 4–7pm) on the second floor,
Navicula Artis (Wed–Sun 3–7pm) on the fourth floor, and the
Techno-Art Centre Gallery 21 (Tues–Sat 3–8pm) on the seventh.
The **Fish Fabriqué** club in the yard between the two blocks is a popular meeting place for musicians and artists.

Around Mayakovskaya metro

Bohemian traditions run deep in the neighbourhood around
Pushkinskaya 10. The poet Mayakovsky (see box on p.234) lends his
name to the nearby **Mayakovskaya metro station** – whose crimson
mosaic platform walls are adorned with his visage – and to **ulitsa
Mayakovskovo** on the other side of the prospekt, where he lived at
no. 52 during 1915–17 to be close to Lili Brik, who lived nearby with
her husband. On the same street, the absurdist writer **Daniil Kharms**
resided for much of his life at no. 11, being known for his affected
English plus fours and pipe, and for bowing to antique lampposts.
His fate was even crueller than Mayakovsky's: arrested by the Soviet
secret police and declared insane, he died in prison. In a Kharms-like

The eastern end of Nevskiy prospekt

Vladimir Mayakovsky

Futurist poet **Vladimir Mayakovsky** was born in Georgia in 1893. An enthusiastic supporter of the Bolshevik cause from an early age – he was elected to the Moscow committee when only 14 years old – Mayakovsky was arrested several times and given a six-month prison sentence in 1909. On his release, he enrolled at the Moscow Institute of Painting, Sculpture and Architecture and became friends with the Futurist painter, David Burlyuk. Together with other **Futurists**, they published a manifesto entitled *A Slap in the Face of Public Taste* and embarked on a publicity tour across Russia. Mayakovsky wore earrings and a yellow waistcoat with radishes in the buttonholes, scrawled obscenities on his face in greasepaint and recited avant-garde verses – the original punk, no less.

He threw himself into the October Revolution, becoming its keenest celebrant and propagandist: as a friend remarked, "Mayakovsky entered the Revolution as he would his own home. He went right in and began opening windows." Though his reputation as a poet rests on his romantic, pre-revolutionary work, he is best known for his later propagandist writing, such as the poem "150,000,000", which pits Ivan against world capitalism. One of the founders of the **Left Front of Art (LEF)**, an agitprop group whose members included Osip Brik and Alexander Rodchenko, Mayakovsky also produced graphic art during the 1920s, including over six hundred giant cartoon advertisements with captions for the Russian Telegraph Agency, ROSTA.

In 1930, five years after condemning the poet Yesenin for his "unrevolutionary" **suicide**, Mayakovsky killed himself in Moscow at the age of 37, with a revolver which he had used twelve years before as a prop in a film called *Not for Money Born*. His last unfinished poem lay beside him. Various motives have been advanced, ranging from despair over his love for Lili Brik to disillusionment with Soviet life, the philistinism of its censors, and hostile reviews of his most recent work. Whatever the truth, thousands filed past his open coffin at the Writers' Union, while a few years later Stalin decreed that "Mayakovsky was and remains the most talented poet of our Soviet epoch. Indifference to his memory and to his work is a crime." From then on, in the words of Pasternak, "Mayakovsky was sold to the people much as Catherine the Great had sold potatoes to the peasants."

twist, his wife – who was long thought to have died in the Blockade – was recently found to be living in Brazil. She hardly remembered him and wondered what all the fuss was about.

Vladimirskaya

Vladimirskaya metro station, south of Nevskiy prospekt, forms the nucleus of the slightly seedy **Vladimirskaya** area, whose sights include Kuznechniy Market, Dostoyevsky's apartment, the Arctic and Antarctic Museum, and the Bread Museum. Further southwest, **Zagorodniy prospekt** cuts through a tract of the inner suburbs associated with Dostoyevsky and Rasputin, to the Technological Institute – the birthplace of the Petrograd Soviet – and the Trinity Cathedral (not to be confused with the cathedral at the Alexander Nevsky Monastery).

Around Kuznechniy pereulok

Coming by metro, you'll either arrive at Dostoevskaya metro, with its elegantly simple marble platforms, or at the older Vladimirskaya metro (to which Dostoevskaya is linked by an underground passage), with ornate lamps and a mosaic of prosperous peasants – before emerging near Kuznechniy Market, situated on the southern side of **Kuznechniy pereulok**. Just around the corner to the left from Vladimirskaya, a newly installed bronze **statue of Dostoyevsky** sits pensively, while peddlers and beggars vie for your custom by the **Vladimir Church** on the corner of Kuznechniy pereulok. A yellow Baroque beauty with five bronze onion domes and a Neoclassical bell tower, the church has now been restored, having served as an ambulance station until 1989. Its upstairs nave has a beguiling raspberry, pistachio and vanilla colour scheme.

The indoor **Kuznechniy Market** (Kuznechniy rynok) is the best-stocked and most expensive market in the city. Also known as the Vladimirskiy Market, it offers fresh produce from all over the former Soviet Union: melons from Kazakhstan, tomatoes from Georgia, farmhouse honey, sour cream, hams and gherkins, not to mention imports such as kiwi fruit. Most vendors offer the chance to taste a sliver before buying – poor pensioners obtain breakfast by visiting a score of stalls.

Kuznechniy Market is open Mon–Sat 11am–8pm. For a list of the city's other markets, see p.310.

The Dostoyevsky Museum

In 1878, Dostoyevsky and his wife Anna moved into an apartment just beyond the market at Kuznechniy pereulok 5 to escape the memory of their previous flat, where their son Alexei had died. On the centenary of the writer's demise the apartment was reconstructed as a **Dostoyevsky Museum** on the basis of photos and drawings. The flat is surprisingly bright and cheerful: thanks to Anna, Dostoyevsky enjoyed a cosy domestic life while he created his brooding masterpieces – the children would push notes under his door, reading "Papa, we love you". Dostoyevsky died of a throat haemorrhage while writing his diary; the clock in the study where he wrote *The Brothers Karamazov* is stopped at the exact time of his death: 8.38pm, on January 28, 1881. Also on display is a printed announcement of Dostoyevsky's exile and a set of prison leg-irons, such as he wore en route to Siberia. At noon on Sundays, Russian **films** of his novels are screened downstairs. The museum also played a leading role in the unofficial art scene in the mid- to late 1980s, offering underground artists a first chance to exhibit their works freely.

The Dostoyevsky Museum is open Tues–Sun 11am–6pm, closed last Wed of the month; $1.75. English audio-guides can be hired for $2.

Dostoyevsky

Born in Moscow in 1821, one of seven children fathered by a violent, alcoholic physician, **Fyodor Dostoyevsky** lost his mother when he was 16 and his father (who was murdered by the family's serfs) two years later. A brief flirtation with Socialist politics ended in Dostoyevsky's arrest and a death sentence, commuted at the last moment to four years' hard labour, plus further service as an ordinary soldier. His first marriage and subsequent affairs were all dismal failures; gambling drained his meagre resources and, to complicate things further, he suffered from epilepsy. In 1866, to meet a tough deadline from a publisher, he hired an 18-year-old stenographer, **Anna Snitkina**, to whom he dictated *The Gambler* in less than a month. Soon afterwards they married and she became his permanent secretary, cured him of gambling, paid off his debts and made him a solid family man for the last quarter of his life.

While posthumously renowned in the West as one of the greatest writers of the nineteenth century, Dostoyevsky's **reputation** inside Russia was long denigrated by the Left, which condemned him for abandoning radicalism and engaging in polemics against the Nihilists. Between the 1930s and 1950s he wasn't even mentioned in Soviet textbooks, although he was eventually rehabilitated as a realist whose flaws embodied the contradictions of his era. None of his descendants dared reveal their identities until the early 1990s, when his great-grandson Andrei emerged from obscurity and undertook a tour of foreign literary societies, whom he disconcerted by his obsession with acquiring a Mercedes – with this, he now scrapes a living as an unregistered taxi driver. Recently, his sister Tatyana appealed for help in an open letter to a weekly newspaper, bitterly comparing her life as a pensioner struggling to survive on $33 a month to the poor of *Crime and Punishment*. None of the six direct descendants of Dostoyevsky still alive in St Petersburg receive any royalties from the millions of his books sold over the years.

The Arctic and Antarctic Museum

The Arctic and Antarctic Museum is open Wed–Sun 10am–5pm; closed last Sat of the month; $2.50.

Across the intersection of Kuznechniy pereulok with ulitsa Marata is the former Old Believers' Church of St Nicholas, which was closed down by the Bolsheviks and reopened in 1937 as the **Arctic and Antarctic Museum**. The Old Believers, of whom there are only about a hundred in St Petersburg, are trying to get the church back, and the outcome is difficult to predict. Meanwhile, the marble-columned nave is filled with stuffed polar wildlife, a mammoth's skull and tusk and the skiplane in which V.B. Shabrov flew from Leningrad to the Arctic in 1930. Off to the sides, at the back, are the leather tent used in the 1937–38 Soviet North Pole expedition and a model of a roomier hut with bunk beds and a portrait of Lenin, used by another group in 1954 – look out for the surgical tools that one explorer used to operate on himself. The dioramas of base camps and re-supply operations are self-explanatory and uncontentious, unlike the exhibits upstairs, which purport to show how Soviet rule improved the lives of the Arctic peoples – a reindeer-skin jacket embroidered with a

Proletarian breaking the shackles of Exploitation sums up the desired impression, while the environmental havoc wrought by the oil and gas industries and the nuclear contamination of Novaya Zemlya and the Kola Peninsula go unmentioned.

The Bread Museum

If your appetite for museums is unsated, carry on to the end of Kuznechniy pereulok and turn right onto Ligovskiy prospekt, where you'll find the **Bread Museum** at no. 73. Located on the fourth floor of a working bread factory permeated by delicious smells, the museum traces the history of a commodity dear to Russian hearts. Believing them to be more advanced in the art of baking, Peter the Great brought Germans over to run the city's first bakeries and then outraged the populace by imposing a hated bread tax. Baking remained a male profession until World War I, when women were employed to alleviate the labour shortage and **bread queues** that were a major cause of the February Revolution. There is a moving section on the Blockade, when the daily bread ration was little larger than a pack of cigarettes and contained ingredients such as sunflower husks and oak bark. If the delicious aromas from the factory give you a craving for the real thing, pay a visit to the museum's **café**, where you can try freshly baked pies, pastries and other delights. For more information, visit the museum's (Russian language-only) Web site at *www.museum.ru/museum/bread*.

The Bread Museum is open Tues–Fri 10am–5pm, Sat 11am–3pm; $1. Tram #19, #25, #44 or #49 along Ligovskiy prospekt.

Along Zagorodniy prospekt

The area around present-day **Zagorodniy prospekt** ("avenue beyond the city") was virgin forest until the middle of the eighteenth century when, in an effort to develop the area, Empress Anna divided it between two regiments of the Imperial Guard: the Semyonovskiy and the Izmailovskiy. Their paths through the woods paved the way for future streets and their massive parade ground (twice the size of Marsovo pole) became the site of St Petersburg's Hippodrome and the Vitebsk Station.

By the latter half of the nineteenth century, Zagorodniy prospekt had developed into a fashionable residential area associated with the city's **musical elite**. The director of the Conservatory, Rubinstein, lived for a while at no. 9 and Tchaikovsky spent a couple of years at no. 14. Just south of the intersection of streets known as the **Five Corners**, which witnessed violent clashes during three revolutions, is the **Rimsky-Korsakov Museum**, located in his former apartment on the third floor of the building in no. 28's courtyard. It contains over 250 items kept by his widow and descendants after his death in 1908, in anticipation of the opening of just such a museum in his honour: among them are two of his conductor's batons and a costume from his opera *The Snow Maiden*, designed by the artist Vrubel. The walls of the study are hung with portraits of composers he admired, including

The Rimsky-Korsakov Museum is open Wed–Sun 11am–6pm, closed last Fri of the month; $1.75. Call ☎113 32 08 for group tours or concert bookings.

one of Glinka, the father of Russian musical nationalism. At musical soirees held in the sitting room Chaliapin would sing, and composers Rachmaninov, Scriabin and Stravinsky would play the piano – concerts still take place in the apartment on a monthly basis. In keeping with Zagorodniy prospekt's musical traditions, the **Jazz Philharmonic Hall** (see p.298) is at no. 27, further along and across the road.

Pionerskaya ploshchad

Southwest of the Rimsky-Korsakov Museum, just to the east of Pushkinskaya metro, is the former stamping ground of the **Semyonovskiy Guards**, the second of the elite regiments founded by Peter before he became tsar. Given almost two hundred years of loyalty to autocracy, the Guards regiments' desertion of Tsarism in February 1917 seems surprising. In fact, the original regiments had already been committed to the front; what remained in Petrograd were the reserve units, composed of disaffected conscripts, whose loyalty was superficial.

In Tsarist times, the regimental parade ground – then known as Semyonovskiy plats – was the scene of the **mock execution of Dostoyevsky** and other members of the Petrashevsky Circle, on December 22, 1849. After eight months' confinement in the Peter and Paul Fortress, the 21 men were brought here to face a firing squad. The first three were tied to a post (Dostoyevsky was in the next batch), hoods were pulled over their faces and the guards took aim. At this point an aide-de-camp rode up with a proclamation, and the general in charge – deliberately chosen for his stutter – read out the commutation of their sentences, most of which were to *katorga* (hard labour). Two days later, fettered at the ankles, the men began their 3000-kilometre trek to Omsk prison in Siberia. It was here, too, that the assassins of Alexander II were hanged in 1881. One of the Nihilists was so heavy that the rope broke twice, whereupon the crowd began calling for a reprieve, but to no avail. Public executions were subsequently discontinued for fear of civil disorder.

In Soviet times the parade ground became a park and was renamed Pionerskaya ploshchad after the Communist youth organization, the Pioneers, and became the site of the **Theatre of Young Spectators** (TYuZ). At the park entrance stands a larger-than-life statue of **Alexander Griboedov** (1795–1829), a soldier and diplomat turned playwright who got into trouble with the censors for his *Woe from Wit* (1824). The following year he was arrested for his Decembrist connections and served a four-month prison sentence, but was subsequently rehabilitated and made an envoy to Persia. Sadly, on their arrival in Tehran, Griboedov and his party were murdered by a mob which sacked the Russian Embassy after an Armenian eunuch had taken refuge there. During Soviet times, his name was bestowed upon the city's loveliest canal, which had previously been named after Catherine the Great.

Rasputin on Gorokhovaya ulitsa

Heading from Zagorodniy prospekt northwest up Gorokhovaya ulitsa (Street of Peas) for 100m brings you to the gloomy residential building at no. 64 that once housed **Rasputin's apartment** – on the third floor at the rear of the courtyard. The apartment was kept under permanent surveillance by the Tsarist secret police and, as noted by their agents, was visited regularly by Rasputin's aristocratic devotees and a host of other women hoping to win favours at court. Rumours abounded of orgies in which the participants formed a crucifix with their naked bodies; though the reality was much cruder: Rasputin swiftly serviced the ladies in a room containing only an icon and an iron bed, before he arose muttering, "Now, now, Mother. Everything is in order."

Rasputin's apartment is now a kommunalka and is not open to the public.

The street is also mentioned in Russian literature. The denouement of Dostoyevsky's *The Idiot* takes place in Rogozhin's house on Gorokhovaya ulitsa, "not far from Sadovaya ulitsa", while the character of Stavrogin in *The Devils* commits his crime on the street. Another fictional resident was the famously indolent Oblomov, in Goncharov's novel of the same name.

Vitebsk Station

Beyond the park stands **Vitebsk Station** (Vitebskiy vokzal), which was the first train terminal in Russia when it opened in 1837, connecting St Petersburg with the palaces at Tsarskoe Selo and Pavlovsk. The existing building, constructed in 1904, is a wonderful Style Moderne edifice containing several halls with elaborate tiling, panelling and stained-glass windows. From its grand lobby, you can ascend a wrought-iron stairway to the ex-Imperial Waiting Room, decorated with murals of the palatial destinations. Near the platforms serving the palaces stands a replica of a nineteenth-century steam train that once operated on the route. An early passenger wrote that "the train made almost one *verst* (kilometre) a minute . . . sixty *versts* an hour, a horrible thought!"

Tekhnologicheskiy Institut

Nowadays chiefly known for its metro station where two lines interchange, the square known as **Tekhnologicheskiy Institut** took its name from the Technological Institute, whose lecture theatre hosted the first meeting of the short-lived St Petersburg Soviet of Workers' and Soldiers' Deputies, created during the 1905 Revolution. Under the leadership of Trotsky, Gorky and others, its executive committee assumed the responsibilities of government, issuing a spate of decrees from the Free Economic Society building across the square (no. 33), now called the **Plekhanov House**. On a lighter note, the square's **hospital** appears in Anthony Burgess's farce, *Honey for the Bears*, wherein the protagonist's wife is persuaded by a Soviet doctor to acknowledge her lesbianism, leaving her husband to confront his own sexuality in Leningrad.

Vladimirskaya

Streets and squares

ploshchad Aleksandra Nevskovo	площадь Александра Невского
Bolshoy Kazechniy pereulok	Большой Казечный переулок
Furshtadtskaya ul.	Фурштадская ул.
Kirochnaya ul.	Кирочная ул.
1ya Krasnoarmeyskaya ulitsa	1-я Красноармейская ул.
Kuznechniy pereulok	Кузнечный переулок
Ligovskiy prospekt	Лиговский проспект
Liteyniy prospekt	Литейный проспект
ul. Marata	ул. Марата
ul. Mayakovskovo	ул. Маяковского
ul. Pestelya	ул. Пестеля
ploshchad Rastrelli	площадь Растрелли
Shpalernaya ul.	Шпалерная ул.
Solyanoy pereulok	Соляной переулок
Tavricheskaya ul.	Таврическая ул.
Vladimirskiy prospekt	Владимирский проспект
ploshchad Vosstaniya	площадь Восстания
Zagorodniy prospekt	Загородный проспект

Metro stations

Ploshchad Aleksandra Nevskovo	Площадь Александра Невского
Chernyshevskaya	Чернышевская
Dostoevskaya	Достоевская
Ligovskiy Prospekt	Лиговский Проспект
Mayakovskaya	Маяковская
Pushkinskaya	Пушкинская
Tekhnologicheskiy Institut	Технологический Институт
Vladimirskaya	Владимирская
Ploshchad Vosstaniya	Площадь Восстания

Museums

Anna Akhmatova Museum	музей Анны Ахматовой
Arctic and Antarctic Museum	музей Арктики и Антарктики
Bread Museum	музей хлеба
Museum of Decorative and Applied Arts	музей Декоративно-прикладного искусства
Museum of the Defence of Leningrad	музей Обороны Ленинграда
Dostoyevsky Museum	музей-квартира Ф.М. Достоевского
Militia Museum	музей истории милиции
Museum of Musical Instruments	музей Музикальны Инструментов
Nekrasov Museum	музей-квартира Н.А. Некрасова
Rimsky-Korsakov Museum	музей-квартира Н.А. Римского-Корсакова
Suvorov Museum	музей А.В. Суворова

The Trinity Cathedral

Last but not least, west along 1ya Krasnoarmeyskaya ulitsa (one stop on tram #28 or #34 from Tekhnologicheskiy Institut, or bus #10 down Voznesenskiy prospekt) stands the huge **Trinity Cathedral** (Troitskiy sobor), whose ink-blue **domes** – visible from all over this part of town – were once spangled with golden stars. The Orthodox configuration of four domes surrounding a larger one dates back to the seventeenth century, when Patriarch Nikon banned tent-roofed churches in favour of a new style, theologically justified as a symbol of the four evangelists and "the seat of the Lord Himself". The cathedral, however, is purely Neoclassical: it was designed in 1828–35 by Stasov, and its only **exterior** decoration consists of a frieze beneath the cornice and a bas-relief above the portico.

In Tsarist times it was the garrison church of the Izmailovskiy Guards, fronted by an enormous column made of captured Turkish cannons. It was here that Dostoyevsky married Anna Snitkina in 1867, four months after he hired her as a secretary (see p.236). The cathedral was closed down in 1938 and only reopened in 1990; its **interior** is still under restoration, although services continue to be held.

Chapter 7

The Southern Suburbs

The **Southern Suburbs** cover a vast area beyond the Obvodniy Canal which was largely open countryside until the mid-nineteenth century. The first buildings here were factories – some of the largest in the Tsarist empire – and the slum housing which grew up around them became home to a militant working class which was instrumental in the revolutions of 1905 and 1917. Following the October Revolution, numerous housing projects were undertaken to replace the slum dwellings, while during the 1930s Stalin planned (and partially completed) a new city centre in these suburbs in an attempt to replace the old one, which was so closely associated in his mind with the ancien régime. Later on, during the Blockade, the front line ran through the working-class Narva and Avtovo districts.

By no stretch of the imagination is this conventional tourist terrain – the distances involved preclude casual sightseeing – but even the little-visited districts reveal fascinating aspects of Petersburg life. You don't have to have an interest in municipal housing to make a visit, either, since there are a couple of sights of more universal appeal, like the **Chesma Church**, one of St Petersburg's most unusual ecclesiastical buildings, and the **Victory Monument**, an awesome sculptural tribute to the city's suffering during World War II. The other target is a series of **cemeteries**, including the fascinating Literatorskie mostki graveyard in the Volkov Cemetery. The southern suburbs are well served by public transport and all the places described, with the exception of the Volkov Cemetery, are within walking distance of a metro station.

Along Moskovskiy prospekt

Moskovskiy prospekt is the longest avenue in the city, a dead-straight six-lane boulevard running from Sennaya ploshchad in the centre of St Petersburg to the Victory Monument on ploshchad Pobedy, 9km to the south. Most visitors only ever see the prospekt on their way to and from the airport and it's an overpowering introduction to the city, built, like the rest of St Petersburg, on an inhumanly large scale. No one in their right mind would suggest walking even part of the way along the prospekt, but there's enough of interest to warrant a selective exploration above ground.

As its name suggests, Moskovskiy prospekt has long been the main road to Moscow – though, in fact, the name dates only from 1956. Before that it was known as International Avenue, then Stalin Avenue; in 1878 it was dubbed Trans-Balkan Avenue, in honour of the Russian troops who had marched down it the previous year en route to fight the Turks in Bulgaria. Conveniently, a **metro** line runs underneath the avenue from Sennaya ploshchad to within walking distance of the Victory Monument, while **tram #29** offers a good surface view of the avenue from Frunzenskaya metro to Moskovskaya ploshchad.

From the Obvodniy Canal to Park Pobedy

One and a half kilometres south of Sennaya ploshchad, run-down apartment buildings give way to hulking factories as Moskovskiy prospekt crosses the **Obvodniy Canal**. Built in the first half of the nineteenth century to help prevent flooding, the canal's eight-kilometre length marked the city's southern limit for many years. Here, at the intersection with Moskovskiy prospekt, one of the most dramatic assassinations of Tsarist times occurred. On July 15, 1904, the SR Fighting Section (see box on p.246) succeeded in blowing up the reactionary interior minister, **V.K. Plehve**, in its third attempt on his life. Yegor Sazanov, dressed as a railway worker and with a seven-kilo bomb wrapped in his handkerchief, was one of four assassins lining the route. Plehve was killed instantly – it took three days to gather up all the pieces of his body – and Sazanov was badly wounded, but the others escaped.

Another one and a half kilometres south of the canal stands the cast-iron **Moscow Triumphal Arch** (Moskovskie vorota), a muddy-green monument modelled on Berlin's Brandenburg Gate. The arch was built by Stasov in the late 1830s to commemorate a whole series of victories against the Persians, Turks and Poles during the first decade of Nicholas I's reign. Along with the Triumphal Arch in Moscow, it was dismantled on Stalin's orders in 1936, only to be re-erected under Khrushchev in 1960. The nearest metro to the monument is Moskovskie Vorota.

The next metro station to the south, **Elektrosila**, whose platforms are peppered with workerist motifs, is named after the nearby electrical engineering factory, founded in 1911 by the German company, Siemens-Schuckert. Between here and Park Pobedy metro station, Moskovskiy prospekt is predominantly residential, lined with Stalinist-era apartment buildings. **Park Pobedy** itself is one of two

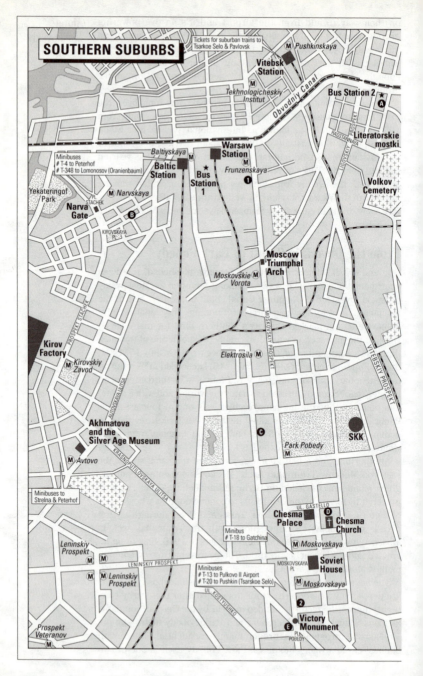

SOUTHERN SUBURBS

Tickets for suburban trains to
Tsarkoe Selo & Pavlovsk

Ⓜ *Pushkinskaya*

Vitebsk Station

Obvodniy Canal

Tekhnologicheskiy Institut

Bus Station 2 ★ Ⓐ

Literatorskie mostki

Baltiyskaya Ⓜ

Warsaw Station

Ⓜ *Frunzenskaya* ❶

Volkov Cemetery

Minibuses
T-4 to Peterhof
T-348 to Lomonosov (Oranienbaum)

★ **Baltic Station**

Bus Station 1

Yekateringof Park

Ⓜ *Narvskaya*

PL. STACHEK

Narva Gate

Ⓑ

KIROVSKAYA PL.

Moscow Triumphal Arch

Moskovskie Vorota Ⓜ

Kirov Factory

Kirovskiy Zavod Ⓜ

PROSPEKT STACHEK

Elektrosila Ⓜ

MOSKOVSKIY PROSPEKT

VITEBSKIY PROSPEKT

Akhmatova and the Silver Age Museum

Ⓜ *Avtovo*

KRASNOPUTILOVSKAYA ULITSA

Ⓒ

Park Pobedy

Ⓜ

● **SKK**

Minibuses to
Strelna & Peterhof

Leninskiy Prospekt Ⓜ

Ⓜ *Leninskiy Prospekt*

LENINSKIY PROSPEKT

UL. GASTELLO

Chesma Palace

Ⓓ ✝ **Chesma Church**

Minibus
T-18 to Gatchina

Ⓜ *Moskovskaya*

MOSKOVSKAYA PL.

Soviet House

Minibuses
T-13 to Pulkovo II Airport
T-20 to Pushkin (Tsarskoe Selo)

UL. KOSTYUSHKO

Ⓜ *Moskovskaya*

❷

Ⓔ **Victory Monument**

Prospekt Veteranov
Ⓜ

PL. POBEDY

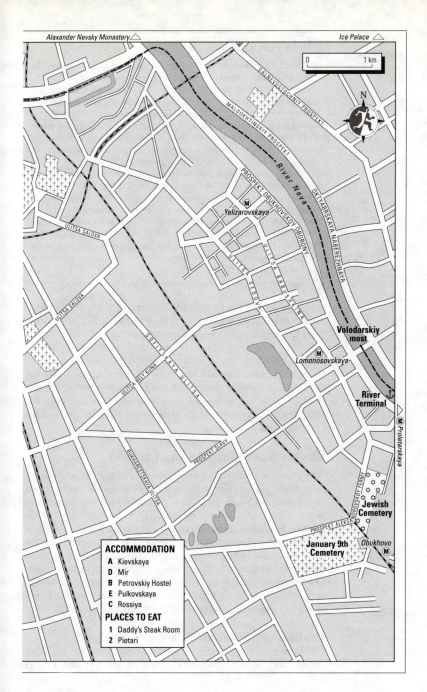

ACCOMMODATION

A Kievskaya
D Mir
B Petrovskiy Hostel
E Pulkovskaya
C Rossiya

PLACES TO EAT

1 Daddy's Steak Room
2 Pietari

The SR Fighting Section

The **Fighting Section** of the Socialist Revolutionary (SR) Party was the main revolutionary terrorist organization during the reign of Nicholas II. Besides the assassination of Plehve, and of Grand Duke Sergei in Moscow, its most spectacular coup was an attempt on the life of Prime Minister Stolypin. On August 12, 1906, an SR suicide squad forced its way into his *dacha* on Aptekarskiy Island and blew up the house, killing themselves and thirty others, and wounding Stolypin's two children. Stolypin himself survived, only to be shot five years later at the Kiev Opera House, in full view of the tsar, by an Okhrana (secret police) double agent.

The Okhrana's policy of infiltrating revolutionary groups was effective, but exposed them to double-crosses. The head of the Fighting Section, **Yevno Azef**, was himself an *okhranik*, but, as a Jew, had every reason to mastermind the killing of Plehve, the architect of the pogroms. Meanwhile, unsuspected by the SRs, Azef betrayed most of them to the Okhrana, while having Father Gapon – who led the march on "Bloody Sunday" – executed for being a double agent; only later was his treachery unearthed by SR counterintelligence. Azef fled to Germany to escape their vengeance and died of natural causes during World War I.

victory parks laid out by volunteer labour in 1945 (the other is on Krestovskiy Island). Flanking its central "Heroes' Alley" are busts of those Leningraders who were either twice awarded the title "Hero of the Soviet Union", or twice decorated with the "Hero of Socialist Labour" medal (including Brezhnev's prime minister, Kosygin). At the eastern end of the park looms the **SKK** (Sportivno-kontsertniy kompleks), a circular sports and leisure complex set in a sterile plaza, reminiscent of Ceausescu's Bucharest. Since its opening in 1980, the SKK has also hosted concerts by leading Russian and foreign musicians (see p.298).

Moskovskaya ploshchad and around

During the 1930s, Stalin toyed with the idea of shifting the centre of Leningrad to the southern suburbs, leaving the historic Tsarist core to wither away. Although plans for a giant ring road were never completed, the intended focus of the new centre was realized in the gargantuan **Moskovskaya ploshchad**, a fascinating legacy of Stalinist urban planning. The square is dominated by the **Soviet House** (Dom Sovetov), begun by Noy Trotsky in 1936, but not completed until after the war. It's a superb, if chilling, gem of Stalinist architecture, topped by a frieze portraying Soviet achievements; similar friezes can also be seen on the surrounding buildings. In 1970 a bronze **statue of Lenin**, by Mikhail Anikushin, was unveiled in the centre of the square.

The Chesma Church and Palace

Within easy walking distance of Moskovskaya ploshchad are a couple of more alluring sights. The first is the **Chesma Church**

(Chesmenskaya tserkov), a stunning red-and-white striped structure, built by Felten in 1777–80; it's situated just off ulitsa Gastello, behind the *Hotel Mir*. The traditional configuration of five Orthodox domes is almost lost in the feast of lanterns and zigzag crenellations which crown this bizarre "pastry Gothick" building. The church's name derives from the Turkish port of Çesme, where, in 1770, the Russians enjoyed one of their greatest naval victories. The building used to house a museum devoted to the battle but it has now reverted to the Church.

The pinkish **Chesma Palace** (Chesmenskiy dvorets), within sight of the church, was built for Catherine the Great as an Imperial staging post en route to Tsarskoe Selo and Pavlovsk. The original building was also designed by Felten, again in a kind of Turkish-Gothic style, but this time utilizing a unique triangular ground plan. Sadly, during the palace's conversion into a hospital for war veterans in the 1830s, it was substantially altered by the addition of three wings and the removal of much of its original decoration. Rasputin's body lay in state here after his murder; today the palace is a home for the elderly and is closed to the public.

The Victory Monument

South of Moskovskaya ploshchad, it's a short walk past the district's main department stores to the **Victory Monument** (officially entitled the "Monument to the Defenders of Leningrad"), which commemorates the hardship that Leningrad's citizens endured during World War II, especially during the Blockade. Paid for by public donations, it was unveiled in 1975 as the centrepiece of **ploshchad Pobedy**. The bowels of the monument consist of a vast broken ring of steel (symbolizing the breaking of the siege) lined with giant medals, in the midst of which flickers an eternal flame. Above the ground rises a 48-metre-high red granite obelisk, fronted by statues of a soldier and a worker. Most striking of all are the larger-than-life blackened bronze tableaux of partisans, salvage workers, nurses and other citizens, facing south towards the enemy. Constructed on a truly grand scale, it was designed to be viewed from a distance or from a passing vehicle (it's on the main road to and from the airport); the Finnish-built **Pulkovskaya Hotel** was deliberately located overlooking the monument, to remind foreign guests of the price that the city paid to defeat the Nazis.

The only reason to get any closer is to visit the subterranean **memorial hall** beyond the eternal flame and accessible via any of the underpasses around the square. Inside the dramatically gloomy marble hall are a few scattered relics from the siege, set in heavy marble sarcophagi, including a violin that was used in a performance of Shostakovich's Seventh Symphony during the Blockade. Its strains alternate with the steady beat of a metronome, a sound which was broadcast over the radio throughout the Blockade, to symbolize the city's heartbeat.

The memorial hall is open Mon, Thurs, Sat & Sun 10am–6pm; Tues & Fri 10am–5pm; closed last Tues of the month; free.

The Narva district

Lying on the road to Peterhof (and Narva, on the Russian–Estonian border), the **Narva district** – west of Moskovskiy prospekt – was once a popular spot for aristocratic *dachas*. In the latter half of the nineteenth century, however, it was developed as one of the city's main industrialized areas. Workers' hovels grew up alongside the factories and docks, and the whole district quickly became one of the breeding grounds of the revolutionary movement. As such, it was one of the first areas to be redeveloped after the Revolution, when it was renamed the Kirov district and endowed with some of the best inter-war architecture in St Petersburg. You can reach the district by taking the **metro** to Narvskaya, whose surface pavilion is built in a highly decorative Neoclassical style typical of the Kirovsko–Vyborgskaya line, which was the first section of the metro to be opened back in 1955.

Ploshchad Stachek

Emerging from the metro, you'll find yourself on **ploshchad Stachek** (Strike Square), scene of the first of the many fatal clashes on "Bloody Sunday" (January 9, 1905). Imperial troops fired without warning on the column of peaceful demonstrators heading for the Winter Palace, who were carrying portraits of the tsar and a white flag emblazoned with the message: "Soldiers! Do not fire on the people."

At the centre of the square is the copper-plated **Narva Gate** (Narvskaya zastava), a diminutive triumphal arch erected to commemorate the Napoleonic Wars. The original arch was hastily designed by Quarenghi in wood, in order to greet the victorious Imperial armies returning from the west, but was later replaced by Stasov's present structure, crowned by a statue of Victory astride her six-horse chariot, painted a martial dark green.

The rest of the surrounding architecture dates from a redevelopment of the late 1920s, when Constructivism was still in vogue. Good examples of the genre are the convex facade of the **Gorky Palace of Culture**, beside the metro station, which was opened on the tenth anniversary of the October Revolution, and the department store opposite – not to mention the heroic **mural** on one of the buildings.

Yekateringof Park

As part of the redevelopment of the late 1920s, a small island to the northwest of ploshchad Stachek was laid out as the Komsomol Park (named after the League of Young Communists). It has now been renamed the **Yekateringof Park** (also known as the Staro Petergofskiy) after the Yekateringof estate founded here by Peter the Great for his wife, Catherine, whose palace unfortunately burnt to

the ground in 1924. A small lake with paddle boats for rent, a fairground with ancient carousels, pony rides, and pensioners playing
chess are just some of the attractions and sights on offer at the weekend. To reach the park head northwest from ploshchad Stachek, then
cross over the stagnant canal to the Komsomol monument which
stands at the park's entrance.

Kirovskaya ploshchad to the Kirov Factory

Five minutes' walk south of Narvskaya metro down prospekt
Stachek, the avenue opens out into the vast megalopolis of
Kirovskaya ploshchad, a Stalinist set piece centred on a huge, six-
teen-metre-tall **statue of Kirov**, the assassinated Party boss (p.204).
The southern side of the square is entirely taken up by a long
Constructivist building, dating from 1926, which now houses a cin-
ema at one end and the district administration offices in the eleven-
storey tower at the other end. The square's other noteworthy
Constructivist edifice is the first **school** to be built in the city after the
Revolution, situated on the northwest corner of the square.
Constructed in 1925–27, it has a convex facade and a ground plan in
the vague shape of a hammer and sickle.

A couple of kilometres further down prospekt Stachek, Kirovskiy
Zavod metro takes its name from a vast heavy engineering plant
known as the **Kirov Factory**, whose origins predate the Bolshevik
Revolution. Founded in 1801 as the Putilov Works, it soon became
the largest industrial enterprise in Russia (employing over 40,000
people) and the cradle of the working-class movement. It was the
dismissal of four *Putilovskiy* workers which sparked off the 1905
Revolution, while the lockout of February 1917 primed the popular
explosion that culminated in the overthrow of Tsarism. During
World War II it was a prime target for Nazi artillery, but production
never ceased during the Blockade, although workers sometimes
had to tie themselves to their benches to avoid fainting through
hunger and exhaustion. After the war, the factory produced nuclear
submarine turbines and other high-tech items relating to the military – a dependency on arms production that brought the Kirov to
the verge of bankruptcy when the defence budget was slashed in
the 1990s. Today, its finances are looking healthier thanks to a
large order for tanks from the Indian government, but much of the
plant still lies idle.

The working-class Avtovo district makes an unlikely setting for the
Akhmatova and the Silver Age Museum. Founded by admirers of
the poetess Anna Akhmatova (see p.218), the display traces the lives
and relationships of the poets and artists of Russia's "Silver Age",
including such luminaries as Blok, Mandelstam, Roerich and Bakst.
The museum is located ten minutes' walk from Avtovo metro station,
at Avtovskaya ulitsa 14.

*The museum is
open Mon–Fri
10am–6pm by
guided tour
only (in
Russian); free.*

ST PETERSBURG

East of Moskovskiy prospekt

The vast tracts of factories and housing estates **east of Moskovskiy prospekt** won't persuade many people to explore this part of town. Indeed, the only conceivable reason for spending any time here is to visit the area's various **cemeteries**, most notably the Literatorskie mostki graveyard in the Volkov Cemetery, where numerous more-or-less famous Russians are buried. To get to the Literatorskie cemetery from the city centre, take any **tram** heading south down Ligovskiy prospekt or a #74 bus from Ligovskiy prospekt metro station, and get off at the end of Rasstannaya ulitsa.

The Literatorskie mostki

*The
Literatorskie
mostki is open
April–Oct
11am–7pm;
Nov–March
11am–5pm;
closed Thurs.
The memorial
hall is open
11am–5pm,
closed Thurs;
free.*

*Numerous
other
illustrious
figures are
buried in the
Tikhvin and
Lazarus
cemeteries in
the Alexander
Nevsky
Monastery
(p.230).*

Packed with notable names from pre-revolutionary Russian culture and politics, the **Literatorskie mostki** graveyard forms an elite enclosure within the Volkov Cemetery and still serves as a place of pilgrimage for many Russians. Among the better-known personalities interred here are the writers **Turgenev** and **Andreyev**, the poet **Blok**, the painter **Petrov-Vodkin** and the scientists **Mendeleyev**, **Popov** and **Pavlov**, not to mention the "Father of Russian Marxism", **Plekhanov**. At the entrance to the graveyard is a **memorial hall** with busts and exhibits devoted to many of the above. There's also a **plan** of the cemetery (in Russian only) on the north wall of the memorial hall. Lenin's mother, two sisters and brother-in-law are buried in a specially landscaped section near the northern wall of the cemetery, and should **Lenin** himself ever be removed from his mausoleum on Red Square, he might end up beside them, as he is said to have requested (though no written evidence has been found to back up this claim).

The Jewish and January 9th cemeteries

The other two major cemeteries are a lot further out, and strictly for hardcore cemetery buffs only. If you're interested, be sure to make the trip early enough so you can be well away by late afternoon, as the 500m route from Obukhovo metro station along prospekt Aleksandrovskoy Fermy passes decrepit garages and factories frequented by aggressive drunks, before you reach the entrance to the city's main **Jewish Cemetery** (Yevreyskoe kladbishche). The accompanying **synagogue**, with its arcaded courtyards, is used occasionally for burial rites, but the graveyard is still in daily use. Unlike so many Jewish cemeteries in Europe, where communities were devastated by the Holocaust, there is a sense of continuity here, notwithstanding the anti-Semitic campaigns of Stalin and the exodus of Russian Jews to Israel.

On the other side of the nearby railway tracks is the Russian Orthodox **January 9th Cemetery** (entrance also via Aleksandrovskoy

Fermy) where the victims of "Bloody Sunday" were secretly buried on that night in 1905 by the Tsarist police. Like the Jewish Cemetery, it remains very much in use, with the most recent graves situated near the church by the western entrance. Russians keep their relatives' graves well tended and the outing often doubles as a family picnic, many plots having benches and tables around them specifically for that purpose.

Streets and squares

prospekt Aleksandrovskoy Fermy	проспект Александровской Фермы
ul. Gastello	ул. Гастелло
Kirovskaya ploshchad	Кировская площадь
Ligovskiy prospekt	Лиговский проспект
Moskovskiy prospekt	Московский проспект
Moskovskaya ploshchad	Московская площадь
Narvskaya ploshchad	Нарвская площадь
ul. Perekopskaya	ул. Перекопская
ploshchad Pobedy	площадь Победы
ul. Rasstannaya	ул. Расстанная
ploshchad Stachek	площадь Стачек

Metro stations

Baltiyskaya	Балтийская
Elektrosila	Электросила
Frunzenskaya	Фрунзенская
Kirovskiy zavod	Кировский завод
Moskovskaya	Московская
Moskovskie Vorota	Московские Ворота
Narvskaya	Нарвская
Obukhovo	Обухово
Park Pobedy	Парк Победы

Museums and sights

Akhmatova and the Silver Age Museum	музей Ахматова Серебхряный век
Chesma Church	Чесменская церковь
January 9th Cemetery	Кладбище Памяти жертв 9-го Января
Jewish Cemetery	Еврейское кладбище
Literatorskie mostki graveyard	Литераторские мостки пекрополь

Chapter 8

Vyborg Side

The industrialized sprawl of the **Vyborg Side** (Vyborgskaya storona), north of the city centre, holds little appeal compared to other parts of St Petersburg, but its contribution to the city's history is undeniable. As **factories** burgeoned along the Bolshaya Nevka embankment and the slums spread northwards, the district became a hotbed of working-class militancy. Despite the forbidding presence of the Moscow Guards regiment, which was stationed in the district, and the notorious **Kresty Prison**, the locals erupted into revolutionary action in 1905 and again in 1917, battling police and troops at the barricades. Fittingly, Lenin was welcomed back from exile at the **Finland Station**, near the Neva embankment, and subsequently hid out in the quarter just before the October Revolution.

In the northern reaches of the Vyborg Side lies a reminder of Leningrad's sufferings during the Blockade: the **Piskarov Memorial Cemetery**, whose mass graves hold 470,000 victims of starvation, cold or shellfire. It requires some effort to get there on your own, as does the district's only other real attraction, the **Buddhist Temple**, across the river from Yelagin Island. Given the distances between the various sights, getting around involves using two separate metro lines and a fair bit of walking.

Finland Station and ploshchad Lenina

The **Finland Station** (Finlyandskiy vokzal) seems an unlikely spot for a momentous, curtain-raising piece of history. Despite efforts by the Soviet government in the 1950s to make the square outside – **ploshchad Lenina** – look suitably imposing, the concrete shed that replaced the old station in the 1950s is hardly an awe-inspiring sight.

Nevertheless, it is possible to imagine the scene when the train carrying the exiles pulled into Finland Station at 11.30pm on April 3,

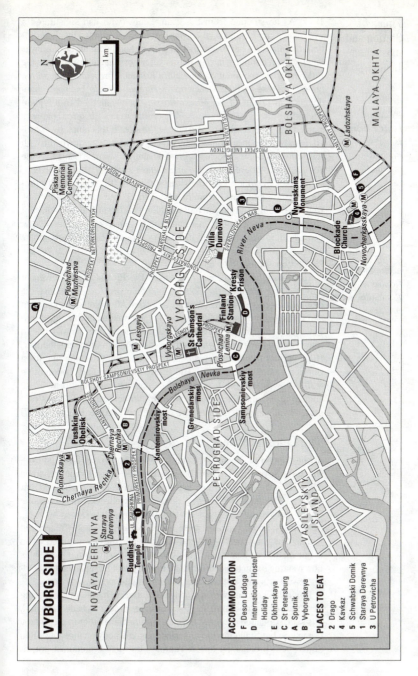

VYBORG SIDE

N | 0 | 1 km

Piskarov Memorial Cemetery

Ploshchad M Muzhestva

NOVAYA DEREVNYA

Pushkin Obelisk

Pionerskaya M

Chernaya Rechka M

Staraya Derevnya

Buddhist Temple M

Kantemirovskiy most

Grenaderskiy most

Bolshaya Nevka

Sampsonievskiy most

PETROGRAD SIDE

St Samson's Cathedral

Vyborgskaya M

Lesnaya

VYBORG SIDE

Villa Durnovo

Finland M Station

Kresty Prison

Ploshchad Lenina M

BOLSHOY SAMPSONIEVSKIY PROSPEKT

PROSPEKT NEPOKORENNYKH

PROSPEKT MARSHALA BLYUKHERA

PISKARYOVSKIY PROSPEKT

River Neva

SVERDLOVSKAYA NAB

KONDRATYEVSKIY PROSPEKT

SHOSSE REVOLYUTSIY

PROSPEKT ENERGETIKOV

BOLSHAYA OKHTA

MALAYA OKHTA

Ladozhskaya M

PROSPEKT METALLISTOV

Nyenskans Monument

Blockade Church

Novocherkasskaya M

VASILEVSKIY ISLAND

ACCOMMODATION
F Deson Ladoga
D International Hostel Holiday
E Okhtinskaya
C St Petersburg
A Sputnik
B Vyborgskaya

PLACES TO EAT
2 Drago
4 Kavkaz
5 Schwabski Domik
1 Staraya Derevnya
3 U Petrovicha

1917. As he stepped from the train, Lenin (who had substituted a workman's cap for his usual bowler hat) seemed stunned by his reception: the platform had been decked with red-and-gold arches and was lined with an honour guard of Kronstadt sailors and a host of cheering Bolsheviks. As the feminist Alexandra Kollantai presented him with a bouquet of roses, a band struck up the *Internationale*, but soon abandoned it in favour of *La Marseillaise*. Lenin emerged to a square packed with tens of thousands of people; torches flickered, banners rippled and searchlights played across the sky. At this point, he boarded the now famous armoured car, which forged its way slowly through the crowd, stopping occasionally for him to shout, "Long live the Socialist Revolution!", and give prizefighter's salutes from its turret.

*Ploshchad
Lenina metro
is next to
Finland
Station.*

The exit by which Lenin left the station is still reverentially preserved (though it now harbours a bookstall), and can be reached by walking through the station hall and along platform 1. In the adjacent "Imperial Waiting Room", Chkheidze, Menshevik president of the Petrograd Soviet, welcomed him with cautious platitudes about the Provisional Government, which Lenin – keen to advance the Revolution – affected to ignore.

*For an
account of the
October
Revolution, see
p.423.*

Three months later, having provoked the Provisional Government into cracking down on the Bolsheviks, Lenin was forced to leave the city, disguised in a wig and labourer's clothes. After hiding out in a barn and lakeside hut near Razliv (see p.382), he was finally smuggled into Finland by train, disguised as a fireman. In the autumn he was able to return by the same train (with the help of its Finnish Communist driver, Hugo Jalava) to persuade his colleagues that the time was ripe for a Bolshevik coup (see p.209). The train's steam engine, **Locomotive #293**, now stands in a special glass pavilion near platform 5. An endearing red-and-black engine with fire tender attached, it was presented by the Finnish government as a gift to the Soviet Union in 1957.

The Lenin statue

At the far end of ploshchad Lenina stands the bronze **Lenin statue**, which on November 7, 1926, became the first Lenin monument to be unveiled in the Soviet Union, setting the tone for the thousands that followed. Designed by Yevseyev, Schuko and Gelfreykh, Lenin has one thumb hooked into his waistcoat and gestures imperiously with his other hand; an oft-repeated pose which inspired the joke "Where did you get that waistcoat?" – "Over there." In time, the city acquired seven major statues of Lenin, each the butt of some witticism. One relates how a statue's arm broke off and the foundry cast its replacement holding a worker's cap, not realizing that the figure already wore one.

Ironically, Lenin abhorred the idea of statues in his honour, believing that "they only gather bird shit". His Last Testament forbade them and, it is said, stipulated a modest burial alongside his mother in the Volkov Cemetery; but Stalin instead enshrined Lenin's body on Moscow's Red Square and proclaimed him a Titan. In the post-Communist era, St

Lenin

Vladimir Ilyich Ulyanov (1870–1924), arguably the greatest revolutionary in modern history, was born in Simbirsk on the Volga. He had a happy, middle-class upbringing; his father was a liberal schools inspector, his ethnic-German mother a strict Lutheran. However, in 1887, his beloved elder brother, Alexander, was arrested and hanged for his part in a student plot to kill the tsar. Vladimir never forgot this, nor the ostracism of the Ulyanovs by their liberal friends – the source of his enduring scorn for "bourgeois radicals". Reading Chernyshevsky's *What Is to be Done?* (a title he would later use for one of his own works) and Marx's *Das Kapital* confirmed him into the faith of **revolutionary socialism**, to which he remained committed for the rest of his life. Even his later alias, Lenin, referred to a cause célèbre (the strike of the Lena River gold-miners), though Party comrades nicknamed him *Starik* (old man), because of his premature baldness.

Exiled to Siberia for Marxist agitation in 1897, he was joined there by **Nadezhda Krupskaya**, whom he probably married in church, despite his own beliefs, to keep her mother happy. In 1900, after his term of exile in Siberia was over, Lenin left Russia to set up the Communist paper *Iskra* (*The Spark*) in Munich: the start of a seventeen-year odyssey around Europe, encompassing genteel poverty in Brussels, Paris, London and Zurich, where Lenin engaged in bitter sectarian battles with fellow exiled Marxists. In 1903 the Russian Social Democratic Labour Party – of which Lenin was a leading member – split into hardline **Bolsheviks** (majority) and moderate Mensheviks (minority), leaving Lenin with a group of radicals to forge into an instrument of his will. Whilst in Paris in 1910, he began a lasting political and romantic relationship with the vibrant French radical, **Inessa Armand**, who spent the war years with Lenin and Krupskaya in Switzerland.

Caught napping by the February Revolution of 1917 in Russia, Lenin hastened to return home from his self-imposed exile. A deal was struck with the German government, which hoped to weaken Russia with "the bacillus of Bolshevism", to convey Lenin and his companions across Europe. Accompanied by the Swiss socialist Fritz Platten, thirty exiles boarded the famous "sealed train" for Stockholm, crossed into Finland on sleighs and eventually transferred to an ordinary Russian train. Lenin stayed up all night quizzing soldiers about the military situation in Petrograd, as the train sped towards the city. He had already decided to take over the Petrograd Soviet and overthrow the Provisional Government: all that mattered was how and when.

Petersburg has been forced to consider a purge of its Soviet monuments and a special commission was established by the Mayor's office to decide which were of intrinsic value and which were too offensive to remain. Fortunately, all the major Lenin statues were spared.

North of Finland Station

Two very long, parallel streets, Lesnoy prospekt and Bolshoy Sampsonievskiy prospekt, run **north from the vicinity of Finland Station**, cutting their way right through an industrial zone. Though neither holds much allure, a surprising amount of history

ST PETERSBURG

pervades the district, which played an important role in the two revolutions.

Factories along Bolshoy Sampsonievskiy prospekt

For most of its length, **Bolshoy Sampsonievskiy prospekt** runs past red-brick **factories** dating from the nineteenth century, which back onto the Bolshaya Nevka embankment. Most were nationalized soon after the Revolution, but the economic demands of the Civil War meant that few benefits accrued to the factory workers until the mid-1920s and early 1930s, when efforts to improve conditions on the Vyborg Side gave rise to some (not especially notable) examples of **early Soviet architecture**.

A case in point is the pair of **Constructivist buildings** at the southern end of the prospekt on the corner with the road that leads to the Sampsonievskiy most. Bartuchev designed the stark building at no. 14 in 1933; the electricity substation that stands next door was built by Schuko and Gelfreykh, who were also partly responsible for the first Lenin statue (see p.254). Further north, opposite ulitsa Smirnova, is the **Russian Diesel Factory**, founded in 1824 by the Swedish immigrant **Emmanuel Nobel**, whose son, Ludwig, began producing pig iron here in 1862. Ludwig's son, Alfred, famously went on to invent dynamite and expiate his guilt by founding the Nobel prizes.

St Samson's Cathedral

The cathedral is open daily 11am–7pm, closed Wed in summer; $8.50. Admission (including a guided tour in English) only by prior arrangement on ☎315 43 61.

About 1km further up the road from the Diesel Factory, **St Samson's Cathedral** (Sampsonievskiy sobor) is an anachronism amidst the smokestacks, being one of the oldest buildings in the city. Completed in 1740, the cathedral is thought to have witnessed the **secret wedding of Catherine the Great and Grigori Potemkin** in 1774, which was attended only by Potemkin's nephew, a lady-in-waiting and a chamberlain. Secret marriages weren't uncommon among the Romanovs: Peter the Great privately wed his mistress before he felt it wise to do so publicly; Empress Elizabeth plighted her troth with Razumovsky, but didn't acknowledge it; while Nicholas I never found out that his daughter Maria had secretly wed a member of the Stroganov family.

The cathedral itself is notable for its Baroque iconostasis and the unusual open galleries on the northern and southern facades. Its ribbed onion domes and cupola conform to the standard Orthodox configuration, but the lofty spired belfry recalls the Lutheran-inspired Peter and Paul Cathedral. In the grounds are the tombs of three courtiers executed on the orders of Empress Anna's paranoid lover, Count Biron. The easiest way to get there is to take the metro to Vyborgskaya and walk around the block.

Lenin on Serdobolskaya ulitsa

A twenty-minute walk west from Chernaya rechka metro station (via
Torzhkovskaya ulitsa) brings you to **Lenin's last secret address** at
Serdobolskaya ulitsa 1, where he stayed in the apartment of Party
member Margarita Sofanova after returning from Finland. While the
Central Committee procrastinated, Lenin feared that the moment for
a coup would pass: on the night of October 24, he departed from
Serdobolskaya ulitsa, leaving a note reading, "I've gone where you
didn't want me to go. Goodbye. Ilyich", and boarded a tram for the
Smolniy. He and his companion, Eino Rahja, managed to bluff their
way through several checkpoints and into the Smolniy Institute, to
join their colleagues.

While the rest may be history, the idea that Lenin instantly
assumed control of a well-planned coup owes much to Soviet propaganda. Though every textbook states that it occurred on October 25,
1917, the exact **date of the Bolshevik Revolution** is by no means
certain. A 1962 conference of distinguished Soviet historians ended
in violent disagreement – with one faction asserting the Revolution
was on the morning of October 24, another, the afternoon of the
same day, and a third, October 22. The implications are that the coup
may have been well under way – if not virtually over – by the time that
Lenin arrived, unannounced, at the Smolniy.

East along the embankment

To the east of Finland Station, Arsenalnaya naberezhnaya – **Arsenal
Embankment** – follows the curve of the River Neva, an unprepos-
sessing grey swathe which cuts between two of the city's most infamous buildings: across the river looms the headquarters of the secret
police, the Bolshoy dom (see p.221); while a little to the east, back
on the Vyborg Side, lies Kresty Prison (see below), whose notoriety
goes back to Tsarist times. During the 1930s and 1940s, the two
places "processed" scores of thousands of people, whose relatives
traipsed between the buildings day after day, trying to discover the
victims' fate. The lack of transport along the Arsenal Embankment
precludes seeing much more than the **Arsenal** itself – a dirty-orange
brick complex belonging to the Army that moved here from Liteyniy
prospekt in the 1840s – and the Kresty Prison beyond, 800m from
Finland Station. The few sights past this are only really worth visiting if you have your own transport.

Kresty Prison

When **Kresty Prison** was first built in the reign of Catherine the
Great, it was considered a model of its kind, taking its name – "Cross"
– from its double cross-shaped configuration. Sporting a Byzantine-
style dome on its Preliminary Investigations Building, it came com-

plete with a chapel for the prisoners, which in Soviet times was turned into the warders' club, with a portrait of "Iron Felix" and the motto *Do as Dzerzhinsky would have done!* where the altar used to be. The chapel has now been handed back to the prisoners and religious services have resumed.

These days Kresty's inmates are "real" criminals, rather than political prisoners. Almost any day, you can see women shouting over the walls to their menfolk inside, who send messages back by blowpipe or slingshot. Poignant though the sight is, it can't compare with the hushed lines that formed during the **purges** of 1934–36, when the poet Anna Akhmatova queued for 21 months outside Kresty, with a host of other women, all seeking news. One day, she was recognized by a stranger, who sidled up and whispered, "Can you describe this?" Akhmatova obliged with *Requiem*, a series of prose poems that opens with an account of the episode and concludes:

> *And from my motionless bronze-lidded sockets,*
> *May the melting snow like teardrops slowly trickle.*
> *And a prison dove coo somewhere over and over*
> *As the ships sail softly down the flowing Neva.*

The Villa Durnovo and the Petrograd Anarchists

Roughly 1500m beyond Kresty, the embankment sweeps past the Neoclassical yellow-and-white mansion of the **Villa Durnovo** at Sverdlovskaya naberezhnaya 22, across the Neva from the Smolniy district. Built for L.P. Durnovo, a wealthy senator and cabinet minister, it was commandeered at the outbreak of the February Revolution by the **Petrograd Anarchists**. Heavily armed and clad in black, they inspired fear by foraying into bourgeois districts, seizing a house, ousting its occupants and installing a colony of their own. Soon after the October Revolution the Anarchists came into conflict with the Bolsheviks, and were decimated in Petrograd and Moscow by the Red Terror – though the Bolsheviks were happy enough to strike deals with provincial Anarchist groups during the Civil War, when much of Ukraine was controlled by the Anarchist Black Army. Following the Bolsheviks' defeat of the Black Army in 1921, and the suppression of the Kronstadt sailors' revolt, Anarchism found itself purged from Soviet history, only re-emerging in the Gorbachev era as anarcho-punks became prominent in the big cities.

On towards the Okhta

Another kilometre along the embankment you come to the **Bezborodko Villa** at no. 40. Set in even larger grounds than Durnovo's mansion, its three-storeyed central building was constructed by the Moscow architect Bazhenov in 1773–77; the semi-circular wings were added by Quarenghi in the 1780s.

From here, you can carry on to the **Okhta district**, on the east bank of the Neva. The Okhta's history dates back to late medieval times when merchants established a waystation here between Novgorod and the markets of the Baltic. Okhta was only incorporated into the city in 1918, before which time it formed a separate community of wood- and metalworkers, who created much of the ironware, bronze work and furniture for the Imperial palaces outside Petersburg. The district has now mushroomed into Bolshaya (Greater) and Malaya (Lesser) Okhta, whose faceless apartment buildings and administrative monoliths are enlivened only by a sprinkling of Mafia-infested restaurants.

Petersburgers have a sentimental regard for the cast-iron bridge, **most Pyotra Velikovo**, which spans the Neva between Okhta and the Smolniy district – officially named after Peter the Great, but popularly known as the "Bolsheokhtinskiy", it was one of the city's lifelines during the Blockade. In the park to the north of the bridge is a recently unveiled granite **monument** to **Nyenskans** – a belated admission that St Petersburg was not created in an uninhabited wilderness, as popular myth has it – since it commemorates the Swedish fortress built here in 1611, round which a town called Nyen existed until it was overrun by Peter the Great's forces in 1703, the year that St Petersburg was founded. One kilometre further south, the embankment is dignified by the **Blockade Church**, a memorial shrine to the dead of the "900 Days", built in the late 1990s in a style that echoes the medieval Russian churches of Pskov.

Life during the Blockade

The Blockade may not have lasted for a full nine hundred days, as legend asserts, but the agonies associated with it defy exaggeration. Between early September 1941 – when the Germans cut off rail links to the city and began bombarding it – and February 7, 1944, when the first train-load of food pulled into Finland Station, Leningrad was dependent on its own resources and whatever could be brought across Lake Ladoga on the icy "Road of Life" in winter. The result was slow **starvation**, as daily rations shrank to 500–600 calories per person. In November 1941, the bread ration was 250 grammes per day for factory workers and 125 grammes for the other two-thirds of the population; the "bread" constituted fifty percent rye flour, the rest being bran, sawdust or anything else to hand. People boiled leather or wallpaper to make broth, and ate cats and dogs. Some even resorted to cannibalism so that citizens feared to walk past alleyways, lest they be garrotted and butchered; if discovered, cannibals were generally executed on the spot.

Although **bombardments** killed seventeen thousand people, far more deaths were caused by starvation and the cold. In winter there was no heating, no water, no electricity and no public transport; amidst blizzards, Leningraders queued for bread, drew water from frozen canals, scavenged for firewood and dragged their dead on sledges to the cemeteries. Eventually, the living grew too weak and the dead too numerous for individual funerals, and corpses were left at designated spots to be collected for burial in mass graves.

ST PETERSBURG

Piskarov Memorial Cemetery

Until 1990, the **Piskarov Memorial Cemetery** (Piskaryovskoe memorialnoe kladbishche), in the city's northern suburbs, used to be the first stop on Intourist excursions – a pointed reminder to visitors of the city's sacrifices in the war against fascism. Today, few tours visit the cemetery, but the grounds are still tidily kept and wreaths are laid every May 9 – Victory Day. Should you wish to pay your respects to the 670,000 citizens who died of starvation during the Blockade, the cemetery lies way out along prospekt Nepokoryonnykh – the "Avenue of the Unconquered". **To get there**, either take the metro to Lesnaya station and then bus #123, or catch bus #107 from the Finland Station to the end of the line and then ride two stops on a #123 or #178 bus; ask to be let off at the cemetery.

The cemetery

The cemetery is officially open daily 10am–6pm, although occasionally it closes around 5pm.

The **origins of the cemetery** lie in the mass burials that took place near the village of Piskarovka from February 1942 onwards. As nobody had the strength to dig the frozen ground, sappers blasted pits into which the unidentified bodies were tipped; some 470,000 people were interred like this. After the war, it took five years of grisly labour to transform the burial ground into a memorial cemetery, which was solemnly opened in 1960. Some might find its poignancy diminished by the regimented layout and cheery flowerbeds, but its sad power is palpable on rainy days and, above all, in winter.

At the entrance are two **memorial halls** containing grim photomontages and personal effects, like a facsimile of the diary of 11-year-old Tanya Savicheva, whose entire family starved to death (she was later evacuated, but also died). On display, too, is the cemetery register, open at a page bearing the entries: "February, 1942: 18th – 3,241 bodies; 19th – 5,559; 20th – 10,043". Further into the cemetery, beyond the trees, an **eternal flame**, kindled by a torch lit from Marsovo pole, flickers on a terrace above the necropolis.

Flanking its 300-metre-long central avenue are 186 low, grassy mounds, each with a granite slab that simply records the year of burial and whether the dead were soldiers (marked by a red star) or civilians (with a hammer and sickle). At the far end, a six-metre-tall, bronze **statue of Mother Russia** by Vera Isayeva and Robert Taurit holds a garland of oak and laurel leaves, as if to place it on the graves of the fallen. The **memorial wall** behind is inscribed with a poem by the Blockade survivor Olga Bergholts, which asserts:

> *We cannot remember all their noble names here,*
> *So many lie beneath the eternal granite,*
> *But of those honoured by this stone,*
> *Let no one forget*
> *Let nothing be forgotten.*

Chernaya rechka

Chernaya rechka – or "Black Stream" – is an appropriate name for what is now a high-rise, industrialized zone; its only claim to fame is that it was in a meadow in this locality that Pushkin's fatal duel with D'Anthès took place, on January 27, 1837. On the centenary of Pushkin's death a granite obelisk was erected on the site of the duel, in what is now a park alongside Kolomyazhskiy prospekt, and a statue of the poet was installed in Chernaya rechka metro station. Lermontov, too, fought a duel here with the son of the French ambassador, de Barantes, but escaped alive, only to be killed in another duel the following year in the Caucasus (where, ironically, he had been exiled for fighting the duel with Barantes).

For more on Pushkin's duel, see p.90.

To the west of the metro station lies the residential **Novaya Derevnya** (New Village) district, which sprawls along the highway opposite the Kirov Islands; the only real reason to make it out this far is to visit the Buddhist Temple.

Streets and squares

Arsenal Embankment	Арсенальная наб.
Bolshoy Sampsonievskiy prospekt	Большой Сампсониевский пр.
Kolomyazhskiy prospekt	Коломяжский пр.
ul. Lebedeva	ул. Лебедева
Lesnoy prospekt	Лесной пр.
Lipova alleya	Липова аллея
prospekt Nepokoryonnykh	пр. Непокорённых
Novosibirskaya ul.	Новосибирская ул.
Primorskiy prospekt	Приморский пр.
Serdobolskaya ul.	Сердобольская ул.
Smirnova ul.	Смирнова ул.
Sverdlovskaya nab.	Свердловская наб.

Metro stations

Chernaya rechka	Чёрная Речка
Lesnaya	Лесная
Ploshchad Lenina	Площадь Ленина
Ploshchad Muzhestva	Площадь Мужества
Staraya Derevnya	Старая Деревня
Vyborgskaya	Выборгская

Sights and monuments

Buddhist Temple	Буддийский храм
Finland Station	Финляндский вокзал
Piskarov Memorial Cemetery	Пискарёвское мемориальное кладбище
St Samson's Cathedral	Сампсониевский собор

The Buddhist Temple

The main attraction in Novaya Derevnya lies way out along Primorskiy prospekt, near the bridge over to Yelagin Island. Secluded in a walled compound, St Petersburg's **Buddhist Temple** (Buddiyskiy khram) has a rough-hewn stone facade tapering skywards, a splendid red-and-gold portico surmounted by totemic statues, and a joss-stick-scented **prayer hall** which exhibits information about the Dalai Lama. Built in 1900–15 at the instigation of Nicholas II's Buddhist physician Pyotr Badmaev, with help from the Lhasa scholar Agwan-Khamba, the building was expropriated after the Revolution and turned into an entomology institute. In 1991, the city council agreed to return it to the Soviet Union's Buddhist community, centred in the Buryat Autonomous Republic of Central Siberia (in what is now the Russian Federation). You can reach the temple (and Yelagin Island) by **minibus** #T-411 or #T-416 from Chernaya rechka metro, or on any bus or minibus heading south along Lipovaya alleya from Staraya Derevnya metro.

Listings

Chapter 9

Accommodation

Anyone travelling on a tourist visa must have **accommodation** arranged before arriving in St Petersburg (see p.21 for more details). However, now that it is easier to obtain business visas (which do not require pre-booked accommodation), independent travellers may be faced with the challenge of finding somewhere to stay on arrival. Most hotels still aren't used to coping with people just turning up – that's not to say they won't have room for you, but the price will be far above the rate charged to pre-booked package tourists, and smaller hotels may not be keen on people without recommendations, especially backpackers.

Anyone travelling on a tight budget will find themselves limited to the dingiest hotels, in which case you'll probably fare much better by opting instead for private accommodation or a hostel.

If you're planning to come during the **White Nights**, it's highly advisable to reserve accommodation as far ahead as possible, as this is the only time of the year that the city's hotels are likely to be full, and hostel or private accommodation may also be in short supply.

Hotels

St Petersburg's **hotels** are still in a state of flux. Having long been controlled (and

---

Accommodation prices

All accommodation in this guide has been given a symbol which corresponds to one of eight **price categories**.

These categories refer to what independent visitors will pay in a hotel for the cheapest available **double room**, which usually includes a private bathroom. For a **single room**, expect to pay around two-thirds the price of a double. When applied to private accommodation or hostels they represent the **rate per person**, unless otherwise stated.

Whilst large hotels take major **credit cards** (marked CC), anywhere else you will have to pay in rubles (except in private accommodation, where dollars are usually preferred). We've indicated where establishments accept credit cards using the following abbreviations: Amex = American Express, DC = Diners Club, MC = Mastercard, EC = Eurocard, JCB = Japanese Credit Bank.

Note also that some of the more expensive hotels quote their prices exclusive of **sales tax** of 23 percent, so make sure you check exactly what the price includes. The prices given in this guide include tax.

① Under $15	③ $30–50	⑤ $100–150	⑦ $200–300
② $15–30	④ $50–100	⑥ $150–200	⑧ Over $300

Accommodation

spoon-fed with guests) by the now defunct Intourist, some are finding the switch to self-management – and the need to attract customers – hard to cope with, whereas others have already teamed up with Western partners in an attempt to improve facilities and business. The buildings themselves range from spartan, low-rise concrete blocks to de luxe Art Nouveau edifices. Some are in prime **locations**, others in grotty suburbs. Given all this, it definitely pays to shop around (or, in the case of package tourists, check in advance where you'll be accommodated).

Although it's still in use, the Intourist system of **rating hotels** with stars should be taken with a pinch of salt, as standards are lower than in the West – the older, lower-rated places are generally a bit shabby, with erratic water supplies and heating; only in the top hotels are you assured of pristine service and overheated rooms. Two-star hotels are mostly 1950s low-rises with matchbox-sized rooms, and are unlikely to have en-suite facilities. Three-star hotels are typically 1960s and 1970s high-rise buildings, equipped with several restaurants, bars and nightclubs. Four- and five-star hotels tend to be either recently refurbished or brand new, and come closest to matching the standards (and prices) of their Western counterparts. Private bathrooms are mandatory in all establishments with three or more stars.

Room rates generally include **breakfast**. When checking in, you will receive a **guest card** which enables you to get past the hotel doorman and claim your room key – don't lose it. The top hotels have electronic card keys for improved security. Most hotels have a **service bureau**, which can obtain theatre tickets, arrange international telephone calls and the like. Each floor is monitored by a *dezhurnaya* or **concierge**, who will keep your key while you are away and can arrange to have your laundry done. However, the presence of a concierge doesn't guarantee security and several hotels are notorious for burglaries.

The hotel listings below are arranged alphabetically and **divided into the**

It is usually possible to book four- and five-star hotel rooms **in advance** from Britain through Utell (☎ 020/7413 8877) reservation systems.

same areas as our guide chapters. You'll find each hotel marked on the corresponding maps throughout the book

Within the Fontanka

If you're looking for a central location within easy walking distance of the major sights, this is the area to be in. The choice is extremely limited, however, and prices reflect the locale – with one exception. The hotels listed in this section are marked on the map on p.66.

Astoria, Bolshaya Morskaya ul. 39 ☎ 210 57 57, fax 210 50 59, *www.spb.astoria*; Nevskiy prospekt/Gostiniy dvor metro. Historic five-star pile overlooking St Isaac's Cathedral, right in the centre, whose guestbook features such names as Lenin, Mrs Thatcher and Chuck Norris. Rooms are light and airy but without A/C. Facilities are shared with the slightly cheaper Angleterre annex, where the poet Yesenin died in 1925. Amex, Visa, MC, DC. ⑦–⑧.

Grand Hotel Europe, Mikhailovskaya ul. 1/7 ☎ 329 60 00, fax 329 60 01, *www.grandhotel-europe.com*; Nevskiy prospekt/Gostiniy dvor metro. St Petersburg's top hotel, just off Nevskiy prospekt. All its A/C rooms are notable for huge bathrooms, and the more exclusive suites are virtual Art Nouveau museum pieces. Clinton, Kohl and Chirac have enjoyed its marbled magnificence and impeccable service since the hotel was refurbished by a Russo-Swedish joint venture in the late 1980s. If you can't afford to stay, at least drop into one of the cafés or restaurants. Amex, Visa, MC, DC. ⑧.

Matisov Domik, nab. reki Pryazhka 3/1 ☎ 219 54 45, fax 219 74 19; bus #22 from Bolshaya Morskaya ulitsa. The least desirable option within the Fontanka, due to its remote location, surly staff, swarms of mosquitoes and abysmal breakfasts – the sole plus is that it's only 10min walk from the Mariinskiy Theatre. ④–⑤.

Nauka, Millionnaya ul. 27 ☎315 86 96, fax 312 31 56; Nevskiy prospekt/Gostiniy dvor metro. Once reserved for guests of the Academy of Sciences, this low-profile establishment now takes tourists as well, if not booked up by visiting academics. Depending on your taste and budget, its unbeatable location (only 150m east of the Hermitage) and rock-bottom rates (cheaper than most hostels) may out-weigh its general shabbiness, shared shower/toilet facilities, and night-time curfew. They may also forbid unmarried couples to share a room. Some rooms have fridges. ②.

Turgenev, Bolshaya Konyushennaya ul. 13 ☎314 45 29, fax 311 51 80; Nevskiy prospekt/Gostiniy dvor metro. Small, friendly, cosy private hotel just off Nevskiy, where they'll serve you break-fast in bed. Guests are met at the airport for free, and don't have to pay for visa support until they arrive. You'll have to book months in advance, however, since there are only four rooms and it's very popular. ③–④.

Vasilevskiy Island

Vasilevsky Island is generally less appealing than "mainland" St Petersburg or the Petrograd Side, and its choice of accommodation is limited. Given the size of the island, proximity to a metro sta-tion is crucial. The hotels listed in this section are marked on the map on p.170.

Pribaltiyskaya, Korablestroiteley ul. 14 ☎356 01 58, fax 356 00 94, *www.pribaltiyskaya.ru*; bus #7 from Nevskiy prospekt or bus #41, #47 or #128 from Vasileostrovskaya metro. Gigantic Swedish-built hotel overlooking the Gulf of Finland, mainly used by Finns on booze-cruises, but also hosts sport and ballroom-dancing competitions. Rooms are on the small size, but have A/C, TV, phone and minibar. Facilities

include a sauna, pool and bowling alley. Amex, Visa, MC, DC. ⑥.

Vergaz, 6–7ya liniya 70 ☎327 88 38, fax 327 88 80; Vasileostrovskaya metro. A good mid-range hotel, only one stop from Nevskiy prospekt by metro. Though the *Pribaltiyskaya* has better facilities, this new Franco-Russian venture is far easier to reach and more stylish, with fourteen large, modern rooms, plus one suite and a self-catering apartment. ④.

Petrograd Side and the Kirov Islands

Petrograd Side is an interesting location, though with fewer hotels than you'd expect. Besides the one listed below, there are a couple of other places that don't take foreign guests, and a major hotel – the *Clarion Severnaya Korona* – that has been due to open for years, but has never quite managed it. The follow-ing hotel is marked on the map on p.188.

Dvorets molodezhi, ul. Professora Popova 47 ☎234 47 14, fax 234 23 61; bus #25 or #134 from Gorkovskaya metro. A reasonably salubrious high-rise with a jungly atrium and fun-oriented facilities (billiards, golf, disco and 24-hour bars). The rooms are smallish and not that comfy, but some have nice views over the Malaya Nevka. Visa, MC. ③–④.

Liteniy, Smolniy and Vladimirskaya

Depending on the locality, the area between the Fontanka and the Obvodniy Canal offers some reasonably priced alternatives to the upmarket hotels with-in the Fontanka, and some others that are inconveniently remote. The hotels listed in this section are marked on the map on p.2160.

Moskva, Alexandra Nevskovo pl. 2 ☎27430 01, fax 274 20 16, *www.hotel-moscow.ru*; Ploshchad Alexandra Nevskovo metro. Enormous, gloomy 1970s hotel that's not as crime-ridden as it used to be but is still renowned for its lousy food and obnoxious security guards. The front-facing rooms suffer from traffic noise, but some overlook the

Accommodation

① *Under $15*
② *$15–30*
③ *$30–50*
④ *$50–100*
⑤ *$100–150*
⑥ *$150–200*
⑦ *$200–300*
⑧ *Over $300*

Accommodation

Alexander Nevsky Monastery. Amex, Visa, MC, DC. ⑤.

Neptun, nab. Obvodnovo kanala 93A ☎324 46 10, fax 274 20 16; 15min walk south of Pushkinskaya metro. A 1990s business-class hotel with decent facilities, but in a fairly grim location on the Obvodniy Canal. Accepts most credit cards. ⑤.

Neva, ul. Chaykovskovo 17 ☎273 25 93, fax 278 05 04; Cherniyshevskaya metro. Agreeable, old-fashioned Soviet-style hotel in a converted nineteenth-century mansion, a 15min walk from the Summer Garden. Most rooms have private bathrooms. Bar and sauna. ②.

Nevsky Palace, Nevskiy pr. 57 ☎275 20 01, fax 301 73 23, *www.ittsheraton.com*; Mayakovskaya metro. Part of the Sheraton chain, this modern five-star hotel is characterless compared to its top-of-the-range rivals the *Astoria* and *Grand Hotel Europe* (see p.268), but popular with business travellers. Secure parking, business centre, plus a sauna and small gym open to non-residents. Amex, Visa, MC, DC. ⑧.

Oktyabrskaya, Ligovskiy pr. 10 ☎277 62 55, fax 315 75 01, *okt@iac.spb.ru*. Ploshchad Vosstaniya/Mayakovskaya metro. A dingy nineteenth-century warren overlooking Moscow Station. All rooms have satellite TV and bathroom (albeit with dodgy plumbing). Its main virtues are its central location, low prices and helpful English-speaking staff. Visa, MC. ②–③.

Rus, Artillereyskaya ul. 1 ☎ 273 46 83, fax 279 36 00; Chernyshevskaya metro. Modern Soviet-style hotel located a few minutes' walk from Liteyniy prospekt. Each room has a VCR, fridge and tiny bathroom. The hotel has an excellent sauna but no dining facilities. Amex, Visa, MC, JCB. ④.

Sovetskaya, Lermontovskiy pr. 43/1 ☎329 01 86, fax 329 01 87, *www.sovietskaya.hotel.service.ru*; 10min walk from Baltiyskaya or Tekhnologicheskiy Institut metro. A 1970s high-rise complex at the grungy end of the River Fontanka. Foreigners are allo-cated rooms of a supposedly higher standard on the "business floor", or in the "Fontanka" annexe around the corner – but other hotels offer a better deal. Amex, Visa, MC. ④–⑤.

The Southern Suburbs

The Southern Suburbs are far from attractive, but some parts are well served by metro, making it more convenient than you'd think. There are hotels to suit most pockets, if not tastes. The hotels listed in this section are marked on the map on p.2440.

Kievskaya, Dnepropetrovskaya ul. 49 ☎166 04 56, fax 166 53 98; trams #10 and #16 or trolleybus #42 from pl. Vosstaniya. A miserable low-rise with tiny rooms, mostly without bathrooms, near Bus Station #2 and the Obvodniy Canal, 15min walk from the nearest metro. Strictly a last resort. ②.

Mir, ul. Gastello 17 ☎108 49 10, fax 108 51 70; 15min walk south of Park Pobedy metro. Similar to the *Kievskaya*, but in a better location off Moskovskiy prospekt. Though definitely overpriced, some of the rooms have been refur-bished with private bathrooms and phones; ask for a room at the back over-looking the Chesma Church. No CCs. ④.

Pulkovskaya, pl. Pobedy 1 ☎123 51 16, fax 264 63 96; 10min walk south of Moskovskaya metro. Clean but some-what shoddy modern hotel, overlooking the impressive Victory Monument en route to the airport. Good facilities, including a sauna, gym and tennis courts; rooms are equipped with A/C and voicemail. Amex, Visa, MC, DC. ⑥.

Rossiya, pl. Chernyshevskovo 11 ☎329 39 09, fax 296 73 03; Park Pobedy metro. A shabby Stalinist pile with 1970s additions such as a pool and sauna, that might close for a refit in 2001. Some rooms have TV, phone and bathroom. Visa, MC. ③.

Vyborg Side

Vyborg Side is the district with the least going for it in terms of ambience, although the *St Petersburg* has the saving grace of being near the cruiser *Aurora*. Otherwise, the only attraction is the cost – and even then there are better deals elsewhere. The hotels listed in this section are marked on the map on p.253.

Deson Ladoga, pr. Shaumyana 26 ☎528 56 28, fax 528 54 48; Novocherkasskaya metro. A clean and pleasant, modern hotel, catering to business travellers, in a seedy location a few stops from the centre by metro. All staff speak English and the restaurant offers European and Chinese cuisine. A morning sauna is included in the price of the room. Visa, MC. ⑤.

Okhtinskaya, Bolsheokhtinskiy pr. 4 ☎227 44 38, fax 227 26 18; tram #7, #23 or #46, trolleybus #7 or #49 from Novocherkasskaya metro. A decent Franco-Russian hotel used by business travellers, with a fine view of the Smolniy Convent across the Neva, A/C rooms with minibar and VCR, and a sauna and Italian deli on the premises. On the downside, there are no baths, only showers, and the hotel is awkward to reach by public transport – for a similar price you could stay at the more accessible and attractive *Vergaz* on Vasilevskiy Island (see p.269). Amex, Visa, DC. ④.

St Petersburg, Pirogovskaya nab. 5/2 ☎542 91 01, fax 248 80 02, *www.spb.hotelspb*; Ploshchad Lenina metro. Vast 1970s eyesore beside a busy road, whose best features are the magnificent view of the Neva from the front-facing rooms and a colossal split-level dining hall. Aside from a sauna and business centre, there are few facilities to boast of. Rooms with double beds cost considerably less than twin-bed rooms. ④.

Sputnik, Staro-Pargolovskiy pr. 34 ☎552 56 32, fax 552 80 84; Ploshchad Muzhestva metro. A cheesy 1960s block plagued by traffic noise day and night. The rooms are clean, with a shower, phone and MTV, but marred by narrow beds and unreliable plumbing. Amex, Visa, MC, JCB. ④.

Vyborgskaya, Torzhovskaya ul. 3 ☎246 91 94, fax 246 81 87; Chernaya rechka metro. Cheap but ugly and half-moribund 1950s hotel in the Novaya Derevnya district, whose only claim to fame is that Vladimir Mashkov – star of the film *The Thief* – once stayed there. Some rooms have showers. No CCs. ②–③.

Accommodation

Private accommodation

Staying in **private accommodation** is probably the most agreeable – if not the cheapest – option for independent (and solo) travellers. The system is still in its infancy, and there is nothing like the kind of assistance that is offered in, say, Prague or Budapest. That said, a handful of **agencies** in the city can arrange rooms at (more or less) short notice, while visitors with Russian friends should be able to tap into the network of **private landlords** catering to foreigners.

The basic choice is between lodging with a Russian family on a B&B or full-board basis, or renting a self-contained apartment; the latter will be cheaper in the long term, but self-catering can be an ordeal until you get the hang of shopping and the language. Rates vary considerably, but usually compare very favourably with hotels, especially if you can strike a deal directly with the homeowner. People may be willing to rent a room and provide three meals a day for as little as $25. But beware when renting from total strangers as you could find all sorts of loopholes and extras added to your bill. Try to rent through friends or through respected agencies such as those recommended below.

Staying with a family

Staying with a Russian family, you will be well looked after and experience the cosy domesticity and tasty home cooking that is the obverse of the scornful indifference and iffy meals you may experience in public. Your introduction to this homely world will be a pair of *tapochki* – the slippers which Russians wear indoors to avoid tramping in mud – followed by a cup of tea or a shot of

① *Under $15*
② *$15–30*
③ *$30–50*
④ *$50–100*
⑤ *$100–150*
⑥ *$150–200*
⑦ *$200–300*
⑧ *Over $300*

Accommodation

vodka. Your room will be clean and comfortable, though it can be disconcerting to discover, in small apartments, that it belongs to one of the family, who will sleep elsewhere for the duration of your stay.

Another, more disagreeable surprise might be that the hot water has been cut off, as happens for up to two weeks during the summer, so that the municipal water company can clean the water mains. Don't blame your hosts should this happen – it's not their fault. All you can do is put up with it, or move to another district of the city that isn't affected at the time.

Most Russians in the habit of renting rooms to foreigners speak some English and obtain paying guests through local agencies such as Ost-West Kontaktservice (see p.273). Depending on who arranges it, and whether all meals or just breakfast are included in the deal, you can **pay** anything from $20 a night for two people up to $60 a day per person. If you book through foreign operators, rates for bed and half-board are likely to be in the region of $60 a day per person (see p.5, p.15 & p.19 for lists of overseas operators who can sort out accommodation for you).

Renting an apartment

You can **rent an apartment** in St Petersburg before you arrive. For UK visitors, Findhorn EcoTravels (p.5) has a comfortable, safe apartment in the city centre which can sleep four and be rented for $250 per week; while firms in St Petersburg such as Alliance and Ost-West Kontaktservice offer a range of flats at competitive rates (see "Accommodation agencies" below). You can also look for ads in the classified section of the *St Petersburg Times* (online at *www.spbtimes.ru*) or contact estate agents listed in the *St Petersburg Traveller's Yellow Pages (www .infoservices.com)*. If you have friends in St Petersburg, another option is to pass the word around that you're looking for a flat. A surprising number of locals have become private landlords, with

apartments scattered across the city, and everyone knows that foreigners can pay premium rates in hard currency. Even so, it's possible to find one- or two-bedroom apartments smack in the centre going for around $250–400 a month. For a really cheap, cheek-by-jowl experience of Russian life, you could rent a room in a **communal apartment**, or *kommunalka*, where up to five or six families share the bathroom, kitchen and phone. Prices are as low as $20 per month. For those who can afford up to $1000 a month, there are plenty of ads for "Euro-standard" apartments with Western fitted kitchens and bathrooms, satellite TV, internet access, CCTV and security guards.

If your budget is more modest, the things to look for are a boiler (*kolkonka*), so you won't be deprived of hot water when the district supply is cut off, a bed that's large enough to be comfortable, and a door that provides some security against burglars. Many apartments have a sturdy outer door, whose lock is operated by pushing in and then retracting a notched metal strip; the inner door is unlocked by conventional keys; while the door from the apartment building onto the street may be locked by a device which requires you to punch in a code. **Door codes** usually consist of three digits; you have to push all three buttons simultaneously to make it work; alternatively, if there's a metal ring, press the numbers in order and pull upwards.

Accommodation agencies

Because **accommodation and visas** are interrelated (see p.21 for details), most of the following local agencies can arrange business visas as well as lodgings, given enough time. If you simply turn up and need a room, Alliance or Ost-West Kontaktservice are probably the best bets.

You should always check exactly how far out of the centre you're going to be staying (and, preferably, insist on seeing the room first) before committing yourself. Note that, legally, you are supposed to register with the PVS (see p.23). An agency can probably arrange this, but a private landlord might baulk at helping you.

Alliance ☎ 987 33 93, *www.apartment.spb.ru*. Apartments on and around Nevskiy prospekt for $25–100 per night, with reductions after three and eight days. Visa support through the International Hostel Holiday (see below).

Host Families Accommodation (HOFA), 193015 Tavricheskaya ul. 5, apt. 25 ☎ & fax 275 19 92, *alexei@hofak.hop.stu.neva.ru*.

Full-board family lodgings for around $53–66 per person, depending on the area; B&B for $25–30 per person. Visa invitation service costs $25 per group, regardless of number of people.

Ost-West Kontaktservice, ul. Mayakovskovo 7 ☎ 279 70 45, fax 327 34 17.

B&B for $20–25 per person, depending on the area; full-board $32–37 per person; flat rental from $600 per month. Business visa support.

St Petersburg Bed and Breakfast ☎ & fax 219 41 16. Arranges B&B family lodgings in all parts of the city, but isn't as reliable as other agencies. No visa support.

Hostels

If you fancy mixing with other foreigners and having knowledgeable help on tap, the city's **hostels** are excellent budget options. The original RYHA (Russian Youth Hostel Association) hostel – the *St Petersburg International Hostel* – was set up by Californian Steve Caron and his Russian partners and is the most backpacker-friendly hostel in the city. It can arrange tourist **visas** for its guests (see "Red tape and visas", p.21), but if you've already obtained your visa it's still advisable to reserve a bed (up to one month ahead during summer) and pre-pay for the first night, as it soon fills up. The *International Hostel Holiday* near Finland

Station is also very good, and able to offer visa support. The quieter *Puppet Theatre Hostel* has fewer facilities but is still perfectly OK, while the downtown *Herzen University Hostel* and the *Petrovskiy Hostel* in the Southern Suburbs are less reliable fallbacks. Note that there is no age limit for guests at any of these hostels.

Accommodation

Herzen University Hostel, Kazanskaya ul. 6 ☎ 314 74 72 or 314 74 68, fax 314 76 59; Nevskiy prospekt/Gostiniy dvor metro (see map on p.68). Mainly used by trainee teachers, but may have summer vacancies. Great location and OK facilities including a solarium and masseur. Double and triple rooms with shared bathrooms ($10 per person).

International Hostel Holiday, ul. Mikhailova 1/9 ☎ & fax 542 73 64 or 327 10 70, *www.hostel.ru*; Ploshchad Lenina metro (see map on p253). A well-run hostel with rooms sleeping three to six people ($18 per person) and private doubles (③) and singles ($40) with shared facilities. Discount of $2 per night after five days. Most rooms have river views, or less attractively overlook Kresty Prison. Offers visa support ($30) and registration. Kitchen, common room and snack bar. English-speaking staff and travel agency. Breakfast included.

Petrovskiy Hostel, Baltiyskaya ul. 26 ☎ & fax 252 53 81; 10min walk from Narvskaya metro (see map on p.244). Russian student hostel affiliated to the RYHA. Simple double and triple rooms with shared bathrooms ($12 per person). Cafeteria and sauna. Little English spoken. Less salubrious and efficient than the *International Holiday Hostel* or the *St Petersburg International Hostel*, but by no means awful.

Puppet Theatre Hostel, ul. Nekrasova 12 ☎ 272 54 01, fax 272 83 61, *puppet@ryh.ru*; 15min from Mayakovskaya or Chernyshevskaya metro (see map on p.216). Sited just off Liteyniy prospekt, within walking distance of the Engineers' Castle, this fifth-floor RYHA hostel is reached via the trade

① *Under $15*
② *$15–30*
③ *$30–50*
④ *$50–100*
⑤ *$100–150*
⑥ *$150–200*
⑦ *$200–300*
⑧ *Over $300*

Accommodation

In addition to hostels, there are basic hotel-cum-sanatoria attached to the Imperial palaces at Peterhof (p.332), Tsarskoe Selo (p.349) and Oranienbaum (p.345), which are in fabulous locations and within commuting distance of the city.

entrance of the puppet theatre next door. Simply furnished but extremely clean, with very friendly, helpful staff, it has five double rooms (③) and a dorm ($16 per person), with toilets and showers in the corridor. Continental breakfast included.

St Petersburg International Hostel, 3ya Sovetskaya ul. 28 ☎ 329 80 18, fax 329 80 19, *www.ryh.ru*; 10min walk from Ploshchad Vosstaniya metro (see map on p.216). Located in a quiet backstreet to the north of Moscow Station. Clean, friendly and well run, with a cybercafé, library and nightly movies. Prices vary from low (Nov–Feb) to high (March–Oct) season. One double room (③) and three- to five-bed dorms ($15–19 per person, low/high season) with shared facilities. On the dorms there's a discount of $1 for ISIC card holders and $3/2 for HI members (only one discount allowed). Breakfast included. Provides tourist visa support ($35) and has its own travel agency, Sindbad travel (*www.sindbad.ru/en*). Reservations can be made through STA in Britain and the USA or at any Hostelling International IBN (International Booking Network) location.

Motels and campsites

Both of St Petersburg's **motel-camp sites** are out along the Vyborg road and chiefly aimed at Finnish motorists. The older Olgino site has a reputation for robberies and prostitution, although it has cleaned up its act somewhat of late; its main virtue, however, is being accessible by bus from the city. If you're arriving by car, Retur Motel-Camping is a far safer bet.

Olgino Motel-Camping, Primorskoe shosse 59, km 18 ☎ 238 36 71, fax 238 37 63; a 40min ride on bus #110, #411 or #416 from Chernaya rechka metro. Low-ranking Mafiosi inhabit the rooms in the main building, while the four-bed cottages in the woods are mainly occupied by Finns. Activities include horseriding, basketball and billiards. ③.

Retur Motel-Camping, Primorskoe shosse 202, km 29 ☎ 437 75 33, fax 437 75 33; same buses as above or a Sestroretsk-bound *elektrichka* train from Finland Station to Aleksandrovskaya Station. A secure campsite (①) with double rooms (②), four-person cottages (④), and the use of a heated pool included in the price. Sauna, tennis and horseriding facilities as well (not included in the room rate).

Chapter 10

Eating and drinking

*When I eat pork at a meal, give me
the whole pig; when mutton, give me
the whole sheep; when goose, the
whole bird. Two dishes are better
than a thousand provided a fellow
can devour as much of them as he
wants.*

Dead Souls, Gogol.

As the above quotation suggests, quantity rather than variety has long characterized the Russian appetite. Especially under Communism, when haute cuisine was wiped out, citizens made a virtue of the slow service that was the norm in Soviet restaurants by drinking, talking and dancing for hours. The Western notion of a quick meal was unthinkable.

Nowadays, the gastronomic scene has improved enormously, with hundreds of new **cafés** and **restaurants** offering all kinds of cuisine and surroundings, aimed at anyone with a disposable income – from mega-rich New Russians and expense-account expatriates to fashion-conscious wealthy teenagers. While some places at the top end of the market can rightfully boast of their haute cuisine, there are lots whose décor and pretensions surpass their cooking, where the clientele's main aim seems to be to flash their money around.

Unlike in the early 1990s, all bars, cafes and restaurants now bill guests and take **payment** in rubles only – though more tourist-oriented places may list prices on their menus in dollars or so-called "Conditional Units" (using the

Cyrillic abbreviation УЕ), which amounts to the same thing. In that case, the total is converted into rubles at the current central bank rate or the rate of exchange advertised on the premises (which may be less favourable). It's often (though not invariably) true that a menu in dollars is an indication that the establishment is overpriced by local standards.

Credit cards are accepted by most top-range or foreign-managed restaurants – we've indicated in our listings which ones are accepted using the relevant abbreviations (Amex = American Express, DC = Diners Club, MC = Mastercard, EC = Eurocard, JCB = Japanese Credit Bank) – but you shouldn't take it for granted. As for paying with travellers' cheques, forget it.

Breakfast, bakeries and snacks

At home, most Russians take **breakfast** (*zavtrak*) very seriously, tucking into calorific dishes such as pancakes (*bliny*) or porridge (*kasha*), with curd cheese (*tvorog*) and sour cream (*smetana*), although some settle simply for a cup of tea and a slice of bread. Hotels will serve an approximation of the "Continental" breakfast, probably just a fried egg, bread, butter and jam; the flashier joints, however, provide a *Shvedskiy stol*, or "Swedish table", a sort of smorgasbord.

Pastries (*pirozhnoe*) are available from cake shops (*konditerskaya*) and some

Eating and drinking

grocers (*gastronom*). Savoury pies (*pirozhki*) are often sold on the streets from late morning; the best are filled with cabbage, curd cheese or rice. It's advisable to steer clear of the meat ones unless you're buying from a reputable café.

Bread (*khleb*), available from bakeries (*bulochnaya*), is one of the country's culinary strong points. "Black" bread (known as *chorniy* or *rzhanoy*) is the traditional variety: a dense rye bread with a distinctive sourdough flavour and amazing longevity. *Karelskiy* is similar but with fruit; *surozhniy* is a lighter version, made with a mixture of wheat and rye. French-style baguettes (*baton*) – white, mixed-grain or plaited with poppy seeds – are also popular. Unfortunately, the old custom, whereby shoppers could test a loaf's freshness with long forks, has gone (people started stealing the forks), but the system of queuing at the *kassa* before queuing for the bread remains.

Like most other Eastern Europeans, the Russians are very fond of **cakes** (*tort*). There are more than sixty varieties, but the main ingredients are fairly standard: a sponge dough, honey and a distinctive spice like cinnamon or ginger or lots of cream and jam. Whatever the season, Russians are always happy to have an **ice cream** (*morozhenoe*), available from kiosks all over town. Much of the locally produced ice cream is cheaper and of better quality than the imported brands; try the popular crème-brûlée or eskimo, a sort of choc-ice. Alternatively, there are a few *Baskin-Robbins* outlets around town.

Most department stores feature a stand-up *bufet*, offering open **sandwiches** with salami, caviar or boiled egg as well as other nibbles. Less appealing buffets can be found in train and bus stations, and around metro stations and markets.

Zakuski

Despite the increasing popularity of fast food, there are signs that Russian culinary traditions are making a comeback,

especially with regard to *bliny* (pancakes), one of the best-loved of Russian **zakuski** – small dishes or hors d'oeuvres, which are often a meal in themselves.

Zakuski traditionally form the basis of the famous *Russkiy stol*, or "Russian table", a feast of awesome proportions, in which the table groans under the weight of the numerous dishes while the samovar steams away. Among the upper classes in Tsarist times, *zakuski* were merely the prelude to the main meal, as foreign guests would discover to their dismay after gorging themselves on these delights. Salted fish, like sprats or herrings, are a firm favourite, as are gherkins, assorted cold meats and salads. Hard-boiled eggs and *bliny*, both served with **caviar** (*ikra*), are also available. Caviar is no longer as cheap as during Brezhnev's era, when people tired of eating so much of it, but it's still cheaper than in the West. There are two basic types: red (*krasnaya*) and black (*chornaya*), with the latter having smaller eggs and being more expensive.

Meals

Russians usually eat their main meal at lunchtime (*obed*), between 1pm and 4pm, and traditionally have only *zakuski* or salad and tea for supper (*uzhin*). Restaurants, on the other hand, make much more of the evening, though some now offer a set-price business lunch to attract extra customers.

Menus are usually written in Russian only, although more and more places offer a short English version. But beware, because the Russian menu is usually typed up every day, whereas the English version will give only a general idea of what might be available. In such cases, you'd probably be better off asking what they recommend (*shto-by vy po rekomendovali?*), which can elicit some surprisingly frank replies.

If your main concern is price, you'll need to stick to **fast-food** outlets or **cafés**, the latter providing some of the best **ethnic food** in the city, including

Armenian (*Armyanskiy*), Georgian (*Gruzinskiy*), and Afghani (*Afganskiy*), as well as traditional Russian cooking.

Russian cuisine owes many debts to Jewish, Caucasian and Ukrainian cooking, but remains firmly tied to its peasant origins. In former times, the staple diet of black bread, potatoes, cabbages, cucumber and onions made for bland eating – *Shchi da kasha, pishcha nasha* ("cabbage soup and porridge are our food") as one saying goes – with flavourings limited to sour cream, garlic, vinegar, dill and a few other fresh herbs. These strong tastes and textures – salty, sweet, sour, pickled – remained the norm, even among the aristocracy, until Peter the Great introduced French chefs to his court in the early eighteenth century.

Most menus start with a choice of soup or *zakuski*. **Soup** (*sup*) has long played an important role in Russian cuisine (the spoon appeared on the Russian table over four hundred years before the fork). Cabbage soup, or *shchi*, has been the principal Russian dish for the last thousand years, served with a generous dollop of sour cream; beetroot soup, or *borsch*, originally from Ukraine, is equally ubiquitous. Soups, however, are often only available at lunchtime and Russians do not consider even the large meaty soups to be a main meal; they will expect you to indulge in a main course afterwards. Chilled soups (*okroshki*) are popular during the summer, made from whatever's available.

Main courses are overwhelmingly based on **meat** (*myaso*), usually beef, mutton or pork, and sometimes accompanied by a simple sauce (mushroom or cheese). Meat may also make its way into *pelmeni*, a Russian version of ravioli, usually served in a broth. As far as regional meat dishes go, the most common are Georgian barbecued **kebabs** (*shashlyk*), or pilau-style Uzbek rice dishes called *plov*.

A wide variety of **fish and seafood** is available in St Petersburg. Pickled fish is a popular starter (try *selotka pod shuby*, herring in a "fur coat" of beetroot, carrot, egg and mayonnaise), while fresh fish often appears as a main course – salmon, sturgeon and cod are the most common choices, though upmarket restaurants may boast lobster and oysters as well. If you're cooking for yourself, the city's fishmongers usually have a wide range of fish; the stores are identifiable by the sign рыба or океан, or by their smell.

In cafés most main courses are served with boiled potatoes and/or sliced fresh tomatoes, but more expensive restaurants willl serve a full selection of accompanying **vegetables**. These are called *garnir* and often have to be ordered and paid for separately. Where the meat is accompanied by vegetables, you may see an entry on the menu along the lines of 100/25/100g, which refers to the respective weight in grams of the meat (or fish) portion, and its accompanying servings of rice/potatoes and vegetable *garnir*. In ethnic restaurants, meat is almost always served on its own. Other vegetables are generally served boiled or pickled, but seldom separately on the menu.

Desserts (*sladkoe*) are not a strong feature of Russian cuisine. Ice cream, fruit, apple pie (*yablochniy pirog*) and jam pancakes (*blinchikiy s varenem*) are restaurant perennials, while in Caucasian restaurants you may get the flaky pastry and honey dessert, *pakhlava* (like Greek or Turkish baklava).

Ethnic food

The former Soviet Union incorporated a vast number of different ethnic groups, each of whom had their own well-known national dishes. Many **Georgian** or **Armenian** dishes, for example, are now standard elements of Russian cooking: there are few restaurants that don't offer *shashlyk*, the Georgian kebab, or *tolma*, Armenian stuffed vineleaves. Georgian is the most easily found ethnic food and has good vegetarian options, such as *lobio* (spiced red or green beans), or aubergine stuffed with ground walnuts. Carnivores can try the *kharcho*, a spicy meat soup, or *satsivi*, a cold dish of chicken in walnut sauce.

A FOOD AND DRINK GLOSSARY

Useful words

завтрак	*zavtrak*	breakfast
обед	*obéd*	main meal/lunch
ужин	*úzhin*	supper
нож	*nozh*	knife
вилка	*vílka*	fork
ложка	*lózhka*	spoon
тарелка	*tarélka*	plate
чашка	*cháshka*	cup
стакан	*stakán*	glass
десерт	*desért*	dessert

Basics

хлеб	*khleb*	bread
масло	*máslo*	butter/oil
мёд	*myod*	honey
молоко	*molokó*	milk
сметана	*smetána*	sour cream
яйца	*yáytsa*	eggs
яичница	*yaichnitsa*	fried egg
мясо	*myáso*	meat (beef)
рыба	*ryba*	fish
фрукты	*frúkty*	fruit
овощи	*ovoshehi*	vegetables
зелень	*zélen*	green herbs
рис	*ris*	rice
овощной	*ovoshchoy*	vegetable
плов	*plov*	plov
плов	*plov*	pilau
пирог	*piróg*	pie
хачапури	*khachapuri*	nan-style bread, stuffed with meat or cheese
сахар	*sákhar*	sugar
соль	*sol*	salt
перец	*pérets*	pepper
горчица	*gorchítsa*	mustard
аджика	*adzhíka*	spicy Georgian relish
пельмени	*pelmeni*	Siberian ravioli

Soups – супы

борщ	*borsch*	beetroot soup
постный борщ	*póstny borsch*	borsch without meat
хаш	*khásh*	tripe soup, traditionally drunk with a shot of vodka as a hangover cure
клёцки	*klyotski*	Belorussian soup with dumplings
бульон	*bulón*	consommé
рассольник	*rassólnik*	brine and cucumber soup
окрошка	*okróshka*	cold vegetable soup
щи	*shchi*	cabbage soup
солянка	*solyánka*	spicy, meaty soup flavoured with lemon and olives
уха	*ukhá*	fish soup

Vegetables – овощи

лук	*luk*	onions
редиска	*redíska*	radishes
картофель	*kartófel*	potatoes
огурцы	*ogurtsy*	cucumbers
горох	*gorókh*	peas
помидор	*pomidóry*	tomatoes
морковь	*morkóv*	carrots
салат	*salát*	lettuce
капуста	*kapústa*	cabbage
свёкла	*svyokla*	beetroot
лобио	*lóbio*	red or green bean stew

Fruit – фрукты

яблоки	*yábloki*	apples
абрикосы	*abrikósy*	apricots
ягоды	*yágody*	berries
вишня	*víshnya*	cherries
финики	*fíniki*	dates
инжир	*inzhír*	figs
чернослив	*chernoslív*	prunes
груши	*grushi*	pears
сливы	*slivy*	plums
виноград	*vinográd*	grapes
лимон	*limón*	lemon
апельсины	*apelsíny*	oranges
арбуз	*arbúz*	watermelon
дыня	*dynya*	melon

Fish – рыба

карп	*karp*	carp
лещ	*leshch*	bream
скумбрия	*skúmbriya*	mackerel
треска	*treská*	chub
щука	*shchúka*	pike
лососина/сёмга	*lososína/syomga*	salmon

Some terms

Note: all adjectives appear in their plural form

отварные	*otvarnye*	boiled
варёные	*varyonye*	boiled
на вертеле	*na vertele*	grilled on a skewer
жареные	*zhárenye*	roast/grilled/fried
тушёные	*tushonye*	stewed
печёные	*pechonye*	baked
паровые	*parovye*	steamed
копчёные	*kopchonye*	smoked
фри	*fri*	fried
со сметаной	*so smetánoy*	with sour cream
маринованные	*marinóvannye*	pickled
солёные	*solyonye*	salted
фаршированные	*farshiróvannye*	stuffed

Eating and drinking

Zakúski – закуски

ассорти мясное	*assortí myasnóe*	assorted meats
ассорти рыбное	*assortí rybnoe*	assorted fish
ветчина	*vetchiná*	ham
винегрет	*vinegrét*	"Russian salad"
блины	*bliny*	pancakes
грибы	*griby*	mushrooms
икра баклажанная	*ikrá baklazhánnaya*	aubergine (eggplant) purée
икра красная	*ikrá krásnaya*	red caviar
икра чёрная	*ikrá chornaya*	black caviar
шпроты	*shpróty*	sprats (like a herring)
колбаса копчёная	*kolbasá kopchonaya*	smoked sausage
маслины	*masliny*	olives
огурцы	*ogurtsy*	gherkins
осетрина с майонезом	*osetrína s mayonézom*	sturgeon mayonnaise
салат из огурцов	*salat iz ogurtsóv*	cucumber salad
салат из помидоров	*salát iz pomidórov*	tomato salad
сардины с лимоном	*sardíny s limónom*	sardines with lemon
сельдь	*seld*	herring
столичный салат	*stolíchniy salát*	meat and vegetable salad
сыр	*syr*	cheese
брынза	*brynza*	salty white cheese
язык с гарниром	*yazyk s garnírom*	tongue with garnish

Meat and poultry – мясные блюда

азу из говядины	*azú iz govyádiny*	beef stew
антрекот	*antrekot*	entrecôte steak
бифстроганов	*bifstróganov*	beef stroganoff
биточки	*bitóchki*	meatballs
бифштекс	*bifshtéks*	beef steak
шашлык	*shashlyk*	kebab
свинина	*svinína*	pork
котлеты по-киевски	*kotléty po-kíevski*	chicken Kiev
кролик	*królik*	rabbit

continues overleaf...

Eating and drinking

Armenian and **Azeri** cuisine is closer to Middle Eastern cooking (with the addition of dried nuts, saffron and ginger), while **Uzbek** features *khinkali* (a spicier kind of *pelmeni*) and sausages made from pony meat (*kazy*). Perhaps the best ethnic treat is **Korean** food, originally introduced by Koreans exiled to Kazakhstan in the 1930s. Marinaded beef dishes like *bulkogi* are fried at your table, accompanied by raw vegetables and hot pickled garlic relish (*kimichi*). One dish often found even in non-Korean eateries is spicy carrot salad (*morkov po-koreyskiy*). **Indian** and **Chinese** cuisine tends to be rather a disappointment for anyone used to the dishes served in such restaurants in the West; either the chefs find it hard to get hold of the right ingredients, or the dishes are toned down to suit Russian tastes.

Among the other cusines represented by at least one restaurant in St Petersburg are American, Brazilian, French, German, Italian, Japanese, Jewish and Mexican.

Vegetarian food

Russia is not a good place for **vegetarians**; meat takes pride of place in the country's cuisine, and the idea of forgoing it voluntarily strikes Russians as absurd. The various non-Russian dishes which find their way onto the menu offer some solace, and if you eat fish you will usually find something to keep the wolf from the door. *Bliny* are a good fallback; ask for them with sour cream, mushrooms or fish if you eat it. If you're not too fussy about picking out bits of meat, *plov* is a possibility, as are *borsch* and *shchi*, but the best dishes

to look out for are *griby s smetanoy* (mushrooms cooked with onions and sour cream), and *okroshka*, the cold summer soup. You could also try asking for *postniy shchi* (meatless, literally "fasting", *shchi*) or *ovoschnoy plov* (vegetable *plov*). *Lobio*, a widely available Georgian bean dish, is also recommended.

In general the **ethnic restaurants** (Georgian, Armenian, Korean, Indian or Chinese) have the most interesting vegetarian options, though many pizzerias run to veggie pizzas and salad bars. The outlook is a lot better if you are **self-catering**, as fresh vegetables are widely available in markets and on the streets, and many supermarkets and shops sell beans, grains and pulses. Note that locally produced fruit and vegetables are available only from June to October; at other times of the year everything is imported and therefore pricier.

Vegetarian phrases

The concept of vegetarianism is a hazy one for most Russians, so simply saying you're a vegetarian may instil panic or confusion in the waiter – it's often better to ask what's in a particular dish you think looks promising. The phrases to remember are *ya vegetarianets/vegetarianka* (masculine/feminine) and *Kakiye u vas yest blyuda bez myasa ili ryby?* (I'm a vegetarian. Is there anything without meat or fish?); for emphasis you could add *ya ne yem myasnovo ili rybnovo* (I don't eat meat or fish).

Drinking

The story goes that the tenth-century Russian prince Vladimir, when pondering which religion to adopt for his state, rejected Judaism because its adherents were seen as weak and scattered; Catholicism because the pope claimed precedence over sovereigns; and Islam because "Drinking is the joy of the Russians. We cannot live without it." A thousand years on, **alcohol** remains a central part of Russian life. The average citizen drinks over a litre of vodka a week, which means many are putting away a lot more than that. And the further north you go the higher the intake, making St Petersburg one of the most drink-sodden cities on earth. However, the city is less boozy than it was a few years ago, mainly owing to the rising costs of alcohol, but also because of the need to work hard now that the security of a state job for life is a thing of the past.

As more and more **cafés** and **bars** open, the choice of drinks and surroundings in which to enjoy them has increased enormously, so that the old spit-and-sawdust Soviet beer halls are now a thing of the past. However, as the price of drinks in these new establishments is at least double that charged by the **street kiosks**, many Russians still prefer to buy booze from them and drink it at home, or on the nearest bench. Partly due to the prevalence of bootlegging (see below), the City Council prohibits the sale of spirits from kiosks, though many continue to sell vodka under the counter. If you're drinking vodka or other spirits in a bar, the usual measures are 50 or 100 grams (*pyatdesyat/sto gram*), which for those used to British pub measures seem extremely generous.

Vodka and other spirits

Vodka (*vódka*) is the national drink – its name means something like "a little

Eating and drinking

Vodka folklore

Russians have a wealth of phrases and gestures to signify drinking vodka, the most common one being to tap the side of your chin or windpipe. The story goes that there was once a peasant who saved the life of Peter the Great and was rewarded with the right to drink as much vodka as he liked from any distillery. Fearing that a written *ukaz* would be stolen while he was drunk, the man begged the Tsar to stamp the Imperial seal on his throat – the origin of the tapping gesture.

Fittingly, the Russian word for drunk – *pyany* – comes from an incident where two columns of drunken soldiers advancing on either side of the Pyany River mistook each other for the enemy and opened fire. Given its long and disreputable role in Russian warfare, it's ironic that the Tsarist government's prohibition of vodka for the duration of World War I did more harm than good, by depriving the state of a third of its revenue and stoking class hatred of the aristocracy, whose consumption of cognac and champagne continued unabated. Stalin knew better during World War II, when soldiers received a large shot of vodka before going into battle.

In Soviet society, vodka was the preferred form of payment for any kind of work outside the official economy and the nexus for encounters between strangers needing to "go three" on a bottle – a half-litre bottle shared between three people was reckoned to be the cheapest and most companionable way to get a bit drunk. Whereas rationing vodka was the most unpopular thing that Gorbachev ever did, Yeltsin's budgets categorized it as an essential commodity like bread or milk. Despite Yeltsin's notorious fondness for vodka, one would rather not believe Shevardnadze's claim to have found him lying dead drunk in the White House during the 1991 putsch, though at the time Shevardnadze told the crowd outside that "I have met the President and he is standing firm in defence of democracy". At least Yeltsin never lent his name and face to his own brand of vodka – unlike Zhirinovsky (who professes not to drink the stuff).

Eating and drinking

drop of water". Normally served chilled, vodka is drunk neat in one gulp, followed by a mouthful of food, traditionally pickled herring, cucumber or mushrooms; many people inhale deeply before tossing the liquor down their throats. Drinking small amounts at a time, and eating as you go, it's possible to consume an awful lot without passing out – though you soon reach a plateau of inebriated exhilaration.

Taste isn't a prime consideration; what counts is that the vodka isn't **bootleg liquor** (*podelnaya*, *falshivaya* or *levnaya* in Russian). At best, this means that customers find themselves drinking something weaker than they bargained for; at worst, they're imbibing diluted methanol, which can cause blindness or even death. To minimize the risk, familiarize yourself with the price of a few brands in the shops; if you see a bottle at well below the usual price it's almost certainly bootleg stuff. Among the hundreds of native brands on the market, Smirnov and the varieties produced under the Liviz and Dovgan labels are probably the best, though many drinkers regard imported vodkas such as Absolut, Finlandia or Smirnoff as more prestigious. To play extra safe, buy vodka from a branded outlet, or *firmeny magazin* – the Liviz distillery has several stores in the city. Otherwise, check that the bottle's seal and tax label are intact, and don't hesitate to pour its contents away if it smells or tastes strange. A litre of decent vodka costs about $4 in the shops.

In addition to standard vodka you'll also see **flavoured vodkas** such as *pertsovka* (hot pepper vodka), *limonaya* (lemon vodka), *okhotnichaya* (hunter's vodka with juniper berries, ginger and cloves), *starka* (apple and pear-leaf vodka) and *zubrovka* (bison-grass vodka). Many Russians make these and other variants at home by infusing berries or herbs in regular vodka.

Other domestic liquors include **cognac** (*konyak*), which is pretty rough compared to French brandy, but easy enough to acquire a taste for. Traditionally, the best brands hail from

Armenia (Ararat) and Moldova (Beliy Aist), but as both states now export these for hard currency, bottles sold in Russia are almost certainly fakes. More commonly, you'll find Georgian or Dagestani versions, which are all right if they're the genuine article, but extremely rough if they're not. Otherwise, you can find imported spirits such as whisky, gin and tequila in many bars and shops, along with Irish Cream, Amaretto and sickly Austrian fruit brandies. Though kiosks are forbidden to sell neat spirits, most of them stock cans of ready-mixed gin and grapefruit or vodka and cranberry juice.

Beer, wine and champagne

Most of the best-selling beers in Russia come from two St Petersburg breweries: Baltika and Vena. **Baltika** beers come in 50cl bottles, numbered from 1 to 9 according to their strength. The most popular are #3, "Classic" lager (ask for *Troika*), #4, "Original" brown ale, and #5, "Porter" stout; #6 and #7 are often found on tap in seedy pool bars, while it doesn't take much #9 to get you slaughtered. **Vena** does two lager-type beers in 30cl bottles or cans: Nevskoe – which many rate as the finest beer in Russia – and Petergof. Other brands include Afanasy, a mild ale brewed in Nizhniy Novgorod, and Sibirskaya Korona (Siberian Crown) lager. You're bound to find one or more of these on tap (*razlivnoe*) in bars, together with foreign imports such as Tuborg, Carlsberg, Holsten, or Guinness, which may also come in bottles or cans in shops. Beer is rarely, if ever, counterfeited, so you needn't worry about drinking it.

The **wine** (*vino*) on sale in St Petersburg comes mostly from the vineyards of Moldova, Georgia and the Crimea, although European imports are increasingly common. Georgian wines are made from varieties of grapes that are almost unknown abroad, so it would be a shame not to sample them, but since the cheapest generic brands in shops and kiosks are either bootlegs or simply disgusting, you should stick to the most expensive versions ($4 and upwards). The ones to look out for are the dry reds Mukuzani and Saperavi, or the sweeter full-bodied reds Kindzmarauli and Khvanchkara, drunk by Stalin. Georgia also produces some fine white wines, like the dry Gurdzhani and Tsinandali (traditionally served at room temperature), as well as the **fortified wines** Portvini (port) and Masala, which are also produced in the Crimea and known in Russian as *baramatukha* or "babbling juice", the equivalent of Thunderbird in the States.

Finally, there's what is still called Soviet **champagne** (*Sovetskoe shampanskoe*), some of which is really pretty good if served chilled, and far cheaper than the French variety. The two types to go for are *sukhoe* and *bryut*, which are both reasonably dry; *polusukhoe* or "medium dry" is actually very sweet, and *sladkoe* is like connecting yourself to a glucose drip. It's indicative of Russian taste that the last two are the most popular of the lot. Like beer, *shampanskoe* is safe to drink as it's difficult to counterfeit.

Tea, coffee and soft drinks

Traditionally, Russian **tea** (*chay*) was brewed and stewed for hours, and topped up with boiling water from an ornate tea urn, or samovar, but nowadays even the more run-of-the-mill cafés tend to use imported teabags. If you're offered tea in someone's home, it may be *travyanoy*, a tisane made of herbs and leaves. Russians drink tea without milk; if you ask for milk it is likely to be condensed. **Milk** (*moloko*) itself is sold in stores and on the streets, along with *kefir*, a sour milk drink.

Coffee (*kofe*) is readily available and of reasonable quality if they use imported espresso brands like Lavazza or Tchibo, though anything called "Nescafé" is likely to be vile. Occasionally you'll be served an approximation of an espresso or, better still, a Turkish coffee – both are served strong and black. Another favourite drink is weak, milky **cocoa**, known as *kakao*, poured ready-mixed from a boiling urn.

Pepsi and Coca-Cola predictably lead the market in **soft drinks**, although they are being challenged by cheaper brands imported from Eastern Europe. Russian lemonades have all but disappeared, though **kvas**, an unusual but delicious thirst-quencher made from fermented rye bread, is making a comeback. Note that

Eating and drinking

Drinks

чай	*chay*	tea
кофе	*kófe*	coffee
с/без сахаром/сахар	*s/bez sákharom/sákhara*	with/without sugar
сок	*sok*	fruit juice
пиво	*pívo*	beer
вино	*vinó*	wine
красное	*krásnoe*	red
белое	*béloe*	white
бутылка	*butylka*	bottle
лёд	*lyod*	ice
минеральная вода	*minerálnaya vodá*	mineral water
водка	*vódka*	vodka
вода	*vodá*	water
шампанское	*shampánskoe*	champagne
брют сухое	*bryut/sukhoe*	extra dry/dry
полусухое сладкое	*polsukhóe/sládkoe*	medium dry/sweet
коньяк	*konyák*	cognac
на здоровье	*za zdaróve*	cheers!

Eating and drinking

draught *kvas* is generally superior to the bottled stuff.

Native **mineral water** is all right, if a bit salty and sulphurous for most Western tastes – Narzan and Borzhomi from the Caucasus are the best-known brands, and seem to have been toned down with a view to launching them on foreign markets. Imported mineral waters are also widely available. Lastly, if you're staying with Russians, you may be offered some **gryb**, a muddy-coloured, mildly flavoured infusion of a giant fungus known as a "tea mushroom".

Fast-food chains

Over the last decade **fast-food chains** have become hugely popular in Moscow and St Petersburg, offering a variety of food and standards of hygiene and ser-

vice infinitely superior to the grimy *stolovaya* (canteens) that were the lot of generations of citizens during Soviet times, but which younger Russians now take for granted. Besides such worldwide giants as *McDonald's* and *Pizza Hut*, there is the Scandinavian chain *Carrol's*, the local *Grill-Master* and other outlets that come and go at intervals. Since most of them are heavily advertised and only too conspicuous (*McDonald's* even sponsors – and appears on – city plans), we haven't bothered to list them under cafés or include them on the maps in this book – but you'll find their details in the box below.

Cafés and bars

Cafés and **bars** in St Petersburg run the gamut from humble eateries to slick

---

The chain gang

Carrol's *Burgers, soups, fries, salads, milkshakes and dessert.* Gostiniy dvor, Gostiniy dvor metro (daily 9am–11pm); Grazdanskiy pr. 41, Akademicheskaya metro (daily 9am–11pm); Kamenoostrovskiy pr. 31, Petrogradskaya metro (daily 9am–11pm); Nevskiy pr. 45, Mayakovskaya metro (daily 9am–11pm); ul. Vosstaniya 5, Ploshchad Vosstaniya metro (daily 8am–11pm); Zanevskiy pr. 71/1, Ladozhskaya metro (daily 9am–11pm).

Grill-Master *Burgers, pizza, fries, salads and cappuccino.* Nevskiy pr. 46; Nevskiy prospekt/Gostiniy dvor metro (daily 8.30am–10pm); Moskovskiy pr. 30, Tekhnologicheskiy Institut metro (daily 10am–10pm); Sadovaya ul. 22, Gostiniy dvor metro (daily 10am–10pm).

McDonald's *Cheaper than everywhere else in Europe, but they don't serve apple pies.* Bolshaya Morskaya ul. 11/6, Nevskiy prospekt metro (open 24hr); Kamenoostrovskiy pr. 39, Petrogradskaya metro (daily

8am–11pm); Moskovskiy pr. 195a, Moskovskaya metro (open 24hr); Sennaya pl. 4/1, Sennaya ploshchad/Sadovaya metro (daily 8am–11pm); Sredniy pr. 29a, Vasileostrovskaya metro (open 24hr); ul. Savushkina 119a, minibus #T-132 from Chernaya rechka metro (open 24hr); Zagorodniy pr. 45a, Pushkinskaya metro (open 24hr).

Patio Pizza *Thin-crust wood-oven pizzas, salad bar, alcohol.* Amex, Visa, MC, EC, DC, Maestro, JCB. Nevskiy pr. 30, Nevskiy prospekt/Gostiniy dvor metro; Nevskiy pr. 182, Ploshchad Aleksandra Nevskovo metro (both daily noon–midnight).

Pizza Hut *Regarded by locals as classy restaurants, with takeaway slice bars.* Amex, Visa, MC, DC, EC. Gorokhovaya ul. 16, on the corner of the Moyka embankment, Sadovaya/Sennaya ploshchad metro; Nevskiy pr. 96, Mayakovskaya/Ploshchad Vosstaniya metro (both Mon–Thurs & Sun noon–10pm, Fri & Sat noon–11pm).

Prices

We have graded all the cafés and restaurants according to probable **prices per person**. In a café, this relates to the cost of a snack or light meal plus a non-alcoholic drink (although in many of them you can have a full meal); for restaurants, it includes a starter, main course and a dessert, but no alcohol, which in many restaurants can easily double your bill.

Cheap	under $10
Inexpensive	$10–20
Moderate	$20–40
Expensive	$40–80
Very expensive	over $80

establishments, and since most places serve alcohol (or beer, at any rate) the distinction between them is often a fine one. Except for establishments in top-

Eating and drinking

class hotels, cafés are generally cheaper than fully fledged restaurants, making them popular with Russians who have some disposable income, but don't ride around in a Mercedes.

Though almost all cafés are private ventures nowadays, some retain the surly habits of Soviet days, when customers counted themselves lucky if they got served at all, and even where they aim to please, you sometimes find inexplicable lapses in standards or decorum. However, you can also find some delicious meals and friendly watering holes if you know where to look, and the number of acceptable places is rising all the time.

Another recent phenomenon is **street cafés** (usually open from May to late Sept), where you can have a coffee and pastry or hamburger, while watching the world go by. The most obvious along Nevskiy prospekt are outside the Lutheran Church at no. 24, by the Portico opposite the *Grand Hotel Europe* (no. 33) and the beer garden in the yard of no.

High-profile horrors

Several flagrant tourist traps flourish along the stretch of Nevskiy prospekt between the Griboedov Canal and the River Moyka. Although no list of offenders can be exhaustive, since new ones crop up every year, some of them have been around for ages. You have been warned.

Chayka (or Tschaika), nab. kanala Griboedova 14; Gostiniy dvor/Nevskiy prospekt metro. Once this was one of the few places in the city where foreigners could get a decent drink and feel comfortable, but nowadays it's not worth bothering to grapple with the arcane house rules, uninspiring food or the prostitutes that stick around hoping for a revival in the place's fortunes. Amex, Visa, MC. Daily 11am–3am. Moderate.

Literaturnoe Café, Nevskiy pr. 18 ☎312 60 57; Gostiniy dvor/Nevskiy prospekt metro. Ghastly Soviet-era tourist trap trading on its Pushkin associations, charging outrageous prices for revolting food, and full of tour groups enduring poncy music and poetry readings whilst moaning about the cover charge. Daily noon–5pm & 7–11pm. Expensive.

Valhall, Nevskiy pr. 22/24 (corner of Malaya Konyushennaya ul.) ☎311 00 24; Gostiniy dvor/Nevskiy prospekt metro. Not as utterly dire as the *Literaturnoe*, but a strong contender. A Viking-theme restaurant serving Scandinavian and Russian "nouvelle" cuisine, which means pretentiously named meat or seafood dishes with a dab of cranberry sauce, served by lethargic staff wearing silly helmets. If you think it couldn't get worse, stay for the floorshow (Wed & Thurs 10pm, Fri–Sun 11pm), featuring a rubber snake being fellated in a jacuzzi. Visa, MC. Daily noon–3am. Expensive.

Eating and drinking

86 – but you'll find them all around the centre and residential districts.

The following selection is listed in alphabetical order under area headings corresponding to the chapters in the guide section. We've provided phone numbers for bars and cafés where it's advisable to phone ahead and reserve a table, particularly if you are planning to eat.

Within the Fontanka

The listings in this section are marked on the map on p.66.

Atrium Café, Nevskiy pr. 25; Nevskiy prospekt/Gostiniy dvor metro. Lots of light and space, juices, tasty soups and crusty bread make the *Atrium* a popular spot for well-dressed Petersburgers to take a break from shopping or the office, amid a mall and business centre by the Kazan Cathedral. Not cheap, but then neither is its clientele. Visa, MC. Daily 10am–11pm. Inexpensive.

Aurora, Nevskiy pr. 60; Gostiniy dvor/Nevskiy prospekt metro. Classical-style patisserie opposite Catherine's Garden, serving creamy pastries, natural ice cream, good coffee, teas and wine, suffused with soft music and a general air of self-indulgence. No CC. Daily 10am–11pm. Inexpensive.

Idiot Café, nab. reki Moyki 82 ☎315 16 75; Nevskiy prospekt/Gostiniy dvor metro. Named after the Dostoyevsky novel, this cosy basement warren is furnished with divans and period junk, and popular with expats and arty Russians. Its (mainly) vegetarian menu is strongest when it comes to *borsch, pelmeni, bliny* and pickled nibbles, and fails when it attempts anything Oriental. Hangover-sufferers should go for the option of a plate of cold snacks with 100g of vodka (equivalent to about 2.5 British measures). They also have cocktails, backgammon and a library of foreign-language books (mostly rubbish). No CC. Daily noon–midnight. Inexpensive.

La Cucharacha, nab. reki Fontanki 39 ☎110 40 46; Gostiniy dvor metro.

Basement Tex-Mex cantina beloved of foreigners and Russians, where the food is tasty and filling, albeit not as authentic as purists might wish. The bill can be reasonable if you don't splurge on margaritas or aged tequila. Reserve a table to avoid queuing after 7pm. Happy hour 6–8pm; live music Tues, Thurs & Fri nights. No CC. Mon–Thurs & Sun noon–1am, Fri & Sat noon–5am. Inexpensive–moderate.

Mezzanine Café, *Grand Hotel Europe*, Mikhailovskaya ul. 1–7; Gostiniy dvor/Nevskiy prospekt metro. Light and airy with comfy armchairs, like a posh hotel in London. The coffee is excellent, but the cakes are disappointing. Amex, Visa, DC, EC, MC. Daily 10am–10pm. Moderate.

Nevskiy 27, Nevskiy pr. 27; Gostiniy dvor/Nevskiy prospekt metro. Decent pastries to eat in or take out. Daily 8am–3pm & 4–8pm (closes 7pm on Sun). Inexpensive.

Nevskiy 40, Nevskiy pr. 40; Gostiniy dvor/Nevskiy prospekt metro. Tourist watering hole with original nineteenth-century *Bierkeller* decor. Does pastries, schnitzel, frankfurters and a few Russian dishes. Nice, but way overpriced by local standards. Daily noon–midnight. Moderate.

Sadko, *Grand Hotel Europe*, ul. Mikhailovskaya 1–7; Gostiniy dvor/Nevskiy prospekt metro. *Sadko's* present forlornness is fitting punishment for its hubris in the past, when security goons excluded anyone but Westerners, hoods and hookers. It now offers reasonable, though overpriced, food, and has a great view of Nevskiy – though they still need to do something about the live music in the evenings. However, Amex, Visa, EC, MC, DC. Daily 10am–10pm. Moderate.

Shamrock, ul. Dekabristov 27; 20min walk from Sadovaya metro. Themed Irish bar opposite the Mariinskiy Theatre, serving draught and bottled foreign beers and hearty pub fare. Live music in the evenings and English premier league football screened on Sat (6pm) and Sun (7pm). Daily noon–2am. Inexpensive–moderate.

Stroganov Yard, Nevskiy pr. 17 ☎315 23 15; Gostiniy dvor/Nevskiy prospekt metro. A glassed-in café in the courtyard of the Stroganov Palace, where each table has a phone for calling diners at other tables, if one is lulled into a flirty mood by the Euro-Russian food and live music in the evenings. Accepts major CC; bureau de change in the yard. Daily 10am–1am. Inexpensive.

Tinkoff, Kazanskaya ul. 7; Nevskiy prospekt/Gostiniy dvor metro. The city's first micro-brewery is a trendy hangout featuring seven varieties of freshly brewed beer (some unfiltered), a stylish sushi bar, hot and cold European dishes, and live music. Visa, MC. Daily noon–2am. Inexpensive–moderate.

Vasilevskiy Island

The listings in this section are marked on the map on p.170.

Bistro Grand, 1ya liniya 36; 15min walk from Vasileostrovskaya metro. There are so few cafés on the island worth mentioning that this decent Russian fast-food outlet really counts for something, with a wide range of soups, salads, stews and vegetarian options. The menu is in English and you can sit outside in the summer. Daily 24hr. Major CC. Inexpensive.

Captain Nemo, pr. Kima 28 ☎350 39 66; 10min walk from metro Primorskaya. Named after the mad submariner of Jules Verne's *20,000 Leagues under the Sea*, this bizarre nautically themed café in the backwaters beyond the Smolensk cemetery is diverting enough if you're in the area, but not worth a special journey. Serves burgers, seafood and Russian staples like *shashlyk*. Daily 11am–10pm. No CC. Inexpensive.

Dialog, Sredniy pr. 66 (corner of 16–17ya liniya) ☎321 59 15; 15min walk from Vasileostrovskaya metro. A cockerel that crows at intervals and all kinds of alpinists' gear hung on the walls add a

kooky touch to this "Bards' Café", where middle-aged Russians sing ballads and meet fellow bards on Thursdays and Fridays. Otherwise the place is pretty dead and the food is poor – but drinks are cheap, and it doesn't attract the lowlife that other bars on the island do. Daily 8–11pm. No CC. Cheap–inexpensive.

Petrograd Side

The listings in this section are marked on the map on p.188.

Café Salkhino, Kronverkskiy pr. 25 ☎ 232 78 91; Gorkovskaya metro. Some of the best Georgian food in town can be had in this small, cosy café hung with paintings by Georgian artists and presided over by the ebullient Ketino and Eka, formerly of the *Rioni* (see p.293). Everything is delicious – the *sulgani* cheese starters, *lobio*, *satsivi* and main courses – and the Georgian wines can be sublime. Daily 11am–11pm. No CC. Inexpensive–moderate.

Kamini, pr. Dobrolyubova 7/2; Sportivnaya metro. A humble, inconspicuous place serving simple vegetarian Russian dishes: *bliny* with mushrooms and sour cream, cabbage soup and pies, and buckwheat *kasha*. No CC. Daily 11am–11pm. Cheap.

Mereti, Shirokaya ul. 12; Gorkovskaya metro. Though not as easy to find as the *Salkhino* (see above), this is another Georgian café well worth investigating, run by relatives of the same extended family and likewise delivering fine Caucasian food in a homely environment. No CC. Daily 11am–11pm. Inexpensive.

Troitskiy most, ul. Malaya Possadkaya 2; Gorkovskaya metro. One of the oldest alternative cafés in St Petersburg, this cheery, laid-back place run by Hare Krishnas has herbal tea and vegetarian snacks. No CC. Daily: summer 24hr; winter 11am–3pm & 4–8pm. Cheap.

Liteniy, Smolniy and Vladimirskaya

The listings in this section are marked on the map on p.216.

Eating and drinking

Eating and drinking

Bagdad, Furshtadtskaya ul. 35; Chernyshevskaya metro. Opened in the Gorbachev era, this relaxed, richly painted basement café serves Central Asian food – try the *plov*, the *manty* (like giant ravioli) or the spicy carrot salad (a Korean dish, but what the hell). No CC. Daily 11am–11pm. Inexpensive.

Bagration Bistro, Liteynit prospekt 8/19; Chernyshevskaya metro. Tiny, austerely chic cellar serving tasty Georgian dishes for a fraction of what you'd pay in the *Bagration* restaurant around the corner. The *lobio*, spicy beef *chashashuli* and cheesy *khachapuri* are a must. No smoking. No CC. Daily 24hr. Cheap.

Baltic Bread (aka Britanskie Pekarnie), 8ya Sovetskaya ul 1; tram #5 or #7 from Ploshchad Vosstaniya metro. A bakery-café selling all kinds of bread, pastries and savoury pies, with a few tables for drinking tea or coffee. A good breakfast spot if you're staying at the *St Petersburg International Hostel* and don't mind walking six blocks to get here. No CC. Daily 10am–10pm. Cheap.

Café Vienna, *Nevsky Palace Hotel*, Nevsky pr. 57; Mayakovskaya metro. Easily the best cakes in town, and as an added bonus the scrumptious cream and chocolate Viennese creations are half-price after 10pm. All major CC. Daily 10am–midnight. Inexpensive.

Football Bar, Mokhovaya ul. 41; Mayakovskaya metro. Basement bar with big-screen TV for sporting and musical events. Draught Irish beers, decent food and a friendly atmosphere. No CC. Daily from 1pm till the last person leaves. Cheap.

Gushe, Nevskiy pr. 47; Mayakovskaya/Ploshchad Vosstaniya metro. A herbalist's and health-food shop with a salad bar and bakery, serving fresh fruit juices and coffee. Tables inside and stools outside for watching life on Nevskiy. No CC. Daily 9am–10.30pm. Cheap.

Khuratok, 3ya Sovetskaya ul. 26; Ploshchad Vosstaniya metro. Two doors along from the *St Petersburg International Hostel*, this friendly café is an excellent place to sample Russian cuisine on the cheap; try the *borsch* or mushroom soup. Menu in English. No CC. Daily noon–11pm. Cheap.

Kolobok, ul. Chaykovskovo 40; Chernyshevskaya metro. Clean self-service place with excellent sweet and savoury *pirozhki* (pies) at ridiculously low prices, and hot meals and salads as well. Discounts for takeouts, before 11am, and for ISIC cardholders. Its early-morning opening makes it ideal for breakfast. No smoking. No CC. Daily 7.30am–8pm. Cheap.

Le Café Bahlsen, Nevskiy pr. 142 ☎271 28 11; Ploshchad Vosstaniya metro. The only German café in town that's not a *Bierstube*. If you're ravenous, the bistro section does a massive grill platter which is cooked at your table and spiced to taste, while the café serves snacks and superior cakes. Daily: bistro noon–10pm; café noon–midnight. Amex, Visa, DC, MC. Moderate.

Liverpool Bar, ul. Mayakovskovo 16 ☎279 20 54; Mayakovskaya metro. A relaxed basement bar playing the music and movies of the Beatles – there's also a pool table. The house speciality is sweet pepper stuffed with fish in wine sauce; the less adventurous can try the baked potatoes and chicken wings, or fish 'n' chips. Discounts on meals noon–4pm; happy hour 4–5pm. No CC. Mon–Thurs 11am–2am, Fri–Sun 11am–5am. Inexpensive.

Metekhi, ul. Belinskovo 3; Gostiniy dvor/Nevskiy prospekt metro. One of the oldest Georgian cafés in town, it wins no prizes for decor or service, but the *khachapuri*, *lobio* and *satsivi* are all spot-on, though the choice gets thin towards the evening. No CC. Daily 11am–9pm. Cheap.

Mollie's Irish Bar, ul. Rubinshteyna 36; Vladimirskaya or Mayakovskaya metro. One of the livelier bars in town, featuring 19 draught beers, 50 cocktails, tasty pub grub, and Irish music and TV sports in the background. Amex, Visa, MC, DC, JCB.

Mon–Thurs noon–2am, Fri & Sat noon–3am, Sun noon–1am. Inexpensive.

Russkie bliny, ul. Gagarinskaya 13; 15–20min from Nevskiy prospekt metro. Very popular, cheap lunchtime spot. Traditional *bliny*, both savoury and sweet – the *bliny* with red caviar or the *blinchiki* (rather like folded and fried *bliny*) with mushrooms or puréed salt fish are wonderful. No smoking or alcohol. Come before 1pm or after 2.30pm to avoid the queues. No CC. Mon–Fri 11am–6pm. Cheap.

Shwarma, Liteyniy pr. 64; Mayakovskaya metro. Probably the best *shwarma* outlet in the city, attracting a diverse clientele (if you can say that about a basement nook with room for six customers to stand) and selling draught Baltika. No smoking. No CC. Daily 24hr. Cheap.

Tuborg Club, Kirochnaya ul. 36; Chernyshevskaya metro. Laid-back café-bar in a courtyard, serving pizzas, pasta and Russian culinary staples, with billiard tables upstairs ($2–$3 per hour). No CC. Daily noon–midnight. Inexpensive.

Wooden Pub, ul. Chaykovskovo 36; Chernyshevskaya metro. Small, friendly basement bar with tables outside in summer. Draught Irish, Danish and Russian beers and a wide range of spirits and French wines, as well as seafood snacks. On Fridays and Saturdays there's a saxophonist and a fiddler. No CC. Daily 11am–2am. Inexpensive.

Zvezdochot (The Astrologer), ul. Marata 35; Vladimirskaya/Dostoevskaya metro. Basement café-bar decorated with runes and zodiac symbols – there's even a resident astrologer. Serves Russian and European food. No CC. Daily noon–11pm. Inexpensive.

Restaurants

St Petersburg's **restaurants** reflect the social revolution of the last decade, as ever more exotic places spring up to pander to the *novie bogatie* (new rich). At the top end of the scale, you'll probably feel uncomfortable if you're not dressed to the hilt – though not many places impose a formal dress code (a jacket and tie for men, a skirt or dress for women). At present, relatively few places include a **service charge** in the bill, so you can tip (or not) as you like. Some places feature **floorshows** consisting of "folk music" and maybe some kind of striptease act (which Russians regard with equanimity), for which there may or may not be a surcharge. At most restaurants it's customary to consign your coat to the *garderob* on arrival; if helped to put it back on later, a small tip is warranted.

As in Moscow, more and more places offer **business lunches** at lower prices than you'd pay dining *à la carte*. Such deals are advertised by signboards outside with the words *biznes lanch* (бизнес ланьч) in Cyrillic, and in the city's foreign-language press, where you may also find details of **food festivals** being held, most frequently at the *Nevsky Palace Hotel*.

We've provided **telephone numbers** for all the restaurants listed, as reserving in advance is always a good idea, particularly if you want to eat after 9pm. Most places now have at least one member of staff with a rudimentary grasp of English. If not, a useful phrase to get your tongue around is *Ya khochu zakazat stol na . . . cheloveka sevodnya na . . . chasov* (I want to reserve a table for . . . people for . . . o'clock today). The following restaurants are listed in alphabetical order under area headings corresponding to the chapters in the guide section.

Within the Fontanka
The listings in this section are marked on the map on p.66.

1001 Nights, ul. Millionnaya 21/6 ☎/fax 312 22 65; Gostiniy dvor/Nevskiy prospekt metro. Delicious Uzbek food, with plenty of salads if you don't fancy specialities such as *kazy* (horse sausage), while the colourful decor, waitresses in silk gowns, Uzbek musicians and beguiling belly dancers (8.30pm & 10pm) make for a memorable evening.

Eating and drinking

Eating and drinking

Finish up with a yummy *Badrok halva.* Daily noon–midnight. No CC. Moderate.

1913 god, Vosnesenskiy pr. 13 ☎315 51 48; bus #22 from Nevskiy pr. to St Isaac's Square. A nondescript exterior conceals one of the best Russian restaurants in town, popular with cultural figures. Generous portions of simple rural dishes like potato pancakes with bacon and sour cream (*draniky*), and richer foreign dishes such as lobster fricassée. Guitar, accordion and violin music after 8pm. Visa, MC. Daily noon–1am. Expensive.

Brasilia, Kazanskaya ul. 24 ☎320 87 77; Nevskiy prospekt or Sennaya ploshchad metro. A cosy, stylish place to enjoy Brazilian food, with an open fire for grilling the house speciality, *rodisio*, consisting of nine kinds of charbroiled meat and fish brought to your table impaled on swords, with a choice of side dressings. Try one of the rum-based long drinks, such as a *majito* or *calerini.* Most CCs. Mon–Thurs & Sun noon–3am, Fri & Sat noon–6am. Moderate.

Caviar Bar, *Grand Hotel Europe*, Mikhailovskaya ul. 1–7 ☎329 60 00; Gostiniy dvor/Nevskiy prospekt metro. An aristocratic haunt before the Revolution, it now panders to the merely wealthy with delicacies such as Kamchatka crab, Siberian *pelmeni* in champagne sauce, sturgeon and salmon mousse, and *bliny* with caviar – all accompanied by champagne or de luxe vodkas. Amex, Visa, MC, DC. Daily 5–11pm. Expensive.

Chopsticks, *Grand Hotel Europe*, Mikhailovskaya ul. 1–7 ☎329 66 30; Gostiniy dvor/Nevskiy prospekt metro. Topnotch Chinese restaurant specializing in Szechuan and Cantonese cuisine, served mild or spicy as desired. The hot and sour soup and Szechuan chicken are especially good, while the service is so attentive that it borders on the slavish. Daily noon–11pm. Amex, Visa, DC, MC, EC. Very expensive.

Dinastiya (Dynasty), Gorokhovaya ul. 11; Gostiniy dvor/Nevskiy prospekt metro. Charming family-run Russian restaurant

whose lengthy menu includes such intriguingly named dishes as "St Petersburg's Secrets" (beef stuffed with apricots and prunes) and "Babushka cake" (sponge cake with hazelnut buttercream or wild blueberry pure). No CC. Daily noon–11pm. Inexpensive.

Dvoryanskoe Gnezdo (The Noble Nest), ul. Dekabristov 21 ☎312 32 05; Sadovaya/Sennaya ploshchad metro. Housed in the summer pavilion of the Yusupov Palace, near the Mariinskiy Theatre, its gourmet creations draw on European, Russian and Asian culinary traditions and are arguably the finest haute cuisine in St Petersburg. Formal dress and reservations essential. Music from 7pm. Daily noon–midnight. Amex, Visa, MC, DC, JCB. Very expensive.

Europe, *Grand Hotel Europe*, Mikhailovskaya ul. 1–7 ☎329 60 00; Gostiniy dvor/Nevskiy prospekt metro. Heavily sauced European and Russian dishes, impeccably served in a sumptuous Art Nouveau setting. Jacket and tie required. Open for breakfast (daily 7–10am) and dinner (Mon–Sat 7–11pm), with a champagne jazz brunch on Sun (noon–4pm). Amex, Visa, EC, DC, MC. Very expensive.

Federico Fellini, Malaya Konyushennaya ul. 24 ☎311 50 78; Gostiniy dvor/Nevskiy prospekt metro. A cinema-restaurant featuring dishes beloved of film stars – Italian, French and Russian – plus a fondue pavilion. The decor is supposed to represent a film set, the menu comes on a film canister, and they show a Fellini film at 9pm (for which there's a surcharge). More swank than substance. Daily noon–1am. Moderate–expensive.

Graf Suvorov, ul. Lomonosova 6 ☎315 43 28; Gostiniy dvor metro. Gourmet Russian and European food served in surroundings of fake luxury. Try the bear filet or deer carpacio and the extensive range of salads, but beware of the stunningly expensive wine list. Also features musical evenings ranging from Gypsy to jazz or Soviet retro, depending on the day of the week. Amex, Visa, MC, DC,

JCB. Daily from noon till the last customer leaves. Very expensive.

Kavkaz Bar, Karavannaya ul. 18 ☎312 16 55; Gostiniy dvor/Nevskiy prospekt metro. The most tourist-oriented of St Petersburg's many Caucasian restaurants, with an interior styled like a Georgian courtyard, waitresses in national costume and live music after 8pm. Café lunch $3.50. Daily: café 11am–8pm; restaurant 11am–1am. Cheap–inexpensive.

La Strada, Bolshaya Konyushennaya ul. 27 ☎/fax 312 47 00; Gostiniy dvor/Nevskiy prospekt metro. A glass-roofed Italian restaurant designed to resemble a pavement café, with a wood-fired oven turning out the best pizzas in town; they also serve Italian nibbles with baked potatoes, a terrific vegetarian lasagne and wonderful tiramisu. No CC. Daily noon till the last customer leaves. Inexpensive–moderate.

Le Français, Galernaya ul. 20 ☎315 24 65; bus #22 from Nevskiy prospekt. A French chef produces fine bistro cuisine from Russian ingredients such as sturgeon and crayfish, accompanied by French cheeses and wines, and served with panache. Pianist Mon–Fri 8pm–1am. Free secure parking. Amex, Visa, MC, DC, EC. Daily 11am–1am; bar until 3am. Moderate.

Milano, Karavannaya ul. 8 ☎314 73 48; Gostiniy dvor metro. Attractive trattoria hung with interesting paintings and offering lots of seafood – the salmon in orange sauce is delicious, as is the pasta in a sauce of capers, garlic and olive oil. Live music Fri & Sat. Amex, Visa, DC, MC. Daily noon–midnight. Moderate.

Nikolay, Bolshaya Morskaya ul. 52 ☎311 14 02; bus #22 from Nevskiy pr. to St Isaac's Square. Though the Russian food is only average, guests can enjoy the walnut-panelled dining room of the House of Architects and ask for a tour of the splendid rooms upstairs (see p.118). No CC. Daily noon–11.30pm. Cheap.

St Petersburg, nab. kanala Griboedova 5 ☎314 49 47; Gostiniy dvor/Nevskiy prospekt metro. This ritzy Russian restau-

rant's menu includes wonderful seafood (try the marinated salmon flavoured with juniper and saffron) and a great beef stroganoff. After 9pm there's a variety show with Peter the Great surrounded by nubile showgirls, or a Russian folk ensemble on Sun, and dancing too. Amex, Visa, MC, DC. Daily noon–2am. Expensive.

Sakura, nab. Kanala Griboedova 10/12 ☎315 94 74; Gostiniy dvor/Nevskiy prospekt metro. Mouthwatering sushi, *nabe*, seafood and meat soups, prepared by a Japanese chef and served by kimono-clad waitresses in *shoji*-screened rooms. Arguably the best Japanese restaurant in the city, and certainly the costliest. Visa, MC. Daily noon–11pm. Very expensive.

Senat Bar, Galernaya ul. 1–3 (by the Bronze Horseman) ☎314 92 53; bus #5 or #22 from Nevskiy prospekt. A popular haunt for suits in a stylishly refurbished basement of the Senate building that once played host to President Clinton, offering good Euro-Russian cuisine and an endless selection of beer and wine. Business lunch $14. Amex, Visa, MC. Daily noon–5am. Moderate–expensive.

Tandoor, Voznesenkiy pr. 2 (by St Isaac's) ☎312 38 86. The oldest and best Indian restaurant in St Petersburg, its decor and atmosphere are fine, but the food is slightly disappointing if you're looking for a curry that bites back, although vegetarians will be heartened by the choice of dishes. Business lunch only $10. Amex, Visa, DC, MC, JCB. Daily noon–11pm. Inexpensive–moderate.

Zolotoy Drakon (Golden Dragon), ul. Dekabristov 62 ☎114 84 41, *www .goldendragon.spb.ru*; 20min walk from Sadovaya/Sennaya ploshchad metro. The multilingual menu boasts 120 Chinese dishes, some of them pretty good, but others toned down for Russian tastes or for lack of authentic ingredients. Daily noon–midnight. Moderate–expensive.

Vasilevskiy Island

The listings in this section are marked on the map on p.170.

Eating and drinking

Eating and drinking

Academia, Birzhevoy prozed 2 ☎ 327 89 42; minibus #T-187 from Nevskiy prospekt. One of a trio of fancy restaurants in the hinterland of the Strelka (the clientele tends to arrive with bodyguards in tow), *Academia* has a faux library-style banqueting hall designed by Andrei Dmitriev (who went on to decorate *Restoran* – see below), and serves light, eclectic Euro-Russian cuisine. The caviar and pasta dishes are delicious, but the wood-oven pizzas don't compare with *La Strada*'s (see p.291). Live music. Guarded parking. Amex, Visa, DC, MC. Daily noon–5am. Expensive.

Kalinka, Sezdovskaya liniya 9 ☎ 328 28 66 or 323 37 18; trolleybus #10 from Nevskiy pr. A stuffed bear and heavy folk-style woodcarvings set the tone for this unabashedly touristy Russian restaurant, where guests are entertained with balalaika music, folk songs and Gypsy dancing. The menu is in English with prices listed in dollars (though you pay in rubles). Amex, Visa, MC, DC, Maestro, JCB. Daily noon–midnight. Expensive.

Restoran, Tamozhniy per. 2 ☎ 327 89 79 or 327 89 75; minibus #T-187 from Nevskiy prospekt. Classical minimalism is the leitmotif of "The Restaurant". The food is traditional Russian, made from the finest ingredients and simply prepared, while the decor is so austere that when the owners came to inspect the premises, they asked the designer "Is that it?" All major CC. Daily noon–midnight. Expensive.

Staraya Tamozhnya. Tamozhniy per. 1 ☎ 327 89 90; minibus #T-187 from Nevskiy prospekt. A doorman dressed as a Tsarist customs official sets the tone for the "Old Customs House", an elegant cellar conversion with an open kitchen. Its Franco-Russian gourmet seafood is superb, and the nightly jazz or dance music lures its Mafiosi clientele onto the dance floor with their girlfriends. Visa, MC. Daily 1pm–1am. Expensive.

Venetsia, ul. Korablestroiteley 21 ☎ 352 54 04; bus #152 from Primorskaya metro. Handy if you're staying at the *Pribaltiyskaya Hotel* but not worth a journey otherwise, this pizza and pasta restaurant pitches itself at moderately affluent locals and visiting Finns, with a floorshow in the evenings. Tues–Sun 12.30pm–11.30am. No CC. Moderate.

Zemchuzhina (Pearl), Shkiperskiy protok 2 ☎ 355 20 63; tram #11 or #40 from Vasileostrovskaya metro. Way out in the wilds of Gavan, St Petersburg's only Jewish restaurant does gefilte fish, goose liver and matzo soup just like Mom used to make, in a cosy setting with Jewish music in the evenings. Visa, MC. Daily noon–11.30pm. Moderate.

Petrograd Side

The listings in this section are marked on the map on p.188.

Austeria, Ioanavskiy ravelin, Peter and Paul Fortress ☎ 238 42 62; Gorkovskaya metro. This nautically themed restaurant in a former officers' mess hall within the fortress walls is stronger on ambience than cuisine, with a working eighteenth-century Dutch music box and live music in the evenings. Go for the sturgeon *shaslyk* on pasta, if anything. Amex, Visa, MC. Daily noon–midnight. Moderate.

Demyanova Ukha, Kronverkskiy pr. 53 ☎ 232 80 90; Gorkovskaya metro. *Ukha* is the Russian equivalent of *bouillabaisse*, and one of the specialities of the house, whose menu features every kind of fish dish in the Russian culinary lexicon – be sure to start with the red caviar *bliny*. Though ideally located for a meal after an afternoon at the Peter and Paul Fortress, bookings are advisable after 7pm. Daily 11am–11pm. Moderate.

Fujiama, Kamennoostrovskiy pr. 54 ☎ 234 49 22 or 327 52 85; Gorkovskaya metro. Decent, affordable sushi and other Japanese dishes served in variously sized rooms, including one where you can dine seated on *tatami* matting. A better deal than *Sakura* in the city centre. Visa, MC. Mon–Thurs & Sun noon–11pm, Fri & Sat noon–1am. Moderate.

Gorniy Orel (Mountain Eagle), by the Zoopark entrance off Kronverkskiy pr.;

Gorkovskaya metro. A lively Georgian place where the *lobio*, *shashlyk* and *chashashuli* are spicier than usual, good homemade wine comes in jugs, and the mingled aromas of zoo animals and grilling meat pervade its garish interior and wobbly outdoor tables. No CC. Daily noon–midnight. Inexpensive.

Grand Café Antwerpen, Kronverkskiy pr. 13/2 ☎ 233 97 46; Gorkovskaya metro. Dutch-Russian joint venture, with a summer terrace and balalaika music in the evening. Offers Russian and European cuisine and De Koninck beer. All major CC. Daily from noon until the last person leaves. Expensive.

Swagat, Bolshoy pr. 91 ☎ 217 44 28; Petrogradskaya metro. The city's second-best Indian restaurant isn't as reliable as *Tandoor* (see p.291), but the service is extremely friendly and prices reasonable. Amex, Visa, MC, DC, JCB. Daily noon–11pm. Moderate.

Zolotoy Drakon na Zooparke, Kronverkskiy pr. 61 ☎ 232 26 43, *www.goldendragon.spb.ru*; 10min walk from Gorkovskaya metro. An offshoot of the *Zolotoy Drakon* near the Mariinskiy Theatre, with the same extensive menu of Chinese dishes tweaked for Russian tastes, pagoda flourishes and waitresses in Suzy Wong dresses. All major CC. Daily noon–midnight. Inexpensive–moderate.

Liteniy, Smolniy and Vladimirskaya
The listings in this section are marked on the map on p.216.

Arirang, 8ya Sovetskaya ul. 20 ☎ 274 04 66; tram #5 or #7 from Ploshchad Vosstaniya metro. Tailor made for RTW travellers staying at the *St Petersburg International Hostel*, five blocks distant, this friendly Korean restaurant features a sushi and sashimi bar (11am–11pm) and nightly karaoke (6pm–5am). No CC. Daily 11am–11pm. Moderate.

California Grill, Nevskiy pr. 176 ☎ 274 24 22; Ploshchad Aleksandra Nevskovo metro. A gaudy temple of Americana at the unfashionable end of Nevskiy

prospekt. Its burgers and Tex-Mex are as good as any in town, but don't bother with the salad bar. Nightly live music; rock 'n' roll party Sun. Amex, Visa, DC, MC, JCB. Daily from 11.30am till the last customer leaves. Moderate.

Imperial, *Nevsky Palace Hotel*, Nevskiy pr. 57 ☎ 275 20 01; Mayakovskaya metro. Diners can enjoy a wonderful view of Nevskiy as they tuck into the buffet of appetizers or the caviar bar, before ordering from the Continental menu. Jazz brunch Sun noon–4pm. Mon–Sat 7–11pm. All major CC. Very expensive.

Landskrona, *Nevsky Palace Hotel*, Nevskiy pr. 57; ☎ 275 20 01; Mayakovskaya metro. Top-floor restaurant with superb views of the city skyline, and a summer terrace. Known for its gourmet Mediterranean specialities and silver service, it matches the *Europe* on food, but can't compete on the interiors. Mon–Fri business lunch $29. Amex, Visa, MC, DC. Daily 12.30pm–1am. Very expensive.

Rioni, ul. Shpalernaya 24 ☎ 273 32 61; trolleybus #3 or #8 from Nevskiy prospekt, or 15min walk from Ploshchad Lenina metro. Discreetly located at the back of an alley opposite the Bolshoy dom, this friendly basement "café" serves some of the best Georgian food in town and has been the launch pad for two others – the *Café Salkhino* and *Mereti* (see p.287) – on the Petrograd Side. Children welcome. No CCs. Mon–Sat noon–11pm. Inexpensive–moderate.

Shinok, Zagorodniy pr. 13, ☎ 311 82 60; Dostoevskaya/Vladimirskaya metro. Unlike its Moscow counterpart, this faux-Ukrainian tavern doesn't have a captive cow and milkmaid for diners to gawp at, but its menu similarly lists two kinds of *borsch*, four varieties of *vareniki* (dumplings) and five types of *salo* (lard) as starters, with suckling pig, chicken or rabbit to follow, accompanied by *gorilka* (Ukrainian vodka) and folk music after 7pm. Amex, Visa, MC, DC. Daily 24hr. Moderate.

Eating and drinking

Eating and drinking

The Southern Suburbs

The listings in this section are marked on the map on p.244.

Daddy's Steak Room, Moskovskiy pr. 73 ☎252 77 44; Frunzenskaya metro. Juicy steaks, salads, seafood and pizzas. Amex, Visa, MC, DC. Daily noon–midnight; bar open until 2am. Expensive.

Pietari, Moskovskiy pr. 222 ☎443 18 09; Moskovskaya metro. Relaxed Finnish-Russian joint venture ("Pietari" is the Finnish name for St Petersburg) offering pasta dishes, reindeer steaks, tiger-prawn salad, sturgeon *solyanka* and pork with prunes. There's no need to reserve for the restaurant (live music 8–11pm) or the beer hall next door. Amex, Visa, MC, DC, JCB, Maestro. Daily 11am–midnight or later. Moderate.

Vyborg Side

The listings in this section are marked on the map on p.253.

Drago, Primorskiy pr. 15 (entrance from ul. Savushkina 20) ☎430 69 84; minibus #T-32 from Chernaya rechka metro. Yugoslav dishes cooked over a charcoal grill amidst mock-baronial splendour that appeals to the gangster-ish clientele. Business lunch $5 (noon–4pm). Guarded parking. All CC. Daily from noon until the last customer leaves. Expensive.

Kavkaz, ul. Stakhanovtsev 5, ☎444 43 09; Novocherkasskaya metro. Like its downtown offshoot, the *Kavkaz Bar*, it serves Georgian specialities such as *khachapuri*, *shashlyk* and marinated meat *basturma*, not to mention a restorative *khásh* on Sun morning. Its café (daily 10am–9pm) has a more limited menu. Visa, MC. Daily noon–midnight. Moderate.

Schwabski Domik, Novocherkasskiy pr. 28/19 ☎528 22 11; Novocherkasskaya metro. The wood-panelled "Swabian Cottage" features hearty German and Czech fare served by waitresses in Swabian costume, and twenty different beers, including some from the Black Forest. Amex, Visa, MC, DC. Daily 11am–1am. Moderate.

Staraya Derevnya, ul. Savushkina 72 ☎431 00 00; tram #2 or #31 from Chernaya rechka metro. Cosy, salon-like interior with traditional Russian home-cooking, and Gypsy and Russian singers (Fri–Sun). No CC. Daily 1–11pm. Moderate.

U Petrovicha, Sredneokhtinskiy pr. 44 ☎227 21 35; tram #7, #23, #46 or bus #174 from Novocherkasskaya metro. Cosy, popular den offering traditional Russian dishes, such as elk, wild boar, rabbit or (the house speciality) suckling pig. Musical duets 7–11pm. Reservations necessary. No CC. Daily noon–5pm & 7pm–midnight. Expensive.

Chapter 11

Nightlife

St Petersburg's **nightlife** is less wild than it was a decade ago, when all restraints were tossed aside following the disappearance of old Soviet ideological taboos. Local **clubs** still come and go but their total number hasn't risen much, and they tend to be tailored to suit the tastes of certain subcultures, from punks to rocka-billies and from cool bohemian types to pop- and porn-loving Mafiosi. The atmosphere can be anything from intellectual to brash and decadent, with theme nights and raunchy floorshows – strip clubs are popular at present, even with staid middle-aged couples. There are also more mainstream **discos** – mostly the province of teenagers – several **jazz** clubs, and a discreet but thriving **gay scene**.

Besides the many clubs that double as **live music venues**, one-off live concerts and/or parties are held in cinemas, palaces of culture and more outlandish venues – including, recently, an abandoned "Plague Fort" off Kronstadt. The listings in *Pulse* and the *St Petersburg Times* generally offer the best guide to **what's on**. Note that although we've listed **admission charges** in dollars, they're payable in rubles.

Clubs

The term *klub* can cover anything from an arthouse café featuring the odd spot of music to a full-blown nightclub with restaurant and casino attached. Owing to licensing laws, some clubs function only at weekends, though they often stay open till dawn. Smart casual dress fits the bill at most venues. If you visit places frequented by Mafiosi, be careful with your money, but don't be too nervous; they are out for a good time and unlikely to be looking for trouble. Men should also be aware that many clubs are full of prostitutes, for whom dancing with guys is just a prelude to business (see p.55).

Africa, nab. reki Moyki 106 ☎114 32 98, *http://africa.zerkalo.ru*; 15min from Sadovaya/Sennaya ploshchad metro. Relaxed Indie club in the Lesgraft Academy of Physical Culture, with live rock, folk, blues or jazz from 7pm to 8pm. Inexpensive drinks and snacks. Thurs–Sun 5pm–1am; $2–3.

Chaplin Club, ul. Chaykovskovo 59, ☎272 66 49 or 272 88 79; Chernyshevskaya metro. A cosy comedy club run by an ardent Chaplin fan, featuring Chaplin movies in the afternoon and cabaret acts such as the mime-comedy troupe Litsedei some evenings ($5–8; table reservations essential); otherwise it's just a place to eat and drink. Daily noon–midnight.

City Club, in the yard of Apraksin dvor (enter under arch on Sadovaya ul. and veer slightly right) ☎310 05 49; Nevskiy prospekt/Gostiniy dvor metro. A mellow hangout for thirtysomethings, above the raucous *Money Honey* (see p.297). Two bars, pool tables and real fireplaces, plus live rock, pop, blues or Latin music. Wed–Sun at 8pm; $1.75.

Nightlife

Fiesta Latina, Smolyachkova ul. 13 ☎542 11 94; Vyborgskaya metro. Not a patch on the old club by Tekhnologicheskiy Institut; the new place has only one dance floor and mean security, which damp its spirits, despite the zesty mix of salsa, flamenco, house and reggae. Fri–Sun 11pm–6am; $2–3.

Fish Fabriqué, Ligovskiy pr. 53 ☎164 48 57; Ploshchad Vosstaniya metro. Once legendary grunge club that's become more of a café for musicians and artists since it moved out into the courtyard of Pushkinskaya 10 (see p.233). Bands still play here, but regulars come for the table-football, cheap food and cult foreign movies (Sun 8pm). Daily 3pm till the last person leaves; $2 for gigs.

Golden Dolls, Nevskiy pr. 60 ☎110 55 70; Gostiniy dvor/Nevskiy prospekt metro. The most in-your-face erotic nightclub on Nevskiy, with bargirls and whores primed to pounce. Russian and European food; all CCs accepted. Daily 3am–6am; $2–5.

Greshniki, nab. kanala Griboedova 28/1 ☎219 42 91; Nevskiy prospekt/Gostiniy dvor metro. You might expect more from a club named "Sinners", but naked dancers and an arthouse strip-show on Fridays are as wild as it gets. Clients have to tally up with the barman and pay on the way out. Daily 6pm–6am; men free till 9pm, $1–2 afterwards; women $5.50.

Griboedov Club, Voronezhskaya ul. 2a ☎164 43 55; Ligovskiy Prospekt metro. A magnet for avant-garde bands, trendsetters and poseurs, set in a deep bomb shelter with a darkened chill-out room and music ranging from jazz-hop to gothic rock; gigs start at 10pm, DJs at midnight. Mon, Wed, Thurs & Sun 6pm–6am, Fri & Sat 6pm–7am; $2.50.

Hali Gali, Lanskoe shosse 15 ☎246 38 27; Vyborgskaya metro. Famous badtaste club aimed at affluent Russians with no inhibitions: waitresses are encouraged to swear and smoke; patrons, to engage in drinking contests or lewd acts. Though you need to understand Russian to get the smutty cabaret,

you might come just for the debauched atmosphere. Nightly show (10pm–1.30am). Daily 6pm–4am; $14.

Hollywood Nites, Nevskiy pr. 46 ☎311 60 77; www.show-cp.ru/hollywood/. Nevskiy prospekt/Gostiniy dvor metro. Heavily advertised American-style nightclub and casino festooned with palm trees and portraits of Hollywood stars. Pricey food and drinks; intimidating clients and security. Wednesday is ladies' night and women get in free; Thursday offers "events and surprises" (anything from erotic shows to competitions); while on Friday to Sunday there are pop concerts and discos. Daily 10pm–6am; casino & restaurant 24hr; $2–5, $8 at weekends.

Konyushenniy dvor (aka Marstall), nab. kanal Griboedova 5 ☎315 76 07; Nevskiy prospekt/Gostiniy dvor metro. The most hassle-free of the city's strip joints, with both male and female acts, girls out for fun, and even middle-aged couples dining at the back. Packed at weekends; empty during the week. Daily noon–6pm; free entry for foreigners with passports.

La Plage, pr. Kosygina 17 ☎525 63 13; tram #10 or #64 from Ladozhskaya metro. Don't bother unless you're keen to see New Russians cavorting in a cheesy "Beach Club" amid the high-rise suburbs. Eurodance, house and Latin American, enlivened by stripping and bottle-spinning barmen and appearances from "the cream of Russian pop". Thurs–Sun 10pm–6am; men $4–6, women $3–4.

Luna, Vosnesenskiy pr. 46 ☎310 36 28; 10min from Sadovaya or Tekhnologicheskiy Institut metro. Typical New Russian hybrid of cheese, sleaze and flashiness, with a casino and floorshow. Fashion shows on Wed; male striptease Thurs; erotic super-show Fri & Sat. Daily 6pm–6am; women free till 11pm (except Fri & Sat), then $7–11, men $9–12.50.

Mama, Malaya Monetnaya ul. 3b ☎232 31 37; Gorkovskaya metro. Minimalist techno club packed with rich teenagers in the latest club wear, dancing to jungle and drum 'n' bass. Not a place to be old or unfashionably dressed. Fri & Sat 11.50pm–6am; $2.

Manhattan (aka Kotyol), nab. reki Fontanki 90 ☎113 19 45, *http://kotel.spb.ru*; Pushkinskaya or Sennaya ploshchad metro. Art club set up for the former underground elite that's now become more open. Pool room and restaurant. Live music three or four nights a week from 10pm. Daily 2pm–5am; $2–3 (Mon free).

Metro, Ligovskiy pr. 174 ☎166 02 04, *www.metro.club.ru*; Ligovskiy Prospekt metro, then any tram south. Sponsored by Coca-Cola, this teenybopper dance club has a varied programme, including disco-house, techno-pop and Eurodance on the third floor (Mon, Wed, Fri & Sat) and "Beer Monday" (free admission with a bottle of Nevsky till 11pm), with raffle and audience-strip on the first floor (1am). Daily 10pm–6am; Mon–Thurs & Sun $1.50–2.50; Fri & Sat $3–4.

Moloko, Perekupnoy per. 12 ☎274 94 67, *http://moloko.piter.net*; Ploshchad Aleksandra Nevskovo metro. One of St Petersburg's best venues for live music – from funk-hop to post-punk – with a friendly bohemian ambience, cheap drinks and no pretensions, though claustrophobics will hate its airless, low-ceilinged tunnels. Thurs–Sun 7–11pm; $1–2.

Money Honey, in the yard of Apraksin dvor (enter the arch on Sadsovaya ul. and veer slightly right) ☎310 05 49; Nevskiy prospekt/Gostiniy dvor metro. A sprawling Texan saloon for local rockabillies to strut their stuff. Rowdy but relaxed; don't forget your leather jacket and quiff. Nightly live music at 8pm & 12.30am ($.150 cover charge). Bar open from 11am daily.

National Hunt, Malaya Morskaya ul. 11 ☎311 13 43; Nevskiy prospekt metro. Widely advertised disco-bar popular with guests at the nearby *Astoria Hotel*, featuring Euro cuisine, dance music, and

strippers after 11pm. Full of hookers, as you'd expect. Daily noon–6am; free entry for foreigners with ID.

Polygon, Lesnoy pr. 65, Bldg. 5 ☎245 27 20, *www.polygonclub.spb.ru*; 10min from Lesnaya metro. Club devoted to "extreme music", from thrash metal to punk – "mostly bad", as its Web site admits. Full of teenagers in leather jackets, getting terminally wasted and leaping offstage. Gigs start at 6pm; $2–3.

Spartak, Kirochnaya ul. 8 ☎273 77 39; 15min from Chernyshevskaya metro. After hours, this arthouse cinema turns into a club with two halls, one for video shows and chilling out, the other for gigs, discos and karaoke. Heavy security. Daily 9pm–2am; $1–10, depending on what's happening.

Tribunal Bar, pl. Dekabristov 1 ☎311 16 90; 15min from Nevskiy prospekt metro. Rowdy New Russian den opposite the Bronze Horseman. Mon is ladies' night; Tues, transvestite show; Wed, disco party; Thurs, Latin night; Sun, topless party. Pricey (but good) beer and snacks, and heavy security. Daily noon–6am; free.

Zoopark, Alexander Park 1 ☎232 31 45, *http://chz.da.ru*; 10min from Gorkovskaya or Sportivnaya metro. Small club in the zoo specializing in live folk and rock, and hosting sporadic festivals. Guests can only enter between 6.30pm and 7pm; events start at 7pm; $1–3.

Gay and lesbian nightlife

Though many of the clubs listed above are popular with gays and lesbians, overt displays of affection can be safely indulged in only at specifically **gay clubs** (there are no lesbian clubs). Details of gay and lesbian events may be posted on the Web site *www.gay.ru*.

Club 69, 2ya Krasnoarmeyskaya ul. 6 ☎259 51 63; Tekhnologicheskiy Institut metro. The city's best-known gay club – though it isn't exclusively gay – with shows, waiters dressed as sailors and a backroom for clandestine encounters. Tues is men only, while Wed & Sun are

Nightlife

Nightlife

For classical and choral music see "The Arts", p.300.

best for dancing; on Thurs there's a mass audience strip, and on Fri & Sat there are male strippers. Daily midnight–6am; men $1–3, women $2–6; free entry 10–11pm Tues, Wed & Sun.

Jungle, ul. Blokhina 8 ☎238 80 33; Sportivnaya metro. Retiring, cheap and unpretentious gay venue in a palace of culture on the Petrograd Side, with a dance hall, "dark maze" and shows from 1.30pm. Fri & Sat 11pm–6am; men $1.50, women $2.50.

Jazz and blues

While other venues might periodically host jazz or blues performances, the scene revolves around the following places. There are also two annual international **festivals**: Jazz Guitar in the spring (☎272 98 50) and the White Nights Swing during June (☎164 98 43). Two useful Web sites with audio links are "Jazz in Russia" (*www.jazz.ru*) – whose text in English includes a section on festivals – and "Blues" (*www.blues.ru*), in Russian only.

Enjoy, Bogatyrskiy pr. 8 ☎393 30 40; Pionerskaya metro. Intimate, attractively designed restaurant hosting concerts by well-known and up-and-coming local musicians. Look out for Yelena Turkina's improvisational jazz ballet and Valery Latman's band Jazz-Comfort. Reservations essential. Daily noon–5am.

Jazz Philharmonic Hall, Zagorodniy pr. 27 ☎164 85 65; Vladimirskaya or Dostoevskaya metro. A rather formal venue founded by the veteran jazz musician David Goloshchokin, who often plays here. The Bolshoy zal is used for mainstream and Dixieland jazz, while the smaller Ellington Hall hosts intimate, candlelit concerts. Tickets available in advance from the box office (2–8pm). Daily 7–11pm ($3–8); Ellington Hall 8–11.30pm ($6–8). Student discount for tickets to the Bolshoy Zal.

JFC Jazz Club, Shpalernaya ul. 33 ☎272 98 50; 10min from Chernyshevskaya metro. A less stuffy venue for all styles of jazz (including the jazz guitar festival)

and excellent Latin nights with cut-price Bacardi. Reservations essential, as the club is tiny and very popular. Located at the back of the courtyard of the block in which it's situated. Daily 7–10pm; $2–3.50.

Jimi Hendrix Blues Club, Liteyniy pr. 33, ☎279 88 13; minibus #T-215 or #T-258 from Nevskiy pr. The liveliest venue in the city for jazz and blues, with two bands playing each night. Decent food and awful service. Daily 24hr; $2.

Kvadrat Jazz Club, ul. Pravdiy 10 ☎315 90 46; Vladimirskaya/Dostoevskaya metro. The foyer of this palace of culture hosts traditional mainstream jazz performed by mainly non-professional bands, followed by jam sessions. Cheap beer and light snacks available. Tues only 8–11pm; $2.

Occasional live venues

The following places occasionally host **rock concerts** by Russian or foreign bands – look out for flyers or in the *St Petersburg Times* or *Pulse* magazine for details.

Lensoviet Palace of Culture, Kamennoostrovskiy pr. 42 ☎346 04 24; Petrogradskaya metro. An increasingly popular venue for veteran bands like Akvarium, or new schlock-rock acts from Moscow.

Oktyabrskiy Concert Hall, Ligovskiy pr. 6 ☎275 13 00 or 275 12 73; Ploshchad Vosstaniya metro. Large mainstream auditorium used by the likes of Alla Pugachova.

SKK, pr. Yuriya Gagarina 8 ☎298 12 11; Park Pobedy metro. Used for concerts by big-name bands. Tickets from any theatre-bookings kiosk (see "The Arts" p.299).

St Petersburg Ice Palace, pr. Pyatiletok 1. New venue, usually used for ice hockey matches, but also for pop concerts.

Yubileyniy Sports Palace, pl. Dobrolyubova 18 ☎238 40 49; Sportivnaya metro. Another occasional venue for big-name bands during summer, not to mention all-night ice-skating discos.

Chapter 12

The Arts

For well over a century, St Petersburg has been one of the world's great centres of **classical music and ballet**, most famously represented by the Mariinskiy opera and ballet company – formerly called the Kirov, the name by which it's still marketed abroad – and also by its fine orchestras and choirs. Although many suffered from the withdrawal of state funding and the exodus of talented artists in the early 1990s, the Mariinskiy has retained its world-class reputation for classical ballet, and acquired new laurels as an opera house.

Despite small drama troupes springing up all over, **theatre** has had a harder time, largely because of the language barrier, which prevents it from attracting richer, foreign audiences. Nevertheless, there are performances that don't require much (if any) knowledge of Russian, such as **mime** and **puppetry**. Sadly, **film**, which once flourished through the local studio Lenfilm, has all but disappeared as a home-grown art form, with most cinemas now showing little more than Hollywood blockbusters and Italian soft-porn, while nearly all the Russian films made nowadays are produced – and financed – in Moscow.

Tickets and information

For most concerts and theatrical performances, you can buy **tickets** from the venue's box office (*kassa*), the many theatre-ticket kiosks (*teatralnaya kassa*) around the city, or from the **central box office** at Nevskiy prospekt 42 – but for ballet or opera at the Mariinskiy Theatre you may have to depend on the tourist service bureaux at the larger hotels, which will add a surcharge.

Unfortunately for visitors, the **two-tier price system** whereby foreigners are charged far more than Russians – which previous applied only to the Mariinskiy and the circus – has now been extended to cover all the city's theatres and concert halls. Although it's easy enough to buy tickets at the Russian price, it's almost impossible to get past the vigilant *babushki* at the Mariinskiy, who send foreigners back to pay the premium charge – though at other venues you might manage to sneak through if you speak Russian or really look the part. Even so, prices are reasonable by world standards: a halfway decent seat at the Mariinskiy can be had for $50, and elsewhere you'll rarely pay more than $10.

Music lovers planning to be in town for some time might buy **abonimenty**, batches of tickets to about ten concerts – by a specific composer, or in a genre such as chamber music – performed at one concert hall or different venues over the course of a month or two. There are various *abonimenty* available, and besides saving you money they can also save you the hassle of queuing for popular concerts if you choose them carefully beforehand.

The *St Petersburg Times* (Fri edition) and *Pulse* both carry **English-language**

The Arts

listings of events at the main concert halls and theatres, although the listings in Russian-language newspapers such as *Chas Pik* (especially its weekly supplement, *Pyatnitsa*) are more comprehensive. Alternatively, you can drop into the Institute for Cultural Relations (ul. Rubinshteyna 8 ☎ 164 75 96) and pick up their detailed monthly bulletin (in Russian only).

You can also look out for posters around town, or ask about current events at the hotels' service bureaux, who can also reserve tickets for a fee. Some hotels, such as the *Grand Hotel Europe*, organize prestigious concerts in places like the Hermitage Theatre or the Yusupov Palace, in which case you can be certain of the quality, though it will come at a price. Lastly, bear in mind that some (though by no means all) theatres and concert halls are **closed in July or August**.

Ballet, opera and classical music

Due to the high demand by visitors, tickets for **ballet** at the Mariinskiy can be hard to obtain, but don't despair if you have no luck, as there are several other respected venues for ballet and opera, and the Mariinskiy isn't the only star act in town. The Eifman Company has won rave reviews for its modern gloss on classical ballet styles and Russian themes, and even performs at the Mariinskiy during the August break, though it's now so popular that getting tickets can be difficult. Another well-known company is Valery Mikhailovsky's Male Ballet, which performs *Swan Lake*

and other classics with more than a *soupçon* of irony. Moreover, many of the Mariinsky's top dancers perform almost daily at the Hermitage Theatre during the Stars of the St Petersburg Ballet festival in June and July.

Under director Valery Gergiev the Mariinskiy has not only nurtured a new generation of great dancers, but has inaugurated a new golden age of **opera**, unseen since the era of Chaliapin. Besides inviting the film director Konchalovsky to stage Prokofiev's *War and Peace*, he has risked disapproval by introducing Wagner to the Mariinskiy's repertoire – a composer never liked in Russia, whose works now take precedence over the Italian and French operas traditionally beloved of Russians. The only negative aspect to this success is that Gergiev, along with star singers like Olga Borodina and Nikolai Putilin, are often abroad – which is great for attracting sponsorship to the Mariinskiy, but means that they're not in St Petersburg as often as their fans – and visiting tourists – would like.

Classical music concerts take place throughout the year, with the largest number during the Stars of the White Nights Festival, when Yelagin Island hosts outdoor performances. In addition to the main venues listed below, there are also concerts in churches and palaces around the city – including Peterhof and Tsarskoe Selo, outside St Petersburg.

You should definitely try to hear some **Russian Orthodox Church music**, which is solely choral and wonderfully in keeping with the rituals of the faith. Splendid choirs perform at the Preobrazhenskiy

---

Folklore shows

A spectacle that might appeal to some are the so-called **folklore shows**, featuring Russian folk songs and high-kicking Cossack dancers, with a bit of ballet thrown in for good measure. Shows are held in the ballroom of the Nikolaevskiy Palace on pl. Truda (☎ 312 55 00 or 311 71 10). You buy tickets ($15) the day before; a vodka, champagne and *zakuski* buffet is included in the price, making it cheaper than splashing out in a restaurant with folkloric acts.

Church near Liteyniy prospekt (daily at 10am & 6pm) and the Alexander Nevsky Trinity Cathedral (6pm daily except Wed). The choir at the former is composed of professional singers from the Kapella Choir. Orthodox services are also held at the St Nicholas Cathedral at 6pm, and at other churches on a less regular basis. Musically speaking, the best services are those on Sat evening and Sun morning. **Military bands** are also worth hearing: they often play in the Alexander Gardens at lunchtime on Sundays during summer, and come out in force on certain public holidays.

Concert halls and opera houses

Bolshoy Concert Hall Oktyabrskiy, Ligovskiy pr. 6 ☎ 275 12 73 or 275 12 75; Ploshchad Vosstaniya metro. The city's largest, most modern concert hall, with comfy seating and unobstructed views of the stage. Used by pop stars like Alla Pugachova, the Eifman and Male Ballet companies, and visiting international acts. Ballet performances are to recorded music.

Children's Philharmonic, Dumskaya ul. 1/3 ☎ 315 39 93; Nevskiy prospekt/Gostiniy dvor metro. Housed in the old City Duma building, this junior orchestra is sure to appeal to kids with an interest in playing a classical instrument. They also stage puppet shows and plays for kids of all ages, which are very popular with Russian families. Closed July.

Hermitage Theatre, Dvortsovaya nab. 34; ☎ 311 34 56 or 341 19 20; Nevskiy prospekt/Gostiniy dvor metro; box office open Tues–Sun 10.30am–5pm. Between May and October, Catherine the Great's private theatre is an exquisite venue for evening concerts by chamber groups from the Philharmonia, and gala performances by Mariinskiy soloists and dancers. It also has its own resident orchestra, the St Petersburg Kamerata. Tickets aren't numbered, so be sure to arrive early to claim a decent seat.

Kapella, nab. reki Moyki 20 ☎ 314 10 58; Nevskiy prospekt/Gostiniy dvor

metro; box office open daily 11am–3pm & 4–7pm. The oldest concert hall in St Petersburg, to the east of the Winter Palace, with its own internationally renowned choir and the State Kapella Orchestra, drawn from students at the Conservatory, who join forces to perform music of varying styles and ages, from Baroque to twentieth century. The international Prokofiev Young Violinists contest is held here in the second half of March.

Male Ballet (Muzhskoy balet), nab. reki Fontanki 90 ☎ 164 78 47; Sennaya ploshchad/Pushkinskaya metro. Valery Mikhailovsky's famous all-male ballet company usually performs at venues such as the Oktyabrskiy, but you can phone their rehearsal studio for details of forthcoming events. Their repertoire includes both classical ballet and modern dance.

Maliy Opera and Ballet Theatre (Maliy operniy teatr, also known as the Mussorgsky Theatre), Mikhailovskaya pl. 1 ☎ 314 37 58; Nevskiy prospekt/Gostiniy dvor metro; box office open 11am–3pm & 4–8pm, closed Tues. Though the ballet and opera at the Maliy aren't as good as at the Mariinskiy, its apricot-and-silver auditorium is no less beautiful. Its repertoire includes mainstream ballets such as *Giselle*, *Les Sylphides* and *Swan Lake*, and Russian operas like *Prince Igor* and *Khovanshchina*. A small museum on the third floor displays designs for the first productions of Prokofiev's *War and Peace* and Shostakovich's *The Nose*. Tickets are easy to come by, except during August when the Mariinskiy is closed and tour groups are forced to come here instead.

Mariinskiy Theatre (Mariinskiy teatr), Teatralnaya pl. 2 ☎ 114 52 64; bus #22 or #43 from Nevskiy prospekt, or tram #5 from Sennaya ploschad/Sadovaya metro; box office open 11am–7pm. Sumptuous nineteenth-century ballet and opera house, better known by its old Soviet title, the Kirov. Unlike the Bolshoy in Moscow, its reputation for ballet is

The Arts

The Arts

undiminished – but the price of success is that the company is obliged to tour for much of the year, leaving lesser dancers behind at the Mariinskiy. The best time to catch the company is during winter, when ballerinas such as Yuliana Lopatkina, Diana Vishneva and Altinai Asilmuratova are around, hopefully accompanied by Farukh Ruzimantov or Igor Zelensky. At this time of the year the Mariinskiy also stages *The Golden Cockerel* for kids, performed by junior members of the Vaganova ballet school. As for opera, Wagner rules at present, but Verdi, Bizet, Mozart and Rossini are still staged. Look out for the baritones Victor Chernomortsev and Nikolai Putilin, or even a rare appearance by Olga Borodina, who's more of a fixture at La Scala, the Met or Covent Garden nowadays. Tickets sell out fast; if you're lucky you might get a cheap standby seat at 6pm on the night of the performance. You may want to dress up to the nines, quaff champagne and promenade with your companion around the Great Hall during the intermission – since that's what everyone else does. Closed Aug.

Philharmonia (Filarmoniya), Mikhaylovskaya ul. 2 ☎110 42 57; Nevskiy prospekt/Gostiniy dvor metro; box office open 11am–3pm & 4–8pm. The grand Bolshoy zal is home to the St Petersburg Philharmonic Orchestra, whose concerts vary depending on the conductor; Mariss Jansons or Yuri Temirkanov are sure to please and sell out fast. The hall is also used by visiting foreign artists, and an orchestra called Klassika that specializes in Strauss waltzes and other lowbrow favourites. The smaller Maliy zal has better acoustics and a separate entrance (at Nevskiy pr. 30) and phone number (☎311 83 33). It's used for solo and chamber recitals, which are usually excellent.

Rimsky-Korsakov Museum, Zagorodniy pr. 28 ☎113 32 08; Vladimirskaya/Dostoevskaya metro. Regular chamber music performances and recitals in the composer's former apartment. Book ahead as seating is limited.

Rimsky-Korsakov Opera and Ballet Theatre (Teatr Opery i Baleta Konservatorii imeni Rimskovo-Korsakova), Teatralnaya pl. 3 ☎312 25 19; bus #22 from Nevskiy prospekt or tram #5 from Sennaya ploschad/Sadovaya metro. The St Petersburg Conservatory's own company of students and teachers stages some fine opera and ballet performances, but the lack of star performers means that tickets are fairly easy to come by.

Smolniy Cathedral, pl. Rastrelli ☎271 76 32; bus #46 from Nevskiy prospekt. Regular performances of orchestral and choral music in what is, outwardly at least, one of the most striking buildings in St Petersburg (see p.226). Its bare, whitewashed interior is a let-down, but the acoustics are superb.

St Petersburg Opera Chamber Music Theatre, Galernaya ul. 33 ☎315 67 69; trolleybus #5 from Nevskiy prospekt. Having finally found a permanent home in a former baronial mansion, the company is set to build upon the success of Yuri Alexandrov's staging of the Pushkin-based operatic trilogy *The Queen of Spades*, *Eugene Onegin* and *Boris Godunov*. Its repertoire also includes Offenbach's operetta *La Belle Hélène*.

Yubileyniy Sports Palace, pl. Dobrolyubova 18 ☎238 40 49. Sports complex on the Petrograd Side with an ice rink that stages "ballet on ice" shows during the winter.

Theatre

St Petersburg prides itself on its dramatic tradition and boasts several sumptuously appointed **theatres**, but at present can't honestly claim superiority over Moscow – unlike in ballet and opera – although a couple of companies have been deservedly acclaimed. Though the fact that shows are invariably in Russian limits its appeal to foreigners, you don't need to understand much to appreciate some of the more experimental productions, puppetry, musicals, mime or the circus. The main events in the theatrical calendar are the **Festival of Russian Theatres**, with performers from all the CIS countries (mid-April), and the **Baltic House Festival** of drama from northern Russia and the Baltic states (Oct). Both are held at the Baltiyskiy dom.

Drama theatres

Akimov Comedy Theatre, Nevskiy pr. 56 ☎ 312 45 55; Nevskiy prospekt/Gostiniy dvor metro; box office open daily noon–3pm & 4–8pm. If your Russian is up to it, this is the place to catch such comic classics as *The Importance of Being Earnest*, Bulgakov's adaptation of Molière's works, and an acclaimed production of Shakespeare's *Twelfth Night*. Closed during the first half of Aug.

Aleksandriinskiy Theatre, pl. Ostrovskovo 2 ☎ 315 44 64; Gostiniy Dvor metro; box office open 11am–3pm & 4–8pm. A beautiful Neoclassical theatre designed by Rossi, with no fewer than four venues, used for opera and ballet as well as drama. Most of the forty-odd plays in its repertoire are by the nineteenth-century dramatist Alexander Ostrovsky, but one can also see Gogol's *The Marriage* and Wilde's *Lady Windermere's Fan*, while the St Petersburg Theatre of Classical Ballet stages favourites such as *The Nutcracker*.

Baltiyskiy dom, Alexander Park 4 ☎ 232 335 39; Gorkovskaya metro. The Baltiyskiy dom's Farce Theatre is the main crowd-puller, while the Small Stage puts on romances and comedies. However, the real attraction is the wealth of talent at the two international drama festivals held here (see above).

BDT (Bolshoy dramaticheskiy teatr), nab. reki Fontanki 65 ☎ 310 92 42; Gostiniy Dvor metro. The city's most heavyweight theatre, whose actors' talents have long been wasted on leaden stagings of Chekhov, Gogol and other Russian classics. More recent productions have included Stoppard's *Arcadia* and Strindberg's *The Father*. At the *malaya stena* (studio theatre) you can see works

in progress, drama competitions and festival shows. During July and August, the main auditorium often hosts ballet performances by soloists from the Mariinskiy.

Eksperiment, Bolshoy pr. 35/75, Vasilevskiy Island ☎ 233 94 28; Vasileostrovskaya metro. Venue for small alternative groups and visiting companies.

Interior Theatre (Interierniy teatr), Nevskiy pr. 104 ☎ 273 14 54; Mayakovskaya metro. Stories and legends from the history of St Petersburg imaginatively enacted for audiences of 5–12-year-olds, plus productions of plays for adults, such as *Hamlet*. Worth visiting just to see the costumes and models, which make the performances here look like Madame Tussaud's redone in the style of *Frankenstein*. Closed mid-July to mid-Sept.

Komissarzhevskiy Drama Theatre (Teatr imeni V.F. Komissarzhevskoy, or KDF), Italyanskaya ul. 19 ☎ 315 53 55; Nevskiy prospekt/Gostiniy dvor metro. Known for intense realist dramas that are particularly inaccessible to non-Russian speakers, the KDF has recently tried to widen its appeal by staging comedies like Bricaire's *French Pranks* and Richardson's *Gallows Humour*. Closed Mon & Tues.

Maliy Dramatic Theatre (Maliy dramaticheskiy teatr), ul. Rubinshteyna 18 ☎ 113 20 39; Mayakovskaya metro. Under director Lev Dodin, this formerly provincial troupe has gained an international reputation and numerous prizes, including an Olivier Award, for its coruscating productions of the classics – though its performances of contemporary works are often less assured. Repertoire includes *The Cherry Orchard*, *Play Without a Name*, *The Possessed*, and *Gaudeamus*.

Open Theatre (Otkrytiy teatr), Vladimirskiy pr. 12 ☎ 117 01 78; Vladimirskaya/Dostoevskaya metro. Wide-ranging repertoire, including some of the more controversial mud-slinging Russian satires.

The Arts

The Arts

Priyut komedianta, Sadovaya ul. 27 ☎310 33 14; Sadovaya/Sennaya ploshchad metro. The "Comedian's Refuge" is renowned for Yuri Tomoshevsky's adaptations of prose and poetry readings from the "Silver Age" of Russian literature, but also features international drama staged by guest directors. Closed June 25–Aug 1.

Theatre on Liteyniy (Teatr na Liteynom), Liteyniy pr. 51 ☎273 53 35; Mayakovskaya metro. Also known as the "Drama and Comedy Theatre", the company features some of St Petersburg's best actors, and won the Critics' Prize in the 1998 Golden Mask awards for O'Neill's *Moon for the Misbegotten*. Shakespeare, Molière and Tolstoy feature in its diverse classical repertoire. The only theatre in the city with wheelchair access. Closed July.

Yusupov Palace Theatre, nab. reki Moyki 94 ☎314 98 83. This gorgeous private theatre occasionally hosts concerts and light opera.

Puppetry, musicals and the circus

Bolshoy Puppet Theatre (Bolshoy teatr kukol), ul. Nekrasova 10 ☎ 273 66 72; 15min from Chernyshevskaya/ Mayakovskaya metro. Children's theatre off Liteyniy prospekt with programmes aimed at kids aged 3–9. Despite its name, it doesn't always stage puppet shows, so it's worth checking beforehand.

Circus at Avtovo (Tsirk na Avtovo), Avtovskaya ul. 1 ☎183 14 98; Avtovo metro. Traditional circus performances and spectacles on specific themes,

including a "Rhapsody on Ice" show with all the performers on iceboards or skates. Shows start at noon, 3pm & 6pm every day except Mon.

Marionette Theatre (Teatr kukol-marionetok), Nevskiy pr. 52 ☎311 21 56; Nevskiy prospekt/Gostiniy dvor metro. Puppet and marionette shows.

Mimigranty Clown-Mime Theatre, 23 Rizhskiy propspekt, Block 2 ☎251 63 28. When they're not clowning around on the streets, Mimigranty can be found in their theatre on the seedy side of the Fontanka. Their repertoire includes *The Circus of Shardam-s*, by the cult writer Daniil Kharms, and an improvisation for clowns entitled *Comedy with Murder*.

Rodina, ul. Karavannaya 12 ☎311 61 31; Nevskiy prospekt/Gostiniy dvor metro. A children's cinema which doubles as a venue for the "Academy of Fools", a clowning and mime troupe.

State Circus (Tsirk), nab. reki Fontanki 3 ☎314 84 78; Nevskiy prospekt/Gostiniy dvor metro; box office open Tues, Wed & Fri–Sun 11am–7pm. Russia's oldest circus, two blocks north of Anichkov most. Trapeze artists, acrobats, illusionists, performing bears and seals – a real old-style show that you'll either love or hate. Tickets can usually be bought on the spot; foreigners pay $9 surcharge, children are admitted for free. Performances at 7pm on Tues, Wed & Fri, and at 11.30am, 3pm & 7pm on Sat & Sun. Closed mid-July to mid-Sept.

Theatre of Young Spectators (Teatr yunykh zriteley, or TYuZ), Pionerskaya pl. 1 ☎112 4102; Pushkinskaya metro. Musicals and dance shows aimed at

---

Mime

Many **mime groups** have no permanent home, so look out for performances at Baltiyskiy dom and Eksperiment. One of the best-known groups is **Derevo**, who produce fascinating shows using influences from Japanese Butto to traditional clowning and mime. The most popular clowns perform with **Litsedei**, who organize mime festivals in St Petersburg, and sometimes appear at the Chaplin Club (see p.295) – while another clown-mime troupe, **Mimigranty**, have their own theatre (see above). Also watch out for **DaNet**, whose use of masks has won them prizes all over Europe.

children and teenagers – no great knowledge of Russian is required. Performances start at 11am & 6pm.

Zazerkalye Children's Theatre, ul. Rubinshteyna 13 ☎312 51 35; Vladimirskaya/Dostoevskaya metro. Colourful, competent opera and ballet "for children", though enjoyable for adults, too. Around New Year, they sometimes do English-language productions.

Film

Despite the city's proud cinematic tradition, virtually all the **films** shown today are Hollywood blockbusters or Euro B-movies, dubbed into Russian with varying degrees of sophistication – a practice that's even applied to foreign films at the city's two arthouse cinemas, Dom kino and Spartak.

To find out **what's showing**, see the weekly list posted outside the Avrora Cinema on Nevskiy prospekt (where several cinemas are located), or the Friday edition of the *St Petersburg Times*. The **Festival of Festivals** in June is the best time to catch new Russian and foreign movies. Except for the Kristall, venues are shabby and old-fashioned – but tickets are cheap. All cinemas are non-smoking, and none take credit cards or phone bookings.

Aurora, Nevskiy pr. 60 ☎315 52 54; Gostiniy Dvor metro. An archetypal Soviet cinema, low on charm and comfort. Besides the main feature in the auditorium, they sometimes show other movies in the café.

Dom kino, Karavannaya ul. 12 ☎314 81 18; Nevskiy prospekt/Gostiniy dvor metro. This wonderful Style Moderne building is the professional clubhouse for the city's filmmakers, and occasionally screens retrospectives.

Kristall Palace, Nevskiy pr. 72 ☎272 23 82; Mayakovskaya metro. The only cinema in St Petersburg with a decent sound system and seating, it mostly screens blockbusters – either Russian or American. Ticket prices can go as high as

$10, though morning shows cost less.

Molodyozhniy, Sadovaya ul. 12 ☎311 00 45; Gostiniy Dvor metro. A run-down complex with two screens; sometimes features retrospectives based on the oeuvre of a single director or actor.

Spartak, Kirochnaya ul 8 ☎272 78 97; Chernyshevskaya metro. Housed in a converted church, the Spartak caters to Petersburgers intent on dissecting the latest Peter Greenaway or a classic film noir, despite the abysmal quality of the prints and soundtrack. A late-night bar and sporadic gigs broaden its appeal and draw mainstream clubbers some nights.

The visual arts

St Petersburg has dozens of **private galleries** and **exhibition halls**, in addition to the temporary displays which can be seen in its museums and state galleries. Most of the private galleries cater for the tourist market and are stuffed to the gills with picture-postcard paintings of the city, alongside *matryoshkas*, balalaikas and other folk objects. However, if you search hard enough there's some fairly decent art on display, too, while at the city's best-known exhibition spaces you're guaranteed to find something interesting at most times of the year – look out especially for temporary exhibitions at the Benois Wing of the Russian Museum (p.164), in the Engineers' Castle. In addition, there are countless **street artists** showing off their talents along Nevskiy prospekt and outside the major tourist attractions.

Borey, Liteyniy pr. 58 ☎273 36 93; Mayakovskaya metro; Tues–Sat noon–8pm. Hosts excellent exhibitions, including shows by experimental artists and work by cult figures such as David Byrne.

Centre of National Cultures, Nevskiy pr. 166 ☎277 12 16; Ploshchad Vosstaniya metro; Tues–Sun 11am–7pm. Solo exhibitions by independent artists, ranging from batiks to handmade toys or plastic carvings. Accepts Visa, MC.

The Arts

The Arts

Golubaya gostinaya, Bolshaya Morskaya ul. 38 ☎315 74 14; Nevskiy prospekt/Gostiniy dvor metro; daily 11am–7pm. Respected contemporary art gallery with a commercial slant (export documentation and a framing service is available on site).

Guild of Masters, Nevskiy pr. 82; Mayakovskaya metro; daily 11am–7pm. High-quality gallery specializing in well-known artists formerly involved in the Stergovlitsi and LOSKh movements.

Manezh, pl. Dekabristov ☎312 81 56; Nevskiy prospekt metro; 11am–5.30pm, closed Thurs. Used for temporary exhibitions by the Artists' Union and others, including an annual showcase of contemporary art in July.

Palitra, Malaya Morskaya ul. 5; Nevskiy prospekt metro; Tues–Fri 11am–7pm, Sat noon–6pm. One of the best-known galleries for painting, graphic art and sculpture by local artists, many of whom were "underground" figures in Soviet times.

Pechatnya, in the Peter and Paul Fortress ☎238 47 82; Gorkovskaya metro; 11am–5pm, closed Wed. Besides the woodcuts, etchings and linocuts on display, you can see artists at work in this refurbished Petrine-era printer's. Accepts Visa and MC.

Petropol, Millionnaya ul. 27 ☎315 34 14; Nevskiy prospekt/Gostiniy dvor metro; daily noon–6pm. Concentrates on sculpture and objets d'art, such as ivory carvings, gems and marquetry, that only the seriously rich can afford.

Pushkinskaya 10, entry through arch of Ligovskiy pr. 53. Studios include FOTO image (Sat 4–7pm) on the second floor; Navicula Artis (Wed–Sun 3–7pm) on the fourth floor; and the Techno Art Centre Gallery 21 (Tues–Sat 3–8pm) on the seventh floor. See also p.233.

Chapter 13

Shops and markets

Consumer goods always had a low priority under the centrally planned Soviet economy, and it wasn't until the 1980s that Western imports began to appear regularly in shops. The early 1990s saw such a flood of imports that local products practically disappeared from the shops, but in the last few years Russian foodstuffs at least have made a comeback, with higher standards of quality and packaging than before – though it's hard to find any clothing or electrical goods that can hold their own. Although the choice of goods and outlets is far wider than in Soviet times, it's still generally true that shopping takes more effort than in the West – so try to be flexible about what you want and always have a shopping bag with you.

Some former state stores still insist on the infuriating system where customers pay at the *kassa* before collecting their goods, which entails queuing at least twice, but most new shops use the one-stop system.

Antiques and memorabilia

These cannot be exported without special permission: if you buy anything of

value and want to take it out of the country, make sure you get an **export licence** from the Ministry of Culture (see p.24).

Apraksin dvor, Sadovaya ul. Two antiques shops and an outlet for Lomonosov porcelain factory seconds make this seedy old arcade worth a visit, while you can occasionally find wonderful 1930–1960s tea and coffee services in the flea market in the yard. Beware of pickpockets.

Ladozhskiy rynok, outside Ladozhskaya metro station. The city's main flea market, Ladozhskiy rynok is way out in Malaya Okhta and only worth the journey after you've thoroughly combed the Apraksin dvor, as the chance of finding something buyable is no better, and pickpockets are equally active. Daily 11am–5pm.

Mebel, ul. Marata 53; Vladimirskaya/Dostoevskaya or Ligovskiy prospekt metros. Mainly tatty furniture, but the department to the left as you go in has inexpensive clocks, cameras, porcelain, and so on.

Opening times

These vary widely, but you can usually count on shops opening from Monday to Saturday at around 10am (9am for food stores), closing for an hour or so between 1 and 3pm, and then reopening until around 7pm. Some department stores stay open until 8pm or 9pm and also open on Sundays (11am–6pm), though this tends to be rather erratic.

Shops and Markets

Peterburgskiy Salon, Nevskiy pr. 54. Very expensive, so for most it's window-shopping only.

Rapsodiya, Bolshaya Konyushennaya ul. 13. Expensive furniture, silverware and ceramics – an antique collector's dream.

Staraya Kniga, ul. Marata 43; Vladimirskaya/Dostoevskaya metro. Small selection of Soviet memorabilia, coins and badges, plus porcelain and the occasional curio.

Bookshops

Glossy **books** about the Hermitage and the Imperial palaces are sold on Nevskiy prospekt and outside the Winter Palace, sometimes at lower prices than in bookstores. Note that you need permission to take books more than twenty years old out of the country (see p.24). All the stores sell art books in English and French.

ABUK, Nevskiy pr. 18. Secondhand Soviet and foreign books, some excellent antique volumes and prints.

Anglia, nab. reki Fontanki 40. Stocks all kinds of books in English, among them a small range of bestsellers and a good selection on Russia, including guidebooks and dictionaries.

Art Shop, Nevskiy pr. 16 & 52. Art books, postcards, maps, prints and watercolours. Standard books are expensive, but you may find some rarer gems tucked away.

Bukinist, Liteyniy pr. 59. Antiquarian books.

Dom knigi, Nevskiy pr. 28. The city's main bookstore, with a good selection of maps and art books on the second floor, and a smattering of cheap novels in English on the first. Also stocks stationery, CD-ROMs and software.

Dom knigi na Liteynom, Liteyniy pr. 30. Secondhand foreign books.

Dom voennoy knigi, Nevskiy pr. 20. Former military bookstore, now with everything from trashy romances and blockbusters to art books and prints.

Mir, Nevskiy pr. 13 & 16. Art books, postcards and some foreign-language paperbacks.

Serebryanniy Vek, Liteyniy pr. 53 (inside the Anna Akhmatova Museum). Top-quality art books. Closed Sat.

CDs, tapes and records

Bootleg CDs and tapes are sold by kiosks in the Nevskiy prospekt underpasses near Gostiniy dvor and in metro stations all over town, alongside properly licensed products, which are better in quality but cost more. You'll even find the odd kiosk where they can record bootleg tapes on request from the sounds in stock; look out for the sign звукозпись. Good-quality Russian-made CDs now run the gamut of classical, folk and pop. If you're interested in Russian bands, tapes, CDs, T-shirts and videos of gigs are available from most of the following outlets:

Karavan, Karavannaya ul. 22; Gostiniy dvor metro. Stocks a wide range of CDs, cassettes and videos.

Klassica, Mikhaylovskaya ul. 2; Nevskiy prospekt metro. One of the best places to buy classical CDs, tapes and LPs.

Music Shock, Bolshoy pr. 52, V.O., Vasileostrovskaya metro; pl. Vosstaniya 13, Ploshchad Vosstaniya/Mayakovskaya metro. Two good outlets for Russian pop, rock and other genres.

Nirvana, Pushkinskaya ul. 10; Mayakovskaya metro. Tiny shop which doubles as a club for rockers from the artists' colony in the same building.

Philharmonia, Mikhaylovskaya ul. 2; Nevskiy prospekt/Gostiniy dvor metro. The Philharmonia's own shop, this is the best place in town for opera CDs.

Rapsodia, Bolshaya Konyushennaya ul. 13; Nevskiy prospekt/Gostiniy dvor metro. Records, sheet music and books.

Rock Island, Kirochnaya ul. 10; Chernyshevskaya metro. In the basement of the courtyard containing the Spartak Cinema.

Rock Shop, ul. Plutalova 25; Petrogradskaya metro. Predictable array of rock and pop CDs, tapes, videos, T-shirts and suchlike.

Severnaya Liniya, Nevskiy pr. 26; Nevskiy prospekt/Gostiniy dvor metro. Sheet music, music books and instruments.

Clothing and accessories

If you've no moral scruples and can afford them, fur hats and coats are the definitive Russian clothing accessory. For a less contentious – though not necessarily much less expensive – look, local designer gear might appeal.

Oxydo, Kamenooskiy pr. One of the trendiest boutiques in the city, with one room for designer sunglasses and goggles, and another with labels like Red or Dead, French Connection and Helmut Lang.

Renegade, nab. Reki Fontanki 50; Gostiniy dvor or Mayakovskaya metro. Small basement outlet for club gear (T-shirts, dayglo puffa jackets) and imported footwear like DMs and Grinders.

Tatyana Parfionova, Nevskiy pr. 5; Mayakovskaya metro. A stylish showroom for the work of Tatyana Parfionova and other Russian designers of women's fashionwear that's worth checking out even if you can't afford to buy anything. Closed Sun.

Department stores

DLT, Bolshaya Konyushennaya ul. 21–23. Wonderful turn-of-the-century department store with good toy sections, although you have to hunt out the Russian goods among the Barbies and Power Rangers. Also sells lingerie, sportswear and shoes – there's even an outlet for Doc Martens.

Gostiniy dvor, Nevskiy pr. 35. An eighteenth-century shopping bazaar divided into numerous little stores selling everything from CDs to lingerie. Includes a branch of the fur hat emporium Red Front, stocking stylish women's hats by the designer Kussenkov.

Moskovskiy univermag, Moskovskiy pr. 205. Conveniently situated on the way to the airport; spend your leftover rubles on fur hats, souvenirs and clothes.

Passazh, Nevskiy pr. 48. Nineteenth-century shopping arcade, with a variety of boutiques and shops selling reproductions of antiques, plus a supermarket in the basement.

Food, drink and consumer goods

Imported goods are available in all shops and department stores, alongside Russian products, which regained a slice of the market after the crash of 1998. So far as **food** is concerned it can be hard to tell them apart, as many foreign brands are now made under licence or counterfeited in Russia – so it pays to examine items before buying. Alternatively, you could stick to one of the expensive foreign stores such as Kalinka Stockmann, where everything is imported. The city's **markets** (see p.310) are also a good place to pick up fresh produce.

Babylon Super, Maliy pr. 54; Chkalovskaya metro. One of the city's largest Western-style supermarkets, selling everything from groceries and, household goods through to DIY materials.

Cosmos, 2ya liniya 61; Vasileostrovskaya metro. Stocks imported groceries, cosmetics and healthcare products.

Liviz, ul. Chaykovskovo 13; Chernyshevskaya metro. The place to buy from the entire range of Liviz vodkas, plus Moldavian, French and Georgian wines and other alcohol, with no fear of encountering any dodgy bootlegs.

Kalinka Stockmann, Finlyandskiy pr. 1; Ploshchad Lenina metro. Food, food and more food – from leeks and broccoli to Worcester sauce – but at a price.

Okhta, Sredneokhtinskiy pr. 5; Novocherkasskaya metro. Luxurious food store for those who can't live without their escargots.

Shops and Markets

Shops and Markets

Sigma, ul. Marata 3; Mayakovskaya metro. Excellent Russian delicatessen with a big range of cheeses, smoked meats and fish, at reasonable prices.

Siwa, Bolshaya Zelenina ul. 14; Chkalovskaya metro. Another vast supermarket on Petrograd Side, and nearer to Chkalovskaya metro than *Babylon Super*.

Spar, pr. Stachek 1; Narvskaya metro. Food, car parts, cosmetics, medicines, plus paints and household fittings.

Yeliseyev's, Nevskiy pr. 56. Fine specialist Russian food store in a gorgeous Style Moderne building, stocking an above-average range of caviar, smoked fish, alcohol and chocolates. Closed Sun.

Markets

While food shops are far better stocked than in Soviet times, the widest selection of fresh produce is still to be found in **markets** (*rynok*), where vendors tempt buyers with nibbles of fruit, cheese, ham, pickles and other homemade delights. Food apart, at some of the markets listed below you'll find an assortment of other goods ranging from Soviet-era bric-a-brac to domestic hardware. Unless specified otherwise, the places listed here are open Tuesday to Saturday 8am to 7pm, Sunday 8am to 4pm. You need to bring cash, as credit cards are useless and there are rarely any ATMs in the vicinity.

Kondratevskiy rynok, Polyustrovskiy pr. 45; trolleybus #3, #12 or #43 from Ploshchad Lenina metro. The city's pet market, where you can also buy fur hats and boots. Closed Sun.

Kuznechniy rynok, Kuznechniy per. 3; Vladimirskaya/Dostoevskaya metro. The best-stocked and most expensive food market in the city. Worth a visit just for the atmosphere.

Ladozhskiy rynok, outside Ladozhskaya metro station. A flea market for clothes, tools, spare parts and household objects, yielding the odd semi-antique or specimen of Soviet kitsch. Beware of pickpockets.

Maltsevskiy rynok, ul. Nekrasova 52; tram #16 or #25 from Ploshchad Vosstaniya. Still better known by its former name, the Nekrasovskiy rynok, this is the best place to buy oriental spices, beans and marinated garlic; fruit and veg is cheaper here than at the Kuznechniy Market.

Sennoy rynok, Moskovskiy pr. 4–6; Sennaya ploshchad metro. Good in summer for seasonal produce, but rather thin at other times of the year.

Sytniy rynok, Sytninskaya pl. 3–5; Gorkovskaya metro. Another rewarding market for Caucasian food produce.

Vasileostrovskiy rynok, Bolshoy pr. 16, Vasilevskiy Island; Vasileostrovskaya metro. Cheap, but less well stocked than other markets.

Souvenirs

Russian **souvenirs** are sold all over the city: along Nevskiy prospekt, Malaya Konyushennaya ulitsa, behind the Church of the Saviour on the Blood, inside, outside the main tourist attractions and hotels, and in countless stores. Those in the Russian Museum

---

Kiosks

In the early years of "wild capitalism", **street kiosks and vendors** sold everything from bootleg booze and videos to frozen chickens. Now there are fewer than before, as the shops contain far more goods and the council has cracked down on unlicensed traders, but kiosks still purvey cigarettes and booze in residential areas, and snacks around metro stations. Aside from the risk of counterfeit liquor (see p.282), food should be treated with caution: ice cream and fruit are usually OK, but sausages and pies should be avoided, particularly from stalls at train stations.

and around the Imperial palaces tend to have particularly good selections. As you'd expect, street traders are generally cheaper than stores.

The most common items are *matryoshka* dolls (either traditional style, or in the form of figures such as Putin, Yeltsin, Gorbachev or Stalin), hand-painted boxes from Palekh, lacquered spoons and bowls from Khokhloma, fur hats, Communist insignia and banners, icons and samovars (though you are unlikely to be able to take the last two out of the country). Small watercolour views of the city are sold on the street outside St Catherine's Catholic Church at Nevskiy pr. 34–36. In department stores, you may also come across lovely blue-and-gold tea services, based on traditional Novgorod designs.

Hotel shops usually take credit cards, but will often charge four or five times the price you'll pay elsewhere.

Farfor, Nevskiy pr. 62; Nevskiy prospekt/Gostiniy dvor metro. Porcelain and crystal glasses.

Heritage, Nevskiy pr. 116; Ploshchad Vosstaniya metro. Souvenirs and art of excellent quality, but pricey.

Iskusstvo, Nevskiy pr. 20; Nevskiy prospekt/Gostiniy dvor metro. Prints by local artists, old postcards and pre-revolutionary banknotes.

Red Front, Bolshaya Morskaya ul. 34; Nevskiy prospekt/Gostiniy dvor metro. Wanna buy a fur hat?

Suveniry, Nevskiy pr. 92; Mayakovskaya metro. Small, but often stocks high-quality goods.

Shops and Markets

Chapter 14

Children's St Petersburg

Although Russians dote on **children**, St Petersburg is not a child-friendly environment, especially for toddlers: parks and playgrounds are littered with broken glass or even syringes, and slides and swings are often unsafe. However, in compensation, there are many specific attractions for kids to see and enjoy. For sporting activities and trips to the steam baths, see the next chapter (p.314). For details on where to find puppet theatres, the children's orchestra, the Rodina Cinema specializing in children's films (which doubles as a venue for clown shows) and the circus, see "The Arts" chapter (p.304).

Attractions

Museums that might interest children of all ages are the Kunstkammer and Museum of Anthropology (p.175), the Railway Museum (p.116) and the Arctic and Antarctic Museum (p.236). Children going through a bellicose phase might also enjoy the *Narodovolets* submarine (p.183), the cruiser *Aurora* (p.201), the Naval Museum (p.172) and the Artillery Museum (p.198). Young girls are more likely to enjoy the costumed waxwork figures in the Beloselskiy-Belozerskiy Palace (p.70) or the Doll Museum (p.185).

Of the **Imperial Palaces** outside the city (see Chapter 17), Peterhof, Tsarskoe Selo and Pavlovsk are probably the most enjoyable for kids, with huge parks, truly fabulous interiors and the

odd amusement park or boating lake. During winter, children can go sledging and skiing at Pavlovsk – see the following chapter for more details.

The run-down **Zoo** (p.197) is only enjoyable for the really young or totally insensitive, though there is the odd pony ride to enliven proceedings. Additionally, there's a **dolphinarium** (*delfinarium*) with an hour-long performance by dolphins and a sea lion (with which kids can be photographed) – though the conditions they're kept in will dismay adults. It's at ul. Sedova 5 ☎560 46 87; bus #8 or trolleybus #14 or #33 from Ploshchad Aleksandra Nevskovo metro, or bus #31, #95 or #114 from Yelizarovskaya metro. Shows Wed–Fri 1pm, 3pm & 5pm, Sat & Sun 11am, 1pm, 3pm, 5pm & 7pm.

You can also hire ponies for a sedate plod around Palace Square, or have a quick ride around the Kazan Cathedral in a horse-drawn trap ($2 per adult; children free).

Parks, playgrounds, and boat trips

Bearing in mind the warnings given above, young children are bound to enjoy **parks** such as the Summer Garden (p.95), the garden behind the Russian Museum, and the Yusupovskiy sad on Sadovaya ulitsa, where they can paddle in the pool. Older kids may be scornful of the old-fashioned **funfairs** and rides at the Tauride Gardens (p.223), Park Pobedy (p.243) and Yekateringof Park (p.248), but tots should be happy enough. Most of the city's **playgrounds** (often in the courtyards of residential blocks) are poorly maintained, but there's a fairly decent public one 100m south of Petrogradskaya metro, on Kamennoostrovskiy prospekt, plus two for local residents which you could get away with using in the gated block at Italyanskaya ul. 27 (leading through to Malaya Sadovaya), and the block between Gagarinskaya ulitsa and the Fontanka, facing the Summer Garden.

A **boat trip** is a good way to pass an hour or so. In addition to the guided tours of the city's river and canals, you can rent a motorboat and explore on your own.

Street entertainment

There are often **buskers and street performers** along Nevskiy prospekt and outside major tourist spots. A journey on one of the city's **trams** is usually a winner: trams #2 and #54 from Sadovaya ulitsa cross the Neva within sight of the Peter and Paul fortress, and during summer antique trams run from Finland Station into the centre in view of the

cruiser *Aurora*. For those children who can keep awake until the early hours, the spectacle of the **bridges** on the Neva opening to let ships through is a memorable one (see p.33 for times).

Toys

Amid the horde of imported **toys** in the DLT (see p.309), you can find simple wooden building blocks in the style of Petersburg palaces or medieval kremlins; cut-out paper dolls in antique Russian costumes; and traditional hand-carved "bears on a see-saw", which are also produced in joke forms such as two bears taking it in turns to work on a computer, or one bear spanking the other with a broom.

Another St Petersburg toy that can't be found anywhere else in the world is the nifty handmade bath toys in the form of sponge cubes (*kyubiki*) that turn into dragons or tortoises when squeezed inside out. They're made by Yuri Lesnik – you can only buy from him directly: call to arrange a meeting (☎930 08 76, *ylesnik@hotmail.com*). A regular-sized *kyubik* costs $2, but giant ones can be carved to order. They make lovely presents for kids up to the age of seven.

Children's
St
Petersburg

For further details of boat trips, see p.35.

Chapter 15

Sport, outdoor activities and bathhouses

In Soviet times, **sport** was accorded high status: a carefully nurtured elite of Olympic medal-winning athletes were heralded as proof of Communism's superiority, while ordinary citizens were exhorted to pursue sporting activities to make them "ready for labour and defence". Consequently, there's no shortage of sports facilities in St Petersburg, though most are for club members only; visitors can either try striking some kind of deal with the staff, or settle for paying much higher rates to use hotel facilities. If you're doing any outdoor activities, including sports such as horseriding and yachting, be sure that they're covered by your **insurance** policy.

For the slothful majority, however, the most popular activity remains visiting the **bathhouse**, or *banya*. Russian bathhouses are a world unto themselves and are the preferred cure for the complaint known locally as "feeling heavy" – which encompasses everything from having flu to being depressed. For a truly Russian experience, a visit to the *banya* is an absolute must.

Bathhouses

The Russian **banya** is as much a national institution as is the sauna in Finland. Traditionally, peasants stoked up the village bathhouse and washed away the week's grime on Fridays; Saturdays were for drinking and Sundays for church – "a *banya* for the soul". Townspeople were equally devoted to the *banya*: the wealthy had private ones, while others visited public bathhouses, favoured as much for their ambience as the quality of their hot room. Today, these traditional bathhouses are classless institutions, where all ages and professions are united in sweaty conviviality.

Before you set off, it's as well to know the procedure when **visiting a banya**. Some bathhouses have separate floors for men and women, while others operate on different days for each sex, but whatever the set-up, there's no mixed bathing, except in special de luxe saunas (available for private rental). The only thing the *banya* will definitely provide (for a modest price) is a sheet in which to wrap yourself. You should **bring** a towel, shampoo, some plastic sandals and possibly a hat to protect your head (towels, flip-flops and weird mushroom-shaped felt hats can be rented at some *banyas*). Expect to pay $3–5 to use a standard *banya*; more at de luxe establishments. At the entrance, you can buy a *venik* – a leafy bunch of birch twigs (or prickly juniper twigs for the really hardy) – with which bathers flail themselves (and each other) in the steam room, to open up the skin's pores and enhance blood circulation. This isn't compulsory.

Hand your coat and valuables to the cloakroom attendant before going into the changing rooms. Beyond these lies a washroom with a **cold plunge pool** or bath; the metal basins are for soaking your *venik* to make it supple. Finally you enter the **hot room** – or *parilka* – with its tiers of benches – the higher up you go, the hotter it gets. Unlike in a sauna, it's a damp heat, as from time to time water is thrown onto the stove to produce steam. Five to seven minutes is as long as novices should attempt in the *parilka*. After a dunk in the cold bath and a rest, you can return to the *parilka* for more heat torture, before cooling off again – a process repeated several times, with breaks for tea and conversation.

Many *banya*-goers cover their heads to protect them from the heat, while others take advantage of traditional health cures and beauty treatments: men rub salt over their bodies in order to sweat more copiously, and women coat themselves with honey, to make their skin softer – you can also throw beer on the stove for a wonderful yeasty aroma. As *banya*-going is a dehydrating experience, it's advisable not to go drunk, with a bad hangover or on a full stomach. Beer is usually on sale in the men's section, but women should bring their own drinks. The traditional farewell salutation to fellow *banya*-goers is "*S lyogkim parom*" – "May the steam be with you".

In addition to those *banyas* listed below in the city, there are several grouped around the lakes in **Ozerki**, to the north of the city (use Ozerki metro station). At these, you can try the Russian custom of leaping through the ice into freezing water in winter rather than just into a cold plunge pool. The *banya* at 84 Bolshaya Ozyornaya ul. (☎553 23 96) is open 24 hours a day and has a sauna, *parilka*, pool, gym and massage.

Banya #13, ul. Karbysheva 29a ☎550 09 85; southwest of Ploshchad Muzhestvo metro. Sauna, solarium and pool. Mon, Tues & Fri–Sun 8am–9pm.

Banya #17, ul. Chaykovskovo 1 ☎272 09 11; near the Bolshoy dom, off Liteyniy prospekt. Pretty run-down, but enjoys a good reputation for its steam room. Wed–Sun 8am–10pm.

Banya #27, ul. Olgi Forsh ☎592 76 22; three blocks west of Grazhdanskiy Prospekt metro. Standard neighbourhood *banya*. Wed–Sun 8am–10pm.

Banya #57, Gavanskaya ul. 5 ☎356 63 51; off the lower end of Bolshoy prospekt on Vasilevskiy Island. Has a private sauna to rent, as well as the public bath. Wed–Sun 8am–10pm. The de luxe section is women only Thurs & Sat; men only Wed, Fri & Sun.

Mytninskie Bani, ul. Mytninskaya 17/19 ☎271 71 19; trolleybus #10 from pl. Vosstaniya. The only wood-stoked *banya* still operating in town and full of atmosphere, despite its poor state of repair. Mon, Tues & Fri–Sun 8am–10pm.

Nevskie Bani, ul. Marata 5/7 ☎311 14 00; Mayakovskaya metro. The cheaper section (open 9am–9pm) is infested with cockroaches, the de luxe (open 24hr) with Mafiosi and call-girls. Sauna, massage, solarium and pool.

Yamskie Bani, ul. Dostoevskovo 9 ☎312 58 36; Vladimirskaya metro. Frequented by the *banya* cognoscenti and well kept by local standards. Thursday is cheap day for pensioners, so there are huge queues. Also has a de luxe section, with private rooms and a gym. Wed–Sun 8am–9pm.

Boating and yachting

A relaxing way to spend a couple of hours is to go **boating** on the serpentine lakes of Yelagin Island. Rowboats are rented out by the hour on the lake near the bridge over to Vyborg Side, but avoid weekends and public holidays, when facilities are oversubscribed, and beware of the wild monkeys on the island in the main lake (see p211).

More ambitiously, you could go **yachting** on the Gulf of Finland, where

Sport, outdoor activities and bathhouses

Sport, Outdoor Activities and bathhouses

strong winds make for fast, exciting sailing, especially during the **St Petersburg Sailing Week** (mid-Aug), a regatta with races in various classes. Most local yachts are Polish copies of US racers, crewed by skilled enthusiasts. Charter trips range from a couple of hours to overnight expeditions to uninhabited islands or sea forts, out in the Gulf. Most yachts sleep six to eight people. Prices depend on the firm or club and what you want to do, so it's definitely worth shopping around the following outfits.

Kronstadt Yacht Club, Leningradskaya pristan ☎276 44 00; hydrofoil from the Tuchkov most. Tucked away in one of the quieter corners of Kronstadt, with a fine view of St Petersburg and the sea forts, this club has a small fleet of yachts and dinghies for rent, but not much English is spoken.

River Yacht Club (aka Tsentralniy Yacht Club), Petrovskaya Kosa, Petrovskiy Island ☎255 66 36; trolleybus #7 from Nevskiy pr. to the end of the line. Though its clubhouse and finances are stuck in a Soviet time-warp, the club once produced teams for the Olympics and was founded as long ago as 1858. Director Yuri Yanin speaks English.

Sunny Sailing, ul. Vosstaniya 55 ☎272 36 63 or 327 35 25, www.sailing.spb.ru; Ploshchad Vosstaniya metro. An upmarket agency with a downtown office, chartering all kinds of boats at premium rates. More clued-up than its rivals, though staff can be rude. The boats are moored at Stelna, near Peterhof; for trips to Valaam they use yachts out of Priozersk.

Bowling and billiards

The city has several well-equipped **bowling** alleys and numerous places with **billiards** or pool tables (roughly $2–6/hr). The main difference between Russian billiards and the English game is that there are no cannons – you can only score points by straightforward pots.

Aquatoria, Vyborgskaya nab. 61 ☎245 20 30; minibus #T-10 from Petrogradskaya metro. Mega entertainment complex near the Kantimirovskiy most, with nine "Brunswick" lanes, "Cosmic Bowling" and lanes for kids, Russian and American billiards, and a disco (Wed–Sun 10pm–6am) with go-go dancers and strippers. Bowling daily noon–6am.

Billiards Blues-Style, ul. Professora Popova 47 ☎234 44 48; bus #25 from Petrogradskaya metro. Billiards, pool and darts, with live blues music, in the *Dvorets molodezhi* – a hotel-cum-youth entertainment centre on Petrograd Side (see "Accommodation", p.269). Daily 10am–7am.

5th Avenue, pl. Konstityutsi 2 ☎123 08 09; Moskovskaya metro. Two blocks west of Moskovskaya ploshchad, with seven lanes for US tenpin bowling, plus Russian and American billiards. Rates are lower during daytime. Mon–Fri from noon, Sat–Sun from 10am, till the last customer leaves.

Fartver, pl. Morskoy Slavy 1 ☎322 69 39; minibus #T-128 from Nevskiy prospekt. A six-lane bowling club near the Sea Terminal on Vasilevskiy Island. Mon–Fri from noon, Sat & Sun from 10am till the last customer leaves.

Trick-Shot, ul. Marata 73 ☎164 98 76; Pushkinskaya metro. Pool tables, bar and restaurant. Takes Visa. Daily 1pm–6am.

Tuborg Club, Kirochnaya ul. 36; Chernyshevskaya metro. Laid-back café-bar with cheap billiard tables upstairs. Daily noon–midnight.

Gyms

While many **gyms** in St Petersburg require expensive membership, the less prestigious setups will let you pay a one-off fee of a few dollars, and most of the top hotels have gyms open to non-residents for a fee.

Astoria Fitness Centre, *Astoria Hotel*, Bolshaya Morskaya ul. 39 ☎210 58 69; bus #22 or #43 from Nevskiy pr. Always phone first as hotel guests have priority. Daily 7am–10pm.

Fitness Factory, Razezhnaya ul. 19 (corner of ul. Dostoevskov) ☎346 80 33; *www.fitnessfactory.spb.ru;* Dostoevskaya/Vladimirskaya metro. Gym, cardio room, aerobics, sauna and solarium. Amex, Visa, MC. Open Mon–Fri 7am–11pm, Sat & Sun 10am–9pm.

Galaxy, Petrovskiy Stadium, Petrograd Side ☎119 57 41; Sportivnaya metro. Sports club with a gym and aerobics room, offering individual computerized programmes for increasing or reducing body mass. Daily 8am–11pm.

Growth Centre, Ispolkomskaya ul. 7 (in the courtyard) ☎277 29 44; Ploshchad Aleksandra Nevskovo metro. A gym specializing in people with back problems; you must be examined by a doctor on the premises first. A season ticket for ten sessions cost about $50. Daily noon–6pm.

Sun & Step Studio, ul. Zhukovskovo 63 (corner of Ligovskiy pr.) ☎346 81 14; *www.fitnessfactory.spb.ru;* Ploshchad Vosstaniya metro. Aerobics, dance classes, sauna, café and solarium. Mon–Fri 9.30am–10.30pm, Sat & Sun 11am–7.30pm.

Too Fort Fitness Centre, pl. Aleksandra Nevskovo 2a (the yard of the *Moskva Hotel)* ☎277 74 91; Ploshchad Aleksandra Nevskovo metro. Gym, swimming pool, sauna. Daily 9am–11pm.

World Class Gym, *Grand Hotel Europe,* Mikhaylovskaya ul. 1–7 ☎329 65 97; Nevskiy prospekt/Gostiniy dvor metro. A rather small gym with a sauna. Mon–Fri 7am–10pm, Sat 9am–9pm.

Zdorovie, ul. Gagarinskaya 32 ☎279 02 26; Nevskiy prospekt or Ploshchad Vosstaniya metro. Aerobics, "shaping" (low-impact aerobics) and sauna. Daily 8am–midnight.

Horseriding

Horseriding in St Petersburg tends to be more serious than just a ten-minute ride across Palace Square, so be prepared for aching muscles the following day.

Proster Equestrian Centre, Krestovskiy Island ☎230 78 73 or 230 78 72; tram #34 from Gorkovskaya metro. Riding lessons, plus *troika* and sleigh rides in winter.

Yumax, ul. Tankistov 5 ☎437 70 17; train from Finland Station to Solechnoe. Out-of-the-city equestrian club with thoroughbreds and trekking ponies for hire, and lessons. Tues–Sun 10am–6pm.

Zaitsev & Anisimov Horse Centre, Primorskiy Park Pobedy, beside the Kirov Stadium ☎235 54 48 or 586 54 48 (ask for Arkadiy Anisimov, who speaks English); bus #71 from Krestovskiy Ostrov metro. Mon–Sun 10am–7pm.

Sport, Outdoor Activities and bathhouses

Ice hockey

SKA St Petersburg is one of the best **ice hockey** teams in Russia, and despite financial difficulties and the loan of top strikers to foreign clubs, they continue to delight crowds at the Yubileyniy Sports Palace on Petrograd Side (☎119 56 12; Sportivnaya metro), or the new and much larger Ice Palace on pr. Pyatiletok in the Malaya Okhta district (Prospekt Bolshevikov metro), constructed for the World Hockey Championship 2000.

Matches are played throughout the year, as listed in *Chas Pik* and *Sport Ekspress*; the latter is the best source of information on all spectator sports.

Rock climbing and bungee jumping

Given St Petersburg's flat topography, local **rock climbing** enthusiasts are obliged to go to the Karelian Isthmus, where participants of any nationality may attend the "Climbing for Everybody" **festival** in early May, held 150km north of St Petersburg; trains from Finland Station run to Kuznechnoe, 15km from the site. For details, contact Sergei Mikheev (*s.mikheev@actor.ru*) well ahead of time, and check out the Web site at *www.city-cat.ru/skala.*

If you really want to get the adrenalin flowing, there's a **bungee jump** at Ozerki, on the northern edge of the city (near Ozerki metro), from a cabin suspended 50m above a lake (daily 2–11pm; one jump costs $14).

You might also visit *www.risk.ru* – an online magazine for Russian hazardous sports enthusiasts.

Skating, sledging and skiing

During winter, Russians dig out their ice skates or skis and revel in the snow. If you can borrow a pair of skates, some picturesque places to go **ice-skating** are the frozen straits between the Peter and Paul Fortress and the Kronverk, the Krasnaya Zarya open-air rink on Lesnoy prospekt, or the lake in the Tauride Gardens; there are other rinks in Park Pobedy near the SKK and by the Kirov Stadium on Krestovskiy Island.
In addition, both the Tauride Gardens and the park behind the Russian Museum are popular nursery slopes, where children learn to ski.

Russia's terrain dictates that cross-country rather than downhill **skiing** is the norm; two popular skiing destinations for locals are the Karelian Isthmus (see Chapter 18) and the park surrounding Pavlovsk Palace (see p.369), where it's possible to rent skis and sledges.

Soccer

St Petersburg's **soccer** fans had to wait ages for the renaissance of Zenit (see p.208), but now that they're firmly in the Premier Division, it's ardently hoped they'll score further victories over hated Muscovite rivals to match the historic cup win of 1999. The big question currently hanging over the club is how they'll cope with the loss of striker Alexander Panov and goalie Roman Berezovsky to St Etienne – though Zenit's top scorer and driving force, Gennady Popovich, remains on the team. Personalities aside, Zenit have undoubtedly benefited from their move to the all-weather Petrovskiy Stadium, which allows the team to train on a full-sized pitch throughout the winter, rather than indoors, as at the old Kirov Stadium.

Their fan club, Nevsky Front, has its headquarters at ul. Nekrasova 25 and a Web site at *www.soccer.ru/zenit*; other sites include the Russian football union's *www.rfs.ru* and *www.russianfootball.com*, which features a schedule of matches for the year.

There are two national competitions: the Russian **Championship**, running from spring to autumn, and the Russian **Cup**, which starts in the summer and ends in the summer of the next year. Games usually begin at 6.30pm and tickets ($2–10) are easy to obtain on the spot.

Kirov Stadium, Krestovskiy Island ☎235 02 43; bus #71 or a 15min walk from Krestovskiy Ostrov metro. Vast, windswept and forlorn now that Zenit have forsaken it, but still an object of some curiosity (see p.212).

Petrovskiy Stadium, Petrovskiy Island ☎233 17 52; near Sportivnaya metro. Refurbished for the 1994 Goodwill Games, with seating for 30,000 and underfield heating, making it the city's premier soccer venue. During the Blockade, soldiers were trained here in unarmed combat and there was an anti-aircraft battery in the centre of the stadium.

Swimming

The seriously hardy can always join the so-called "walruses", who swim in all weathers in the polluted Neva by the Peter and Paul Fortress. For mere mortals, the choice is rather limited, with most Russians opting instead for a trip to the *banya*. The major problem for foreigners is that to use public **swimming pools** you are supposed to have a health certificate (*spravka*) from a Russian doctor; furthermore, pools tend to limit bathers to only half an hour in the water and close from July to September anyway. Hotel pools do not have the same restrictions, but it can be difficult for non-residents to gain access to them as pools are small and guests get priority.

Dinamo, pr. Dinamo 44 ☎235 47 17; Krestovskiy Ostrov metro. Indoor pool in the Dinamo sports complex. Daily 8am–8pm.

LDM, ul. Professora Popova 47 ☎234 97 72; bus #25 from Petrogradskaya metro. Fun pool with slides and waterfalls, next to *Billiards Blues-Style* and the *Dvortets molodezhi*. A certificate is required in theory, but seldom asked for in practice. Daily 8am–8pm.

Railway Institute Sports Centre, Kronverkskiy pr. 9 ☎232 66 14; Gorkovskaya metro. Clean Olympic pool, and you can often persuade them that you "forgot" your health certificate.

Spartak Pool, Konstantinovskiy pr. 19 ☎235 07 33; tram #17 or #34 from Chkalovskaya metro. Olympic pool with slide, sauna, gym, shower and massage, on Krestovskiy Island. Officially a certificate is required, but you can usually get round this.

Tennis

As a keen **tennis** player, Yeltsin did much to promote the sport in Russia, which became chic in a way that would have been inconceivable in Soviet times – while the photogenic Anna Kournikova has further raised the game's profile. But whereas Moscow lures top players to the international Kremlin Cup with over $1 million in prize money, St Petersburg is nowhere on the world tennis circuit.

If you want to play yourself, **courts** can be rented over summer at the following places, mostly on Krestovskiy Island. Prices vary widely, from $5 per hour upwards.

Yelagin Ostrov, near the palace on Yelagin Island ☎430 11 21; tram #20, #37 or #46 from Chkalovskaya metro. Floodlit outdoor courts. Daily 8am–midnight.

Dinamo Sports Centre, Dinamo pr. 44, Krestovskiy Island ☎235 00 35; tram #26 or #34 from Chkalovskaya metro. Clay, synthetic and indoor courts. Advance booking essential; some English spoken.

Kirov Stadium, Krestovskiy Island ☎235 48 77; bus #71 from Krestovskiy Ostrov metro. Indoor courts.

Molniya, Primorskiy pr. 50 ☎430 75 09; tram #2, #31 or #37 from Chernaya Rechka metro. Clay courts; book well in advance.

Sport, Outdoor Activities and bathhouses

Out of the City

Chapter 16

Introduction

At the weekend the city can seem quite deserted as Petersburgers leave in droves for the surrounding countryside. It was the tsars who first established the tradition of retreating from the urban bustle to enjoy the woods and lakes outside the city, where they built magnificent palaces set in sprawling, landscaped grounds. The aristocracy soon followed suit, and small towns and garrisons began to grow up around the Imperial estates, which subsequently became popular summer resorts for city dwellers, who built or rented *dachas* (country homes) there. Today, making a trip into the countryside around St Petersburg is relatively easy due to the city's minibuses, hydrofoils and extensive suburban railway network. Count on spending an extra couple of days in St Petersburg if you just want to see one or two outlying palaces; more like two weeks if you are determined to visit everything covered in the following three chapters.

The most popular destinations are the **Imperial palaces** (chapter 17), to the south and west of St Petersburg, to whose building or enlargement every tsar since Peter the Great contributed. **Peterhof** was the first to be created, and remains most people's first choice to visit, thanks to the sheer variety of different palaces erected there over the years. It's also the only Imperial estate which makes full use of the sea – arriving by hydrofoil is an unforgettable experience. Catherine the Great's preferred residence, **Tsarskoe Selo**, runs Peterhof a close second, sporting another fabulous main palace and huge grounds with numerous follies. Also in the town is the school which the poet, Alexander Pushkin, attended for six years. Nearby **Pavlovsk** is famed more for its landscaped park and pavilions than its comparatively modest and intimate palace, though the latter makes a welcome change from the heavy Baroque splendours of Tsarskoe Selo. **Oranienbaum**, **Gatchina** and **Strelna** can muster less in the way of splendid architecture, but the lack of crowds at all three is a distinct advantage. All the palaces are ideal places to take children: there's plenty of space to run around and a variety of museums and buildings to engage their interest.

Out in the Gulf of Finland, off the coast of Oranienbaum, the eighteenth-century island fortress of **Kronstadt** (chapter 18) – famous for its role in several Russian revolutions – has been opened to foreigners after decades of being off limits. Also covered in chapter 18 is the forested **Karelian Isthmus**, which stretches northwest from St Petersburg to the Finnish border. Its **Gulf coast** – awash with small pebbly coves and rocky headlands – is *dacha* country par excellence, while the region's history is writ large in the medieval town of **Vyborg**, near the border. On the eastern side of the isthmus, **Lake Ladoga** is far too large to get to grips with on a short trip, barring a visit to the infamous prison fortress of **Schlüsselburg**, but with more time and money you could sign up for a short cruise to the beautiful **Valaam** archipelago and the fabulous wooden churches of **Kizhi** island, on Lake Onega.

If St Petersburg is the country's "window on the West", **Novgorod** (chapter 19), a three-hour bus ride south, is an archetypal medieval Russian city. It boasts a Kremlin (fortified inner city), Russia's oldest cathedral and numerous onion-domed stone churches, as well as an open-air museum of wooden architecture located by the Yuryev Monastery, on the outskirts. At a push, Novgorod is near enough to visit on a long day-trip from St Petersburg, but is better appreciated as a weekend break from the city.

Practicalities

Accommodation in the various towns is limited to a few hotels or hostels – you'll find suggestions on where to stay in the text. Good **meals** are even less easy to come by, so you may wish to prepare a picnic before you set out.

Transport out of St Petersburg is relatively easy. You can reach almost all the places described in the following chapters by minibus or train; specific details are provided with each account. Services are very regular throughout the year, the system is extremely cheap, and distances are not particularly vast. There's no need to book tickets in advance, though be aware that summer weekends (especially in Aug) see huge crowds descending on the most popular spots at weekends.

Chapter 17

The Imperial palaces

The Russian Imperial Court was the largest and most extravagant in Europe, and the **Imperial Palaces**, established around the city during the eighteenth century, are its most spectacular legacy. During the golden age of autocracy, the Imperial estates grew ever more ostentatious, demonstrating the might of the Romanov dynasty through the sheer luxuriance of its palace buildings. Largely designed by foreign architects, but constructed by Russian craftsmen using the Empire's vast natural resources of gold, marble, malachite, porphyry, lapis lazuli and amber, the palaces now count among the most important cultural monuments in Russia.

The peripatetic nature of **court life** meant that each ruler divided his or her time between several palaces, adding to and remodelling them as they saw fit. Initially, the palaces functioned as magnificent stage sets, against which scenes of murder, passion and intrigue were played out, but as St Petersburg grew ever more politically volatile, they became a place of refuge for the country's rulers. After the Revolution, the palaces were opened and ordinary citizens were invited to feast their eyes on the awesome facades and opulent interiors – the fruits of centuries of exploitation.

During **World War II**, all of the palaces except Oranienbaum lay within Nazi-occupied territory. For three years, the Germans set about destroying everything they could lay their hands on: thousands of trees were felled, and palaces and pavilions dynamited. This "cultural destruction" was one of the charges brought against the Nazis at the Nuremburg Trials by Soviet prosecutors who set up a special commission to assess the damage. It was years before any of the palaces were reopened to the public, and the fact that they were reconstructed at all seems even more incredible than their creation.

Peterhof and **Tsarskoe Selo** are the most elaborate and popular of the palaces, followed – roughly in order of merit – by **Pavlovsk**, **Gatchina**, **Oranienbaum** and Peter the Great's wooden palace at **Strelna**. All the palaces (but not the towns in which they stand) have reverted to their pre-revolutionary **names** (as used in this chapter), but the Soviet titles of three of them are still often used by Russians:

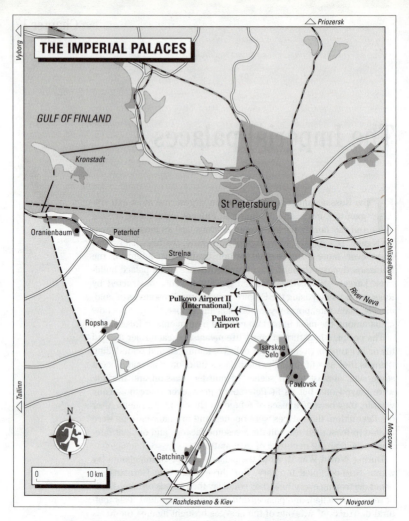

THE IMPERIAL PALACES

GULF OF FINLAND

Kronstadt

St Petersburg

Vyborg

Priozersk

Schlüsselburg

River Neva

Oranienbaum

Peterhof

Strelna

Pulkovo Airport II
(International)

Pulkovo
Airport

Ropsha

Tsarskoe
Selo

Pavlovsk

Tallinn

Moscow

N

Gatchina

0   10 km

Rozhdestveno & Kiev

Novgorod

Petrodvorets (Peterhof), Pushkin (Tsarskoe Selo) and Lomonosov (Oranienbaum). These replaced the original names, which were considered to be too reactionary or too Germanic, although the names of Gatchina and Strelna, lacking any ideological undertones, were never altered.

Visiting the palaces

Minibuses are the easiest way to reach most of the palaces: the points of departure for services to Stelna, Peterhof, Tsarskoe Selo, Oranienbaum and Gatchina are all located close to metro stations, and shown on our map of the Southern Suburbs (p.244). Services run every 20–30 minutes, and since you buy a ticket on board, there's no need to queue or worry about finding the right ticket kiosk – which certainly isn't the case with the electrified **suburban train** system (*prigorodniy poezd* or *elektrichka*). Though trains are nearly as frequent as minibuses on weekday mornings and week-ends, they are less so around midday, and foreigners are liable to be confused by the fact that the ticket kiosks (*prigorodniy kassy*) for these services are in a separate side hall, or outside the station. The only palace that's easier to reach by train is Pavlovsk, which isn't accessible by minibus from St Petersburg. Last but not least are the **hydrofoils** that zoom across the Gulf to Peterhof during the summer – a highly scenic approach.

Full transport details for each palace can be found in the "Practicalities" boxes accompanying each account.

It's also possible to visit the more popular palaces on **organized tours**, which range from upmarket excursions offered by the inter-national hotels ($25 per person and upwards) to inexpensive trips on tour buses which depart from outside the Winter Palace and Gostiniy dvor ($4–7, payable in rubles). As the latter cater to locals, the com-mentary is in Russian only.

At all the palaces, dual **ticket prices** apply: low for Russians; much higher for foreigners, ranging from $2 to $8 and payable in rubles. Since a separate ticket is required for each sight or section within a palace, the entrance fees soon mount up, so if you have one it pays to take your student card (or assert "*Ya student*" and hope for the best); if you wish to take **photographs** or use a **video camera** indoors, you'll need to buy a permit. The *kassa* will often be away from the palace itself, in a little wooden booth or kiosk. On entry, many of the palaces require you to put on felt overshoes (*tapochki*) to protect their parquet floors.

Guided tours are on offer at most palaces, though invariably only in Russian; although you're expected to join a group, it's easy enough to catch up with the one in front, or fall behind to enjoy the rooms in peace. If you really want a tour in English it's sometimes possible to tack onto a pre-paid group and listen in to their guide. Keep an eye out, too, for the palaces' various **temporary exhibitions**, featuring anything from Fabergé Eggs to hitherto neglected aspects of Tsarist history.

Strelna

Only 23km from St Petersburg along the Gulf of Finland, **Strelna**, built on land wrested from Sweden during the Northern War, was the site of Peter the Great's original attempt to create a seaside palace to rival Versailles. Dating from 1715, the **Wooden Palace** was built for Peter to live in while overseeing work on the great stone **Konstantin Palace** and its grounds, criss-crossed with canals and girdled by reservoirs. After five years' work, however, he realized that it was

impossible to create the high-spurting fountains he desired without installing pumps, and that the palace's sea canal was prone to silt up – and therefore turned his attention to another site further east, which became Peterhof.

Thereafter, Strelna's Wooden Palace served as an overnight halt for journeys along the Gulf, while the stone palace remained unfinished until the reign of Empress Elizabeth. Today, the two buildings stand in stark contrast to one another, with the former now restored under the aegis of the Peterhof Museum Reserve while the latter remains ravaged by war and neglect. Though Strelna has far less to offer visitors than the other Imperial residences, it does provide a unique opportunity to step back in time and gain an idea of what the other Tsarist palaces looked before their restoration following World War II.

The Wooden Palace

The Wooden Palace is open Tues–Sun 10.30am–5pm, closed Mon & last Tues of the month; $3.

Situated on a ridge overlooking the Gulf, Peter's **Wooden Palace** (Derevyanniy dvorets) is a charming, two-storey building painted yellow and white. While its decor is largely of the Petrine era – when wallpaper was a fashionable novelty – the palace's furnishings span almost two hundred years, since it was also used by later rulers. One of the finest exhibits is the travel chest of Alexander III, incorporating a slide-out bed, folding desk, chairs, washstand, kitchen and homeopathic pharmacy, plus all kinds of implements including a device for stretching gloves.

Another room is devoted to pastimes: Peter loved chess and draughts, while his female successors preferred cards (playing for money was forbidden, so courtiers gambled for diamonds instead). In the **dining room**, with its beautiful tiled stove, notice the unique samovar with two taps belonging to Catherine the Great, who drank her tea with milk in the English fashion. Peter's **bedroom** has a four-poster curtained in green felt, with a patchwork quilt sewn by his wife, Catherine I, while his **study** contains a device for warming his feet while he worked at the desk. The final rooms are more formal, presaging the second-floor **Upper Hall**, adorned with Chinese vases, Japanese bronzes and European paintings. As in Peter's time, visitors are greeted by a caged songbird on the upstairs landing.

Outside, the **garden** sports flowerbeds, glazed urns and fountains on its seaward side, and an apiary and vegetable plots to the rear which once supplied the palace with food. It was here, during the reign of Empress Anna, that potatoes were first grown in Russia – initially just for their flowers, which were worn at balls as a fashionable accessory. A little further on, a wooden cross and shrine mark the site of a church and bell tower, destroyed during the war, which may be rebuilt in time for St Petersburg's tercentenary. Sadly, nothing remains of Peter the Great's treehouse, where he used to enjoy smoking a pipe and watching ships on the Gulf in the evenings.

The Konstantin Palace

Turn left outside the entrance to the grounds of the Wooden Palace and follow a track beside a pond to reach a ruined gateway through which you'll find the gigantic **Konstantin Palace** (Konstantinovskiy dvorets), sited on a lofty terrace overlooking a wild park stretching to the shores of the Gulf. This derelict edifice is both awesome and pathetic, distinguished by a huge triple archway whose coffered ceiling is quite well preserved – unlike the interior, which retains nothing of its former splendour, having been turned into a College of the Arctic during Soviet times, when its elegant tiled stoves were replaced by ugly boilers and the rooms and corridors painted in bilious shades of blue and pink. Although volunteers have partly restored the great **ballroom**, designed by Stackenschneider, repairing the whole palace will require massive state investment – this is actually said to be on the cards, though some feel that the palace should be left as it is.

The Konstantin Palace is usually open Sat & Sun 11am–6pm; $3. To check, call ☎ 156 77 07 (Mon–Fri) or ☎ 421 48 42 (Sat & Sun) and ask to speak to Galina Yeregina.

Guided **tours** focus on a single room chronicling Strelna's owners since Tsar Paul gave it to his second son, Konstantin, and on its heyday under several later grand dukes with similar forenames or patronymics – the last, Dmitri Konstantinovich, renounced the palace after the February Revolution and moved into a house in the grounds, but was nonetheless shot by the Bolsheviks in 1919. Strelna is best known, however, for its association with his brother, **Konstantin Konstantinovich** (1858–1915), a poet, translator and playwright under the *nom de plume* of "K.R." (Konstantin Romanov), who fathered nine children but was also a secret homosexual, as his diaries posthumously revealed.

If you can't persuade the staff to let you up into the rickety **tower,** then a balcony emblazoned with the Soviet crest affords an enticing view of the **park**, bisected by a great canal choked with waterlilies.

Practicalities

Strelna is easily reached from St Petersburg or Peterhof either by **train** (alight at Strelna station and follow Frontovaya ulitsa to the Petersburg highway, then turn right and keep going till you cross the canal – the Wooden Palace lies across the road), or on any of the **minibuses** that shuttle between Peterhof and Avtovo metro station in St Petersburg. The latter method is quicker (45min), cheaper and easier, with the added advantage that it affords glimpses of other former palaces and monasteries en route. If you opt for a minibus, ask to be dropped off at the Wooden Palace rather than the stone one, which isn't as visible from the highway. As there are no cafés in Strelna, you should bring a **picnic** or eat at Peterhof – though calls of nature can be satisfied at the Wooden Palace, whose staff boast of their "Euro standard" toilets.

Strelna

Most of the old bridges still survive as skeletal frames, but the island at the far end is now inaccessible, and nothing remains of the *dacha* once owned by the ballerina Mathilda Kshesinskaya (see p.200), whom K.R. privately regarded as "a trollop".

Peterhof (Petrodvorets)

As the first of the great Imperial palatial ensembles to be established outside St Petersburg, **Peterhof** embodies nearly three hundred years of Tsarist self-aggrandizement. As you'd expect from its name (meaning "Peter's Court" in German, and pronounced "Peter*gof*" in Russian), its founder was **Peter the Great**. Flushed with triumph from the Northern War against Sweden, he decided to build a sumptuous palace and town beside the Gulf, following the construction of his island fortress of Kronstadt, which secured the seaborne approaches to the city.

After an abortive attempt at Strelna, Peterhof was selected as the site due to its more favourable hydrography and coastline, which permitted the great fountains and access by water that Peter desired. Architects scrambled to keep up with the stream of projects issuing from his pen, while visiting ambassadors were often obliged to join the tsar in labouring on the site. Even so, Peterhof's existing Great Palace wasn't built until the reign of **Empress Elizabeth**, when court life became more opulent, reaching its apogee during the reign of **Catherine the Great**, whose acquaintance with Peterhof dated back to her loveless marriage to Peter III (see p.344). Although Catherine's immediate successors preferred other palaces, **Nicholas I** returned the court to Peterhof, building the Cottage Palace in the Alexandria Park, where the Imperial family lived with minimal pomp, reflecting the later Romanovs' creeping embourgeoisement.

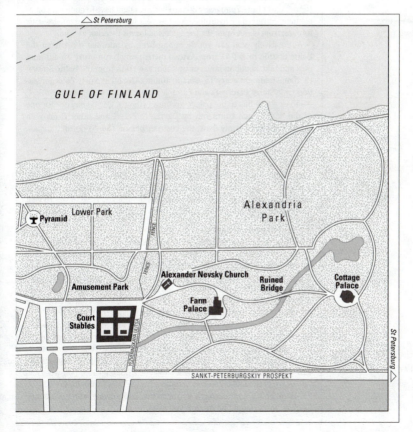

Peterhof

Practicalities

When to go is a tricky question. Although Peterhof's grounds are open daily (9am–9pm), its fountains only operate from June to October (11am–5pm; 8pm at weekends), while the various museum palaces are each closed on different days, namely: the Great Palace (Mon & last Tues of the month); Monplaisir (Wed & last Thurs); Catherine Wing (Thurs & last Fri); Marly Palace (Tues & last Wed); and Cottage Palace (Fri & last Tues). This makes weekends – when it is predictably the most crowded – the only time when everything is certain to be open. Moreover, opening days in winter are further limited: Monplaisir is closed from October to May and the Catherine Wing, Marly Palace and Cottage Palace are only open at weekends from October to April.

Getting there from St Petersburg is fairly straightforward. From late May to mid-September (weather permitting), Raketa **hydrofoils** (30–40min; $7 one way) speed across the Gulf of Finland to Peterhof, a trip that offers the bonus of a splendid first glimpse of the Great Palace and a distant view of Kronstadt. The hydrofoils leave St Petersburg from the jetty outside the Hermitage (11am–7pm; every 30min) but you might have to queue. If you're planning to return by hydrofoil, don't leave it too late, as long queues start forming from about 5pm; the last hydrofoil leaves Peterhof at 8pm.

Alternatively, you can get there and back by **minibus** #T-4 from the Baltic Station or #T-4a from Avtovo metro, which run every 15–20 minutes and take about an hour; or by **suburban train** from the Baltic Station (5.45am–midnight every 15–30min; 40min). Get off at Noviy Petergof station (*not* Stariy Petergof) and catch a #350, #351, #352, #353, #354, #355 or #359 bus to the palace grounds (10min). Or you can opt for one of the daily **coach tours** run by Davranov Travel and other firms with kiosks outside Gostiniy dvor; the cost per person ($4–5) doesn't include admission.

Visitors need separate **tickets** to enter Peterhof's grounds (sold near the jetty and the Benois Wing) and each palace (sold in situ). If you haven't got much time, the highlights are the Great Palace, Monplaisir, the Lower Park and the Cottage Palace. The Grand Cascade, the jewel in Peterhof's crown, can be enjoyed for free, though you have to pay to visit the Grotto.

Eating and accommodation

Providing you're not pushed for time, the best place **to eat** is the *Café Trapeza* (Tues–Sun noon–10pm), just to the east of the Upper Garden, a surprisingly classy but reasonably priced café serving delicacies such as grilled prawns. In the left wing of the palace is a branch of the *Schwabski Domik* (Tues–Sun 11am–6pm), which serves Germanic snacks and beer. Alternatively, you can buy cheaper beer and sausages from the outdoor cafeteria near the landing stage and eat them under the trees.

Given the regular transport between Peterhof and St Petersburg, there's no need **to stay** overnight unless you fancy hitting the sights before the day-trippers arrive, in which case try the Spartan but clean *Petrodvorets Sanatorium* (open all year) next door to the Benois Wing. Foreigners pay $15 a head whether they occupy a single or a double room (showers and toilets are in the hall). You can book in advance (☎427 50 98, fax 427 50 21; 9am–5pm), and although you may not find anyone who speaks any English, there should be room if you just turn up.

In 1944, after Peterhof had been liberated from Nazi occupation, the authorities decided that its Germanic name was no longer appropriate and replaced it with its Russian equivalent, "Petrodvorets" (pronounced "Petrodvaryets"). In 1992, however, the palace officially reverted to its former name, Peterhof – although the **town** itself is still called **Petrodvorets**.

Unsurprisingly, the palace and park are the setting for several **festivals**, including the opening and closing of the "fountain season" (see the Grand Cascade account below) and concerts and ballet in the grounds and the throne room of the palace during the White Nights in June. The latter are held under the aegis of the "Palaces of St Petersburg" festival, which also involves Tsarskoe Selo. For details, see the *St Petersburg Times* or *Where St Petersburg*.

The Marine Canal and Grand Cascade

As you arrive by hydrofoil, the Great Palace rises like a golden curtain at the far end of the **Marine Canal** (Morskoy kanal), which flows through Peterhof's Lower Park and once formed an approach route for yachts. The granite-banked canal is flanked by 22 marble basins spurting water, whose splashing noises mingle with the whir of videos and the oom-pah of a brass band dressed in Petrine-era costumes. Follow the canal southwards from the hydrofoil jetty and you'll come to the **Voronikhin Colonnades**, named after the architect who designed this pair of Neoclassical pavilions that flank the enormous circular basin below the Grand Cascade.

Peterhof's grounds are open daily 9am–9pm; $4. Tickets are sold near the jetty and at the park gates beside the Benois Wing.

The **Grand Cascade** (Bolshoy kaskad) is the pride of Peterhof, with water cascading over the blue-and-yellow ceramic steps and 142 jets spurting from 64 sources, including gilded **statues** and bas-reliefs. In the circular basin at the bottom, the glittering muscular figure of Samson rending the jaws of a ferocious lion symbolizes Russia's victory over Sweden in the Northern War: the lion is the heraldic beast of Sweden and the decisive battle of Poltava occurred on St Samson's Day (June 27) in 1709.

It's worth buying a ticket to visit the split-level **Grotto** beneath the Cascade. The uppermost grotto is lined with tufa rocks and was used for informal parties, while in the lower grotto jets of water are triggered to squirt anyone tempted by the fruit on the table. The giant pipes that feed the fountains were originally made of wood and were maintained by a special "Fountain Corps" of men and boys – the latter being employed to crawl through the pipes to repair them.

Tickets for the Grotto are sold from the window facing the upper terrace; $3.

The **fountains** at Peterhof only operate during the summer, with **ceremonies** marking the opening and closing of the "fountain season" (normally on the first Sunday in June and the first Sunday in October), featuring music in the park, outdoor ballet performances and evening fireworks. On weekdays, the fountains are turned off at 5pm.

The Great Palace

The Great Palace is open Tues–Sun 11am–5pm, closed last Tues of the month; $8.

The yellow, white and gold **Great Palace** (Bolshoy dvorets) above the Cascade is far removed from that originally designed for Peter by Le Blond in 1714–21. Peter's daughter, Empress Elizabeth, employed Bartolomeo Rastrelli to add a third storey and two wings terminating in pavilions with gilded cupolas, while much of the interior was later redesigned by Vallin de la Mothe and Yuri Felten, with further alterations made in the mid-nineteenth century. Yet there's a superb cohesion at work, a tribute both to the vision of the palace's original creators and to the skills of the experts who rebuilt Peterhof after World War II.

The palace is entered from the terrace above the Cascade. Tour groups are admitted according to a signposted rota, but individuals are supposedly allowed to enter at any time. **Tickets** for tours of the rooms are sold inside; foreigners buy them at a desk beyond the *tapochki* lobby, where you are issued with your felt overshoes. At the time of writing, the set **itinerary** through the palace leads from the "public" state rooms into the Imperial Suite, as if you were a courtier granted intimate access to the monarch. Though this is likely to continue to be the case, your own route might differ slightly from the one described below, as newly restored rooms are opened to the public.

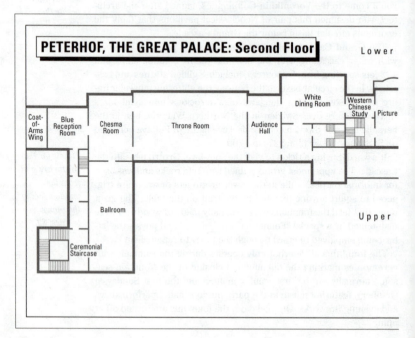

PETERHOF, THE GREAT PALACE: Second Floor

Lower

Coat-of-Arms Wing — Blue Reception Room — Chesma Room — Throne Room — Audience Hall — White Dining Room — Western Chinese Study — Picture

Ballroom

Ceremonial Staircase

Upper

The State Rooms

Visitors ascend to the **state rooms** via Rastrelli's **Ceremonial Staircase**, just as ambassadors and courtiers did in Tsarist times. Aglow with gilded statues and vases, beneath a ceiling fresco of Aurora and Genius chasing away the night, it rivals the Jordan Staircase in the Winter Palace for sheer splendour. Once upstairs, you pass through an exhibition on the restoration of Peterhof before reaching the silk-papered **Blue Reception Room**, where the Imperial secretary once vetted visitors to the rooms beyond.

The **Chesma Room** takes its name from the Russian naval victory against the Turks at Chesma Bay in 1770, scenes from which decorate the walls. When Count Alexei Orlov, commander of the Russian squadron, saw Philippe Hackert's preliminary sketches, he criticized the depiction of a ship exploding in flames as unrealistic and arranged for a frigate to be blown up before the artist's eyes, as a model. Off to the right, you can gaze into the recently reopened **Ballroom**, glittering with mirrors and encrusted with gilded candelabras – Empress Elizabeth nicknamed it the Kuptsi (merchant's) Hall because "they love gold", and had her favourite architect, Rastrelli, create a similar hall in the Catherine Palace at Tsarskoe Selo (see p.353). From here, you proceed into the **Throne Room**, the largest hall at Peterhof, once used for gala receptions and balls. Designed by Felten, its white-and-turquoise mouldings are offset by

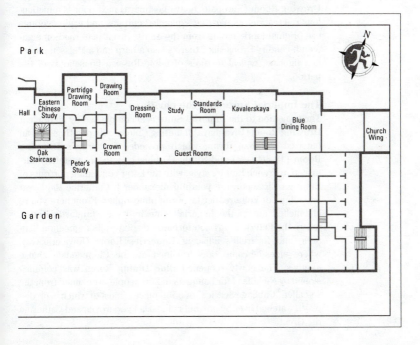

scarlet curtains, crystal chandeliers and a magnificent parquet floor. Amidst all this opulence, the throne at the far end is an almost humble addendum, overlooked by a portrait of Catherine the Great in the green uniform of the Preobrazhenskiy Guards.

Ladies-in-waiting once primped and preened in the mirrored **Audience Hall** (Audientszal) next door, where gilded cherubs and garlands festoon every frame and cornice. Beyond lies the **White Dining Room** (Belaya stolovaya), its dazzling stucco work garnished with touches of green; the long table is set with the 196-piece Catherine Dinner Service, made in Staffordshire, England, for the empress.

Next comes the **Western Chinese Study**, one of a pair of rooms designed by de la Mothe in the 1760s, when chinoiserie was all the rage. Sumptously decorated in red, green and gold lacquer, it contains a suitably Oriental tea service. From here, you pass into the **Picture Hall** (Kartinny zal) at the centre of the palace, overlooking the park and gardens. Also dubbed the "Room of Fashion and Graces", its walls are lined with 368 portraits of eight young court ladies wearing national costumes.

The **Eastern Chinese Study** (Vostochniy Kitayskiy kabinet) originally looked quite different, its walls and furniture covered in white satin rather than the existing lacquer work (notice how the parquet clashes with the pseudo-Ming stove). Conversely, the **Partridge Drawing Room** (Kuropatochnaya gostinaya) next door is a meticulous re-creation: its partridge-spangled curtains and wall coverings use original fabric dating from the 1840s (itself patterned on eighteenth-century Lyons silk); there's also a harp and a Meissen porcelain figurine, typical features of noble Russian households of the period.

The Imperial Suite and the pavilions
The transition to the **Imperial Suite** is accomplished by an opulent **Drawing Room** (Divannaya) flaunting Chinese silk paintings and an outsized Ottoman divan, which precedes Catherine's **Dressing Room** (Tualetnaya) and **Study** (Kabinet). Both are tastefully furnished in French Empire style, with the latter containing portraits of Empress Elizabeth, the youthful Alexander I, Catherine the Great and a bust of Voltaire, her favourite philosopher. From here you're channelled out of the Imperial Suite into the **Standards Room**, where the Peterhof garrison formerly displayed its regimental banners, and Rastrelli's adjacent **Equerries Room** (Kavalerskaya), where aides-de-camp once reclined on the Chippendale chaise longues. The newly reopened **Blue Dining Room** was commissioned by Nicholas I for banquets of 250 people, who dined from the so-called "Cabbage Service" of 5550 pieces (most of which is on display), watched over by portraits of Maria Fyodorovna and Catherine the Great.

With the palace's east wing still under restoration, the tour then does a U-turn, returning to the Imperial Suite via a series of **guest rooms**. Recreated using Felten's original drawings as a guide, the bedchamber is a joyous mismatch of gilded swags and chinoiserie wallpaper, with the bed ensconced in a curtained alcove. Its soubriquet, the **Crown Room**, derived from Paul I's habit of mounting his crown on a stand in the middle of the room, as if to derive reassurance from the sight.

The last room visited is one of the oldest – and newest – in the palace. Designed by Le Blond at Peterhof's inception, the oak-panelled **Study of Peter the Great** reflects the tsar's enthusiasms, carved with nautical, military and festive motifs. Only eight panels survived the war, the rest being modern reproductions which took up to eighteen months' work apiece to complete. At the top of the **Oak Staircase**, by which visitors leave the Imperial Suite, hang Peter's "Rules for Guests", forbidding them to arrive without invitation, abuse other guests or take their bedding. Nobody could stay without a card showing the number of their bed in the palace; sleeping in any other bed was prohibited. Visitors who broke the rules either faced a drubbing from the tsar or his jester, Washo (who was entitled to buffet anyone, however illustrious), or were forced to drain the "Great Eagle Cup" (see "Monplaisir", p.338).

For more on Peter's partying habits, see p.97.

Leaving the building, it's worth stepping back to admire the gorgeous **pavilions** at the end of each wing, a crowning touch by Rastrelli. Each is named after the finial atop its gilded coronet (as are the wings): the **Coat-of-Arms Wing** is magnificently surmounted by the double-headed eagle of the Romanovs, while an Orthodox cross glitters above the **Church Wing**.

Monplaisir and the Catherine Wing

Peter the Great's favourite haunt, **Monplaisir** (French for "my pleasure"), is the major attraction at Peterhof after the Great Palace. Situated beside the Gulf of Finland, with a distant view of St Petersburg, it is both homely and extravagant, its modest facade hiding a roisterous past. If you come on Wednesday, when Monplaisir is closed, the adjacent **Catherine Wing** affords some consolation. Both are on the edge of the Lower Park, an easy walk from the Great Palace, past the Roman Fountains (see p.340).

Monplaisir

Designed by the tsar himself (with the assistance of several architects), the low, brick **Monplaisir** palace reflects the influence of Holland, where Peter learned shipbuilding in 1697. Even after the Great Palace was finished, he lived and entertained at Monplaisir whenever possible. Here, too, he interrogated his son Alexei before confining him to the Peter and Paul Fortress on suspicion of treason. The main wing, on the seafront, is discreetly shuttered, and visitors

Monplaisir is open June–Sept 10.30am–5pm; closed Wed & last Thurs of the month; $6.

have to buy **tickets** and then enter around the back of the eastern side, from where **tours** commence every ten minutes.

Starting with Peter's **art collection** (the first in Russia), you progress through the **Eastern Gallery**, with its sixteen glazed doors, into the extraordinary **Lacquered Study**. A feast of black, gold and red, its 94 lacquered panels were originally created by icon-painters who spent months studying Chinese techniques but couldn't resist imparting a Russian flavour to their work. The originals were chopped up and used as firewood by the Nazis, and what you see today was re-created from the evidence of three surviving panels.

In the **State Hall** beyond, the ceiling fresco depicting Apollo sur-rounded by figures from the *commedia dell'arte* must have swum before the eyes of those guests forced to drink from the dreaded Great Eagle Cup, holding 1.25 litres of fortified wine, which had to be drained in one gulp by anyone who broke Peter's rules. Envoys who passed out were roused next day and either issued with axes and ordered to join him in a bout of tree felling or taken for a bracing sail on the Gulf. Peter's wife, Catherine I, entered into the spirit of things by cooking meals in the Dutch-tiled **Pantry**, and inviting guests to help themselves to *zakuski* in the **Buffet**.

On the other side of the State Hall is Peter's small **Naval Study**, with its tile-inlaid wainscotting and inspirational view of the Gulf. Their **Bedroom** is equally small and homely, and Peter's nightcap can be seen on the bedside table on the far side of the four-poster. The tour concludes in the **Western Gallery**, decorated with an alle-gorical fresco and seascapes (including one of Zaandam, where Peter lived with a Dutch blacksmith while working at the local shipyards).

Thirty years after Peter's death, Monplaisir was home to the future Empress Catherine the Great during her marriage to Tsar Peter III. When he took a mistress, Countess Vorontsova, Catherine started an affair with Stanislaw Poniatowski (later to become the last king of Poland) and soon the Imperial couple were living apart: Peter's preferred residence was at Oranienbaum and Catherine chose to live in a pavilion called the Tea House, beside Monplaisir. There, on July 28, 1762, she learned from Alexei Orlov that the coup against her husband was under way and hastened to Petersburg to rally her supporters. By nightfall she had become Empress of All the Russias.

The Catherine Wing

The adjacent **Catherine Wing** (Yekaterininskiy Korpus) was added to Monplaisir by Empress Elizabeth in the 1740s to accommodate court balls and masquerades. Catherine the Great apparently felt no sentimental attachment to the nearby Tea House, for it was knocked down when Quarenghi remodelled the wing for her in the 1780s. Its simple Baroque exterior defers to Monplaisir's, while the interior is plush but not overly opulent.

The Catherine Wing is open May–Sept 10.30am–5pm, closed Thurs & last Fri of the month; Oct–April Sat & Sun 10.30am–5pm; $3.

Tours usually begin in the **Blue Drawing Room** (occasionally from the Green Drawing Room), which dates from the same period as Alexander I's **Study**. The latter is ornamented with knick-knacks relating to the 1812 Napoleonic invasion and a portrait of Alexander's murdered father, Paul. Next you enter Alexander's **Bedroom**, which contains a magnificent "boat" bed with fantastic candelabras mounted on the headboard; some ivory piquet cards belonging to Catherine the Great are preserved in a case by the far wall. Next door is the **Heating Room** – easily mistaken for a kitchen – where plates were kept warm during banquets. The blue-and-gold dinner service comes from Ropsha, where Catherine's husband, Peter III, was murdered. Proceeding through the **Green Drawing Room**, full of walnut furniture, and the stuccoed, mirrored **Blue Hall**, you enter the glittering **Yellow Hall**, its table set for a banquet of 45 guests. The red-and-gold Guryev Service comprises several thousand pieces and was made in St Petersburg early last century. Portraits of Alexander I and Catherine the Great are usually accompanied by a giant tapestry depicting Peter the Great at the helm of a storm-wracked dinghy, his companions cowering astern (the picture is based on a real event), but the tapestry is currently away on tour.

The terrace, garden and bathhouse

Monplaisir backs onto a seafront **terrace** from where Peter liked to watch naval manoeuvres. Between the Catherine Wing and Monplaisir lies a **garden**, centred on the **Wheatsheaf Fountain**, whose 25 jets of water resemble heads of grain. A composition designed by Peter himself flanks the Wheatsheaf Fountain on four sides, consisting of gilded fountain-statues of Psyche, Apollo, Bacchus and a faun with a kid – collectively dubbed "the Bells". He also commissioned a **joke fountain** that squirts anybody who treads on a certain part of its gravel plot – always good for a laugh. The building nearby is the **Bathhouse Wing** (Baniy Korpus) of Monplaisir, built for Catherine I.

The Upper Garden and the Lower Park

Having visited the Great Palace and Monplaisir, you'll have seen something of Peterhof's grounds and will probably have been tempted to stray by the **fountains** (*fontany*) glimpsed down every path. There are five in the formal Upper Garden – behind the Great Palace – and dozens in the wooded Lower Park. While the Upper Garden rates a brisk circumambulation, the Lower Park deserves a longer ramble, though most of its best fountains are either clustered between the Chessboard Hill Cascade and Monplaisir, or ennoble the approaches to the Marly Palace. Providing you keep this in mind, it doesn't matter which of the many routes you take – the account below is one of many possibilities.

While comparing site plans with what's on the ground can be a little confusing, it's hard to get lost for long, since there are so many obvious landmarks. Treat the signposts with suspicion, however, as many point in entirely the wrong direction: the Marine Canal and the east–west avenue leading to the Marly Palace are surer aids to orientation.

The Upper Garden and Peter and Paul Cathedral

Framed by borders and hedges, the ornamental ponds of the expansive **Upper Garden** (Verkhniy sad) commence with the so-called **Square Ponds** near the Great Palace, sporting marble statues of Venus and Apollo. Next comes the **Oak Fountain**, a complete misnomer for a statue of Cupid donning a tragic mask in a circular pool ringed by allegorical figures. The garden's focal point is the **Neptune Fountain**, made in Nuremberg in 1650–58 to mark the end of the Thirty Years' War. The fountain turned out to require too much water to operate and spent years in storage until it was snapped up by Tsarevich Paul for 30,000 rubles in 1782. Stolen by the Nazis, it was tracked down in Germany and reinstalled in 1956. Lastly there's the **Mezheumny**, whose strange name (meaning "a bit of this, a bit of that") alludes to the many alterations it's undergone over the years, resulting in a plump dragon and four dolphins; an alternative translation, however, has it meaning "neither here nor there", and refers to its location.

Beyond Peterhof's Upper Garden, on the far side of Sankt-Peterburgskiy prospekt, is the five-domed **Peter and Paul Cathedral** (sobor Petra i Pavla), though it's nothing like its namesake in St Petersburg, resembling instead a medieval Russian church and embodying the Slavophilism of the 1890s. Turned into a cinema after the Revolution and only returned to the Orthodox Church in the 1990s, its interior has now been refurbished, and the acoustics remain superb.

The Lower Park

Stretching down to the sea from the palace, the 102-hectare **Lower Park** (Nizhniy park) is laid out with symmetrical avenues linking the lesser palaces and fountains, the latter fed by water from the Ropsha Hills, 22km away. In total, Peterhof's **hydraulic system** has 50km of pipes, 22 locks and 18 lakes, discharging 100,000 cubic metres of water every day during summer. In the winter, the fountains are turned off and the statues encased in insulated boxes, to prevent them from cracking in the subzero temperatures.

East of the Grand Cascade's Samson statue stands the **Triton Fountain**, which honours the Russian naval victory over Sweden at Hangö, while further along the path is a piazza dominated by two **Roman Fountains**, resembling giant cake stands. The **Chessboard Hill Cascade** (Shakhmatnaya gorka) to the south boasts three dragons from which water spouts down a chequered chute flanked by statues of Greek and Roman deities. Between the Roman Fountains and Monplaisir are several more **joke fountains** (*shutikhi*), still primed to soak but too leaky to surprise anyone. The **Umbrella Fountain** starts raining when you sit underneath it, as does the **Spruce Fountain**, which resembles trees. To the east of the Umbrella is the **Pyramid Fountain**, whose 505 jets rise in seven tiers to form an apex.

Heading west towards the Marly Palace you'll first encounter the **Adam Fountain**, with Adam gazing soulfully over the rooftops of two Greco-Chinese pavilions, followed by the **Eve Fountain** – Eve with apple and figleaf in hand – beyond the Marine Canal. From there you can detour northwards to the Hermitage or press on past the **Lion Cascade** (resembling a Greek temple) to the Marly Palace. The southern side of the park is flanked by the **Triton Bells Fountain**, named after the fish-tailed Triton boys who hold cups full of sculpted bells amidst clouds of spray. These precede the **Menazherny Fountains**, which use less water than their powerful jets suggest – their name derives from the French word *ménager*, meaning "to economize". Beyond rises the **Golden Hill Cascade** (Zolotaya gorka), a flight of waterfalls issuing from gilded orifices. Like the Chessboard Hill Cascade, it is flanked by allegorical statues and offers a ravishing view of the park.

The Hermitage and Marly Palace

En route between Monplaisir and the Marly Palace visitors can make a detour to the **Hermitage** (Ermitazh), near the shore, a moated, two-storey pavilion with round-headed windows and Corinthian pilasters gracing its orange-coloured facade. Designed for Peter the Great, but only completed after his death, it was intended for dining *sans* servants: guests ate upstairs, with a lovely view of Peterhof and the Gulf, and ordered dishes by placing notes on the table, which was lowered by pulleys to the kitchen below and then returned laden with delicacies. In 1797, the pulley chair by which guests were hoisted upstairs was replaced by a flight of stairs after a cable snapped, stranding Tsar Paul between floors. The upstairs **Dining Room** is hung with paintings, while the **Buffet** downstairs displays Japanese and Chinese porcelain and Russian crystalware.

The Hermitage is currently closed for repairs.

Built around the same time as Monplaisir, the **Marly Palace** takes its name and inspiration from the hunting lodge of the French kings at Marly le Rois, which Peter the Great visited during his Grand Tour of Europe. More of a country house than a palace, it is entered from around the back, where Catherine the Great once fed her goldfish from a platform overlooking four ponds. **Tickets** for the Marly must be bought at the wooden hut nearby and visits are by guided tour only, lasting about fifteen minutes.

The Dutch-tiled **Kitchen** connects directly with the **Buffet**, so that dishes arrived hot at the table – an innovation that Peter was especially proud of. As usual, the four-poster in his **Bedroom** is far too

The Marly Palace is open May–Sept 10am–4pm, closed Tues & last Wed of the month; Oct–April Sat & Sun 10am–4pm; $3.

short – Peter was 2.3 metres tall – and there's a small den where he drew plans and fiddled with instruments. Upstairs are guest rooms exhibiting Petrine memorabilia and a **Dining Room** with a superb view of the avenues converging on the palace.

The Benois Wing and Court Stables

The Benois Wing is open May–Sept Tues–Sun 10.30am–5pm, closed last Tues of the month; Oct–April Sat & Sun 10.30am–4pm; free.

The Benois family's connection with Tsarist Russia dates back to 1794, when Louis Benois arrived from France to work as a chef for Paul I. He married a Russian woman and had eighteen children (seventeen of whom died when they were very young). Their only surviving son Nikolai was "adopted" by Empress Maria Fyodorovna. He then trained as an architect and fathered six children, all of whom became artists or architects. Nowadays their former summer home, the **Benois Wing** (Korpus Benua), just to the east of the Great Palace, proudly exhibits evidence of their talents, with displays ranging from architectural plans to surrealist paintings. Surprisingly, there are also cinema posters and photographs of the British actor **Peter Ustinov** – a grandson of Leonty Benois, who designed the annexe of the Russian Museum – and a number of architectural sketches by Ustinov's son Igor, who lives in Paris. There may also be other, **temporary exhibitions**, for which a small entrance charge is levied.

To the east of the Benois Wing, en route to the Alexandria Park, you can't miss the **Court Stables** (Pridvornye konyushni), a sprawling complex modelled on Hampton Court in England. The stables were designed by Nikolai Benois, and the building now houses a sanatorium, which is, sadly, partly derelict.

The Alexandria Park

Landscaped in a naturalistic English style by Adam Menelaws, the **Alexandria Park** surrounds the Cottage Palace of Nicholas I and Alexandra Fyodorovna (after whom the park is named). Finding Peterhof's Great Palace "unbearable", she pressed Nicholas to build a home suited to a cosier, bourgeois lifestyle, where they lived *en famille* with few servants and no protocol, but heavily guarded. The Cottage Palace (see below) is definitely worth the fifteen-minute walk through the overgrown park (no ticket required). As the gates from Peterhof's Lower Park are locked, you must enter via the road alongside the small amusement park and Court Stables (see above); keep your ticket if you intend to return to the main buildings at Peterhof. Just inside the park is a spiky neo-Gothic **Alexander Nevsky Church**, which was used by the court as a private chapel.

The **Farm Palace** (Fermerskiy dvorets), further east beyond the church, is past saving, but remains picturesquely derelict. Built as a combined stables, stud farm and hothouse, it appealed to Nicholas and Alexandra's son, Alexander II, a keen weekend farmer. The path carries on to a whimsical **Ruined Bridge** beside a gully that once fed the park's lake. Having scrambled down and up the other side, you'll see the Cottage Palace straight ahead.

The Cottage Palace

Sited on a bluff overlooking the Alexandria Park, the **Cottage Palace** (dvorets Kottedzh) is a two-storeyed gingerbread house that's rarely visited by foreigners; you'll have to join a Russian group for a guided tour, or you can phone ahead and book a tour in English.

Designed in 1826–29 by Adam Menelaws in the pseudo-Gothic style then fashionable, the **interior** is notable for its richly carved jambs and moulded tracery ceilings. As you enter the lobby, notice the stone covered with Arabic script, above the inner door: a trophy from the fortress of Varna in Bulgaria, captured during the Russo-Turkish War of 1828–29. The **Tsaritsa's Study** has a stained-glass screen and a sensuous frieze around the window bay, while the adjacent **Grand Drawing Room** (Bolshaya gostinaya) boasts a starburst ceiling as intricate as lace, and a clock modelled on the facade of Rouen Cathedral. In the burgundy-coloured **Library** (Biblioteka) are a mother-of-pearl and ivory model of a castle near Potsdam and a screen decorated with German knights – reminders that Empress Alexandra was born Charlotte, princess of Prussia, while Nicholas had a German mother. From the **Grand Reception Room**, you pass into a **Dining Room** (Stolovaya) bisected by Gothic pillars and flanked by pew-like chairs. Its long table is set with Alexandra's dinner service of 314 porcelain and 353 crystal pieces, specially commissioned for the cottage.

The **Staircase** is a triumph of *trompe l'oeil* by G.B. Scotti, who painted Gothic arches, vaults and windows all over the stairwell in subtle tones of grey and blue. On the floor above are the **family rooms**, modestly sized and decorated by Tsarist standards. First comes the suite of rooms belonging to Crown Prince Alexander, comprising a bathroom (Vannaya), classroom (Uchebnaya komnata) and a valet's room. In the tsar's **Dressing Room** scenes from the Russo-Turkish War hang alongside a marble-topped washstand and a screened-off shower. Next door is the **Tsar's Study**, followed by the **Blue Room** (Golubaya gostinaya), which belonged to Nicholas's daughter, Maria Nikolayevna. The room is furnished with Sèvres and Meissen porcelain and also contains a clock with 66 faces, one for each province of Russia (including "Russian America", as Alaska was known until 1867).

Entering the next room you skip a generation, for after Alexander II's assassination, the crown passed to his son, Alexander III, whose wife, Maria Fyodorovna, made this her **Drawing Room**. A sad tale lies behind the **Nursery** (Detskaya), beyond. Prepared decades earlier during Maria Nikolayevna's pregnancy, it was sealed up after she died in childbirth, its fabulous Doll's Tea Service left there for the baby that died with her.

The Cottage Palace is open May–Sept 10.30am–5pm, closed Fri & last Tues of the month; Oct–April Sat & Sun 10.30am–4pm; $5. Tours in English can be booked on ☎ 420 00 73.

Peterhof

Before leaving, nip upstairs to Nicholas I's **Naval Study**, a garret with a balcony overlooking the Gulf, from where he observed exercises off Kronstadt through a spyglass and gave orders to the fleet by telegraph or speaking trumpet.

Oranienbaum (Lomonosov)

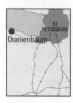

For more on Menshikov, see p.179.

Prince Menshikov began work at **Oranienbaum** in 1713, shortly after his master, Peter the Great, started Peterhof, 12km to the east. Typically, the ostentatious Menshikov set out to build a palace which would surpass even Peterhof, planting orange trees in the lower park ("Oranienbaum" is German for "orange tree") – the ultimate in conspicuous consumption, given the local climate. The building of Oranienbaum bankrupted Menshikov and in 1728 the whole estate passed into the hands of the Crown, whereupon it was used as a naval hospital until Empress Elizabeth gave it to her nephew, the future Tsar Peter III and husband of Catherine the Great.

Catherine hated life at Oranienbaum – "I felt totally isolated, cried all day and spat blood," she wrote in her memoirs. Conversely, Peter

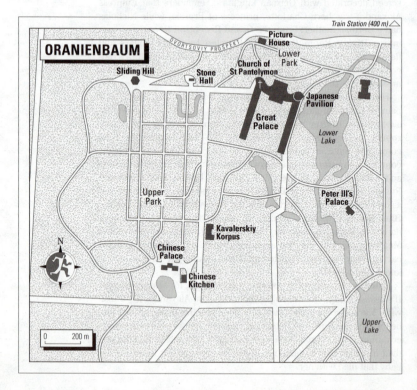

had a wonderful time, putting his valets through military exercises or spending hours playing with lead soldiers on the dining tables. He was also fond of inflicting his violin-playing on those around him, although, according to Catherine, "He did not know a single note . . . for him the beauty of the music lay in the force and violence with which he played it."

Unlike the other Imperial palaces around St Petersburg, Oranienbaum never fell into the hands of the Germans, although it suffered constant bombardment as a tiny enclave held by the Russians throughout the Blockade. After the war, both town and palace were renamed **Lomonosov**, after the famous Russian polymath who founded a glass factory in the area. Although Oranienbaum's palaces are quite bare and ruined compared to those at Peterhof and Tsarskoe Selo, the site is peaceful and uncrowded and the parks are lovely, with meadows full of wild flowers. It's hoped to establish an annual festival here (every July or August), called the **"Golden Orange"** and featuring the latest period-costume films by Russian directors, plus a fashion show. Call ☎ 423 16 13 for information.

Practicalities

The easiest way of getting to Oranienbaum is by **minibus #T-348** or suburban **train** from St Petersburg's Baltic Station (see map on p.244); both run every 15–20 minutes, but you don't need to queue for a ticket for the minibus, and the journey is quicker. Moreover, many of the train stations en route don't have signs on the platforms, so passengers seated at the rear of the train won't be able to see such few signs as there are at Oranienbaum – the station is four stops after Noviy Petergof, immediately after you first glimpse the Gulf of Finland, and serves as the terminal for minibuses.

To reach the palace grounds from the station, cut across the small park towards the grey-domed Church of Archangel Michael; the entrance to the Lower Park is just across the road beyond the church. There are several **snack stands** near the station, and a **market** near the church sells fresh produce. Within the palace grounds there's an old-fashioned Soviet-style **café** in the Kavalerskiy Korpus near the Chinese Palace, which also has **rooms** with one to four beds (☎ 423 16 32; ②), and a **sauna** for guests, should you want to stay the night.

Tickets, orientation and opening hours

Since all Oranienbaum's palaces are out of sight of one another, and signposts are few and far between, you'll need to use the plan on p.344 for **orientation**. With just four buildings open to the public, it's possible to see everything comfortably in a day, including the grounds. There's no entrance charge for the grounds themselves, but visitors need separate tickets for each building (sold individually from each building's *kassa*). The grounds are open all year (daily 7am–7pm), but as none of the buildings at Oranienbaum is heated they open only from May to October. All have the same **opening hours** (Mon 11am–4pm, Wed–Sun 11am–5pm; closed Tues and last Mon of the month).

The Lower Park and palaces

Oranienbaum

Entrance to the Great Palace is $1; guided tours in Russian can be arranged by calling ☎423 16 27.

To reach the **Great Palace** (Bolshoy dvorets), enter the **Lower Park** (Nizhniy park) through the gates on Dvortsoviy prospekt and bear right past the Lower Lake. Built in 1713 by the architect Schnadel, Menshikov's rival to the Great Palace at Peterhof perches on a lofty terrace which could once be approached from the sea via a canal. Its concave central block is upstaged by the massive domed **pavilions** at either end; the one on the western end previously contained the Church of St Pantelymon; the one on the eastern end is the so-called Japanese Pavilion. Menshikov was arrested for treason in 1727 and subsequently exiled to Siberia; the following year the crown took possession of the estate, but not before Menshikov's bitter enemies, the Golitsyns, had stripped the colossal palace of its valuables.

Boats can be rented on the Lower Lake.

Today the palace is in a sorry state and more impressive for its sheer size and presence than its interiors: rooms that hosted royalty in the nineteenth century now lie bare and devoid of glamour under damp-stained ceilings. The melancholy array of **portraits** of Oranienbaum's owners includes Peter III, who abdicated here under duress shortly before he was murdered at Ropsha. The latest casualty is the **Japanese Pavilion**, which took its name from the shelves of Japanese ceramic figures that it used to house, but is now in danger of collapse. The military still occupy the lengthy side wings of the Great Palace, hidden behind high wooden fences. Near the bottom of the Lower Park stands Peter III's **Picture House**, once home to Peter's art collection and venue of the first operas to be staged in St Petersburg.

Peter III's Palace

Admission to the palace is $3. The apartments can be visited on a guided tour (in Russian only).

Peter III's Palace (dvorets Petra III), situated in the southeast corner of the Lower Park, was originally surrounded by barracks, fortifications and a moat, though all that remains of them now is a decrepit ceremonial archway. The palace itself is a modest two-storey structure built by Rinaldi for Peter before his marriage to Catherine, which accounts for the small size of Peter's bachelor apartments on the upper floor. One of the few memorable rooms is the **Picture Hall** (Kartinniy zal), covered in a patchwork of 58 paintings by eighteenth-century European masters. Chinese elements are also present, most notably in the silk hangings, lacquer paintings and dress cabinets. Scenes of life in Peter's military encampment appear on the stucco-work ceiling of his **Boudoir**. On a more personal note, evidence of Peter's diminutive physique can be seen in his uniform **dress coat**, which looks the right size for a twelve-year-old.

The Upper Park

Beyond the Great Palace lies the **Upper Park** (Verkhniy park), whose intricate network of minor paths is now lost in undergrowth, although the basic grid remains. It was Catherine's favourite part of

Peter III

Peter III inherited his love of military affairs from his father, the duke of Holstein. Happiest in the company of men, Peter couldn't cope with assertive, aristocratic women – least of all his wife, the future Catherine the Great – and the marriage wasn't consummated for several years. "When he left the room the dullest book was a delight," she recalled in her memoirs. In the first few months of his reign, Peter managed to offend the Russian clergy by his continued adherence to Lutheranism and the military by introducing Prussian uniforms and spending more time with his Holstein bodyguards than with the Imperial Guards. It became common knowledge at court that he was planning to send Catherine to a nunnery and enthrone his mistress, Countess Elizabeth Vorontsova.

In June 1762, just seven months into Peter's reign, Catherine launched a pre-emptive **coup**, marching on Oranienbaum with her lover, Grigori Orlov, and twenty thousand Imperial Guards. Peter rushed to Peterhof and tried to escape to Kronstadt, but the garrison there had already defected and he was forced to return to Oranienbaum, where, in the words of his idol, Frederick the Great, he abdicated "like a child who is sent to bed". Stripped of his Prussian uniform, Peter fainted from shock and was carted off to the palace at Ropsha, where he soon met his death. The announcement on July 7, 1762 blamed "a terrible colic", though his demise was universally ascribed to the Orlov brothers, who reputedly strangled him after he refused to drink poisoned wine.

the estate and is still by far the loveliest stretch of the park to wander through, with canals, bridges and ponds scattered about the mixed woodland of firs, limes, oaks and silver birch. After Peter's death, Catherine commissioned Rinaldi to build the two finest buildings at Oranienbaum here: the Sliding Hill and the Chinese Palace. En route from the Great Palace to the Sliding Hill you'll pass the **Stone Hall**, from where Catherine the Great, dressed as Minerva, would sally forth in a chariot for costume balls.

The Sliding Hill

From the Stone Hall, it's a short stroll west along the northern border of the Upper Park to the **Sliding Hill** (Katalnaya gorka). Painted ice-blue and white, and looking like an oversized slice of wedding cake, this three-storey pleasure pavilion is all that remains of a fantastic **rollercoaster** that once stretched for just over half-a-kilometre along Upper Park. The rollercoaster was flanked on both sides by raised drives on which guests could race their horses. In winter, sledges were used; in summer, wheeled carts, offering a unique sensation of height and speed in a flat landscape, where nothing else moved faster than a horse could gallop. Such constructions were very popular in eighteenth-century Russia and were a regular feature in public fairgrounds, later spreading to Europe and America and giving rise to the mechanized versions seen today.

To get a better idea of how it once looked, buy a ticket from the *kassa* and climb the staircase to the second floor, where a scaled-

The Sliding Hill is only open in the summer; $1.

down model of the original rollercoaster is on display. The top-floor rooms are largely devoid of furniture and the central domed hall's main point of interest now is its artificial marble floor. Off the hall is the **Porcelain Room** (Farforoviy kabinet), its gilded stucco work sprouting animalistic sconces which provide niches for some outrageously kitsch Meissen pottery, depicting "Chinese" and mythological scenes symbolizing Russia's victory over Turkey. The **White Room** (Beliy kabinet) – actually duck-egg blue and white – was Rinaldi's first venture into Neoclassicism after working in the Rococo style for many years. From its windows you can see Kronstadt Island: the Sliding Hill's curators claim they can foretell the weather from the visibility of Kronstadt's Naval Cathedral.

The Chinese Palace

The Chinese Palace is only open in summer; $6.

From the Sliding Hill or Stone Hall, any of the paths or avenues leading south will take you to the **Chinese Palace** (Kitayskiy dvorets). Catherine liked to call it "Her Majesty's private *dacha*", though she spent only 48 days here in the course of her 34-year reign. Unlike the Chinese follies at Peterhof, Rinaldi's palace shows only a few traces of the Orient. The weathered exterior is a quietly understated Baroque, while the luxurious yet intimate **interior** is decorated in a more fanciful Rococo style, with pink, blue and green *faux marbre*, ceiling frescoes by Venetian painters and particularly ornate parquet floors. The decor is completely European until the **Buglework Room** (Steklyarusniy kabinet) with its touch of Oriental exotica – the walls depict peacocks, pheasants and other birds fashioned from beads produced at the Lomonosov factory.

Only in the last two rooms of the west wing do Chinese elements begin to emerge more clearly. Despite the proximity of Russia to the East, "Chinese Rococo" reached St Petersburg via Europe, where it had become a passion in the mid-eighteenth century. The first signs are in the **Small Chinese Room** (Maliy Kitayskiy kabinet), though even here they are confined to the wallpaper and a handful of Oriental vases. The **Large Chinese Room** (Bolshoy Kitayskiy kabinet) shows no such restraint: its walls are covered with Chinese landscapes of wood and walrus-ivory marquetry work, large Chinese lanterns hang in two of its corners, and a fresco of the union of Europe and Asia (bizarrely represented as a European bride surrounded by Asiatic warriors and mandarins) adorns the ceiling. The wonderfully carved full-sized billiard table was made in England.

East of the pond outside the palace lies a small pavilion known as the **Chinese Kitchen**. Like the Chinese Palace itself, the pavilion conceals a smattering of chinoiserie behind its Baroque exterior.

Tsarskoe Selo (Pushkin)

Of all the Imperial palaces, none is more evocative of both the heyday and twilight years of the Romanovs than those at **Tsarskoe Selo** (Royal Village), 25km south of St Petersburg. This small town flanks

Practicalities

There's no point in coming on Tuesday (or the last Mon of the month), when the Catherine and Alexander palaces and the Lycée are closed, as are several of the museums (which are also closed on either Mon or Wed). Any day from Thursday to Sunday is fine unless you're planning to combine Tsarskoe Selo with a visit to Pavlovsk, whose palace is closed on Friday.

Tsarskoe Selo is accessible by minibus #T-18 from Moskovskaya ploshchad (every 15–20min; 45min), or suburban train from Vitebsk Station (every 20–30min; 30min). (In the station, look out for a replica Tsarist-era steam train, off the concourse, and the ex-Imperial Waiting Room in the main building, decorated with scenes of Tsarskoe Selo before the Revolution.)

Alighting at the town's station (still named Detskoe Selo), you can catch several buses to the palace grounds from across the forecourt: #370 or #378 drops you three stops later at the end of Oranzhereynaya ulitsa; #382 stops on Leontyevskaya ulitsa, slightly nearer the palace; while #371 follows a longer route via the Egyptian Gates, terminating near the Church of the Sign. If you're traveling on to Pavlovsk, it's easier to catch a #370 bus from Oranzhereynaya ulitsa, which goes directly to Pavlovsk Palace, rather than going by train.

Orientation and tickets

Starting at the Catherine Palace, it's easy to orientate yourself in relation to everything else. It takes several hours to do justice to the Catherine Park and Palace, and you should plan on spending the whole day here if you want to visit the Lycée and the Alexander Palace as well. If you're intending to combine Tsarskoe Selo with Pavlovsk, there won't be time to see more than the main palaces at each and something of the grounds.

During the summer, you need to buy an admission ticket for the Catherine Park as well as a ticket for the palace once you're inside the grounds. No tickets are required for the Alexander Park; tickets for the palace are sold on the spot.

Eating and accommodation

Right opposite the Lycée, the *Café Tsarskoe Selo* (11am–midnight; closed Tues) sells pizzas and hamburgers, while a smarter café on the first floor of the Catherine Palace's southern wing (noon–8pm) has soup, pies, pastries, ice cream and beer. For a full meal, the *Tsarskoe Selo* restaurant (noon–11pm) at the train station is marginally better than the overpriced and lacklustre *Admiralty* in the tower by the Great Pond, though it's surprising that the town doesn't run to anything better.

While few visitors bother **staying overnight**, simple two- or three-bed rooms are available in the *Baza Otdykha*, in a side wing of the Catherine Palace (☎470 56 75; ①). Facilities are fairly basic and the staff aren't accustomed to foreign tourists, but the location and low prices are unbeatable. Alternatively, you can book a room in the *Kochubey Dacha* (☎465 21 55; ③) on the south side of the park, which has en-suite rooms and guarded parking.

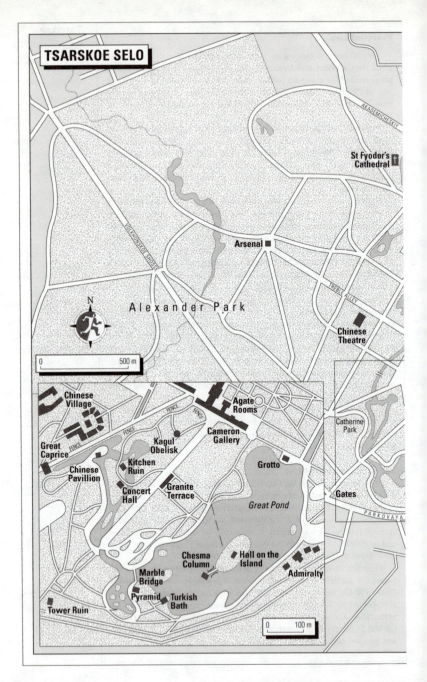

TSARSKOE SELO

St Fyodor's Cathedral

Arsenal

Alexander Park

Chinese Theatre

N

0 ——— 500 m

Chinese Village

Agate Rooms

Great Caprice

Kagul Obelisk

Cameron Gallery

Chinese Pavillion

Kitchen Ruin

Grotto

Concert Hall

Granite Terrace

Great Pond

Catherine Park

Gates

Chesma Column

Hall on the Island

Marble Bridge

Admiralty

Pyramid

Turkish Bath

Tower Ruin

0 ——— 100 m

AKADEMICHESKIY

TREBLE ALLEY

PARKOVAYA

VOLCHANSKOE SHOS.

FENCE

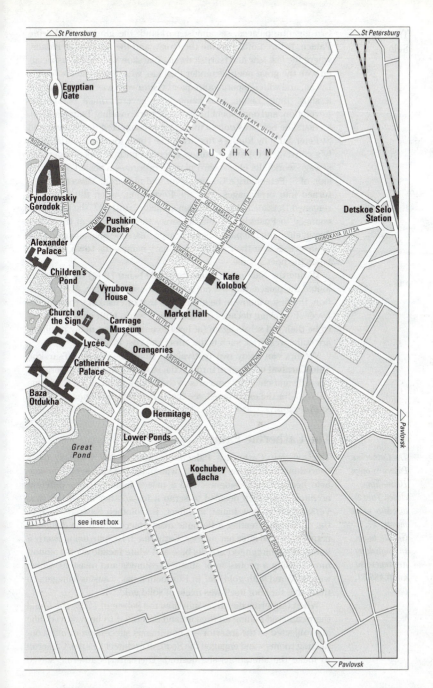

two gigantic palaces, set amidst parkland: the glorious **Catherine Palace**, beloved of Catherine the Great, and the **Alexander Palace**, where the last tsar and tsaritsa dwelt. Tsarskoe Selo is also associated with the great poet Alexander Pushkin, who studied at the town's **Lycée**; and with Rasputin, a frequent visitor who was buried here for a short time. Lenin, too, came here several times before the Revolution, and once spent hours in the park, evading Tsarist agents.

Tsarskoe Selo was once a model town connected to Pavlovsk and St Petersburg by Russia's first train line (built for the Imperial family's convenience), and featuring electric lighting, piped water and sewage works. Its chessboard plan incorporates a scaled-down version of St Petersburg's Gostiniy dvor and numerous villas that were turned into orphanages after the Revolution, when the town was renamed Detskoe Selo – "Children's Village". In 1937, the name was changed to **Pushkin**, to commemorate the centenary of the poet's death; although the palace is now called Tsarskoe Selo again and the main streets bear their pre-revolutionary names, the **town** itself still bears the poet's name.

During the **Nazi occupation** (Sept 1941–Jan 1944) the Germans looted the palaces and left not a single house habitable. After liberation, the first window to be glazed was that of Pushkin's room in the Lycée. Following decades of **restoration** work, both palaces appear to be their old selves again (at least externally), but many pavilions are still unrestored, such is the effort and cost involved.

Visitors can enjoy two **festivals** in June: the one-day **Tsarskoe Selo Carnival** procession through the streets of town, and a series of operatic and chamber **concerts** in the throne room of the Catherine Palace – for the exact dates, see the *St Petersburg Times* or *Where St Petersburg*.

The Catherine Palace

The Catherine Palace is open 10am–5pm; closed Tues & last Mon of the month; $7. Guided tours in English by arrangement on ☎ 465 53 08.

The existing **Catherine Palace** (Yekaterininskiy dvorets) owes everything to Empress Elizabeth, who made the village of Tsarskoe Selo her summer residence, had a palace built by three different architects and then decided to scrap it for another one, fit to rival Versailles. Her new Italian architect, Bartolomeo Rastrelli, rose to the challenge, creating a Baroque masterpiece which the delighted empress named after her mother, Catherine I. Despite being nearly a kilometre in circumference, its blue-and-white **facade** avoids monotony by using a profusion of atlantes, columns and pilasters, which were covered with gold leaf in Elizabeth's day, causing villagers to think that the roof itself was made of solid gold.

When Catherine the Great inherited the palace in 1762, she found the weathered gilding an eyesore and ordered it to be removed. She also objected to the **interior** – a continuous succession of interconnecting rooms – and engaged the Scottish architect Charles Cameron to make the alterations she desired. Thereafter, Catherine stayed every summer, living quite informally unless diplomatic protocol required otherwise.

After Catherine's death, her son Paul spurned Tsarskoe Selo and appropriated many items for his own palaces at Pavlovsk and Gatchina. Although the palace gained a new lease of life under her grandson, Alexander I, who celebrated Russia's victory over Napoleon by employing Viktor Stasov to redesign several rooms (and repair fire damage after 1820), subsequent monarchs preferred Peterhof's Cottage Palace or the Alexander Palace as summer residences.

Intended to be approached from the northwest, the palace's grandest sweep faces the Alexander Park across a vast courtyard sporting ornamental gates. Nowadays, visitors see the opposite side first, while the full glory of its 306-metre-long facade is only apparent if you step back a little way. The **state rooms** are on the upper floor. You have to enter with a group but it's easy to break away once inside. Bear in mind that with rooms constantly opening or closing as restoration continues, your itinerary may differ from the one outlined below.

Visitors ascend by the **State Staircase**, installed in the 1860s, with its elegantly balustraded double flights of steps; notice the ornate barometer and thermometer, inset on either side. At the top of the stairs are two marble reclining cupids; the one on the east side, which is lit by the rising sun, is rubbing his eyes as he awakes; the one on the west, where the sun sets, is asleep.

The southern wing

While restoration continues, only two state rooms in the **southern wing** are open, both of them devised by Rastrelli for Elizabeth. First, however, you enter two small unrestored rooms with models and engravings of the palace at various stages, including photographs of its ruined state after the war. Next is Rastrelli's **Great Hall** (Bolshoy zal), which was used for balls. Elizabeth liked costume balls, where she dressed as a Dutch sailor or a Chevalier Guard; the only costumes forbidden were those of a harlequin or a pilgrim (respectively deemed to be indecent and profane). The hall is 48m long and fabulously ornate, glittering with mirrors and windows, its walls encrusted with gilded cherubs and garlands. Across the vast ceiling, a fresco entitled *The Triumph of Russia* glorifies the nation's achievements in war, the arts and sciences.

On the other side of the Great Hall, but closed to the public, are three great antechambers where those waiting to be received by Catherine cooled their heels (which one they waited in depended on their rank). These are currently being restored, though so far only the paintings on the ceilings are nearing completion, while the walls are still bare brick. **Catherine's private apartments**, which lie beyond, are just empty shells. Designed by Cameron, these included a Lyons Hall swathed in yellow silk; Arabian and Chinese halls; a Silver Room; and a bedroom with porcelain walls and violet pilasters.

You return to the staircase via the white-and-gold **Kavalerskaya Dining Room**, which was used by Elizabeth's gentlemen-in-waiting.

Into the northern wing

The doorway on the far side of the staircase leads into the **State Dining Room**, whose discreet parquet and opulent mouldings find an echo in the next two salons, the **Green** and **Raspberry Pilaster Rooms**, named after their gilt-edged pilasters. These are followed by a **Portrait Hall**, in which hangs a rather good painting of Catherine I. Next stop is the famous **Amber Room** (Yantarnaya komnata), which is expected to be fully restored by the summer of 2001, after thirty years of labour by Russian artists. The priceless amber panels of the original chamber were stolen by the Nazis and have yet to be recovered, although a small mosaic portion turned up in Bremen in 1997 and a furniture restorer in Leipzig admitted to working on an amber commode during the Communist era. The original panels were a gift

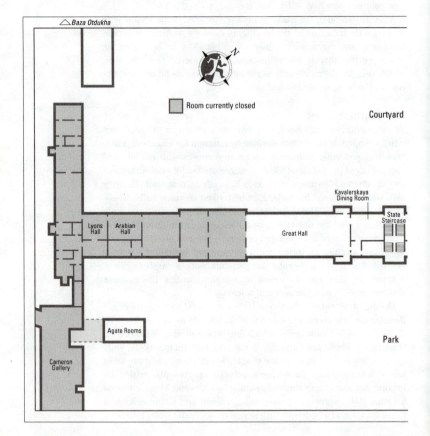

from Frederick I of Prussia to Peter the Great, and mounted in the room by Rastrelli in 1775. As they weren't quite large enough, he used mirrored insets and trompe l'oeil to complete the decor.

From here you enter a **Picture Hall** (Kartinniy zal). Of the 130 canvases displayed here before the war, 114 were saved. Mostly Flemish, French and Italian works of the seventeenth and eighteenth centuries, they're offset by two huge tiled wall-stoves and a parquet floor inlaid with pink and black palm wood. Next you pass through the **Small White Dining Room** into **Alexander I's Drawing Room** (Gostinaya Aleksandra I), with its collection of small portraits of those who ruled before Catherine the Great, and large portraits of Catherine and her favourite grandson, Alexander I.

The Cameron Rooms and the Chapel

Through the **Buffet** you enter the **Green Dining Room** (Zelionaya stolovaya), the first of a suite of salons created in the 1780s by

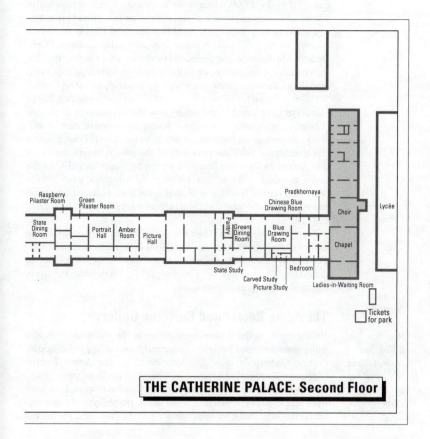

THE CATHERINE PALACE: Second Floor

Cameron, on Catherine's orders, for her son Paul and his wife Maria
Fyodorovna. You immediately sense Cameron's love of Classical
motifs, though it was Ivan Martos who actually sculpted the figures,
garlands and cameos. The following suite of rooms is sometimes
closed, due to staff shortages.

On the other side of the **Waiters' Room** (Ofitsiantskaya), which
contains a selection of Romantic landscapes, is the fine **Blue
Drawing Room** (Golubaya gostinaya), with its magnificent painted
ceiling, floral-patterned silk wallpaper, blue-crystal floor lamps and
turquoise inlays. From there, you'll pass into the **Chinese Blue
Drawing Room**, an intimate salon papered in silk hand-painted with
Chinese landscapes. Both the silk and Cameron's fireplace are reproductions, based on surviving fragments of the originals, while the
decor is supplemented by a painting by Johann Groot of Elizabeth as
Flora, goddess of flowers.

In olden days before entering the chapel, the court would have
gathered in the **Predkhornaya**, or anteroom, which is papered in
golden silk interwoven with pheasants and swans. From here a narrow stairway descends to the royal blue-and-gold **Chapel** (currently
closed), whose gilded onion domes rise above the palace rooftops.
Designed by Rastrelli and renovated by Stasov after the fire of 1820,
the chapel suffered further when the Nazis stole its ceiling fresco and
mouldings, as well as 96 icons, which are gradually being replicated.

Passing through the simply decorated **Ladies-in-waiting Room**
(Kameryungferskaya) you emerge into the magnificent **Bedroom**
(Opochivalnya), with its slender columns and sense of elegant intimacy. Returning via the **Picture Study** to the **Green Dining Room**
you then move down the park side of the palace, stopping to look
into Alexander I's **State Study**, designed by Stasov in 1817. As the
tsar's personal effects (left undisturbed after his death) were
destroyed during World War II, they have been replaced by period
pieces, such as the vase that depicts him entering Paris with his army
in 1814.

From here you cross a rather shabby back staircase to enter a suite
of unrestored rooms housing exhibitions of furniture and paintings.
The last five rooms as you return to the main staircase contain an
exhibition, "The Orient at Tsarskoe Selo", comprising furniture,
objets d'art, carpets and weaponry.

*The Agate
Rooms are
open
May–Sept Mon
& Wed–Sun
11am–4.30pm;
Nov–April Sat
& Sun
11am–4pm;
$2.50.*

The Agate Rooms and Cameron Gallery

Jutting out from the southeastern corner of the Catherine Palace, a
whitewashed cloister leads to a nondescript two-storey building concealing Cameron's most fabulous creation: the **Agate Rooms**
(Agatovye Komnaty). Designed as a summer pavilion, these chambers flaunted all the mineral wealth of the Russian Empire, fashioned
from agate, jasper, malachite, lapis lazuli, porphyry and alabaster.
Catherine often held intimate dinner parties here, and the rooms

connected directly to her private apartments on the upper floor of the palace. There's nothing left of the original bathhouse on the lower level, whose rooms now display **temporary exhibitions**. On the upper level, the **Agate Room** proper sports a magnificent parquet floor from the palace that Catherine was building for her last lover, Lanskoy, before his untimely death. The **Great Hall** beyond features malachite columns and a bronze coffered ceiling, and was originally lit by candelabras held by four marble maidens. A door leads directly to Catherine's private **Hanging Garden**, on a level with her private apartments and the upper storey of the Cameron Gallery.

The **Cameron Gallery** is a perfect Neoclassical foil to the Baroque palace. Cameron reputedly doffed his hat to Rastrelli's Catherine Palace every time he passed it on the way to work, and continuously modified his own design of the gallery to harmonize with Rastrelli's creation. Among the antique statues installed beneath the arcades was a bust of Charles James Fox, arch enemy of British Prime Minister Pitt the Younger, whom the empress despised.

The Catherine Park

The 566-hectare **Catherine Park** (Yekaterininskiy park) is characterized by three styles of landscape gardening: French, English and Italian. Directly behind the Catherine Palace, the original nucleus of the park – commissioned by Elizabeth – was laid out geometrically, with pavilions and statues at the intersections. Sadly, you can't see inside the **Upper Bath**, which was reserved for royalty, or the **Lower Bath**, used by the courtiers. Nor can you enter the derelict **Hermitage** pavilion, whose Baroque facade echoes that of the Catherine Palace at the opposite end of the avenue. Between the baths and the **Fish Canal** (which once supplied food for banquets) are marble statues of **Adam** and **Eve**, similar to those at Peterhof.

The park is open daily 6am–11pm; winter free, summer $2

Chamber music concerts are held in summer outside the Upper Bath.

Around the Great Pond

One of the more alluring sights in the park is the **Great Pond**, the focal point of the romantic "English Park" below the Cameron Gallery. Here, the court floated on gilded boats, watching regattas of gondolas and sampans, or pyrotechnic battles between miniature warships. Its designer, John Bush, exploited the hilly terrain to create ravishing perspectives which Catherine's architects embellished with pavilions and follies. The island in the middle of the lake is accessible by a ferry ($3.50) pulled by an underwater cable, which enables you to visit the **Hall on the Island**, where musicians once played, and the **Chesma Column**, honouring the Russian naval victory at Chesma Bay and modelled on the Rostral Columns in St Petersburg.

A clockwise circuit of the pond takes about thirty minutes, starting with the so-called **Grotto**, a domed pavilion once decorated inside with 250,000 shells. Further on, you can wander off to the **Lower**

Ponds and the marble **Column of Morea** (commemorating Russian victories in Greece in 1770), or head straight for the **Admiralty** – two Dutch-style boathouses flanking a tower (now a café). Further along are a former **Turkish Bath**, resembling an Ottoman mosque, the stone **Pyramid** where Catherine buried her favourite dogs, and Cameron's **Marble Bridge**, a copy of the Palladian bridge at Wilton House in England.

Towards the Chinese Village

West of the Great Pond lies the "**Italian Park**", whose canals and hillocks are interlaced with paths meandering from one folly to another. Catherine liked to stroll here with her dogs, unaccompanied by courtiers; in *The Captain's Daughter*, Pushkin relates how the heroine of the tale, Maria Ivanovna, unknowingly encountered the empress and interceded for her betrothed. Even more fancifully, Catherine is supposed to have once told a sentry to stand watch over a violet that she wanted to pick, but then forgot about it. As the order was never revoked, a guard was posted on the spot for decades afterwards.

A zigzag trail taking in the park's highlights starts either at the **Granite Terrace** above the Great Pond, or the **Kagul Obelisk** beyond the Cameron Gallery. On an island further south are a small **Concert Hall** and **Kitchen Ruin**, the latter designed to look picturesque rather than for cooking purposes. On another islet, visible from the bridge, stands a **Chinese Pavilion** flying metal flags. Also known as the "Creaking Pavilion" because it was designed to creak whenever someone entered, it is now derelict and closed.

From the Great Caprice head north and cross one of the pagoda-arched Chinese Bridges to reach the Alexander Park (see p.360).

Heading west, you'll soon spot the colourful **Chinese Village** (Kitayskaya derevnya), a series of Oriental pavilions in an overgrown corner of the park – though you can't reach them unless you climb over the fence beside the main avenue. Originally a whimsical folly, the village was turned by Catherine into a home for serfs who had run away from their oppressive masters. Ravaged during World War II, the pavilions have now been restored and turned into luxury apartments for nouveaux riches; the income is being used to repay the restoration costs. Their upturned roofs are as gaudy as circus tents, and crowned with dragons. From here, a path continues on to the **Great Caprice**, a massive humpback arch topped by a pagoda.

Around the Lycée

Across Sadovaya ulitsa from the Catherine Palace stands the famous Imperial **Lycée** where **Alexander Pushkin** once studied. Established to provide a modern education for the sons of distinguished families, it proved more attractive to the poorer nobility than to great aristocrats, who refused to send their children away to boarding school. The 12-year-old Pushkin was a member of the first class presented to Alexander I at the inauguration ceremony on October 19, 1811.

During his six years at the Lycée, he grew bold and lyrical, drank punch and wrote poetry, culminating in a bravura recital of his precocious *Recollections of Tsarskoe Selo* in the assembly hall, on June 9, 1817.

Guided tours show you around the classrooms, music room and the physics laboratory – all equipped as in Pushkin's day. Upstairs in the dormitories, the cubbyhole labelled *No. 14. Alexander Pushkin* is reverentially preserved. If you understand Russian, you'll hear much about the influence of his favourite teacher, Kunitsyn (to whom he dedicated several poems), and his crafty valet, Sazanov, who secretly committed several murders and robberies in the two years that he was employed by Pushkin.

Most visitors then head for the **statue of Pushkin** daydreaming on a bench, created in 1900 by Robert Bach – it's just beyond the **Church of the Sign** (tserkov Znameniya) of 1734, the oldest building in Tsarskoe Selo. Back on Sadovaya ulitsa, a sign points you into a courtyard containing the royal stables, now a **Carriage Museum**, while further along are the **Orangeries**, a vast complex now used by the Horticultural Faculty of St Petersburg University.

Lastly, look out for the former **house of Anna Vyrubova** (not open to the public), on the corner of Tserkovaya and Srednaya ulitsa just north of the Church of the Sign. Alexandra's closest friend, Vyrubova introduced her to Rasputin and was rumoured to participate in his orgies. After the February Revolution she tried to clear her name by submitting to a medical examination and was found to be a virgin; she later emigrated and wrote a book entitled *Memories of the Russian Court*.

The Alexander Palace

Heading north past the Church of the Sign, you'll soon reach the **Alexander Palace** (Aleksandrovskiy dvorets), a Palladian pile that's regarded as Quarenghi's masterpiece. Commissioned by Catherine the Great for her grandson, the future Alexander I, it later became the summer home of a succession of Imperial heirs, each of whom left their mark on the building. It is especially associated with the last tsar and tsaritsa, Nicholas II and Alexandra, who made it their principal residence until the end of the monarchy, whereupon it became a museum of the Romanov dynasty.

The sympathetic impression this museum made on visitors irked the Bolsheviks, however, who sold off much of the contents in the late 1920s – although it remained a museum until the outbreak of war, when the Nazis looted the palace and turned it into an SS hospital. After the war, the government decided not to reopen the museum and gave the palace to the navy as a training college. However, one wing has been partly restored and was opened to the public in 1997, with the support of the Alexander Palace Association of Russian and foreign admirers, whose official Web site (*www.alexanderpalace.org*) is a mine of information.

Tsarskoe Selo

The Lycée is open Mon & Wed–Sun 10.30am–5.30 pm by guided tour in Russian only; $1.

The Carriage Museum is open summer Mon & Thurs–Sun 11am–5pm; winter Sat & Sun 11am–5pm; $2.50

The Alexander Palace is open Mon & Wed–Sun 10am–4.30pm; $4.

Though few of the palace's half-dozen rooms can compare with the Catherine Palace for magnificence, they have a poignancy that other Imperial residences lack, due to the almost tangible presence of Nicholas, Alexandra and their children, some of whose **personal effects** are on display. Particularly moving are the uniforms that Tsarevich Alexei and his sisters wore in their capacity as honorary colonels of various regiments, and the fanciful headgear and harness of Alexei's pet donkey, accompanied by photos of him playing. The finest chambers are Nicholas's **New Study**, with its Art Nouveau columns, friezes and billiard table, and the **Reception Room**, with its oak ceiling, wainscotting and huge, hooded fireplace. It's possible that some of the **state rooms** currently occupied by the navy will be opened to visitors in the future, such as the Semi-Circular Hall, from which the family left the palace for the last time on August 1, 1917, or the so-called Mountain Hall, with its enormous wooden slide, used by generations of Romanov children.

The Alexander Park and around

West of the Alexander Palace spreads the extensive **Alexander Park** (Aleksandrovskiy park), altogether wilder than the Catherine Park, with dank thickets, rickety bridges and algae-choked ponds. Although you don't need a ticket to enter, access is limited to a handful of gates, including one in the vicinity of the Alexander Palace. Among the park's features are a Chinese Theatre, a Dragon Bridge, and a wooded hillock, romantically dubbed Mount Parnuss. It's worth heading northwards to find the amazing **Fyodorovskiy Gorodok**, built in neo-Russian style as a barracks for the tsar's bodyguard on the 300th anniversary of the Romanov dynasty in 1913. Walled and turreted like a medieval Kremlin, with fairytale carvings around its portals, various parts of the building have been taken over by diverse organizations, including the local church administration and the Cossack Society.

Just to the west, above the trees, rise the dull bronze domes of **St Fyodor's Cathedral**, where Empress Alexandra often prayed in the crypt, lamenting the murder of Rasputin. **Rasputin's grave** was originally situated near the village of Alexandrovskaya, further west, but on the night of Tsar Nicholas's abdication the body was exhumed by soldiers, who stole the icon that the tsaritsa had placed in the coffin and burned the corpse to ashes (thus fulfilling one of Rasputin's own prophecies). The ashes were eventually reburied at Pargolovo, to the north of St Petersburg, and the icon sold to an American collector.

Alternatively, from the Alexander Palace you can bear right along Kuzminskaya ulitsa to reach the **Pushkin dacha**, a charming period residence where the poet and his wife spent the summer of 1831.

The Pushkin dacha is open Wed–Sun 10am–4.30pm; $1. To arrange a guided tour (in Russian only), call ☎ 476 69 90.

Pavlovsk

In 1777, in an unusually affectionate gesture, Catherine the Great gave 607 hectares of land along the River Slavyanka to her son, the future Tsar Paul, to reward him for the birth of a grandson who would continue the dynasty. The area – virgin forest used by the tsars for hunting – was named **Pavlovsk**, after Paul (*Pavel* in Russian), though the style of the Great Palace here is more a reflection of the tastes of his second wife, the German-born Maria Fyodorovna, who outlived her husband by 28 years and made numerous modifications after his death.

The Great Palace aside, Pavlovsk has nothing to compare with the numerous fine buildings to be seen at Peterhof or Tsarskoe Selo. Instead, it's the beauty of **Pavlovsk Park**, one of the largest landscaped parks in the world, which has drawn crowds for a century. With the completion of Russia's first railway line, from St Petersburg to Pavlovsk, the place quickly became one of the most popular daytrips from the capital. Tolstoy was a frequent visitor, though as he confessed in his diary, he hated himself for it: "Went to Pavlovsk. Disgusting. Girls, silly music, girls, mechanical nightingale, girls, heat, cigarette smoke, girls, vodka, cheese, screams and shouts, girls, girls, girls!"

Pavlovsk's beauty was obliterated during the Nazi occupation, during which fifteen thousand locals were deported to labour camps in Germany and three years of vandalism concluded with a final orgy of destruction. Although Soviet bomb-disposal experts defused the high-explosive devices left in the charred shell of the palace, its dome and roof had already been ruined, seventy thousand trees felled, and bridges and pavilions dynamited. It was five years before the park was reopened to the public and over a decade before any of the palace rooms could be visited.

The enormity of Pavlovsk's **restoration** is conveyed by the fact that over forty thousand fragments of plaster had to be salvaged and pieced together merely to recreate the sumptuous mouldings inside its central dome. All in all, the whole task of restoration took 26 years, an epic undertaking described in the book *Pavlovsk: The Life of a Russian Palace*, whose author, Suzanne Massie, has "adopted" Pavlovsk and established a foundation to support further restoration efforts now that state funding has dried up. One result of her efforts has been the creation of an official Pavlovsk **Web site** (*www.pavlovskart.spb.ru*); you'll also find further information on this and other Imperial palaces at *www.alexanderpalace.org*.

The Great Palace

The **Great Palace** (Bolshoy dvorets) has come a long way since its rather modest central building was erected in 1782–86 by Charles

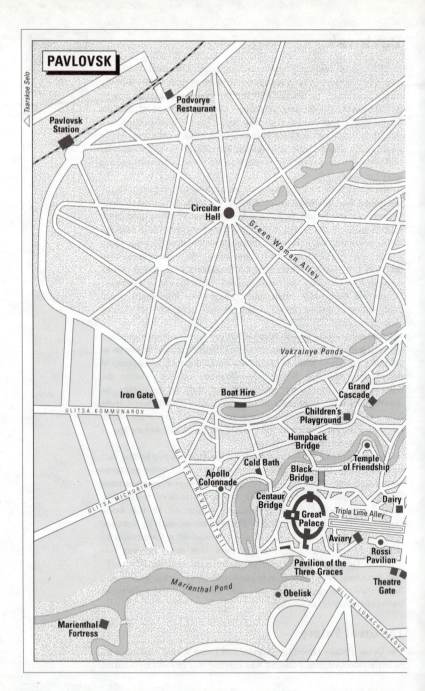

PAVLOVSK

Tsarskoe Selo

Podvorye
Restaurant

Pavlovsk
Station

Circular
Hall

Green Woman Alley

Vokzalnye Ponds

Iron Gate

ULITSA KOMMUNAROV

Boat Hire

Grand
Cascade

Children's
Playground

Humpback
Bridge

Cold Bath

ULITSA REVOLYUTSII

ULITSA MICHURINA

Apollo
Colonnade

Black
Bridge

Temple
of Friendship

Centaur
Bridge

Great
Palace

Dairy

Triple Lime Alley

Aviary

Rossi
Pavilion

Pavilion of the
Three Graces

Theatre
Gate

Marienthal Pond

Obelisk

ULITSA LUNACHARSKOVO

Marienthal
Fortress

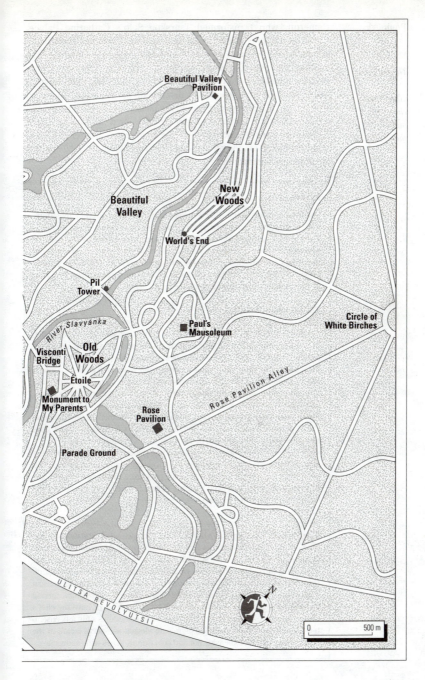

Beautiful Valley
Pavilion

Beautiful
Valley

New
Woods

World's End

Pil
Tower

River Slavyanka

Paul's
Mausoleum

Circle of
White Birches

Visconti
Bridge

Old
Woods

Étoile

Monument to
My Parents

Rose Pavilion Alley

Rose
Pavilion

Parade Ground

ULITSA REVOLYUTSII

0   500 m

Pavlovsk

The palace is open 10am–5pm, closed Fri & last Mon of the month; $6.50.

Cameron, who transformed Tsarskoe Selo's Catherine Palace. Cameron was one of the few architects to win Catherine the Great's lasting admiration, and she therefore foisted his talents upon her son as well. Pretty soon, however, Cameron's Palladian fixation and concern for minutiae began to clash with Paul's and Maria Fyodorovna's tastes, and he was eventually dismissed, his assistant, Vincenzo Brenna, being employed to extend the palace into a much larger and more elaborate complex. Some of the best architects in St Petersburg were recruited to decorate its interior – Quarenghi, Rossi and Voronikhin among others – and the overall Neoclassical effect is surprisingly homogenous.

Practicalities

Pavlovsk is 30km south of St Petersburg, a 35-minute journey by **suburban train** (departures every 20–30min) from Vitebsk Station. Since Pavlovsk is only 5km south of Tsarskoe Selo, it's possible to visit both in succession if you choose the right day, but to do justice to either really requires a full day each. Whatever you decide, bear in mind the opening times for the Great Palaces at Pavlovsk (10am–5pm; closed Fri & first Mon of the month) and Tsarskoe Selo (see p.349).

Tickets and orientation

From outside Pavlovsk Station – one stop after Detskoe Selo – it's either a short ride on bus #370, #383 or #383a to right outside the Great Palace, or a twenty-minute walk southeast through the park. If you're planning on seeing Pavlovsk only, it's probably best to take the bus, view the Grand Palace first and then explore the grounds, and walk back to the station. If you're intending to combine Pavlovsk with Tsarskoe Selo, you could walk through the grounds to the Great Palace, then catch a bus on to Tsarskoe Selo (#370 will drop you at the end of Oranzhereynaya ulitsa, while bus #383 passes along Moskovskaya ulitsa, three blocks north of the Catherine Park). Alternatively, catch bus #473 from Pavlovsk Station, which goes along Parkovaya ulitsa, south of Tsarskoe Selo's Catherine Park.

With over 607 hectares of woodland to explore, it's easy enough to get lost in Pavlovsk Park, especially given the unreliable signposting. You need to buy an admission **ticket** for the park from the *kassa* opposite the train station; you'll also need separate tickets for the Great Palace and any of the pavilions which happen to be open.

Eating

If you want to eat cheaply, it's best to bring your own picnic and head off into the park. For more substantial fare, try *Podvorye* (daily noon–11pm; book ahead on ☎465 13 99 to be sure of a table), a fancy restaurant in the style of an *izba* (a traditional wooden peasant cottage), 200m from the station (turn left as you come off the platform), which serves traditional Russian food with a flourish and includes Prince Charles and President Chirac among its satisfied customers. You can eat well for under $15, or have the chef's choice (a bit of everything) for $25; there's also sometimes a fun folk ensemble playing. In the palace itself there's an elegant self-service café in the south wing, serving expensive hot and cold drinks, cakes and sandwiches.

Life at Pavlovsk was conducted according to the whims of Paul and Maria. While he drilled his troops all day, she painted and embroidered. Guests generally found the social life extraordinarily dull, consisting of interminable gatherings where only banalities were exchanged. The palace was intended to be approached from the east, from where you get the best overall view off the great sweep of Brenna's semicircular wings. At the centre of the courtyard is a **statue of Paul** dressed in the Prussian military uniform he loved so much. The *kassa* (ticket kiosk) is in the north wing; foreigners and tour groups enter the palace here, while Russians enter nearer the middle of the main building. Whichever side they enter from, visitors are issued with their *tapochki* and sent off on a tour of the state rooms, each of which contains a black-and-white photograph documenting its ruination during the war.

The State Rooms

Built during the era of the European Grand Tour and the first great archeological digs, the palace contains numerous motifs from antiquity, beginning with the **Egyptian Vestibule** (Yegipetskiy vestibyul) on the first floor, which is lined with pharaonic statues and zodiac medallions. From here, visitors are ushered upstairs to the second-floor **state rooms** via the main **staircase**, designed by Brenna and using martial motifs to pander to Paul's military pretensions. The northern parade of rooms reflect his martial obsessions, the southern ones the more domesticated tastes of Maria Fyodorovna. The striking thing about all the rooms, though, is their relatively human scale – you could just about imagine living here – unlike those of the Great Palaces of Peterhof and Tsarskoe Selo.

At the top of the stairs is the domed **Italian Hall** (Italyanskiy zal), which extends upwards into the palace's central cupola. The decor, intended by Cameron to evoke the atmosphere of a Roman bathhouse, is uniformly Neoclassical, with rich helpings of trompe l'oeil and stucco, and a fine collection of candelabras shaped like French horns. From here you pass through the small Valet's Room and Dressing Room into **Paul's Study**, hung with a portrait of Peter the Great and lined with busts of Roman emperors. At the far end is Paul's modestly proportioned **Hall of War** (Zal voyny), an explosion of gilded *objets de guerre*, in which even the candlesticks symbolize war spoils – although Paul himself never saw any military action. The bas-reliefs below the ceiling represent the Trojan Wars and *The Odyssey*.

The palace wing of the tsar is connected to that of the tsaritsa by Cameron's green-coloured **Grecian Hall** (Grecheskiy zal), designed to resemble the interior of a Greek temple. It's undoubtedly the most ornate room in the palace, featuring a set of exquisite jasper urns and series of wooden divans; the fireplaces were taken from the Engineers' Castle after Paul's death. Maria's suite of rooms begins

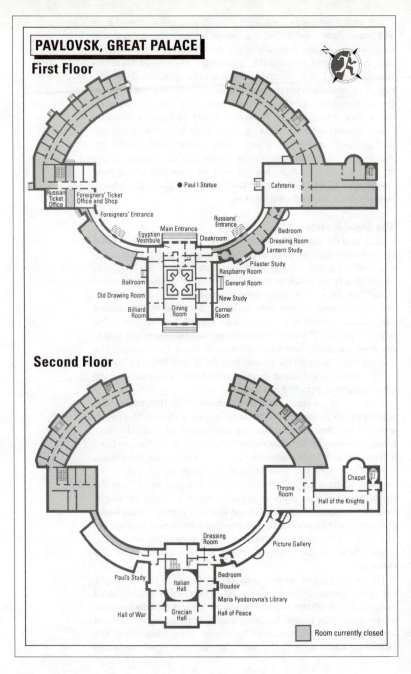

PAVLOVSK, GREAT PALACE

First Floor

Russian Ticket Office
Foreigners' Ticket Office and Shop
Foreigners' Entrance
Paul I Statue
Cafeteria
Egyptian Vestibule
Main Entrance
Russians' Entrance
Cloakroom
Bedroom
Dressing Room
Lantern Study
Pilaster Study
Raspberry Room
General Room
New Study
Corner Room
Ballroom
Old Drawing Room
Billiard Room
Dining Room

Second Floor

Throne Room
Hall of the Knights
Chapel
Dressing Room
Picture Gallery
Paul's Study
Italian Hall
Bedroom
Boudoir
Maria Fyodorovna's Library
Hall of War
Grecian Hall
Hall of Peace

Room currently closed

with the **Hall of Peace** (Zal mira), the perfect antidote to Paul's Hall of War, though no less gilt-laden, the symbols of war replaced instead by floral motifs, musical instruments and images of fecundity.

Maria Fyodorovna's Library is considered by many to be Voronikhin's masterpiece, not the least of whose treasures is the desk chair he designed for the tsaritsa, its back rest flanked by two fluted horns containing potted plants. The parquet flooring, inlaid with twelve different varieties of wood, is exceptional, while the bay study is surrounded by numerous books on botany, the tsaritsa's favourite hobby. Though you can't hear it in action, the table in her **Boudoir** plays melodies from Bach and Beethoven whenever its drawers are opened. In her **Bedroom**, two golden putti stand at the end of the canopied gilt bed and opposite is a glass cabinet containing the 64-piece toilette set given to the tsaritsa by Marie Antoinette, with whom she got on famously while in Paris. Neither the bed nor the toilette set was ever used, their function being merely to impress visitors. Next is Maria's **Dressing Room** (Tualetnaya), featuring an unusual steel dressing table with matching accessories, all studded with "steel diamonds".

Paul I

Given the eccentricities and shortcomings of the rest of the Romanovs, it's rather unfair that **Paul I** (1754–1801) should be the only one tagged "the mad tsar". Rumours of illegitimacy plagued him throughout his life, though his boorish temperament and obsession with all things military suggest that Peter III might have been his real father after all. However, his mother, Catherine the Great, had already taken Sergei Saltykov as a lover when she became pregnant, so people drew the obvious conclusion.

Paul saw very little of Catherine during **childhood**, and was just eight years old when his father was deposed with her consent. Although she immediately designated Paul as her legitimate successor, he never forgave her for his father's murder. A sickly child, Paul suffered from digestive problems, vomiting and diarrhoea, and in later life from insomnia, tantrums and paranoia. His first **marriage** was a disaster: his wife was seduced by his best friend and died in childbirth; but the second one proved happier, despite the fact that Maria Fyodorovna reputedly had an affair with her Scottish physician, Dr Wilson, who may have been the real father of Tsar Nicholas I.

After Catherine's death, Paul deliberately sought to destroy everything she had stood for, sacking those who had enjoyed her favour and elevating those whom she had disgraced. Besides those embittered by their fall, he also caused widespread resentment among the nobility by attempting to curtail their abuses of power. He abolished the 25 years' military service that oppressed the peasantry; planned to reform the country's corrupt financial institutions; and almost managed to secure Malta as a Russian naval base – to the alarm of England, whose ambassador subsequently played a hidden role in Paul's **assassination** (see p.99). After his death, Paul's worthy intentions were forgotten, and his faults and foibles emphasized – as he himself once remarked, "Anecdote pushes out History".

The southern wing

At this point, you leave the palace's original building and pass through a couple of tiny lobbies to enter the **southern wing**, whose rooms were designed by Brenna on a much grander scale. The **Picture Gallery** (Kartinnaya galereya) is a case in point: a long, curving hall with green ruched curtains, it was built to display the collection of seventeenth- and eighteenth-century paintings which Paul and his wife purchased on their grand shopping tour of Europe. Whilst not outstanding, the collection includes works by Angelica Kauffmann, Tiepolo, Salvatore Rosa and a small sketch by Rubens.

Beyond lies the Great Dining Hall, also known as the **Throne Room** (Tronniy zal), whose most arresting feature is a giant ceiling fresco, designed by the Russo-Italian set designer Pietro di Gottardo Gonzago, which struggles to achieve some sort of false perspective from the flat and rather low ceiling (the painting was in fact only executed during the postwar renovation, following the chance discovery of Gonzago's plans by Soviet restorers). The 606-piece Gold Dinner Service, made by the St Petersburg porcelain factory, is laid out on three large dining tables – otherwise the room is barely furnished. An orchestra used to play in the adjacent room on special occasions, which contains marble sculptures of two of Paul and Maria's daughters, who died during childhood.

After Napoleon seized Malta, the island's Chivalric Order of Knights fled to Russia, where they promptly deposed the current Grand Master and elected Paul in his place. Paul was a wise choice in terms of position and wealth, but as an Orthodox believer, his election wasn't recognized by the pope. Nevertheless, he built the lime-green **Hall of the Knights** (Kavalerskiy zal) to receive his charges. The hall contains lashings of lapis lazuli and a collection of Classical sculptures, but the only reference to the knights themselves is the small Maltese cross on the ceiling.

From here, you enter the **Imperial Chapel**, which is totally non-Orthodox in its design, with sculptural decoration and no icons. The paintings are copies of seventeenth- and eighteenth-century Western European works in the Hermitage. Paul's throne stands in the corner of the gallery.

Back through the Picture Gallery, you come to a staircase up to the **top floor**, which contains an interesting exhibition of furniture and interiors from the 1800s to the Revolution. Rooms typical of each period have been recreated to give a real sense of how people actually lived – unfortunately, this part of the palace is often closed due to staff shortages.

The private apartments

Returning down the staircase to the **first floor** of the north wing brings you to the tsar and tsaritsa's **private apartments**, designed on a more cosy scale than the state rooms, though no less ornate in their decor. First is the **Raspberry Room** (Malinoviy kabinet), so called for the colour of the upholstery and draperies, followed by the **General Room** (Obshchiy kabinet), where Paul and his family used to gather. Such gatherings were seldom happy for, as Chancellor Rostopchin observed, "Alexander hates his father, Konstantin fears him, the daughters, under their mother's influence, loathe him, and they all smile and would be glad to see him ground to powder."

Beyond lies Paul's formal **New Study** (Noviy kabinet), designed on simple, Neoclassical lines by Quarenghi and hung with a series of engraved copies of Raphael's frescoes for the papal chambers of the Vatican. Next comes the **Corner Room** (Uglovaya gostinaya), sporting lilac-tinted false marble walls and Karelian birch furniture. The room was designed by Carlo Rossi, who began his illustrious career here in 1803, redesigning fire-damaged rooms. The largest room on the first floor is the Cameron-designed **Dining Room** (Stolovaya), whose austerity was in keeping with Paul's liking for simple food – his favourite dish was cabbage.

Passing through the Billiard Room, whose table was destroyed during the war, you reach the **Old Drawing Room** (Staraya gostinaya). Its pale blue walls are adorned with tapestries given to Paul by Louis XVI following his visit to Paris, which originally hung in Paul's palace at Gatchina (see p.374). Altogether more satisfying, though, is the cheerful sky-blue and gold **Ballroom** (Tantsevalniy zal), restored to Cameron's original design after the war and dominated by two huge scenes of Rome by the French artist Hubert Robert. The procession of private apartments in the **southern wing** is currently being renovated.

Pavlovsk Park

The walk from the train station to the Great Palace gives only the briefest of glimpses of **Pavlovsk Park** (Pavlovskiy park), which stretches for several kilometres either side of the River Slavyanka. The park was laid out by the architects Cameron and Brenna, with help from the stage designer Gonzago; Voronikhin and Rossi also contributed, and some say that Capability Brown actually devised the original plan. Whatever the truth, the park's distinguishing feature is its naturalistic landscaping, with gently sloping hills, winding paths, a meandering river and hectares of wild forest – it's especially lovely in the autumn, due to its richly coloured and variegated foliage.

The park is open daily 9am–8pm; $2.

Most of Cameron's and Rossi's **architectural diversions** are concentrated in the more formal gardens around the palace and in the immediate vicinity of the river, which flows north through the middle of the park. You could cover a large number of these fairly comfortably in an afternoon; a more thorough exploration of the park would take the best part of a day. There are no hard-and-fast rules about which route you should take through the park; the following account is a guide to the highlights.

Pavlovsk

From the Private Garden to the Marienthal Fortress

Southwest of the Great Palace, separated from the rest of the park by a high iron railing, the tsar and tsaritsa's **Private Garden** was laid out by Cameron in a formal Dutch style, with flowerbeds that explode with colour in summertime. At the far end of the garden, by the main road, Cameron's Greek-style **Pavilion of the Three Graces** takes its name from the central statuary group representing Joy, Flowering and Brilliance. The only access to the Private Garden is through the palace itself, but it is rarely included in the guided tour.

On the other side of the main road, the upper section of the River Slavyanka forms the large **Marienthal Pond**, in an area once known as the "Russian Switzerland" (various other sections of the park were landscaped in emulation of France, Italy and England – a popular conceit of the time). Cameron's **Obelisk** on the southern shore of the pond commemorates the foundation of Pavlovsk in 1782, while at the far western end of the water stands the **Marienthal Fortress**, a toy Gothic castle built by Brenna in 1795 to flatter the new tsar's military pretensions.

North of the Slavyanka

From the terrace to the west of the Great Palace, you can view the wide sweep of the Slavyanka valley. High up on the opposite bank, Cameron's **Apollo Colonnade** was left a picturesque ruin after being struck by lightning and then damaged by a landslide during a storm in 1817. Down to the right, steps descend to the **Centaur Bridge**, guarded by four centaurs, which leads to a **Cold Bath** (Kholodnaya banya) that occasionally serves as a venue for small exhibitions. From here, there's a superb view uphill to the palace.

Several more bridges cross the Slavyanka downstream from the Cold Bath – including the **Humpback Bridge** and the **Black Bridge** – with a monumental staircase running down from the palace to meet them. Beyond, set in a sharp bend in the slow-moving river, lies the largest and most eye-catching of Cameron's pavilions, the circular **Temple of Friendship** (Khram Druzhby), the first building in Russia to use the Doric order. Commissioned as a diplomatic gesture in an effort to cement the shaky relationship between Maria Fyodorovna and Catherine the Great, it is studded with medallions illustrating the themes of platonic and romantic love.

On the plateau to the north of the Slavyanka valley, the **Vokzalnye Ponds** are a popular spot for a bit of lazy **boating**, with boats available for rent on the north side of the ponds. Their name derives from the train station (*vokzal*) that was once situated to the northeast of Rossi's **Iron Gate**, the official entrance to Pavlovsk.

Along the Triple Lime Valley

Immediately to the east of the palace, the **Triple Lime Alley** stretches for 300m through a more formal section of the park. The north side of the avenue is designed as a parterre, made up of two **Great**

Circles, with early eighteenth-century marble statues of Peace and Justice at their centres. To the south, Cameron built an **Aviary** (Voler), used for small receptions and meals, and now prettily strewn with vines. On the other side of the ornamental box-hedge maze stands a **Pavilion**, designed by Rossi but erected only on the eve of World War I, within which lurks a statue of Maria Fyodorovna. Finally, at the far end of the alley lies a common **grave** for the Soviet soldiers killed clearing Pavlovsk of mines.

Towards the Old and New Woods

Paul's favourite hobby was drilling his regiments in the **Parade Ground** laid out to the northeast of the Triple Lime Alley, which was later transformed into parkland. In his bid to Germanize and "civilize" Russia's upper classes, the police were ordered to scour the park, destroy all the traditional round Russian hats they could find and cut the lapels off coats and cloaks – as the English ambassador was mortified to discover.

North of the Parade Ground is the area known as the **Old Woods**, where a circle of twelve paths forms an *étoile*. At its centre stands Apollo, chief patron of the Muses, while the entrance to each path is marked by a bronze statue of a muse or mythological figure. The path leading west takes you to the **Monument to My Parents**, a pavilion erected by Maria Fyodorovna in memory of her father and mother, the duke and duchess of Württemburg, whose profiles appear on the marble pyramid within.

To the northeast of the *étoile* stands **Paul's Mausoleum**, built by Thomas de Thomon on the tsaritsa's instruction. Despite the difficulties of their marriage, she always took her husband's side in the intrigues of Catherine's last years, and the dedication – "To My Husband and Benefactor" – is probably sincere. Head a kilometre of so east from here to reach one of the most beautiful and isolated areas of the park, Gonzago's **Circle of White Birches**.

Paul is actually buried alongside the other Romanovs in the Peter and Paul Cathedral (p.194).

If you've got time to spare, longer walks are possible along the **Beautiful Valley** and the **New Woods**, to the north of Paul's mausoleum. A few scattered monuments serve as points of orientation – the "ruined" Pil Tower, the World's End column and the Beautiful Valley Pavilion – though none is architecturally outstanding.

Gatchina

In 1776, Catherine the Great gave **Gatchina** and its neighbouring villages to her lover, Grigori Orlov, as a reward for helping her to depose (and dispose of) her husband, Peter III. Its enormous palace wasn't completed by Rinaldi until 1781; by then Orlov – tormented by visions of Peter's ghost – was on the verge of insanity and had only two miserable years to enjoy it before he died, whereupon Catherine promptly passed it on to her son, Paul, who thus inherited

Gatchina

Gatchina from his own father's murderer. Paul had Vincenzo Brenna remodel the palace during the 1790s, raising the height of its semi-circular galleries and side blocks, and installing cannons and sentry boxes to make it look even more like a feudal castle or a barracks – which suited Paul's interests perfectly.

During its heyday, five thousand people were employed at Gatchina (most of them carefully selected from families that had served the Romanovs for generations), while its kennels included every breed of dog from borzois to bulldogs (used for bear-hunting). Some thirty years after Paul's murder, Gatchina became the residence of Nicholas I, who had both side blocks reconstructed and his own living quarters installed in the Arsenal Block, while the late-eighteenth-century state rooms in the central block were restored. The next Romanovs to spend any time here were Alexander III and his wife Maria Fyodorovna, who fled here for security reasons immediately after Alexander II's funeral, and henceforth left Gatchina only for official engagements in the Winter Palace. Finding Gatchina "cold, disgusting and full of work-men", with drawing rooms large enough to hold a regiment and ceilings too high to allow the intimate atmosphere then *de rigueur*, they occupied the servants' quarters on the first floor. Their English governess refused to bring up their baby under such conditions, however, so the nursery was installed upstairs in a vast drawing room hung with tapestries. For almost two years after his accession, Alexander lived in seclusion, wearing the costume of a *muzhik*, shovelling snow and cutting wood. When a visitor expressed surprise, the tsar retorted: "Well, what else can I do till the Nihilists are stamped out?"

In October 1917, Gatchina witnessed the ignominious "last stand" of the Provisional Government, whose leader **Kerensky** fled here in an American embassy car on the morning of October 25, thus escaping arrest at the Winter Palace. After lunch he drove on to Pskov and persuaded a cavalry unit to return with him to Gatchina, whose curator lamented that "the prospect of lodging an entire Cossack division in the palace was not a happy one". In the event, Kerensky refused to accompany them into battle, remaining in his room "lying on the couch, swallowing tranquillizers," until he slipped away disguised as a sailor (*not* a female nurse, as alleged by the Soviets) on October 31.

Like the other Imperial palaces, Gatchina was ravaged by the Nazis during World War II, though its staff managed to evacuate four train-loads of treasures before the Germans arrived. Turned into a naval college after the war, restoration work didn't begin until 1985, and even then it was accorded a far lower priority than Peterhof or Tsarskoe Selo – hence the small number of rooms that have been restored and the fact that work is still continuing. Restorers have been helped, however, by a collection of 1870s' watercolours by Edward Hau and Luigi Premazzi, which recorded many of the rooms in meticulous detail. For a sample, check out the half-dozen rooms illustrated on the **Web site** at *www.alexanderpalace.org/gatchina*.

Practicalities

Located about 50km south of St Petersburg, Gatchina is best reached by #T-18 **minibus** from Moskovskaya metro, which takes about 45 minutes and terminates outside Gatchina-Baltiyskaya train station, two minutes' walk from the palace – it's faster, cheaper and less hassle than taking a **suburban train** (every 40min; 6.30am–midnight) from St Petersburg's Baltic Station to the same destination. Gatchina may also be reached by train from the Warsaw Station, calling at the Tatyanino and Gatchina-Varshavskaya stations on the other side of town from the palace, which entails a much longer walk and isn't recommended – although you can use either station to continue on towards the Nabokov family estate at Rozhdestveno (see p.118).

Besides a café in the palace itself, there are several nondescript places **to eat** on Sobornaya ulitsa, ten minutes' walk from the palace in the centre of town. In the unlikely event that you want **to stay**, the *Hotel Gatchina* (☎1 14 58; ①) on the corner of Krasnaya ulitsa and Chkalova ulitsa has basic rooms and shared bathrooms, but hot water is only available during winter.

The palace

In contrast to the other Imperial palaces, whose brick and stucco facades are ornamented and painted in bright colours, Gatchina is built of monochromatic limestone with walls of such thickness – up to two metres in places – that they resisted all attempts by the Germans to destroy them. Restoration work has been confined to the central section, and the interiors of the Arsenal and Kitchen blocks will probably never be renewed, since paintings and photographs of their decor perished at the same time as the originals – though some idea of what they looked like can be gained from a historical exhibition on the first floor. Here you'll also find an **Exhibition of Weaponry**, with 1100 items that were either brought back as booty, received as gifts or purchased by the tsars, displaying extraordinary craftsmanship and a generous use of gold, silver, ivory and coral.

Until the **Grand Staircase** has been fully restored, visitors reach the second floor via a spiral stairway within the **Signal Tower** – originally one of 150 such towers, which were capable of transmitting messages all the way from St Petersburg to Warsaw in twenty minutes using a heliographic relay system. Like guests of old, you then approach the state rooms via an **Antechamber** decorated with armorial mouldings and a ceiling fresco of the Virgin and infant Jesus, illuminated by chandeliers in drum-like casings. Paul's love of the military is also echoed by the trumpet-shaped candelabras within the columned **Marble Dining Room**, which Nicholas I's wife later used as a bathroom. Beyond lies Paul's **Throne Hall**, with its huge red velvet and gilt throne and pistachio-coloured walls hung with Gobelin tapestries presented by Louis XVI of France – one represents Asia

The palace is open Tues–Sun 10am–5pm, closed first Tues of the month; $8.

and depicts a lion savaging a zebra; the other Africa, showing a tribal chieftain in a litter.

The **Crimson Drawing Room** was once adorned by three Gobelin tapestries illustrating scenes from *Don Quixote*, of which only one – showing Sancho Panza's arrival on the isle of Baratana – now hangs in situ, the other two being held at Pavlovsk, and unlikely to return soon. (In an episode worthy of Gogol's satires, the director of Gatchina wrote to the Ministry of Culture requesting the tapestries' return. Shortly afterwards he was appointed director of Pavlovsk, in which capacity he received his own request, and rejected it.) In Paul's **State Bedroom**, gilded mirrors create the illusion of a corridor receding to infinity, while a disguised door beside his bed leads to the secret passage beneath the palace.

Finest of all is the **White Hall**, or ballroom, its parquet floor inlaid with nine kinds of rare wood and its ceiling festooned with elaborate stucco garlands. Notice the lion and the lobster above the doorways, representing the astrological symbols for the months of July and August, when the palace was used as a Imperial residence. The last room was once Maria Fyodorovna's Throne Hall, but now serves as a picture gallery, as do half-a-dozen rooms on the floor above. Most of the **paintings** are of historical rather than artistic merit, such as the scenes of life at Gatchina during Nicholas I's reign; portraits of Catherine the Great as a young bride and an old woman; and Paul's daughter Anna, who was wooed by Napoleon – whom Maria Fyodorovna dismissed as "that Corsican show-off" – and later married into the Greek royal family (making her an ancestor of Britain's current Prince of Wales).

Finally, visitors return to the first floor and are ushered into the long, dank **subterranean passage** that runs from the palace to the Silver Lake – it's not, as you might imagine, a product of Paul's fear of assassination, but was actually created during Orlov's time as a kind of romantic folly. Its acoustics are such that a word spoken at one end clearly echoes back from the far end, 200m away.

The park and town

The wildest of all the palace grounds, Gatchina's **park** is what draws most visitors, particularly in the autumn, when its sense of uncontrolled nature reclaiming a man-made setting is at its most vivid. Although the tsars' private **Dutch Garden** is inaccessible, visitors may roam more or less everywhere else – unless, as sometimes happens, vandals wreck one of the bridges that connect the chain of islands between the **White and Silver lakes**. The former never freezes over, and provided a testing ground for the first Russian submarine in 1879. On its far side, a lovely little **Temple of Venus** stands on the Island of Love, where pleasure boats once docked. The **Birch Cabin** resembles a stack of logs from the outside, but contains a palatial suite of mirrored rooms within.

The Birch Cabin is open May–Sept Tues–Sun 10am–6pm; $8, including a guided tour (in Russian only) of the park's other pavilions.

Besides the geometric **Silvia Park**, there are two ex-hunting grounds: to the north, **Menagerie Park** is where Alexander III took his children to follow animal tracks in summer and dig paths through the snow during winter; in the other direction lies the **Priory Park**, named after the **Priory Palace** overlooking the **Black Lake**. This Germanic-looking edifice was built for Prince Conday, Prior of the Maltese Knights of St John, who never actually lived there. It is slowly being restored, but isn't open to the public yet.

Finally, the town itself boasts two imposing buildings: the Baroque **Pavlovskiy Cathedral** and the pseudo-medieval **Cathedral of the Assumption**, plus some folksy **wooden houses** along ulitsa Chkalova.

Palaces and parks

Peterhof	Петергоф
Petrodvorets	Петродворец
Alexandria Park	Парк Александрия
Bathhouse Wing	Баный корпус
Benois Wing	Корпус Бенуа
Catherine Wing	Екатерининский Корпус
Cottage Palace	Коттедж
Great Palace	Большой дворец
Hermitage	Эрмитаж
Lower Park	Нижний парк
Marly Palace	Марли
Monplaisir	Монплезир
Upper Garden	Верхний сад
Oranienbaum	Ораниенбаум
Lomonosov	Ломоносов
Chinese Palace	Китайский дворец
Great Palace	Большой дворец
Japanese Pavilion	Японский павильон
Lower Park	Нижний парк
Peter III's Palace	дворец Петра III
Sliding Hill	Катальная Горка
Upper Park	Верхний парк
Tsarskoe Selo	Царское село
Pushkin	Пушкин
Alexander Palace	Александровский дворец
Alexander Park	Александровский парк
Catherine Palace	Екатерининский дворец
Catherine Park	Екатерининский парк
Pavlovsk	Павловск
Great Palace	Большой дворец
Pavlovsk Park	Павловский парк
Gatchina	Гатчина
Gatchina Park	Гатчинский парк

Chapter 18

Kronstadt and the Karelian Isthmus

The island fortress and naval base of **Kronstadt** was established soon after St Petersburg was founded. Sited on Kotlin Island in the Gulf of Finland, the fortress was the linchpin of the city's defences against seaborne invasion and the home port of the Baltic Fleet, yet would later become the state's Achilles heel when its forces revolted against tsar and commissar alike. Off limits to foreigners for decades, this curiously time-warped town now welcomes tourists, but is likely to appeal mainly to those keen on maritime history or bizarre urban landscapes.

A more mainstream attraction is the **Karelian Isthmus** between the Gulf of Finland and Lake Ladoga, where Petersburgers relax at their *dachas* between bouts of sunbathing, swimming in lakes and mushroom-picking. It's a soothing landscape of silver birches and misty hollows, with spectacular sunsets reflected in limpid water, the mosquitoes being the only drawback. You'll need a car, however, to really explore the region. Relying on public transport, you're limited to the towns **along the Gulf coast**: Razliv, where Lenin hid out in 1917; Repino, which houses the delightful memorial house of the artist Repin; and historic **Vyborg**, with its castle and Nordic houses. On the southern shore of **Lake Ladoga**, on the other side of the isthmus, the infamous Tsarist penal island of **Schlüsselburg** is also reasonably accessible. Requiring a greater investment of time and money are cruises from St Petersburg to the **Valaam** archipelago in Lake Ladoga, and the amazing wooden churches of **Kizhi**, on Lake Onega.

Historically, the Karelian Isthmus has been a bone of contention between Russia and its Baltic neighbours since medieval times. In 1812 it passed to the Grand Duchy of Finland (then a semi-autonomous part of the Tsarist Empire), with the frontier drawn to the east of Kronstadt. In 1917, during the turmoil of revolution, the Finns seized the opportunity to declare independence and the isthmus remained Finnish territory until the Winter War of 1939–40,

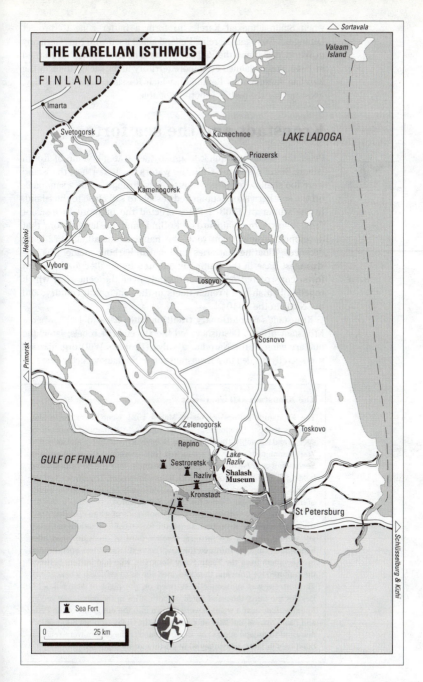

THE KARELIAN ISTHMUS

FINLAND

Imarta

Svetogorsk

Kuznechnoe

Priozersk

LAKE LADOGA

Sortavala

Valaam Island

Helsinki

Kamenogorsk

Vyborg

Losovo

Primorsk

Sosnovo

Zelenogorsk

Toskovo

Repino

Lake Razliv

GULF OF FINLAND

Sestroretsk

Shalash Museum

Razliv

Kronstadt

St Petersburg

Schlüsselburg & Kizhi

Sea Fort

0   25 km

N

when Stalin annexed Karelia to form a buffer zone to protect Leningrad. To regain Karelia, Finland allied itself with Nazi Germany in World War II and the Red Army was driven out; when it returned in 1944, Stalin claimed even more territory in the far north (now the Karelian Autonomous Republic), which Russia retains to this day, insisting that the matter is non-negotiable.

Kronstadt and the sea forts

Peter the Great was quick to grasp the strategic value of Kotlin Island, 30km out in the Gulf: the waters to the north of the island were too shallow for large ships to pass through, while a sandbank off the southern shore compelled vessels to sail close to the island. In the winter of 1703–4 Peter erected the offshore Kronschlot Fort, followed by a shipyard on Kotlin Island; the large colony that developed around them took the name Kronstadt in 1723. Its defences, floating batteries and naval harbour made this the strongest base in the Baltic, augmented by smaller *forty*, or sea forts, constructed on outlying islands over the centuries, which repelled British and French fleets in the nineteenth century, and the Nazis in the 1940s.

Kronstadt's **revolutionary tradition** dates back to 1825, when a Kronstadt officer, Bestushev, led the Decembrist rebels; later, the military wing of the Narodnaya Volya (People's Will) organization was secretly headed by a Kronstadt sailor, Sukhanov. As the first rev-

---

The Kronstadt sailors' revolt

The **Kronstadt sailors' revolt** of March 1921 went under the slogan "Soviets without Communism". Their manifesto demanded freedom of speech and assembly, the abolition of Bolshevik dictatorship and an end to War Communism. Only the ice-locked Gulf prevented the rebel cruisers *Sevastopol* and *Petropavlovsk* from steaming into the Neva basin and holding St Petersburg hostage. With a thaw imminent, Trotsky warned the rebels: "Only those who surrender unconditionally can count on the mercy of the Soviet Republic" – but few of them responded.

Two hours before dawn on March 8, thousands of white-clad Red Army troops advanced on Kronstadt, across the frozen Gulf, unnoticed until they got within 500m of the fortress, when a third of them drowned after Kronstadt's cannons ruptured the ice. The next assault was spearheaded by volunteers from the Tenth Party Congress, who laid ladders between the ruptured ice floes and then swarmed across to establish a beachhead. The fortress was subsequently stormed on the night of March 16–17. Besides the thirty thousand killed on both sides in the battle, any sailors found with or near a weapon were thrown into the dungeons of the Peter and Paul Fortress and later shot or sent to the Gulag (though 8000 sailors managed to escape across the ice to Finland). The sailors were rehabilitated only in 1994, when they were posthumously pardoned.

olutionary wave crashed over Russia, the Kronstadt sailors mutinied in 1905 and 1906, avenging years of maltreatment by throwing their officers into the ships' furnaces. After the fall of Tsarism in 1917, the sailors declared their own revolutionary Soviet and then an independent republic. The Bolsheviks could never have carried out the October Revolution, or survived the Civil War, were it not for the Kronstadt sailors, whom they deployed as shock troops: "the pride and glory of the Revolution". The world was therefore stunned when they revolted yet again in 1921 – this time, against the Bolsheviks (see box on p.378).

Kronstadt

Until 1992, foreigners could visit **Kronstadt** only by the risky expedient of being smuggled in disguised as a Russian. Today the island is freely accessible even to solo tourists, but you would still be unwise to **photograph** any warships or barracks, or to drink the local **water**, which is even more polluted than St Petersburg's due to an unfinished **tidal barrage** that spans the neck of the Gulf. Intended to protect the city from flooding, its massive sluice gates loom above the road atop the barrage that connects Kronstadt to the northern shore of the mainland. It is planned eventually to built a road to the southern side of the Gulf as well – in the meantime, locals wishing to reach Oranienbaum during winter simply drive across the ice.

Arriving by hydrofoil or ferry (see p.381) in Kronstadt's Middle Harbour, you'll see warships of the Baltic Fleet at anchor before disembarking near Petrovskiy Park, centred on a swashbuckling **statue of Peter the Great**, inscribed: "To defend the fleet and its base to the last of one's strength is the highest duty". Such sentiments are repeated on monuments to sailors or submariners in every park and square, juxtaposed with surreal installations like the sea-mine used as a charity collection box on prospekt Lenina, the submarine conning tower on ploshchad Roshalya, and the gun turret guarding the bridge to Yakornaya ploshchad.

The latter square also harbours the splendid **Naval Cathedral** – a massive Neo-Byzantine edifice containing a **Museum of the Kronstadt Fortress**, whose highlight is a dramatic diorama of the town under Nazi bombardment – and a lovely Art Nouveau **monument to Admiral Makarov**, whose distinguished career was crowned by disaster with the decimation of the Baltic Fleet at the battle of Tsushima in 1905. Statues in other parks honour Faddei Bellinghausen, who explored Antarctica during 1820–21, and Pavel Pakhtusov, the discoverer of Novaya Zemlya.

The Museum of the Kronstadt Fortress is open Tues–Sun 11am–6pm; $2.

The remainder of the town largely consists of decaying factories, barracks and oily eighteenth-century canals and dock basins that crisscross the centre, their names redolent of faraway lands. In Petrine times these were lined with taverns and brothels where sailors caroused – a steamy past whose only contemporary echoes are the

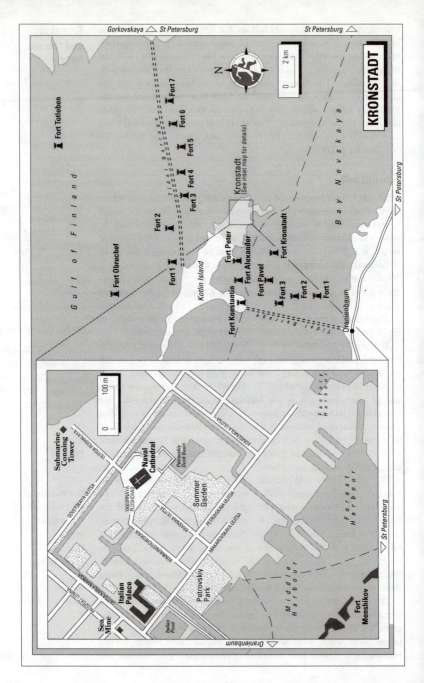

KRONSTADT

Gorkovskaya △ St Petersburg   St Petersburg △

Gulf of Finland

N

0   2 km

Fort Totleben

Fort 7
Fort 6
Fort 5
Fort 4
Fort 3
Fort 2
Fort 1

Fort Obruchef

Tidal Barrage

Kotlin Island

Kronstadt
(See inset map for details)

Fort Peter
Fort Alexander
Fort Kronstadt

Fort Konstantin
Fort Pavel
Fort 3
Fort 2
Fort 1

Tidal Barrage

Oranienbaum

Bay Nevskaya

▽ St Petersburg

Submarine Conning Tower

0   100 m

Naval Cathedral

OKTYABRSKAYA AVE.
SOVIETSKAYA ULITSA
YAKORNAYA PLOSHCHAD
Petrovskiy Duck Basin
KOMSOMOLA ULITSA

KOMMUNISTICHESKAYA
KRASNAYA ULITSA
PETROVSKAYA ULITSA
MAKAROVSKAYA ULITSA

Summer Garden

Italian Palace

PR. LENINA
UL. KARLA MARKSA

Petrovskiy Park

Sea Mine

Italian Pond

Factory Harbour

Forest Harbour

Middle Harbour

Fort Menshikov

▽ Oranienbaum

▽ St Petersburg

Sailors' Club in the decrepit **Italian Palace** on Makarovskaya ulitsa and the International Customs Terminal at Fort Konstantin (see below).

Practicalities

During **summer**, the best way of reaching Kronstadt is by **hydrofoil**: services depart daily from the Tuchkov most jetty near the eastern end of Vasilevskiy Island every hour between 7am and 9pm; the journey takes thirty minutes and costs only $0.50. There is also a **car ferry** (every 1–2hr) from Oranienbaum on the southern shore of the Gulf; bus #6 runs from Oranienbaum train station to the ferry (*parom*) landing stage, from where the crossing takes 45 minutes.

At other times of the year, Kronstadt is accessible only by road: the #510 **bus** from Staraya Derevnya metro on St Petersburg's Vyborg Side runs every forty minutes, taking an hour, or you can hire an unofficial **taxi** from the nearby Chernaya rechka metro for $5–6. When it comes to the **return journey**, note that tickets for the hydrofoil and ferry only go on sale fifteen minutes before departure, in a log cabin beside the park near the landing stage. Taxis for St Petersburg wait behind the Gostiniy dvor near the northern end of prospekt Lenina, beyond a few **cafes**, the best of which is *Skazka*, at no. 33. On weekdays, there's a **currency exchange** in the cinema on the corner of Sovetskaya ulitsa and ulitsa Roshalya, while during summer you can stay in cosy cabins on the **hotel-ship** *Fort Konstantin* (☎ 439 18 04; ①) – though it doesn't run to showers.

The sea forts

Aficionados of maritime life or naval history might consider visiting some of the old *forty* – or **sea forts** – built on man-made islands in the Gulf, which last saw active service during World War II. Two of the so-called **Numbered Northern Forts** are actually accessible on foot from the tidal barrage to the mainland, while the larger complex of **Fort Konstantin** can be reached by car via the unfinished southern barrage (a taxi from town will cost $1–2). There has been a half-hearted attempt to turn the latter into a tourist marina, which so far amounts to two café-bars, a hotel-ship and the chance to fire a naval cannon into the Gulf ($14) – ask to *vystrel iz pushki* if you're interested.

You can also hire a motorboat to reach **Fort Alexander**, 600m offshore, a sinister, kidney-shaped bastion where the scientist Mechnikov devised a bubonic plague vaccine – hence its nickname: the Plague Fort (*Chumnoy*). Foreigners pay $50 an hour for the motorboat out there, though it might be affordable for a group or if you can manage to join a Russian party. For those with more time and money, it's also possible to hire a yacht with crew to reach **Obruchef** or **Totleben**, two large forts with concrete casements and harbours built early last century between Kotlin Island and Sestroretsk. Visits to both involve an overnight stay with a *shashlyk* barbecue. Compare quotes from Sunny Sailing and the River Yacht Club in St Petersburg, or the locally based Kronstadt Yacht Club (see p.316).

ST PETERSBURG

Along the Gulf coast

The **Gulf coast** of the Karelian Isthmus begins on the edge of St Petersburg, from where a ribbon of urban development extends northwest along the water as far as Zelenogorsk. Happily, for most of the way high-rise buildings are less in evidence than clapboard *dachas*, painted in bold colours and decorated with intricate fretwork gables. Although rocky headlands and sandy coves can be glimpsed through the pine trees, Russian holidaymakers are equally fond of the birch woods and lakes that lie inland. **En route to Razliv**, some 30km from the city, there are a few places at which you may like to stop off: **Olgino** has a motel and campsite (p.274), while **Dubki** and **Lisiy Nos** both have bathing lakes nearby.

Transport

With a car you can stop wherever looks promising along the coast, or venture into the interior. **Public transport** is less flexible, but by using trains and buses you should be able to see a fair amount. *Elektrichka* **trains** from Finland Station (Ploshchad Lenina metro) run every thirty minutes. There are two lines, the direct, inland Vyborgline, and the Krugovoy or round-coast line. Bear in mind, however, that not all trains stop at all stations.

Buses #416 (to Sestroretsk) and #411 (to Zelenogorsk) run with similar regularity along the coastal road, starting from St Petersburg's Primorskiy prospekt, near Chernaya rechka metro. Both forms of transport are more frequent in the morning, so it pays to make an early start. There are also **minibuses** to Olgino (#T-210 & #T-210a), Sestroretsk (#T-T25 & #T-25a) and Zelenogorsk (#T-411) from Novaya Derevnya metro station.

Razliv

In Soviet times, tourists and schoolchildren were regularly bussed into **Razliv** to view two hideouts used by Lenin before the Revolution, both reverentially preserved as memorial museums. Now, only true believers and curiosity-seekers bother to come, and Razliv is otherwise just a residential satellite of Sestroretsk, further up the road. Of the two, the Shalash Museum is hard to reach without a car, though the Sarai Museum is easily accessible by public transport – minibuses and buses stop at several points along the road through Razliv, or you can come by *elektrichka* train, getting off at the Tarkhovka halt. Either way, the journey from St Petersburg takes about 45 minutes.

The Sarai Museum

The **Sarai Museum** is at ulitsa Yemelyanova 2, a signposted ten-minute walk from the *elektrichka* stop. Lenin arrived here by train on the night of July 10, 1917, a fugitive from Petrograd, where the

Provisional Government had begun cracking down on the Bolsheviks. His host was a local munitions worker and secret Party member, Nikolai Yemelyanov, whose family were then living in a small barn (*sarai*) while their house was being repaired. Lenin was installed in the loft, reached by a steep ladder, until he found other quarters (see below).

The year after Lenin's death in 1924, the barn was given concrete underpinning, impregnated with protective resins and later shielded from the elements by a glass screen, resulting in the surreal building that you see today. On the first floor are the family's possessions; in the loft above, copies of the chairs and samovar which Lenin used (the originals were formerly displayed in the main Lenin Museum in Leningrad). The **house** opposite the barn exhibits photographs of various Bolsheviks in disguise and copies of the articles that Lenin wrote while staying here.

The Shalash Museum

Four kilometres north of the main road through Razliv, the turn-off to the lakeside **Shalash Museum** is signposted by a large Soviet monument. In 1917, the far shore of Lake Razliv was only accessible by boat and offered greater concealment than the barn, where Lenin was liable to be spotted by government spies. Yemelyanov told his neighbours that he planned to raise a cow and had hired a Finn to cut the hay. Under this pretext, Lenin moved into a hut (*shalash*) made of branches and thatch, built in a clearing by the lake. In this "green study" he wrote articles such as *On Slogans* and *The Answer*, and began *The State and Revolution*. After a fortnight, however, even this hideout seemed too risky, and on August 8 Lenin was smuggled into Finland disguised as a steam-engine fireman.

What used to be a meadow is now laid out with paths and features a granite **monument** with a stylized representation of the hut. Being made of perishable hay – and occasionally set alight by vandals – the **hut** itself is rebuilt every year. In the nearby glass-and-concrete **pavilion** you can see copies of the peasant's smock and scythe that Lenin used, a blue notebook containing his notes for *The State and Revolution*, and Vladimir Pinchuk's statue, *Lenin in Razliv*.

Between Razliv and Repino

Lake Razliv (which means "flood") was actually created as a reservoir for Russia's first armaments factory, founded by Peter the Great at **Sestroretsk**, 33km from St Petersburg. Like the city's Vyborg Side, the township was once noted for its working-class militancy, though its factory now produces nothing more dangerous than television screens (though in Russia even these can be fairly lethal, since certain models are liable to explode). Between here and the next settlement, **Solechnoe**, are two sanatoria formerly reserved for the Party elite: *Duny* (☎437 47 67; ④, pool and sauna extra) is a quiet

Along the Gulf coast

The Sarai Museum is usually open 10am–6pm, closed Wed; free. Call ☎434 61 45 if you want to confirm opening times.

The Shalash Museum is usually open 10am–6pm, closed Wed; $0.25. Call ☎437 30 98 if you want to confirm opening times.

place with facilities for those suffering from cardiac problems, though it now caters to anyone who can afford its bed-and-board rates, and also has a golf course (☎437 38 74). The similar *Belyie Nochy* rest centre (☎437 31 93; ④, includes treatment) next door was once visited by Gorbachev and Mrs Thatcher.

Repino

Repino, 47km northwest of St Petersburg, is what Russians call a *poselok*, or small urban-type settlement, named after the eminent painter **Ilya Repin** (1844–1930), who built a house near what was then the village of Kuokkala and lived there permanently from 1900. Repin showed no inclination to leave even after Kuokkala became Finnish territory in 1917, but continued to receive visitors and honours from Soviet Russia until his death. Turned into a museum after the Soviet annexation of Karelia, the house was burned to the ground by the Nazis in 1944 and then painstakingly re-created in the post-war era. If you arrive **by train**, head from the station down towards the sea and then, after 600m, turn left onto ulitsa Repina – the brightly coloured gates of Repin's estate are 500m further along. The #411 **bus** from St Petersburg stops right outside: ask to get off at Penaty.

Repin's house: Penaty

Penaty is usually open May–Sept 10.30am–5pm; Oct–April 10.30am–4pm; closed Tues; $2. Call ☎231 68 34 if you want to confirm opening times.

Repin's house is named **Penaty** after the household gods of ancient Rome, the Penates, a title that suits its highbrow domesticity. The picturesque wooden building has a steep glass roof and an abundance of windows, while the **interior** reflects the progressive views of Repin and his wife, Natalya Nordman. A sign in the cloakroom advises: "Take off your own coats. Don't wait for servants – there aren't any." On Wednesdays, when the Repins held open house, guests were expected to announce their own arrival by ringing a gong.

Only intimates were admitted to Repin's **study**, which contains a huge jasper paperweight and statues of Tolstoy and the critic Stasov. The drawing room is hung with autographed pictures of Gorky and Chaliapin, and there's a painting of the Repins' artist son, Yuri. Repin himself also dabbled in sculpture: his statue of Tolstoy occupies the glassed-over winter veranda. The dining room features a round table with a revolving centre. Guests had to serve themselves (without asking others to pass anything) and stow the dirty dishes in the drawers underneath; anyone who didn't was obliged to mount the lectern in the corner of the room and deliver an impromptu speech. Only vegetarian food was served.

Repin's paintings can be seen in the Russian Museum in St Petersburg (p.162) and the Tretyakov Gallery in Moscow.

The best room in the house is Repin's **studio**, upstairs, filled with light and cluttered with *objets* and sketches. Notice the metre-long brushes and the special palette-belt, which the ageing artist used to compensate for his long-sightedness and atrophying muscles. By the stove are various props used in his famous painting of *The Zaporodzhe Cossacks Writing a Mocking Letter to the Sultan*, and Repin's last self-portrait, painted at the age of 76. Finally, you go up to the top floor to view a touching home movie of Repin and his friends throwing snowballs in the grounds of Penaty.

The grounds behind the house contain two follies, the **Temple of Osiris and Isis** and the **Tower of Scheherazade**, both built of wood. **Repin's grave** is on top of a hillock by an oak tree, as stipulated in his will – follow the path leading off to the right to reach it.

Vyborg

After decades of Soviet neglect, the historic town of **Vyborg**, 174km northwest of St Petersburg and just 30km from the Finnish border, is looking to Finland to revive its fortunes – an ironic reassertion of past leanings, given that the Finns regard Vyborg (which they call Viipuri) as theirs by right. Architecturally, at least, they have a point, as its old quarter consists of Baltic merchants' houses and Lutheran churches, while the centre is defined by Finnish Art Nouveau and Modernist architecture, interspersed with newer Soviet eyesores. Demographically, however, Vyborg is definitely Russian, not least because most of its Finnish population fled in 1944 – though Russians have lived here since the town's earliest days. In Soviet times, Vyborg's port, paper mills and optics factory employed half the population; today, its economy is heavily dependent on cross-border tourism, smuggling and prostitution, and is in a parlous state – to the extent that many outlying settlements are without gas and hot water in the depths of winter.

With luck, your visit might coincide with one of Vyborg's annual **festivals**: the Zvonkiy solovushka children's festival in May; the Rytsarskiy turnir historical pageant in June; the yacht regatta in July; or the "Window of Europe" film festival in August.

The Town

The town is spread out over the series of rocky peninsulas that enclose Vyborg Bay, on the Gulf of Finland. Ignoring the industrial suburbs, basic **orientation** is fairly simple; from the **train** and **bus stations** on the northern mainland, a grid of streets spreads around the central square and west to the old quarter, huddled on the peninsula's cape. The castle, situated on an island off the end of the peninsula, is easily recognizable by its lofty tower, visible from all around the bay. Vyborg itself is compact enough for visitors to see everything on foot in a couple of hours except for Monrepos park, outside town, for which you'll need to take a taxi.

From Krasnasya ploshchad to the old town

A five-minute walk from the train station will bring you to **Krasnaya ploshchad**, notable for its unusually corpulent **statue of Lenin**.

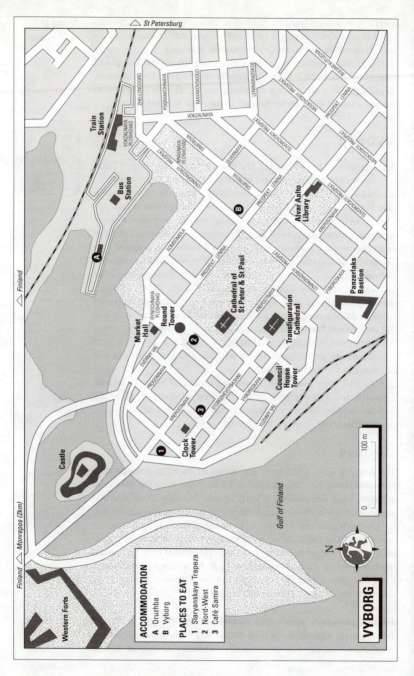

△ St Petersburg

Train Station

Bus Station

Finland △

△ Finland

Market Hall

Round Tower

Castle

Clock Tower

Cathedral of St Peter & St Paul

Transfiguration Cathedral

Alvar Aalto Library

Panzerlaks Bastion

Council House Tower

Western Forts

Finland △   Monrepos (2km) △

Gulf of Finland

N

0   100 m

ACCOMMODATION
A Druzhba
B Vyborg

PLACES TO EAT
1 Slaryanskaya Trapeza
2 Nord-West
3 Café Samira

VYBORG

Carry on to prospekt Lenina and bear right across the park to reach the **Alvar Aalto Library**, an early work by the famous Finnish architect, fronted by a bronze bull elk. Completed in 1935, when Aalto was in his thirties, its boxy, light simplicity established him as a Modernist. Sadly, in Soviet times the library was clumsily "renovated" and a granite facade reminiscent of Lenin's mausoleum added – Aalto himself, revisiting the library shortly before his death in 1976, disclaimed the building as his own work.

Head northwest along prospekt Lenina to reach **Rynochnaya ploshchad**, where stalls selling clothes, souvenirs, and binoculars and sniper-scopes from the optics factory presage an orange-brick, neo-Gothic **Market Hall**. Nearby stands the squat, sixteenth-century **Round Tower** (Kruglaya bashnya), crowned by an iron cupola and spike – formerly part of a belt of fortifications girdling the entire peninsula, it now contains a restaurant.

The market is open Mon–Sat 9am–7pm.

From here you can head into the picturesquely decrepit old quarter, known as the **Stone City**, where Krepostnaya ulitsa leads eastwards to the yellow Lutheran **Cathedral of SS Peter and Paul**, built in the 1790s, and the pink, blue-domed Orthodox **Cathedral of the Transfiguration** that catered to Vyborg's Russian population during its Finnish era. Beside the nearby cinema, ulitsa Titova leads downhill towards the octagonal **Council House Tower** (Bashnya Ratushi) – another remnant of the old fortifications – or you can walk along ulitsa Storozhevoy bashni to the massive seventeenth-century **Clock Tower**, or head down towards the docks to find the **Panzerlaks** (Shield of the Lakes) **bastion**, which now contains a bar.

Vyborg Castle

Vyborg Castle – known as the *zamok* or *krepost* – occupies an island in the bay below the Stone City. Protected by five-metre-thick walls and numerous bastions, it was originally built by the Swedes in 1293 after they had assumed control of what had been a Russian trading port ("Wiborg" means "holy fortress" in Swedish). Captured by Peter the Great in the Northern War, the fortress's military significance declined after 1812, when Vyborg was transferred to the Grand Duchy of Finland, and the castle served as a prison until its brief reversion to active service during World War II. Nowadays its citadel contains two **museums** devoted to military history and period artefacts including prints, maps and weaponry, but the real attraction is the 48-metre-high **tower**, which affords a stunning view of the whole town and far out into the Gulf of Finland.

The castle is open Tues–Sun: summer 10.30am–5pm; winter 10.30am–4pm; $1, plus an additional $1 to climb the tower.

Monrepos

Vyborg's final and perhaps finest attraction is **Monrepos** park, beside the Gulf of Finland, 2km beyond the castle. Though not accessible by public transport, you can take a taxi there ($1) and arrange for it to pick you up again later. Entered by a massive wooden Neo-

The park is open daily 10am–8pm; $0.50.

Vyborg

Gothic gateway, the park uses the mossy, red granite crags and boulders of the Karelian shoreline to stunning effect, enhanced by dwarf firs and spruces that give it something of the look of a Japanese garden, embellished by Classical pavilions and Gothic follies – though sadly it's rather run-down due to lack of funds. Laid out 1759 by Commandant Stupishin, the park attained its apotheosis under Baron Nikolai, whose family is buried in a mock castle on the rocky **Isle of the Dead** (accessible by rowing boat). The isle lies off to the left beyond the boarded-up wooden **palace** of Count Wurtemburg – currently being restored by Finns – while further to the west, a spring gushes pure water.

Practicalities

Aside from signing up for a day-long **coach excursion** ($7) at the Turservis kiosk outside Gostiniy dvor, the easiest way of reaching Vyborg from St Petersburg is by *elektrichka* **train** from Finland Station – preferably one of the *komerchiskaya* expresses, which take one hour and forty-five minutes, rather than a regular train. There are two expresses on Monday, Tuesday, Thursday and Friday (departing at 7.57am & 6.28pm), plus an additional service (12.48pm) at weekends, but only one on Wednesday. The two daily **coaches** from Petersburg to Helsinki (book through Finnord, Italyanskaya ul. 37) both call at Vyborg after dark, so aren't much use unless you're willing to spend the night there. **Motorists** have a choice of three routes: the coastal road, the A-125 from Zelenogorsk or, quickest of all, the A-122, which runs furthest inland.

There are two **hotels** within walking distance of the train station. The *Druzhba* (☎ & fax 278/257 44; ④), just past the bus station, is conspicuous by its pyramidal shape and the two replica Viking longships on the quay outside. It's more comfortable here than at the *Vyborg* (☎278/223 83, fax 278/261 96; ④), at Leningradskiy pr. 14 – though both have en-suite rooms, plus a sauna, bar and restaurant. **Eating** out costs less than in Petersburg: try the Korean *Café Samira* (daily 11am–midnight) on the corner of Novoy zastavy and Storozhevoy bashny, or the Russian *Slavyanskaya Trapeza* in a

---

Onward travel to Finland

If you're **travelling on to Helsinki**, there are three trains and coaches daily. Coach tickets can be bought on board, or at the *Druzhba* on weekdays; services depart from the bus station. Keep your passport handy, as there are several checkpoints before the customs post, which is enlivened by Finns stocking up on booze, cigarettes, CDs and videos before going home – note that most of the vodka is counterfeit. Motorists must be sure to get a stamp from Russian customs before reaching the border guards, 5km down the road – or you'll be sent back. In any case, expect to spend at least an hour in a queue of vehicles on each side of the border.

---

cellar at ul. Yuzhniy val 4/2 (daily noon–2am). Other options include the Round Tower – whose **bar** is open till dawn – and the *Nord-West*, just behind it. You'll find a 24-hour **currency exchange** office in the *Druzhba*, and an ATM upstairs in the train station.

Lake Ladoga

The eastern shore of the Karelian Isthmus is much rockier than the Gulf coast, reflecting the stormy nature of **Lake Ladoga** (Ladozhskoe ozero). Covering 187,726 square kilometres, Ladoga is Europe's largest lake, and also the source of the River Neva. Frozen over for up to six months of the year, it became famous during World War II for its **"Road of Life"**, which enabled Leningrad to survive the Blockade. Whenever the ice was thick enough, convoys drove across the lake through the night, hoping to avoid the Luftwaffe. In this way, 1,500,000 tonnes of supplies and 450,000 troops reached the city, and 1,200,000 civilians were evacuated.

For visitors, Ladoga holds two main attractions. At its southern end, the Tsarist prison fortress of **Schlüsselburg** makes an interesting day-trip in summer, and the frozen lake itself is well worth seeing during winter (though the fortress is closed then). Those with time and money to spare might consider a summer cruise from St Petersburg to **Valaam**, an archipelago in the north of Lake Ladoga, perhaps continuing to the fabulous wooden churches of **Kizhi** (p.396) on Lake Onega, even further north.

Schlüsselburg (Schlisselburg)

The island fortress known as **Schlüsselburg** was born of rivalry between the medieval rulers of Novgorod and Sweden, who realized that the River Neva's outflow from Lake Ladoga held the key to the lucrative trade route between Russia and the Baltic. First fortified in 1323 by Georgy of Novgorod, the island – known to the Russians as **Oreshek** (from the word for "little nut") and to the Swedes as Noteborg – constantly changed hands until its definitive recapture in 1702 by Peter the Great, who renamed it Schlüsselburg (meaning "Key Fortress" in German).

Having lost its military significance after Peter's victory over Sweden in the Northern War, the fortress became a prison for political offenders, while the lakeside **town** – also called Schlüsselburg – continued to trade with the Russian interior. After the Bolshevik Revolution, the prison was turned into a museum devoted to the infamies of Tsarism – a few years later, Ladoga itself became the gateway to a chain of waterways and penal camps reaching to the Arctic Circle, where thousands died building the canal that links the lake to the White Sea. Although the town fell to the Nazis in 1941, the fortress held out for 500 days until the Blockade of Leningrad was broken. In honour of this feat, the town was renamed Petrokrepost (Peter's Fortress) – a name that's still used in everyday speech, notwithstanding its official reversion to **Schlisselburg** (a Russified form of the original name) in 1990.

The island fortress

The fortress is usually open mid-May to mid-Sept daily 10am–5pm; $1. Call ☎238 46 79 if you want to confirm opening times.

From mid-May to mid-September, hourly **ferries** sail from the town's jetty, across the sluice gates from the bus terminal, out to Oreshek – a tongue of rock 700m offshore, whose angular Kremlin **walls** enclose a dark mass whose ruined skyline still shows the scars of heavy shelling during the Blockade. Approaching from the southwest, like generations of prisoners, you enter the maw of the **Tsar's Tower**. Inside, to the left, a door opens onto a secret passage, while further along looms the red-brick **citadel**.

The penal quarter begins with the **Secret Castle** (Sekretny zamok) built by Peter the Great, whose **Tower of Cells** – the oldest prison in Russia – originally held his first wife, Evdokiya, and their daughter (who died there). Later, Prince Golitsyn was imprisoned here by Empress Anna (whose favourite, Biron, suffered likewise after her demise); Empress Elizabeth incarcerated Ivan VI here (he was killed in 1764 following an attempt to escape); Catherine sent the publisher and Freemason Novikov here; and Nicholas I found room for several Decembrists and the Anarchist Bakunin. In the **courtyard** beyond, Lenin's brother, Alexander Ulyanov, was hanged for attempted regicide in 1867.

Further along the spit of land stands the **New Prison**, built in 1884 to hold members of the Nihilist organization Narodnaya Volya who had previously been confined in the Peter and Paul Fortress. Conditions were so harsh that seventeen of the twenty-one prisoners died within four years of moving to Schlüsselburg. Later, the famous revolutionary Vera Figner survived many years in cell no. 26. Although the fortress's post-revolutionary role as a museum was inevitable, ex-prisoners, asked whether they wanted it preserved as a monument to tyranny, answered: "We have suffered enough, let the foul place crumble to ruin."

The town and lake

Aside from a statue of Peter the Great near the jetty, the only sight in town, right next to the bus stop, is the eighteenth-century **Church of the Annunciation**, an imposing Baroque edifice, fetchingly painted apricot and white, but derelict since it was closed in the 1930s. Although returned to Orthodox hands in 1990, there is no money available for restoration, so services are held in the smaller **Church of St Nicholas** nearby (itself converted into a factory during Stalinist times).

In winter, a far more impressive sight is the **frozen lake**. Where icebreakers have smashed a channel for ferries, the piled pack ice resembles a scene from Antarctica. Meanwhile, scores of Russians sit out fishing through holes in the ice, their improvised plastic "tents" the only shelter against the driving sleet and subzero temperatures. In 1997, 75 fishermen were rescued after nine hours on an ice floe that had broken adrift, but made light of the experience as a "normal hazard" of their sport. With similar insouciance, locals dub the **mosquitoes** that appear over summer "Swedes", because "they're blonde and don't bite".

Practicalities

The easiest way of reaching Schlüsselburg from St Petersburg is **by car**. From Murmanskoe shosse in the Okhta district, head 60km east along the M-18 highway and turn north after crossing the River Neva. Failing that, catch **bus #○575** or **#575** from outside Ulitsa Dybenko metro station in Petersburg's southern suburbs, which arrives in the centre of Schlüsselburg one hour later. *Elektrichka* **trains** from Finland Station depart less frequently, take longer, and drop you on the far shore of the lake, from where there is no direct access to the island and only two ferries a day to the town itself, across the bay. Finally, Davranov Travel in St Petersburg run **excursions** by coach ($5) every fortnight or so – check the schedules posted in their kiosks outside Gostiniy dvor (see p.84).

The town's amenities boil down to a basic **canteen**, or *stolovaya* (Mon–Sat 11am–2pm & 3–5pm, Sat till 6pm), on the corner near the bus stop serving hot soup, with a bar in the basement. Since there's no tourist accommodation, bear in mind that **buses** back to St Petersburg are less frequent after 5pm; the last one leaves shortly before 11pm.

Valaam

Some 250km from St Petersburg, towards the northern end of Lake Ladoga, the islands of the **Valaam** archipelago have a unique history and society, shaped by mystics, exiles and nature. Despite being ice-bound for five months of the year, Valaam is blessed with a favourable micro-climate, enjoying twice as much sunshine as St Petersburg and abounding in berries, mushrooms, wild flowers, butterflies and songbirds. It remains almost as quiet now as it was when Avram of Rostov – the founder of Valaam's hermetic tradition – arrived in 960, and heard a leaf fall in the forest. It's a far cry from St Petersburg, and to go mushrooming or fishing is a perfect way to absorb the island's natural beauty, while the cruise there and back (see box on p.393) is also fun.

For Orthodox believers, Valaam is a **holy isle** of saints and hermits, whose shrines echo Christ's Passion in the Holy Land; a "Jerusalem of the North", offering redemption to the sinful and miracles to the faithful. The monastery's own resurrection has been remarkable, for until six monks returned in 1989 there had been none on Valaam since 1940, when its brethren and treasures were

Lake Ladoga

evacuated to Finland as Stalin occupied Karelia. In the meantime, Valaam had served as a dumping ground for disfigured war veterans, isolated from Soviet society until 1967, when it became a tourist destination for Leningrad's intelligentsia, and both sides were shocked by the gulf in living standards and horizons.

Over the past decade the **monastery** has partly recovered its former *de facto* sovereignty over Valaam. The restoration of the monastery is the only building work currently allowed on the island, whose 500 inhabitants are disgruntled that their promised new housing hasn't materialized – symptomatic of a gulf between the monks and the locals, who already do without electricity and supplies from the mainland for weeks at a time, and would probably leave if the monastery banned liquor and tobacco, as in Tsarist times. The Patriarch of the Russian Orthodox Church (who was once a monk on Valaam) has even ensured that the local army garrison consists of true believers, with leave to fast and attend holy festivals.

The monastery

The origins of the **Monastery of the Transfiguration of the Saviour** (Spaso-Preobrazhensiy Valaamskiy monastyr) are obscure, but there

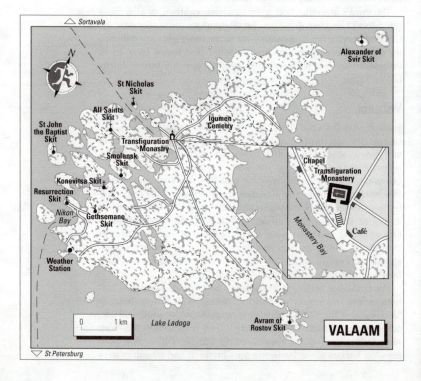

OUT OF THE CITY: CHAPTER 18

Cruises to Valaam and Kizhi

From May to September, **cruise boats** depart every few days from St Petersburg's River Terminal (Rechnoy vokzal) at prospekt Obukhovsoy obornony 95, near Proletarskaya metro. East German-built boats like the *M/S Kronstadt* and *M/S Sankt Petersburg* have en-suite cabins, a restaurant and bar-disco, and are used by foreign tour operators (see p.5) and local firms alike – the only difference being the quality of the meals and the cost of the cruise. Older, less salubrious Russian vessels such as the *M/S Popov* are used by less fastidious agencies and poorer Russian tourists.

You can buy **tickets** for the *Kronstadt* and *Sankt Petersburg* from Itus-Tour (Ligovskiy pr. 64 ☎164 99 56, fax 112 20 13), the Central Travel Agency (Bolshaya Konyushennaya ul. 27 ☎315 30 74), Sindbad Travel (3-ya Sovetskaya ul. 28 ☎327 83 84, *sindbad@sindbad.ru*) or Sputnik (ul. Chapygina 4 ☎234 35 00). July, August and weekends are the most expensive times to travel, but even then fares aren't exorbitant: for one person sharing a twin cabin, a trip to Valaam lasting one day and two nights is about $70; $109 buys an extra day on the island; while a three-or four-day cruise, with one or two days at Kizhi as well, costs from $156 to $200. If you're prepared to settle for the *Popov*, tickets can go as low as $55 for a two-day cruise, or $82 for four days. Foreigners pay a **surcharge** on all tickets of $21 for Valaam, or $30 for Valaam and Kizhi.

The package includes all **meals** except dinner the first night (which costs extra) and breakfast on return to Petersburg (which isn't provided), but vegetarians need to bring alternatives to the meaty, Soviet canteen-style fare. Passengers are assigned a shift (*smena*) for meals and excursions; your table-number will be posted in your cabin. Drinks are inexpensive, so everyone makes the most of the bar and disco. As there are no facilities for exchanging **money** or using credit cards, you should bring enough rubles to cover expenses.

seems to have been a cloister here even before Avram's arrival, and legend attributes the conversion of the pagans of Valaam to none other than the Apostle Andrew, the "First Called". From the fourteenth century onwards the monastery was often sacked by the Swedes, and also served as a fortress against them. Laid waste in 1611, it was rebuilt a century later with funds from Peter the Great, and reached its apogee in the late nineteenth century, when the existing cathedral and residential blocks were built, hermitages were rebuilt or founded, and there were nearly a thousand monks in residence. Although 600 were conscripted and all but two hermitages closed during World War I, the monastery had the good fortune to end up on Finnish territory and escape the scourging of the Church in Russia – while monks who fled Karelia in 1940 were able to establish the New Valaam Monastery in Finland, whose rejection of Patriarchal authority during the Soviet era continues to this day (a rejection reciprocated by the Russian Church, which derides them as mere Finns who follow the Gregorian calendar and therefore can't possibly be true Orthodox believers).

Religious processions at Valaam

For monks and pilgrims, **processions** affirm the true faith and its unity
with the rocks and waters of Valaam. Icons are borne forth and liturgies
sung in slow procession from one shrine to another. Tourist spectators are
tolerated, but expected to observe the proprieties of dress and behaviour,
including not photographing the monks.

May 19 A procession by water from Monastery Bay to the Nicholas Skit
on the day of the transportation of St Nicholas's relics.

All Saints' Day A procession from the monastery to the All Saints' Skit,
and a celebration in its lower church.

July 11 A procession around the monastery in memory of SS Sergei and
German.

August 14 From the monastery to the bay, for the consecration of the
water.

The 100-odd monks on Valaam maintain their own **"time zone"**,
synchronized to Jerusalem and the Holy Land rather than Moscow.
Many of the **monks** are in their early thirties, including an ex-
Moscow DJ, a Socialist Realist artist turned icon-painter, and an
actor who found God through a stage adaptation of Dostoyevsky's
The Possessed. Rising at 5.30am, they spend as much as ten hours a
day praying in the **cathedral**, whose lower church contains the relics
of St German and St Sergei, and the icon *Our Lady of Valaam*. The
huge upper church is currently under repair, its exterior swathed in
scaffolding below a blue spire and cupola, visible all around
Monastery Bay. Tall service blocks surround the compound, housing
monks' cells and local families with nowhere else to live. A burly
monk ensures that nobody enters the holy precincts improperly
dressed, and others speed around the island's dirt roads in jeeps like
an occupying army.

Visitors are told not to photograph the monks, and that entry to
churches is conditional on men wearing long trousers and women
full-length skirts and headscarves. Women in trousers may be offered
a black, wraparound skirt to pass muster, but shouldn't count on it –
the monks would prefer that only pilgrims disturbed their sanctuary.
The monastery's **Web site** (*www.karelia.ru/~valaam*) is one of
many devoted to Valaam and its saints – the movement is especially
strong in America, where eighteenth-century missionaries from
Valaam made converts and founded churches and monasteries as far
afield as Alaska.

The skits

The **skit** (pronounced "skeet") or hermitage – the domicile of a few
monks living under stricter vows than their monastic brethren, such
as continual silence and prayer, or a vegan diet – is a leitmotif of
Valaam's landscape and religious life. The first skits were founded by

Abbott Nazary in the 1790s, with rock-cut cells in emulation of bygone, solitary hermits like Avram or Alexander of Svir, but these proved so harmful to the health that Abbott Damaskin (known for sleeping in a coffin) built brick living quarters, so that the larger skits came to resemble miniature monasteries.

The **Resurrection Skit**, overlooking Nikon Bay, was built during the 1890s where a hermit of the previous century had lived in a cave with snakes, and where St Andrew is said to have raised a stone cross only 28 years after the death of Christ. Its tidy quadrangle of brick dwellings could be mistaken for a private school, but for the monastery guides who greet visitors disembarking from cruise ships in the bay.

Ten minutes' walk inland, the **Gethsemane Skit** is a simple cream-coloured wooden church near a picturesquely dark lake, offset by the sky-blue roofs and spires of surrounding buildings – the cabins where the monks live are strictly off-limits, as a sign proclaims. From here you can follow a path through the woods to the **Konevitsa Skit** – a wooden chapel, only used on holy days, in a wonderful location atop the sheer cliffs of a narrow bay. A trail with stretches of timber baulks circumvents **Lake Igumen** and the **Black Lake**, with one route returning to the main road between the Resurrection Skit and the monastery, and the other forging on for 3km across a peninsula, an island and two bridges, to reach All Saints' Skit on Saints' Island, the smallest of the three main islands in the archipelago.

The **All Saints' Skit** is the oldest of Valaam's hermitages and the most romantic-looking, with a stone church and cells on the spot where St Alexander of Svir once lived, surrounded by brick dwellings, walls and towers, amid a sheltered clearing whose shallow soil is quickly warmed by the sun, enabling the monks to grow water melons as well as vegetables. At present there are five monks, observing a rule that forbids milk on non-Lenten days, and any con-tact with women except on All Saints' day. The dirt road that links the island to the monastery, 3km away, passes "**Shishkin's Fir**", the model for *A Fir-Tree on Valaam* by Shishkin, one of the many Romantic painters drawn to Valaam in the nineteenth century.

The other hermitages are only accessible by car or boat. Visitors who sign up for the organized boat trip from Nikon Bay to the monastery will get a distant view of the **John the Baptist Skit** and a closer one of the **Nicholas Skit** at the mouth of Monastery Bay, whose monks formerly acted as customs officials, searching incom-ing vessels for alcohol and tobacco. But you'll need to charter your own boat to land there, let alone catch sight of the hermitages of **Avram of Rostov** and **Alexander of Svir**, both located on remote islands.

Practicalities

Valaam is situated 170km north of Schlüsselburg and 250km from St Petersburg by boat – the only way of getting there when the lake isn't frozen over. Cruise boats moored in Nikon Bay offer their passengers a free **guided walk** from the Resurrection to the Konevitsa Skit to ensure that nobody gets lost, while after lunch there's a motorboat ride ($3 per person) around the coast to visit the monastery. There's nothing to stop you exploring the island for yourself, however: the walk to the Konevitsa Skit is easily done with the aid of a map, while local people offer transport around the island (at group, not individual, rates). A **jeep-ride** to the monastery (6.5km) and back costs $3 per vehicle if you arrange it yourself with a local driver (rather more if you let the cruise-boat operators organize it for you); a ninety-minute tour of several skits about $7; and private **boat trips** to beaches, lakes or islands about $14 per hour. You can even charter a boat, sleeping up to ten people, for trips of several days exploring the remoter islands, maybe spotting some of Valaam's twenty wild **elks**. Talk to Dmitri Soshkin, who owns one of the jeep-taxis, if you're interested. You can buy smoked fish, berries, mushrooms and honey from the islanders, and beer and vodka from the stall near the landing stage.

Kizhi

Kizhi island is about 250km from Valaam as seabirds fly, but nearly twice as far by boat, from Lake Ladoga up the River Svir into the green, glacial **Lake Onega**. Kizhi, its archipelago and the shore of the lake are collectively known as **Zaonezhe**, or "Beyond the Onega", formerly the domain of the pagan Ves and Saami peoples of Karelia until they were absorbed by the kingdom of Novgorod in the twelfth century – the name Kizhi is thought to derive from the ritual games (*kizhat*) which they held on the island. Kizhi remained the religious and commercial centre of the region under Russian rule: its domain numbered 130 villages by the sixteenth century and was rich in timber, furs and foodstuffs, though it was repeatedly invaded by Swedes, Poles and Lithuanians until Russia's victory in the Northern War brought peace, and an upsurge in construction across the region gave rise to some of the finest **wooden architecture** in Europe.

Wildlife of Kizhi

The **wildlife** of the Kizhi archipelago includes 190 species of birds, 36 kinds of mammal, and seven amphibians and reptiles. Elks, bears, alpine hares and foxes, badgers, martens, lynxes and otters can be seen in the spruce woods, which also harbour wood grouse, hazel hens and eagle owls. Other birds are at home on the cliffs and beaches of the skerrries – golden and white-tailed eagles, grey cranes, lesser black-throated gulls and ospreys – while the inland bogs abound in rare plants such as water lobelia, rockrose and lady's slipper.

Due to Kizhi's remoteness, both the buildings and the folk culture that sustained them survived into the twentieth century, but were deteriorating as a result of the declining and ageing population, and the impact of modernization. From 1948 onwards, Soviet ethnographers studied the villages, identified outstanding monuments and began moving them to Kizhi to create what is now the **Open-air Museum of History, Architecture and Ethnography** – a folklore reservation of both genuine and reconstructed villages housing a population whose lifestyle isn't so different from their grandparents, though their aspirations are higher. While tourism offers an economic lifeline, the number of visitors has been limited to 130,000 a year to minimize damage to the environment. The nucleus of the museum is the amazing *pogost*. From here, trails lead north and south to the villages, each of which contains at least one house designated as a **folk museum**. A single **ticket** ($10) is valid for all the sites on the island. For a preview, check out the museum's **Web site** at *www.karelia.ru* or visit *http://kizhi.karelia.ru*.

All the folk museums are open daily: mid-May to June 9am–4pm; June–Aug 8am–8pm; Sept to mid-Oct 9am–4pm.

Kizhi festivals

If you can, time your visit to catch one of the local **festivals**. The Festival of Kizhi Volost (Aug 23) features folk music, dancing and handicrafts, while other events are mainly religious, but still end in feasting and drinking – such as the Easter gatherings, the festivals of Christ's Transfiguration (Aug 19) and the Intercession of the Virgin (Oct 14), and the chapel feast of the Dormition at Vasilevo (Aug 28). Similar chapel feasts occur in other villages, only accessible by motorboat: SS Peter and Paul's at Volkostrov (June 12), SS Kirik and Ulita's at Vorobiyi (July 28), and St Ilya's day at Telyatniko (Aug 2).

The pogost

Built over three centuries by local carpenters, the *pogost* comprises an extraordinary ensemble of disparate wooden structures enclosed by a wooden stockade. The *pogost* was begun in 1714 with the 37-metre-high **Church of the Transfiguration** – a magnificent edifice twice as tall as St Basil's in Moscow, with 22 onion domes upon tiers of *bochka* (barrel) roofs, inset one above another to form a cascade of shingles reaching almost to the ground. Its dramatic silhouette is enhanced by the contrast between its dark fir timbers and the shingles (called *cheshui* – or "fish scales" – in Russian) carved from moist aspen, which ages from a golden hue to silver. Though the church's 30,000 shingles were designed to channel rainwater away, and there was also an inner flush roof to catch any leaks and carry them into a drain, these precautions didn't prevent rot from affecting its beams over the centuries, and the interior is now supported by a metal cage and off limits to visitors.

Kizhi

Despite the legend that, after its completion, master carpenter Nestor cast his axe into the lake, vowing "There has not been, nowhere is and never will be a church like this!", the inhabitants of Kizhi had another go fifty years later, erecting the **Church of the Intercession**, whose boxy, nine-domed silhouette offsets the pyramidal Church of the Transfiguration. Meant for winter use, it became the only place of worship after 1937, till services were banned entirely after World War II, when the open-air museum was established – though they resumed in 1997, its trapezium still contains an exhibition on the Kizhi peasants' revolt of 1769–71 and icons of the Onega region. A tall, freestanding **bell tower** of 1874 completes the *pogost*.

The villages

After the *pogost*, most visitors head for the **reconstructed village** at the southern end of the island, whose buildings encapsulate the traditional Zaonezhe way of life. The village has two farmsteads that once belonged to middling-affluent peasants, combining home and barn under one roof, with spacious, functional living quarters full of artefacts – the house from Seredeka contains an interesting collection of boats and sleighs. Nearby are a threshing barn, a windmill, a watermill and two diminutive churches. The **Church of the Resurrection of Lazarus** – originally from the Muromskiy Monastery in northern Karelia – is the oldest wooden church extant in Russia (1390), while the octagonal tent-roofed **Chapel of the Archangel Michael** was taken from Lelikozero in the Kizhi skerries. During the tourist season there are demonstrations of traditional crafts, and islanders come to make hay in the surrounding meadows.

The islanders live in two original, rather than reconstructed, villages (though some of the buildings in them, such as the Sergin house, have been transplanted from other sites): **Vasilevo**, on the western side of the island, boasts the finest secular building on Kizhi: the enormous, rambling **Sergin house** that once accommodated a family of 22. Taken from the village of Munozero, it now shares the limelight with the **Sergeeva house** from Lipovitsy, the abode of the Vasilevs, one of the most prosperous local families a century ago. Nearby is the earliest native church on the island, the seventeenth-century **Assumption Church**, whose large octagonal bell tower originally doubled as a watchtower.

Yamka, on the other side of the island, lacks any outstanding houses but epitomizes the traditional Zaonezhne village, with houses running along the shore facing the lake, fields and kitchen gardens out back, barns and granaries nearby, and a windmill, threshing barn and wayside cross further on. As with all Kizhi's timber structures, the logs were felled in the late autumn after the final ring of the tree had hardened, and left on the ground until late spring. By using axes instead of saws, the grain of the wood was closed rather than left open to moisture; and nails were dispensed with in favour of notches or mortise and tenon joints, which are better suited to the climate.

Should you walk from Yamka to Vasilevo, a distance of 5km, the trail passes within sight of the **Chapel of St Veronica's Veil** on Naryina Hill, whose picturesque witch's hat belfry with a broad frill adorns the highest point on Kizhi. Further north, another **reconstructed village** represents the **Pudozh** region of Karelia, noted for cultivating superb flax which was exported as far away as England, Holland and Belgium – some fine textiles are displayed in the **Belaev house**, one of three farmsteads in the village. From here, a trail continues to the **Chapel of Three Sanctifiers** at the northern end of the island, which once served as a watchtower in the village of Kavgora, and is intended to be the focus of another reconstructed village dealing with the Finnish Ludiki folk culture.

The skerries

The dozens of islands, or **skerries**, off the Zaonezhskiy peninsula are dotted with a handful of villages, tenuously connected to the mainland by motorboat – one of the few signs of modernity in a time-warped waterworld. Kizhi's open-air museum offers three **motorboat excursions** around the skerries. **Tour #1** covers the southern skerries, where there's the greatest concentration of islands, with landings at nesting sites and the village of Lelikovo, interspersed by a short hike and a picnic by a lake. On **tour #2**, offshore views of several villages north of Kizhi are followed by a 1.5km hike to Lake Vekhozero and a visit to the archeological excavations and lime-pit on Yuzhniy Island. **Tour #3** lasts twice as long as the others, and involves walking across Bolshoy Klimentskiy Island from Sennaya Guba to Cape Voinavolok, via woods, meadows and beaches, offering a chance to see all kinds of wildlife.

Kizhi	Кижи
Kronstadt	Кронштадт
Petrokrepost	Петрокрепость
Razliv	Разлив
Repino	Репино
Schlüsselburg	Шлиссельбург
Sestroretsk	Сестрорецк
Solnechnoe	Солнечное
Valaam	Валаам
Vyborg	**Выборг**
Krasnaya ploshchad	Красная площадь
ul. Krasnoarmeyskaya	ул. Красноармейская
Krepostnaya ul.	Крепостная ул.
prospekt Lenina	пр. Ленина
prospekt Pobedy	пр. Победы
ul. Ushakova	ул. Ушакова
Vokzalnaya ul.	Вокзальная ул.
Zheleznodorozhnya ul.	Железнодорожная ул.

Chapter 19

Novgorod

Despite its name, **Novgorod** – or "New Town" – is Russia's oldest city, founded, according to popular belief, by the Varangian (Scandinavian) Prince Rurik in 862 AD. By the end of the tenth century it had developed into an important commercial centre thanks to its favoured position on the River Volkhov, which flows north into Lake Ladoga and on to the Gulf of Finland – part of an ancient trade route stretching from Scandinavia to Greece.

Novgorod was traditionally ruled over by the eldest son of the prince of Kiev, though power later devolved to the town meetings or *veche*, dominated by wealthy local landlords who had a healthy disdain towards the prince – "if the prince is no good, into the mud with him" was their motto. Novgorod was the only important city in Russia that was not captured by the Tatars in the thirteenth century and was the administrative seat of a principality that stretched west to Poland and north to the White Sea. During its most successful period – from the twelfth to the fifteenth century – Novgorod's republican-minded nobles bestowed a fantastic architectural legacy upon the town, much of which survives to this day, including a complete fortified inner city, or **Kremlin** (akin to the one in Moscow), and over a hundred Byzantine-style **churches** (of which some forty remain). The cultural life of the city also flourished. Icon painters in the town's monasteries formed their own school and examples of their work can be seen in the **Novgorod Museum** and in St Petersburg's Russian Museum. In addition, the 750 texts inscribed on birch bark that were found during excavations testify to the fact that the level of literacy in Novgorod was unmatched anywhere else in Russia.

The city remained proudly independent until Tsar Ivan III first brought it under the administrative control of Muscovy in 1478. Just under a century later, in 1570, Novgorod was subdued once and for all by **Ivan the Terrible**, who marched on the town and built a high timber wall around it to prevent anyone from leaving. Every day for five weeks, hundreds of the imprisoned inhabitants were put to death in front of the tsar and his depraved son Ivan: grisly stories tell of dozens being fried alive in a giant metal pan. Estimates of the number of Novgorodians slaughtered range from 15,000 to 60,000.

Misfortune again overtook the city during its **occupation by the Swedes** in the early seventeenth century, but the stubborn inhabitants rebuilt it and restored the fortifications, which played a vital role in the defence against Swedish attack for decades afterwards.

Things remained relatively peaceful until **World War II**, during which 98 percent of Novgorod's buildings were ruined and its population decimated as the front rolled back and forth over the city. As a matter of patriotic pride the Soviets determinedly rebuilt the Kremlin walls, the churches and the rest of the town from scratch. Nowadays, Novgorod seems genteel and crime-free in comparison to St Petersburg, and in a reassertion of past economic ties now belongs to the Hanseatic League of northern European cities, though its former trading links are less important to the local economy than the Dovgan vodka distillery, one of the town's chief industries.

The Old Town

While the bulk of the city, which has a population of 240,000, is architecturally undistinguished, the **old town** possesses many historic buildings dating from the fifteenth and sixteenth centuries and is divided neatly in two by the wide sweep of the River Volkhov. The left bank, known as the **Sophia Side** (Sofiyskaya storona), is focused on the walled Kremlin, where the prince and later the archbishop resided. This oval-shaped fortress, which predates its more famous namesake in Moscow, is the most obvious place to begin a tour of Novgorod.

On the opposite bank is the **Commercial Side** (Torgovaya storona), site of the old marketplace and once home to the city's rich

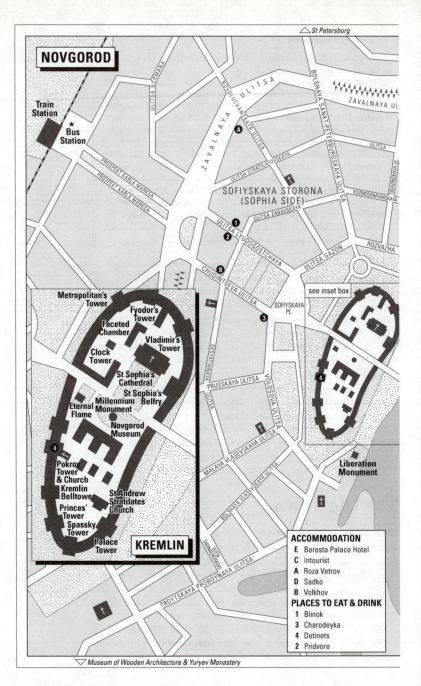

NOVGOROD

△ St Petersburg

Train Station

★ Bus Station

ULITSA GERMANA

PROSPEKT KARLA MARKSA

PROSPEKT KARLA MARKSA

ZAVALNAYA ULITSA

NOVOLUCHANSKAYA ULITSA

A

BOLSHAYA SANKT-PETERBURGSKAYA ULITSA

ZAVALNAYA UL

ULITSA

TIKHVINSKAYA UL

KOZMODEMYANSKAYA

ULITSA STRATILATOVSKAYA

SOFIYSKAYA STORONA
(SOPHIA SIDE)

1
2

ULITSA ZABAVSKAYA

ULITSA LYUDOGOSTCHAYA

ULITSA GAZON

ROZVAZHA

CHUDINTSEVA ULITSA

B

see inset box

SOFIYSKAYA PL

3

4

Metropolitan's Tower

Faceted Chamber

Clock Tower

Fyodor's Tower

Vladimir's Tower

St Sophia's Cathedral

St Sophia's Belfry

Eternal Flame

Millennium Monument

Novgorod Museum

4

Pokrox Tower & Church

Kremlin Belltower

Princes' Tower

Spassky Tower

St Andrew Stratilates Church

Palace Tower

KREMLIN

PESTALNAYA ULITSA

PRUSSKAYA ULITSA

VOLOSOVA ULITSA

MALAYA VLASEVSKAYA ULITSA

BOLSHAYA VLASEVSKAYA ULITSA

Liberation Monument

TROYTSKAYA PROBOYNAYA ULITSA

ACCOMMODATION
E Beresta Palace Hotel
C Intourist
A Roza Vetrov
D Sadko
B Volkhov

PLACES TO EAT & DRINK
1 Blinok
3 Charodeyka
4 Detinets
2 Pridvore

▽ Museum of Wooden Architecture & Yuryev Monastery

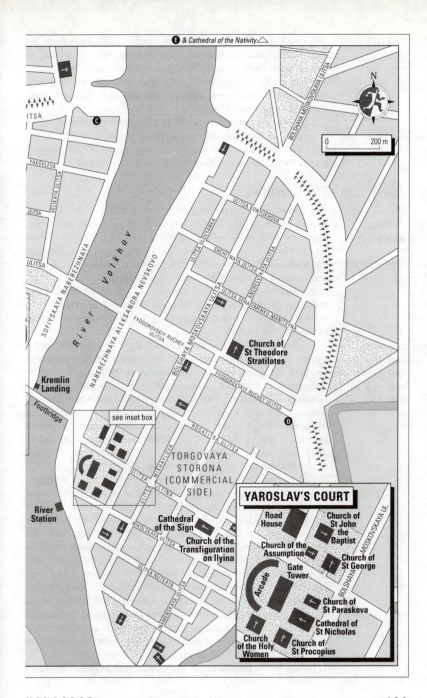

& Cathedral of the Nativity △

N

0   200 m

River Volkhov

SOFIYSKAYA NABEREZHNAYA

NABEREZHNAYA ALEKSANDRA NEVSKOVO

YAKOVLEVA

VELIKAYA ULITSA

ULITSA

ULITSA

BOLSHAYA MOSKOVSKAYA ULITSA

ULITSA KONYUKHOVA

ULITSA OLOVYANKA

SHCHITNAYA ULITSA

ANDREEVSKAYA

ULITSA GERASIMENKO-MANITSYNA

FYODOROVSKIY RUCHEY ULITSA

BOLSHAYA MOSKOVSKAYA ULITSA

FYODOROVSKIY RUCHEY ULITSA

Church of St Theodore Stratilates

Kremlin Landing

Footbridge

see inset box

ROGATITSA ULITSA

MIKLAYLOVA

ULITSA ILYINA

TORGOVAYA STORONA (COMMERCIAL SIDE)

River Station

NIKOLSKAYA ULITSA

ULITSA NUTNAYA

ILYINA

ZNAMENSKAYA ULITSA

Cathedral of the Sign

Church of the Transfiguration on Ilyina

YAROSLAV'S COURT

Road House

Church of St John the Baptist

Church of the Assumption

Gate Tower

Church of St George

Arcade

BOLSHAYA MOSKOVSKAYA UL

Church of St Paraskeva

Cathedral of St Nicholas

Church of the Holy Women

Church of St Procopius

merchants. Much of the present layout of the city dates from the reign of Catherine the Great, when the existing medieval network of narrow streets was replaced by a series of thoroughfares radiating out from the Kremlin on the left bank and running at right angles to the river on the right bank. The two sides are linked by a pedestrian footbridge and a road-bridge.

Excursions around the Kremlin and the town's churches can be arranged through the Novgorod Museum Reserve (☎ & fax 1622/737 70), whose Web site (*http://eng.novgorod-museum.ru*) contains many images of Novgorod's historic buildings.

The Kremlin

The Kremlin is open 6am–midnight; free.

The impressive, nine-metre-high red-brick walls of the **Kremlin** (known locally as the "Detinets"), crenellated and punctuated at regular intervals by bulky towers, date from the fifteenth century, when they formed the inner ring of a series of earthen ramparts. The original wooden ramparts were erected by Prince Vladimir in 1044 AD, and replaced by stone walls from 1302 onwards. As many as eighteen churches and 150 houses were once crammed inside these walls, though much of the Kremlin now consists of open space. The walls are best seen from the east, along the river, as they are hidden by trees on the western side.

St Sophia's Cathedral is open daily noon–1pm & 2.30–6pm; $1.30.

Inside the walls, **St Sophia's Cathedral** (Sofiyskiy sobor) is the earliest and by far the largest of all the churches in Novgorod, and has been the Kremlin's main landmark since its completion in the mid-eleventh century. Commissioned by Yaroslav the Wise, this Byzantine cathedral resembles its namesake in Kiev, which Yaroslav had erected a decade earlier – it may in fact have been constructed by the same Greek master builders. As such it represents the peak of princely power in Novgorod, and afterwards became a symbol of great civic pride: "Where St Sophia is, there is Novgorod" mused Prince Mstislav as Novgorod held out against the Tatars.

The cathedral's five bulbous domes cluster around a slightly raised, golden helmet dome topped by a stone pigeon. Legend has it that if the pigeon ever falls, Novgorod will suffer a calamity; so far the worst fate to befall it was being hit by a bullet shortly before the town was occupied by the Germans in 1942. In Soviet times the cathedral was classified as a museum and worship forbidden but, like many churches in Novgorod, it was returned to the Orthodox Church in 1991. Now plastered and painted white, the cathedral was originally bare brick, as can be seen on a small patch on the northern side. The only original exterior decorative features which survive are on the western facade, which sports a faded fresco, and on the splendid bronze twelfth-century **Magdeburg Doors**, made in Germany and covered with little figures in high relief (the sculptors themselves are depicted in the bottom left-hand corner).

Inside, on the far side of the nave, a fragment of eleventh-century

fresco survives – a portrait of the Byzantine Emperor Constantine
and his mother Helen. Here you can also see part of the original
floor, nearly 2m below the level of the current floor. Other minor
patches of frescoes can be seen in the cupola and on the embrasures,
but most of these date from the end of the nineteenth century. The
well-preserved iconostasis is one of the oldest in Russia and includes
works from the eleventh to seventeenth century; to the right of the
altar, encased in a box, is the famous **Icon of the Sign**, with its damaged eye (see p.408). Note also the vast chandelier, which was a present from Tsar Boris Godunov, and the ornately carved wooden
chapel where Ivan the Terrible used to pray before he ravaged
Novgorod.

Rising up to the west of the cathedral is the minaret-like **Clock
Tower** (Chasozvon), a fifteenth-century structure which served as a
watchtower for the archbishop. The tower's famous bell, which used
to call the citizens to meetings of the *veche*, was carried off to
Moscow by Ivan III after he had revoked the city's charter of self-government. Alongside the tower are the old law courts and the
Archbishop's Courtyard (Vladychniy dvor), with the **Faceted
Chamber** (Granovitaya palata) on the west side. Its nondescript
exterior hides a wonderful rib-vaulted, fifteenth-century reception
hall, now a high-security museum of ecclesiastical treasures comprising jewelled crosses, mitres and icon covers from the sixteenth to
nineteenth century. The building alongside contains an **Embroidery
Museum** that includes life-sized "portrait shrouds" of St Valaam and
Christ – the latter was ceremonially taken out of the cathedral at
Easter to symbolize his resurrection.

*The Faceted
Chamber is
open 10am–
6pm, closed
Wed; $1.30.*

To the east of the cathedral stands **St Sophia's Belfry** (Sofiyskaya
zvonnitsa), constructed during the fifteenth to seventeenth century,
but drastically altered in the nineteenth century. The giant bells
which once tolled from its upper gallery are now displayed below in
their dismantled state.

*The
Embroidery
Museum is
open
10am–6pm;
closed Wed &
last Fri of the
month; $1.30.*

Around the Millennium Monument

South of the cathedral, at the centre of the Kremlin, is the vast, bell-
shaped **Millennium Monument**, cast in iron by an English company
and unveiled in 1862 on the thousandth anniversary of Rurik's arrival
in Novgorod. Figures representing Mother Russia and the Orthodox
Church crown the monument's giant globe, while around it (clockwise from the south) stand Rurik, Prince Vladimir, the tsars Michael
(the first Romanov), Peter the Great and Ivan III, and lastly Dmitri
Donskoy trampling a Tatar. A frieze around the base of the monument
contains more than a hundred smaller figures, including Catherine
the Great, Alexander Nevsky, Pushkin, Lermontov and Glinka, as well
as sundry other military and artistic personages. The Nazis dismantled the 65-tonne monument during World War II, intending to transport it to Germany, but thankfully never got around to doing so.

To the west of the Millennium Monument, the Soviet regime erected its own monument, centred on an **eternal flame**, commemorating those who died during the fight to liberate Novgorod from Nazi occupation. Like the Tomb of the Unknown Soldier by the Kremlin walls in Moscow, it is a traditional spot for newlyweds to lay flowers and have their photographs taken.

Behind the Millennium Monument is a block of early nineteenth-century administrative offices, the largest building in the Kremlin – the radical writer Alexander Herzen worked here in the 1840s during one of his many periods of internal exile. Now home to the **Novgorod Museum**, its first floor is devoted to historical artefacts, ranging from birch-bark texts and an original segment of tree-trunk pavement from the fifteenth century to a bullet-holed bust of Tolstoy that received its wounds during the Nazi occupation. On the upper floor you'll find a splendid collection of icons from the Novgorod school, including *The Battle Between Novgorod and Suzdal*, which dates from the 1560s – somewhat later than the version in the Russian Museum in St Petersburg (see p.153).

*The Novgorod
Museum is
open Mon &
Wed–Sun
10am–6pm,
closed last
Thurs of the
month; $1.30.*

The Commercial Side

From the river bank on the east side of the Kremlin, there's a great view of the **Commercial Side** (Torgovaya storona), site of Novgorod's medieval market. More than any other Russian city, Novgorod developed a middle class of artisans and merchants thanks to its unique access to trade routes with the rest of northern Europe. During the city's medieval heyday, numerous wooden and masonry churches were built on this side of the river, funded increasingly by the rich mercantile class, and the market once boasted 1500 stalls selling everything from silver and bone to honey and fur – though all that remains now is a long section of the old seventeenth-century **arcade**, and beyond it, from the same period, a **gate tower**.

The foundation of St Petersburg in 1703 dealt a major blow to Novgorod's commercial prosperity, and the final straw came in 1851, when the new railway linking Moscow and St Petersburg bypassed the town entirely. By the mid-nineteenth century, an English traveller found "no life left in the bazaar; customers are so rare. The principal trade seems to be that of icons."

Yaroslav's Court

The densest cluster of surviving medieval buildings is to be found immediately behind the arcade, where the palace of Yaroslav the Wise once stood in a grassy area still known as **Yaroslav's Court** (Yaroslavovo dvorishche). Its most important surviving building is the **Cathedral of St Nicholas** (Nikolskiy sobor), which once enshrined an icon that reputedly cured Yaroslav of an illness. Built in 1113 in a Byzantine style that was a deliberate challenge to St Sophia's, it originally sported a full complement of five domes, which unfortunately received a bashing in World War II. The only interior feature worth mentioning is a graphically gruesome but severely damaged fresco of Job afflicted with boils.

The neighbouring **Church of St Paraskeva** (Tserkov Paraskevy Pyatnitsi) was commissioned a century later by the newly ascendant local merchants and dedicated to the patron saint of commerce, but was then rebuilt in 1345. Its distinctive style – large, round-arched porches flanked by clusters of thin columns supporting a single-domed, gabled roof – was probably executed by craftsmen from Smolensk and represented a dramatic shift in the Novgorodian style. Nowadays, sadly, it has fallen into a state of disrepair and is closed to the public.

On the other side of the Cathedral of St Nicholas are two sixteenth-century *trapeznie* churches – churches that included a refectory (*trapezna*) at the west end – which heralded the beginning of a new period of building by the Muscovite merchants who controlled Novgorod following Ivan III's occupation. The **Church of the Holy Women** (Tserkov Zhon-mironosits), nearest to the cathedral, built in 1510 by the merchant Ivan Syrkov, is a classic example, with an arcaded refectory and a series of *kokoshniki*, or decorative wooden gables. In 1529, Syrkov's son began the slightly smaller **Church of St Procopius** (Tserkov Prokopiya) next door. Like the Church of the Holy Women, the decorative detailing around the arches and drum departs slightly from the austere norm of Novgorod, reflecting the more fanciful tastes of its Muscovite patron.

A short step north of the Church of St Paraskeva is a trio of churches, the two oldest of which are the **Church of St John the Baptist** (1127) and the **Church of the Assumption** (1135), both begun by Prince Vsevolod shortly before he and his family were hounded out of Novgorod by the local nobility in 1137. Today, however, most of the churches detailed above either serve as shops of one kind or another or are undergoing restoration prior to reopening for services.

Beyond Yaroslav's Court

A good half a kilometre east of Yaroslav's Court, along ulitsa Ilyina, is one of Novgorod's finest creations, the **Church of the Transfiguration on Ilyina** (Tserkov Spasa Preobrazheniya na Ilyine), built in 1374 by the *ulichani*, or street community, which kept its bank vault on the upper floor. Designed as a standard single-dome structure with a tall drum (the steeply pitched roof is modern), the big surprise here is the mixture of pagan and Christian symbolism on the whitewashed exterior: sun symbols and anthropomorphic crosses, either indented or in relief. The **interior** contains fragmentary fourteenth-century frescoes, the only documented paintings in Novgorod by Theophanes the Greek, Andrei Rublev's teacher. The best preserved are those on the upper levels, depicting the Trinity,

The church is open Mon–Fri 10am–3pm, closed last Thurs of the month; $1.30.

*The cathedral
is open
Tues–Sun
10am–5pm,
closed first
Thurs of each
month; $1.30.*

*The Icon of the
Sign is now
displayed in St
Sophia's
Cathedral (see
p.405).*

*The Cathedral
of the Nativity
is open
Tues–Sun
1–8pm; closed
first Wed of the
month; free.*

the saints David, Daniel, Semyou the older and younger, and Olympus, all seated on pillars. The frescoes were badly damaged in the war, when the Germans used the church as a machine-gun nest.

Across the road stands the **Cathedral of the Sign** (Znamenskiy sobor), built in the seventeenth century's state-approved Muscovite style, although its surrounding outbuildings make it look more like a monastic complex. It is now used as a concert hall, owing to its superb acoustics, but visitors can go inside to view the wonderful frescoes in hues of russet, pink and blue. To the right of the doorway, look out for the one of Peter the Great (in a green suit) awaiting judgement for his reforms of the Orthodox Church. The cathedral's predecessor on this site was built to house the famous **Icon of the Sign**, which was carried to the walls of Novgorod's Kremlin when the town was besieged by the Suzdalians in 1169. Legend has it that when one of the enemy's arrows pierced the icon's right eye, the Virgin turned her face away to weep and the Suzdalian soldiers went blind and started killing each other in a frenzy.

Both churches stand at the crossroads of ulitsa Ilyina and **Znamenskaya ulitsa**, which is lined with the sort of picturesque wooden houses that characterized the majority of towns and villages in Russia before 1917, though the ones that you see here were built shortly after World War II. There are too many other churches scattered around the Commercial Side to describe them all, but two deserve special mention. On the north side of Fyodorovskiy ruchey ulitsa stands the **Church of St Theodore Stratilates** (Tserkov Fyodora Stratilata), the prototype for the Church of the Transfiguration on Ilyina, built by the widow and son of a wealthy merchant. It's a classic example of fourteenth-century Novgorodian architecture, a single-domed cubic structure, modestly decorated on the outside, and containing valuable fourteenth-century frescoes within – though unfortunately it's not currently open to the public.

Last but not least is the **Cathedral of the Nativity** (Rozdenstvenskiy sobor), located at the far northern end of Bolshaya Moskovskaya ulitsa, 500m beyond the *Beresta Palace* (bus #4 or #19). This was once the centrepiece of the Antonov Monastery (whose buildings are now occupied by Novgorod University), founded in 1125 by Anthony the Roman, who is said to have floated all the way from Rome to Novgorod on a rock. Most of the frescoes in the cathedral date from the nineteenth century; those in the hall flanking the southern side of the nave depict the life of Anthony, whom the Russians call Antonni Rimylani.

Around the Yurev Monastery

If you want to explore a little further afield, it's only a three-kilometre journey south to the shores of **Lake Ilmen**. Here you'll find the **Yurev Monastery** – the largest surviving complex of its kind in Novgorod – and the wonderful **Museum of Wooden Architecture**, which is also the venue for two annual festivals (see box on p.401). **To get there**, take bus #7 or #7a from outside the train station or from near the *Charodeyka* café on Volosova ulitsa. However, if you are content just to see the lake, a more relaxing alternative may be a trip down the River Volkhov – boats depart from the Kremlin landing stage for a one-hour return trip ($2).

The Yurev Monastery

At their peak, there were over twenty monasteries around Novgorod, many of them small towns in themselves. Although a convent and several hermitages on the shores of Lake Ilmen are now being revived, the only one that's readily accessible is the **Yurev Monastery** (Yuryev monastyr), founded by Prince Vsevolod in 1117. Surrounded by massive white walls and with a 52-metre-high bell tower above the entrance, the monastery grounds are now being cultivated again with the aid of a cow and a tractor, and the ten resident monks have restored one of the wings of cells, though the other (used as flats in Soviet times) is still derelict.

The monastery is open daily 10am–6pm; there's an admission charge ($1) to enter the cathedral. Visitors must dress appropriately: long trousers for men, and headscarves and full-length skirts for women.

At the heart of the complex is the majestic **Cathedral of St George** (Georgievskiy sobor), built by a "Master Peter" who is renowned as the first truly Russian architect. As one of the final great churches to be built by the Novgorod princes, it was a last-ditch attempt to surpass St Sophia, which was by then in the hands of the archbishop. During his rape of Novgorod, Ivan the Terrible personally wrenched the icons from its iconostasis. Although twelfth-century frescoes survive here and there, most date from the nineteenth century. On the west wall is a splendid Last Judgement, with the Devil seated on the Beast of the Apocalypse and the dead being raised from their graves; another fresco depicts a crocodile and elephant from Noah's ark.

The Museum of Wooden Architecture

Five hundred metres back down the road to Novgorod, in the woods to the west of the Yurev Monastery, the **Museum of Wooden Architecture** was established on the site of an ancient village in the 1960s to display old timber buildings from the Novgorod region. Wood was the most practicable and readily available building material in northern Russia – from the earliest times, the Novgorodians were derided by others as mere "carpenters".

The museum is open daily: mid-April to mid-Sept 10am–6pm; mid-Sept to mid-April 10am–4pm; $1.30.

The oldest buildings here date from the sixteenth century, including a wonderful **Church of the Nativity from Peredeiki** encircled by a raised gallery where the villagers would gossip after services. Most of the houses feature large lean-to barns, although the actual living quarters were much smaller, with benches on opposite sides of the room for the adults to sleep on, men on one side and women on the other. As the children slept just below the roof and grandparents above the stove, opportunities for procreation were limited to the weekly visit to the *banya* (bath house).

Practicalities

Novgorod is 190km south of St Petersburg, a three-hour journey by
bus, train or tourist coach. If you don't mind the restrictions of an
organized tour, it's probably easiest to take your pick of the rival
companies whose kiosks stand outside Gostiniy dvor, offering day-
trips to Novgorod for $7.50–$9. The price doesn't include admission
charges to the museums and churches, and commentary will be in
Russian only, but it's far cheaper than the car-plus-interpreter deals
offered by tourist agencies and top hotels. Just be sure to check
exactly which sites are featured on the itinerary.

Alternatively, you could go it alone by **bus**. There are departures
roughly every two hours from Bus Station #2, at naberezhnaya
Obvodnovo kanala 36. The first bus leaves at 6.50am; the last bus
returns from Novgorod at 7.30pm. **Trains** are less convenient,
departing in the late afternoon. **Tickets** for both trains and buses can
be bought from the stations right up to the moment of departure,
though it's wiser to book in advance, especially for early-morning
buses. In Novgorod, the **bus and train stations** are adjacent to each
other, northwest of the centre and a fifteen-minute walk from the
Kremlin.

Accommodation

You can just about see Novgorod on a long day-trip, but it's much
easier if you spend the night. If you fancy staying with a local
English-speaking family, **B&B lodgings** (②) can be pre-booked in St
Petersburg through HOFA (see p.273). Alternatively, there are several **hotels** in town of varying quality. The best value is the *Roza
Vetrov*, at Novoluchanskaya ul. 27a (☎ & fax 1622/720 33; ②), a
ten-minute walk from the train station; bookings can be made
through *International Hostel Holiday* in St Petersburg (see p.273).
The *Volkhov*, at ulitsa Frolovskaya 24 (☎1622/115 07; ②), is less
homely but more central, while another good bet at the budget end
of the scale is the *Sadko*, at Fyodorovskiy Ruchey ulitsa 16 on the
Commercial Side (☎ & fax 1622/943 82; ②). For a marginally higher standard of comfort, there's the riverside *Intourist* (☎1622/750
89, fax 741 57; ④), while if money's no object, the four-star *Beresta
Palace* (☎1622/333 15, fax 317 07; ⑤) is perhaps the finest hotel
in Russia outside of Moscow and St Petersburg.

Eating and drinking

If you're on a tight budget, *Blinok* at Lyudogostchaya ulitsa 3 serves
delicious, cheap pancakes, and also sells beer in the sit-down section. For a proper meal, the *Pridvore* across the road (daily
noon–midnight) does excellent Russian food, but you'd do best to eat
in the bar (which has a separate entrance) rather than the restaurant,
where the service is rather slapdash. Another option is the medieval-
style *Detinets* in the Kremlin (daily 11am–6pm & 7–11pm, Mon

opens at noon), which specializes in ancient Russian recipes and drinks like beef-in-the-pot, carp, *medovukha* (honey mead) and *sbittern* (a herbal concoction, served warm). In contrast, the *Charodeyka*, on the corner of Volosova ulitsa, is all chrome and glass, with a Euro-oriented menu (pizzas, steaks, chicken dishes, fish kebabs) and imported drinks only (which pushes up the price). On the Commercial Side, there's a choice between two hotel restaurants: the decent but unexciting place in the *Sadko*, and the extremely ritzy dining room in the *Beresta Palace* – expect to pay around $50 per head.

While you can also **drink** at any of the above venues, the liveliest nightspot in Novgorod is the nameless bar at the entrance to the Kremlin bus park on Sofiyskaya ploshchad, just to the west of the Kremlin, which features live music and karaoke competitions and attracts a young crowd.

The Old Town

Novgorod	Новгород
Streets	
ul. Chudnitsa	ул. Чудница
ul. Gazon	ул. Газон
ul. Ilyina	ул. Ильина
Troytskaya Proboynaya ul.	Троицкая Пробойная ул.
Znamenskaya ul.	Знаменская ул.
Sights	
Faceted Chamber	Грановитая палата
Museum of Wooden Architecture	музей Деревянного Зодчества
St Sophia's Cathedral	Софийский собор
Yurev Monastery	Юрьевский монастырь

Contexts

A History of St Petersburg

For a city less than three hundred years old, St Petersburg has experienced more than its fair share of upheaval. Founded by Peter the Great as a "window on the West", and steeped in culture and bloodshed, it was admired and despised in equal measure as the Imperial capital of the Romanov dynasty and the most European of Russian cities. As the cradle of three revolutions, St Petersburg has a history inseparable from that of modern Russia, whose own travails are reflected in the city's changing names: from Tsarist St Petersburg to revolutionary Petrograd, and from Soviet Leningrad back to post-Communist St Petersburg. The city will celebrate its tercentenary in 2003.

Peter the Great

The foundation of St Petersburg was the work of Tsar Peter I, a giant in body and spirit better known as **Peter the Great** (1682–1725), one of the three "great despots" of Russian history (the other two being Ivan the Terrible and Stalin). After a disturbed and violent childhood – at the age of ten he witnessed the murder of many of his closest relatives by the Kremlin Guards – he became obsessed with all things military and nautical, drilling regiments during his early teens and learning the art of shipbuilding at first hand in Dutch shipyards during his famous "Great Embassy" to Western Europe in 1697.

Following his tour, where he had been gripped by what he saw, Peter embarked upon the forced

westernization of his backward homeland. He changed the country's name from Muscovy to Russia, replaced the Orthodox calendar with the Julian calendar, and further departed from the xenophobic traditions of Old Muscovy by inviting foreigners to settle in Russia. He forced the sons of landowners into the military or civil service and, aided by his jester, shaved off the beards of his courtiers, also making them smoke tobacco and wear Hungarian or German dress. Not content to stop there, he broke the power of the Church by replacing the self-governing Orthodox Patriarchate with a Holy Synod, essentially a secular ministry of religion subordinate to the tsar.

These reforms were extremely unpopular with most Russians and were accompanied by repressive measures borrowed straight from old Muscovite traditions. It was Peter who first introduced the internal passport system, later so beloved of the Communists, and who organized forced labour gangs to build his great projects. When faced with opposition or rebellion, he was ruthless, even overseeing the torture and death of his own son, Alexei, whom he suspected of conspiring against him. War characterized much of Peter's reign and many of his reforms were fashioned simply to keep Russia's military machine running smoothly. The quest for a sea port dominated his military thinking and in 1700 a peace treaty with Turkey left Peter free to pursue his main objective: the foundation of a new capital with trading access to the West via the Baltic Sea.

The major Baltic power of the day was Sweden and the war between the Russians and Swedes, known as the **Great Northern War**, lasted from 1700 to 1721. In 1700, at Narva, 150km west of present-day St Petersburg, the 18-year-old Swedish king, Charles XII, put the Russians to flight in blizzard conditions, but failed to follow up his victory with a march on Moscow, concentrating instead on subduing the rebellious Poles. Peter took advantage of the break in hostilities to strengthen his position around the Gulf of Finland.

The foundation of St Petersburg

Although popular legend has it that prior to the foundation of St Petersburg the Neva delta was an uninhabited wilderness, in fact there already existed a Swedish trading town, **Nyen**, in what is now the Okhta district, which had to be overrun before Peter could establish his new capital. Nonetheless, the site he chose was so exposed that it can fairly be termed a settlement in the wilderness – a fetid marshland chronically prone to flooding, with few natural or human resources nearby. On May 16, 1703, Peter is said to have snatched a halberd from one of his soldiers, cut two strips of turf, laid them across each other, and declared, "Here there shall be a town!"; though, of course, Pushkin's version of Peter's speech – "By nature we are fated here to cut a window through to Europe" – is more famous. Either way, **Sankt Pietr Burkh** (as it was originally called in the Dutch fashion) soon became known as the "city built on bones". Thousands of Swedish prisoners-of-war were press-ganged into work, joined by numerous other non-Russians from the far reaches of the Empire. Conditions were dire: there was a shortage of basic tools; earth had to be carried in the workers' clothing; and thousands died of starvation, cold, disease and exhaustion.

Nevertheless, in less than five months, a wooden fortress had been built on a small island. Next a wooden church was erected, along with a modest wooden cottage, which served as Peter's residence, and an inn, the *Four Frigates*, which doubled as the town hall. Within a year, there were fifteen houses on nearby Petrograd Island, where Peter first intended to base his new city, and the beginnings of the Admiralty on the mainland, then little more than a shipyard.

In the summer of 1706, with St Petersburg barely on the map, Charles XII invaded Russia from Poland. Again, within an ace of victory, he made the fateful decision not to march on Moscow, but to concentrate his efforts on Ukraine. Charles's supply and baggage train was attacked and defeated en route from Estonia in October 1708. The Russian winter inflicted yet more casualties on the Swedes and on June 27, 1709, at the **Battle of Poltava**, Peter trounced Charles, forcing him to flee to Turkey. The Great Northern War dragged on for another twelve years, but, as Peter put it, "Now the final stone has been laid in the foundation of St Petersburg."

Russia's victory at Poltava greatly strengthened the position of St Petersburg. In 1710, the Imperial family moved to the new city, together with all government institutions, and in 1712, Peter declared St Petersburg the Russian capital. Due to the shortage of masons, a decree was issued forbidding building in stone anywhere in the Empire outside St Petersburg; forty thousand workmen a year were sent from the provinces, while small landowners and nobles were obliged to resettle in the city and finance the building of their own houses. Encampments larger than the city itself rose up to absorb the incoming labour force. Floods still plagued the islands – at one point Peter himself nearly drowned on Nevskiy prospekt – and wolves roamed the streets after dark, devouring anyone foolish enough to go outside.

Peter the Great's successors

Having killed his only natural heir, Peter was forced to issue a decree claiming the right to nominate his successor, but when he died in 1725, he was so ill that he was unable to speak. Initially his wife, **Catherine I** (1725–27), was hailed as tsaritsa but she died after a reign of less than two years. Peter's grandson, **Peter II** (1727–30), then became tsar and moved the capital and the court back to Moscow in 1728, leaving St Petersburg in decline.

Peter II's sudden death from smallpox in 1730 left the throne wide open. In desperation, the Supreme Privy Council turned to the widowed Anna Ivanovna, a German-born niece of Peter the Great. Empress **Anna** (1730–40) re-established St Petersburg as the capital and brought with her an entourage of unpopular German courtiers. Her ten-year reign was characterized by cruelty and decadence, best illustrated by the Ice Palace that she ordered to be built on the River Neva (see p.88). Affairs of state were carried out by her German favourite, Ernst-Johann Biron, whose rule of terror, known as the *Bironovshchina*, involved the execution of thousands of alleged opponents.

Anna died childless in 1740, leaving the crown to her great-nephew, **Ivan VI** (1740–41), who – because of his youth – was put under the regency of his mother, Anna Leopoldovna. However, real power remained in the hands of the hated Biron, until a coup, backed by the powerful Preobrazhenskiy Guards and financed with French money, elevated Peter the Great's daughter Elizabeth to the throne.

Empress Elizabeth and Peter III

Like her father, **Elizabeth** (1741–61) was stubborn, quick-tempered and devoted to Russia, but, unlike him, she detested serious occupations and "abandoned herself to every excess of intemperance and lubricity". Elizabeth was almost illiterate and her court favourite, Razumovsky (a Cossack shepherd turned chorister whom she secretly married), couldn't write at all. She liked dancing and hunting, often stayed up all night, spent hours preening herself and lived in chaotic apartments, the wardrobes stacked with over fifteen thousand dresses, the floors littered with unpaid bills. Her peregrinations from palace to palace and from hunting parties to monasteries resulted in a budget deficit of eight million rubles by 1761.

Although Elizabeth hated the sight of blood, she would order torture at the slightest offence – or throw her slipper in the offender's face. Yet she abolished the death penalty and was sensible enough to retain as one of her principal advisors the enlightened Count Shuvalov, who encouraged her in the foundation of Moscow University and the St Petersburg **Academy of Arts**. Indeed, the spectacular achievements of Catherine the Great were based more than Catherine liked to admit on the foundations laid in Elizabeth's reign. In foreign affairs, Elizabeth displayed a determined hostility towards Prussia, participating in both the War of Austrian Succession (1740–48) and the Seven Years' War (1756–63), during which Russian troops occupied Berlin.

On Elizabeth's death in 1761, the new tsar – her nephew, **Peter III** – adopted a strongly pro-Prussian policy, forcing the army into Prussian uniforms and offending the clergy by sticking to the Lutheran faith of his Holstein homeland. The one concession to the nobility during his six-month reign was the abolition of the compulsory 25-year state service. It was a decree of great consequence, for it created a large, privileged leisured class, hitherto unknown in Russia. Childish, moody and impotent, Peter was no match for his intelligent, sophisticated wife, Sophia of Anhalt-Zerbst, who ingratiated herself with her subjects by joining the Orthodox Church, changing her name to Catherine in the process. Their marriage was a sham, and in June 1762 she and her favourite, Grigori Orlov, orchestrated a successful coup with the backing of the Imperial Guard regiments. Peter was imprisoned in the palace of Ropsha, where he was later murdered by the Orlov brothers.

Catherine the Great

The reign of **Catherine the Great** spanned four decades (1762–96) and saw the emergence of Russia as a truly great European power. Catherine was a woman of considerable culture and learning and a great patron of the arts. Many of St Petersburg's greatest architectural masterpieces – including the Winter Palace, the Smolniy Cathedral and the Tauride Palace – were completed during her reign, while Catherine's art collection still forms the core of the Hermitage. Inevitably, however, she is best known for her private life; her most prominent favourite courtier, Count Potemkin, oversaw one of the most important territorial gains of her reign – the annexation of Crimea in 1783, which secured the Black Sea coast for Russia.

After consolidating her position as an autocrat – after all, she had no legitimate claim to the throne – Catherine enjoyed a brief honeymoon as a liberal. French became the language of the court, and with it came the ideas of the Enlightenment. Catherine herself conducted a lengthy correspondence with Voltaire, while the first great Russian polymath, Lomonosov, was encouraged to standardize the Russian language. However, the lofty intentions of her reforms were watered down by her advisors to little more than a reassertion of "benevolent" despotism. When it came to the crucial question of the emancipation of the serfs, the issue was, not for the first or last time, swept under the carpet. And when writers like Radishchev began to take her at her word and publish critical works, she responded by exiling them to Siberia.

Catherine's liberal leanings were given a severe jolt by the **Pugachev Revolt**, which broke out east of the River Volga in 1773, under the leadership of a Don Cossack named Pugachev. Encouraged by the hope that, since the nobility had been freed from state service, the serfs would likewise be emancipated, thousands responded to Pugachev's call for freedom from the landowners and division of their estates. For two years, Pugachev's Cossack forces conducted a guerrilla campaign from Perm in the Urals to Tsaritsyn on the Volga, before being crushed by Imperial troops. The French Revolution of 1789 killed off what was left of Catherine's benevolence and in her later years she relied ever more heavily on the powers of unbridled despotism.

Paul and Alexander I

On Catherine's death in 1796, her son **Paul** became tsar. Not without good reason, Paul detested his mother and everything associated with her, and immediately set about reversing most of her policies: his first act was to give his father, Peter III, a decent burial. Like his father, Paul was a moody and militarily obsessed man, who worshipped everything Prussian. He offended the army by forcing the Guards' regiments back into Prussian uniforms, earned the enmity of the nobility by attempting to curtail some of the privileges they had enjoyed under Catherine, and reintroduced the idea of male hereditary succession that had been abandoned by Peter I.

Paul was strangled to death in March 1801 (see p.99), in a palace coup which had the tacit approval of his son, **Alexander I** (1801–25). Alexander shared Catherine's penchant for the ideas of the Enlightenment, but also exhibited a strong streak of religious conservatism. His reign was, in any case, dominated by foreign affairs and, in particular, the imminent conflict with Europe's dictator, Napoleon. His anti-Napoleonic alliance with Austria and Prussia proved a dismal failure, producing a series of Allied defeats which prompted Alexander to switch sides and join with Napoleon – an alliance sealed by the Treaty of Tilsit in 1807, but which proved to be only temporary.

The Patriotic War

In June 1812, Napoleon crossed the River Niemen and invaded Russia with his Grand Army of 600,000 men – twice the size of any force the Russians could muster. Progress was slow, with the Russians employing their famous "scorched earth" tactics to great effect, while partisans harassed the French flanks. Patriotic fervour forced the Russian general, **Kutuzov**, into fighting a pitched battle with Napoleon, despite having only 100,000 men at his disposal. The **Battle of Borodino**, which took place outside Moscow, resulted in horrific casualties on both sides, but produced no outright victor. Napoleon continued on his march, entering Moscow in September; the following day, the city was consumed in a fire. The popular Russian belief at the time was that the French were responsible, though the governor of Moscow – determined to avoid the capture of his city – was actually the culprit.

Despite abandoning Moscow to the French, Alexander steadfastly refused to leave St Petersburg and meet with Napoleon, leaving the latter no choice but to forget his conquest and begin the long retreat home. Harassed by Russian regulars and partisans, and unprepared for the ferocity of the Russian winter, the

Napoleonic Grand Army was reduced to a mere thirty thousand men when it finally recrossed the Niemen. The Russians didn't stop there but pursued Napoleon all the way back to Paris, which they occupied in 1814. At the Congress of Vienna, the following year, Russia was assured of its share of the spoils of the post-Napoleonic carve-up of Europe.

The Decembrists

The whiff of reform in the early years of Alexander's reign was quickly expunged by the reactionary minister, Arakcheev, to whom the tsar deferred in almost all matters of state from 1815 onwards. This came as a particularly big disappointment to the victorious Russian troops returning from their civilizing experience of life in Western Europe. Several underground groups were formed by Guards' officers and liberal members of the nobility. The principal organizations in the early 1820s were the "Southern Society", under the leadership of Colonel Pestel, whose aim was to establish a classless republican state; and the "Northern Society", which favoured a constitutional monarchy. Both societies were involved in secret propaganda and recruitment from 1823 onwards, and planned to assassinate the tsar in 1826.

When Alexander conveniently died in November 1825, without leaving a male heir, the plotters sought to take advantage of the dynastic crisis that ensued. The Imperial Guards initially swore allegiance to Alexander's brother, Constantine, who was next in line for the throne, but who had secretly given up his right to the succession. The plotters hurriedly devised a coup, to be staged on December 14, the day the soldiers were to swear a new oath of allegiance to Alexander's younger brother, Nicholas. Word got out about the Decembrists, as they became known, and on the day, their nerve failed. For six hours, loyalist troops and Decembrists faced one another across what is now ploshchad Dekabristov, with neither side prepared to fire the first shot. As dusk fell, Nicholas gave the order to clear the square: two hours and several hundred casualties later, the job was done.

Nicholas I

In the aftermath of the Decembrist uprising, things took a turn for the worse. **Nicholas I** (1825–55) adopted a more "hands-on" approach to government than Alexander, personally interrogating many of the plotters. Five ringleaders were executed and more than a hundred exiled to Siberia. No mention of the revolt was allowed in the press, which was even more strictly censored than before, and every effort made to expunge the memory of this "horrible and extraordinary plot" (as Nicholas described it). Yet, despite this, and the fact that the plotters were exclusively officers and aristocrats, the Decembrists became an inspiration for subsequent generations of revolutionaries.

The reign of Nicholas I was epitomized by the slogan "Orthodoxy, Autocracy, Nationality", coined by one of his ministers. The status quo was to be maintained at all costs: censorship increased, as did police surveillance, carried out by the infamous **Third Section** of the tsar's personal Chancellory. A uniformed gendarmerie was created and organized along military lines, while an elaborate network of spies and informers kept a close watch on all potential subversives. The most intractable problem, as ever, was serfdom, "the powder-magazine under the state", as Nicholas's police chief dubbed it. Serfs accounted for four-fifths of the population, and during the late 1820s there were a number of abortive serf rebellions, though none approached the scale of the Pugachev revolt. The economic position of Russia's serfs remained more or less stagnant throughout Nicholas's reign, and hampered the industrialization of the country, which was mostly confined to developments in the cotton and beet-sugar industries.

Perhaps the greatest social change in Russia took place in the upper echelons of society. In the 1840s, the deferential admiration in which the educated classes normally held the tsar was replaced by increasingly bitter criticism. The best known of the various secret societies was the St Petersburg-based **Petrashevsky Circle**, among whose number was the writer, Dostoyevsky. Their platform of democratic reforms was to be achieved through peasant rebellion, though there was little real hope of organizing one. The European revolutions of 1848 had made the tsar even jumpier than before – Russian troops were instrumental in putting down the Hungarian uprising – and in early 1849, more than a hundred of the Petrashevsky Circle were arrested. Fifteen, including Dostoyevsky, were subjected to a mock execution before being exiled to Siberia (see p.238).

In early 1854, the **Crimean War** broke out and Russia found itself at war with Britain, France and Turkey. The war went badly for the Russians and

served to highlight the flaws and inadequacies inherent in the Tsarist Empire: Russian troops defending Sebastopol faced rifles with muskets; Russian sailing ships had to do battle with enemy steamers; and the lack of rail-lines meant that Russian soldiers were no better supplied than their Allied counterparts, who were thousands of miles from home. The Allied capture of Sebastopol in 1855 almost certainly helped to accelerate the death of the despondent Nicholas, whose last words of advice to his son and successor were "Hold on to everything!"

The Tsar Liberator: Alexander II

In fact, the new tsar, **Alexander II** (1855–81), had little choice but to sue for peace, and for those who hoped for change in Russia, the defeats of the Crimean War came as a blessing. The surviving Decembrists and Petrashevsky exiles were released, police surveillance eased and many of the censorship restrictions lifted. But as far as democratic reforms were concerned, Alexander remained true to his dynastic inheritance, believing wholeheartedly in unadulterated autocracy.

In 1861, Alexander II signed the historic decree allowing for the **emancipation of the serfs**, thus earning himself the soubriquet of "Tsar Liberator". In reality, the Emancipation Act was a fraud, replacing the landowner's legal ownership with a crushing economic dependence in the form of financial compensation, which the freed serfs were forced to pay their landlords over a period of 49 years. However, Alexander did push through a number of other **reforms** which represented a significant break with the past. He reduced military service from twenty-five years to six (nine with the reserves); created a limited form of local self-government through appointed regional *zemstva* (assemblies); and reformed the judicial system, introducing trial by jury and a trained judiciary.

Populists and assassins

Alexander's reforms stopped short of any major constitutional shift from autocracy, thus disappointing those who had hoped for a "revolution from above". As a result, the 1860s witnessed an upsurge in peasant unrest and a marked radicalization of the opposition movement which had formed among the educated elite. From the ranks of the disaffected intelligentsia came the amorphous "**Populist**" (Narodnik) movement, which gathered momentum throughout the late 1860s and early 1870s. The Populists' chief ideologue, Nikolai Chernyshevsky, was committed to establishing a Socialist society based around the peasant commune, without the intervening stage of capitalism. There were, however, widely differing views on the best means of achieving this end. The "Nihilists" – as the writer Turgenev dubbed them in his novel *Fathers and Sons* (1862) – led the charge in the 1860s, most famously with the first attempt on the tsar's life, carried out in April 1866 by the clandestine organization, "Hell".

The other school of thought believed in taking the Populist message to the people. This proselytizing campaign reached a climax in the "crazy summer" of 1874, when thousands of students, dressed as simple folk, roamed the countryside attempting to convert the peasantry to their cause. Most of these exhortations fell on deaf ears, for although the peasantry were fed up with their lot, they were suspicious of all townspeople and, for the most part, remained blindly loyal to the tsar. The authorities were nevertheless sufficiently convinced of the danger of this agitation to make mass arrests, which culminated in the much publicized trials of "the 50" and "the 193", which took place in St Petersburg in 1877–78.

The failure of the 1874 propaganda campaign signalled a return to more conspiratorial methods. Following what was probably Russia's first mass political demonstration, outside St Petersburg's Kazan Cathedral in 1876, a new terrorist organization was founded, called "Land and Liberty". This group had not been in existence long before an argument over the use of violence split the movement in two. Land redistribution was the major aim of the "Black Partition", one of whose leaders, Plekhanov, went on to found the first Russian Marxist political grouping; the other main splinter group was the "People's Will" (Narodnaya Volya), who staged a number of spectacular terrorist acts, before successfully assassinating the tsar himself in March 1881 (see p.91).

Alexander III and industrialization

The assassination of Alexander II failed to stir the Russian people into revolution, and the new tsar, **Alexander III** (1881–94), was even less inclined than his predecessor to institute political change. Assisted by his ultra-reactionary chief advisor, Pobedonostsev, the tsar shelved all constitutional

reforms, increased police surveillance and cut back the powers of the *zemstva*. The police stood idly by during a wave of pogroms against Russian Jews in 1881–82, Pobedonostsev subsequently instituting a series of harsh anti-Semitic laws.

The 1880s brought considerable economic and social change to Russia. **Industrialization** had increased considerably since the Emancipation Act – Russia's rate of growth outstripped that of all the other major European powers – while during Alexander III's reign foreign investment more than doubled. In St Petersburg, huge factories sprang up in the suburbs, drawing in more and more peasants from the countryside, which resulted in the creation of an increasingly large urban working class. Although this new class wouldn't make an impact in politics until the late 1890s, it had an immediate effect on St Petersburg, whose population swelled to almost half a million (making it the fourth largest city in Europe), with all the attendant desperate poverty, child beggars and prostitution described in *Crime and Punishment.*

Nicholas II

When Alexander III died in 1894, the throne passed to his son, **Nicholas II** (1894–1917), the last of the Russian tsars. On his accession, Nicholas signalled his intention to continue his father's policies by denouncing the constitutional reforms proposed by the *zemstvo* of Tver as "senseless dreams". In the same year, the tsar married the German-born princess Alexandra of Hesse, whose autocratic tendencies and extreme religious Orthodoxy wielded an unhealthy influence. At the tsar's Moscow coronation in May 1896, 1300 people were killed in a stampede – an inauspicious start to a doomed reign.

The failure of terrorism to ignite the spark of revolution in Russia had temporarily discredited the Populist cause. It wasn't until the late 1890s that a new Populist force, the **Socialist Revolutionary Party**, or SR, emerged, once more publicizing their cause through acts of terrorism. In the run-up to 1905, the party's terrorist wing, the SR Fighting Section, succeeded in assassinating the interior minister, Sipyagin, and the tsar's chief minister, Vyacheslav von Plehve (see p.243), but still failed to attract the mass of the peasantry to its cause.

Meanwhile, a section of the Russian intelligentsia had begun to shift its ideological stance towards **Marxism**, which pinned its hopes on the newly emerging urban proletariat, rather than the peasantry, as the future agent of revolution. The first Marxist organization, "Emancipation of Labour", was founded in 1883 by a handful of ex-Populist exiles in Switzerland, including the "father of Russian Marxism", **Georgy Plekhanov**. The group was so small that, when out boating on Lake Geneva, Plekhanov once joked, "Be careful: if this boat sinks, it's the end of Russian Marxism."

Plekhanov teamed up with (among others) Vladimir Ilyich Ulyanov – later known as **Lenin** – to form the **Russian Social Democratic Labour Party** (RSDLP), which was founded (and immediately suppressed) in 1898. Forced underground, divisions quickly began to appear concerning the nature of the party; Lenin argued for a conspiratorial, disciplined party, while his chief rival, Martov, wanted a more open, mass membership. In the split that followed, Lenin managed to claim for his supporters the description **Bolsheviks** (meaning "majority" in Russian), while his opponents became known, somewhat unfairly, as **Mensheviks** ("minority", with all its connotations of weakness).

At the turn of the century, a third force in Russian politics emerged, representing the interests of the liberal bourgeoisie. Its chief spokesman was Professor Milyukov, who later founded the Constitutional Democratic Party, better known as the **Kadet Party**. The liberals' demands for freedom of the press, assembly and association – modest enough in any other European country – were positively revolutionary in the context of Tsarist Russia.

The 1905 Revolution

The economic boom of the late 1890s came to an abrupt end in 1900 and was followed by a slump which put many of the new working class out of work. In addition, there was unrest in the countryside, compounded by a series of anti-Semitic pogroms initiated by Plehve, while the tsar's hope of a quick military victory in the **Russo-Japanese War** ended in disaster at Port Arthur. Back in the capital, St Petersburg, a strike broke out at the giant Putilov engineering plant and quickly spread to the numerous other factories that now encircled the city.

On January 9, 1905 – **Bloody Sunday** – 150,000 striking Petersburgers and their families converged on Palace Square to hand a petition to the tsar, demanding basic civil rights and labour laws. Under the leadership of Father Gapon, who was head of a police-sponsored trade union, the crowd marched peacefully from different parts of the city, carrying portraits of the tsar and singing hymns. In a series of separate incidents, the Imperial Guards fired on the crowd to disperse the protestors, killing as many as one thousand demonstrators and wounding several thousand others. For the rest of his reign, the tsar would never quite shake off his reputation as "Bloody Nicholas".

When the first wave of strikes petered out, the tsar clung to the hope that a reversal of fortune in the Far East would ease his troubles. However, the destruction of the Russian Baltic Fleet at Tsushima Bay in May 1905, and the mutiny of the crew of the battleship *Potemkin*, forced the reluctant tsar to make peace with Japan and, at home, propose the establishment of a consultative assembly – **the Duma** – which was to be elected by a restricted suffrage. However, this last-minute concession was insufficient to prevent a printers' strike in St Petersburg in late September from developing into an all-out general strike. Further mutinies occurred among the troops and the countryside slid into anarchy.

By the middle of October, Nicholas II had little choice but to grant further concessions. In the **October Manifesto**, the tsar granted a future Duma the power of veto over any laws, promised basic civil liberties and appointed Count Witte as Russia's first prime minister. Meanwhile, in the capital, the workers seized the initiative and created the **St Petersburg Soviet**, made up of some 500 delegates elected by over 200,000 workers. Under the co-chairmanship of **Trotsky** (who had yet to join the Bolsheviks), the Soviet pursued a moderate policy, criticizing the proposed Duma, but falling far short of calling for an armed uprising – as the Russian middle classes feared would happen.

From 1905 to World War I

Since the October Manifesto had split the opposition movement (into those who did and didn't wish to participate in the Duma) and the emergence of the Petersburg Soviet was alarming the bourgeoisie, Nicholas II had the perfect excuse for a clampdown. In December, the leaders of the Soviet were arrested and a Bolshevik-inspired uprising in Moscow was easily crushed. During 1906, there were further mutinies in the army and navy, and mayhem in the countryside, but the high point of the revolution had passed. Notwithstanding the continuing activities of the SR Fighting Section, the workers' movement began to decline, while the revolutionary elite languished in Tsarist prisons or, like Lenin, was forced to endure an impotent exile in Europe.

The main task facing the tsar was how to confront the new Duma. The first nationwide elections in Russian history were successfully held. The franchise was broad-based, though a long way from universal suffrage, with the Kadets emerging as the largest grouping. Nevertheless, the opening of the **First Duma**, which took place in St Petersburg's Tauride Palace on May 10, 1906, was attended by diverse figures, from grand dukes to peasants' and workers' deputies in overalls and muddy boots, whose faces impressed the Dowager Empress with their "strange, incomprehensible hatred". After ten weeks of debate, the issue of land distribution reared its ugly head, prompting the tsar to surround the palace with troops and dissolve the Duma. The succeeding Second Duma suffered a similar fate.

The most positive post-revolutionary repercussions took place within **the arts**. From 1905 to 1914, St Petersburg (and Moscow) experienced an extraordinary outburst of artistic energy: Diaghilev's Ballets Russes dazzled Europe; Chekhov premiered his works in the capital; poets and writers held Symbolist seances in city salons; while Mayakovsky and other self-proclaimed Futurists toured the country, shocking the general public with their statements on art.

Witte's successor as prime minister, **Pyotr Stolypin**, crushed any lingering thoughts of insurrection by liberal use of the gallows, which were nicknamed "Stolypin's necktie"; the **Third Duma**, elected on a much narrower franchise, dutifully ratified Stolypin's package of minor reforms in 1907. The tsar, who disapproved of constitutional reform of any kind, abandoned the capital for the security of the Imperial Palaces outside St Petersburg. He and his wife shunned court life and fell further under the influence of the notoriously debauched religious charlatan, **Rasputin**, who they believed held the key to the survival of their only son, Alexei, who suffered from haemophilia.

World War I

In the nationalistic fervour that accompanied the outbreak of **World War I**, the name of the capital, St Petersburg, was deemed too Germanic for comfort and replaced by the more Russian-sounding **Petrograd**. Yet serious deficiencies in the structure of army and military production were barely acknowledged, let alone tackled. The first Russian offensive ended in defeat at the Battle of Tannenberg in August 1914, with estimated casualties of 170,000. From that moment onwards, there was rarely any good news from the front; in the first year alone, around four million soldiers lost their lives. In an attempt to prove that everything was under control, the tsar foolishly assumed supreme command of the armed forces – a post for which he was totally unqualified.

By the end of 1916, even out-and-out monarchists were voicing reservations about Nicholas II. The tsar's German-born wife, who dismissed minister after minister, was openly accused of treason, while the tsar's advisor, Rasputin, was assassinated by a group of aristocrats desperate to force a change of policy. Firmly ensconced with his weakling son in the Imperial headquarters at Mogilev, Nicholas refused to be moved. As inflation spiralled and food shortages worsened, strikes began to break out once more in Petrograd. By the beginning of 1917, everyone from generals to peasants talked of an imminent uprising.

The February Revolution

On February 22, there was a lockout of workers at the Putilov works in Petrograd – the **February Revolution** had begun. The following day (International Women's Day), thousands of women and workers thronged the streets attacking bread shops, singing the *Marseillaise* and calling for the overthrow of the tsar. Soldiers and Cossacks fraternized with the demonstrators and when the Volhynia Guards obeyed orders and fired on the crowds, the Petrograd garrison mutinied. On February 27, prisons were stormed and the Fourth Duma was surrounded by angry demonstrators and mutinous troops. The Duma, which the tsar had formally prorogued, approved the establishment of a Provisional Committee "for the re-establishment of order in the capital", while Trotsky and the Mensheviks quickly re-established the Petrograd Soviet. On March 2, en route to the capital, the tsar was finally persuaded to abdicate in favour of his brother, Grand Duke Michael, who gave up his claim to the throne the following day: the Romanov dynasty had ended.

Out of the revolutionary ferment, a system of "dual power" arose. The **Provisional Government**, under the presidency of the wealthy liberal, Count Lvov, attempted to assert itself as the legitimate successor to Tsarist autocracy. Freedom of speech and a political amnesty were immediately decreed; there were to be elections for a Constituent Assembly, but there was to be no end to the war. This last policy pacified the generals, who might otherwise have attempted to suppress the Revolution, but quickly eroded the Provisonal Government's popularity. The other power base was the **Petrograd Soviet**, dominated by Mensheviks, which was prepared to give qualified support to the "bourgeois revolution" (they were less enthusiastic about the war) until the time was ripe for the establishment of Socialism. The Soviet's most important achievement was the effecting of "Order No. 1", which called for the formation of Soviets throughout the army, whose existence gradually undermined military discipline.

After ditching some of its more right-wing elements, the Provisional Government co-operated more closely with the Petrograd Soviet. **Alexander Kerensky** became the minister of war and toured the front calling for a fresh offensive against the Germans, which commenced in late June. The attack began well but soon turned into a retreat, while discontent in St Petersburg peaked again in a wave of violent protests known as the **July Days**. Soldiers and workers, egged on by the city's Anarchists and some Bolsheviks, marched on the Petrograd Soviet, calling for the overthrow of the Provisional Government. Lenin, who had returned from exile in April, was bitterly opposed to the government, but felt that the time was not right for an armed uprising; the Soviet also proved unwilling to act. In the end, troops loyal to the government arrived in St Petersburg and restored order. Trotsky and others were arrested, Lenin was accused of being a German spy and forced once more into exile, and the Bolsheviks as a whole were branded as traitors.

Kerensky used the opportunity to tighten his grip on the Provisional Government, taking over as leader from Count Lvov and making the fateful decision to move into the Winter Palace. If the July Days were a blow to the Left, the abortive **Kornilov Revolt** was an even greater setback for the Right. In late August, the army's commander-in-chief, General Kornilov, attempted to march on Petrograd and crush Bolshevism once and for all. Whether he had been encouraged in this by Kerensky remains uncertain, but in the event, Kerensky decided to turn on Kornilov, denouncing the coup and calling on the Bolsheviks and workers' militia to defend the capital. Kerensky duly appointed himself commander-in-chief, but it was the Left who were now in ascendance.

The October Revolution

During the course of September, the country began to slide into chaos: soldiers deserted the front in ever greater numbers, the countryside was in turmoil, while the "Bolshevization" of the Soviets continued apace. By mid-September, Lenin, who was still in hiding in Finland, began to urge an armed uprising. This was, however, not a move supported by the majority of the Bolshevik leadership until mid-October. Through the auspices of the Military Revolutionary Committee, which had been established by the Petrograd Soviet to defend the city against the threat of counter-revolution, Trotsky skilfully prepared the Bolshevik Red Guards for an armed coup, using the Smolniy Institute as their headquarters.

The **October Revolution** is thought to have begun in the early hours of the 25th, with the occupation of all the key points in Petrograd by the Committee's Red Guards. Kerensky fled St Petersburg, ostensibly to rally support for the government; it was in fact his final exit. Meanwhile, posters announcing the overthrow of the Provisional Government appeared on the streets at 10am, though it wasn't until 2am the following day that the government's ministers were formally arrested in the Winter Palace. It was an almost bloodless coup (in Petrograd at least), though it unleashed the most bloody civil war and regime in Russia's history.

The coup had been deliberately planned by Trotsky to coincide with the Second All-Russian Congress of Soviets, which convened at the Smolniy Institute on the night of the uprising. At the Congress, the Bolsheviks had a majority, further enhanced when the Mensheviks and right-wing SRs staged a walkout in protest at the coup. Lenin delivered his two famous decrees: the first calling for an end to the war and the second approving the seizure of land by the peasants. An all-Bolshevik **Council of People's Commissars** was established, headed by Lenin, with Trotsky as Commissar for Foreign Affairs. A spate of decrees was issued, the most important of which were those calling for the institution of an eight-hour working day, the abolition of social classes and the nationalization of all banks and financial organizations.

Conditions in Petrograd were, if anything, even worse than before the coup. Food was scarcer than ever, while rumours of anti-Bolshevik plots abounded. As early as December 1917, Lenin decided to create a new secret police, under the official title of the "All-Russian Extraordinary Commission for Struggle against Counter-Revolution, Speculation and Sabotage", known as the **Cheka** (aptly meaning "linchpin" in Russian). Although the Bolsheviks had reluctantly agreed to abolish the death penalty in October, the Cheka, under its leader Felix Dzerzhinsky, reserved the right to "have recourse to a firing squad when it becomes obvious that there is no other way".

On November 12–13, elections were held for the long-awaited **Constituent Assembly**, which met for the first and only time on January 5, 1918, in the Tauride Palace. As the first Russian parliament elected by universal suffrage, this was meant to be "the crowning jewel in Russian democratic life", but Lenin already privately regarded it as "an old fairytale which there is no reason to carry on further". Having received only a quarter of the vote, the Bolsheviks surrounded the palace the following day, preventing many delegates from entering; Red Guards eventually dismissed those inside the building with the words, "Push off. We want to go home."

The Civil War 1918–20

More pressing than the internecine feuds of the Russian Socialist parties was the outcome of the peace negotiations with Germany. In mid-February of 1918, talks broke down between the two powers, and the Germans launched a fresh offensive against the Russians. Eventually, on March 3, Trotsky signed the **Treaty of Brest-Litovsk**, which handed over Poland, Finland, Belarus, the Baltics and – most painfully of all – Ukraine, Russia's bread basket. Following the treaty, the Bolsheviks transferred the **capital** from

Petrograd to **Moscow** – leaving the city more exposed than ever to foreign attack. Within two years, Petrograd's population had shrunk by 65 percent, to 799,000.

At the Seventh Party Congress, at which the Social Democratic Labour Party was renamed the **Communist Party**, the left-inclined SRs walked out in protest at the peace treaty. On July 6, the German ambassador was assassinated by an SR member and the following day the Left-SRs staged an abortive coup. In August, they struck again, with the assassination of the Petrograd Cheka chief, Moses Uritsky, plus an unsuccessful attempt on Lenin's life. The Bolsheviks responded with a wave of repression which became known as the **Red Terror**. Declaring "an end to clemency and slackness", the Cheka immediately shot 512 "hostages" in Petrograd and 500 at Kronstadt. While Dzerzhinsky's deputy, Yakov Peters, complained that "the number of executions has been greatly exaggerated; in no way does the total exceed 600", another aide, Martyn Latsis, made the famous pronouncement that one look at a suspect's hands would suffice to determine his class allegiance.

By the time the Red Terror hit Petrograd, the **Civil War** was already raging. In a vain attempt to force Russia back into the war against Germany, but also out of a genuine fear of Bolshevism spreading, the Western powers sent troops to fight the Reds. **Foreign intervention** peaked in late 1918: Czechoslovak troops, who were being evacuated from the country, seized control of much of the Trans-Siberian Railway; British troops landed in Murmansk in Karelia and Baku in Azerbaijan; US, Japanese, French and Italian forces took over Vladivostok; while the Germans controlled the vast tracts of land given to them under the Brest-Litovsk treaty. Fearing that the Czechoslovak Legion would free the Imperial family from captivity in Yekaterinburg, Lenin ordered local Bolsheviks to execute the tsar and his relations on July 16–17.

With the end of World War I, foreign troops began to return home, leaving the Reds and the **Whites** (anti-Soviet forces) to fight it out. What the Reds lacked in terms of military experience, they made up for in ideological motivation and – thanks to the influence of Lenin and Trotsky – iron discipline. The disparate anti-Soviet forces, on the other hand, represented every type of political movement from monarchists to SRs. The sides were evenly matched in numbers and rivalled each other in ferocity when it came to exacting revenge on collaborators. Ultimately, the Reds prevailed, though not without a few close calls: during the autumn of 1919, a White force of 20,000 men was prevented from capturing Petrograd only by the personal intervention of Trotsky, who rallied the Red Army and turned the tide of the battle.

Not only did the Civil War cost the lives of millions, but it also promoted the militarization of Soviet society, under the rubric of "**War Communism**". Workers' control in the factories and the nationalization of land had plunged the Soviet economy into chaos just as the Civil War broke out. In an attempt to cope, the Bolsheviks introduced stringent economic centralization, replacing workers' control in the factories with labour discipline of a kind not seen since the pre-trade union days of Tsarism. With inflation spiralling and the currency almost worthless, the peasants had little incentive to sell their scarce produce in the cities. Red Guards were sent into the countryside to requisition food by force and "committees of the poor" were set up in the villages to stimulate a class war against the richer peasantry, or *kulaks*.

The Kronstadt revolt and the NEP

By 1921, Soviet Russia was economically devastated – the population of Petrograd alone had been reduced by two-thirds in just three years. The Communists found themselves confronted with worker unrest and, for the first time, serious divisions began to appear within the Party itself. The most outspoken faction to emerge was the **Workers' Opposition**, led by two lifelong Bolsheviks, Alexandra Kollontai and Alexander Shlyapnikov. Their main demands were for the separation of the trade unions from the Party and for fewer wage differentials. In February 1921, even the Kronstadt sailors – who had been among the Bolsheviks' staunchest supporters from 1905 onwards – turned against the Party. The **Kronstadt sailors' revolt** precipitated a general strike in Petrograd when troops once more refused to fire on the crowds. Rejecting calls for negotiations, the Bolsheviks accused the Kronstadt sailors of acting under the orders of a White general and, after a bloody battle, succeeded in crushing the rebellion (see p.378).

At the same time as the Kronstadt revolt was underway, Lenin was presiding over the **Tenth Party Congress**, at which he declared a virtual end to democratic debate within the Party and officially banned all Party factions. Those SRs still at large were rounded up and either exiled or subjected to the first Soviet show trial, which took place in 1922. From now on, real power was in the hands of the newly emerging Party bureaucracy, or **Secretariat**, whose first general secretary, appointed towards the end of 1922, was none other than the Georgian Communist, **Stalin**.

At the Party Congress, Lenin unveiled his **New Economic Policy** (NEP), which marked a step back from the all-out confrontation with the peasantry that had been the hallmark of War Communism. The state maintained control of the "commanding heights" of the economy, while reintroducing some form of free market for agricultural produce, thus providing the peasants with an incentive to increase productivity. It was a compromise formula which greatly favoured the peasantry (who still formed the majority of the population) over the working class: the NEP was popularly dubbed "New Exploitation of the Proletariat".

The rise of Stalin

Following **Lenin's death** on January 24, 1924, an all-out power struggle began. Trotsky, the hero of the Civil War, and Bukharin, the chief exponent of the NEP, were by far the most popular figures in the Party, but it was Stalin, as head of the Secretariat, who held the real power. Stalin organized Lenin's funeral and was the chief architect in his deification, which began with the renaming of Petrograd as **Leningrad**. By employing classic divide-and-rule tactics, Stalin picked off his rivals one by one, beginning with the exile of Trotsky in 1925, followed by the neutralization of Zinoviev, the Leningrad Party boss, and Bukharin in 1929.

Abandoning the NEP, in the first Five-Year Plan (1928–32), Stalin embarked upon the **forced collectivization** of agriculture and industrialization on an unprecedented scale. Declaring its aim to be "the elimination of the *kulak* as a class", the Party waged open war on a peasantry who were overwhelmingly hostile to collectivization. The social and economic upheaval wrought on the country has been dubbed the "Third Revolution" – indeed, it transformed Russian society more than any of the country's previous revolutions. The peasants' passive resistance, the destruction of livestock and the ensuing chaos all contributed to the **famine of 1932–33**, which resulted in the death of as many as five million people from starvation and disease.

The purges and the show trials

Realizing that some retrenchment was necessary, Stalin ascribed the consequences of collectivization to Party cadres "dizzy with success" (as his speech in *Pravda* put it), and advocated more realistic goals for the second Five-Year Plan (1933–37). In 1934, at the Seventeenth Party "Congress of Victors", Stalin declared that the Party had triumphed, pronouncing that "Life has become better, Comrades. Life has become gayer". Of the two thousand or so delegates who applauded, two-thirds would be arrested in the course of the next five years.

On December 1, 1934, the **assassination of Sergei Kirov**, Leningrad Party boss and the most powerful figure in the ruling Politburo after Stalin, took place in the Smolniy Institute in St Petersburg. Stalin, who probably planned the murder, began a **mass purge of Leningrad**: some 30,000–40,000 citizens were arrested in the spring of 1935 alone, while historians suggest that one-quarter of the city's population may have been purged within a year – the majority of them destined for the **Gulag**, or "Corrective Labour Camps and Labour Settlements".

In the summer of 1936, the first of the great **show trials** took place, during which the old Bolsheviks, Kamenev and Zinoviev, "confessed" to Kirov's murder and (along with fourteen others) were executed. At the beginning of 1937, the head of the NKVD (secret police), Genrikh Yagoda, was arrested and replaced by Nikolai Yezhov, who presided over the darkest period in Russian history, the Yezhovshchina, or **Great Terror**, of 1937–38.

Exact figures are impossible to ascertain, but the total number of people arrested during the purges is thought to have been in the region of eight million, of whom at least a million were executed, while countless others died in the camps. In December 1938, Yezhov himself was replaced by Lavrenty Beria – a clear signal from Stalin that the worst was over, for the moment at least.

World War II and the Blockade

On June 22, 1941, Hitler abandoned the short-lived Nazi–Soviet non-aggression pact and invaded the Soviet Union, starting what is known in Russia as the **Great Patriotic War**. Despite advance warnings from numerous sources, Stalin was taken by surprise and apparently suffered a nervous breakdown, withdrawing to his *dacha* outside Moscow while his subordinates attempted to grapple with the crisis. In the first days of the war, over a thousand Soviet aircraft were destroyed on the ground; whole armies were encircled and captured; and local Party officials fled from the advancing *Blitzkrieg*. In some regions the population welcomed the Germans as liberators – until Nazi brutality flung them back into the arms of Stalin.

The position of **Leningrad** soon became critical. By September 1941, it was virtually surrounded by German forces, whose operational directive read: "The Führer has decided to wipe the city of Petersburg off the face of the earth. It is proposed to tighten up the blockade of the city and level it to the ground by shelling and continuous bombing from the air." So began the terrible "900 Days" of starvation and bombardment, known to Russians as **the Blockade** (*blokada*).

No preparations had been made for the Blockade: indeed, shortly before it began, food had actually been sent out of Leningrad to the forces at the front. The only supply line lay across Lake Ladoga, to the east of the city, where trucks could cross the icy "**Road of Life**" when the lake was frozen in winter. Yet, despite heroic improvisations, Leningrad came close to collapse in the winter of 1941–42, when 53,000 people died in December alone. By the second winter, supplies were better organized and the population had developed a powerful sense of solidarity, but even so, 670,000 citizens died before the Blockade was finally broken in January 1944. In recognition of its sacrifices, Leningrad was proclaimed a "**Hero City**" of the Soviet Union; its shops were supplied with the best food in the country and every child born in the city received a special medal.

Stalin's final years

After the enormous sacrifices of the war – in which 27 million Soviet citizens had perished – people longed for a peaceful, freer life. However, Stalin's advanced years prompted an intensification of the power struggle, which brought with it a fresh wave of arrests and show trials. The most powerful figure among his would-be successors was **Andrei Zhdanov**, who had been in charge of Leningrad during the Blockade. His rivals, Malenkov and Beria, were desperate to discredit him and in the summer of 1946 they pronounced him "guilty of a lack of ideological vigilance". Zhdanov counterattacked with a clampdown on "anti-patriotic elements" and "kow-towing" to the West. Leningrad was once more singled out for special attention; Zhdanov launched a vitriolic attack on two local journals and accused the city's beloved poet, Anna Akhmatova, of being "half-nun, half-whore".

When Zhdanov died (or was poisoned) in 1948, his rivals in the Politburo fabricated the "**Leningrad Affair**", in which Zhdanov's closest allies – many of them from Leningrad – were accused of trying to seize power and were executed. Thousands of Leningraders fell victim to the witch-hunt that followed the trial of the Zhdanov group and wound up in the Gulag. Stalin's final show trial was the "Doctors' Plot", in which a group of (mostly Jewish) physicians "confessed" to the murder of Zhdanov. Thankfully, the death of Stalin two months into the charade, on March 5, 1953, brought an end to the proceedings and the charges were subsequently dropped.

Khrushchev and the "thaw"

Following Stalin's death, the power struggle within the Soviet leadership continued unabated. Beria, the odious secret police chief, was the first to be arrested and executed, in July 1953; Malenkov lasted until 1955, before he was forced to resign; whereas Foreign Minister Molotov hung on until 1957. The man who was to emerge as the next Soviet leader was **Nikita Khrushchev**, who, in 1956, when his position was by no means unassailable, gave a "**Secret Speech**" to the Twentieth Party Congress, in which Stalin's name was for the first time officially linked with Kirov's murder and the sufferings of millions during the Great Terror. So traumatic was the revelation that many delegates had heart attacks on the spot. In the same year, thousands were rehabilitated and returned from the camps. Yet for all its outspokenness, Khrushchev's **de-Stalinization** was strictly limited in scope – after all, he himself had earned the nickname "Butcher of the Ukraine" during the Yezhovshchina.

The cultural **thaw** that followed Khrushchev's speech was equally selective, allowing the publication of Solzhenitsyn's account of the Gulag, *One Day in the Life of Ivan Denisovich*, but rejecting

Pasternak's *Doctor Zhivago*. Khrushchev emptied the camps, only to add a new twist to the repression, by sending dissidents to psychiatric hospitals. In **foreign affairs**, he was not one to shy away from confrontation, either. Soviet tanks spilled blood on the streets of Budapest in 1956, while Khrushchev oversaw the building of the Berlin Wall and, in October 1962, took the world to the edge of the nuclear precipice during the Cuban Missile Crisis. He also boasted that the Soviet Union would surpass the West in the production of consumer goods within twenty years, and pinned the nation's hopes on developing the so-called "Virgin Lands" of Siberia and Kazakhstan.

By 1964, Khrushchev had managed to alienate all the main interest groups within the Soviet hierarchy. His emphasis on nuclear rather than conventional weapons lost him the support of the military; his de-Stalinization was unpopular with the KGB; while his administrative reforms struck at the heart of the Party apparatus. As the Virgin Lands turned into a dust bowl, his economic boasts rang hollow and the Soviet public was deeply embarrassed by his boorish behaviour at the United Nations, where Khrushchev interrupted a speech by banging on the table with his shoe. In October 1964, his enemies took advantage of his vacation at the Black Sea to mount a bloodless coup, and on his return to Moscow, Khrushchev was presented with his resignation "for reasons of health". It was a sign of the changes since Stalin's death that he was the first disgraced Soviet leader to be allowed to live on in obscurity, rather than being shot.

The Brezhnev era

Under Khrushchev's ultimate successor, **Leonid Brezhnev**, many of the more controversial policies were abandoned. Military expenditure was significantly increased, attacks on Stalin ceased and the whole era of the Great Terror was studiously ignored in the media. The show trial of the writers, Sinyavsky and Daniel, which took place in February 1966, marked the official end to the "thaw", and was followed by a wave of renewed repression in all the major urban centres, including Leningrad. The crushing of the Prague Spring in August 1968 showed that the new Soviet leaders were as ruthless in stamping out opposition as their predecessors.

Thanks to public indifference and press censorship, most Russians knew little of **Alexander**

Solzhenitsyn when he was exiled to the West in 1974, and even less of **Andrei Sakharov**, the nuclear physicist sentenced to internal exile for his human-rights campaigns. Yet despite the activities of the KGB, the Brezhnev era is now remembered in Russia as a rare period of peace and stability. With many goods heavily subsidized by the state, ordinary citizens could bask in the knowledge that meat and bread cost the same as they had done in 1950 (even if you did have to queue for it), while those with money had recourse to the burgeoning black market. The new-found security of the Party cadres, who were subjected to fewer purges than at any time since the Soviet system began, led to unprecedented levels of corruption.

As sclerosis set in across the board, industrial and agricultural output declined to new lows. By 1970, the average age of the Politburo was over seventy – embodying the geriatric nature of Soviet politics in what would later be called the **Era of Stagnation** (*zastoy*). Amongst the Politburo members tipped to succeed Brezhnev was **Grigori Romanov**, the Leningrad Party secretary who allowed the city to fall into decay and abused his position; it was rumoured that he once borrowed a priceless Imperial dinner service from the Hermitage for his daughter's wedding party.

Gorbachev's reforms

Brezhnev died in November 1982 and was succeeded by **Yuri Andropov**, the former KGB boss, who had hardly begun his anti-corruption campaign when he too expired, in February 1984. The Brezhnevite clique took fright at the prospect of yet more change and elected the 73-year-old **Konstantin Chernenko** as general secretary, but when he also died, in March 1985, it was clear that the post required some new blood.

Mikhail Gorbachev – at 53, the youngest member of the Politburo – was chosen as Chernenko's successor with a brief to "get things moving". The first of his policies to send shock waves through Soviet society – a campaign against alcohol – was probably the most unpopular and unsuccessful initiative of his career. This was followed shortly afterwards by the coining of the two famous buzz words of the Gorbachev era: **glasnost** (openness) and **perestroika** (restructuring). The first of these took a battering when, in April 1986, the world's worst nuclear disaster – at

Chernobyl – was hushed up for a full three days, before the Swedes forced an admission out of the Soviet authorities. Similarly, Gorbachev denied the existence of political prisoners right up until Sakharov's unexpected release from exile in the "closed" city of Gorky, in December 1986.

Regardless, Gorbachev pressed on with his reforms, shaking up the bureaucracy and launching investigations into numerous officials who had abused their positions in the Brezhnev years. One of the most energetic campaigners against corruption was the new Moscow Party chief, **Boris Yeltsin**, whose populist antics, such as exposing black market dealings within the state system, infuriated the old guard. In October 1987, Yeltsin openly attacked Gorbachev and the hardline ideologist, Yegor Ligachev, and then dramatically resigned from the Politburo; shortly afterwards, he was sacked as Moscow Party leader.

Yeltsin's fate was a foretaste of things to come, as Gorbachev abandoned his balancing act between left and right and realigned himself with the hardliners. In the summer of 1988, radicals within the Party formed the **Democratic Union**, the first organized opposition movement to emerge since 1921. Gorbachev promptly banned its meetings and created a new Special-Purpose Militia unit – the **OMON** – to deal with any disturbances. Meanwhile, in the Baltic republics, nationalist **Popular Fronts** emerged, instantly attracting a mass membership. Estonia was the first to make the break, declaring full sovereignty in November 1988 and raising the national flag in place of the hammer and sickle in February of the following year.

1989 and all that

In the **elections** for the Congress of People's Deputies of March 1989, Soviet voters were, for the first time in years, allowed to choose from more than one candidate, some of whom were even non-Party members. Despite the heavily rigged selection process, radicals – including Yeltsin and Sakharov – managed to get themselves elected. When the congress met in May, a Latvian deputy started the proceedings with a call for an enquiry into events in Georgia, where Soviet troops had recently killed 21 protestors. When Sakharov called for an end to one-party rule, his microphone was switched off – a futile gesture by Gorbachev, since the sessions were being broadcast live on Russian TV.

Gorbachev's next crisis came with the **miners' strike** in July, when thousands walked out in protest at shortages, safety standards and poor wages. Gorbachev managed to entice them back to work with various promises, but the myth of the Soviet Union as a workers' state had been shattered for ever. The events which swept across the satellite states in Eastern Europe throughout 1989, culminating with the **fall of the Berlin Wall** and the Velvet Revolution in Czechoslovakia, were another blow to the old guard, but Gorbachev was more concerned about holding together the Soviet Union itself. That Communism now faced its greatest crisis at home was humiliatingly made plain by unprecedented counter-demonstrations during the October Revolution celebrations on November 7, 1989: one of the banners read: "Workers of the World – we're sorry".

The beginning of the end

1990 proved no better a year for Gorbachev or the Party. On January 19, Soviet tanks rolled into the Azerbaijani capital, Baku, to crush the independence movement there – more than a hundred people were killed that night. In February, Moscow witnessed the largest **demonstration** since the Revolution of 1917, with scores of thousands converging on Red Square, calling for an end to one-party rule and protesting against the rising anti-Semitic violence that had resulted in several murders in Leningrad. Gorbachev attempted to seize the initiative by agreeing to end one-party rule and simultaneously electing himself president, with increased powers to deal with the escalating crisis in the republics.

The voters registered their disgust with the Party at the March **local elections**. In the republics, nationalists swept the board and declarations of independence soon followed, while in Russia itself, the new radical alliance, **Democratic Platform**, gained majorities in the powerful city councils of Leningrad and Moscow. Gavril Popov became chairman of the Moscow council, while an equally reformist law professor, **Anatoly Sobchak**, was eventually elected to the leading post in Leningrad. May Day, 1990, was another humiliation for Gorbachev, who was jeered by sections of the crowd in Red Square. By the end of the month Yeltsin secured his election as chairman of the Russian parliament and, two weeks later, in imitation of the Baltic States,

declared **Russian independence** (June 12).

In July 1990, the Soviet Communist Party held its last ever congress. Yeltsin tore up his Party card in full view of the cameras – two million had done the same by the end of the year. The economic crisis, spiralling crime and chronic food shortages put Gorbachev under renewed pressure from Party hardliners. The first ominous signs came as winter set in, with a series of leadership reshuffles that gave the Interior Ministry and control of the media back to the conservatives. On December 20, the liberal Soviet foreign minister, Edvard Shevardnadze, resigned, warning that "dictatorship is coming".

The effects of Gorbachev's reshuffle became clear on January 13, 1991, when thirteen Lithuanians were killed by Soviet troops as they defended – unarmed – the national TV centre. Yeltsin immediately flew to the Baltics and signed a joint declaration condemning the violence. A week later in Latvia, the OMON stormed the Latvian Interior Ministry in Riga, killing five people. Hours before this attack, Moscow witnessed its largest ever demonstration – 250,000 people came out to protest against the killings. The Russian press had a field day, going further than ever before, mocking Gorbachev and backing the Balts. Gorbachev responded by threatening to suspend the liberal press laws, while adding more hardliners to the Politburo and giving wider powers to the security forces.

In June, the citizens of Leningrad narrowly voted in a referendum to rename the city **St Petersburg**, to the fury of Gorbachev, who refused to countenance it (the decision was only ratified by parliament after the putsch). At the same time, both Moscow and St Petersburg voted in new radical mayors (Popov and Sobchak) to run the reorganized city administrations. Popular disgust with Party rule was manifest in the overwhelming majority of votes cast for Yeltsin in the **Russian presidential election** of June 12, despite efforts to block his campaign. As Russia's first ever democratically elected leader, he could claim a mandate for bold moves and within a month had issued a decree calling for the removal of Party "cells" from factories. It was the most serious threat yet to the dominance of the Communist Party in Soviet life. Three days later, leading hardliners published a lengthy appeal for action "to lead the country to a dignified and sovereign future". Another indication of what might be in store came at the end of July, when seven Lithuanian border guards were shot dead in one of the continuing Soviet army attacks on Baltic customs posts.

The Putsch

On Monday August 19, 1991, the Soviet Union woke up to the soothing sounds of Chopin on the radio and *Swan Lake* on television. A **state of emergency** had been declared, Gorbachev had resigned "for health reasons" and the country was now ruled by the self-appointed "State Committee for the State of Emergency in the USSR". The main participants included many of Gorbachev's most recently appointed colleagues, under the nominal leadership of Gennady Yenayev, whose election as vice-president Gorbachev had obtained only after threatening his own resignation. Gorbachev himself, then on holiday in the Crimea, had been asked to back the coup the previous night, but had refused (to the surprise of the conspirators) and was consequently under house arrest. So began what Russians call the **Putsch**.

In Moscow, tanks appeared on the streets from mid-morning onwards, stationing themselves at key points, including the Russian parliament building, locally known as the **White House**. Here, a small group of protestors gathered, including Yeltsin, who had narrowly escaped arrest that morning. When the first tank approached, he leapt aboard, shook hands with its commander and appealed to the crowd (and accompanying radio and TV crews): "You can erect a throne using bayonets, but you cannot sit on bayonets for long." The Afghan war hero, Alexander Rutskoy, turned up and started organizing the defence of the building, making it harder for regular troops to contemplate attacking it. Actually, the role of storming the White House had been allocated to the crack KGB Alpha Force, but, for reasons unknown, they never went into action. News of the standoff – and Yeltsin's appeal to soldiers not to "let yourselves be turned into blind weapons" – was broadcast around the world and beamed back to millions of Russians via the BBC and the Voice of America.

In Leningrad, the army stayed off the streets and Mayor Sobchak kept his cool, quoting the constitution to the local coup commander at Military District headquarters. He warned them, "If you lay a finger on me, you will be put on trial like the rest of the Nazis." It was pure bravado,

but it worked: the local commander agreed to keep his forces in their barracks. The putsch had been badly planned from the start, with no preparatory round-up of opponents, nor any effort to sever international and domestic telephone lines. By Monday evening, Sobchak had appeared on local television and denounced the putsch – in Leningrad, it was effectively over on day one, though the citizens who gathered to defend City Hall had an anxious night awaiting tanks that never materialized. The following day, 200,000 Leningraders massed on Palace Square in protest against the putsch, while the eyes of the world were on Moscow.

On Tuesday, the defenders of the White House were heartened by the news that one of the coup leaders, Pavlov, had resigned due to "high blood pressure" (he had been drinking continuously) and the crowd grew to 100,000 in defiance of a curfew order. Around midnight, an advancing armoured column was stopped and firebombed on a Moscow ring road and three civilians were shot dead. Next morning it was announced that several military units had decamped to Yeltsin's side and on Wednesday afternoon the putsch collapsed as its leaders bolted. One group flew to the Crimea in the hope of obtaining Gorbachev's pardon and were arrested on arrival. Yenayev drank himself into a stupor and several others committed suicide.

The end of the Soviet Union

Gorbachev flew back to Moscow, not realizing that everything had changed. At his first press conference, he pledged continuing support for the Communist Party and Marxist-Leninism, and openly admitted that he had trusted the conspirators as men of "culture and dialogue". He was, by now, totally estranged from the mood of the country and marooned by the tide of history. The same day, jubilant crowds toppled the giant statue of Dzerzhinsky which stood outside the Lubyanka in Moscow. On Friday, Gorbachev appeared before parliament and was publicly humiliated by Yeltsin in front of the television cameras. Yeltsin then decreed the Russian Communist Party an illegal organization, announced the suspension of pro-coup newspapers such as *Pravda* and had the Central Committee headquarters in Moscow sealed up.

The failure of the putsch spelt the **end of Communist rule** and the **break-up of the Soviet**

Union. Any possibility of a Slav core remaining united was torpedoed by loose talk of re-drawing the border between Russia and Ukraine, and the new-found goodwill between Russia and its former satellites quickly evaporated. In December, Ukraine voted overwhelmingly for independence; a week later the leaders of Russia, Belarus and Ukraine formally replaced the USSR with a **Commonwealth of Independent States** (CIS), whose nominal capital would be Minsk; the Central Asian republics declared their intention of joining. On December 25, Gorbachev resigned as president of a state which no longer existed; that evening the Soviet flag was lowered over the Kremlin and replaced by the Russian tricolour.

The new Russia

On January 2, 1992, Russians faced their New Year hangovers and the harsh reality of massive price rises, following a decree by Yeltsin that lifted controls on a broad range of products. The cost of food rose by up to 500 percent and queues disappeared almost overnight. According to the Western advisors shaping Russia's new economic policy, this would stimulate domestic production and promote the growth of capitalism in the shortest possible time. Initially, **inflation** was limited by keeping a tight rein on state spending, in accordance with the monetarist strategy of Prime Minister **Yegor Gaidar**, but despite Yeltsin's defence of his painful and unpopular measures the policy soon came unstuck after the Central Bank began printing vast amounts of rubles to cover credits issued to state industries on the verge of bankruptcy. Inflation soared.

Meanwhile, **St Petersburg** also had other concerns. On March 25, an accident at the nuclear reactor at **Sosnovy Bor**, on the Gulf of Finland, caused concern around the world. The reactor was of the same type as the one that blew up at Chernobyl and initial reports suggested that St Petersburg had been contaminated. In fact, no radiation was released, but the accident highlighted environmental worries, including the **pollution** of the city's water supply by industrial effluents discharged into Lake Ladoga and the Neva, exacerbated by the half-finished tidal barrage across the Gulf. While Mayor Sobchak toured the West to raise funds to invest in St Petersburg, unscrupulous foreign companies tried to take advantage: one firm offered to build the

city a free ring-road if only they could bury rubbish beneath it, neglecting to mention that they had highly toxic waste in mind.

By the autumn of 1992, Russia's economic policy was in dire straits and Yeltsin was forced to replace Gaidar with the veteran technocrat **Viktor Chernomyrdin**, in December 1992. Chernomyrdin surprised parliament by immediately reneging on earlier promises both to increase subsidies to industry and to restore them for vital foodstuffs (including vodka). For much of 1993 there was a **"War of Laws"** between the government and parliament, with each flouting or repealing the other's decrees and budgets. Parliament's speaker, **Ruslan Khasbulatov**, exercised such influence over the deputies that articles in the press suggested he had them under some form of hypnosis – although as a leader Khasbulatov suffered the political handicap of being a non-Russian (born in Chechnya), and few believed that his defence of parliamentary privilege was anything but self-serving. Another erstwhile Yeltsin ally who now found himself in opposition was Vice-President **Alexander Rutskoy**, who denounced Gaidar's team as "boys in pink pants", and railed against the government as "scum" and "faggots".

In March 1993, Congress reneged on its earlier promise to hold a **referendum** on a new constitution. Yeltsin declared that he would hold an opinion poll anyway, which he hoped would provide evidence of popular support for himself, although it would have no legal force. On March 20, Yeltsin appeared on TV to announce the introduction of a special rule suspending the power of Congress and called for new elections. In the meantime, there was a nationwide vote of confidence in the president and vice-president, plus a referendum on the draft constitution, and new electoral laws were passed. At this point Congress and Rutskoy attempted to impeach Yeltsin. The impeachment was narrowly avoided and a referendum was held. This seemed largely to vindicate Yeltsin and his economic policies, but not his calls for early parliamentary elections.

The uneasy stalemate lasted until September, when Yeltsin brought things to a head by dissolving Congress under a legally dubious decree. In response, **deputies occupied the White House**, refusing to budge as Yeltsin cut off their electricity and finally blockaded them in. The crisis deepened as Rutskoy gathered an armed force around the building and appeared on TV handing out guns. Who fired the first shot is still disputed, but the result was a series of battles, which lasted two days and left more than a hundred people dead. Snipers picked people off on the streets, Rutskoy ordered his supporters to storm the Moscow council building and the TV centre, and national television went off the air. Yeltsin responded by ordering tanks to shell the White House into submission on the morning of October 4.

With his parliamentary foes behind bars Yeltsin turned on the local councils who had supported Congress out of sympathy for their approach or simply as elected representatives. Councils all over Russia were abolished and new elections declared, leaving power concentrated in the hands of local mayors and their bureaucrats. While Yeltsin was determined to be re-elected and rewrite the constitution, he bewildered many supporters by distancing himself from the party created to represent his government in the forthcoming elections, which bore the presumptuous name of **Russia's Choice** and campaigned as if its triumph was a foregone conclusion.

Vladimir Zhirinovsky and "Tsar Anatoly"

The result of the December 1993 elections to the new parliament or Duma was a stunning rebuff for Russia's Choice, which won only 14 percent of the vote, compared to 23 percent for the so-called Liberal Democratic Party of **Vladimir Zhirinovsky**, an ultra-nationalist with a murky past who threatened to bomb Germany and Japan and to dump radioactive waste in the Baltic States. His success owed much to a superbly run TV campaign, whose effects lasted just long enough to get the LDP into parliament, beside the "red-brown" alliance of other ultra-nationalists and Communists.

While Russian liberals and world opinion were aghast, evidence later emerged of systematic voting fraud in Zhirinovsky's favour, which could only have been organized at the highest level. For Yeltsin, the crucial point was that Zhirinovsky supported the new **Constitution**, giving unprecedented powers to the president, and backed Yeltsin's government in the Duma, despite his aggressive rhetoric. Even so, it seemed a humiliating rebuff when the Duma promulgated an amnesty for the participants in the October "events", and the organizers of the 1991 putsch too.

In the wake of the elections, the government backpedalled on further economic reforms and tried to improve its nationalist credentials by taking a sterner stand on the rights of Russians in the ex-republics, or "Near Abroad". Resurgent **nationalism** was evident across the board in foreign policy, from warnings against expanding NATO into Eastern Europe or the Baltics to arguments with Ukraine over Crimea, and increasingly blatant interventions in civil wars in the Caucasus and Central Asia. The Russian Army's new strategic doctrine identified regional wars as the chief threat to national security and defending the old borders of the USSR as a top priority.

In **St Petersburg**, the election of a new city council in March 1994 returned only half the required number of deputies, as apathetic and confused voters stayed at home. This allowed Sobchak to take sole command and pursue his strategy of boosting St Petersburg's international reputation by hosting conferences and the **Goodwill Games** and attracting state visits by Prince Charles and Queen Elizabeth: his fondness for ceremonies and VIPs led to him being dubbed "Tsar Anatoly the First". Although further elections finally produced a new council at the end of 1994, it was so divided that most of its energies went on feuding. Sobchak himself spent much of his time on foreign trips, and his reputation also suffered from rumours that members of his family had profited from shady property deals – factors that would contribute to his electoral defeat less than two years later.

The war in Chechnya

In December 1994 the Kremlin embarked on a **war in Chechnya** to subdue the breakaway Caucasian republic. The Chechens put up fierce resistance in their capital Grozny, which Defence Minister Grachev had boasted could be taken by a regiment of paratroops in two hours, but in fact only fell after weeks of bombardment, leaving the city in ruins and up to 120,000 dead – including tens of thousands of Russian conscripts. Back home, the debacle was attributed to the so-called "**Party of War**", a shadowy alliance of figures within the military, security and economic ministries, whose geopolitical or personal interests coincided. It was even said that Grachev and other commanders deliberately sacrificed their own troops to write off hundreds of armoured vehicles, in order to cover up the illicit sale of

1600 tanks from the Soviet Army in East Germany.

As the war dragged on throughout 1995, there was a massive protest vote for the Communists in the December parliamentary elections, which boded ill for Yeltsin's chances in the **Presidential election** of June 1996. Fearing the consequences of a victory by the Communist leader **Gennady Zyuganov**, Russia's financiers and journalists gave unstinting support to Yeltsin, with television, in particular, demonizing Zyuganov and denying the Communists any chance to state their case. Yeltsin's campaign was masterminded by Deputy Prime Minister **Anatoly Chubais**, who banked on the anti-Yeltsin vote being split between Zyuganov and the ex-paratroop general **Alexander Lebed** – as indeed happened. Having gained half the vote, Yeltsin co-opted Lebed by offering him the post of security overlord, and subsequently ordered him to end the war in Chechnya. Lebed duly negotiated the withdrawal of Russian forces – leaving the issue of Chechen independence to be resolved at a future date – only to be sacked from the government soon afterwards, having served his purpose.

Yeltsin's second term

With the Communist threat dispelled, the **oligarchs** behind Yeltsin's re-election soon fell out over the remaining spoils. **Vladimir Potanin** acquired thirty percent of the world's nickel reserves for a mere $70 million and a controlling stake in the telecom giant Svyazinvest due to the intervention of Chubais – enraging **Boris Berezovsky**, whose TV station ORT aired a 29-minute diatribe against Potanin during a news show. Along with the banking and media moguls **Vladimir Gusinsky** and **Mikhail Khodorovsky**, and oil or gas barons such as **Rolan Abramovich**, they became synonymous with a series of scandals – including "book advances" to Chubais and his privatization chief Alfred Kokh which were patently bribes. After Chubais had to resign as a sop to public opinion (he became boss of the electricity monopoly), Berezovsky's influence in the Kremlin grew even greater, and he was widely seen as the "kingmaker" of Russian politics.

Meanwhile, St Petersburg's 1996 mayoral election saw Sobchak ousted by his own deputy, **Vladimir Yakovlev**, following a bitter campaign dominated by allegations of corruption and nepotism. Though it didn't seem important at the

time, one of Sobchak's protégés – an ex-KGB officer, Vladimir Putin – reacted to this by leaving St Petersburg politics to work in the Kremlin, where he would soon become noticed and destined for greater things. At the time, however, all eyes were on Yakovlev as he assumed the new post of governor and tried to grapple with the city's chaotic finances and decrepit infrastructure. His first year in office was marked by bungles and U-turns, but by 1997 he found the nerve to double municipal rents and service charges, paving the way for a balanced budget that helped St Petersburg to float a $300 million Eurobond issue, bringing in new funds for development.

Property was (and is) a vital issue. The privatization of municipal real estate yielded vast profits for speculators and corrupt officials, who were assumed to have ordered the 1997 assassination of St Petersburg's Vice-Governor **Mikhail Manevich**, after he began investigating fraudulent city property deals. Even more shocking was the murder of the widely admired **Galina Starovoitova** in November 1998. An outspoken democrat and human-rights campaigner, who opposed the war in Chechnya and was untainted by corruption, she was mourned by many as the last true democratic politician in Russia.

The 1998 crash

The late 1990s saw prime ministers and cabinets change with bewildering frequency, as Yeltsin manoeuvred to build or neutralize coalitions in the Duma and its upper house, the Federation Council (dominated by regional governors), and find scapegoats for Russia's economic problems. First he encouraged Russia's creditors by appointing the energetic reformer **Boris Nemtsov** to the cabinet – only to sacrifice him a few months later to placate Chernomyrdin and the Duma, whose featherbedding of the gas, industrial and collective farm lobbies ensured that the state budget went into deficit, obliging it to rely on short-term "hot" loans. By April 1998 Russia's foreign debt stood at $117 billion, workers were owed $9 billion in unpaid wages, and pensioners over $13 billion. With a crisis imminent, Yeltsin stunned the world by dismissing Chernomyrdin's entire cabinet and nominating 35-year-old **Sergei Kirienko** as prime minister. A low-profile technocrat with no power base, his nomination was twice rejected by the Duma, until Yeltsin warned deputies that their Moscow flats and sinecures would be forfeit if they did so a third time.

Unfortunately, Kirienko's rescue plan depended on a "final loan" from the International Monetary Fund, at a time when the collapse of economies across Asia raised fears of a global crash, and pushed down the price of Russia's chief exports, oil and gas. As the IMF loan stalled and hard currency reserves evaporated, the pressure to default or devalue became intolerable, until the Central Bank caved in. In August, the **ruble crashed** and many banks and businesses went into liquidation; the capitalist bubble had burst. Kirienko was promptly sacked and replaced by the veteran diplomat and spymaster **Yevgeny Primakov**, a "safe" candidate accepted across the political spectrum, and also internationally. The US sent three million tonnes of emergency food aid, to avert the possibility of food riots during the winter.

Yet the crash had some positive results. With imports so costly, shoppers switched back to domestic products, rewarding firms that survived the crisis with a larger share of the market. It also cut a few of the oligarchs down to size – though others seized the chance to snap up rivals' assets or dump all their own liabilities. By the end of the decade, these changes combined with arms sales and the rising price of gas and oil to produce a modest economic revival, which would contribute to the groundswell of support for Russia's next leader.

Yeltsin's endgame

While his government grappled with governing, Yeltsin was preoccupied with ensuring his own future – if not by running for President again in 2000, then by choosing a successor who would safeguard "**The Family**" – a term widely used to describe his inner circle of advisors and relatives, whose backroom deals with Berezovsky were the source of constant speculation in parts of the media they didn't control. With his health so uncertain that even Prime Minister Primakov expressed doubts as to whether Yeltsin could function as president – for which Primakov was sacked in January 1999 – Yeltsin had no alternative but to find a successor whom he could trust to guarantee the Family's security after they left the Kremlin. There would be no mercy if the Communists won, nor any sympathy from Lebed,

while Moscow's Mayor Luzhkov and the recently dismissed Primakov offered little hope either – but any of them could win the next election.

Yeltsin's chosen successor emerged as suddenly and mysteriously as the apartment-block **bombings** that killed over 300 people in Moscow and other cities in September. Coming only a month after a Chechen warlord seized thousands of hostages in Daghestan, most Russians believed the government's claim that Chechen terrorists were responsible (though foreign journalists speculated that the FSB was behind the bombings), and demanded action.

It was then that the new acting prime minister, **Vladimir Putin**, made his name by pledging "We will wipe the terrorists out wherever we find them – even on the toilet". Within weeks Russia launched a **second war in Chechnya**, using overwhelming firepower from the start. By December eighty percent of Grozny was in ruins and the plight of its besieged civilians was an international issue, but in Russia most greeted the city's fall as just revenge for Russia's defeat five years earlier. Berezovsky's media went into overdrive, casting Putin as the resolute, honest leader that Russia required, while tarring Luzhkov as hand-in-glove with the Mafia, and Primakov as old and sick. A new party nicknamed "Bear" materialized overnight to back Putin's candidacy, and was soon riding high in the polls.

The final masterstroke was **Yeltsin's surprise resignation** during his New Year message to the nation on the last night of the old millennium, when Russians would be more inclined to raise a rueful toast than ponder how power had so swiftly passed to Putin. His first decree as acting president was to grant Yeltsin and his family lifelong immunity from arrest, prosecution or seizure of assets, and confer on Yeltsin the title of "First President" in perpetuity.

President Putin

Ensconced in the Kremlin as acting president, Putin enjoyed every advantage in the forthcoming election, which most of his opponents tacitly conceded was a foregone conclusion. His inauguration on May 5, 2000 was heralded as the first peaceful democratic transfer of power in Russian history, replete with ceremonial trappings harking back to Tsarist times, invented for the occasion. His pledge to restore Russia's greatness was followed by decrees doubling military spending, increasing the powers of the security agencies, and appointing seven "Super Governors" to oversee the regions. The drive to strengthen the state and **centralize authority** after an era of dissolution is one of the leitmotifs of Russian history, exemplified by Ivan the Terrible, Peter the Great, Lenin and Stalin. While stressing his commitment to democracy and the rule of law, Putin's view of Russian history embraced the Soviet, Tsarist and post-Soviet eras as equally worthwhile – symbolized by his decision to restore the Tsarist eagle as the state symbol, and the old Soviet national anthem (with revised words).

For those who feared that totalitarianism was creeping back, an early warning sign could be found in the **campaign against NTV** and other elements of the Media-MOST group, which had infuriated the Kremlin by revealing human-rights abuses in Chechnya and casualties among Russian troops. Media-MOST's boss, Gusinsky, was arrested and spent several days in Moscow's notorious Butyurka prison, in what was seen by liberals as a warning to other media moguls, but welcomed by most Russians as a blow against the hated oligarchs. Putin then convened a meeting of the oligarchs that pointedly excluded Gusinsky, Berezovsky and Abramovich, where the invitees reportedly pledged to pay more taxes and quit meddling in state affairs. Gusinsky prudently left Russia, soon to be followed by Berezovsky.

Besides alleging that millions of dollars had been embezzled to finance Putin's election campaign, Berezovsky also implied that he had paid the Chechen warlord to invade Daghestan and thus set the stage for a new war in Chechnya and Putin's subsequent rise to power.

However, Putin's reputation suffered more from a spate of high-profile **disasters** – a bomb in a Moscow subway that killed twelve and injured scores; a fire in Moscow's Ostankino TV Tower that blacked out national television for several days; and, most notably, the loss of 118 men aboard the submarine *Kursk*, a tragedy which cast both navy and Kremlin in the role of villains after they had rejected offers of foreign help at a time when it was still possible to save some survivors. Nonetheless, Putin's political objectives were broadly accepted by the Duma and the public, foreign heads of state queued up to meet him, and his tour of Asia yielded a promise from North Korea that defused fears of a nuclear arms race in the region and negated the supposed justification for the US "Son of Star Wars" anti-ballistic missile system. Given US claims that Russia has deployed short-range nuclear missiles in the Baltic enclave of Kaliningrad, and the ascension of George W. Bush to the White House, it seems that **arms racing** is set to return as a major issue in relations between the two states (not to mention Europe and China).

Books

The number of books available about Russia and the old Soviet Union is vast. We have concentrated on works specifically related to St Petersburg and on useful general surveys of Russian and Soviet history, politics and the arts. Where two publishers are given, they refer to the UK and US publishers respectively; for books published in one country only, the publisher is followed by the country; if a book has the same UK and US publisher, only the publisher's name is given. Books that are out of print are denoted "o/p".

General accounts, guides and illustrated books

Baedeker's Handbooks (Baedeker, o/p). The 1914 *Baedeker's Handbook to Russia* was a stupendous work that almost bankrupted the company, with dozens of maps and reams of information that were soon rendered irrelevant by the Revolution. A facsimile edition was produced in the 1970s, but today this too is almost as rare as the original, copies of which sell for up to £500 in antiquarian bookshops.

Marshall Berman, *All That is Solid Melts into Air: The Experience of Modernity* (Verso/Penguin). A wide-ranging study of modernism with a superb chapter on St Petersburg, covering Pushkin, Gogol, and Chernyshevsky amongst others. Thought-provoking stuff.

Kathleen Berton Murrell, *St Petersburg: History, Art and Architecture* (Troika, Moscow/Flint River Press, UK). Informative text by a long-term resident in Russia, although the photographs follow no apparent logical order.

James H. Billington, *The Icon and the Axe* (Vintage, US). Dated in many of its perceptions, but still the most comprehensive and readable study of Russian culture from medieval to Soviet times.

Robert Byron, *First Russia, Then Tibet* (Penguin, UK). A classic travel account of the 1930s with a well-honed chapter on Leningrad (though it is the Tibetan section that really shines).

Marquis de Custine, *Empire of the Czar* (Anchor). Another vintage masterpiece, and the first book by a Westerner to get to grips with Russia, which de Custine visited during the 1830s.

Michael Dohan (ed), *St Petersburg Traveller's Yellow Pages* (Infoservices International, US). Annual listings book on sale all over St Petersburg in its Cyrillic edition, and less widely in the English one. The previous year's edition is available online at *www.infoservices.com*.

Duncan Fallowell, *One Hot Summer in St Petersburg* (Vintage, UK). Sex, drugs and tears during the torrid White Nights, as an English writer gets into the St Petersburg demi-monde and falls in love with a naval cadet. Some good descriptions, amidst a lot of hyperbolic waffle.

Prince George Galitzine, *Imperial Splendour* (Viking, UK). Palaces and monasteries of old Russia, presented by a member of the Russian nobility who lived most of his life in London, but made regular trips back to St Petersburg from the early 1960s.

Katya Galitzine, *St Petersburg: The Hidden Interiors* (Hazar Publishing, UK). A bit of a misnomer, since most of the buildings featured are well known, but Leonid Bogdanov's photographs make this an irresistible coffee-table book.

Vadim Gippenreiter & Alexei Komech, *Old Russian Cities* (Laurence King, o/p). Colour photos of the loveliest towns and cities in Russia, carefully staged to exclude any Soviet architecture. Among the dozens of places featured are St Petersburg, Novgorod and the Imperial palaces.

Mikhail Iroshnikov et al., *Before the Revolution: St Petersburg in Photographs 1890–1914*

(Abrams, o/p). Evocative black-and-white photographs (many never published before) of the city in the last decades of its Tsarist incarnation, with a historical text by four eminent St Petersburg academics.

Ian Jack (ed), *Russia: the Wild East* (Granta, UK). A disturbing anthology of pieces on Russian life by writers such as Orlando Figes, Colin Thubron and Vitaly Vitaliev, ranging from St Petersburg to Siberia, and vodka to the war in Chechnya.

Pavel Kann, *Leningrad: A Guide* (Planeta, Moscow). The last in a classic Soviet series of city guides, giving pride of place to Lenin memorial sites and the like; the 1988 edition is blissfully impervious to perestroika. It's sold by street vendors along Nevskiy prospekt.

Lawrence Kelly, *St Petersburg: A Traveller's Anthology* (Constable & Atheneum, o/p). Amusing descriptions of court life, eyewitness accounts of historic events and excerpts from books long out of print. Stops short of Petrograd and the Revolution, though.

Evgenia Kirichenko & Mikhail Anikst, *The Russian Style* (Laurence King, UK). A coffee-table book of Russian interiors, ranging from the palatial to the humble, including famous writers' homes, amazing Style Moderne mansions and glittering palace halls.

Prince Michael of Greece, *Imperial Palaces of Russia* (IB Tauris/St Martin's Press). Lavishly illustrated survey of all the major palaces in and around St Petersburg, by the "heir" to a royal family that the Greeks rejected in 1974.

Suzanne Massie, *Land of the Firebird*; *Pavlovsk: The Life of a Russian Palace* (both Hearttree Press, US). The first is a colourful tour of pre-revolutionary Russian culture; the second sweeps over three centuries of history as embodied by Pavlovsk Palace, its inhabitants and its restorers, accompanied by wonderful illustrations.

John Nicholson, *The Other St Petersburg*. Absurdity, drinking and courtyards loom large in these amusing character sketches of Petersburg as it was before capitalism changed everything. You can buy this self-published book in the duty-free at Pulkovo-2 airport or some bookshops on Nevskiy, or read excerpts online at *www.other.spb.ru*.

Anthony Ross, *By the Banks of the Neva* (Cambridge University Press). A history of the British community in eighteenth-century St Petersburg and their contribution to the city as engineers, artists, governesses, soldiers and sailors – the list is endless.

Colin Thubron, *Among the Russians* (Penguin, UK); *In Siberia* (Chatto & Windus, UK). The first includes a chapter on Leningrad, a visit to which formed part of Thubron's angst-ridden journey around the USSR in the early 1980s; the second is as lapidary and insightful and even more gloom-inducing, given such locales as Kolyma and Vorkuta, the worst hells of the Gulag.

Solomon Volkov, *St Petersburg: A Cultural History* (Free Press). A scholastic tour de force, ranging from architecture and music to fashion and philosophy.

Various, *St Petersburg: A Guide to the Architecture* (Bibliopolis, St Petersburg). A compact guide to who built what and where, illustrated with black-and-white photographs. Though widely available on Nevskiy, it's only worth buying if you're especially interested in architecture.

History, politics and society

John T. Alexander, *Catherine the Great: Life and Legend* (Oxford University Press). Just what the title says, with rather more credence given to some of the wilder stories than in Vincent Cronin's book (see below).

Antony Beevor, *Stalingrad* (Viking Penguin). Epic tale of one of the most decisive battles of World War II, told in all its gory details from the standpoint of ordinary soldiers on both sides and the citizenry caught in the middle.

Robert Conquest, *Stalin: Breaker of Nations* (Weidenfeld & Nicolson/Viking Penguin); *The Great Terror: A Reassessment* (Pimlico/Oxford University Press). The first is a short, withering biography of the Soviet dictator; the second, perhaps the best study of the Terror. In 1990 this was revised after new evidence suggested that Conquest's tally of the number of victims of the Terror was an underestimate; previously he had been accused of exaggeration.

Steve Crawshaw, *Goodbye to the USSR: The Collapse of Soviet Power* (Bloomsbury, UK). A clear and insightful account of the Gorbachev era by the *Independent's* Eastern European editor, covering the period from 1985 up to Gorbachev's resignation in the aftermath of the putsch.

Vincent Cronin, *Catherine, Empress of all the Russias* (Harvill/HarperCollins). Salacious rumours are dispelled in this sympathetic biography of the shy German princess who made it big in Russia.

Isaac Deutscher, *Stalin* (Penguin, UK). Classic political biography, sometimes criticized for being too sympathetic towards its subject.

Harold Elletson, *The General Against the Kremlin* (Little, Brown). An intriguing biography of the maverick soldier-turned-politician Alexander Lebed up until his dismissal by Yeltsin in 1996, since when his star has waned.

Marc Ferro, *Nicholas II: The Last of the Tsars* (Oxford University Press). A concise biography by a French historian who argues that some of the Imperial family escaped execution at Yekaterinburg.

Orlando Figes, *A People's Tragedy: The Russian Revolution 1891–1924* (Pimlico/Viking Penguin). Vivid, detailed, anecdotal, closely argued and sure to infuriate Marxists and monarchists alike. A tour de force.

Stephen Handleman, *Comrade Criminal: The Theft of the Second Russian Revolution* (Yale University Press). Fascinating study of how organized crime spread through every level of Russian society and how Communist *apparatchiki* transformed themselves into gangster-capitalists.

Adam Hochschild, *The Unquiet Ghost: Russians Remember Stalin* (Serpent's Tail/Penguin). A searching enquiry into the nature of guilt and denial, ranging from the penal camps of Kolyma to the archives of the Lubyanka. Hochschild concludes that the road to hell is paved with good intentions and that few people living under the Terror would have behaved any better.

Dominic Lieven, *Nicholas II* (St Martin's Press, US). Another post-Soviet study of the last tsar that draws comparisons both between the monarchies of Russia and other states of that period, and the downfall of the Tsarist and Soviet regimes.

Robert Massie, *Peter the Great* (Abacus/Ballantine); *Nicholas and Alexandra* (Indigo/Dell). Both the boldest and the weakest of the Romanov tsars are minutely scrutinized in these two heavyweight, but extremely readable, biographies – the one on Peter is especially good, and contains much about the creation of St Petersburg.

William Millinship, *Front Line* (Methuen, o/p). Interviews with diverse women in the new Russia by the Moscow correspondent of Britain's *Observer*. By turns vivid, gripping, moving and appalling – a fascinating slice of Russian life.

Edvard Radzinsky, *Rasputin: The Last Word* (Weidenfeld, UK). The most recent and comprehensive biography of the "mad monk" who hastened the fall of tsarism, using newly discovered files from the archives of the Provisional Government.

John Reed, *Ten Days that Shook the World* (Penguin). The classic eyewitness account of the 1917 Bolshevik seizure of power, which vividly captures the mood of the time and the hopes pinned on the Revolution. The book of the film *Reds*.

David Remnick, *Lenin's Tomb* (Penguin/Random House); *Resurrection: The Struggle for a New Russia* (Picador, UK). *Lenin's Tomb* remains the most vivid account of the collapse of the Soviet Union, though some of its judgements seem simplistic with hindsight. *Resurrection* is also riveting, but the jury is still out on Remnick's analysis of the Yeltsin era.

Harrison Salisbury, *Black Night, White Snow; The Nine Hundred Days* (both Da Capo Press, US). The events of the 1905 and 1917 revolutions and the wartime siege of Leningrad are vividly related in these two books by a veteran American journalist. Both are highly recommended.

Jonathan Steele, *Eternal Russia: Yeltsin, Gorbachev and the Mirage of Democracy* (Faber/Harvard University Press). *The Guardian*'s former Moscow correspondent provides a thought-provoking and incisive look at the evolution of the new Russia, which he sees very much as a product of a deep-rooted authoritarian tradition.

Henri Troyat, *Alexander of Russia* (Dutton). Study of the "Tsar Liberator", Alexander II, sympathetically profiled by a French historian.

John Ure, *The Cossacks* (Constable, UK). A lively history of the freebooting warriors who rocked the Romanov dynasty but also served as its most faithful instrument of repression, by a former British diplomat who began his career in Russia.

Dimitri Volkogonov, *Stalin: Triumph and Tragedy* (Prima Publishing, US). Weighty study of the Soviet dictator, drawing on long-withheld archive material, by Russia's foremost military historian.

Edmund Wilson, *To the Finland Station* (Penguin). A classic appraisal of Lenin's place in the Russian revolutionary tradition, first published in 1940, combining metaphysics and political analysis with waspish characterization.

The arts

Anna Benn & Rosamund Bartlett, *Literary Russia: A Guide* (Picador, UK). Comprehensive guide to Russian writers and places associated with their lives and works, including such famous Petersburgers as Dostoyevsky and Akhmatova along with figures who are less well known abroad, such as the cult author Daniil Kharms.

Alan Bird, *A History of Russian Painting* (Phaidon/Macmillan). A comprehensive survey of Russian painting from medieval times to the Brezhnev era, including numerous black-and-white illustrations and potted biographies of the relevant artists.

John E. Bowlt (ed), *Russian Art of the Avant Garde* (Thames & Hudson/Penguin). An illustrated volume of critical essays on this seminal movement, which anticipated many trends in Western art that have occurred since World War II.

Leslie Chamberlain, *The Food and Cooking of Russia* (Penguin). Informative and amusing cookbook, full of delicious – if somewhat vague – recipes.

Matthew Cullerne Brown, *Art Under Stalin* (Phaidon/Holmes & Meier); *Contemporary Russian Art* (Phaidon, UK). The former is a fascinating study of totalitarian aesthetics, ranging from ballet to sports stadia and films to sculpture; the latter covers art in the Brezhnev and Gorbachev eras.

John Drummond (ed), *Speaking of Diaghilev* (Faber). What may prove to be a definitive work, given that it consists of over twenty interviews with Diaghilev's few remaining contemporaries. Dancers, conductors, choreographers and contemporary observers give their thoughts and memories of the impresario behind the *Ballets Russes*.

Camilla Gray, *The Russian Experiment in Art 1863–1922* (Thames & Hudson). A concise guide to the multitude of movements that constituted the Russian avant-garde, prior to the imposition of the dead hand of Socialist Realism.

George Heard Hamilton, *The Art and Architecture of Russia* (Yale University Press). An exhaustive rundown of the major trends in painting, sculpture and architecture in Russia, from Kievan Rus to the turn of this century.

Jay Leyda, *Kino* (Princeton University Press). A weighty history of Russian and Soviet film to the early 1980s.

Roberta Reeder, *Anna Akhmatova: Poet and Prophet* (Allison & Busby, UK). Comprehensive and well-researched biography of one of the greatest poets of Russia's "Silver Age", with accounts of the artists, poets and events that influenced her life and work.

Artemy Troitsky, *Back in the USSR: The True Story of Rock in Russia* (Omnibus, UK). First-hand account of 25 years of rock music inside Russia by the country's former leading music journalist and critic, who later edited the Russian edition of *Playboy* magazine.

Russian fiction and poetry

Anna Akhmatova, *Selected Poems* (Penguin). Moving and mystical verses by the doyenne of Leningrad poets, whose *Requiem* cycle spoke for a generation traumatized by the purges. Essential reading.

Andrei Bely, *Petersburg* (Penguin, US). Apocalyptic novel set in 1905, full of *fin-de-siècle* angst and phantasmagorical imagery, by St Petersburg's equivalent of Prague's Kafka.

Andrei Bitov, *Pushkin House* (Harvill/Random House). A bittersweet tale about growing up in Leningrad during the post-Stalin years, partly based on the author's own experiences at university.

Fyodor Dostoyevsky, *Poor Folk and Other Stories; The Brothers Karamazov; The Gambler; The House of the Dead; The Idiot* (all Penguin); *Crime and Punishment* (Penguin/Random House); *Notes from the Underground* (Penguin/Bantam); *The Possessed* (Vintage/NAL-Dutton). Pessimistic, brooding tales, often semi-autobiographical (particularly *The Gambler* and *The House of the Dead*). His masterpiece, *Crime and Punishment*, is set in Petersburg's infamous Haymarket district.

Daniil Kharms, *Incidences* (Serpent's Tail, UK). Literary miniatures by the legendary St Petersburg absurdist. In his home city you can find other works in Russian, including Kharms's irreverent "Pushkin stories", illustrated with his own cartoons.

Vladimir Nabokov, *Invitation to a Beheading; Laughter in the Dark; Look at the Harlequins!; Nabokov's Dozen; Speak, Memory* (all Penguin/Random House). Though best known abroad for his novel of erotic obsession, *Lolita*, Nabokov is chiefly esteemed as a stylist in the land of his birth. His childhood home stands just off St Isaac's Square, and is vividly recalled in his autobiographical *Speak, Memory*.

Boris Pasternak, *Doctor Zhivago* (HarperCollins/Ballantine). A multi-layered story of love and destiny, war and revolution, chiefly known in the West for the film version. Russians regard Pasternak as a poet first and a novelist second.

Victor Pelevin, *A Werewolf Problem in Central Russia and Other Stories; Omon Ra; The Blue Lantern: Stories* (all New Directions, US); *Buddha's Little Finger* (Viking, US); *The Life of Insects* (Penguin); *The Clay Machine-Gun* (Faber, UK). Digital-age fables by the literary voice of Russia's "Generation P", for whom Pepsi, not the Party, set the tone. Essential reading.

Aleksandr Solzhenitsyn, *August 1914* (Penguin); *Cancer Ward* (Vintage/Random House); *First Circle* (Harvill/Northwestern University Press); *The Gulag Archipelago* (Harvill/HarperCollins); *One Day in the Life of Ivan Denisovich* (Vintage/Knopf). Russia's most famous modern dissident – the last two books listed here constitute a stunning indictment of the camps and the purges, for which Solzhenitsyn was persecuted by the state in Brezhnev's time and feted in the West (at least before he lambasted its decadence).

Literature by foreign writers

Malcolm Bradbury, *To The Hermitage* (Overlook Press, US). Witty and intriguing story interweaving St Petersburg in the time of Catherine the Great and in 1993, with French encyclopédiste Diderot as the central character.

Celia Brayfield, *White Ice* (Penguin, UK). A tale of passion and greed involving a diamond necklace and four disparate characters, in a story that ranges from pre-revolutionary St Petersburg to Thatcher's Britain, via Leningrad and London in the 1960s.

Alan Brien, *Lenin: The Novel* (Paladin & Morrow, o/p). Masterly evocation of Lenin's life and character, in the form of a diary by the man himself, whose steely determination and sly irascibility exude from every page.

Anthony Burgess, *Honey for the Bears* (Norton, US). An amusing tale of misadventure, sexual discovery and black-marketeering in 1950s Leningrad. An early work by the prolific British polymath, whose interest in Russia ran deep.

Bruce Chatwin, *What Am I Doing Here* (Picador/Penguin). A memorable account of visiting Russia with the art collector George Ortiz and a lively essay on Russian Futurism are only two of the gems in this collection of travel pieces and *pensées*.

J. M. Coetzee, *The Master of Petersburg* (Minerva/Penguin). Brooding novel centred on Dostoyevsky, who gets drawn into the nefarious underworld of the St Petersburg nihilists after the suspicious suicide of his stepson.

Tom Hyman, *Seven Days to Petrograd* (Penguin & Bantam, o/p). Thriller about an attempt to avert the Bolshevik Revolution by killing Lenin aboard the "sealed train", featuring an unlikely romance between the would-be assassin and Lenin's soul mate, Inessa Armand.

Michael Ignatieff, *The Russian Album* (Vintage & Penguin, o/p). An evocative family history dating back to before the Revolution by the émigré scion of an old Russian family with roots in St Petersburg.

John le Carré, *The Russia House* (Hodder/Knopf). Well-intentioned but overlong attempt to exorcize the ghosts of the Cold War by the world's best-known spy novelist. His snapshots of Leningrad and Moscow in the days of perestroika are less illuminating than the author's own perspective as a former spy.

Philip Kerr, *Dead Meat* (Vintage/Bantam). Edgy, atmospheric thriller set in a Mafia-infested St Petersburg, where the lugubrious detective Grushko tries to uncover the truth behind a journalist's murder. Made into a three-part BBC television series.

Language

common second languages, though few Russians know more than a phrase or two of either, and any attempt to speak Russian will be heartily appreciated. At the very least you should try to learn the Cyrillic alphabet so you can read the names of metro stations and the signs around the city. For more detail, check out the *Rough Guide Russian Phrasebook*, set out dictionary-style for easy access, with English-Russian and Russian-English sections, cultural tips for tricky situations and a menu reader.

Russian is a highly complex eastern Slav language and you're unlikely to become very familiar with it during a brief visit to St Petersburg. English and German are the most

The Cyrillic alphabet

Contrary to appearances, the **Cyrillic alphabet** is the least of your problems when trying to learn Russian. There are several different ways of **transliterating**

CYRILLIC CHARACTERS

Аа	a	Ий	y	Уу	u	Ьь	a silent "soft
Бб	b	Кк	k	Фф	f		sign" which
Вв	v	Лл	l	Хх	kh		softens the
Гг	g*	Мм	m	Цц	ts		preceding
Дд	d	Нн	n	Чч	ch		consonant
Ее	e*	Оо	o	Шш	sh	Ъъ	a silent "hard
Ёё	e	Пп	p	Щщ	shch		sign" which
Жж	zh	Рр	r	Ыы	y*		keeps the
Зз	z	Сс	s	Ээ	e		preceding
Ии	i	Тт	t	Яя	ya		consonant hard*

*To aid pronunciation and readability, we have also introduced a handful of exceptions to the above transliteration guide:

Гг (g) is written as v when pronounced as such, for example Горкого – Gorkovo.

Ее (e) is written as Ye when at the beginning of a word, for example Елагин – Yelagin.

Ыы (y) is written as i, when it appears immediately before и (y), for example Литейный – Liteyniy.

Note: just to confuse matters further, hand-written Cyrillic is different again from the printed Cyrillic outlined above. The only place you're likely to encounter it is on menus. The most obvious differences are:

б which looks similar to a "d"

г which looks similar to a backwards "s"

и which looks like a "u"

т which looks similar to an "m"

A RUSSIAN LANGUAGE GUIDE

Accents over letters indicate the stressed vowel/syllable. For vocabulary relating to food and drink, see p.278.

Basic words and phrases

Yes	*da*	да
No	*net*	нет
Please	*pozháluysta*	пожалуйста
Thank you	*spasíbo*	спасибо
Excuse me	*izviníte*	извините
Sorry	*prostíte*	простите
That's OK/it doesn't matter	*nichevó*	ничего
Hello/goodbye (formal)	*zdrávstvuyte/do svidániya*	здравствуйте/до свидания
Good day	*dóbriy den*	добрый день
Good morning	*dóbroe útro*	доброе утро
Good evening	*dóbriy vécher*	добрый вечер
Good night	*spokóynoy nochi*	спокойнойночи
See you later (informal)	*poká*	пока
Bon voyage	*schastlívovo putí*	счастливого пути
Bon appetit	*priyátnovo appetíta*	приятного аппетита
How are you?	*kak delá*	как дела
Fine/OK	*khoroshó*	хорошо
Go away!	*ostavte menya!*	оставте меня
Help!	*na pómoshch*	на помощь
Today	*sevódnya*	сегодня
Yesterday	*vcherá*	вчера
Tomorrow	*závtra*	завтра
The day after tomorrow	*poslezávtra*	послезавтра
Now	*seychás*	сейчас
Later	*popózzhe*	попозже
This one	*éta*	это
A little	*nemnógo*	немного
Large/small	*bolshóy/málenkiy*	большой/маленький
More/less	*yeshché/ménshe*	ешё/меньше
Good/bad	*khoróshiy/plokhóy*	хороший/плохой
Hot/cold	*goryáchiy/kholódniy*	горячий/холодный
With/without	*s/bez*	с/без

Getting around

Over there	*tam*	там
Round the corner	*za uglóm*	за углом
Left/right	*nalévo/naprávo*	налево/направо
Straight on	*pryámo*	прямо
Where is. . . ?	*gde*	где
How do I get to Peterhof?	*kak mne popást v Petergof*	как мне попасть в Петергоф
Am I going the right way for the Hermitage?	*ya právilno idú k Ermitazhu*	я правильно иду к Эрмитажу
Is it far?	*etó dalekó*	это далеко
By bus	*avtóbusom*	автобусом
By train	*póezdom*	поездом
By car	*na mashine*	на машине

On foot	*peshkóm*	пешком
By taxi	*na taksi*	на такси
Ticket	*bilét*	билет
Return (ticket)	*tudá i obrátno*	туда и обратно
Train station	*vokzál*	вокзал
Bus station	*avtóbusniy vokzal*	автобусный вокзал
Bus stop	*ostanóvka*	остановка
Is this train going to Novgorod?	*étot póezd idét v Nóvgorod*	этот поезд идёт в Новгород
Do I have to change?	*núzhno sdélat peresádku*	нужно сделать пересадку
Small change (money)	*meloch*	мелочь

Questions and answers

Do you speak English?	*Vy govoríte po-anglíyski*	вы говорите по-английски
I don't speak German	*ya ne govoryú po-nemétski*	я не говорю по-немецки
I don't understand	*ya ne ponimáyu*	я не понимаю
I understand	*ya ponimáy u*	я понимаю
Speak slowly	*govoríte pomédlenee*	говорите помедленее
I don't know	*ya ne znáyu*	я не знаю
How do you say that in Russian?	*kak po-rússki*	как по-русски
Could you write it down?	*zapishíte éto pozháluysta*	запишите это пожалуйста
What . . .	*chto*	что
Where	*gde*	где
When	*kogdá*	когда
Why	*pochemú*	почему
Who	*kto*	кто
How much is it?	*skólko stóit*	сколько стоит
I would like a double room	*ya khochú nómer na dvoíkh*	я хочу номер на двоих
For one night	*tólko sútki*	только сутки
Shower	*dush*	душ
Are these seats free?	*svobódno*	свободно
May I . . . ?	*mózhno*	можно
You can't/it is not allowed	*nelzyá*	нельзя
The bill please	*schet pozháluysta*	счёт пожалуйста
Do you have . . . ?	*u vas yest*	у вас есть
That's all	*eto vsé*	это всё

Some signs

Entrance	*vkhod*	ВХОД
Exit	*výkhod*	ВЫХОД
Toilet	*stualét*	ТУАЛЕТ
Men's	*múzhi*	МУЖСКОЙ
Women's	*zhény*	ЖЕНСКИЙ
Open	*otkrýto*	ОТКРЫТО
Closed (for repairs)	*zakrýto (na remont)*	ЗАКРЫТО НА РЕМОНТ
Out of order	*ne rabótaet*	НЕ РАБОТАЕТ
No entry	*vkhóda net*	ВХОДА НЕТ
No smoking	*ne kurít*	НЕ КУРИТЬ
Drinking water	*piteváya vodá*	ПИТЬЕВАЯ ВОДА
Information	*správka*	СПРАВКА
Ticket office	*kássa*	КАССА

continues overleaf...

A RUSSIAN LANGUAGE GUIDE contd.

Days of the week

Monday	*ponedélnik*	понедельник	Friday	*pyátnitsa*	пятница
Tuesday	*vtórnik*	вторник	Saturday	*subbóta*	суббота
Wednesday	*sredá*	среда	Sunday	*voskreséne*	воскресенье
Thursday	*chetvérg*	четверг			

Months of the year

January	*yanvár*	январь	July	*iyúl*	июль
February	*fevrál*	февраль	August	*ávgust*	август
March	*mart*	март	September	*sentyábr*	сентябрь
April	*aprél*	апрель	October	*oktyábr*	октябрь
May	*may*	май	November	*noyábr*	ноябрь
June	*iyún*	июнь	December	*dekábr*	декабрь

Numbers

1	*odín*	один	50	*pyatdesyát*	пятьдесят
2	*dva*	два	60	*shestdesyát*	шестьдесят
3	*tri*	три	70	*sémdesyat*	семьдесят
4	*chetýre*	четыре	80	*vósemdesyat*	восемьдесят
5	*pyat*	пять	90	*devyanósto*	девяносто
6	*shest*	шесть	100	*sto*	сто
7	*sem*	семь	200	*dvésti*	двести
8	*vósem*	восемь	300	*trísta*	триста
9	*dévyat*	девять	400	*chetýresta*	четыреста
10	*désyat*	десять	500	*pyatsót*	пятьсот
11	*odínnadtsat*	одиннадцать	600	*shestsót*	шестьсот
12	*dvenádtsat*	двенадцать	700	*semsót*	семьсот
13	*trinádtsat*	тринадцать	800	*vosemsót*	восемьсот
14	*chetýrnadtsat*	четырнадцать	900	*devyatsót*	девятьсот
15	*pyatnádtsat*	пятнадцать	1000	*týsyacha*	тысяча
16	*shestnádtsat*	шестнадцать	2000	*dve týsyachi*	две тысячи
17	*semnádtsat*	семнадцать	3000	*tri týsyachi*	три тысячи
18	*vosemnádtsat*	восемнадцать	4000	*chetýre týsyachi*	четыре тысячи
19	*devyatnádtsat*	девятнадцать			
20	*dvádtsat*	двадцать	5000	*pyat týsyach*	пять тысяч
21	*dvádtsat odín*	двадцать один	10,000	*désyat týsyach*	десять тысяч
30	*trídtsat*	тридцать	50,000	*pyatdesyát týsyach*	пятьдесят тысяч
40	*sórok*	сорок			

Cyrillic into Latin script (for example "Chajkovskogo" or "Chaykovskovo" for Чайковского). In this book, we've used the Revised English System, with a few minor modifications to help pronunciation. All proper names appear as they are best known, not as they would be transliterated; for example "Tchaikovsky" not "Chaykovskiy".

The list below gives the Cyrillic characters in upper and lower case form, followed simply by the Latin equivalent. In order to pronounce the words properly, you'll need to consult the pronunciation guide below.

Vowels and word stress

English-speakers find it difficult to pronounce Russian accurately, partly because letters which appear at first to have English equivalents are subtly different. The most important rule to remember, however, is that Russian is a language which relies on **stress**.

The stress in a word can fall on any syllable and there's no way of knowing simply by looking at it – it's something you just have to learn, as you do in English. If a word has only one syllable, you can't get it wrong; where there are two or more, we've placed accents over the stressed vowel/syllable, though these do not appear in Russian itself. Once you've located the stressed syllable, you should give it more weight than all the others and far more than you would in English.

Whether a **vowel** is stressed or unstressed sometimes affects the way it's pronounced, most notably with the letter "o" (see below).

а – a – like the *a* in father

я – ya – like the *ya* in yarn, but like the *e* in evil when it appears before a stressed syllable

Э – e – always a short *e* as in get

е – e – like the *ye* in yes

и – i – like the *e* in evil

й – y – like the *y* in boy

о – o – like the *o* in port when stressed, but like the *a* in plan when unstressed

ё – e – like the *yo* in yonder. Note that in Russia, this letter is often printed without the dots

у – u – like the *oo* in moon

ю – yu – like the *u* in universe

ы – y – like the *i* in ill, but with the tongue drawn back

Consonants

In Russian, **consonants** can be either soft or hard and this difference is an important feature of a "good" accent, but if you're simply trying to get by in the language, you needn't worry. The consonants listed below are those which differ significantly from their English equivalents.

б – b – like the *b* in bad; at the end of a word like the *p* in dip

в – v – like the *v* in van but with the upper teeth behind the top of the lower lip; at the end of a word, and before certain consonants like *f* in leaf

г – g – like the *g* in goat; at the end of a word like the *k* in lark

д – d – like the *d* in dog but with the tongue pressed against the back of the upper teeth; at the end of a word like the *t* in salt

ж – zh – like the *s* in pleasure; at the end of a word like the *sh* in bush

з – z – like the *z* in zoo; at the end of a word like the *s* in loose

л – l – like the *l* in milk, but with the tongue kept low and touching the back of the upper teeth

н – n – like the *n* in no but with the tongue pressed against the upper teeth

р – r – trilled as the Scots speak it

с – s – always as in soft, never as in sure

т – t – like the *t* in tent, but with the tongue brought up against the upper teeth

х – kh – like the *ch* in the Scottish loch

ц – ts – like the *ts* in boats

ч – ch – like the *ch* in chicken

ш – sh – like the *sh* in shop

щ – shch – like the *sh-ch* in fresh cheese

There are of course exceptions to the above pronunciation rules, but if you remember even the ones mentioned, you'll be understood.

Glossary

Russian words

Note: accents denote stress, and are not usually shown.

bánya bathhouse

báshnya tower

bulvár boulevard

dácha country cottage

dom kultúry communal arts and social centre; literally "house of culture"

dvoréts palace

górod town

kanál canal

kassa ticket office

kládbishche cemetery

kommunalka communal flat, where several tenants or families share the bathroom, kitchen and corridor

krépost fortress

monastyr monastery or convent; the distinction is made by specifying *muzhskóy* (men's) or *zhenskiy* (women's) *monastyr*

most bridge

muzhík before the Revolution it meant peasant; it now means masculine or macho

náberezhnaya embankment

óstrov island

ózero lake

pámyatnik monument

pereúlok lane

plóshchad square

prospékt avenue

reká river

restorán restaurant

rússkiy/rússkaya Russian

rynok market

sad garden/park

shossé highway

sobór cathedral

storoná district

teátr theatre

tsérkov church

úlitsa street

vokzál train station

vystavka exhibition

zal room or hall

zámok castle

Art and architectural terms

Art Nouveau French term for the sinuous and stylized form of architecture – known as Style Moderne in Russia – dating from the turn of the century to World War I.

Atlantes Supports in the form of carved male figures, used instead of columns to support an entablature.

Baroque Exuberant architectural style of the seventeenth and early eighteenth centuries that spread to Russia via Ukraine and Belarus. Characterized by heavy, ornate decoration, complex spatial arrangement and grand vistas.

Caryatids Sculpted female figures used as a column to support an entablature.

Constructivism Soviet version of modernism that pervaded the arts during the 1920s. In architecture, functionalism and simplicity were the watchwords.

Empire style Richly decorated version of the Neoclassical style, which prevailed in Russia from 1812 to the 1840s. The French and Russian Empire styles both derived from Imperial Rome.

Entablature The part of a building supported by a colonnade or column.

Fresco Mural painting applied to wet plaster, so that the colours bind chemically with it as they dry.

Futurism Avant-garde art movement glorifying machinery, war, speed and the modern world in general.

Grisaille Painting in grey monotone used to represent objects in relief.

Icon Religious image, usually painted on wood and framed upon an iconostasis.

Iconostasis A screen that separates the sanctuary from the nave in Orthodox churches, typically consisting of tiers of icons in a gilded frame, with up to three doors that open during services. The central one is known as the Royal Door.

Nave The part of a church where the congregation stands (there are no pews in Orthodox churches).

Neoclassical Late eighteenth- and early nineteenth-century style of architecture and design returning to classical Greek and Roman models as a reaction against Baroque and Rococo excesses.

Neo-Russian (also known as Pseudo-Russian) Style of architecture and decorative arts that drew inspiration from Russia's medieval and ancient past, folk arts and myths.

Pilaster A half column projecting only slightly from the wall.

Portico Covered entrance to a building

Putti Cherubs

Rococo Highly florid, fiddly but occasionally graceful style of architecture and interior design, forming the last phase of Baroque.

Sanctuary (or Naos) The area around the altar, which in Orthodox churches is always screened by an iconostasis.

Stalinist Declamatory style of architecture prevalent from the 1930s up to the death of Stalin in 1953 that returned to Neoclassical and neo-Gothic models as a reaction against Constructivism and reached its "High Stalinist" apogee after World War II.

Stucco Plaster used for decorative effects.

Style Moderne Linear, stylized form of architecture and decorative arts influenced by French Art Nouveau, which took its own direction in Russia.

Trompe l'oeil Painting designed to fool the onlooker into believing that it is actually three-dimensional.

Political terms and acronyms

Apparatchiki A catch-all term to describe the Communist Party bureaucrats of the Soviet era.

Bolshevik Literally "majority"; name given to faction who supported Lenin during the internal disputes within the RSDLP during the first decade of this century.

Cheka (Extraordinary Commission for Combating Counter-revolution, Speculation and Delinquency in Office) Bolshevik secret police, 1917–21.

CIS Commonwealth of Independent States – loose grouping which was formed in December 1991 following the collapse of the USSR. Most of the former Soviet republics have since joined, with the exception of the Baltic States.

Civil War 1918–21 War between the Bolsheviks and an assortment of opposition forces including Mensheviks, SRs, Cossacks, Tsarists and foreign interventionist armies from the West and Japan.

Decembrists Those who participated in the abortive coup against the accession of Nicholas I in December 1825.

Duma The name given to three parliaments in the reign of Nicholas II, and the lower house of the parliament of the Russian Federation since 1993 (its upper chamber is called the Federation Council).

February Revolution Overthrow of the tsar in February 1917.

Five-Year Plan Centralized masterplan for every branch of the Soviet economy. The first five-year plan was promulgated in 1928.

FSB (Federal Security Service) The name of Russia's secret police since 1993.

GIBDD Traffic police.

GPU Soviet secret police, 1921–23.

Gulag Official title for the hard labour camps set up under Lenin and Stalin.

Kadet Party Liberal political party in operation from 1905 to 1917.

KGB Soviet secret police 1954–91.

Menshevik Literally "minority"; name given to faction opposing Lenin during the internal disputes within the RSDLP during the first decade of this century.

Metropolitan Senior cleric, ranking between an archbishop and the patriarch of the Russian Orthodox Church.

MVD Soviet secret police from 1946 to 1954; now runs the regular police (Militia) and the OMON (see below).

Narodnaya Volya (People's Will) Terrorist group that assassinated Alexander II in 1881.

New Russians (*novye russkie*) Brash nouveaux riche of the post-Soviet era, mocked by countless New Russian jokes.

NKVD Soviet secret police, 1934–46.

October Revolution Bolshevik coup d'état which overthrew the Provisional Government in October 1917.

OGPU (Unified State Political Directorate) Soviet secret police 1923–34.

Okhrana Tsarist secret police.

Oligarchs Immensely rich and shady financiers who emerged during the Yeltsin era.

OMON Paramilitary force established in 1988, now used for riot control and fighting civil wars within the Russian Federation.

Patriarch Head of the Russian Orthodox Church.

Petrine Anything dating from the lifetime of Peter the Great (1672–1725).

Populist Amorphous political movement of the second half of the nineteenth century advocating Socialism based on the peasant commune, or *mir*.

Purges Name used for the mass arrests of the Stalin era, but also for any systematic removal of unwanted elements from positions of authority.

RSDLP (Russian Social Democratic Labour Party) First Marxist political party in Russia, which rapidly split into Bolshevik and Menshevik factions.

SR Socialist Revolutionary.

Tsar Emperor. The title was first adopted by Ivan the Terrible.

Tsaritsa Empress; the foreign misnomer Tsarina is better known.

Tsarevich Crown prince.

Tsaraevna Daughter of a Tsar and Tsaritsa.

USSR (Union of Soviet Socialist Republics). Official name of the Soviet Union from 1923 to 1991.

Whites Generic term for Tsarist or Kadet forces during the Civil War, which the Bolsheviks applied to almost anyone who opposed them.

Index

Stay in touch with us!

ROUGHNEWS is Rough Guides' free newsletter. In three issues a year we give you news, travel issues, music reviews, readers' letters and the latest dispatches from authors on the road.

I would like to receive ROUGHNEWS: please put me on your free mailing list.

NAME ....

ADDRESS ....

Please clip or photocopy and send to: Rough Guides, 62–70 Shorts Gardens, London WC2H 9AH, England or Rough Guides, 375 Hudson Street, New York, NY 10014, USA.

ROUGH GUIDES: Travel

Alaska
Amsterdam
Andalucia
Argentina
Australia
Austria

Bali & Lombok
Barcelona
Belgium &
 Luxembourg
Belize
Berlin
Brazil
Britain
Brittany &
 Normandy
Bulgaria
California
Canada
Central America
Chile
China
Corsica
Costa Rica
Crete
Croatia
Cuba
Cyprus
Czech & Slovak
 Republics

Dodecanese &
 the East Aegean
Devon &
 Cornwall
Dominican
 Republic
Dordogne & the
 Lot
Ecuador
Egypt
England
Europe
Florida
France
French Hotels &
 Restaurants
 1999
Germany
Goa
Greece
Greek Islands
Guatemala
Hawaii
Holland
Hong Kong &
 Macau
Hungary

Iceland
India
Indonesia
Ionian Islands
Ireland

Israel & the
 Palestinian
 Territories
Italy
Jamaica
Japan
Jordan
Kenya
Lake District
Languedoc &
 Roussillon
Laos
London
Los Angeles
Malaysia,
 Singapore &
 Brunei
Mallorca &
 Menorca
Maya World
Mexico
Morocco
Moscow
Nepal
New England
New York
New Zealand
Norway
Pacific
 Northwest
Paris
Peru
Poland
Portugal
Prague
Provence & the
 Côte d'Azur
The Pyrenees
Romania
St Petersburg
San Francisco

Sardinia
Scandinavia
Scotland
Scottish
 highlands and
 Islands
Sicily
Singapore
South Africa
South India
Southeast Asia
Southwest USA
Spain
Sweden
Switzerland
Syria

Thailand
Trinidad &
 Tobago
Tunisia
Turkey
Tuscany &
 Umbria
USA
Venice
Vienna
Vietnam
Wales
Washington DC
West Africa
Zimbabwe &
 Botswana

AVAILABLE AT ALL GOOD BOOKSHOPS

ROUGH GUIDES: Mini Guides, Travel Specials and Phrasebooks

MINI GUIDES

Antigua
Bangkok
Barbados
Beijing
Big Island of Hawaii
Boston
Brussels
Budapest
Cape Town
Copenhagen
Dublin
Edinburgh

Florence
Honolulu
Ibiza & Formentera
Jerusalem
Las Vegas
Lisbon
London Restaurants
Madeira
Madrid
Malta & Gozo
Maui
Melbourne
Menorca

Montreal
New Orleans

Paris
Rome
Seattle
St Lucia
Sydney
Tenerife
Tokyo
Toronto
Vancouver

TRAVEL SPECIALS

First-Time Asia
First-Time Europe
Women Travel

PHRASEBOOKS

Czech
Dutch
Egyptian Arabic
European
French
German
Greek

Hindi & Urdu
Hungarian
Indonesian
Italian
Japanese
Mandarin
  Chinese
Mexican
  Spanish
Polish
Portuguese
Russian
Spanish
Swahili
Thai
Turkish
Vietnamese

AVAILABLE AT ALL GOOD BOOKSHOPS

ROUGH GUIDES:
Reference and Music CDs

REFERENCE

Blues:
  100 Essential CDs
Classical Music
Classical:
  100 Essential CDs
Country Music
Country:
  100 Essential CDs
Drum'n'bass
House Music
Hip Hop
Irish Music
Jazz

Music USA
Opera
Opera:
  100 Essential CDs
Reggae
Reggae:
  100 Essential CDs
Rock
Rock:
  100 Essential CDs

Soul:
  100 Essential CDs
Techno
World Music

World Music:
  100 Essential CDs
English Football
European Football
Internet
Money Online
Shopping Online
Travel Health

ROUGH GUIDE MUSIC CDs

Music of the Andes
Australian Aboriginal
Bluegrass
Brazilian Music
Cajun & Zydeco
Music of Cape Verde
Classic Jazz
Music of
  Colombia
Cuban Music
Eastern Europe

Music of Egypt
English Roots Music
Flamenco
Music of Greece
Hip Hop
India & Pakistan
Irish Music
Music of Jamaica
Music of Japan
Kenya & Tanzania
Marrabenta
  Mozambique
Native American
North African
Music of Portugal
Reggae
Salsa
Samba
Scottish Music
South African Music
Music of Spain
Sufi Music
Tango

Tex-Mex
West African Music
World Music
World Music Vol 2
Music of Zimbabwe